Judicial Review Proc

A practitioner's guide

Jonathan Manning was called to the Bar in 1989 and joined Arden Chambers in London as a founder member in 1993, where he specialises in administrative, housing and local government law. He is an author of *Local Government Constitutional and Administrative Law; A Guide to the Greater London Authority* and *Housing Law Pleadings in Practice* (respectively 1999, 2000 and 2003 [2nd edn], Sweet & Maxwell); a contributor to *Human Rights Act 1998: A practitioner's guide* (1998, Sweet & Maxwell) and *The Home Lawyer* (2003, Guardian Books) and a former editor of the *Local Government Law Reports*, the digest of the *Journal of Local Government Law* and the *Encyclopaedia of Local Government Law* (all Sweet & Maxwell). He regularly lectures on judicial review.

The Legal Action Group is a national, independent charity which campaigns for equal access to justice for all members of society. Legal Action Group:
- provides support to the practice of lawyers and advisers
- inspires developments in that practice
- campaigns for improvements in the law and the administration of justice
- stimulates debate on how services should be delivered.

Judicial Review Proceedings

A practitioner's guide to advice and representation

SECOND EDITION

Jonathan Manning

Legal Action Group
2004

Second edition published in Great Britain 2004
by LAG Education and Service Trust Limited
242 Pentonville Road, London N1 9UN
www.lag.org.uk

© Jonathan Manning

First published 1995

British Library Cataloguing in Publication Data
a CIP catalogue record for this book is available from the British
Library.

ISBN 1 903307 17 1

Typeset and printed by Hobbs the Printers,
Totton, Hampshire SO40 3WX

Foreword

To the first edition by the Right Honourable Lord Justice Laws (formerly the Hon Mr Justice Laws)

There are nowadays quite a lot of text books about judicial review. Sir William Wade's *Administrative Law*, now in its 7th edition, has as every practitioner knows been very influential in the development of our public law. A new edition of de Smith's *Judicial Review of Administrative Action* is forthcoming, edited by Lord Woolf and Professor Jeffrey Jowell. And there are others. But Mr Manning's new book fills a real place; it is a relatively short, and extremely clear, introduction to the subject which I think will be of very great use, particularly to practitioners who are not public law specialists but may have to work in this area from time to time.

There is an excellent balance between the author's treatment of the substantive law, in chapters 1 to 8, and the later chapters (together with the appendices) dealing with procedure. I would particularly commend chapter 6 (Grounds on which judicial review may be sought): just over 20 pages long, it is an admirable account of an aspect of the subject which is, plainly, at its very centre. And in practical terms, the precedents given in appendix 1 will be of great value to busy practitioners who have to draft documents for submission to the court, often in a hurry: and of value to the court too, if it means that the documents are likely to say as much, but no more, than they should – as it certainly will, if Mr Manning's book obtains the currency it deserves.

Mr Manning has done a real service to the profession in writing this book. I hope it will be widely used; I think it should be recommended reading for pupils in public law chambers, and for trainees in solicitors' firms practising in this field, and it is an excellent vade mecum for non-specialists. I hope it enjoys every success.

Preface

In the preface to the first edition of this book, I said that my aim was to provide a comprehensive introduction to the law and practice of judicial review proceedings and to explain in a 'relatively' straightforward manner the principles of this notoriously complex and constantly evolving area of law. That remains the aim of this second edition, although things seem to have become rather more complicated since 1995, the book having grown from 125 to 440 pages of text.

In part, this is a reflection of developments in the subject matter of judicial review. The enactment and effect of the Human Rights Act 1998, the power struggle between *Wednesbury* unreasonableness and proportionality, the new procedural regime introduced by Civil Procedure Rules Part 54 and the pre-action protocol (to name but a few of the developments of the last few years) have all demanded inclusion and discussion. I have tried, additionally, to improve upon the first edition, and have therefore attempted to be rather more comprehensive in my coverage of European law (both EU and human rights), the role of judicial review in relation to various substantive areas of law (which could have been a book – or many – in itself) and, indeed, in all aspects of my treatment of the subject. Chapter 6, grounds on which review may be sought, commended for its brevity in Mr Justice Laws' (as he then was) Foreword to the first edition has grown from 20 to 60 pages.

I hope that these changes have improved the book; giving it bigger muscles rather than just a big stomach (which, spookily, mirrors the development of my own physique) and without it losing the 'relative' straightforwardness of explanation which, I hope was a strength of the first edition and which is a major part of the point of an introductory work.

Anyway, the law is stated as at 1 October 2003, although I have tried to take account of later developments where possible.

Jonathan Manning
Arden Chambers
London

Acknowledgements

I have made so many people's lives a misery in so many ways during the preparation of this edition that it is difficult to know where to start.

I must first express my gratitude (and admiration) to the publishers, past and present, at the Legal Action Group, who have worked with me on the second edition. I am aware of what I put them through and am extremely grateful for their perseverance, constant help and support, and for good humour above and beyond the call of duty. I should also like to thank everyone else at LAG who has worked on this edition.

I must also thank Lindsay Johnson, Amy Baker and Tina Conlan at chambers who researched and wrote first drafts of chapters 8 to 16 (the 'areas of law' chapters). Lindsay also assisted with chapter 1 ('Sources of law'). Without their help, and that of Simon Strelitz at proof stage, this edition would still not be finished.

On a personal note, I should like to thank my wife for patiently accepting the horrors of living with me, generally and while I was writing this, and for clearing out the basement by herself, my parents for all they have done for me, and Andrew Arden QC for 14 years of guidance and support (including introducing the first edition of this book to LAG in 1994).

There are many other people who have given help and support and still more who have refrained from telling me just how annoyed they are with me, and to all of them I offer my sincere thanks.

For Claire-Louise

Contents

Table of cases

Table of statutes

Table of statutory instruments

Table of European legislation

Abbreviations

ADR	Alternative dispute resolution
AJA 1999	Administration of Justice Act 1999
CDS	Criminal Defence Service
CFI	Court of First Instance
CLS	Community Legal Service
CPR	Civil Procedure Rules
DPA	Data Protection Acts
EC Treaty	Treaty of Rome 1957, establishing the European Community
ECHR	European Court of Human Rights
ECJ	European Court of Justice
EU	European Union
HRA 1998	Human Rights Act 1998
IR	Immigration Rules
LEA	Local education authority
LSC	Legal Services Commission
NIAA 2002	Nationality, Immigration and Asylum Act 2002
PACE 1984	Police and Criminal Evidence Act 1984
PD	Practice Direction
RSC	Rules of the Supreme Court
RSL	Registered social landlord
SCA 1981	Supreme Court Act 1981
SENDIST	Special Educational Needs and Disability Tribunal
SENT	Special Educational Needs Tribunal
SSA 1998	Social Security Act 1998
SSCBA 1992	Social Security Contributions and Benefits Act 1992
SSFA 1998	Schools Standards and Framework Act 1998
TCPA 1990	Town and Country Planning Act 1990
Treaty on EU	Maastricht Treaty 1992 on European Union

Introduction

I.1 Introduction

Introduction

I.1   Judicial review is the process by which the High Court scrutinises the legality of acts or decisions of public bodies, tribunals and inferior courts (magistrates' courts, county courts, coroners' courts and in some circumstances Crown Courts). The bodies that are susceptible to judicial review are not only those exercising judicial or quasi-judicial functions, but they must be public bodies and so will not include those exercising a solely 'domestic', or contract-based, function (such as religious courts, private disciplinary tribunals, the Jockey Club, the Football Association and private bodies exercising purely private law functions). Judicial review is used to correct errors of law or decisions, in a public law context, which are perverse or have been taken without proper regard to any procedural protection conferred by common law or statute.

I.2   Traditionally analysed,[1] the judicial review jurisdiction is supervisory rather than appellate. It is concerned with procedure and the decision-making process and not the merits of the original case. It is not a system of appeal, and the court will not substitute its own decision for that of the body under review:[2]

> The Court of King's Bench has an inherent jurisdiction to control all inferior tribunals, not in an appellate capacity, but in a supervisory capacity. This control extends not only to seeing that the inferior tribunals keep within their jurisdiction, but also to seeing that they observe the law ... The King's Bench does not substitute its own views for those of the tribunal, as a Court of Appeal would do. It leaves it to the tribunal to hear the case again, and in a proper case may command it to do so. When the King's Bench exercises its control over tribunals in this way, it is not usurping a jurisdiction which does not belong to it. It is only exercising a jurisdiction which it has always had.[3]

1   Though in recent (especially post Human Rights Act 1998) times, the approach of the court has been more interventionist than the traditional analysis would permit even, on occasion, resembling that of an appeal where fundamental rights have been at stake: see, eg, *R (Daly) v Secretary of State for the Home Department* [2001] 2 AC 532, HL; *R (Wilkinson) v Broadmoor Special Hospital Authority* [2001] EWCA Civ 1545; [2002] 1 WLR 419; (2002) 5 CCLR 121; *R (Mullen) v Secretary of State for the Home Department* [2002] EWHC 230 (Admin); [2002] 1 WLR 1857. See also, procedurally, Civil Procedure Rules (CPR) r54.19, which enables a court, in appropriate circumstances, to take the decision itself rather than remit it back to the decision-maker.

2   Save in particular circumstances: see CPR r54.19 (above) and, eg, *Edwards v Bairstow* [1956] AC 14, HL.

3   *R v Northumberland Compensation Appeal Tribunal ex p Shaw* [1952] 1 KB 338, CA, per Denning LJ at 346–347.

1.3   Accordingly, if an application for judicial review is successful, the court will usually quash the decision complained of (or declare it to be unlawful) and may remit the matter back to the relevant body to take a fresh decision in accordance with the law. If, however, a body or tribunal, properly directing itself, having regard only to relevant considerations, etc, could only have come to one lawful decision, then the High Court may itself substitute that proper decision for the decision of the body under review.[4]

1.4   The following remedies may be available in judicial review proceedings:[5]

Quashing Order (certiorari) – an order to quash the decision complained of. The court may in some circumstances then direct the body or tribunal in question to reach a decision in accordance with the court's finding. This does not, however, necessarily mean that the applicant will succeed in obtaining a different or more favourable decision.

Mandatory Order (mandamus) – an order requiring the performance of a specified act or duty. The court will generally not order a public body to reach a particular result, but only to reconsider the matter in accordance with the law.

Prohibiting Order (prohibition) – an order preventing the decision-maker concerned from acting or continuing to act in excess of his or her jurisdiction.

Declaration – a determination by the court of the rights of the applicant in relation to the matter under challenge.

Injunction – an order requiring the defendant to do, or to refrain from doing, a specified act. It is frequently sought as an interim remedy.

Damages – damages may only be awarded in judicial review proceedings in two situations. First, if the claimant would, had the claim been brought as a private law action, have been entitled to damages; second, if damages are claimed for breach of the claimant's rights under the Human Rights Act 1998.

---

4   See *Edwards v Bairstow* [1956] AC 14, HL.
5   The subject of remedies is considered in detail in chapter 5.

I.5   In addition to the above, the court has certain ancillary powers, which are dealt with in more detail elsewhere.[6]

I.6   The current rules governing judicial review are to be found in Supreme Court Act (SCA) 1981 s31, Civil Procedure Rules (CPR) Part 54, Practice Direction 54, a Practice Statement and some Guidance Notes. The procedure for making an application is in two stages:

(a) the application for permission to apply for judicial review; and
(b) the full, or substantive, application, made if permission has been granted.

I.7   The granting of a remedy is discretionary and does not issue as of right, even if the court accepts that a decision was unlawful on administrative law principles. Consequently, it is necessary for advisers to act without delay, and to consider whether other, alternative remedies have been exhausted before commencing a claim, as these factors will be relevant to the court's exercise of its discretion.

I.8   Judicial review has always been a politically sensitive remedy (central government's attitude to scrutiny of its decisions by the courts is ambivalent at best and frequently hostile[7]). Coupled with this, it is generally perceived as an expensive and sometimes inconvenient remedy, given that it requires a large amount of preparation and paperwork, it takes place in the High Court, only in London, and it may well not lead to the granting of the substantive remedy which is, in reality what the claimant seeks, but rather only to the reconsideration of the matter by the decision-maker who will frequently have the right to reach the same decision on the merits, if that decision is approached lawfully. The court's powers are circumscribed by the constitutional limits to the remedy – as stated above, it is not for the court to re-take the decision itself, but simply to scrutinise the decision which was taken to ensure that it was lawful.

I.9   Perhaps for these reasons, Parliament has sought to remove some of the most common types of claim from the Administrative Court, or at any rate from the judicial review procedure as it is described in this book. Homelessness challenges were removed to the county court by way of a newly created right to appeal against such decisions on a point of law.[8] More recently, challenges to decisions of the Immigration

---

6   At chapter 5, below at paras 5.34–5.74.
7   As in the Home Secretary's tirade against Collins J following the decisions in *R (Saadi) v Secretary of State for the Home Department* [2001] EWHC Admin 670.
8   Housing Act 1996 s204. *Tower Hamlets LBC v Begum (Nipa)* [2000] 1 WLR 306, CA, confirmed that the county court would, on a section 204 appeal, simply apply judicial review principles.

Appeal Tribunal, long susceptible to judicial review and another major source of work for the Administrative Court have become subject to a new 'statutory review' procedure which precludes any oral consideration of the permission application and imposes stricter time-limits and limitations on the documentary evidence which may be put before the court.[9]

I.10 At the same time, pressure has arisen from a different source for the courts to address one of the issues referred to above – the restraints on the extent to which the court may intervene in the decision and the degree of scrutiny which it is permissible for them to apply. The source of this pressure has been the enactment of the Human Rights Act 1998, and in particular the obligation which it has imposed on the courts, in cases involving human rights issues, to have regard to the jurisprudence of the European Court of Human Rights,[10] and the requirements of article 6[11] for a claimant to have a right of access to a court of full jurisdiction.[12]

I.11 In response to this pressure, the courts have begun to develop a new, more interventionist model of judicial review. Under this new model, the court is entitled to apply the European doctrine of 'proportionality' and thereby subject decisions to a much closer scrutiny, requiring the decision-maker to advance a positive objective justifcation for the decision and considering that justification for itself.[13] There have even been concessions to the heretical idea that the court has power to conduct a 'full-merits' review where fundamental rights are at stake and the circumstances require it.[14]

---

9 See Nationality, Immigration and Asylum Act 2002 s101(2), and CPR Part 54 Section II (in force from 1 April 2003).

10 Human Rights Act 1998 s2.

11 Human Rights Act 1998 Sch 1, art 6.

12 The argument was that the judicial review court did not have full jurisdiction because of its inability to investigate the merits of the decision under challenge. A recent House of Lords decision appears now to have finally resolved this issue (at least so far as the UK courts are concerned), in terms that the judicial review jurisdiction will almost inevitably be considered sufficient to comply with the requirements of article 6: see *Runa Begum v Tower Hamlets LBC* [2003] UKHL 4; [2003] 2 WLR 388.

13 See,eg, *R (Daly) v Secretary of State for the Home Department* [2001] 2 AC 532, HL; *R v Secretary of State for the Home Department ex p Mahmood* [2001] 1 WLR 840, CA.

14 See *R (Wilkinson) v Broadmoor Special Hospital Authority* [2001] EWCA Civ 1545; [2002] 1 WLR 419; (2002) 5 CCLR 121 at [36] and [83]; *R (Mullen) v Secretary of State for the Home Department* [2002] EWHC 230 (Admin); [2002] 1 WLR 1857. Compare *Adan v Newham LBC* [2001] EWCA Civ 1919; [2002] 1 WLR 2120.

1.12   This model is still not fully developed. Given that it has arisen from the human rights legislation, it has currently only been applied in human – or what have been called 'fundamental' – rights cases. It does seem unlikely, however, that such a distinction is maintainable indefinitely. The Court of Appeal recently referred to the conceptual difficulties of attempting to keep the *Wednesbury* unreasonableness doctrine[15] and that of proportionality separate, describing it as 'unnecessary and confusing' to seek to keep them both in play, while in separate compartments. The court went on to express the view that the traditional *Wednesbury* test of perversity should now be laid to rest altogether, whether or not fundamental rights were involved, in favour of proportionality which is far more 'precise and sophisticated'.[16]

1.13   At the same time as these conceptual issues, which go to the heart of the remedy, have been in play, the procedure for making judicial review claims has been completely revised, with CPR Part 54 replacing Rules of the Supreme Court (RSC) Order 53. It is at the permission stage where the majority of the changes have been made. It is now no longer a 'without notice' procedure (although this is largely a formalisation of what had become the practice under Order 53), with defendants now required to submit a summary of their reasons for resisting the claim prior to the permission decision being made – on the papers, now, in all cases (but subject to a right to renew the application in open court).

1.14   It can therefore be seen that much has changed and is still changing in judicial review. The following chapters set out in more detail the sources and concepts of public law, the grounds on which challenges may be brought, and the bodies against whom they may be brought, together with consideration of the remedies which may be available, and the procedure which is to be followed in what can seem a thoroughly confusing and arcane area of law.

---

15   *Associated Provincial Picture Houses v Wednesbury Corporation* [1948] 1 KB 223, CA.

16   *Association of British Civilian Internees – Far Eastern Region v Secretary of State for Defence* [2003] EWCA Civ 473, at [34]. The Court of Appeal recognised that only the House of Lords could abolish the *Wednesbury* doctrine (but refused leave to appeal to the House of Lords).

CHAPTER 1

Sources of law

Introduction

1.1 There are three main legal sources that feed into the law of judicial review. The first is common law – judicial review is a common law remedy. The second and third sources derive from Europe: European Community law and human rights law. In this chapter, each will be briefly examined.

Common law

1.2 The power of the High Court to entertain challenges to the decisions of government and other public bodies has been developed by the courts themselves. The provisions of the Supreme Court Act 1981 and rules of court do not create the jurisdiction, but merely regulate it in essentially procedural terms.

1.3 Indeed, the courts have consistently rejected parliamentary attempts to limit or remove its supervisory jurisdiction. An example of this has been the attitude of the courts to ouster, finality and 'no certiorari' clauses.[1]

1.4 The courts do, however, accept constitutional limits to their powers. Hence, Acts of Parliament are not susceptible to review, nor are certain exercises of royal prerogative[2]. In addition, where Parliament provides a different form of remedy, such as a statutory right of appeal, the courts do accept that judicial review will generally not lie.[3]

European Community and human rights law

1.5 Public law in England and Wales is no longer comprehensible without an understanding of the principles and effect of European Community law and European human rights law, which engage with domestic law at a number of points and on different levels. The majority of these

---

1 See, eg, *Anisminic Ltd v Foreign Compensation Commission* [1969] 2 AC 147, HL; *R v Medical Appeal Tribunal ex p Gilmore* [1957] 1 QB 574, CA. See below paras 7.43–7.50.

2 See below, paras 2.42–2.51.

3 See generally, on alternative remedies, paras 7.9–7.20. Examples of statutory rights of appeal which have effectively replaced judicial review are: Town and Country Planning Act 1990 s189; Housing Act 1996 s204. The existence of a right of appeal does not always rule out judicial review, however: see, eg, Tribunals and Inquiries Act 1992 s11 and *Ellis & Sons Fourth Amalgamated Properties v Southern Rent Assessment Panel* (1984) 14 HLR 48, QBD, in which the court held that judicial review was a preferable remedy to the statutory right of appeal.

engagements are discussed elsewhere in (and throughout) this book as part of the treatment of the substantive topics to which they relate. The starting-point to this explanation of the interaction between domestic law and law from Europe is, however, to be found in the following sections of this chapter. The next section contains a basic outline of the institutions and principles of Community law. The final section introduces European human rights law and the Human Rights Act 1998.

Community law

Institutions of the European Union

The Council of the European Union

1.6   The Council of the European Union comprises representatives from each member state, who must be authorised to 'commit' the government of that state.[4] Usually, the minister responsible for the particular matter under discussion will be the state's representative. The Council meets whenever convened by the President of the Council, whether of his own motion or at the request of either a member state or of the Commission.[5] Each member state holds the presidency of the council for six months, during which time its representative will arrange, set the agenda for and chair meetings, and may well initiate policies in areas of concern to the state in question or to the Council as a whole.

1.7   The Council's functions are set out in article 202 of the EC Treaty. Most important among these is to decide whether legislative proposals from the Commission (see para 1.10 below) will become law. Such decisions are taken by vote, requiring either unanimity or a qualified or simple majority depending upon the provisions of the treaty article governing the subject matter in question. The Council may ask the Commission to formulate proposals for legislation that it considers desirable for the attainment of common objectives.[6] It may also delegate to the Commission power to pass further regulations on any particular matter, although this may be subject to the condition that such regulations are acceptable to a committee (or committees) comprised of representatives of the member states, to ensure that such regulations accord with the Council's own wishes.

4   Treaty of Rome 1957 (EC Treaty) art 203.
5   EC Treaty art 204.
6   EC Treaty art 208.

1.8   The Council has additional powers relating to the police and judiciary in criminal matters.[7]

The European Council

1.9   This consists of the member states' heads of government, together with the President of the Commission, assisted by the members' foreign ministers and other Commission officials. It must meet at least twice a year under the chairmanship of the member whose state currently holds the presidency of the Council, and must submit a report to the European Parliament after each such meeting, and an annual report on the progress achieved by the Union. Its role is to provide the Union with 'the necessary impetus for its development' and to 'define the general political guidelines thereof'.[8]

The Commission

1.10   The most important aspect of the Commission's role is the initiation of legislation, upon which the Council of the European Union acts, and the shaping of general policy strategies for the Community as a whole. The Commission also exercises powers, delegated from the Council, to make subordinate legislation in the form of regulations.[9] Its main administrative function is to oversee the implementation of legislation by the member states to ensure that the rules are commonly and uniformly applied. The Commission also plays an important role in the formulation of the EU's budget and in external relations.

1.11   The Commission is comprised of 20 commissioners[10] who must be persons 'whose independence is beyond doubt' and who 'shall neither seek nor take instructions from any government or from any other body.'[11] Commissioners are nominated by national governments, each member state being entitled to either one or two commissioners, subject to a vote of approval by the European Parliament. The President of the Commission is nominated by common accord by the national governments.[12]

1.12   There is also an extensive Commission bureaucracy, organised into Directorates General, each covering one of the major fields of activity. Each is headed by a Director General, under whom serve

---

7   Maastricht Treaty 1992 (Treaty on EU) art 34.
8   Treaty on EU art 4.
9   EC Treaty art 211.
10   The number may be increased by the Council: EC Treaty art 213(1).
11   EC Treaty art 213.
12   EC Treaty art 214(2).

several Directors who run the various directorates within the Directorate General.

The European Parliament

1.13 The Parliament is an autonomous body, currently comprising 626 Members of the European Parliament (MEPs), who are directly elected representatives of each member state, elected according to the state in question's own national electoral procedures. The distribution of seats broadly reflects the distribution of population across the Union. Members are elected for a term of five years, and sit in political rather than national groupings. The Parliament determines its own methods of operation and adopts its own rules of procedure.[13] It elects its own President together with 14 vice-presidents for two-and-a-half-year terms, who form the Bureau of Parliament.

1.14 The Parliament has no power to initiate legislation, but does have various roles in the legislative process. In some cases, it must be consulted before legislation can be adopted, and a failure to wait for its opinion can result in the measure being anulled,[14] though the Council is not obliged to act in accordance with its opinion. In other cases, the Council can only adopt the legislative measure if the Parliament has approved it or failed to take a decision within three months. Alternatively, the Parliament can reject or propose amendments to the proposal by absolute majority. If the measure is rejected, it can only be adopted by unanimous vote of the Council. If it is amended, the Commission must reexamine it, in the light of the amendments, and the Council may then adopt or further amend the Commission's amendments by unanimity, and adopt the measure by qualified majority. In yet other cases, the Parliament has an effective right of veto if it votes by an absolute majority to reject the measure. If it proposes amendments, these must be reexamined by the Commission and the Council, in a similar manner to that described above.

The European Court of Justice

1.15 The European Court of Justice (ECJ) currently consists of 15 judges, assisted by eight Advocates General. They are appointed by agreement of the member states for a term of six years. Attached to the ECJ is a Court of First Instance (CFI), which has jurisdiction to hear and

---

13 EC Treaty art 199.
14 See, eg, *European Parliament v Council (Generalised Tariff Preferences)* [1995] ECR I–643.

determine (subject to appeal on a point of law to the ECJ) certain classes of action.

1.16   Currently, the CFI has power to hear all actions brought by 'non-privileged' parties, ie, parties other than member states or Community institutions, as well as staff disputes within those institutions and appeals against some Commission decisions. It has no power, however, to give preliminary rulings, and the ECJ retains its exclusive and final interpretive jurisdiction.

1.17   The ECJ is the final court of appeal of the European Union (EU). Its most important function is to 'ensure that in the interpretation and application of [the EC Treaty], the law is observed.'[15] The court has used this provision to extend its jurisdiction over bodies not expressly subject to it (such as the European Parliament) and over functions beyond those referred to in the EC Treaty. It also now has power to impose pecuniary penalties against member states which have failed to comply with previous judgments against them.[16]

The Court of Auditors

1.18   This body has the status of the 'fifth Community institution', since the enactment of the Treaty of the EU.[17] Its principal role is to scrutinise the finances of the Community and ensure sound financial management. It also assists the Parliament and the Council in the control of the implementation of the budget.

Types of EU legislation

1.19   There are three main types of legislative instrument: regulations, decisions and directives. Article 249 of the EC Treaty provides that:

> In order to carry out their task and in accordance with the provisions of this Treaty, the European Parliament acting jointly with the Council, the Council and the Commission shall make regulations and issue directives, take decisions, make recommendations or deliver opinions.
>
> A regulation shall have general application. It shall be binding in its entirety and directly applicable in all member states.
>
> A directive shall be binding, as to the result to be achieved, upon each Member State to which it is addressed, but shall leave to the national authorities the choice of form and methods.

15   EC Treaty art 220. For the court's jurisdiction generally, see EC Treaty arts 226–243.

16   EC Treaty art 228.

17   EC Treaty art 7. Its role is set out in arts 246–248.

A decision shall be binding in its entirety upon those to whom it is addressed.

Recommendations and opinions shall have no binding force.

Regulations

1.20 In most instances, the Treaty does not specify the form in which legislation is to be made. Regulations are the form of legislation most akin to national primary or subordinate legislation. They apply to all member states and are directly applicable. This latter term has two meanings. First, they take effect as part of the member states' national legal systems without the need for any national legislation to incorporate them. Indeed, national legislation purporting to enact them would be contrary to Community law, as it would 'jeopardise the simultaneous and uniform application in the whole of the Community',[18] and may 'affect the jurisdiction of the court to pronounce on any question involving the interpretation of Community law ... which means that no procedure is permissible whereby the Community nature of a legal rule is concealed from those subject to it.'[19]

1.21 Second, the term has been interpreted by the ECJ as meaning that regulations create rights which individuals can enforce through their own national courts.[20]

1.22 The ECJ will decide whether what purports to be a regulation is in fact a regulation in substance. If it is not, it will take effect as a decision.

Decisions

1.23 Decisions may be addressed to member states or to companies (for instance in competition cases), but they are binding in their entirety upon their addressees, taking effect when notified to them. The Council may delegate to the Commission the power to take decisions which the Council itself could take.[21]

Directives

1.24 Directives do not necessarily bind all member states; only those to whom they are addressed. Moreover, while they are binding as to the result to be achieved, they leave it to the individual state to determine the form and method of implementation. The ECJ has held, however, that like regulations, directives have direct effect enabling individuals

18 *Commission v Italy Case* 39/72 [1973] ECR 101.
19 *Variola v Amministrazione delle Finanze Case* 34/73 [1973] ECR 981.
20 See paras 1.33–1.44 below.
21 EC Treaty art 202.

to rely on them in actions against the state (though not necessarily in other types of action).[22] A state may be liable in damages for failing to implement a directive, even if it was not directly effective at the time.[23]

Recommendations and opinions

1.25   The fact that these measures have no binding force does not prevent a member state from seeking a ruling from the ECJ as to their validity or interpretation.[24]

Effect of EU law

Interpretation

1.26   Significant areas of UK law enforced by the UK courts now comes into play directly from Europe.[25] In this context, it is appropriate to draw attention to the different approach taken under European law – and, importantly, by UK courts when considering either primary or secondary legislation intended to implement European directives[26] – from that traditionally taken under domestic law. When considering European provisions, a predominantly purposive, or teleological, interpretation is to be applied, designed to give effect to the spirit rather than the letter, even filling in gaps as they may appear.[27]

1.27   It may be that, with the advance of the purposive approach to construction in English law, the distinction between the approaches may gradually erode but, *Pepper v Hart*[28] notwithstanding, there can be no

22   *See, eg, Van Duyn v Home Office* [1974] ECR 1337.
23   *Francovich v Italy Case C–6/90; Bonifaci v Italy Case C–9/90* [1991] ECR I-5357.
24   See, eg, *Grimaldi v Fonds des Maladies Professionelles Case C–322/88* [1989] ECR 4407.
25   Some of the best known, outside the commercial arena, arise in the context of employment, social security and consumer law.
26   *Litster v Forth Dry Dock Engineering Co Ltd* [1990] 1 AC 546, HL.
27   *HP Bulmer Ltd v J Bollinger SA* [1974] Ch 41, CA; *R v Henn* [1981] AC 850, HL.
28   [1993] AC 593, HL, and subsequent cases, eg, *Sidhu v British Airways plc* [1997] AC 430, HL. In *Pepper v Hart*, the House of Lords accepted for the first time, on strict conditions, it would be permissible for the court, construing the meaning of a statutory provision, to have regard to statements which were made during parliamentary debates, reported in *Hansard*. The conditions are (a) that the statutory provision in question is ambiguous or obscure (which means more than that the parties disagree as to its meaning); (b) that the statement referred to was made by the sponsor of the Bill; and (c) that the statement is sufficiently clear.

doubt that, at present, the starting points are different: in English law, the court starts with the wording, resorting to additional material – whether or not including *Hansard* – where necessary to seek an alternative interpretation; in European law, and when implementing it, the court will start with the purpose or intention and apply the wording accordingly.

Supremacy of Community law

1.28 The European Communities Act 1972 gives Community law primacy over national law.[29] The courts are required to interpret national law in accordance with EU legislation, whether that legislation was enacted before or after the national legislation.[30] Community law must also be given primacy over any incompatible domestic legislation.[31]

1.29 It is for national courts to determine how to protect an individual whose rights under Community law have been infringed.[32] While the ECJ does not require national courts to create new remedies for the enforcement of Community rights, which would not be available under national law,[33] nevertheless rights derived from Community law must be protected with remedies no less favourable than those applicable to analogous rights arising under domestic law.[34] The penalties imposed by member states for breach of European provisions must, however, be proportionate.[35] The ECJ has also held that if the right to seek judicial review is to be an effective remedy, it will generally be required that reasons are given for a decision curtailing or denying a Community right, and that the applicant (or other person seeking to do so) be able to defend the Community right under the 'best possible conditions.'[36]

29 Section 2(1) concerning existing law and section 2(4) on subsequent law. See also *McCarthys v Smith* [1979] 3 All ER 325, CA at 328; *R v Secretary of State for Transport ex p Factortame* [1990] 2 AC 85, HL.

30 *Marleasing SA v La Comercial Internacional de Alimentacion SA* [1990] ECR I-4135, ECJ (considered below at para 1.45).

31 *Costa v ENEL* [1964] ECR 585; *Administrazione delle Finanze dello Stato v Simmenthal SpA* [1978] ECR 629, ECJ.

32 *Rewe-Zentralfinanz eG and Rewe-Zentral AG v Landwirtschaftskammer fur das Saarland Case* 33/76 [1976] ECR 1989, ECJ.

33 *Rewe-Handelgesellschaft Nord mbH v Hauptzollamt Kiel Case* 158/80 [1981] ECR 1805.

34 It is because of this that a Community right will be brought into the public law forum and will be enforceable by public law remedies by way of judicial review. See *Burgoin SA v Minister of Agriculture, Fisheries and Food* [1986] QB 716, CA.

35 *Sagulo, Brenca and Bakhouche Case* 8/77 [1977] ECR 1495.

36 *UNECTEF v Heylens Case* 222/84 [1987] ECR 4097 at para 15.

1.30   A certain tension has arisen, however, between the principle that member states need not create new remedies ('national autonomy'), and the principle that Community rights must be given effective protection ('effectiveness'). In *R v Secretary of State for Transport ex p Factortame Ltd (No 2),*[37] the ECJ held that any provision of a national legal system, and any legislative, administrative or judicial practice which impaired the effectiveness of Community law by withholding from the national courts the power to do everything necessary to set aside national legislative provisions, which might prevent, even temporarily, Community rules from having full force and effect are incompatible with the requirements of the EC Treaty. This was as much the case where the rule prevented the grant of relief in any given circumstances, including interim relief. Accordingly, 'a court which in those circumstances would grant interim relief, if it were not for a rule of national law, is obliged to set aside that rule'. It appears, therefore, that the principle of 'effectiveness' must take precedence over the principle of national autonomy.

1.31   In addition, in *Francovich*,[38] the ECJ held that each member state must make provision to permit claims for compensation against the state for breach of Community law. The court gave very little guidance concerning the circumstances in which such a remedy must be available, and such guidance as it did give related only to the non- or mis-implementation of directives: that the directive should entail the grant of rights to individuals; that it should be possible to identify the content of those rights from the provisions of the directive; and that there must be a causal link between the breach of the state's obligation and the harm suffered. The court has since added a further condition that the breach must be sufficiently serious.[39]

1.32   The UK courts have demonstrated a willingness to apply direct effective provisions directly, even if this involves setting aside an inconsistent Act of parliament, as in *R v Secretary of State for Transport ex p Factortame Ltd (No 2)* where the House of Lords spelt out that the operation of a statute may be suspended pending the resolution of a European challenge.[40] Judicial review of an inconsistent Act is also, now, possible.[41] In the case of non-directly effective provisions, the

37   [1991] 1 AC 603, HL.
38   *Francovich v Italy Case* C–6/90; *Bonifaci v Italy Case* C–9/90 [1991] ECR I–5357.
39   *Brasserie du Pecheur SA v Germany Case* C–46/93; *R v Secretary of State for Transport ex p Factortame Ltd and others* (No 3) C–48/93 [1996] ECR I–1029.
40   [1991] 1 AC 603, ECJ and HL.
41   *Equal Opportunities Commission v Secretary of State for Employment* [1995] 1 AC 1, HL.

courts have shown themselves willing to apply domestic legislation in conformity with them, even where this is not the prima facie meaning of the words used.[42]

Direct effect

1.33 This doctrine applies to treaty provisions, regulations and certain directives. It was first enunciated by the ECJ in the case of *Van Gend en Loos*.[43] In that case, which related to the imposition of import duties on goods imported from Germany to the Netherlands, the applicant appealed against payment of the duty, contending that it was in contravention of article 12 of the EC Treaty. The national court referred to the ECJ the question whether that article had direct application, in the sense that nationals of a state could use it as the basis of a claim to rights which the court must protect. The ECJ held that the Community constituted a new system of international law:

> ... for the benefit of which states have limited their sovereign rights, albeit within limited fields, and the subjects of which comprise not only member states but also their nationals. Independently of the legislation of member states, Community law therefore not only imposes obligations on individuals but is also intended to confer upon them rights which become part of their legal heritage. These rights arise not only where they are expressly granted by the Treaty, but also by reason of obligations which the Treaty imposes in a clearly defined way upon individuals as well as upon the member states and upon the institutions of the Community.[44]

1.34 The conditions for direct effect, laid down by the ECJ in *Van Gend en Loos*, were that the provision laid down a clear and unconditional prohibition, which was a negative obligation, not qualified by any reservation on the part of states and not requiring any legislative intervention by them.[45] The fact that the subjects of the obligation under article 12[46] were the member states themselves did not imply that their nationals could not benefit from the obligation.

1.35 The ECJ has extended this principle in subsequent cases. In *Reyners v Belgium*,[47] for example, it stated that the principles of freedom

---

42 See, eg, *Webb v EMO Air Cargo (UK) Ltd* [1993] 1 WLR 49; *Pickstone v Freemans* [1989] 1 AC 66, HL.

43 *NV Algemene Transporten Expeditie Onderneming van Gend en Loos v Nederlandse Administratie der Belastingen* Case 26/62 [1963] ECR 1.

44 [1963] ECR 1 at 12.

45 [1963] ECR 1 at 13.

46 Now EC Treaty art 25.

47 *Case* 2/74 [1974] ECR 631.

of movement and establishment by self-employed workers, and of non-discrimination were directly effective, even though the Community legislation implementing the relevant articles of the EC Treaty[48] had not yet been adopted. The rule of equal treatment with nationals was one of the fundamental legal provisions of the Community. It required the achievement of a precise result, made easier by implementing measures but not dependent upon them. The directives provided for by the EC Treaty were superfluous with regard to implementing the rule on nationality, as the treaty provisions had direct effect.[49]

1.36   The principle of direct effect also applies to regulations.[50] Th ECJ has also held that decisions, which apply only to their addressees, could be directly effective, notwithstanding that no reference is made in the EC Treaty to 'direct applicability' in respect of them. In *Franz Grad v Finanzamt Traunstein*,[51] the ECJ held that:

> Particularly in cases where, for example, the Community authorities by means of a decision have imposed an obligation upon a member state or all the member states to act in a certain way, the effectiveness ... of such a measure would be weakened if the nationals of that state could not invoke it in the courts and the national courts could not take it into consideration as part of Community law. Although the effects of a decision may not be identical with those of a provision contained in a regulation, this difference does not exclude the possibility that the end result, namely the right of the individual to invoke the measure before the courts, may be the same as that of a directly applicable provision of a regulation.[52]

1.37   The obligation imposed by the decision was sufficiently unconditional, clear and precise to be capable of having direct effect.

1.38   Directives always require implementation by the individual states, since they are binding as to their result, but allow the national state to determine the form and method of achieving that result.[53] This has not prevented the ECJ from ruling that directives are also capable of having direct effect, depending upon whether the nature, general

---

48 EC Treaty arts 43, 44 and 47 (formerly articles 52, 54 and 57).

49 See also *Defrenne v Societe Anonyme Belge de Navigation Aerienne Case* 43/75 [1976] ECR 455, in which the court held that the core principle of equal pay for equal work was directly effective, in a case where it was conceded that the female applicant, an air stewardess, was doing the same work as her male colleagues.

50 *Commission v Italy Case* 39/72 [1973] ECR 101; *Variola v Amministrazione delle Finanze Case* 34/73 [1973] ECR 981.

51 *Case* 9/70 [1970] ECR 825.

52 [1970] ECR 825 at [5].

53 See para 1.24 above.

scheme and wording of the provision in question are capable of having direct effects on the relations between member states and individuals. Moreover, article 234[54] – which enables national courts to refer to the ECJ questions concerning the validity and interpretation of all acts of the Community institutions, without distinction – implied that these acts may be invoked by individuals in the national courts.[55]

1.39   In a subsequent case, the ECJ emphasised that a member state should not be able to rely, as against individuals, on its own failure to implement the measures required by a directive within the prescribed period.

> It follows that a national court requested by a person who has complied with the provisions of a directive not to apply a national provision incompatible with the directive not incorporated into the internal legal order of a defaulting member state, must uphold that request if the obligation in question is unconditional and sufficiently precise.[56]

1.40   It was only once the prescribed period for implementation of the directive had expired, however, and in the event of default, that the directive could have direct effect. Until then, the member state remained 'free in the field'.[57]

Limits to the doctrine of direct effect

1.41   In order to have direct effect, the provision of the directive must be sufficiently clear, precise and unconditional. If there is any discretion left to the member state with regard to the particular provision, that provision will not be sufficiently precise and unconditional. In *Francovich*[58] the court had to determine whether Directive 80/987 on the protection of employees in the event of their employers' insolvency was sufficiently precise. Member states were required to set up guarantee institutions to protects employees' rights, but Italy had not done so within the stipulated time limit. The court held that the relevant provisions of the directive, which stated: 'member states shall lay down detailed rules for the organisation, financing and operation of the guarantee institutions ...' were not sufficiently precise. Member states enjoyed a wide discretion with regard to the organisation, the functioning and the financing of guarantee institutions. While the beneficiaries and the

---

54 Formerly EC Treaty art 177.
55 *Van Duyn v Home Office Case* 41/74 [1974] ECR 1337.
56 *Pubblico Ministero v Tullio Ratti Case* 148/78 [1979] ECR 1629.
57 [1979] ECR 1629.
58 *Francovich v Italy Case* C–6/90; *Bonifaci v Italy Case* C–9/90 [1991] ECR I–5357.

content of the guarantee could be determined, the provisions did not identify the institutions liable under the guarantee.

1.42   In *Marshall v Southampton and South-West Hampshire AHA (Teaching)*,[59] the ECJ held that the binding nature of a directive only existed in relation to 'each member state to which it is addressed'. It followed that a directive may not of itself impose obligations on an individual and that a provision of a directive may not be relied upon as against such a person, but only in an action against the state. The Court of Appeal, however, held that the plaintiff could rely on the directive in her claim against the Health Authority, on the basis that the authority was an emanation, or organ of the state.[60]

Organs of the state

1.43   The impact of the *Marshall* decision – that directly effective provisions could only be relied on in actions against the state – has been somewhat lessened by the broad definition of 'state', which the ECJ has adopted for the purpose of the enforcement of directives. It has been held that the 'state' will include 'all organs of the administration, including decentralised authorities such as municipalities.'[61] This is because directives are binding upon all the authorities of the member state.

1.44   For this purpose, then, local authorities and various other bodies are organs of the state, themselves required to apply the provisions of directly effective but unimplemented Community law in preference to inconsistent provisions of national law. In *Foster v British Gas plc*[62] it was held that:

> ... a body, whatever its legal form, which has been made responsible, pursuant to a measure adopted by the state, for providing a public service under the control of the state and has for that purpose special powers beyond those which result from the normal rules applicable in relations between individuals, is included in any event among the bodies against which the provisions of a directive capable of having direct effect may be relied upon.

Indirect effect

1.45   The ECJ has also held that even where directives cannot have direct effect, national law must be read and interpreted in the light of them and in such a way as to conform to their provisions, even in a case

59   *Case* 152/84 [1986] ECR 723.
60   [1986] 1 CMLR 688, CA.
61   *Fratelli Costanzo SpA v Comune di Milano Case* 103/88 [1989] ECR 1839.
62   *Case* 188/89 [1990] ECR I–3313.

between two private individuals, so that there was no organ of the state who could be held responsible for non-implementation of the directive.[63]

European public law doctrines

1.46 The doctrine of proportionality is one of a number of European law doctrines[64] for determining the legality of administrative action, which is only now finding acceptance in English law where fundamental rights are at stake, and potentially even where they are not.[65] It involves a closer level of scrutiny than the traditional tests available to the court in judicial review and has the potential, therefore, to facilitate a more interventionist approach. A full discussion of the principles of the European public law doctrines can be found elsewhere in this book.[66]

European human rights law

European Court of Human Rights jurisprudence

Interpretation of Convention rights

1.47 The European Court of Human Rights (ECHR) distinguishes between two kinds of complaint: those where what is alleged is an 'interference' with a right (ie, a positive, detrimental act of interference); and those where it is claimed that positive action is required in order to guarantee the right. In either case, it is necessary, first, to establish on the true construction of the European Convention on Human Rights (the Convention), whether the right relied on is even capable of protecting the applicant from the conduct complained of. For this purpose, the court utilises a number of different methods of construction: such as

---

63 *Marleasing SA v La Comercial Internacionale de Alimentacion SA Case C–106/89* [1990] ECR I–4135.

64 Including that of the margin of appreciation.

65 See *R (Alconbury Ltd) v Secretary of State for the Environment, Transport and the Regions* [2001] UKHL 23, [2001] 2 All ER 929 per Lord Slynn at [51]; *R (Daly) v Secretary of State for the Home Department* [2001] UKHL 26; [2001] 2 AC 532, per Lord Cooke at [32]; *Association of British Civilian Internees – Far Eastern Region v Secretary of State for Defence* [2003] EWCA Civ 473, per Dyson LJ at [34].

66 See below, paras 1.52–1.60 in the context of European human rights law, and paras 6.14–6.33 in the context of the approach of the UK courts since enactment of the Human Rights Act 1998.

taking the ordinary meaning of the words used in the provisions;[67] or subjecting the Convention to a grammatical analysis, which involves comparing the English and French versions of the text;[68] considering the importance of the provision in the context of the whole Convention and attempting to ascertain the meaning of the provision in question by analysing its position in the Convention.[69]

1.48   Use may be made of the background papers, or *travaux preparatoires*, of the Convention,[70] but not if the meaning of the words used in the Convention are sufficiently clear and in keeping with the purpose of the Convention.[71] Their use may also be limited if the court is employing an 'evolutive' or purposive approach.

Purposive approach to construction

1.49   Most important among these methods of construction is the purposive approach.[72] The court will construe the Convention by considering its aim, which is the protection of individual rights:

> In interpreting the Convention, regard must be had to its special charac-
> ter as a treaty for the collective enforcement of human rights and funda-
> mental freedoms ... Thus the object and purpose of the Convention as an
> instrument for the protection of individual human beings require that its
> provisions be interpreted and applied so as to make its safeguards practi-
> cal and effective ... In addition, any interpretation of the rights and freedoms
> guaranteed has to be consistent with 'the general spirit of the Conven-
> tion, an instrument designed to maintain and promote the ideals and
> values of a democratic society.'[73]

1.50   The ECHR has emphasised in a number of decisions[74] that the Convention is a living document, and that interpretation of its meaning must be considered in the light of prevailing conditions at the time of the alleged breach, rather that at the date of drafting of the Convention itself. Having said that, the court cannot, by means of such

---

67   *Johnston v Ireland* (1986) A–112; (1987) 9 EHRR 203.

68   *Lawless v Ireland* (1961) A–3; *Brogan v United Kingdom* (1988) A–145-B.

69   *Klass v Germany* (1978) A–28.

70   *Johnston v Ireland* (1986) A–112; (1987) 9 EHRR 203; *Glasenapp v Federal Republic of Germany* (1986) A–104.

71   *Lawless v Ireland* (1961) A–3.

72   See paras 1.26–1.27 above, in relation to the ECJ approach.

73   *Kjeldsen, Busk Madsen and Petersen v Denmark* (1976) A–23, para 53.

74   For example, *Marckx v Belgium* (1979) A–31; *Johnston v Ireland* (1986) A–112.

an evolutive approach, derive from the Convention and the protocols a right which was not present at the outset.[75]

1.51 If the Convention right relied on, on its true construction, is not capable of protecting the applicant from the conduct complained of, that is plainly an end of the matter. If it is so capable, the court then looks to see whether that conduct did, in fact, violate the right relied on. The approach of the ECHR to the question brings into play a number of other legal concepts, and is of particular relevance in the context of the responsibilities of public authorities.

European public law doctrines[76]

Margin of appreciation

1.52 National authorities are accorded a 'margin of appreciation' in the manner in which they guarantee the Convention rights of their citizens. The wider the variations between the practices of different signatory states, the wider this margin of appreciation is likely to be. Thus, in *Johnston*[77] the court held, in respect of the applicant's claim that under article 8 of the Convention, he had a right to be able to obtain a divorce, that:

> ... the notion of 'respect' is not clear-cut: having regard to the diversity of the practices followed and the situations obtaining in the contracting states, the notion's requirements will vary considerably from case to case. Accordingly, this is an area in which the contracting parties enjoy a wide margin of appreciation in determining the steps to be taken to ensure compliance with the Convention with due regard to the needs and resources of the community and of individuals ...[78]

Balance

1.53 The language of the court's reference to the 'needs and resources of the community and of individuals' is in terms of a balance. The court has emphasised the balancing exercise to be undertaken:

---

75 See, eg, *Johnston v Ireland* (1986) A–112; (1987) 9 EHRR 203.

76 This is considered elsewhere at paras 6.14–6.33, in the context of the application of the doctrine by the UK courts since the enactment of the Human Rights Act 1998.

77 *Johnston v Ireland* (1986) A–112; (1987) 9 EHRR 203.

78 (1986) A–112 at para 55(c).

... regard must be had to the fair balance that has to be struck between the general interest of the community and the interests of the individual, the search for which balance is inherent in the whole of the Convention.[79]

1.54   This balancing exercise may even fall to be undertaken in cases where the Convention does not itself allow for limitations or restrictions on rights. In *Soering v United Kingdom*,[80] it was alleged that the UK was in breach of article 3 of the Convention (which – as the court emphasised – makes provision for no exceptions or derogations) by deciding to extradite the applicant to the United States where he was to be tried for capital murder in Virginia. The applicant thus ran the risk of exposure to the 'death row phenomenon', which was alleged to be inhuman and/or degrading treatment and/or punishment.

1.55   The ECHR held that, in interpreting and applying the notions of inhuman or degrading treatment or punishment, one of the factors to be taken into account – indeed inherent in the whole of the Convention – was:

> ... [a] search for a fair balance between the demands of the general interest of the community and the requirements of the protection of the individual's fundamental rights. As movement about the world becomes easier and crime takes on a larger international dimension, it is increasingly in the interest of all nations that suspected offenders who flee abroad should be brought to justice. Conversely, the establishment of safe havens for fugitives would not only result in danger for the state obliged to harbour the protected person but also tend to undermine the foundations of extradition.[81]

Proportionality

1.56   Consideration of proportionality may take a number of forms, and arise in a number of different contexts relating both to the interference itself, and/or to any number of subsidiary questions which the ECHR is required to answer in order to arrive at a conclusion.[82]

1.57   A challenge, for example, by a lawyer to the Belgian legal professional requirement to undertake pro bono work for clients who could not afford to pay, on the basis that this amounted to forced or com-

---

79   See, in other contexts, among others, *James v United Kingdom* (1986) 1986 A–98, para 50, and *Sporrong and Lönnroth v Sweden* (1982) A–52, para 69; *Rees v United Kingdom* (1986) A–106, para 37.

80   (1989) 11 EHRR 439.

81   (1989) 11 EHRR 439 at [89].

82   See, eg, *Soering v United Kingdom* (1989) 11 EHRR 439 at [104] and [110] where the proportionality was considered in a number of different contexts.

pulsory labour in contravention of article 4 of the Convention, failed, in part because the court did not consider the burden imposed by this requirement to be disproportionate. The amount of time the applicant was required to spend on pro bono work allowed sufficient time for the performance of his paid work.[83]

1.58   In *Gaskin v United Kingdom*,[84] it was alleged that the UK was, by article 8 of the Convention, under a positive obligation to allow the applicant access to personal records concerning his having been taken into care. The court held that the UK system of allowing access to such records with the consent of the contributor was in principle 'compatible with the obligation under article 8, taking into account the State's margin of appreciation'.

1.59   Such a system, however, must also secure the right of access where a contributor was not available to consent or withheld that consent improperly:

> Such a system is only in conformity with the principle of proportionality if it provides that an independent authority finally decides whether access has to be granted in cases where a contributor fails to answer or withholds consent.[85]

1.60   Accordingly, a breach of the Convention was established.

United Kingdom courts' approach prior to the Human Rights Act 1998

1.61   In a series of cases in the 1970s, the Court of Appeal came close to giving effect to the Convention in domestic law, even though (subsequently) this approach was renounced. In *R v Secretary of State for the Home Department ex p Phansopkar*,[86] Lord Scarman held that it was the duty of public authorities administering the law, as well as the courts, to have regard to the Convention:

> It may, of course, happen under our law that the basic rights to justice undeferred and to respect for family and private life have to yield to the express requirements of a statute. But in my judgment it is the duty of the courts, so long as they do not defy or disregard clear unequivocal provision, to construe statutes in a manner which promotes, not endangers, those rights. Problems of ambiguity or omission, if they arise under the language of an Act, should be resolved so as to give effect to, or at the very

---

83   *Van der Mussele v Belgium* (1983) A–70, para 39.

84   (1989) A–160.

85   *Gaskin v United Kingdom* (1989) A–160 at [49].

86   [1976] QB 606, CA.

least so as not to derogate from the rights recognised by Magna Carta and the European Convention.[87]

1.62   Similarly, in *R v Secretary of State for the Home Department ex p Bhajan Singh*,[88] Lord Denning MR stated that both immigration officers and the secretary of state should take account of the principles set out in the Convention when carrying out their duties, since they were under a public law duty to act fairly and the Convention was a statement of the principles of fair dealing.

1.63   There followed a period of retrenchment by the courts, most famously in *R v Secretary of State for the Home Department ex p Brind*[89] in which the House of Lords confirmed that the Convention was no part of English law, and so a failure to act in accordance with it would not give rise to a ground for judicial review. While the presumption that Parliament intended to legislate in conformity with it might be resorted to in order to resolve an ambiguity or uncertainty in a statutory provision, there was no presumption that the Secretary of State's discretion must be exercised in accordance with it.[90]

1.64   An alternative view, which found favour in *Brind* in the Court of Appeal,[91] and to some extent in *Porter v Magill* in the Divisional Court,[92] was that the protections afforded to the individual by the common law were coterminous with those afforded by the Convention. Moreover, in *R v Ministry of Defence ex p Smith*[93] it was held by the Court of Appeal that Convention could be used as an aid to the construction of the common law as well as statute.

The Human Rights Act 1998

1.65   The Human Rights Act (HRA) 1998 is the vehicle for introducing Convention rights into domestic law. The Act does not, however,

---

87   [1976] QB 606 at 626F–G.

88   [1976] QB 198, at 207F.

89   [1991] 1 AC 696, HL.

90   [1991] 1 AC 696 at 748 per Lord Bridge; at 760–762 per Lord Ackner. See also *Derbyshire CC v Times Newspapers Ltd* [1994] AC 534, HL, per Lord Keith of Kinkel at 550–551.

91   *R v Secretary of State for the Home Department ex p Brind* [1991] 1 AC 696, HL, per Lord Donaldson MR at 717E.

92   (1998) 30 HLR 997, DC, where the court held that there was no distinction which could be drawn between the rights conferred by article 6 of the Convention (see paras 6.115–6.133 below) and those conferred by the common law. See now the decision of the House of Lords at [2001] UKHL 67; [2002] AC 357.

93   [1996] QB 517, CA.

incorporate the Convention. Instead, it includes the majority (but not all) of such rights in its Schedule 1, as rights incompatibly with which public authorities must not act, and compatibly with which the courts must construe legislation if it is possible to do so. While the Act does not require challenges to the conduct of public authorities to be brought by way of judicial review, this is nevertheless the most appropriate method of challenge in most cases, not least because the claimant is likely to be seeking one or more of the public law remedies available only on judicial review and is likely also to wish to raise other public law grounds of challenge.

Acting compatibly

1.66   Human Rights Act 1998 s6(1) is the provision that renders it unlawful for a public authority to act in a way which is incompatible with any of the Convention rights contained in Schedule 1. 'Acting' includes a failure to act.[94] The definition of 'public authority', for these purposes and more generally is considered elsewhere.[95]

1.67   The general prohibition on acting incompatibly with Convention rights is subject to two defences, provided by HRA 1998 s6(2). The language used to create these defences is as follows:

(2) Subsection (1) does not apply to an act if –
    (a) as a result of one or more provisions of primary legislation, the authority could not have acted differently;
    or
    (b) in the case of one or more provisions of, or made under, primary legislation which cannot be read or given effect in a way which is compatible with the Convention rights, the authority was acting so as to give effect to or enforce those provisions.

1.68   In *R (Bono) v Harlow DC*,[96] it was held that the HRA 1998 s6(2)(b) defence would only save an act carried out under the requirements of subordinate legislation if the subordinate legislation itself could not have been framed in terms which would have complied with the Convention because of incompatible primary legislation. It was not sufficient that the subordinate legislation did not comply (if it could have done) and was in force to require the authority's compliance with it.

---

94   HRA 1998 s6(6).
95   Chapter 2, paras 2.53–2.74.
96   [2002] EWHC 423 (Admin); [2002] 1 WLR 2475.

Reading legislation compatibly

1.69   In addition, the courts are obliged to read and give effect to primary and subordinate legislation so far as they can in a way that is compatible with the Convention rights.[97] If this is not possible, the validity of the legislation is not affected, but the court may be able to make a declaration of incompatibility in appropriate circumstances.[98]

1.70   The court has no power to strike down incompatible primary legislation, only to declare it to be incompatible. Such a declaration, if made, does not affect the validity or continued enforceability of the legislation. Nor does it affect the rights of the parties to the claim in which the declaration is made. In the case of subordinate legislation, the courts may strike it down unless the primary legislation under which it was made prevents the removal of the incompatibility. In the latter case, again, a declaration of incompatibility is all that is available.[99]

Interpreting Convention rights

1.71   In approaching their tasks under the HRA 1998, the courts are obliged to have regard to the jurisprudence of the ECHR.[100] They are not, however, bound by it or obliged to adopt or follow it even on the construction or effect of Convention rights. As Laws LJ has stated:

> But I should say that I think it important to have in mind that the court's task under the HRA, in this context as in many others, is not simply to add on the Strasbourg learning to the corpus of English law, as if it were a compulsory adjunct taken from an alien source, but to develop a municipal law of human rights by the incremental method of the common law, case by case, taking account of the Strasbourg jurisprudence as HRA section 2 enjoins us to do.[101]

---

97   HRA 1998 s3.

98   HRA 1998 ss3 and 4.

99   HRA 1998 s4, and see *R (Bono) v Harlow DC* [2002] EWHC 423 (Admin); [2002] 1 WLR 2475.

100   HRA 1998 s2(1). Account must be taken of any judgment, decision, declaration or advisory opinion of the court, any opinion of the Commission in a report adopted under art 31 of the Convention, and decision of the Commission in connection with art 26 or art 27(2) of the Convention, and any decision of the Committee of Ministers taken under art 46 of the Convention.

101   *Runa Begum v Tower Hamlets LBC* [2002] EWCA Civ 239; [2002] 1 WLR 2491, per Laws LJ at [17]. (The House of Lords decision on appeal is at [2003] UKHL 5; [2003] 2 AC 430).

The courts' response to the Human Rights Act 1998

1.73   The courts' response to and treatment of the Human Rights Act (HRA) 1998 has been mixed. On the one hand, and looked at as a whole, the body of substantive rights and protections conferred by UK law in relation to the specific matters addressed by the European Convention do not look very different three years after the 1998 Act came into force than they did before its enactment. The courts have in general not applied the Act to expand the content of rights available to people in their dealings with public authorities.

1.74   In contrast, the court's response to the HRA 1998 – in terms of its effect on the process of judicial review itself, including the kinds of issues which the court may review, the degree of judicial scrutiny which should be applied on that review and the principles which govern the application of that scrutiny – has been quietly revolutionary. It entails, at least where 'fundamental rights' are at stake, a considerably more interventionist model of judicial review (based on the doctrine of proportionality) and an objective assessment by the court of the positive justification for the decision under challenge which has to be offered by the defendant. Even the possibility of a 'full-merits' review, ie, review of the facts, has become accepted in some contexts.[102] Recently, the Court of Appeal has suggested dispensing with the doctrine of *Wednesbury*[103] unreasonableness altogether, whether or not there were any human rights of European flavour to the challenge, in favour of the more precise and sophisticated model of judicial review offered by proportionality.[104]

1.75   The detail of this latter response, in so far as it has affected the very essence of judicial review, is described elsewhere throughout this book, in relation to each of the substantive public law concepts and issues which are considered in the following chapters. It should

---

102   See, in particular, *R v Secretary of State for the Home Department ex p Mahmood* [2001] 1 WLR 840, CA; *R (Daly) v Secretary of State for the Home Department* [2001] UKHL 26; [2001] 2 AC 532; *R (Wilkinson) v Broadmoor Special Hospital Authority* [2001] EWCA Civ 1545; [2002] 1 WLR 419; (2002) 5 CCLR 121. See also the general overview, in the Introduction at pp5–6 above and the cases cited there.

103   *Associated Provincial Picture Houses v Wednesbury Corporation* [1948] 1 KB 223, CA.

104   *Association of British Civilian Internees – Far Eastern Region v Secretary of State for Defence* [2003] EWCA Civ 473, at [34]. The Court of Appeal recognised that only the House of Lords could abolish the *Wednesbury* doctrine (but refused leave to appeal to the House of Lords).

certainly not be thought that UK law and Strasbourg law are now in any sense identical in relation to these issues. Nevertheless, probably the most striking aspect of the courts' response to the Human Rights Act 1998 has been the complete reversal of the judicial antipathy towards proportionality, in favour of its wholehearted embracement.

CHAPTER 2

Bodies amenable to judicial review

Bodies amenable to review

2.1 In general terms, there are three types of body whose decisions may be challenged by way of judicial review:

(a) inferior courts;
(b) tribunals; and
(c) other bodies performing public acts and duties, including local authorities.

2.2 Broadly, the same categories of body are public authorities for the purposes of the Human Rights Act 1998,[1] with the obvious difference that superior courts as well as inferior courts are included within that definition.

Inferior courts

2.3 These are the county courts, magistrates' courts, coroners' courts and, in some circumstances, the Crown Court.

County courts

2.4 The High Court has long asserted a supervisory jurisdiction to control the county court,[2] even where Parliament had, on the face of it, sought to oust such jurisdiction.[3]

2.5 In *R (Sivasubramaniam) v Wandsworth County Court*,[4] the Court of Appeal considered again the principles applicable to the availability of judicial review in respect of decisions of the county court. The appellant had brought judicial review proceedings against two decisions of a circuit judge.

2.6 The first decision challenged was a refusal of permission to appeal from a decision of the district judge. By virtue of the Access to Justice

---

1 Human Rights Act 1998 s6. The definition of 'public authority' under this section is discussed below at paras 2.62–2.74.

2 *R v HHJ Sir Shirley Worthington-Evans ex p Madan* [1959] 2 All ER 457; *R v Keighley County Court ex p Home Insulation Ltd* [1989] COD 174; *R v HHJ Sir Donald Hurst ex p Smith* [1960] 2 All ER 385; *R v Wandsworth County Court ex p Munn* (1994) 26 HLR 697, QBD; *In re Racal Communications Ltd* [1981] AC 374.

3 See, eg, County Courts Act 1959 s107.

4 [2002] EWCA Civ 1738.

Act 1999 and Civil Procedure Rules (CPR) Pt 52,[5] there is no further right of appeal from a refusal of permission to appeal. The second was the circuit judge's refusal to set aside an award made by the District Judge in arbitration proceedings which had been concluded some years previously. Permission to apply for judicial review was refused. The claimant appealed to the Court of Appeal.

2.7   On the appeal, the Lord Chancellor was permitted to intervene to contend that either: (a) the CPR Pt 52 procedure impliedly ousted the court's supervisory jurisdiction or that (b) in any event, judicial review should be refused on principle by the court, given that Parliament had legislated so that the right of litigants to seek a review of judicial decisions is limited to the CPR Pt 52 procedure (including the unavailability of any further right of appeal from a refusal of permission to appeal).[6] It would be contrary to this clear legislative policy to permit it to be circumvented by entertaining judicial review applications in respect of refusals of permission to appeal.

2.8   The Court of Appeal dismissed both of the appellant's appeals. Regarding the refusal to set aside the award, the appellant had an alternative remedy, by way of a right of appeal under CPR Pt 52, which he ought to have utilised. The only exception to the general rule that judicial review of a discretionary decision would not be permitted where there was an alternative remedy, was where the alternative remedy was less satisfactory than judicial review. Usually, however, a right of appeal would be more convenient and judicial review would be refused, save in exceptional cases (an example of which the Court of Appeal could not envisage).[7]

2.9   In the situation where permission to appeal had been refused, the Court of Appeal rejected the argument that Access to Justice Act (AJA) 1999 s54(4) had impliedly ousted the court's power to entertain judicial review proceedings in an appropriate case. There was a clear line of authority that only the clearest words could have effect to oust certiorari,[8] which left no room for implied ouster. It was, nevertheless,

---

5   Access to Justice Act 1999 s54(4) provides that no appeal may be made against a decision of a court to grant or refuse permission to appeal. See also Access to Justice Act 1999 ss54(1), (3) and 56(1); The Access to Justice Act 1999 (Destination of Appeals) Order 2000 SI No 1071 (in force from 2 May 2000); and CPR rr52.3 and 52.13.

6   That is, by Access to Justice Act 1999 s54.

7   *R (Sivasubramaniam) v Wandsworth County Court* [2002] EWCA Civ 1738; [2003] 1 WLR 475, per Lord Phillips of Worth Matravers MR at [47]–[48].

8   See, eg, *R v Medical Appeal Tribunal ex p Gilmore* [1957] 1 QB 574, per Denning LJ at 585.

contrary to principle for litigants to be able to circumvent the legislative policy of the AJA 1999 by the use of judicial review proceedings. Parliament, while not having ousted the court's jurisdiction, had not contemplated the spate of applications of this sort, and it was disproportionate and inappropriate for the Administrative Court judges to be required to deal with such matters where one judge (ie, on the application for permission to appeal) had already reviewed the decision complained of and found there to have been no grounds for appeal.

2.10   Accordingly, judges should summarily refuse permission to apply for judicial review in such cases in the exercise of their discretion, for the reason that the CPR Pt 52 procedure was proportionate and sensible, and all issues regarding the legality of the decision sought to be appealed could be raised on an application for permission to appeal. The same reasoning would apply to any judicial review claim in respect of a grant of permission to appeal, should such a claim be brought.[9]

2.11   Judicial review would only be available in exceptional circumstances such as in the rare case where the challenge to the decision was founded on a claim of old-style jurisdictional error (ie, where the error arose outside – rather than from – the reasons given for refusing permission to appeal, the judge having stepped outside or misunderstood his powers) or where a procedural irregularity had occurred of a kind that constituted a denial of the claimant's right to a fair hearing.[10] This did not affect the susceptibility to judicial review of refusals of permission to appeal by the Immigration Appeal Tribunal, which was based on 'special factors' specifically applicable to immigration appeals.[11]

Magistrates' courts

2.12   In relation to decisions made by magistrates' or county court circuit judges, judicial review may, on occasion, be a more appropriate remedy than appeal, although in general, both remedies may be available. Although the position is, in principle at least, analogous to that in

---

9   *R (Sivasubramaniam) v Wandsworth County Court* [2002] EWCA Civ 1738; [2003] 1 WLR 475, at [53]–[55].

10   [2002] EWCA Civ 1738 at [56].

11   [2002] EWCA Civ 1738 at [52]. The judicial review jurisdiction has, anyway, now been replaced by a 'statutory review' procedure: see CPR Pt 54, Section II and below at paras 18.148–18.154.

Sivasubramaniam[12] in so far as the right to appeal magistrates' decisions will constitute an alternative remedy which generally ought to be used, nevertheless, judicial review of the magistrates' is far more common and widely accepted than of the county court.

2.13 Where, in particular, the essence of the challenge is not to the substance of the court's decision but to the manner in which it was reached, judicial review can be the proper procedure to use.[13] Where a court has been asked to state a case and has refused, *Sivasubramaniam* could, by analogy, apply to preclude judicial review. On the other hand, judicial review of a refusal by magistrates to state a case on the ground that it is 'frivolous' has long been accepted as permissible.

2.14 There are signs, however, that the courts are moving towards a more strict requirement that rights of appeal should be used, where they are available. In *R (Clark-Darby) v Highbury Magistrates' Court*,[14] the making by the magistrates' court of a council tax liability order was challenged by way of judicial review. The claimant alleged that she had not received notice of the hearing and so had not been able to put her defence. The local authority challenged the use of judicial review procedure, suggesting that the claimant ought to have appealed to the Divisional Court by way of case stated.

2.15 The court held that it was bound by the decision in *R v Hereford Magistrates' Court ex p Rowlands*,[15] which had decided that the claimant was entitled to use judicial review. The judge, Sir Richard Tucker, nevertheless suggested that where points of 'pure' law were concerned, as distinct from breaches of natural justice, the appropriate route and the one primarily intended by Parliament for the correction of errors of law is an appeal by way of case stated to the Divisional Court.

2.16 It has been held that the High Court is not concerned with a miscarriage of justice arising on the evidence, and that quashing, mandatory or prohibiting orders should only be made if:

- the court has failed properly to exercise its jurisdiction;

---

12 *R (Sivasubramaniam) v Wandsworth County Court* [2002] EWCA Civ 1738. The comments of the court concerning the permissibility of a challenge to a refusal of permission to appeal do not apply, because there is no requirement of permission to appeal in criminal cases: Supreme Court Act 1981 s18; Access to Justice Act 1999 s54(2).

13 See, eg, *R v Bristol Magistrate' Court ex p Rowles* [1994] COD 137, DC; but see also *R v Folkestone Magistrates' Court ex p Bradley* [1994] COD 138.

14 [2001] EWHC Admin 959.

15 [1998] QB 110.

- some error of law appears on the face of the record, or
- there has been a breach of the principles of natural justice, etc.[16]

Quashing orders[17]

2.17   So long as the justices have not exceeded their powers, certiorari cannot be used to challenge the exercise of their discretion, for example, a decision on how much weight to give a piece of evidence, or an acquittal after a trial on the merits.[18] If, however, there has been an error in procedure, such as where an order has been made or sentence passed which is not authorised by law, or where there has been an invalid committal for sentence, then quashing orders can be used effectively. In *K v Hendon Justices ex p Director of Public Prosecutions*,[19] it was held that an order of certiorari (quashing order) would lie to quash an acquittal where the information had been dismissed for want of prosecution, due to the late attendance at court of the prosecutor, ie, without a trial on the merits.[20]

2.18   If, moreover, the High Court considers that a convicted person's sentence was in excess of the magistrates' jurisdiction, it may substitute the proper sentence which the lower court did have power to impose. It appears that a sentence which is so harsh and oppressive that no reasonable tribunal could have passed it may be regarded as in excess of jurisdiction.[21] A defendant should, however, appeal against sentence to the Crown Court before seeking permission to apply for judicial review.[22]

Mandatory orders

2.19   A mandatory order requires a judge or justices to do an act relating to the duties of their office. It will not be granted where some form of appeal exists which would be equally effective. Such an order will only

16   For example, *R v Bristol Magistrate' Court ex p Rowles* [1994] COD 137, DC; but see also *R v Folkestone Magistrates' Court ex p Bradley* [1994] COD 138. See also *In re Racal Communications* [1981] AC 374, HL, per Lord Diplock at 383.

17   For a more detailed consideration of the remedies available in judicial review proceedings, see chapter 5 below.

18   *R v Dorking Justices ex p Harrington* [1984] AC 743, HL.

19   [1993] COD 61, DC.

20   See also *R v Stipendiary Magistrates ex p Director of Serious Fraud Office* [1994] COD 509, DC, where it was held that judicial review was appropriate where the magistrates' decision contained serious errors of law on its face. It was not necessary to state a case.

21   *R v St Albans' Crown Court ex p Cinnamond* [1981] QB 480, DC.

22   *R v Battle Justices ex p Shepherd and Another* (1983) 5 Cr App R (S) 124, DC. See generally chapter 7 below.

be appropriate where there has been a wrongful refusal of jurisdiction, rather than an error in the exercise of that jurisdiction.[23] It will, therefore, not be appropriate where, for instance, there has been a refusal to receive admissible evidence or to allow a line of cross-examination. In such a situation, the justices, although perhaps acting wrongly, are not acting outside their jurisdiction.

2.20   A mandatory order may, however, be sought, for example, in relation to a decision to refuse to grant public funding for extraneous reasons or a refusal to consider each case on its merits. In *R v Brown*,[24] magistrates who refused to try an information on the basis that other persons ought also to have been charged were compelled by mandamus to do so.

Prohibiting orders

2.21   These will only be appropriate where the proceedings to be reviewed are not yet concluded and so there is a possibility of correcting the alleged defect. A classic example is where there has been inordinate delay in bringing a matter to trial and the justices have ordered that the trial go ahead, failing to consider who caused the delay and whether the defendant has been prejudiced by it.[25]

Ultra vires as a defence[26]

2.22   Public law challenges may also be used as a shield. An individual, for example, charged with an offence of contravening subordinate legislation or a decision of a public body, or acting without a relevant licence may wish to raise as a defence to those proceedings the invalidity of the measure or decision that he is charged with contravening.

2.23   In *Boddington v British Transport Police*,[27] the defendant was convicted of a charge of smoking in a railway carriage where smoking was prohibited, contrary to a railway byelaw.[28] He sought to defend himself on the basis that the relevant byelaw was ultra vires and void, but was not permitted to do so. The House of Lords held that a defendant to a criminal charge was entitled as a matter of right to raise such

23   See *In re Racal Communications* [1981] AC 374, HL and *R (Sivasubramaniam) v Wandsworth County Court* [2002] EWCA Civ 1738; [2003] 1 WLR 475.

24   (1857) 7 E&B 757.

25   *R v West London Stipendiary Magistrate ex p Anderson* (1984) 148 JP 683, QBD.

26   See, in general, chapter 3 below.

27   [1999] 2 AC 143, HL.

28   Contrary to byelaw 20 of the British Railways Board's Byelaws 1965, made under the authority of Transport Act 1962 s67(1).

a defence, absent a clear parliamentary intention to the contrary. The presumption, moreover, that a legislative measure was valid until a court ruled otherwise did not affect the principle that once a court decided it to be ultra vires, it was void from the start and would be treated as never having had any legal effect.[29]

Crown Court

2.24   The Crown Court, which is not an inferior court, is nonetheless susceptible to judicial review except in matters relating to trial on indictment.[30] In the main, Crown Court decisions in respect of the court's appellate jurisdiction from the magistrates' court, or where there has been a committal for sentence, will be reviewable. In *R v Wolverhampton Crown Court ex p Crofts*,[31] the prosecution successfully applied for judicial review of a decision by the Crown Court to allow an appeal from the magistrates, where the evidence on which the appeal had been allowed had been shown to the Crown Court to be false.

2.25   In *R v Harrow Crown Court ex p Dave*,[32] however, the court took the view that decisions of the Crown Court exercising its appellate jurisdiction should not be challenged by way of judicial review when it is clear from the decision that the issue could be resolved on an appeal by way of case stated.[33] In fact, in *ex p Dave* itself, the court quashed the decision in question, and held that when sitting in an appellate capacity, the court must give sufficient reasons to demonstrate that it had identified the main issues in contention in the case and how it had resolved each of them.

2.26   In *R v Inner London Crown Court ex p Bentham*,[34] a local authority admitted the offence of statutory nuisance, on a prosecution brought by one of its tenants.[35] The magistrates made a nuisance order requiring the carrying out of specified works. The authority appealed to the Crown Court against the order. The Crown Court refused an application for legal aid by the prosecutor (ie, the tenant – the victim of the nuisance). The basis for the refusal was that she did not fall within the relevant

29   [1999] 2 AC 143 per Lord Irvine of Lairg LC, at p155B–D. See further at paras 7.28–7.31 below.

30   Supreme Court Act 1981 s29(3).

31   [1983] 1 WLR 204, QBD.

32   [1994] 1 WLR 98, DC.

33   [1994] 1 WLR 98 at 107E.

34   [1989] 1 WLR 408, CA.

35   The prosecution was brought under the Public Health Act 1936, now Environmental Protection Act 1990 s82.

provisions of the Legal Aid Act 1974, as she was not a person resisting an appeal by a person convicted or sentenced by the magistrates. The applicant successfully applied to quash that decision, as the Crown Court had erred in law in its interpretation of the Act.

Matters relating to trial on indictment

2.27 The general exclusion of judicial review of matters relating to trial on indictment has been given a relatively narrow construction by the courts.[36]

2.28 In *Re Smalley*,[37] the House of Lords, while declining to prescribe in the abstract any precise test, offered a 'helpful pointer' to the legislative purposes behind the provision, namely to exclude review:

> ... of any decision affecting the conduct of a trial on indictment, whether given in the course of the trial or by way of pre-trial directions.[38]

2.29 A further helpful pointer was offered by Lord Browne-Wilkinson in *R v Manchester Crown Court ex p Director of Public Prosecutions*,[39] where he said:

> It may ... be a helpful further pointer ... to ask the question 'Is the decision sought to be reviewed one arising in the issue between the Crown and the defendant formulated by the indictment (including the costs of such issue)?' If the answer is 'Yes', then to permit the decision to be challenged by judicial review may lead to delay in the trial: the matter is therefore probably excluded from review by the section. If the answer is 'No', the decision of the Crown Court is truly collateral to the indictment of the defendant and judicial review of that decision will not delay his trial: therefore it may well not be excluded by the section.[40]

2.30 In *R v Maidstone Crown Court ex p Harrow LBC*,[41] the Divisional Court held that the provisions of Supreme Court Act (SCA) 1981 s29(3) did not bite where the Crown Court had acted entirely without jurisdiction. In that case, the defendant had pleaded not guilty by way of insanity. The judge had neither held a trial of that issue before the jury, nor had the defendant been convicted of the offence. The judge

---

36 See especially *Re Smalley* [1985] AC 622, HL and *In re Sampson* [1987] 1 WLR 194, HL.

37 [1985] AC 622, HL.

38 [1985] AC 622 per Lord Bridge of Harwich at 642F.

39 [1993] 4 All ER 928; [1993] 1 WLR 1524, HL.

40 [1993] 4 All ER 928 at 933J–934A.

41 [2000] QB 719; [2000] 2 WLR 237, DC.

nevertheless, without jurisdiction, imposed an order requiring the defendant to be supervised by Harrow LBC's social services department for two years. There was no right of appeal, the defendant not having been convicted.

2.31   The Divisional Court held that in such a case, it was entitled to accept jurisdiction notwithstanding that the order which had been made was unarguably a matter relating to trial on indictment, which would not ordinarily be amenable to judicial review. Where the foundation of the judicial review application was absence of jurisdiction, as distinct from a challenge to the quality of a decision that was within jurisdiction, the court would not decline jurisdiction just because of SCA 1981 s29(3). The court enjoyed a supervisory jurisdiction over all Crown Court decisions save where the Crown Court exercised its jurisdiction relating to trial on indictment; Parliament cannot have intended, however, in enacting SCA 1981 s29(3), that decisions wholly outside the Crown Court's jurisdiction which were also unappealable, would remain effective and uncorrected.[42]

2.32   Supreme Court Act 1981 s29(3) has been held to be compatible with Convention rights under the Human Rights Act 1998. In *R (Shields) v Liverpool Crown Court*,[43] the Divisional Court held that a defendant's right to appeal against conviction provided an effective remedy for the purposes of article 6 (right to a fair trial). There was no requirement under the European Convention on Human Rights that a remedy must be provided at an earlier stage. Accordingly, there was no right to seek judicial review of the judge's refusal to extend legal aid to enable the defendant to instruct Queen's Counsel.

2.33   The court reached the same conclusion in *R v Canterbury Crown Court ex p Regentford Ltd*,[44] holding that SCA 1981 s29(3) precluded an acquitted defendant challenging by judicial review the judge's refusal to make a costs order in its favour, and that although there was no right of appeal against that decision, the exclusion of judicial review was not incompatible with any Convention right, as there was no Convention right to have decisions reviewed by judicial review.[45]

---

42   See also *R (Kenneally) v Snaresbrook Crown Court* [2001] EWHC Admin 968; [2002] QB 1169, DC.

43   [2001] EWHC Admin 90; [2001] ACD 325, DC.

44   [2001] HRLR 18.

45   The court considered, however, that the failure of English law to provide any remedy, may well conflict with article 13 of the European Convention on Human Rights and therefore the UK's treaty obligations, although article 13 was not included in Schedule 1 to the Human Rights Act 1998.

2.34 The following types of order have been held to fall within the SCA 1981 s29(3) exclusion of judicial review:

- an order relating to the composition of a jury;[46]
- an order that certain counts on an indictment be stayed on the ground of delay;[47]
- an order quashing an indictment on the basis that the charges it contained fell outside the Crown Court's jurisdiction;[48]
- an order that an acquitted, legally-aided defendant contribute to the costs of his own defence;[49]
- orders concerning costs in general;[50]
- a decision not to hold a trial of the issue whether the defendant was fit to plead;[51]
- the imposition of a mandatory life sentence;[52]
- a refusal to lift a stay of proceedings against the applicant;[53]
- a decision not to impose reporting restrictions in relation to the conviction of a minor;[54]
- a decision that documents were relevant and not covered by public interest immunity and so ought to be disclosed to the defence.[55]

2.35 In contrast, the following have been held to be amenable to judicial review:

- an order forfeiting the recognizance of a surety;[56]

---

46 *R v Sheffield Crown Court ex p Brownlow* [1980] QB 530, CA.

47 *In re Ashton* [1994] AC 9, HL.

48 *R v Crown Court at Manchester ex p Director of Public Prosecutions* [1993] 4 All ER 928; [1993] 1 WLR 1524, HL.

49 *In re Sampson* [1987] 1 WLR 194, HL.

50 *Meredith, ex p* [1973] 1 WLR 435, DC; *R v Cardiff Crown Court ex p Jones* [1974] QB 113, DC (doubted in *Re Smalley* [1985] AC 622, HL); *R v Smith (Martin)* [1975] QB 531, CA. See also *R v Canterbury Crown Court ex p Regentford Ltd* [2001] HRLR 18, QBD (Admin Ct).

51 *R v Crown Court at Bradford ex p Bottomley* [1994] COD 422, DC. The court held that 'nothing could be plainer' than that the question related to trial on indictment.

52 *R v Daniella Lichniak in the Court of Appeal* [2001] QB 296. (Affirmed by the House of Lords: [2002] UKHL 47, [2003] 1 AC 903.)

53 *R v Plymouth Crown Court ex p Withey* (1999) 11 October (unreported); *R v Central Criminal Court ex p Raymond* [1986] 1 WLR 710.

54 Under Children and Young Persons Act 1933 s39. *R v Winchester Crown Court ex p B (A Minor)* [1999] 1 WLR 788, DC.

55 *R (Customs and Excise Commissioners) v Leicester Crown Court* [2001] EWHC Admin 33; (2001) *Times* 23 February.

56 *Re Smalley* [1985] AC 622, HL.

- a decision to refuse bail;[57]
- an order dismissing charges before arraignment on the ground of insufficient evidence for a jury to convict;[58]
- a decision concerning the listing of a trial which may affect its validity;[59]
- a costs order made against the Crown after an acquittal;[60]
- an order purporting to control proceedings which were continuing in the magistrates' court.[61]

2.36   It can be seen from these examples that the Crown is frequently the claimant in such cases, having limited rights of appeal itself.

2.37   Where SCA 1981 s29(3) precludes the grant of one of the prerogative orders, the court has no jurisdiction to grant a declaration.[62]

Tribunals

2.38   It has been clear for many years that the decisions of all types of tribunal are reviewable in respect of any error of law.[63] In some cases, the empowering legislation provides a statutory appeal to the High Court or elsewhere on a point of law (eg, council tax charge and valuation tribunals, appeals from planning inspectors to the High Court, homelessness appeals to the county court). Where this is so, judicial review, strictly so called, may be excluded.[64]

2.39   Tribunals and Inquiries Act 1992 s11 provides that an appeal to the High Court on a point of law lies from a number of other statutory

---

57   *R (O) v Harrow Crown Court* [2003] EWHC 868 (Admin); (2003) *Times* 29 May.

58   *R v Central Criminal Court ex p Director of the Serious Fraud Office* [1993] 1 WLR 949, DC. Though only in exceptional circumstances. See also *R v Crown Court at Snaresbrook ex p Director of the Serious Fraud Office* (1998) 95(44) LSG 35; (1998) 42 SJLB 263; (1998) *Times* 26 October, QBD.

59   *R v Southwark Crown Court ex p Commissioners for Customs and Excise* [1993] 1 WLR 764, DC (but see comments in *In re Ashton* [1994] AC 9, HL).

60   *R v Wood Green Crown Court ex p Director of Public Prosecutions* [1993] 1 WLR 723, DC.

61   *R (Customs and Excise Commissioners) v Canterbury Crown Court* [2002] EWHC 2584 (Admin); [2003] Crim LR 195, DC.

62   *R v Chelmsford Crown Court ex p Chief Constable of Essex* [1994] 1 WLR 359, DC.

63   See *Anisminic Ltd v Foreign Compensation Commission* [1969] 2 AC 147; [1969] 1 All ER 208, HL.

64   Town and Country Planning Act (TCPA) 1990 ss284–289; Housing Act 1996 s204 and see *Tower Hamlets LBC v (Nipa) Begum* [2000] 1 WLR 306; (2000) 32 HLR 445, CA.

tribunals (eg, rent assessment committees). This, however, does not necessarily exclude judicial review.[65] In other cases, statute has set up an appeal structure rendering review less important (eg, employment tribunals and the Employment Appeal Tribunal; adjudicators and the Immigration Appeal Tribunal).

2.40   Where there is no right of appeal of any kind, judicial review will, in any event, generally be available. It is not proposed to set out here any detailed provisions relating to the availability of, or interrelationship between, statutory appeals and judicial review in the context of tribunal decisions, nor on the conduct of or procedure concerning statutory appeals.[66]

Other bodies performing public acts and duties

2.41   This last category is somewhat nebulous, but decisions over the last 15 years or so have dramatically expanded the range of bodies whose decisions fall within the scope of the Administrative Court. Moreover, with the increasing influence of European law and principles, even those certainties which used to exist are no longer so clearly correct.

The Crown

2.42   Traditionally, the Crown itself is not amenable to the prerogative orders,[67] although its servants are. This is no longer a safe assumption, however. Where a challenge to a statute is based on an overriding provision of European law,[68] the operation of the statute may, and in some circumstances must, be suspended pending the resolution of the challenge, and the offending provisions of the Act can be held invalid.[69] Where the provision of an Act of Parliament is

---

65   See, eg, *Ellis & Sons Fourth Amalgamated Properties v Southern Rent Assessment Panel* (1984) 14 HLR 48, QBD, in which the court held that judicial review was a preferable remedy to the statutory right of appeal.

66   For further information on these matters see: Wade and Forsythe, *Administrative Law* (9th edn, forthcoming 2004, OUP); Richard Gordon, *Judicial Review and Administrative Court Practice* (2nd edn, forthcoming 2004, Sweet & Maxwell).

67   See chapter 5 below.

68   See chapter 1 above at paras 1.28–1.32.

69   *R v Secretary of State for Transport ex p Factortame (No 2)* [1991] 1 AC 603, ECJ and HL, especially per Lord Bridge of Harwich at 658–659, see also *Equal Opportunities Commission v Secretary of State for Employment* [1995] 1 AC 1, HL.

incompatible with Convention rights granted by the Human Rights Act 1998, the courts cannot quash the offending provision, but can only declare it incompatible.[70]

2.43   A declaration has always been available against the Crown. In terms of interim relief, a stay may be granted pending the outcome of the application for review, and/or an injunction.[71] The Court of Appeal has also held that a stay may be ordered not only of judicial proceedings but also of decisions of the secretary of state and the process by which such decisions have been reached; the term 'stay' is simply the public law description of what; in private law, is called an injunction, as in judicial review proceedings the claimant and the decision-maker are not in any true sense opposing parties.[72] For the principles upon which the court will decide whether to grant a stay, see chapter 5 below.

Prerogative powers

2.44   Traditionally, the courts would not review the exercise of prerogative powers. However, in *Council of Civil Service Unions v Minister of State for the Civil Service*,[73] the House of Lords held that the exercise of such powers was reviewable, so long as the subject-matter of the power was justiciable. For example, the courts would not review the exercise of treaty-making powers, honours, mercy, etc, because these were not matters suitable to be ruled on by a court. The number of such powers which the courts will now regard as justiciable may be increasing. For instance, in *R v Secretary of State for the Home Department ex p Bentley*,[74] where the secretary of state had refused to grant a pardon, the court held that the prerogative power of mercy was amenable to review in an appropriate case, and requested the minister to reconsider the matter, while declining to make any order on the judicial review application itself.

70   Human Rights Act 1998 s4.

71   *In re M* [1994] AC 377, HL; see also, in a European context, *R v Secretary of State for Transport ex p Factortame (No 2)* [1991] 1 AC 603, ECJ and HL, which was overruled in part, ie, in relation to domestic (non-EC) disputes, by *In re M* [1994] AC 377, HL.

72   *R v Secretary of State for Education ex p Avon CC* [1991] 1 QB 558, CA, per Glidewell LJ.

73   [1985] AC 374, HL.

74   [1994] QB 349; [1994] 2 WLR 101, DC. See also *R v Secretary of State for Foreign and Commonwelath Affairs ex p Everett* [1989] 1 QB 811, CA, where the court entertained a challenge to (but upheld) the policy of the secretary of state to refuse a passport to a person in respect of whom there was an outstanding arrest warrant, especially per Taylor LJ at 820; *R v Secretary of State for Foreign and Commonwealth Affairs ex p Rees-Mogg* [1994] QB 552, QBD.

2.45 More recently, the court has considered again the question of justiciability and extent of so-called 'forbidden areas' within which exercises of the prerogative will not be reviewable. In *R (Campaign for Nuclear Disarmament) v The Prime Minister*,[75] the claimant sought an advisory declaration that UN Security Council Resolution 1441 did not authorise military action to be taken against Iraq and that any such action without the obtaining of a second UN resolution would be unlawful as a matter of international law.

2.46 A three-judge Administrative Court held that it had no jurisdiction to entertain the claim. The court would not make a declaration on the meaning of an international instrument which had no domestic existence having not been incorporated into UK law, and where no determination fell to be made regarding the rights of people in the UK which would require that instrument to be construed by the court.[76] In any event, the subject matter of the claim was not justiciable as it involved matters of international relations, defence and national security and so should not be determined by a court. The defendant contended that it would be damaging to the public interest for the court even to consider the issue, as that would oblige the defendant to justify its position which would itself harm the public interest. A question would not be justiciable where for the court even to determine it would damage the public interest in areas of international relations, national security or defence.[77]

2.47 In any event, moreover, the court would not act to make advisory declarations unless there was a good reason to do so, which was not the case here.[78] The issues, however, were so obviously important that permission to apply would be granted and the substantive claim dismissed on these preliminary issues.

2.48 In *R (Abbasi) v Secretary of State for Foreign and Commonwealth Affairs*,[79] the Court of Appeal was prepared to entertain an application

---

75 [2002] EWHC 2759 (Admin); [2003] CP Rep 28; (2002) *Times* 27 December.

76 [2002] EWHC 2759 (Admin) per Simon Brown LJ at [36]–[40]. See also *R v Lyons* [2002] UKHL 44; [2003] 1 AC 976, in which it was held that the English courts have no jurisdiction to interpret or apply international treaties, as they do not form part of English law. In that case, the House of Lords applied this principle to refuse to quash convictions entered prior to the coming into force of the Human Rights Act 1998 on the ground that the ECHR had held that they had not enjoyed a fair trial for the purposes of article 6 of the European Convention on Human Rights.

77 *R (Campaign for Nuclear Disarmament) v The Prime Minister* [2002] EWHC 2759 (Admin), per Simon Brown LJ at [41]–[45]; per Richards J at [55]–[60].

78 [2002] EWHC 2759 (Admin) at [46].

79 [2002] EWCA Civ 1598.

for judicial review, seeking an order to require the Foreign Secretary to intervene with the US authorities in relation to the continued administrative detention of the claimant, a British citizen, at Camp Delta on Guantanamo Bay, Cuba.

2.49   The court held that where fundamental human rights of British citizens were at stake, the courts would be prepared to review the actions of a foreign sovereign state. The claimant had been and continued to be detained arbitrarily, and indefinitely, with no opportunity to challenge the legitimacy of that detention before any court or tribunal. While this treatment was objectionable, however, the court could provide no direct remedy. The claimant was outside the jurisdiction of the UK for the purposes of his Convention rights, given that there was no act by any UK body which had caused his current situation, nor which had violated any of his rights. Nor did the UK authorities have any control over his detention.

2.50   Having said this, the Court of Appeal refused to accept the defendant's contention that judicial review was excluded where there had been a refusal to lend diplomatic assistance to a British citizen whose human rights were violated by the conduct of a foreign state, as this involved an exercise of prerogative power. The question was not whether the source of Foreign Office power was prerogative, but whether the subject matter of the claim was justiciable.

2.51   There was a legitimate expectation that the authorities would properly consider a request for such assistance. The decision whether or not to accede to such a request would be reviewable if it were irrational or contrary to that legitimate expectation. The court was therefore entitled to investigate whether such a request had properly been considered. If it had, but the defendant refused the request for assistance, the court could not properly entertain a challenge to that refusal, as that decision involved issues of foreign policy which were matters for governmental decision. For the court to seek to determine such matters would involve entering the 'forbidden areas' of non-justiciable discretion. In the circumstances of the case, the request for assistance had been properly considered and it would be inappropriate to order the secretary of state to express a view as to the legality of the claimant's detention or to make any specific representations to the United States government, as to do so would plainly have an impact on the conduct of foreign policy at a particularly delicate time.[80]

---

80   [2002] EWCA Civ 1598 per Lord Phillips of Worth Matravers MR at [106]–[107].

Other decisions

2.52 A person or body exercising powers delegated by prerogative power may also be susceptible to review. Moreover, it seems that an administrative recommendation to a minister may be susceptible to review.[81] In *Tower Hamlets LBC v Secretary of State for the Environment*,[82] a declaration was granted to the effect that two paragraphs of the secretary of state's Homelessness Code of Guidance were wrong in law. The secretary of state did not argue, in the Court of Appeal, that the nature of the code rendered judicial review inappropriate, which the Court referred to as a 'correct and responsible position'.[83] The activities of the Parliamentary Ombudsman are, it appears, also amenable to review, although the court will not readily be persuaded to interfere with the exercise of his discretion.[84]

Other bodies

2.53 A non-statutory body whose authority derives solely from contract, such as an employer's disciplinary tribunal, falls outside the scope of review.[85]

2.54 In recent years, however, the courts have shifted the emphasis from the traditional test based solely on the source of the body's powers to one founded on both the source and also the nature of the functions performed or powers exercised by the body.[86] Accordingly, non-statutory bodies set up to undertake public functions have been held to fall within the scope of review.

2.55 In *R v Panel on Takeovers and Mergers ex p Datafin*,[87] the Court of Appeal held that the source of power and functions performed were

---

81 *R v Secretary of State for Transport ex p APH Road Safety Ltd* [1993] COD 240, QBD; but see *R v Secretary of State for the Home Department ex p Westminster Press Ltd* [1992] COD 303, DC, where it was held that a government circular to police chiefs concerning information to be given to the media was not reviewable.

82 (1994) 25 HLR 534, CA.

83 (1993) 25 HLR 524 per Stuart-Smith LJ at 532.

84 *R v Parliamentary Commissioner for Administration ex p Dyer* [1994]1 WLR 621, DC.

85 See *R v British Broadcasting Corporation ex p Lavelle* [1983] 1 WLR 23, QBD; *R v East Berkshire Health Authority ex p Walsh* [1985] QB 152, CA; compare *R v Secretary of State for the Home Department ex p Benwell* [1985] QB 554, QBD.

86 See, eg, *Council of Civil Service Unions v Minister of State for the Civil Service* [1985] AC 374, HL.

87 [1987] QB 815, CA.

both relevant factors, to be given different weight in different circumstances:

> In all the reports it is possible to find enumerations of factors giving rise to the [supervisory] jurisdiction, but it is a fatal error to regard the presence of all those factors as essential or as being exclusive of other factors. Possibly the only essential elements are what can be described as a public element, which can take many different forms, and the exclusion from the jurisdiction of bodies whose sole source of power is a consensual submission to its jurisdiction.[88]

2.56   It seems, then, that in broad terms, a body is amenable to judicial review if, on consideration of the source and nature of its powers, it has an essential public law element or 'nexus'. Without falling into the fatal error referred to above, it may be said that a body may have such a public law element where, for example, the elements suggested in *Datafin* itself can be identified:

- it performs or operates in the public domain as an integral part of a regulatory system which performs public law duties;
- it is non-statutory by government decision but is established 'under the authority of government';[89]
- it is supported by a periphery of statutory powers and penalties;
- it is embraced by government and performs functions that government would otherwise perform; and/or
- it is under a duty in exercising what amount to public powers to act judicially;
- the source of the body's power must not derive exclusively from a consensual submission to jurisdiction.[90]

2.57   It does not necessarily follow from this that a public body's decision will inevitably fall outside the scope of the remedy if it involves an employment, or other, contractual relationship. The essential question is that of the existence of a public law nexus in the issue that has been raised.[91]

---

88   [1987] QB 815, per Sir John Donaldson MR at 838E.
89   [1987] QB 815 per Lloyd LJ at 849D.
90   [1987] QB 815 at 849D. see also *R v Insurance Ombudsman ex p Aegon Life Insurance Ltd* [1994] COD 426: the Insurance Ombudsman's decisions were not reviewable; his jurisdiction was purely contractual. Whether this case would be decided in the same way today is not entirely clear. The Financial Services Ombudsman, who has replaced him (with a broader jurisdiction) has been the subject of judicial review.
91   See further paras 2.64–2.74 below.

If one is to be found, such as the use of a contractual power for an improper purpose,[92] then, especially if no remedy is available in private law,[93] it is likely that judicial review will still be available.

2.58 Since *Datafin*, it has been held that state school governors are susceptible to review,[94] as is a district valuer,[95] the Parliamentary and Local Government Ombudsmen,[96] the National Health Service,[97] a hospital ethics committee,[98] an electricity board,[99] the police,[100] a Code of Practice Committee[101] and registrars of births, deaths and marriages.[102]

2.59 Conversely, those bodies held to be outside the scope of review include the Insurance Ombudsman,[103] the Jockey Club,[104] the Football Association,[105] the Chief Rabbi,[106] and the Independent Broadcasting

---

92 In *R v Liverpool CC ex p Ferguson* (1985) *Times* 20 November, DC, a decision to dismiss school teachers was a direct consequence of a decision to set an unlawful rate, which meant that it was not properly or legitimately taken in the furtherance of the authority's duty as an education authority. See also, eg, *Roberts v Hopwood* [1925] AC 578, HL.

93 *R v Hammersmith and Fulham LBC ex p National Association of Local Government Officers* [1991] COD 397, DC, where it was considered that there would be no remedy in the industrial tribunal.

94 And governors of a city technology college: *R v Governors of Haberdashers' Aske's College Trust ex p T* [1995] ELR 350; but not independent school governors: *R v Fernhill Manor School ex p A* [1994] ELR 67.

95 *R v Kidderminster District Valuer ex p Powell* (1992) 4 Admin LR 193.

96 *R v Parliamentary Commissioner for Administration ex p Dyer* [1994] 1 WLR 621; *R v Local Commissioner for Administration for the South, etc, ex p Eastleigh BC* [1988] QB 855.

97 *Re Walker's Application* (1987) *Times* 25 November 25.

98 *R v Ethical Committee of St Mary's Hospital (Manchester) ex p Harriott* [1988] 1 Federal Law Reports 512 (FC), an Australian case.

99 *R v Midlands Electricity Board ex p Busby* (1987) *Times* 28 October.

100 *R v Commissioner of Police for the Metropolis ex p P* (1996) 8 Admin LR 6.

101 *R v Code of Practice Committee of British Pharmaceutical Society ex p Professional Counselling Aids Ltd* [1991] COD 228, QBD.

102 *R v Registrar of Births, Deaths and Marriages ex p Minhas* [1977] QB 1.

103 Whose jurisdiction is purely contractual (by agreement between insurance companies): *R v Insurance Ombudsman ex p Aegon Life Insurance Ltd* [1994] CLC 88; [1994] COD 426.

104 *R v Disciplinary Committee of the Jockey Club ex p Aga Khan* [1993] 1 WLR 909; *R v Jockey Club ex p RAM Racecourses Ltd* [1993] 2 All ER 225, DC; *R v Disciplinary Committee of Jockey Club ex p Massingberd-Mundy* [1993] 2 All ER 207, DC; *R v Disciplinary Committee of the Jockey Club* [1993] 1 WLR 909, CA.

105 *R v Football Association Ltd ex p Football League Ltd* [1993] 2 All ER 833, QBD.

106 *R v Chief Rabbi of the United Hebrew Congregation of Great Britain and the Commonwealth ex p Wachmann* [1992] 1 WLR 1036, QBD.

Authority.[107] As stated above, a non-statutory body whose authority derives solely from contract, such as an employer's disciplinary tribunal, falls outside the scope of review.[108]

2.60   There is a clear tendency towards focus on the nature of the function rather than the body, although it goes too far to suggest that the latter is irrelevant.[109] Neither of the *Datafin* propositions (ie, 'essential public law element' and 'no consensual submission to jurisdiction') has ever been tested in the House of Lords.[110] Having said this, the process of adopting a 'functions-based' test, rather than the traditional 'source of powers' test, was one that started in the House of Lords with *Council of Civil Service Unions*,[111] and it seems unlikely that the modern House of Lords will revert to traditional orthodoxy.

2.61   The functions-based test does create uncertainties about which bodies are and are not susceptible to review. The examples above[112] – of bodies not so susceptible – are as explicable on the basis of function as they are by reference to the nature of the body. Nevertheless, in *R v Derbyshire CC ex p Noble*,[113] Woolf LJ stated that 'the courts have, over the years, by decisions in individual cases, indicated the approximate divide'. In *R v Legal Aid Board ex p Donn & Co (a firm)*,[114] Ognall J took the view that the 'answer must ... fall to be decided as one of overall impression, and one of degree. There can be no universal test'.

107   Acting under its articles of association: *R v Independent Broadcasting Authority ex p Rank Organisation plc* (1996) *Times* 14 March.

108   See, eg, *R v British Broadcasting Corporation ex p Lavelle* [1983] 1 WLR 23; *R v East Berkshire Health Authority ex p Walsh* [1985] QB 152, CA; compare *R v Secretary of State for the Home Department ex p Benwell* [1985] QB 554.

109   The nature of the body and its functions was the close focus of the Court of Appeal in the recent cases of *Poplar HARCA v Donoghue* [2001] EWCA Civ 595; [2001] QB 48; [2001] 3 WLR 183; [2001] 4 All ER 604; (2001) 33 HLR 823; *R (A) v Partners in Care Ltd* [2002] EWHC 592 (Admin); [2002] 1 WLR 2611; (2002) 5 CCLR 330 and *R (Heather and others) v Leonard Cheshire Foundation and HM Attorney General* [2002] EWCA Civ 366; [2002] 2 All ER 936; (2002) 5 CCLR 317. These were all cases concerning the very closely related question of whether the bodies were 'public authorities' for the purposes of Human Rights Act 1998 s6 (see further paras 2.62–2.74 below). The Court of Appeal applied the *Datafin* principles in answering this question. See also *Hampshire County Court v Graham Beer (t/a Hammer Trout Farm)* [2003] EWCA 1056.

110   See Wade and Forsythe, *Administrative Law* (9th edn, forthcoming 2004, OUP); Alder and Handy, *Housing Associations: the law of social landlords* (3rd edn, 1997), Sweet & Maxwell, p31.

111   *Council of Civil Service Unions v Minister of State for the Civil Service* [1985] AC 374, HL.

112   para 2.59.

113   [1990] ICR 808, CA, at 814.

114   [1996] 3 All ER 1, QBD, at 11.

'Public authorities' in human rights cases – the analogous issue

2.62   The Human Rights Act 1998 defines a 'public authority' as including: (a) a court or tribunal, and (b) any person with functions of a public nature.[115] In relation to a particular act, however, a body will not be a public authority for the purposes of the Act by virtue only of (b) above if the nature of the act is private.[116] It can be seen that all courts fall within this definition, whether or not they are inferior.[117]

2.63   In judicial review cases involving human rights issues, the range of bodies whose decisions may be open to challenge could have been held to be significantly wider than in cases which have no human rights element. Indeed, on the wording of the Act itself, it seems to have been open to the courts to adopt a purely functions-based test.

2.64   To date, this has not occurred. In *Poplar HARCA v Donoghue*,[118] the Court of Appeal was faced with the issue whether a Registered Social Landlord (RSL) was a public authority, for the purpose of challenging a decision it had made to seek a possession order in respect of a property it had let under an assured tenancy, on the mandatory ground available under the Housing Act 1988.[119] The court held that while Human Rights Act (HRA) 1998 s6 required a generous interpretation, it was clearly inspired by the approach adopted by the courts in judicial review proceedings following *Datafin*.[120]

2.65   The Court of Appeal observed that the fact that a body performs functions which a public body would otherwise be obliged to perform cannot necessarily render the function a public function. Public bodies can use private bodies to perform their functions without the nature of the function thereby inevitably being considered public so as to turn the private body into a public authority for the purposes of HRA 1998 s6. Otherwise every bed and breakfast hotel which provided temporary accommodation for homeless persons would be obliged to comply with the Human Rights Act 1998.[121]

---

115   Human Rights Act 1998 s6(3).

116   HRA 1996 s6(5).

117   See paras 2.3–2.23 above.

118   [2001] EWCA Civ 595; [2002] QB 48; [2001] 3 WLR 183; [2001] 4 All ER 606; (2001) 33 HLR 823.

119   Housing Act 1988 Sch 2, ground 8.

120   *Poplar HARCA v Donoghue* [2001] EWCA Civ 595; [2001] QB 48, per Lord Woolf CJ at [58].

121   [2001] EWCA Civ 595.

2.66   In holding, nonetheless, that the RSL was a public authority, the court took account of the following features:

- in transferring its housing stock to the RSL, the local authority had not transferred its primary duties. The RSL was simply the means by which the local authority performed those duties;
- the act of providing accommodation is not, without more, a public function for the purposes of HRA 1998 s6, irrespective of the section of society for whom that accommodation is provided;
- the fact that a body does not conduct its activities for profit, but is motivated in doing so by its perception of the public interest does not point to the body being a public authority;
- what can make an act which would otherwise be private into a public act is a 'feature or combination of features which impose a public character or stamp on that act'.[122] Statutory control over the act can at least help to mark it as private, as can the extent of control over it exercised by another public authority. The mere fact of supervision by a regulatory body does not render the acts done public acts, but the more closely the acts in question are enmeshed with the activities of a public body, the more likely those acts are to be public. This was analogous to the position in judicial review where a regulator may be deemed public but supervise the private activities of those it regulates;
- the closeness of the relationship between the RSL and the local authority: the local authority had created the RSL for the purpose of taking a stock transfer; five of the RSL's board members were councillors of the local authority; the RSL was subject to the guidance of the local authority in its acts towards the tenants;
- at the time of the stock transfer, the tenant was a tenant of the local authority and it was intended that she would be treated no better and no worse after the transfer than if she had remained a tenant of the local authority. The RSL therefore stood in relation to her in very much the position that had previously been occupied by the local authority.[123]

2.67   The court emphasised that, in addition to taking account of these factors, it was desirable to step back and look at the situation as a whole. Lord Woolf CJ stated:[124]

---

122   *Poplar HARCA v Donoghue* [2001] EWCA Civ 595, per Lord Woolf at [65].
123   [2001] EWCA Civ 595 at [65].
124   [2001] EWCA Civ 595 at [66].

As is the position on applications for judicial review, there is no clear demarcation line which can be drawn between public and private bodies and functions. In a borderline case, such as this, the decision is very much one of fact and degree. Taking into account all the circumstances, we have come to the conclusion that while the activities of housing associations need not involve the performance of public functions in this case, in providing accommodation for the defendant and then seeking possession, the role of Poplar is so closely assimilated to that of Tower Hamlets that it was performing public and not private functions ... We emphasise that this does not mean that all of Poplar's functions are public ...

2.68   In *R (Heather) v Leonard Cheshire Foundation*,[125] the Court of Appeal reached the opposite conclusion where a challenge was brought by a resident of a residential home, placed there pursuant to the local authority's obligations under National Assistance Act 1948 s21, to the defendant's decision to close it.

2.69   The defendant was manifestly not performing public functions. While the degree of public funding for an otherwise private body can be relevant to the question of whether or not the functions performed were public in nature, this was not the case here. There was no distinction other than the funding of the activities in question, between what was happening to those residents who were privately funded to reside in the home and those who were being funded by the local authority. Nor was there any other evidence of any public flavour to the defendant or its functions. The defendant was not standing in the shoes of the local authority: the National Assistance Act 1948 authorised the actions of the local authority but did not give the defendant any powers; nor were any other statutory powers being performed by the defendant when performing functions for the residents.[126]

2.70   The situation might have been different if the local authority could divest itself if its article 8 Convention obligations by contracting out its duties under the National Assistance Act 1948. In such a case, the court would have a responsibility to approach the interpretation of Human Rights Act 1998 s6(3), in relation to the definition of 'public authority' to ensure that the residents' article 8 rights were protected. That was not the case, however. The local authority remained under an article 8 obligation to the residents, who also enjoyed contractual rights against the defendant.[127]

---

125   [2002] EWCA Civ 366; [2002] 2 All ER 936; [2002] HLR 49; (2002) 5 CCLR 317.

126   *R (Heather) v Leonard Cheshire Foundation* [2002] EWCA Civ 366 per Lord Woolf CJ at [35].

127   [2002] EWCA Civ 366 at [33].

2.71   In *R (A) v Partnerships in Care Ltd*,[128] a patient detained in a private psychiatric hospital under Mental Health Act 1983 s3(1), sought judicial review of the hospital managers' decision to change the focus of her specialist ward from the care and treatment of people with personality disorders to the care and treatment of mentally ill people. The claimant alleged that this caused her no longer to receive the treatment she required. The hospital contended that changing the focus of the ward did not amount to a public function which could render them a public body amenable to judicial review or a public authority for the purposes of the Human Rights Act 1998.

2.72   Keith J held that the hospital was amenable to judicial review and a public authority. Although not part of the National Health Service, it was registered as a mental nursing home under Registered Nursing Homes Act 1984 Part II. The Nursing Homes and Mental Nursing Homes Regulations 1984,[129] moreover, applied to it, so that the secretary of state acting through the relevant health authority was accorded a measure of control and supervision over the hospital. More importantly, the regulations imposed obligations directly on the hospital, in particular those of providing adequate professional staff and adequate treatment facilities.[130] The Mental Health Act 1983, in addition, laid down a comprehensive statutory regime governing the admission and treatment of detained patients and, indeed, provided for their compulsory detention.[131]

2.73   Given these important statutory functions, which were devolved to the managers of the hospital itself and the specific statutory underpinning of their decisions concerning the facilities and staff to be provided, given also the public interest in the care and treatment of the hospital's patients so as not to prolong their detention by reason of their not receiving the necessary care and treatment, the managers' decision did have a public flavour and the managers were a functional public authority.[132]

2.74   The functional nature of the test in relation to *hybrid* bodies, as those bodies who exercise some public and some private functions have come to be called, under Human Rights Act 1998 s6, can be seen from these cases, although the courts have (as shown above),

---

128   [2002] EWHC 529 (Admin); [2002] 1 WLR 2610; (2002) 5 CCLR 330, QBD.
129   SI No 1578.
130   Regulation 12(1).
131   *R (A) v Partnerships in Care Ltd* [2002] EWHC 529 (Admin) per Keith J at [16]–[17].
132   [2002] EWHC 529 (Admin) at [24]–[25].

continued to regard the source of the powers as a critical part of the test whether the body is a public authority in relation to a particular activity. In *Parochial Church Council of the Parish of Aston Cantlow v Wallbank*,[133] the House of Lords concluded that a church council's decision to require a lay rector pay for chancel repairs did not amount to the discharge of a function of a public nature within the meaning of Human Rights Act 2003 s6(3)(b). Lord Nicholls of Birkenhead suggested that 'public function' in this context should be given generous interpretation so as to further the statutory aim of protecting human rights, and observed that there could be no universal test of what is a public function:

> ... given the diverse nature of governmental functions and the variety of means by which these functions are discharged today. Factors to be taken into account include the extent to which in carrying out the relevant function the body is publicly funded, or is exercising statutory powers, or is taking the place of central government or local authorities, or is providing a public service.

2.75   In *Hampshire County Court v Graham Beer (t/a Hammer Trout Farm)*,[134] the Court of Appeal expressed surprise that no reference was made to either the *Donoghue* or the *Heather* case in the speeches in *Aston Cantlow*. Notwithstanding the House of Lords' decision, *Donoghue* and *Heather* remained authoritative on this issue. The *Hampshire* case itself concerned the question of whether a private company set up by the county council to run farmers' markets which had previously been run by the council was a public authority and amenable to judicial review in respect of its decision to refuse the claimant access to a farmer's market.

2.76   The Court held that the company was acting as a public authority and that its decision was amenable to judicial review, for the following reasons: (a) the decision concerned a right of access to a public market held on public land, which factor alone was arguably sufficient; (b) the company owed its existence to the council and was set up using statutory powers; (c) the company had stepped into the shoes of the council; and (d) the council had assisted the company since its incorporation, eg, by providing offices, a discretionary grant and personnel to it. These factors, taken in combination (particularly (b) and (c)) compelled the conclusion that the company's decision was amenable to judicial review.

---

133   [2003] UKHL 37; [2003] 3 WLR 283.
134   [2003] EWCA Civ 1056; (2003) *Times* 25 August; (2003) 31 EG 67 (CS).

Emanation or organ of the state

2.77 In this context, it may be recalled[135] that similar issues arise in relation to the question of whom should be considered an 'emanation of the state', for the purposes of Community law and, in particular, directly effective provisions of Community legislation. The European Court of Justice (ECJ), holding that the (then nationalised) gas utility, British Gas, was an emanation of the state,[136] posed a similar, yet significantly different, test to that in *Datafin* and *Poplar:*[137]

> ... a body, whatever its legal form, which has been made responsible, pursuant to a measure adopted by the state, for providing a public service under the control of the state and has for that purpose special powers beyond those which result from the normal rules applicable in relations between individuals, is included in any event among the bodies against which the provisions of a directive capable of having direct effect may be relied upon.

---

135 See paras 1.42–1.44 above.
136 *Foster v British Gas* [1990] ECR I–3313; [1991] 1 QB 405 at 427G–H.
137 *R v Panel on Takeovers and Mergers ex p Datafin* [1987] QB 815, CA; *Poplar HARCA v Donoghue* [2001] EWCA Civ 595; [2001] QB 48; [2001] 3 WLR 183; [2001] 4 All ER 604; (2001) 33 HLR 823.

CHAPTER 3

Reviewable decisions

Public and private law

3.1   As has already been seen, judicial review is concerned, primarily, with the improper exercise of public powers and duties. It is, therefore, only decisions or actions in a public law context which may be subject to review (and not even all of those[1]). This is so even though the body which took the decision may be classified as a public or a private body. The discussion of the *Datafin*[2] and *Poplar*[3] cases in the previous chapter[4] indicates the potentially complex interrelationship between the true classification of the act and the nature and form of the body which performed it. As to whether a body is a public authority for the purposes of the Human Rights Act 1998,[5] in particular, the form and structure of the body will have a considerable effect on whether the act under challenge can properly be classified as a public or private act; likewise the classification of the act as public or private will frequently determine the issue as to whether a body is a public authority.

3.2   Until it is accepted that in many cases it may be impossible to disentangle the two issues, the process undertaken by the courts may appear to be quite circular: the classification of the act (particularly under the Human Rights Act 1998) determines the status of the body as a public authority (or not), but the nature of the body informs the classification of the act. These issues have been discussed elsewhere.[6]

3.3   In other cases, there will be no dispute that the decision-maker is a public body, such as central government or a local authority. It is still necessary, however, to analyse the nature of the decision or act, in such cases, to decide whether it is properly classified as existing in public or private law, given that for judicial review to be the appropriate form of challenge, it is necessary that the decision or act exists in public law. Public bodies perform private law acts all the time in respect of which they can sue and be sued in private law proceedings: breaches of contract and covenants in leases and tenancy agreements, nuisance and negligence, employment of staff, personal injury, etc.

3.4   The importance of the correct identification of an act or decision as existing in public or private law has been considerable, not least because

---

1   See paras 3.46–3.53 below.
2   *R v Panel on Takeovers and Mergers ex p Datafin* [1987] QB 815, CA.
3   *Poplar HARCA v Donoghue* [2001] EWCA Civ 595; [2001] QB 48; [2001] 3 WLR 183; [2001] 4 All ER 604; (2001) 33 HLR 823.
4   See paras 2.55–2.67 above.
5   Human Rights Act 1998 s6(3)(b).
6   See paras 2.55–2.67.

the potential consequences of misidentification and therefore challenge by the wrong procedure were, under the old rules,[7] severe. A private law action would be liable to be struck out as an abuse of the process of the court if brought to challenge an act that the court considered to be a public law act. Judicial review would likewise be refused to challenge a private law matter except in very limited circumstances where the court was able to permit the claim to proceed as a private law action.[8]

3.5   The consequences of such mistakes may no longer be so significant. Civil Procedure Rules (CPR) r54.20 confers on the court a comprehensive power to transfer cases out of or into the Administrative Court, much broader in its effect than the equivalent provision under the old rules.[9] The courts, in addition, unhappy for years about the amount of time and public money frequently devoted to debates concerning the form of proceedings rather than dealing with the substantive dispute[10] have recently expressed the view that the new rules are sufficiently flexible to accommodate justifiable errors of procedure without resort to the draconian remedy of strike out.[11]

3.6   In spite of this welcome and sensible development, the distinction between public law rights and duties and those which exist in private law is still important. In domestic law, there is no right to damages for breach of a public law obligation;[12] the classification of the act will also be likely to determine whether any remedy under the Human Rights Act 1998 will be available; the procedure and time limits for, as well as the remedies available in relation to public and/or private law matters are of course significantly different. Leniency by the courts in relation to use of the incorrect procedure is less likely where the error is one which ought not to have been made.

---

7 Rules of the Supreme Court (RSC) Order 53.
8 See RSC Ord 53 r9(5). See also, eg, *BBC v Lavelle* [1983] 1 WLR 23, QBD.
9 See RSC Ord 53 r9(5). See also, eg, *BBC v Lavelle* [1983] 1 WLR 23, QBD.
10 *Roy v Kensington and Chelsea Family Practitioner Committee* [1992] 1 AC 625, HL, per Lord Lowry at 651; *Trustees of the Dennis Rye Pension Fund v Sheffield CC* [1998] 1 WLR 840, CA.
11 See, eg, *Clark v University of Lincolnshire and Humberside* [2000] 1 WLR 1988, CA; *R (Heather) v Leonard Cheshire Foundation* [2002] EWCA Civ 366; [2002] 2 All ER 936; [2002] HLR 49; (2002) 5 CCLR 317.
12 See, eg, *R v Northavon DC ex p Palmer* (1994) 26 HLR 572, QBD, and *O'Rourke v Camden LBC* [1998] AC 188, HL, where claims for damages for alleged breaches of the duties owed to homeless persons under the Housing Act 1985 Part III (now Housing Act 1996 Part VII) were dismissed on the basis that such duties existed in public law only.

Classification of acts and decisions

O'Reilly v Mackman and the general rule

3.7   Two points may be noted. First, it can be difficult to distinguish between public and private law rights, as the jurisprudence of English law never formally evolved distinctions of this kind until the House of Lords did so (without analysing such distinctions) in O'Reilly v Mackman.[13] Second, it does not automatically follow from the classification of a duty, power or right as existing solely in the realm of public law that issues concerning that power, duty or right cannot be litigated in an ordinary private action if they are in some way linked to a private law right (see further below).

3.8   In O'Reilly, the House of Lords held that, as a 'general rule', it was contrary to public policy and an abuse of the process of the court to permit a dissatisfied applicant to proceed by way of an ordinary action (ie, in modern procedural parlance, to bring a CPR Pt 7 claim and avoid Pt 54 procedure), when the substance of the complaint was founded in public law. This would enable the applicant to evade the provisions of the rules of court governing judicial review claims,[14] which are designed to afford safeguards for public authorities against groundless and unmeritorious applications, in the interests of good administration. The safeguards referred to by Lord Diplock in O'Reilly were the requirement for permission to apply and the strict time limits (preventing tardy applications), the need for sworn evidence[15] making full and frank disclosure of all relevant facts and the court's discretionary control over both disclosure and cross-examination.[16] Accordingly, the courts may insist on challenge by judicial review, by striking out any other action.

3.9   The difficulties referred to above tend to arise in cases where there is a mixture of public and private law rights, and/or where there is more than one possible analysis of the position. This can often be where contractual obligations are superimposed upon those imposed by statute.

---

13 [1983] 2 AC 237 (see further below).

14 That was then RSC Order 53; now CPR Pt 54.

15 Now a pleaded statement of facts verified by a statement of truth: CPR rr54.6 and 22.1; Practice Direction 54, para 5.6.

16 O'Reilly v Mackman [1983] 2 AC 237 at 280G–281D and 284B. See also Cocks v Thanet DC [1983] 2 AC 286, HL, per Lord Bridge of Harwich at 294E–H. As to these procedural requirements, see below, chapters 18 and 19.

Applying *O'Reilly*: public or private?

3.10   In *Cocks v Thanet District Council*,[17] decided on the same day as *O'Reilly*, the distinction between public and private law rights was considered again by the House of Lords. Lord Bridge held that the general rule expounded in *O'Reilly* applied where it was necessary, as a condition precedent to the enforcement of a statutory private law right, to impugn an authority's public law decision. He referred to a 'dichotomy' between the 'decision-making' and 'executive' functions of an authority. The former involved the exercise of discretionary powers invested in the authority by Parliament and which are for the authority to exercise rather than for the court. Those functions could only exist in public law. The latter functions were no more than the implementation of the public law decision and could be enforced by private action.[18] Thus, the decision whether an applicant fulfilled the statutory conditions to entitle him to housing were a matter of public law. The actual obligation to house a qualifying applicant would be a matter of private law, however, enforceable by an action for injunction and damages. The decision challenged fell within the 'decision-making' category.

3.11   In *O'Rourke v Camden LBC*,[19] the House of Lords disapproved this approach, rejecting the classifications of 'decision-making' or 'executive' as a basis for the distinction between duties which do, and those which do not, give rise to a private law right of action. Such a distinction would give rise to the anomaly that an authority who accept that a duty is owed but who discharge it inadequately would be liable in damages, while an authority who perversely refuse to accept that they are under any duty at all would not be so liable.[20] That would be contrary to principle.

3.12   The House of Lords held that the question whether any private law duty exists depends, rather, on whether on a correct construction of the statute such a duty has been intended by Parliament. This is the same test as applied to the courts to the related question whether there has been a breach of statutory duty which gives rise to a private law claim for damages.[21]

---

17 [1983] 2 AC 286, HL.
18 *Cocks v Thanet DC* [1983] 2 AC 286, HL, per Lord Bridge at 292D–293B; *Mohram Ali v Tower Hamlets LBC* [1993] QB 407, CA, per Nolan LJ at 413G–414B.
19 [1998] AC 188, HL.
20 [1998] AC 188 at 196G.
21 For, still, the leading authority on the principles applicable to the question whether a statutory duty is owed, see *X (Minors) v Bedfordshire CC* [1995] 2 AC 633, HL. See also *Stovin v Wise* [1996] AC 923, HL.

3.13   Accordingly, where the existence of a duty is dependent upon 'a good deal of judgment' on the part of the authority, and the authority enjoy a wide discretion about the discharge of any duty which does arise, it is unlikely that Parliament will have intended errors of judgment to give rise to a private law right of action for breach of statutory duty, and so the duty will exist in public law.[22] Where the duty arises under a comprehensive statutory scheme which also contains a detailed, self-contained and exhaustive procedure for enforcing the duties of the authority, this is likewise indicative of a Parliamentary intention not to create such a private law right of action.

Applying *O'Reilly*: exceptions

3.14   That there may be exceptions to the mandatory use of the judicial review procedure was envisaged by Lord Diplock in *O'Reilly* itself, particularly where the invalidity of the decision arises as a collateral issue in a claim for infringement of a right of the plaintiff arising under private law.[23] His Lordship also accepted that it may be permissible for the parties to proceed (by consent) by way of ordinary action rather than seeking review.[24] Whether or not further exceptions should be made should be decided on a case-by-case basis. These matters have been considered extensively by the courts, in a series of cases from which the following principles have emerged.[25]

3.15   The first category of exception found to exist by the court, almost immediately after *O'Reilly*, is where the public law element of the claim is merely peripheral; in such cases that element may not be sufficient to justify proceeding by way of judicial review.[26] If the public and private law elements are inextricably linked, moreover, then it appears that matters can proceed either way. In *An Bord Bainne*

---

22   *O'Rourke v Camden LBC* [1998] AC 188, HL, per Lord Hoffmann at 194B–E.

23   *O'Reilly v Mackman* [1983] 2 AC 237 at 285F.

24   *O'Reilly v Mackman* [1983] 2 AC 237 and see, eg, *Gillick v West Norfolk and Wisbech Area Health Authority and the Department of Health and Social Security* [1986] AC 112, HL.

25   See especially *Cocks v Thanet DC* [1983] 2 AC 286, HL; *Wandsworth LBC v Winder* [1985] AC 461, HL; *Mohram Ali v Tower Hamlets LBC* [1993] QB 407, CA; *Tower Hamlets LBC v Abdi* (1992) 91 LGR 300, CA; *Hackney LBC v Lambourne* (1992) 25 HLR 172, CA; *O'Rourke v Camden LBC* [1998] AC 188, HL; *Trustees of the Dennis Rye Pension Fund v Sheffield CC* [1998] 1 WLR 840, CA. See also *R v Northavon DC ex p Palmer* (1994) 26 HLR 572, QBD.

26   See *Davy v Spelthorne BC* [1984] AC 262, HL.

Co-operative Ltd (Irish Dairy Board) v Milk Marketing Board,[27] Sir John Donaldson MR allowed a private action to continue on the basis that although the matter could be said to be one of public law, private rights were involved and it could cause injustice to require the use of the public law procedure.

3.16 Throughout the 1990s, the courts became increasingly frustrated at the large quantity of satellite litigation which the decision in *O'Reilly* spawned, as public bodies frequently applied to strike out proceedings taken against them, such litigation often reaching the Court of Appeal and House of Lords. In one of those cases, *Roy v Kensington and Chelsea Family Practitioner Committee,*[28] the issue arose whether *O'Reilly* laid down a rule applicable to all cases or only those where private rights were not also at stake. Lord Lowry, with whom the rest of the House agreed, declined to decide between the two approaches but much preferred the broader approach:[29]

> ... which is both traditionally orthodox and consistent with the *Pyx Granite principle* [1960] AC 260, 286, as applied in *Davy v Spelthorne Borough Council* [1984] AC 262, 274 and in *Wandsworth London Borough Council v Winder* [1985] AC 461, 510. It would also, if adopted, have the practical merit of getting rid of a procedural minefield.

3.17 Even adopting the narrow approach, however, for the purposes of the appeal, there were many indications in favour of a liberal attitude towards the exceptions to the rule contemplated but not spelt out by Lord Diplock and concluded:[30]

> In conclusion, my Lords, it seems to me that, unless the procedure adopted by the moving party is ill-suited to dispose of the question at issue, there is much to be said in favour of the proposition that a court having jurisdiction ought to let a case be heard rather than entertain a debate concerning the form of the proceedings.

3.18 The courts have built on this approach in subsequent cases. In *Trustees of the Dennis Rye Pension Fund v Sheffield City Council,*[31] the Court of Appeal held that the statutory code for the approval of housing grants[32] entitled a person to payment of the grant once he had complied with

---

27 (1984) 128 Sol Jo 417, CA.
28 [1992] 1 AC 625, HL.
29 [1992] 1 AC 625 at 653.
30 [1992] 1 AC 625 at 651.
31 [1998] 1 WLR 840, CA.
32 Then, Housing Grants, Construction and Regeneration Act 1993 Part I.

statutory conditions for payment, and that there was no reason why he could not bring a private law action to recover the amount of the unpaid grant as an ordinary debt.

3.19   In the course of his judgment, Lord Woolf MR suggested the following guidance. Where it is not clear whether judicial review or an ordinary private action is appropriate, it is safer to apply for judicial review because there could then be no question of any abuse of process by seeking to avoid the protection it offered to public bodies. In most cases, it should not be necessary for procedural reasons to become involved in 'arid arguments' about whether the issues are correctly treated as involving public or private law or both (though it may be necessary to consider this for reasons of substantive law). If judicial review is used when it should not be, the court can safeguard its resources by directing either that the case should proceed as if begun by private action, or else that it should be heard by a non-Administrative Court judge.

3.20   If a case is brought by an ordinary private law action and an application is made to strike it out on the basis that it should have been brought by way of judicial review, the court should ask itself, if the correct procedure is not clear, whether permission would have been granted if the judicial review procedure had been used. If so, that would indicate that the avoidance of the protections conferred by the judicial review procedure has done no harm. The court should consider, in addition, which procedure would be the most appropriate to try the case. If an ordinary action is equally or more appropriate than a judicial review claim, that would be a further indication that the case should not be struck out.

3.21   Where it is not clear whether proceedings have been properly brought by ordinary action, it should be remembered that, by consultation with the Administrative Court Office, the case could be transferred to the Administrative Court as an alternative to being struck out.[33]

3.22   This topic was revisited by the Court of Appeal, and Lord Woolf MR, in *Clark v University of Lincoln and Humberside*.[34] In that case, the court felt free to reconsider Lord Diplock's guidance in *O'Reilly* in the

---

33 [1998] 1 WLR 840, per Lord Woolf MR at 848E–849B. See also *Mercury Communications Ltd v Director General of Telecommunications* [1996] 1 WLR 48, per Lord Slynn of Hadley at 57.

34 [2000] 1 WLR 1988, CA.

light of the new Civil Procedure Rules, even though CPR Pt 54 was not yet in force. In Lord Woolf's judgment, he highlighted the importance of these procedural changes and in particular the enhanced control which the court would exercise in relation to all proceedings, not just those brought by way of judicial review. The intention of the CPR was to harmonise procedures as far as possible and avoid barren procedural disputes.[35]

3.23   In particular, if ordinary actions under CPR Pt 7 or Pt 8 were brought raising public law issues, they would now be subject to the provisions of CPR Pt 24 which enabled the court to give a summary judgment on a claim or an issue, whether of its own motion or on application, where it considered the claimant to have no real prospect of success. Accordingly, the distinction between judicial review proceedings and ordinary actions was now limited – in judicial review claims, the claimant requiring permission needed to establish a real prospect of success; in ordinary actions, the defendant making a CPR Pt 24 application needed to establish that the claimant had no real prospect of success.[36]

3.24   The courts would today be flexible in their approach to abuse of process arguments, in the light of the changes brought about by the CPR. Those changes include a requirement that parties must act reasonably both before and after they have commenced proceedings. They are under an obligation to assist the court to further the overriding objective which includes ensuring that cases are dealt with expeditiously and fairly. They should not allow the choice of procedure to achieve procedural advantages.[37]

3.25   The courts, moreover, were now entitled to consider delay in commencing proceedings within the limitation period, outside judicial review cases, in deciding whether those proceedings were abusive. In cases where judicial review would usually be the appropriate procedure, the court would be entitled to consider whether there has been unjustified delay in commencing the proceedings. The court could also consider the nature of the claim. Delay in bringing proceedings for a discretionary remedy has always been a factor that could be taken into account. If the claim would affect the public generally, the court would adopt a stricter approach than if only the immediate parties were

---

35   *Clark v University of Lincolnshire and Humberside* [2000] 1 WLR 1988 per Lord Woolf MR at [37].
36   [2000] 1 WLR 1988 at [27]–[28].
37   [2000] 1 WLR 1988 at [33]–[34].

affected. Where a claim was brought in contract where it could more appropriately have been brought by way of judicial review, the court would not strike it out solely because of the procedure adopted but would consider whether in all the circumstances, including delay, there had been an abuse of the CPR. This was the same approach as would be adopted on an application under CPR Pt 24.[38]

3.26   He concluded that since O'Reilly, the emphasis had changed:

> What is likely to be important ... will not be whether the right procedure has been adopted but whether the protection provided by Order 53[39] has been flouted in circumstances which are inconsistent with the proceedings being able to be conducted justly in accordance with the general principles contained in Part 1. Those principles are now central to determining what its due process.[40]

3.27   In R (Heather) v Leonard Cheshire Foundation,[41] the Court of Appeal (Lord Woolf CJ) having concluded that the defendant was not a public authority for the purposes of Human Rights Act 1998 s6, because it had not been exercising a public function in deciding to close a residential care home which it operated, turned to deal with a contention which the defendant had raised, namely that proceedings ought not to have been brought by way of judicial review.

3.28   Lord Woolf CJ was clearly unimpressed by the raising of the issue, describing it as '... an echo of the old demarcation disputes as to when judicial review was or was not appropriate under Order 53. CPR Part 54 is intended to avoid any such disputes which are wholly unproductive.'[42]

3.29   He again emphasised the scope for using the judicial review procedure:

> In a case such as the present where a bona fide contention is being advanced (although incorrect) that LCF [Leonard Cheshire Foundation] was performing a public function, that is an appropriate issue to be brought to the court by way of judicial review.'[43]

---

38 [2000] 1 WLR 1988 at [35]–[38].
39 Now CPR Pt 54.
40 *Clark v University of Lincolnshire and Humberside* [2000] 1 WLR 1988 per Lord Woolf MR at [39].
41 [2002] EWCA Civ 366; [2002] 2 All ER 936; [2002] HLR 49; (2002) 5 CCLR 317.
42 [2002] EWCA Civ 366 per Lord Woolf CJ at [38].
43 [2002] EWCA Civ 366 at [38].

3.30 Lord Woolf also emphasised the flexibility of the CPR:

> We wish to make clear that the CPR provides a framework which is sufficiently flexible to enable all the issues between the parties to be determined. Issues if any as to the private law rights of the claimants have not been determined. A decision had to be reached as to what happened to these proceedings. In view of the decisions of [the judge below] and this Court the claimants have no public law rights ... In view of a possibility of a misunderstanding as to the scope of judicial review we draw attention to this and the powers of transfer under Part 54.'[44]

Applying *O'Reilly*: end of the road for abuse of process?

3.31 In the light of the decisions set out above, the scope for disputes on the correct forum for a claim is likely to be significantly reduced, but is unlikely to disappear. The substantive importance of the distinction between public and private law rights, referred to by Lord Woolf in *Dennis Rye*,[45] will still have certain procedural consequences, particularly where what is at stake is not a mixture of public and private law rights and obligations, but one or the other. It seems, for example, that a private law action claiming damages for breach of what, on analysis, is a public law obligation (leaving aside human rights cases)[46] will still be abusive because it is hopeless.

3.32 Accordingly, it would be premature to cast aside the principles enunciated in the following cases on abuse, relating specifically to challenges, by individuals, to the institution – or threat – of private law proceedings by public bodies.

3.33 In *Mohram Ali v Tower Hamlets LBC*,[47] decided after *Roy*, but before *O'Rourke*,[48] the Court of Appeal held that a homeless person was not entitled to challenge the suitability of the council's offer of permanent accommodation under the Housing Act 1985 s65(2),[49] by way of a civil action in the county court, but only by judicial review.

3.34 The approach of the court in *Ali* illustrates some of the factors which the court may consider in concluding whether a duty owed is in the sphere of public or private law, factors which are echoed in

---

44 [2002] EWCA Civ 366 at [39].
45 See paras 3.18–3.21 above.
46 On damages for which, see chapter 5 below, at paras 5.19–5.33.
47 [1993] QB 407, CA.
48 *O'Rourke v Camden LBC* [1998] AC 188, HL.
49 Now, so far as there is an equivalent, Housing Act 1996 s193(2) (as amended).

O'Rourke, and therefore whether an act or decision may be challenged by ordinary action. Nolan LJ said:

> The closing words of [Housing Act 1985 s69(1)] seem to me to call unmistakably for the exercise by the local authority of a subjective judgment as to what constitutes suitable accommodation ... I take this view of the matter the more readily because of the subject-matter of the judgment which is required. In many, if not most cases, the suitability of particular accommodation for a particular applicant is a matter upon which differing views may honestly and reasonably be held. The particular accommodation offered will inevitably depend upon what is available to the local authority from its own resources, or from the accessible resources of others. The amount of available accommodation will constantly vary. It is of the greatest importance that the suitable accommodation required by the homeless applicant should be provided with least possible delay. All of these factors seem to point to the desirability of the judgment being exercised by the local authority, with its unique knowledge of the facts, rather than by the courts.[50]

3.35   On the other hand, in *Hutchings v Islington LBC*[51] it was held that a former local government officer could bring proceedings for a declaration as to his superannuation entitlement, notwithstanding the statutory underpinning of the local government pension scheme or the appellate jurisdiction conferred on the secretary of state by the relevant provisions.[52] The right to claim payment of the pension, whether contractual or statutory, was a private law right enforceable by action against the authority; the issue arose from the former contract of employment, or at any rate the pension right did so; the superannuation provisions comprised a private law statutory right to receive a pension in accordance with the scheme.[53]

3.36   Subject to any specific statutory inhibition, a defendant could presumably defend a private action on the basis of a breach of a right conferred by the European Convention on Human Rights (the Convention) without needing to seek judicial review, as, under the Human Rights Act 1998, such matters can be litigated in 'any legal proceedings'.[54]

---

50   [1993] QB 407, CA, at 413G–414B.
51   (1998) 1 LGLR 1, CA.
52   Superannuation Act 1972 and Local Government Superannuation Regulations 1986 SI No 24 regs 99–104.
53   *Hutchings v Islington LBC* (1998) 1 LGLR 1, Pill LJ dissented.
54   See Human Rights Act 1998 s7(1)(b).

Applying *O'Reilly*: defending private law proceedings

3.37 Where a person is defending a private action against a public body, it is permissible to raise a public law defence and/or counterclaim in those proceedings without seeking an adjournment to apply for judicial review, provided such public law defence or counterclaim is linked to a private law defence. Accordingly, in *Wandsworth LBC v Winder*,[55] the House of Lords permitted a secure local authority tenant to defend the authority's possession proceedings based on rent arrears, on the basis that the only rent unpaid related to an unlawful and perverse rent increase. If the defence were made out, the tenant would have established a defence on the merits: that he was not liable to pay the sum claimed and so there were no rent arrears, and no ground for possession could be established. The tenant, furthermore, had not chosen the forum of the proceedings, and it would be a strange use of language to describe his behaviour as abusive.[56]

3.38 If, however, a defendant seeks to raise by way of a defence only matters which only exist in public law (such as a challenge to the decision to institute the proceedings, based on an allegation that that decision was improper due to an alleged breach of a public law duty) the proper procedure is to apply for an adjournment of the private action to enable an application for judicial review to be made or, if made already, to be resolved.[57] An adjournment will generally not be granted unless there is a real possibility that permission will be granted. The permission application must, in any event, be made promptly, ie, in relation to the public law decision challenged, not in relation to the conduct of the private law proceedings.

3.39 Accordingly, in numerous cases, the courts have held that a defence to private law proceedings was not properly relied on, where the only ground of defence was alleged to be the perversity of the decision to bring the proceedings. In *Tower Hamlets LBC v Abdi*,[58] and *Hackney*

---

55 [1985] AC 461, HL.

56 Per Lord Fraser, at 509E. See also *Leeds CC v Spencer* [2000] BLGR 68, where the Court of Appeal approved the circuit judge's decision that the defendant could defend debt proceedings by arguing the illegality of the claimant authority's statutory notice requiring the defendant to take steps, the defendant's failure to comply with which had led to the claimant taking the steps itself and claiming the cost of so doing from the defendant.

57 *Avon CC v Buscott* [1988] 1 All ER 841, CA. See also *West Glamorgan CC v Rafferty* [1987] 1 WLR 457.

58 (1992) 91 LGR 300, CA.

LBC v Lambourne,[59] a challenge to the suitability of long-term accommodation could not be raised as a defence to proceedings brought by the local authority for possession of insecure, interim accommodation (secured by the authority for the defendant pending the provision of the long-term accommodation) when the defendant had refused the long-term accommodation whose suitability was under challenge.

3.40   Even if the 'defence' was established, and it was shown that the local authority had failed to comply with its obligation to secure suitable long-term accommodation, and even if that entailed a continuing right on the part of the defendant to some interim accommodation secured by the authority, this still did not give the defendant any private law right to remain in the specific interim accommodation possession of which was sought, so as to defeat that claim on the merits. That interim accommodation had been let on a bare contractual basis with no security of tenure and a valid notice to quit had been served. The authority was accordingly entitled, as a matter of private law, to recover possession of it

3.41   Indeed, in *Lambourne* the Court of Appeal rejected the submission that a challenge, on public law grounds, to the decision to serve a notice to quit could be raised by way of defence. Although if the defendant succeeded in having the notice to quit quashed, he or she would have a private law right to remain in the temporary accommodation, to allow the validity of the notice to quit to be questioned in this way would be to circumvent the reasoning and policy of the decisions in *Ali* and *Abdi*. The defence was therefore struck out.

3.42   Similarly, in *Waverley DC v Hilden*,[60] travellers were not permitted to raise a defence to proceedings for possession of a copse based solely on allegations that the decision to take proceedings was procedurally defective and perverse, and in *Manchester City Council v Cochrane*,[61] the defendant introductory tenants, could not raise a defence to the possession proceedings against them based on an allegedly procedurally defective review which the local authority had carried out, when the governing legislation did not permit the county court to entertain any such defence.

---

59   (1992) 25 HLR 172, CA.
60   [1988] 1 WLR 246, ChD.
61   [1999] 1 WLR 809, CA.

Applying *O'Reilly*: defending criminal proceedings

3.43   It is now clear that a person charged with a criminal offence may raise, as a defence to the prosecution, the invalidity, whether procedural or substantive, of the measure pursuant to which the prosecution was brought. In *Boddington v British Transport Police*,[62] the House of Lords held that there was no proper basis for the distinction which the cases had previously drawn between procedural invalidity (which could form the basis of the defence) and substantive invalidity (which could not).[63] Accordingly, in *Boddington*, the defendant had been entitled to defend himself in a prosecution for smoking on a train in breach of a railway byelaw, by contending that the byelaw was invalid and a nullity, although on the merits, the defence failed.

Express indication of appropriate forum

3.44   Some statutes give clear indications of the most appropriate forum for litigation. For instance, under Housing Act 1985 s110, any question arising under Part IV of the Act (relating to public sector security of tenure) may be determined by the county court. This clear indication that such matters are more appropriately litigated in the county court (and implicitly therefore less appropriately by way of judicial review proceedings) is reinforced by a costs penalty provision in section 110(3). This states that if proceedings are brought in the High Court which, by virtue of the section, could have been brought in the county court, the person bringing them shall not be entitled to recover any costs. Identical provisions also appear in Housing Act 1996 ss138 (3) and 143N(4).

Summary

3.45   It can be seen, then, that notwithstanding the courts' plain reluctance to become embroiled in purely tactical use of procedural provisions, it remains essential to be aware of the distinctions discussed above. If there is genuine doubt, when acting for a claimant, about the appropriate way to proceed, it should be remembered that in genuinely difficult cases, the courts have demonstrated their unwillingness to permit

---

62   [2000] 2 AC 143, HL.
63   See, eg, *Bugg v DPP* [1993] QB 473.

technical arguments over the proper form of an action to result in the striking out of an otherwise meritorious and responsibly brought case.[64] The court does now have the power to transfer cases into and out of the Administrative Court.[65]

Non-reviewable public law decisions

Target duties

3.46   There is an important class of powers and duties which, although existing in public law, are not enforceable at the suit of an individual. They have become known as 'target' duties, meaning that they set a target for the authority to aim at, but failure to achieve which will not ordinarily entitle an individual to seek judicial review. The duty is owed to society as a whole or a specific section of it. Parliament has not intended to confer specific rights upon which an individual may rely.[66]

3.47   In *R v Inner London Education Authority ex p Ali*,[67] the Divisional Court held that the authority's obligation to secure that there were sufficient schools available in their area for providing primary and secondary education was a target duty.[68] Woolf LJ stated[69] that a 'degree of elasticity' was built into the duty. While a number of standards must be achieved by the authority, 'the setting of those standards is, in the first instance, for the local education authority alone to determine so long as those standards are not outside the tolerance provided by the section'.

3.48   This does not necessarily take the decision-maker outside the scope of judicial review altogether, if the decision can be shown to have been taken in contravention of the established principles of public law, such as the obligation to take account of all relevant matters, ignore the irrelevant, not to fetter a discretion, not to act perversely, etc. There is, nevertheless, no specific duty enforceable at the suit of the

---

64   See the discussion above at paras 3.18–3.30.
65   See CPR Pt 30; Rule 54.20 and see *R (Heather) v Leonard Cheshire Foundation* [2002] EWCA Civ 366; [2002] 2 All ER 396; [2002] HLR 49; (2002) 5 CCLR 317.
66   *R(A) v Lambeth LBC* [2003] UKHL 57, upholding [2001] EWCA Civ 1624; [2002] HLR 13; (2001) 4 CCLR 486.
67   (1990) 2 Admin LR 822, QBD.
68   Education Act 1944 s8.
69   (1990) 2 Admin LR 822 at 828D.

individual. Thus, in *R (A) v Lambeth LBC*,[70] the House of Lords confirmed that the obligation of a local authority under Children Act 1989 s17(1)[71] was a target duty only.[72]

Other decisions

3.49 In some circumstances, it has been held that review can only be sought of a decision which has already been taken; a belief that a certain decision will be taken is insufficient.[73] It may be, moreover, that a decision has no effect on individual rights and so does not engage public law principles or a right to seek a remedy from the courts.[74] In other cases, however, the absence of a decision has not been an obstacle to judicial review.[75]

3.50 Some interim decisions may be challengeable in their own right,[76] even though the claimant is entitled to wait until the conclusion of the proceedings. Others, however, may not be challenged: the claimant may only bring a challenge after the conclusion of the proceedings, or process, in which it was taken. An example of this class of case is where, for example, a formal decision-making process exists, which

---

70 [2003] UKHL 57. See specifically Lord Hope of Craighead at [85]–[91]; Lord Millett at [107]–[109] and Lord Scott of Foscote [113]–[119] and [135]. See also Lord Nicholls of Birkenhead, dissenting in part, at [25]–[30], with whom Lord Steyn agreed, at [64].

71 To safeguard and promote the welfare of children in their area who are in need and, so far as is consistent with that duty, to promote the upbringing of children by their families by providing a range and level of services appropriate to those children's needs.

72 See also, eg, *R v Islington LBC ex p Rixon* [1997] ELR 66; (1998) 1 CCLR 119, QBD; *R v Bath Mental Healthcare NHS Trust ex p Beck* (2000) 3 CCLR 5, QBD; *R v Kensington and Chelsea RLBC ex p Kujtim* [1999] 4 All ER 161; (2000) 32 HLR 579; 2 CCLR 340, CA.

73 See, eg, *R v Leicestershire Education Authority ex p Cannon* [1991] COD 120, DC. See also *R v Secretary of State for the Home Department ex p Wynne* [1993] 1 WLR 115.

74 See, eg, *R (Campaign for Nuclear Disarmament) v Prime Minister* [2002] EWHC 2759 (Admin) (2002) *Times* 27 December; *R (A) v Chief Constable of C* [2001] 1 WLR 461, QBD; *R (Southall) v Secretary of State of Foreign and Commonwealth Affairs* [2003] EWCA Civ 102; [2003] ACD 321.

75 See, eg, *R v Secretary of State for Transport ex p Richmond Upon Thames LBC (No 3)* [1995] Env LR 409, QBD; *R v Secretary of State for the Home Department ex p Tower Hamlets LBC* [1993] QB 632, CA.

76 See, eg, the consideration of this issue in *R (Burkett) v Hammersmith and Fulham LBC* [2002] UKHL 23; [2002] 1 WLR 1593, per Lord Steyn at [42].

Parliament intended to be used in its entirety prior to judicial review being sought.[77]

3.51   Where a prohibiting order is sought, the principles may differ. In particular, it would of course be contrary to the nature of the order for the claimant to await the outcome of the process which it is sought to stop.[78]

3.52   There is a conceptual distinction between decisions which it is not appropriate to challenge by way of judicial review and those where there is simply another more appropriate alternative remedy which the courts will require claimants to utilise. On the other hand, in practical terms, the two are so closely related that such distinctions may become blurred such that the distinction is without a difference. In *Re C (Adoption: Religious Observance)*,[79] Wilson J held that judicial review was wholly inappropriate to challenge a local authority's decisions concerning a child where care proceedings were already underway and could be resolved within those proceedings.

3.53   Similarly, in *R (X and Y) v Gloucestershire CC*,[80] the parents of an unborn baby were refused an injunction to restrain the local authority from bringing emergency protection proceedings in relation to the baby. Munby J held that judicial review proceedings to restrain the issue of proceedings could only be appropriate in exceptional circumstances, such as: where the court would have no jurisdiction to hear those other proceedings; or they would be vexatious or otherwise an abuse of process; or a party to existing proceedings would be severely prejudiced by the issue of further proceedings. In addition, judicial review should not be used where another equally effective remedy is available; it is a blunt and unsatisfactory tool to deal with such sensitive and difficult matters as care and similar cases; and it would

---

77 See, eg, *R (AM) v Head Teacher of St George's Catholic School and others* [2002] EWCA Civ 1822; [2003] ELR 104, CA, where the court refused relief on judicial review, on the basis that it was inappropriate to have brought the claim challenging a decision to exclude a child from school, confirmed at the first stage of the statutory appeals process, because Parliament intended the remaining stages of that 'tailor-made' process to be exhausted. See also, eg, *R v Association of Futures Brokers and Dealers Ltd ex p Mordens Ltd* [1991] COD 40, QBD.

78 See above, chapter 2 and below, chapter 5.

79 [2002] 1 FLR 1119. See also *Re L (Care Proceedings: Human Rights Claims)* [2003] EWHC 665, per Munby J at [36], where he applied the same principle to the raising of human rights challenges in judicial review proceedings rather than in the existing care proceedings.

80 [2003] EWHC 850 (Admin).

be intolerable if the court should deny a child the protection it urgently needed because it felt inhibited from taking steps which may impinge on the judicial review claim.

Powers and duties

3.54 Reviewable decisions or actions will be taken pursuant either to a duty imposed on the decision-maker in question or a power conferred upon her or him. Most of the cases in this area of the law concern the exercise by bodies of discretionary powers, or of duties which include some discretionary elements: where statute imposes a straightforward duty on a body, a private law right to the discharge of that duty may well be conferred upon the intended beneficiaries of the duty, giving rise to a private action for an injunction and/or damages for breach of statutory duty.[81]

3.55 Accordingly, judicial review is more frequently concerned with two kinds of duty, each of which involves elements of discretion or judgment to be exercised by the body discharging the duty. The first type is where the duty only arises if certain subjective criteria are satisfied (eg, '... if it appears to the authority that ... then the authority shall...'). The second is where the duty itself contains subjective elements (eg, the duty to secure that 'suitable' accommodation becomes available).[82]

3.56 Such duties may be treated in the same way as pure discretions (eg , '... if the authority is satisfied that ... it *may* ...)[83] in so far as review is sought of the discretionary element(s) of the duty – for instance, the 'suitability' of the accommodation offered. The same factors – relevant and irrelevant considerations, motives, fettering of discretion, etc – will need to be considered, whether the decision is taken pursuant to a power or a duty.[84]

3.57 If review is sought of a failure to comply with the duty at all, one basis of review, leaving aside bad faith, would generally be that the authority had misdirected itself in law or, in other words, applied the wrong test. This may occur, for instance, if, in a homelessness case, an authority were to write in terms that notwithstanding the fact that an applicant satisfied all the criteria, the authority did not intend to secure that any accommodation at all became available.

---

81 See *X (Minors) v Bedfordshire CC* [1995] 2 AC 633, HL.

82 Housing Act 1996 ss193(2) and 206.

83 See, as an example, Housing Act 1996 s198(1).

84 See chapter 6 – Grounds on which review may be sought.

3.58   It is important to note, and can be seen by studying any Act which creates public law duties and powers, that in so far as the discretionary elements are concerned, some decisions require a higher degree of certainty than others on the part of the decision-maker regarding whether the criteria for the making of the decision are fulfilled. Some powers may be exercisable 'if it appears to the authority', others 'if the authority is satisfied', yet others 'if the authority has reason to believe'.

3.59   It is now clear that no power, however subjectively worded, is unfettered, unreviewable or exercisable unreasonably. Nevertheless, it will be easier to show that a decision-maker could not have had 'reason to believe' that certain facts were so on the evidence before her or him, than that the same facts could not have 'appeared' to be so to the same decision-maker.[85]

---

85 For grounds for review and the effect of subjective wording, see chapter 6, at paras 6.6–6.7, especially *Padfield v Minister of Agriculture, Fisheries and Food* [1968] AC 997, HL; *Secretary of State for Education and Science v Tameside BC* [1977] AC 1014, HL, and the dissenting speech of Lord Atkin in *Liversidge v Anderson* [1942] AC 206. HL.

CHAPTER 4

Parties

4.1   There are three potential parties to judicial review proceedings: the claimant; the defendant; and an interested party.

The claimant – sufficient interest

4.2   The claimant must be someone with 'sufficient interest' in the matter to which the application relates.[1] This is commonly referred to as *locus standi* or 'standing'.

4.3   What constitutes a sufficient interest is a matter of mixed fact and law. In the leading authority, *R v Inland Revenue Commissioners ex p National Federation of Self-Employed and Small Businesses Ltd (NFSSB)*,[2] the House of Lords held that the issue is relevant both at the permission stage and on the substantive hearing. A different test, however, is to be applied at each: on a permission application, standing is merely a 'threshold' question for the court, designed only to turn away hopeless or meddlesome applications and prevent abuse by busybodies, cranks and other mischief-makers. A ruling at this stage in favour of the claimant is, however, only provisional and may be revised on further consideration by the court hearing the full application. The test at the full hearing is whether the claimant can show a strong enough case on the merits, judged in relation to his or her own concern with the subject matter of the application. This is because the merits of the case and the standing of the claimant are inextricably linked. It is wrong, therefore, to treat the question of standing as a preliminary issue: it cannot be considered in the abstract or as an isolated point but must be taken together with the legal and factual context. The reason for this seems to be that the test at the second stage is of a sufficient interest in *the matter to which the application relates*.[3]

Examples

4.4   In most cases, it will be clear whether or not an applicant has sufficient interest to bring an application. However, it has been held that an applicant did not have sufficient standing to challenge a decision of the Serious Fraud Office relating to his wife.[4] Similarly, parents were not

1   Supreme Court Act 1981 s31(3).
2   [1982] AC 617, HL.
3   [1982] AC 617 especially per Lord Wilberforce at 630C–E; Lord Diplock at 643G–644B; Lord Scarman at 653G.
4   *R v Director of the Serious Fraud Office ex p Johnson (Malcolm Keith)* [1993] COD 58, QBD.

entitled to challenge the refusal of an army board of inquiry to disclose to them its report relating to the death of their son.[5] In *Feakins v Secretary of State for Environment, Food and Rural Affairs*,[6] the court held that although the claimant did not have sufficient interest in the subject matter of the claim, the court would nevertheless consider the merits of the case on the basis that if the decision challenged was unlawful, it would be in the public interest for the court to indicate this. In *R (Davies) v Secretary of State for Environment, Food and Rural Affairs*,[7] the court struck out a claim as an abuse of the process of the court where the named claimant was a company which had ceased to exist and had no interest in the proceedings, and the individual who was purporting to pursue the claim on behalf of the company had no authority to do so.

4.5 In a housing law context, see *R v Manchester City Council ex p Baragrove Properties Ltd*,[8] where the landlord of housing benefits claimants was held to have standing to challenge the local authority's decision to treat the benefit applicants – the tenants of the claimant – as not liable to make payments in respect of their tenancies, and therefore not entitled to any benefit.[9] This was because the claimant's own conduct was central to the authority's decision: the authority's view had been that the claimant was deliberately seeking tenants who were eligible for benefit in order to charge high rents which would be paid in housing benefit.

A more appropriate challenger?

4.6 The availability of another, more appropriate, party to bring a challenge may influence the decision as to whether or not a claimant should be accorded standing. In *Durayappah v Fernando*,[10] the House of Lords remarked that if the person principally affected by a decision chose to take no action to challenge it, there seemed no reason why anybody else should be permitted to challenge it.[11] In *R (Bulger) v Secretary of State for the Home Department*,[12] the court refused standing to the

5 *R v Secretary of State for Defence ex p Sancto* (1993) 5 Admin LR 673, QBD.
6 [2002] EWHC 2574 (Admin); [2003] EHLR 7.
7 [2002] EWHC 2762 (Admin); [2003] ACD 34.
8 (1991) 23 HLR 337, QBD.
9 Under Housing Benefit (General) Regulations 1987 SI No 1971 reg 7(b). Now reg 7(1)(b).
10 [1967] 2 AC 337, HL.
11 See also *R v Bow County Court ex p Pelling* [1999] 1 WLR 1807.
12 [2001] EWHC Admin 119; [2001] 3 All ER 449, QBD.

father of a murdered child to apply for judicial review of a decision of the Lord Chief Justice to reduce the tariffs of the sentences being served by the children who had committed the murder. Since the Crown or a defendant would be able to challenge the decision, it was unnecessary and undesirable for a third party to seek to intervene. The Lord Chief Justice's invitation to the claimant to make representations to him did not confer standing on the claimant to challenge the tariff.

Education

4.7   In education cases, such as those relating to refusals of admission or school closure or re-organisation, there has been judicial consideration of whether the parent or the child (or both) would have standing to bring a challenge. In the context of school admissions cases, it has been held that while the child may well have a sufficient interest to mount a challenge, nevertheless the parent(s) should usually be named as the claimant(s) as the only reason for bringing a challenge in the name of the child is usually to be able to obtain public funding for the challenge and to protect the parents in costs should the challenge fail. This was an abuse and a device and reason for refusing permission to apply for judicial review.[13]

4.8   In relation to school closure, however, the position appears to be somewhat different. In *R (WB and KA) v Leeds School Organisation Committee*,[14] Scott Baker J held that issue was relevant not to standing but to abuse and therefore the court's discretion. Both parents and children had a sufficient interest to bring judicial review proceedings in school closure or re-organisation cases, and while in many cases it may be the parents who had the real interest and while it may be an abuse of process to name the child as the claimant for the purposes of obtaining funding and protection against a possible costs order, clear evidence would be needed to establish such an abuse. The school admissions cases, referred to above, were distinguished on the basis that the appellate regime under consideration made it clear that the right of appeal was that of the parent and not the child. There was no indication that the court's decisions in those cases were intended for any wider application.[15]

---

13   *R v Richmond LBC ex p JC* [2001] ELR 13, and *B v Head Teacher of Alperton Community School* [2001] ELR 359.
14   [2002] EWHC 1927 (Admin); [2003] ACD 5.
15   [2002] EWHC 1927 (Admin) at [32]–[37].

Capacity

4.9　It has been held that, in addition to standing, the claimant must also have capacity (on ordinary civil law principles) to bring litigation;[16] the issue to be determined at the permission stage.[17] More recently, the courts appear to have relaxed this requirement somewhat. In a number of cases, unincorporated associations have brought challenges successfully.[18]

4.10　In *R v Traffic Commissioner for the North Western Traffic Area ex p 'Brake'*,[19] the court suggested that there may be no requirement for capacity in public law claims, which were different from private actions. In a claim concerning breach of a private right, such a right had to be shown to exist and this could only be so if the claimant was a legal person who could enjoy such a right. In public law claims, however, the focus was on the decision of the public body. The dispute, at least technically, was between the Crown and the public body[20] and the issue was whether the act challenged was unlawful, and whether the claimant could show a sufficient interest to bring the challenge. It was not in every case that a claimant would have to show, therefore, that a right of his or hers had been infringed, but rather that the illegality of the public body's act had in some way affected her or him.

4.11　In *R v Ministry of Agriculture, Fisheries and Food ex p British Pig Industry Support Group*,[21] it was held that there was no reason in principle why an unincorporated association should not be entitled to bring judicial review proceedings, so long as proper provision was made for the defendant to be protected in costs. It may not be possible to make an order of security for costs against a party who was not a corporate body,[22] and if that were so, it may be that the court ought, as a condition of the grant of permission, to require that a legal person be joined as a party for the purpose of ensuring that an effective costs order can be made where appropriate should the defendant succeed.

16　*R v Darlington BC ex p Association of Darlington Taxi Owners* [1994] COD 424, QBD (unincorporated association lacked capacity).

17　*R v Darlington BC ex p Association of Darlington Taxi Owners* [1994] COD 424, QBD.

18　See, eg, *R v Gloucestershire CC ex p Barry* [1996] 4 All ER 421 (in the Court of Appeal); *R v Liverpool CC ex p Baby Products Association* (2000) 2 LGLR 689; [2000] BLGR 171, QBD.

19　[1996] COD 248.

20　But see, on this point, *R (Ben-Abdelaziz) v Haringey LBC* [2001] EWCA Civ 803; [2001] 1 WLR 1485.

21　[2000] Eu LR 724, QBD.

22　See CPR r25.13(2)(c).

Public interest challenges

4.12 Public interest challenges have been described as having the 'essential characteristics' that they raise issues of general importance in circumstances where the challenger has no private interest in the outcome of the case.[23] In *NFSSB*,[24] Lord Diplock expressed the view that traditional tests of standing may be too restrictive in such cases:

> It would, in my view, be a grave lacuna in our system of public law if a pressure group … or even a single public-spirited taxpayer were prevented by outdated technical rules of *locus standi* from bringing the matter to the attention of the court to vindicate the rule of law and get the unlawful conduct stopped … It is not … a sufficient answer to say that judicial review of the actions of officers or departments of central government is unnecessary because they are accountable to Parliament for the way in which they carry out their functions. They are accountable to Parliament for what they do so far as regards efficiency and policy, and of that Parliament is the only judge; they are accountable to a court of justice for the lawfulness of what they do, and of that the court is the only judge.[25]

4.13 The courts have, in recent times, adopted a more liberal approach to standing in such cases.[26] Mere busybodies will not have sufficient interest,[27] although clearly there is some room for difference of opinion on where the line may properly be drawn between busybodies and the 'public-spirited' people of whom Lord Diplock spoke with approval in *NFSSB*.[28] In *R v Her Majesty's Treasury ex p Smedley*,[29] a claimant in his capacity of elector and taxpayer was permitted to challenge (albeit unsuccessfully) the government's undertaking to pay by Order in Council its contribution of £121 million to the European Community.

---

23 *R v Lord Chancellor ex p Child Poverty Action Group* [1999] 1 WLR 347.

24 *R v Inland Revenue Commissioners ex p NFSSB* [1985] AC 617, HL.

25 At 644E.

26 The decision of Schiemann J in *R v Secretary of State for the Environment ex p Rose Theatre Trust Company* [1990] 1 QB 504, QBD has not been followed. In that case, he held that a person could not obtain sufficient interest simply by writing to the decision-maker and receiving a reply. Nor would a group of individuals each without sufficient interest in a matter acquire a sufficient interest simply by forming themselves into a group or company, purporting to have such an interest, used as their 'campaign's vehicle'; see 521C–E.

27 See, eg, *R v Monopolies and Mergers Commission ex p Argyll Group plc* [1986] 1 WLR 763, CA.

28 For example, *R v Legal Aid Board ex p Bateman* [1992] 1 WLR 711, CA, where standing was accorded to a 'responsible' person.

29 [1985] QB 657, CA.

In *R v Secretary of State for Foreign and Commonwealth Affairs ex p Rees-Mogg*,[30] the claimant's long-standing and 'sincere interest in constitutional affairs' was held to be a sufficient basis for according him standing to challenge the implementation of the Maastrict treaty (although the claimant was also a taxpayer).

4.14 Pressure and public interest groups also appear to have the requisite standing in suitable cases (and see above[31] in relation to the requirement or otherwise for legal capacity). The Child Poverty Action Group has been held to have standing in an application to challenge the manner in which the secretary of state was administering the law to the alleged detriment of claimants of benefits.[32] The standing of interest groups was considered in more detail in *R v HM Inspectorate of Pollution and Ministry of Agriculture, Fisheries and Food ex p Greenpeace Ltd*.[33] Otton J held that the claimant pressure group did have sufficient interest to challenge the decision of the inspectorate to vary authorisations granted to British Nuclear Fuels Ltd to discharge certain forms of radioactive waste from Sellafield, to permit the testing of the THORP plant.

4.15 The question of standing was, he held, primarily one of discretion and it was appropriate to take into account, in considering the matter, the nature of Greenpeace and the extent of its interest in the issues raised in the application, the remedy it sought to achieve and the nature of the relief sought. Considering these matters, the judge noted the level of support Greenpeace enjoyed worldwide, its consultative status with several United Nations bodies and the fact that it was a respectable and responsible body with a genuine concern for the environment and a bona fide interest in BNFL's activities at Sellafield and the discharge of radioactive waste. In particular, he had regard to the fact that 2,500 of the body's UK supporters came from the Cumbria region and it would be to ignore the blindingly obvious for the court to disregard the concern and perception of danger to their health and safety from any additional radioactive discharge, which such people inevitably felt. In addition, Greenpeace had been treated as one of the consultees during the consultation process and had been invited to comment on the Inspectorate's letter in which it had stated it was 'minded to vary' BNFL's existing authorisations.

---

30 [1994] QB 552, QBD.

31 At paras 4.9–4.11.

32 *R v Secretary of State for Social Services ex p CPAG* (1984) *Times* 16 August, QBD.

33 [1994] 4 All ER 329, QBD (see also, on appeal [1994] 1 WLR 570, CA).

4.16   If Greenpeace were denied standing, moreover, those it represented might not have an effective way of bringing these issues before the court. It was unlikely that an individual neighbour or employee of BNFL would command the expertise which was at the disposal of Greenpeace, and so a less well-informed challenge might be mounted which would stretch, unnecessarily, the court's resources and would not afford the court the assistance it required to do justice between the parties. In addition, if an individual applicant was legally aided, the respondents would have no effective remedy in costs.

4.17   As to relief, while the House of Lords had held in *NFSSB*[34] that the seeking of an order of mandamus (a mandatory order) may be a reason to decline jurisdiction, here certiorari (a quashing order) was sought, and the injunction claimed, if the decision were quashed, would still be in the discretion of the court. It was not to be assumed, however, that Greenpeace or any other interest group would automatically possess standing in any application for judicial review. The matter must be decided on the facts of each individual case as a matter of discretion.

Control of public interest challenges

4.18   While the courts have generally adopted a liberal approach to standing in relation to challenges brought by public interest groups,[35] it has nonetheless been suggested that they will require strict compliance with the rules in such cases which, although now accepted and indeed a 'greatly valued dimension of the judicial review jurisdiction' are open to potential abuse, meaning that delay will be tolerated less readily.[36] This should not be seen as creating too high a hurdle, however, nor as encouraging premature applications. In *R v Secretary of State for Trade and Industry ex p Greenpeace*,[37] the court could not envisage many cases where on the same facts a public interest challenge would be refused because of delay where a private claimant would be permitted to proceed.

---

34   *R v Inland Revenue Commissioners ex p NFSSB* [1985] AC 617, HL.

35   See, eg, *R v Secretary of State for Foreign and Commonwealth Affairs ex p World Development Movement* [1995] 1 WLR 386, DC, where the claimant was success-ful in challenging aid for the building of the Pergau Dam; *R v Secretary of State for the Environment ex p Kirkstall Valley Campaign Ltd* [1996] 3 All ER 304.

36   *R v Secretary of State for Trade and Industry ex p Greenpeace Ltd* [1998] Env LR 415, per Laws J at 425.

37   [2000] Env LR 221.

Standing in Human Rights Act 1998 cases

4.19 In human rights cases, there is a different test for standing. The European Convention on Human Rights[38] and the Human Rights Act (HRA) 1998[39] frame the test in terms that the person seeking review must be a 'victim' of the act or decision complained of.

4.20 The jurisprudence of the Strasbourg Court has been relatively elastic as to who may properly be considered a 'victim' – article 34 does not define the term – though it is clear that there must be some connection between the claimant and the injury or violation complained of. In other words, the claimant must show he or she has been, or that there is a reasonable likelihood that he or she will be, directly affected in some way. In *Cullen v Chief Constable of the Royal Ulster Constabulary*,[40] Lord Millett noted that a person could qualify as a victim, in accordance with Strasbourg case-law, even if the alleged breach of her or his rights had caused no damage.[41]

4.21 More importantly, the Convention does not provide for applications in the form of a 'popular action'. Thus, although in other respects the Strasbourg jurisprudence is merely something to which due regard must be paid, in relation to the definition of 'victim' Convention law appears to be decisive.[42] It is unlikely in the extreme that a pressure group will be able to assert that it is a victim for the purposes of the Human Rights Act 1998 even though it may well represent victims. Accordingly, on issues arising under the HRA 1998, there would seem to be no alternative to the old approach in judicial review proceedings of selecting a 'test claimant'.[43] The pressure group itself, however, may well be able to appear as an interested party.[44]

The position of the Crown

4.22 In *R (Ben-Abdelaziz) v Haringey LBC*,[45] the Court of Appeal held that the position of the Crown in judicial review proceedings (given that it is

38 Article 34.
39 Human Rights Act 1998 s7(1).
40 [2003] UKHL 39; [2003] 1 WLR 1736.
41 [2003] UKHL 39 at [81].
42 Human Rights Act 1998 s7(6).
43 For example, *R v HM Treasury ex p Smedley* [1985] QB 657.
44 See paras 4.26–4.28 below. See also chapter 20 below at para 20.31.
45 [2001] EWCA Civ 803; [2001] 1 WLR 1485.

listed as a party in every claim) was best described as 'nominal'. In reality, the claim was a contest between the claimant, who brought and pursued it, and the defendant; the proceedings were not brought by the Crown or at the Crown's instigation. The requirement for permission could not be construed as having any effect on this position.[46]

The defendant

4.23   As stated above, the defendant must be an inferior court, a tribunal or some other public body. It must, in addition, have been acting in a public law rather than a private law capacity in relation to the act or decision under challenge.[47]

Claimant and defendant

4.24   On occasion, public bodies, especially local authorities, have sought judicial review of decisions they themselves have taken. While, conceptually, this would seem to pose difficulties, the courts have generally adopted a relaxed attitude, especially where the alternative to such actions is even less attractive, such as permitting clearly unlawful conduct to continue in circumstances where there is no other available mode of challenge and/or no other claimant likely to come forward.

4.25   In *R v Birmingham City Council and Fitzpatrick ex p Birmingham City Council*,[48] the court permitted the authority to challenge a decision of its own housing benefit review board, in circumstances where the board's decision – that the housing benefit applicant was entitled to benefit – clearly contravened the Housing Benefit Regulations and was unlawful. Similarly, the leader of an authority has been entitled to seek judicial review of a decision of his authority's planning

---

46 This may seem rather a strange matter for the court to be asked to determine in the 21st century. In fact, it concerned rather an ingenious attempt to circumvent the provisions of Human Rights Act 1998 s22(4) to enable a claimant to claim compensation for an act that was completed prior to the Act coming into force, by arguing that the judicial review proceedings they had brought were proceedings brought by a public authority (the Crown).

47 See chapter 2 above, regarding identifying a public body amenable to review, and chapter 3 above, on reviewable decisions.

48 (1992) 24 HLR 279.

committee on the ground of bias/fraud,[49] and the adoption of a new constitution by an authority has been quashed on the application of the authority's chief executive where a procedural error had the effect that, by statute, all of the authority's elected members had ceased to be members of the authority.[50]

Third parties

4.26   Interested third parties have a right to be served with the application and appear on the hearing of the application.[51] In certain circumstances, such as in a human rights case where a declaration of incompatibility is to be sought, the Crown must be served as an interested third party. It will usually be for the claimant to give informal notice to the Crown, and for the court to decide whether the making of a declaration is sufficiently likely to render formal notice necessary.[52]

4.27   Any person, even if not served, may apply to the court to file evidence and/or to make representations at the hearing of the judicial review claim.[53] Such an application should be made by letter to the Administrative Court Office, setting out who the applicant is and why and in what form he or she wishes to participate in the proceedings. If a prospective costs order is sought, the letter should also set out the type of, and grounds for the, order sought. Applications of this type sought must be made at the earliest reasonable opportunity as it will usually be essential not to delay the hearing of the claim.[54] Where all parties consent, the court may deal with such an application without a hearing.[55] The court may give permission on conditions and may also give case management directions.[56]

---

49 *R v Bassetlaw DC ex p Oxby* [1998] BLGR 283.

50 *R (Meredith) v Merthyr Tydfil County Borough Council* [2002] EWHC 634 (Admin).

51 CPR rr54.7 and 54.17. See further below at paras 18.07 and 20.31.

52 *Poplar HARCA v Donoghue* [2001] EWCA Civ 595; [2001] QB 48; [2001] 3 WLR 183; [2001] 4 All ER 604; (2001) 33 HLR 823.

53 CPR r54.17.

54 CPR Practice Direction 54, paras 13.3–13.5.

55 CPR PD 54, para 13.1.

56 CPR PD 54, para 13.2.

4.28   These provisions are considerably wider than their equivalents under the old procedural regime.[57] Under the old rules, however, interested third parties frequently participated. It was held, however, that there was no general right for a third party to be heard on appeal, even if he or she had taken part at first instance,[58] though this did not preclude the appellate court in its discretion from allowing such a person to be heard. Whether the court would take the same approach under the CPR is not clear.[59]

57   RSC Ord 53 r9(1).

58   *R v Licensing Authority ex p Smith Kline & French Laboratories Ltd* [1990] 1 AC 64, HL.

59   But see the comments of Brooke LJ in *Thurrock BC v Secretary of State for the Environment, Transport and the Regions* [2001] EWCA Civ 226; (2001) EGCS 3 at [23] to the effect that as the CPR created a new procedural code, old authorities relating to procedural issues may be of little use and could even be positively misleading.

CHAPTER 5

Remedies available in judicial review

continued overleaf

5.1   The following remedies may be available in judicial review proceedings:

- an order of certiorari (now known as a 'quashing order')[1]
- an order of mandamus (now known as a 'mandatory order')[2]
- an order of prohibition (now known as a 'prohibiting order')[3]
- a declaration
- an injunction
- damages.

5.2   Certiorari, mandamus and prohibition are the names given to these remedies in Supreme Court Act 1981 ss29–33, which have not been repealed, and are known as the 'prerogative' orders, as they derive from the prerogative writs of the same names,[4] which were traditionally used by the common law courts to control the use and abuse of powers. In accordance with the philosophy of the Civil Procedure Rules, to modernise legal language including, among other things, avoiding the use of Latin, they are now known as quashing, mandatory and prohibiting orders.

5.3   In addition to those remedies listed above, the court has certain ancillary powers, and it is possible to apply for interim relief (see below). It should be remembered that the grant of a remedy is discretionary, even if the court is satisfied that the decision under challenge was reached improperly.[5]

The quashing order (certiorari)

5.4   As its new name states, a quashing order results in the quashing of the decision or order under challenge. In some cases, the court may remit the matter back and direct that the body or tribunal reach a conclusion in accordance with the court's findings.[6] In others, the court may take the decision itself.[7]

---

1 CPR r54.1(2)(d).
2 CPR r54.1(2)(b).
3 CPR r54.1(2)(c).
4 See Supreme Court Act 1981 s29(5).
5 Traditionally, the discretionary nature of relief was reflected in judicial review terminology – 'relief' was 'sought' not 'claimed'. This use of language has been continued in the new judicial review Claim Form (N461) section 6, but not in CPR r54.6(1)(c). See further below, as to the discretionary nature of relief, chapter 7, paras 7.1–7.25.
6 See para 5.34 below.
7 See para 5.35 below.

5.5   It follows from the nature of this remedy, and indeed of judicial review as a whole, that although a claimant may succeed in obtaining a quashing order, this does not necessarily mean that he or she will succeed in obtaining a different or more favourable decision when the matter is reconsidered by the decision-maker in question. It may well be that when the matter is reconsidered in accordance with the law, the decision-maker could quite lawfully reach the same decision again.

5.6   A stay or injunction is likely to be available, in principle, as an interim measure, pending the full hearing.[8]

The mandatory order (mandamus)

5.7   A mandatory order is an order requiring the performance of a specified act or duty. A claimant will not usually be entitled to claim a mandatory order requiring the defendant to do the substantive act or to reach the substantive decision which the claimant desires (ie, to decide in the claimant's favour).

5.8   Unless: (a) there exists an absolute duty, as distinct from a mere discretion or a duty arising only upon the defendant being satisfied regarding certain facts; or (b) the defendant has already decided in the claimant's favour all the issues necessary to impose a duty to do that which the claimant seeks; or (c) only two decisions were possible and, of those two, the one made by the defendant has been held to be perverse by the court, leaving only one lawful option available, it will not be possible to seek a mandatory order requiring the body to act in accordance with the claimant's wishes. All that may be sought is an order with the effect of requiring that the defendant reconsider the application, this time in accordance with the law, and without making the errors (or any others) which led to the first decision being quashed.

5.9   In many cases the courts are reluctant to grant mandatory orders, as it is generally presumed (with good cause) that if the court has ruled a decision to be unlawful, the defendant will comply with – and give effect to – that ruling by reconsidering the matter without the need for such a draconian order. Accordingly, it is often advisable for an applicant to seek a declaration in addition or in the alternative (see paras 5.11–5.14 below).

8   See paras 5.45–5.49 below.

The prohibiting order (prohibition)

5.10 A prohibiting order prevents the decision-maker concerned from acting or continuing to act in excess of jurisdiction. As with mandatory orders, however, the court may well consider that it is sufficient to grant a declaration in terms that the proposed action is in excess of the decision-maker's jurisdiction, or otherwise improper, unless the claimant can demonstrate why this is not so and that prohibition is actually necessary. A stay or injunction is available as an interim measure.

Declaration and injunction

5.11 A declaration is not a prerogative order, nor is it a remedy in the same sense as the others discussed in this chapter. It does not quash anything nor require anyone to do or refrain from doing anything, but is simply a determination by the court of the respective rights and obligations of the parties (or in some circumstances of the error into which the decision-maker has fallen[9]). In judicial review proceedings, the court, in its discretion, frequently grants declarations instead of mandatory relief, on the basis that public bodies comply with decisions of the court without the necessity of a mandatory order.

5.12 A declaration or injunction will only be granted where one of the prerogative writs could have been granted,[10] although this does not prevent a claimant from seeking such remedies instead of a prerogative order. Indeed, where a declaration of unlawful conduct is necessary in order to facilitate a claim for damages, the court will generally be willing to allow a claim to proceed, even where no substantive relief is required.[11]

---

9 See, eg, *R v Secretary of State for Social Security ex p Association of Metropolitan Authorities* (1992) 25 HLR 131, QBD.

10 *R v Inland Revenue Commissioners ex p National Federation of Self-Employed and Small Businesses* [1982] AC 617, HL, per Lord Scarman at 648; cited in *Davy v Spelthorne DC* [1984] AC 262, HL, per Lord Wilberforce at 278D; see also *R v Chelmsford Crown Court ex p Chief Constable of Essex* [1994] 1 WLR 359, DC, and Supreme Court Act 1981 s31(2).

11 See, eg, *R v Northavon DC ex p Palmer* (1993) 25 HLR 674, QBD. On the hearing of the damages claim (1994) 26 HLR 572, QBD, the court held that the matters complained of gave rise to no right to damages. As to the right to claim damages, see further paras 5.15–5.18 below. See also: *O'Rourke v Camden LBC* [1998] AC 188, HL; *O'Rourke v United Kingdom* (2001) 26 June (unreported) and *R (Morris) v Newham LBC* [2002] EWHC 1262 (Admin). But compare *R v Blandford Justices ex p Pamment* [1990] 1 WLR 1490, CA.

5.13   A declaration or injunction may be granted where the court considers it just and convenient to do so, taking account of the matters in
respect of which relief is sought, the nature of the persons and/or
bodies against whom relief is sought and to all the circumstances of the
case.[12] This will not always be the case. In *R (Campaign for Nuclear
Disarmament v Prime Minister,*[12a] for example, the Court declined to
grant an advisory declaration as to whether UN resolution 1441 authorised military action to be taken against Iraq, on the basis that it was not
appropriate for the court to grant declarations on the meaning of international instruments which had no existence in UK law, where no
rights of any UK citizen were affected by it. Similarly, in *R (Southall)
v Secretary of State for Foreign and Commonwealth Affairs,*[13] the Court of
Appeal refused permission to appeal a refusal of permission to move
for judicial review where the claimant sought a declaration that the
government must hold a referendum or general election prior to
approving any European constitution. The court held that the declarations sought were inappropriately vague and that the case was unarguable, but that in any event, as a matter of discretion the court would
refuse a declaration where there was no draft treaty in existence
to which all the relevant governments had consented and so it
was impossible to evaluate what domestic constitutional effect the
implementation of such a treaty would have.

5.14   By CPR r54.3, the Part 54 procedure may, but need not, be used
for judicial review claims where all that is sought is a declaration
and/or an injunction. An application for an injunction, however, which
seeks to restrain a person from acting in any office in which he or she
is not entitled to act, must be made in Part 54 proceedings.[13a]

Damages (other than claims under the Human Rights Act 1998)

5.15   A judicial review claim may include a claim for damages but may not
seek damages alone.[14] An award of damages is discretionary, and the
court may only make one, other than in human rights cases which
are considered separately below, if it is satisfied that if the claim had

---

12   Supreme Court Act (SCA) 1981 s31(2).
12a [2002] EWHC 2759 (Admin); (2002) *Times* 27 December.
13   [2003] EWCA Civ 1002; [2003] ACD 321.
13a SCA 1981 s30 and CPR r54.2(d).
14   CPR r54.3(2).

been brought as a private law action, begun at the same time as the judicial review claim, the claimant could or would have been awarded damages. In other words, a damages claim may only be included in order to bring a valid private law claim for damages in the same proceedings as the public law challenge.

5.16   The court enjoys no wider jurisdiction to award damages to a claimant than it would enjoy if a damages claim came before it in the usual way, nor does a claimant acquire any additional cause of action for damages in respect of a breach of a public law duty.[15] In numerous cases, the court has refused a claim for damages on the ground that the duty breached existed in public law only and so gave rise to no private law right to damages.[16]

5.17   Under the old procedural rules, any loss and damage claimed had to be fully particularised,[17] and although there is no specific equivalent provision contained in CPR Part 54, it is advisable that any claimant wishing to include a claim for damages should give as much information in the claim form concerning the grounds for and amount of the claim as he or she would if bringing a CPR Part 7 claim.

5.18   In practice, if a claim for judicial review has been successful, a course frequently taken by the court is to order, at the conclusion of the substantive hearing, that the damages claim proceed as if commenced by private action and stand adjourned, sometimes to the Queen's Bench Division and sometimes even to the county court, for an assessment of damages hearing. Given the difficulty of adjudicating on factual disputes in the Administrative Court, it is unusual for the judicial review court to hear the damages claim, or to assess the quantum, itself.[18]

Damages in human rights cases

5.19   Damages for any act or proposed act by a public authority, which the court finds unlawful may only be awarded by a court that has power to award damages or order the payment of compensation in civil

---

15   SCA 1981 s31(4), and see *Calveley v Chief Constable of Merseyside Police* [1989] QB 136, CA.

16   See the cases referred to above at note 11.

17   RSC Ord 53 r7(2) applying RSC Ord 18 r12.

18   See, eg, *R v Lambeth LBC ex p Campbell* (1994) 26 HLR 618, and the cases noted above at note 11.

proceedings.[19] The court's jurisdiction to award damages is confined by the requirements of Human Rights Act 1998 s8(3), which provides that:

> (3) No award of damages is to be made unless, taking account of all the circumstances of the case, including –
>   (a) any other relief or remedy granted, or order made, in relation to the act in question (by that or any other court),
>   and
>   (b) the consequences of any decision (of that or any other court) in respect of that act,
>   the court is satisfied that the award is necessary to afford just satisfaction to the person in whose favour it is made.

5.20　In *Cullen v Chief Constable of the Royal Ulster Constabulary*,[20] Lord Millett stated that the significance of the limitation applied by this provision should not be overlooked. 'It means that Parliament has contemplated that there would be cases where breach of a Convention right did not automatically give rise to an award of damages, and this is inconsistent with the notion that such an award is necessary to vindicate the right'. The most obvious example of such a case was where no damage had been suffered.[21]

5.21　In addition, in determining whether to make an award and if so, the amount of such an award, the court is obliged to take account of the principles applied by the European Court of Human Rights in relation to compensation awards under article 41 of the Convention.[22] The European Court has adopted a somewhat cautious approach to the issue of damages, both in terms of the circumstances in which it will make an award and of the amount of such awards as it does make. Financial compensation tends only to be awarded where it is impossible to reverse all the consequences of the breach of the Convention right in question, ie, where the claimant cannot be put back in the position in which he or she ought to have been had the breach not occurred.

5.22　The often contradictory decisions of the European Court in this context, however, may well leave the field clear for the domestic courts to derive their own principles for awarding damages, on the basis that taking account of the European Court principles takes the matter no

---

19　Human Rights Act 1998 s8(2).
20　[2003] UKHL 39; [2003] 1 WLR 1736.
21　[2003] UKHL 39 at [84]. The comments of Lord Millett on this subject were strictly speaking obiter dicta, as the alleged wrong had been committed prior to the coming into force of the Human Rights Act 1998.
22　Human Rights Act 1998 s8(4).

further. This would seem to be particularly so in relation to the availability of damages to compensate non-pecuniary loss.[23]

5.23 In *Cullen*,[24] Lord Millett noted that it was difficult to discern any consistent principles from the jurisprudence of the European Court, but that where a claimant cannot establish either pecuniary or non-pecuniary loss, the decision of the court that the conduct complained of constitutes a breach of a convention right will generally be considered to be sufficient just satisfaction. Given the court's power to make appropriate declarations there was little reason for making an award of nominal damages, which would be both inconsistent with the principles applied by the European Court and unnecessary. To make such an award would probably also be inconsistent with Human Rights Act 1998 s8(3).[25]

5.24 It follows from the above that the court will only have power to award damages for breaches of Convention rights if the combination of other remedies which the claimant has been awarded in legal proceedings, and/or other action taken by any court is insufficient to compensate the claimant properly in respect of the breach. Damages are therefore very much a secondary remedy.

5.25 Notwithstanding the above, the courts have indicated that damages in the context of breach of Convention rights may extend a claimant's right to be compensated further than would be permissible on ordinary common law principles. In particular, the availability of damages for breach of Convention rights may well extend their ambit into areas of public authorities' activity that might traditionally have been regarded as existing in public law only and so conferring no right to compensation.[26]

5.26 It must be remembered, however, that the position, in judicial review proceedings, remains governed by Supreme Court Act 1981 s31(4), which provides that damages can only be claimed in judicial review proceedings if they would have been awarded in a private law

23 See, in particular, *R (KB and others) v Mental Health Review Tribunal* [2003] EWHC 193 (Admin); [2003] 3 WLR 185; (2003) 6 CCLR 96, per Stanley Burnton J at [33]–[41], and the European cases there cited.

24 *Cullen v Chief Constable of the Royal Ulster Constabulary* [2003] UKHL 39. See also *R (KB and others) v Mental Health Review Tribunal* [2003] EWHC 193 (Admin) at [41].

25 *Cullen v Chief Constable of the Royal Ulster Constabulary* [2003] UKHL 39 per Lord Millett at [78]–[83].

26 But see *R (Ben-Abdelaziz) v Haringey LBC* [2001] EWCA Civ 803; [2001] 1 WLR 1485.

action brought by the claimant at the time of commencing the judicial review claim.[27]

Principles of awarding damages

5.27   In *R (KB and others) v Mental Health Review Tribunal*,[28] Stanley Burn-ton J described the object of an award of damages as 'to provide com-pensation for injury: no more, no less.'[29] It was not the function of awards to mark the court's disapproval of the conduct complained of nor to compel future compliance with Convention rights. Even though there may be a discernible tendency on the part of the European Court to make larger awards where it disapproved of the conduct in question or where there had been repeated breaches, this was not expressly reflected in any principle applied by the court.[30] Human Rights Act 1998 s9(3) expressly prohibits an award of non-compensatory dam-ages in relation to a judicial act done in good faith. Accordingly, exem-plary damages were not available[31] (although aggravated damages may be). Nor were damages for loss of a chance, as such an award would be contrary to the principles applied by the European Court.[32]

5.28   Regarding distress and inconvenience, damages would not be avail-able for every feeling of frustration or distress, particularly given that domestic law did not usually recognise such losses as free-standing heads of damage, and the court should be reluctant to create anomalies between damages recoverable for breach of Convention rights and those for other civil wrongs. Thus, while full account must be taken of the claimant's state of health, including his or her mental health, for damages under this head to be available, the frustration and distress must be significant and of such intensity that it would justify an award of compensation for non-pecuniary damage.[33]

5.29   In *Marcic v Thames Water Utilities Ltd*,[34] the Court of Appeal sug-gested that where a statutory undertaker carries on an undertaking for the benefit of the community as a whole (in that case operating a sewerage system) an obligation to pay damages under the Human Rights Act 1998, where an individual suffers damage thereby, may be

---

27 See paras 5.15–5.18 above and see *R (Ben-Abdelaziz)* (above).
28 [2003] EWHC 193 (Admin); [2003] 3 WLR 185; (2003) 6 CCLR 96.
29 [2003] EWHC 193 (Admin) at [50].
30 [2003] EWHC 193 (Admin) at [50].
31 [2003] EWHC 193 (Admin) at [60].
32 [2003] EWHC 193 (Admin) at [64].
33 [2003] EWHC 193 (Admin) at [71]–[73].
34 [2002] EWCA Civ 64; [2002] QB 929; [2002] 2 WLR 932.

more extensive than would be the case solely on the basis of their obligations imposed by the law of nuisance and of breach of statutory duty. In order for an interference with the individual's article 8 Convention rights to be justified under article 8(2), it may be necessary for compensation to be paid to the individual, to achieve a fair balance between the individual's interests and those of the local community as a whole which benefits from the undertaking.[35] In *Anufrijeva v Southwark LBC*,[35a] Lord Woolf CJ stressed the importance of keeping human rights damages awards within modest bounds, in the context of allegations by asylum-seekers that they had not received the benefits to which they were entitled due to maladministration. Public resources were limited and the paying of substantial damages awards would deplete the resources available to the public for primary care. The following procedures should be therefore be applied: (i) the court should look critically at any claim for Human Rights Act damages for maladministration unless brought by way of judicial review; (ii) even if judicial review was not possible, such as where damages only were claimed, claims should still be brought in the Administrative Court as ordinary claims; (iii) before permission was granted, the claimant should be required to explain why it was not more appropriate to use an internal complaints procedure or make a complaint to the relevant ombudsman; (iv) if there was a legitimate claim for other relief, the permission decision in respect of the damages claim should possibly be adjourned, or that claim stayed until the claimant had made appropriate use of alternative dispute resolution (ADR). Where the court must hear such a claim, decisions should be made in a summary manner, the hearing limited to half a day save in exceptional circumstances, and citing more than three authorities justified.

Measure of damages

5.30   In *R (Bernard) v Enfield LBC*,[36] a local authority's unexplained failure to make arrangements, under National Assistance Act 1948 s21, for the provision of suitably adapted accommodation for a disabled claimant or to act in accordance with its social services department's recommendations in this regard, was held to breach the claimant's article 8 Convention rights. She had been obliged to remain in unsatisfactory

---

35   [2002] EWCA Civ 64, per Lord Phillips MR at [112]–[118]. See also *S v France* (1990) D&R 250.

35a [2003] EWCA Civ 1406; (2003) 6 CCLR 411; (2003) *Times* 17 October.

36   [2002] EWHC 2282 (Admin); [2003] HRLR 4; (2002) 5 CCLR 577.

(because unadapted) living conditions and the authority's 'failure to enable the claimant to live as normal a family life as possible showed a singular lack of respect for her private and family life and condemned her to living in conditions which made it virtually impossible to have any meaningful private or family life'.[37] Damages of £10,000 were awarded because a refusal to do so would not have afforded the claimant just satisfaction and would have been 'unjust'.

5.31   As to the measure of damages, the judge rejected the parties' submissions that it would be appropriate to assess the quantum of the award by reference to personal injury cases or housing disrepair cases. The consequences of such matters were not truly comparable with the humiliating conditions the claimant had endured for some 20 months, and there were different considerations of policy in play. There was no reason why the award should not be comparable with (or should be lower than) an award for tortuous conduct, even though there was no comparable tort. Accordingly, the measure of damages was most appropriately assessed by reference to awards recommended by the Local Government Ombudsmen, because the breaches of duty found by the judge amounted, in essence, to an extreme example of maladministration.[38]

5.32   In *R (KB and others) v Mental Health Review Tribunal*,[39] the claimants successfully contended that repeated adjournments in their applications to the Mental Health Review Tribunal were unjustified and breached the right to a speedy hearing under article 5(4) of the Convention. They now claimed damages for distress, deprivation of liberty, damage to mental health and loss of chance of earlier discharge.

5.33   As to the measure of damages, the court held that it should take account of awards made by the European Court but be free to depart from them in order to award adequate, but not excessive, damages in UK terms.[40] Only very general principles could be identified from the European Court decisions. There was no basis for awarding less under the Human Rights Act 1998 'just satisfaction' jurisdiction than would have been awarded for a comparable tort. Racial and sexual discrimination cases did not provide reliable analogies. In those cases, the discrimination was likely to be intended to be hurtful, whereas there was no intention on anyone's part here to cause distress.[41]

---

37   [2002] EWHC 2282 (Admin) per Sullivan J at [34].
38   [2002] EWHC 2282 (Admin) at [60].
39   [2003] EWHC 193 (Admin); [2003] 3 WLR 185; (2003) 6 CCLR 96.
40   [2003] EWHC 193 (Admin) at [47].
41   [2003] EWHC 193 (Admin) at [74].

Remission back to decision-maker

5.34   Where the court quashes a decision, it may also remit the matter back to the decision-maker, with a direction to reconsider it in accordance with the findings of the court.[42] This would not seem appropriate in cases where there are disputes on the facts and evidence or where the complaint concerns a procedural flaw in the decision. In such cases, the decision-maker would generally be expected to reconsider the decision from the beginning. It may be appropriate, however, where the decision-maker has been guilty of an error of law.

Retention of the decision

5.35   CPR r54.19(3) provides that, on quashing a decision, where the court considers that there is 'no purpose to be served' in remitting the matter back to the decision-maker, it may take the decision itself, subject to any statutory provision. It continues that '[w]here a statutory power is given to a tribunal, person or other body it may be the case that the court cannot take the decision itself'. It seems unlikely, therefore, that this much hedged-around power is intended to – or can – make any major change to the general constitutional position that on quashing a decision, the court will leave it to the decision-maker to take a new one. It is after all one of the hallmarks of a public law function that the statutory designate of that function is in a much better position to exercise it than would be the court.[43]

Proceedings to continue as if begun by private action

5.36   The court now has broad powers to order that a judicial review claim should continue as if it had not been brought using the CPR Part 54 procedure and, if it does so, to give directions about the future management of the claim.[44] This replaces the considerably more circumscribed powers available under the old rules.[45]

5.37   One of the situations in which the court will exercise its powers is where damages are claimed. The court may, having granted the

---

42   CPR Rule 54.19(2).

43   See, eg, *Mohram Ali v Tower Hamlets LBC* [1993] QB 407, CA, especially per Nolan LJ at 413G–414B.

44   CPR r54.20.

45   RSC Ord 53 r9(4)–(5).

application, order that the action continue as if begun by writ, and then adjourn the assessment of damages to the master or even transfer it to the county court.[46] There were conflicting judicial statements under the old rules on whether, if the judicial review application was misconceived but the claim for damages arguable, the court would exercise its power or refuse the claim,[47] but in the light of recent comments by the Lord Chief Justice regarding the flexibility of the Civil Procedure Rules to permit claims to be heard in the most effective manner and to avoid the old technical procedural disputes, it seems likely that if the claim is, in all the circumstances, appropriate to be heard, the court will make the necessary orders to permit this to happen.[48]

5.38   It was held to be inappropriate under the old rules, and presumably would remain so, for a defendant who had filed no evidence to apply for an order that a claim should proceed as if begun by private action in order to seek to gain a further opportunity to defend the claim.[49]

5.39   In *R v Blandford Justices ex p Pamment*,[50] the Court of Appeal considered a case where damages were claimed in an application for judicial review of a criminal cause or matter. The court indicated that in criminal causes, given that there is no appeal from the Divisional Court to the Court of Appeal, the best course where the actual judicial review application is academic, in that its sole or main purpose is to facilitate a damages claim (as was the position in *Pamment* itself), would be for the Divisional Court to decline, as a matter of discretion, to deal with the application for judicial review, and to allow the damages claim to proceed as if commenced by writ. That way the claim for damages could be heard without any pre-judgment as to the legitimacy of the order challenged and there would be a clear route to the Court of Appeal (Civil Division).[51]

46   See, for example, *R v Sandwell MBC ex p Thomas* (1992) 22 December (unreported), where the latter course was taken.

47   See *Calveley v Chief Constable of Merseyside Police* [1989] QB 136, CA; compare *R v Secretary of State for the Home Office ex p Dew* [1987] 1 WLR 881, QBD.

48   See *R (Heather) v Leonard Cheshire Foundation* [2002] EWCA Civ 366; [2002] 2 All ER 936; (2002) 5 CCLR 317; *Clark v University of Lincolnshire and Humberside* [2000] 1 WLR 1988, CA.

49   *R v Justices of the Peace for the Petty Sessional Division of Reading; Chief Constable of Avon and Somerset; Intervention Board for Agricultural Produce ex p South West Meat Ltd* [1992] COD 224, DC.

50   [1990] 1 WLR 1490, CA.

51   [1990] 1 WLR 1490 at 1496D. Compare *R v Northavon DC ex p Palmer* (1993) 25 HLR 674, QBD. Whether or not damages may be available in a criminal context is another matter: see, eg, *Olotu v Home Office* [1997] 1 All ER 385.

Power to vary sentence

5.40   In criminal cases, where judicial review is sought of a sentence which the sentencing court had no power to pass, the court may vary the sentence itself. It does this by substituting a sentence which the court under challenge would have had power to pass, rather than granting a quashing order, quashing the sentence.[52] This applies only to sentences passed by the magistrates' court or by the Crown Court on committal for sentence or on appeal from the magistrates.[53] There is no power to review sentences passed on indictment.[54] This is a matter for the Court of Appeal (Criminal Division).

Dismissal of application

5.41   The application may, of course, also be dismissed. It is for the claimant to prove his or her case to the ordinary civil standard of proof, save in rare situations such as illegal entrant cases. Where the Home Secretary asserts that a person is an illegal entrant, it is for him to prove the facts relied on by the immigration officer as justifying that conclusion.[55]

Interim relief

5.42   An application may be made for an interim order at any stage in proceedings, although it is usual to do so at the permission stage. On, or even before, the grant of permission,[56] the court has power to grant interim remedies in accordance with CPR Part 23. In practice, the most important types of application are likely to be for an interim injunction, for disclosure, or for cross-examination.

5.43   By CPR r54.10(2), where permission is granted, the court has power to grant a stay of proceedings to which the claim relates. Temporary injunctions may be granted at any stage, even after judgment. Cross-undertakings in damages ought, usually, to be required. If acting for a

---

52   Supreme Court Act 1981 s43(1).
53   Supreme Court Act 1981 s43(1).
54   Supreme Court Act 1981 s29(3).
55   *Khawaja v Secretary of State for the Home Department* [1984] AC 74, HL.
56   *Re M* [1994] 1 AC 377.

defendant, it must be remembered to request such an undertaking, if appropriate, and for what it may be worth, as such matters are frequently overlooked.

5.44　　If interim relief is sought, after the substantive application has been dismissed, pending appeal, it will be necessary to show that the appeal has good prospects of success.

Injunction

5.45　Traditionally, an interim injunction was not available against the Crown.[57] If, however, it has acted contrary to Community law, the Crown is susceptible to this remedy. This is because if injunctive relief is necessary to ensure full effectiveness of Community law, a national rule preventing such a remedy (such as Crown Proceedings Act 1948 s21(2)) must not be applied.[58] In *In re M*,[59] the House of Lords held that as, historically, prerogative orders had been made against the Crown and its officers, Crown Proceedings Act 1948 s21 did not prevent injunctions issuing against ministers and other officers of the Crown in similar circumstances.

5.46　　The courts also have jurisdiction to grant interim injunctions against ministers and other officers of the Crown,[60] although this power should only be exercised in limited circumstances.

5.47　　As with other interim injunctions, the principles set out in *American Cyanamid Company v Ethicon Ltd*[61] will apply, although the courts have modified the considerations to some extent. In *R v Secretary of State for Transport ex p Factortame (No 2)*,[62] Lord Goff of Chieveley stated that where a judicial review claim involves a public authority seeking to enforce the law, damages would not usually be an adequate remedy for either party. Accordingly, in considering the balance of convenience, the court must also take account of the interests of the public in general to whom the authority owes duties. In such a case, the claimant is not required to show a strong prima facie case that the law which the authority seeks to enforce is invalid. The matter is one for the discretion of the court. The court should not restrain the authority from enforcing the law, however, unless satisfied that the challenge to its

57　Crown Proceedings Act 1948 s21(2).
58　See chapter 1, paras 1.28–1.32 above.
59　[1994] 1 AC 377, HL.
60　Supreme Court Act 1981 s31(2).
61　[1975] AC 396, HL.
62　[1991] 1 AC 603, ECJ and HL.

validity is sufficiently firmly based to justify that exceptional course being taken.[63] In general, it seems that it will be more difficult to establish that the balance of convenience favours the granting of an injunction.[64]

5.48 Where a mandatory injunction is sought, it will generally be necessary to show a strong prima facie case.[65] The court has not always applied such a test however. In *R v Cardiff City Council ex p Barry*,[66] a lower test and, arguably, a more practical line was suggested by the court, which it continued to follow at least in homelessness cases until most such cases were removed from the judicial review jurisdiction.[67] In *Barry*, the court held that where permission is granted, an injunction requiring the authority to provide temporary accommodation (or at least allow the applicant to remain in the currently provided temporary accommodation) would generally follow, unless, for example, the defendant was prepared to agree to that course without such an order being made.

Stay

5.49 The court has power to order a stay, not only of judicial proceedings, but also of decisions of ministers and of the process by which such decisions were reached.[68] It is a precondition of the exercise of this power, however, that permission is granted.[69]

5.50 The case of *R v HM Inspectorate of Pollution, Ministry of Agriculture, Fisheries and Food ex p Greenpeace Ltd*[70] is illustrative of the principles to be applied when considering a stay, particularly where the applicant is an interest group. On granting permission to apply for judicial review, Brooke J considered an application for an interlocutory stay to prevent the commissioning of the THORP plant at

---

63 [1991] 1 AC 603 at 674.
64 See *Smith v Inner London Education Authority* [1978] 1 All ER 411, CA.
65 See *R v Kensington and Chelsea RLBC ex p Hammell* [1989] QB 518, CA.
66 (1989) 22 HLR 261, QBD.
67 By the Housing Act 1996 s204 which created a right of appeal on a point of law to the county court in respect of most decisions taken in homelessness cases (such decisions being listed at Housing Act 1996 s202).
68 *R v Secretary of State for Education ex p Avon County Council* [1991] 1 QB 558, CA.
69 CPR r54.10, and see *R (H) v Ashworth Hospital Authority* [2002] EWCA Civ 923; [2003] 1 WLR 127; (2002) 5 CCLR 390, per Dyson LJ at [47].
70 [1994] COD 56, QBD; see paras 4.14–4.17 above, for the report of the substantive hearing.

Sellafield, pending the full hearing of the claimant's challenge. The defendant and British Nuclear Fuels Ltd (BNFL) submitted that very considerable losses would be suffered if a stay was granted, amounting to £2 million per week. The claimant had current assets of just under £1 million and liabilities of £1.2 million. A further difficulty was that BNFL, against whom the stay was sought, was not a party to the application.

5.51   The judge undertook the conventional *American Cyanamid* balancing exercise, stating that it was a difficult balancing exercise to perform. He took into account the fact that the claimant would still have to establish at the full hearing that it had standing to bring the application (although the courts were more and more willing these days to entertain applications by such bodies). The judge was also considerably influenced by the likely financial loss to BNFL and the claimant's likely inability to pay for it. The Inspectorate's view, moreover, was that the effect of the planned testing of the plant would be minimal, although that was plainly not the claimant's view. Should the applicant succeed at the full hearing, BNFL would have to bear the cost of decommissioning the plant. Accordingly, a stay was refused.

5.52   The court considered the principles upon which a stay should be granted in the context of what was essentially a commercial dispute in *Scotia Pharmaceuticals International Ltd v Secretary of State for Health and Norgine Ltd*.[71] Application was made by Norgine to discharge a stay which had been imposed on the grant to Norgine of a product licence. The stay had been granted at the application of Scotia, pending a reference of the litigation between them to the European Court of Justice. The court held that the principles applicable to challenges to primary or secondary legislation were inappropriate to a trade dispute and that it should ask only whether there was a serious question to be tried. Having decided that there was, the well-known *American Cyanamid* principles[72] were applicable, and the application to remove the stay dismissed.

5.53   In *R (H) v Ashworth Hospital Authority*,[73] the Court of Appeal held that the court had power to order a stay of a Mental Health Review

---

71 [1994] COD 241, DC.

72 *American Cyanamid Company v Ethicon Ltd* [1975] AC 396, HL. An injunction will be granted to preserve the status quo where there is doubt whether damages would provide an adequate remedy.

73 Joined with *R (Ashworth Hospital Authority) v Mental Health Review Tribunal for West Midlands and North West Region* [2002] EWCA Civ 923; [2003] 1 WLR 127; (2002) 5 CCLR 390.

Tribunal decision to discharge a compulsorily detained patient, even where that decision had already been fully implemented.[74] That power should only be used, however, if there was a strong and not merely an arguable case that the tribunal's decision had been unlawful, together with cogent evidence that the patient posed a risk to her or himself or to others and/or was dangerous. Where a stay is ordered, it is essential that the validity of the tribunal's decision should be determined by the court with the greatest possible speed.[75]

5.54   On judicial review of the magistrates' refusal to stay a criminal prosecution as an abuse of process, the court's powers will be strictly limited. This is, however, a different aspect of the stay jurisdiction, not related to interim relief.[76]

Disclosure

5.55   The ability of claimants to obtain disclosure of documents containing personal information about themselves is now wider and more comprehensive than was previously the case, given the general rights conferred by Data Protection Act 1998 s7.[77]

5.56   Other than as stated above, however, disclosure is not obtainable as of right in judicial review proceedings, but only at the discretion of the court. Generally, the courts have restricted the circumstances in which disclosure will be ordered. In *O'Reilly v Mackman*,[78] Lord Diplock stated that neither disclosure nor cross-examination would usually be ordered except to the extent that justice in the individual case required it. In the *NFSSB* case[79] Lord Scarman stated that for disclosure to be ordered, first, there must be evidence revealing reasonable grounds for believing that there has been a breach of a public law duty and, second, disclosure should be strictly limited to documents relevant to the issue arising from the affidavits.

---

74   In *H*, the patient had been discharged but had remained in hospital as a voluntary patient having nowhere else to go.

75   [2002] EWCA Civ 923 per Dyson LJ at [47].

76   See, eg, *R v Barry Magistrates' Court ex p Malpas* [1998] COD 90, DC applying *R v Willesden Justices ex p Clemmings* (1988) 87 Cr App R 280.

77   There will be specific rights referable to information held by public bodies when the Freedom of Information Act 2001 comes into force (see below, paras 14.35–14.48).

78   [1983] 2 AC 237 at 282–283.

79   [1982] AC 617 at 654. See also, generally, chapter 4, para 4.3.

5.57   The court will not allow an application for disclosure to be used to fill gaps in the claimant's evidence,[80] or which amounts to a 'fishing expedition'. The Court of Appeal has held that it would be improper to allow disclosure of documents to permit the claimant who seeks to go behind the defendant's evidence to ascertain whether it is correct, unless there is some material outside the evidence which suggests that in some material respect it is inaccurate, misleading or in a material respect incomplete.[81] Nor will the court permit an application for disclosure to see, in effect, whether disclosure has been properly given. That is not the function of disclosure and is impermissible.[82]

5.58   It has also been held, on the other hand, that the grant of permission may, in an appropriate case, raise a sufficient inference of irrationality for there to be room for an order for production of a relevant document.[83] In *R v Governor of Pentonville Prison ex p Herbage (No 2)*,[84] it was held that disclosure will be ordered where necessary to advance the justice of the case and/or for the fair disposal of the matter. If an application for judicial review is bound to fail, disclosure should not be ordered.

5.59   The courts have, more recently, indicated that the position concerning disclosure may not be so strict in human rights cases, or under the Civil Procedure Rules, Part 31 of which applies to judicial review as to all other kinds of civil proceedings.[85]

Oral evidence and cross-examination

5.60   The courts have been similarly restrictive in defining the circumstances in which they will permit the cross-examination of witnesses and oral evidence generally. Lord Diplock in *O'Reilly v Mackman*,[86]

---

80   See *R v Inland Revenue Commissioners ex p Taylor* [1988] COD 61, QBD.

81   *R v Secretary of State for the Environment ex p Islington LBC and London Lesbian and Gay Centre* [1992] COD 67, CA. See also *R v Secretary of State for Education ex p J* [1993] COD 146, QBD, and *R v Arts Council of England ex p Women's Playhouse Trust* (1997) *Times* 20 August.

82   *R v Secretary of State for Transport ex p Factortame Ltd* [1997] COD 432, DC, referring to *Berkeley Administration Inc v McClelland* [1990] FSR 381.

83   *R v Secretary of State for Transport ex p APH Road Safety Ltd* [1993] COD 150, QBD.

84   [1987] QB 1077, CA.

85   See *R v Ministry of Defence ex p Smith* [1996] QB 517, CA, per Henry LJ at 543. See also *R (S) v Plymouth City Council* [2002] EWCA Civ 388; [2002] 1 WLR 2583.

86   [1983] 2 AC 237, HL, at 282G.

stated that although the grant of leave to cross-examine is governed by the same principles as apply in any action begun by originating summons,[87] and should be permitted whenever the justice of the case requires, it would be rare that the issues arising on judicial review would call for cross-examination. The reason for this is that the decision-maker's factual findings are not generally open to review by the court.[88] To allow cross-examination, Lord Diplock said:

> ... presents the court with a temptation, not always easily resisted, to substitute its own view of the facts for that of the decision-making body upon whom the exclusive jurisdiction to determine facts has been conferred by Parliament ...

5.61   Allegations of breach of natural justice or of procedural unfairness are, he said, in general, exceptions to this.

5.62   In *R v Reigate Justices ex p Curl*,[89] the court held that it would not generally hear oral evidence of what had occurred in an inferior court, even where a breach of natural justice was alleged, as this would involve the magistrates in attending the High Court to justify the decisions they took during the hearing before them.

Oral evidence and cross-examination in fundamental rights cases

5.63   There is some indication that the court will be considerably more willing to permit cross-examination, and even to decide the facts for itself, where it is necessary to do so.

5.64   In *R (Wilkinson) v Broadmoor Special Hospital Authority*,[90] the claimant, detained in hospital under Mental Health Act 1983 s3, sought to challenge by way of judicial review, the decision of the defendant to administer anti-psychotic drugs to him without his consent. On the grant of permission, he applied for an order that the doctors who had approved the treatment should attend the substantive hearing to be cross-examined as to their belief that the claimant was not mentally capable of refusing consent to the treatment.

---

87   The nearest CPR equivalent of which is the Part 8 claim.
88   This may not apply in *Edwards v Bairstow* [1956] AC 14 type situations (see chapter 6).
89   [1991] COD 66, DC.
90   [2001] EWCA Civ 1545; [2002] 1 WLR 419; (2002) 5 CCLR 121. See also *S v Airedale NHS Trust* [2002] EWHC Admin 1780; [2003] Lloyd's Rep Med 21.

5.65   On appeal from the judge's refusal of such an order, the Court of Appeal held that, since the Human Rights Act 1998 was in force, the court could, where a claimant's fundamental human rights were at stake, decide for itself an issue of fact, namely in that case, whether the claimant was capable of giving (and so also withholding) consent to the medical treatment which the defendant wished to carry out. The court could carry out a full merits review if appropriate, and for that purpose order the attendance of doctors to be cross-examined at the full hearing.

5.66   While a majority of a differently constituted Court of Appeal rejected the suggestion that *Wilkinson* was authority for the proposition that the court could, on judicial review, undertake a review of the facts where Parliament had decided that a particular body – not the court – should be the decision-maker of fact,[91] a third court, in *R (Mullen) v Secretary of State for the Home Department*,[92] observed that *Wilkinson* 'amply demonstr ates' that the court on judicial review can and will, if necessary, assess relevant facts for itself, even to the extent of ordering cross-examination of witnesses.

5.67   In *R(PG) v Ealing LBC*,[93] Munby J held that *Wilkinson* plainly indicates that there will be judicial review cases in which cross-examination is not only appropriate, but essential, and that there will be cases in which the intensity of the review demanded by a challenge based on an alleged breach of Convention rights, will require cross-examination to be ordered so that the court complies with its own obligations under the Convention. Notwithstanding *Wilkinson*, however, recourse to such powers could be expected to be very much the exception. The 'overwhelming' bulk of judicial review cases would continue to be determined without oral evidence.

Expedition or abridgement of time for evidence

5.68   A potentially important interlocutory tool for claimants is to ask for an expedited hearing and/or the abridgement of time for the service of the defendant's evidence. This will be particularly relevant where an application for an interim injunction cannot be made or has been refused, as current waiting times in the Administrative Court for a full hearing,

91   *Adan v Tower Hamlets LBC* [2001] EWCA Civ 1919; [2002] 1 WLR 2120.
92   [2002] EWHC 230 (Admin); [2002] 1 WLR 1857. In fact, Simon Brown LJ gave the leading judgment in both *Wilkinson and Mullen*. Hale LJ, who gave a concurring judgment in *Wilkinson* dissented in *Adan*.
93   [2002] EWHC 250 (Admin); [2002] ACD 48.

following the grant of permission, can still be many months, even given the new procedural code.[94]

Bail

5.69   The High Court has a fairly wide power, arising from its inherent jurisdiction, to grant bail. This power arises on the adjournment of a permission application as well as on the grant of permission itself, although not where permission is refused. The Court of Appeal has power to grant bail on an appeal against a refusal of permission, and a refusal by the single judge to grant bail may itself be appealed to the Court of Appeal.[95] RSC Order 79 r9[96] governs the procedure for making bail applications in criminal cases to the High Court.

5.70   In immigration cases, the court's approach appears to be slightly different.[97] Where a person is detained pending a decision about whether to grant him or her leave to enter the UK, the immigration adjudicator has jurisdiction to grant bail, on terms if appropriate, and application should be made by that route rather than to the High Court. Where a person is detained pending removal from the UK, the Home Secretary can grant temporary admission, but cannot attach terms to it. In such cases, if the Home Secretary refuses to do so and opposes bail, the courts will not grant bail unless it can be shown that, in refusing temporary admission, the Home Secretary has erred in principle, or that decision is unreasonable in the *Wednesbury* sense.[98] Where the Home Secretary has refused temporary admission but would not oppose bail on terms, the court would usually grant conditional bail.

Remedies against third parties

5.71   In *R v HM Inspectorate of Pollution, Ministry of Agriculture, Fisheries and Food ex p Greenpeace Ltd,*[99] the Court of Appeal confirmed the

---

94   See *Practice Statement*, Scott Baker J, 1 February 2002 [2002] 1 All ER 633. See also the annual Practice Statement for 2003 which can be found at the Court Service website at www.courtservice.gov.uk.

95   See *R v Secretary of State for the Home Department ex p Turkoglu* [1988] QB 398

96   Retained in force at CPR Sch 1.

97   *Re Vilvarajah's application for bail* (1987) *Times* 31 October, CA.

98   *Associated Provincial Picture Houses v Wednesbury Corporation* [1948] 1 KB 223, CA; and see below, chapter 18.

99   [1994] 1 WLR 570, CA.

decision of Brooke J[100] that where a stay was sought which would affect a third party whom it was not sought to make a party to the action, the correct approach was still to follow the usual principles applied when an interlocutory injunction was sought against another party.

5.72   In *R (Prokopp) v London Underground Ltd,*[101] the claimant sought to prevent the first defendant from undertaking demolition works in connection with a proposed extension of one of its railway lines. He sought judicial review against them, and against the two relevant local authorities, whose decisions not to take enforcement action against the railway company he challenged on the basis that the railway company did not have planning permission for the demolition. (The permission which had been granted had expired because, due to a mistake in its implementation rendering that implementation unlawful, it had not been *lawfully* implemented within the requisite five-year period.) The claimant obtained an interim injunction against the railway company prohibiting them from commencing work, notwithstanding concerns about his standing as a private individual to seek to enforce breaches of planning control in circumstances where the authorities charged with doing so had decided not to take action.

5.73   The court held that it could be appropriate to grant interim relief to a private individual against a developer, to prevent the taking of irrevocable steps which the claimant contended to be unlawful but which were not being enforced by the local planning authority. In such a case, while the claim would initially be brought against the developer, the local authority must be added as a defendant and the claim would proceed against the authority with the developer taking part as an interested party. A private individual could not, however, obtain a permanent injunction in a public law claim, which would, in effect, amount to the enforcement action which was the responsibility of the local authority and which carried with it procedural safeguards for the developer such as a right of appeal.

5.74   The Court of Appeal reversed the judge's decision on other grounds, and did not comment on these issues.[102]

---

100 Discussed at paras 5.50–5.51 above.
101 [2003] EWHC 960 (Admin), [2003] 19 EGCS 119. Hackney LBC and Tower Hamlets LBC were the second and third defendants.
102 [2003] EWCA Civ 961; (2003) *Times* 28 August.

Habeas corpus ad subjiciendum

5.75   Examination of this related remedy is beyond the scope of this book. It is a prerogative remedy, whereby the detention of the individual pursuant to administrative orders may be supervised by the court. If granted, the writ requires the release of the applicant from detention.

5.76   The use of this remedy is significantly less important now than was the case in former years, as it now appears to be treated simply as a branch of judicial review. The same legal principles apply to *habeas corpus* as to judicial review. The remedy is now used predominantly in immigration and mental health cases.

5.77   Applications are governed by CPR Sch 1 and RSC Ord 54, which together with its Practice Direction,[103] sets out the procedure to be adopted. In essence, the rules have retained the old procedure, forms and practice directions applicable to the making of such applications prior to 26 April 1999.[104]

103 Practice Direction RSC PD 54.
104 RSC PD 54, in particular at paras 2.2, 3.1, 4.1 and 7.1.

CHAPTER 6

Grounds on which review may be sought

continued overleaf

Vires

6.1   The term 'ultra vires' is frequently used in judicial review, usually to describe a decision taken, or a policy adopted, by a public body which was outside the powers of that body. The concept of 'vires', meaning jurisdiction or power, is the central concept of administrative law.[1] A decision-maker with statutory powers has, of definition, only those powers which Parliament has conferred, and may only act 'within the four corners of' those powers.[2] Any act done or decision made outside, or in excess of, such powers will be ultra vires and generally void.[3]

6.2   Accordingly, to give a basic example, if a body with power to decide to build roads, were to decide to build a railway line, that decision would be ultra vires: there would be no power in the body in question to make it.[4] In this sense, the question of whether or not an act or decision is ultra vires may simply be a matter of construing the power in question, contained in the empowering legislation, and ascertaining whether or not it authorised the act or decision under challenge.

6.3   Vires has, however, been given a broader meaning in the context of judicial review. In *Anisminic v Foreign Compensation Commission*,[5] the House of Lords held that no tribunal has jurisdiction to make any error of law.

> Lack of jurisdiction may arise in various ways ... [W]hile engaged on a proper inquiry, the tribunal may depart from the rules of natural justice; or it may ask itself the wrong questions; or it may take into account matters which it was not directed to take into account. Thereby it would step outside its jurisdiction. It would turn its inquiry to something not directed by Parliament and fail to make the inquiry which Parliament did direct. Any of these things would cause its purported decisions to be a nullity ...

6.4   In this way, all errors of law may be errors which can be said to render the resulting decision ultra vires. In the example given above, if the body determined to build a road but, in reaching that decision, took account

---

1   See, eg, *Boddington v British Transport Police* [2000] 2 AC 143, HL, per Lord Steyn at 171F–G (citing with approval a passage in Wade and Forsyth, *Administrative Law* (OUP, 7th edn, p41).

2   See, for example, *Associated Provincial Picture Houses Ltd v Wednesbury Corporation* [1948] 1 KB 223, CA, per Lord Greene MR at 233–234.

3   Regarding the difficult question of the status of ultra vires decisions, see below, chapter 7, paras 7.26–7.31.

4   See, for example, the unsuccessful challenge in *Westminster Corporation v London and North Western Railway Co* [1905] AC 426, HL, below at para 6.90.

5   [1969] 2 AC 147, HL, per Lord Pearce at 195.

of an irrelevant consideration, or failed to consider something relevant, the resultant decision could be termed ultra vires: the body only has power to make a *lawful* decision to build a road. It has no more power to reach a decision to build a road taking the wrong factors into account than it does to decide to build a railway. In *R v Hull University Visitor ex p Page*,[6] Lord Browne-Wilkinson stated:

> If the decision-maker exercises his powers outside the jurisdiction conferred, in a manner which is procedurally irregular or is *Wednesbury* unreasonable, he is acting ultra vires his powers and therefore unlawfully.

6.5   For this reason, each of the potential grounds for review set out below may be considered to involve aspects of the principles of vires and ultra vires.

Ultra vires and the basis of challenge

6.6   A reviewable decision may arise from the exercise, or failure to exercise a public law power or duty. The fact that such a power or duty may well be worded in subjective terms (such as 'if it appears to the authority'; 'if the Secretary of State considers'; 'if the tribunal has reason to believe') does not exclude the remedy of judicial review. Public law powers may only validly be used in accordance with the administrative law principles described in this chapter. The concepts of a discretion unfettered by the rule of law and indeed of unreviewable administrative action have always been firmly rejected by the courts as anathema to a constitutional system based on the rule of law. The relevant questions are therefore not whether a decision is reviewable at all, but about the scope and intensity of that review (or, to put it another way, the breadth of the discretion conferred), the answers to which questions will depend on the intention of Parliament, the context, and the importance of the rights at stake.[7]

---

6   [1993] AC 682, at 701.

7   See, eg, *Tower Hamlets LBC v Chetnik Developments Ltd* [1988] AC 858, HL, especially per Lord Bridge of Harwich at 872A–873G, citing with approval Wade, *Administrative Law*, (5th edn, 1982), pp55–356. See also *Secretary of State for Education and Science v Tameside MBC* [1977] AC 1014, HL, and, eg, *R (Daly) v Secretary of State for the Home Department* [2001] UKHL 26; [2001] 2 AC 532, per Lord Steyn at [27]; *R (Mahmood) v Secretary of State for the Home Department* [2001] 1 WLR 840. Always interesting is the dissenting speech of Lord Atkin in *Liversidge v Anderson* [1942] AC 206.

6.7   While, therefore, the decision-maker's judgment will not itself be impugned by the courts so long as it is made in accordance with the principles of administrative law outlined above, this is simply another way of stating the proposition that the court will not substitute its own view for that of the decision-maker. It does not exclude the court's supervision of the way in which the decision was reached.[8]

6.8   The classic statement of the grounds for judicial review remains that of Lord Greene MR in *Associated Provincial Picture Houses Ltd v Wednesbury Corporation*,[9] although there has been recent judicial criticism to the effect that it adopts an overly restrictive approach.[10] Lord Greene said:

> Bad faith and dishonesty stand by themselves. A decision-maker must also direct himself properly in law ... I will summarise once again the principle applicable. The court is entitled to investigate the action of the local authority with a view to seeing whether they have taken into account matters which they ought not to take into account, or, conversely, have refused to take into account or neglected to take into account matters which they ought to take into account. Once that question is answered in favour of the local authority, it may still be possible to say that although the local authority have kept within the four corners of the matters which they ought to consider, they have nevertheless come to a conclusion so unreasonable that no reasonable authority could ever have come to it.[11]

6.9   In *Council of Civil Service Unions (CCSU) v Minister of State for the Civil Service*,[12] Lord Diplock reformulated the grounds for seeking review under three heads:

(a) illegality;
(b) irrationality; and
(c) procedural impropriety.

---

8   See *Secretary of State for Education and Science v Tameside MBC* [1977] AC 1014, HL. See also, eg, *Mercury Ltd v Director General of Telecommunications* [1996] 1 WLR 48, HL, per Lord Slynn of Hadley at 58G–H.

9   [1948] 1 KB 223,CA.

10   See *R (Daly) v Secretary of State for the Home Department* [2001] UKHL 26; [2001] 2 AC 532 per Lord Cooke of Thorndon at [32], in which he described *Wednesbury* as an 'unfortunately retrogressive decision in English administrative law' a description of the case that may have surprised lawyers at the time (and subsequently); *R (Association of British Civilian Internees (Far East Region)) v Secretary of State for Defence* [2003] EWCA Civ 473; (2003) *Times* 19 April, per Lord Phillips of Worth Matravers at [34]–[35].

11   [1948] KB 223, at 233–234.

12   [1985] AC 374, HL.

By 'illegality', I mean that the decision-maker must understand correctly the law that regulates his decision-making power and must give effect to ... By 'irrationality', I mean ... 'Wednesbury' unreasonableness ... I have described the third head as 'procedural impropriety' rather than a failure to observe the basic rules of natural justice.[13]

6.10   It has not been entirely clear, however, where the lines fall to be drawn between these three categories. Clearly irrationality can be equated with *Wednesbury* unreasonableness, and was by Lord Bridge of Harwich in *R v Secretary of State for the Environment ex p Hammersmith and Fulham LBC*.[14] *Wednesbury*, however, also classified as 'unreasonable' misdirections of law and having regard to irrelevant matters, which *CCSU* and *Hammersmith and Fulham* classified as 'illegality'. Procedural irregularities could, in one sense, themselves be classified within 'illegality' given that to fall into procedural error is, in terms of *Anisminic*,[15] to commit an error of law.

6.11   In *Leeds CC v Spencer*[16] Brooke LJ stated:

> ... it seems to me that to speak of '*Wednesbury* unreasonableness' and link this phrase exclusively with perversity or with a decision which defies logic tends to muddy the waters. In deciding whether to serve such a notice and the identity of the person(s) on whom it should serve it, the council was bound to take into account all relevant considerations, and if it failed to do so, the cases show that it could be castigated for acting unreasonably in the *Wednesbury* sense. In terms of strict legal analysis it would be abusing the power given to it by Parliament by failing to take into account all the matters it should have taken into account, and its act would be ultra vires.

6.12   The extent to which, in practical terms, the correct classification of a ground for review as falling within one or other(s) of the *CCSU* categories is, perhaps, open to doubt. While, in *Boddington*,[17] Lord Steyn spoke of categorisation as an 'indispensible tool in the search for rationality and coherence in law', it was recognised by Lord Greene

---

13   [1985] AC 374 at 410.
14   [1991] 1 AC 521 at 597F.
15   *Anisminic v Foreign Compensation Commission* [1969] AC 426, HL. See also, on this point, *Begum (Nipa) v Tower Hamlets LBC* [2000] 1 WLR 306, CA.
16   [2000] BLGR 68, CA, at 75.
17   *Boddington v British Transport police* [2000] 2 AC 143, HL at 170F. This was in the different context of whether it was possible to draw a rational distinction between the 'substantive' and 'procedural' invalidity of a byelaw.

MR in *Wednesbury* itself that the different grounds tend to 'run into each other' and are not hermetically sealed one from the other.[18]

6.13   Thus, while the traditional grounds of intervention fall broadly within certain categories, such grounds and categories are, at best, really only examples of the reasons for the court's intervention in different cases. They are by no means rigid, self-contained, or mutually exclusive. It may well be possible to characterise an error made by a decision-maker as unlawful for a number of reasons, and on several 'grounds'.

Fundamental rights cases

Common law 'anxious scrutiny'

6.14   Even before the coming into force of the Human Rights Act 1998, the judicial review courts had begun to develop the principles of review enshrined by *Wednesbury* and *CCSU*, as they applied in cases where human rights were at stake. In *R v Ministry of Defence ex p Smith*,[19] where the secretary of state's policy of not permitting gay men and women to serve in the armed forces was challenged, the Court of Appeal held that it was not appropriate to adopt a basic *Wednesbury* approach to reviewing the secretary of state's policy. Instead, the conventional *Wednesbury* approach must be adapted to a human rights context. The court would give 'anxious scrutiny' to the policy under challenge (also referred to as a 'super-*Wednesbury*' approach).[20]

6.15   The effect of this approach was to require the secretary of state to show an important competing public interest which he could reasonably judge sufficient to justify the policy. The court would only strike the policy down if satisfied that this justification was perverse. The more substantial the interference with human rights, the more that would be required by way of justification before the court would

---

18   See also, eg, *Wheeler v Leicester CC* [1985] AC 1054, per Lord Roskill at 1078B–C; *R v Secretary of State for the Environment ex p Nottinghamshire CC* [1986] AC 240, HL, per Lord Scarman at 249D–E; *R v Panel on Take-overs and Mergers ex p Guinness plc* [1990] 1 QB 146, per Lord Donaldson MR at 160A–C; *Boddington v British Transport Police* [1999] 2 AC 143, per Lord Steyn at 170E.

19   [1996] QB 517, CA.

20   See *Vilvarajah v United Kingdom* (1991) 14 EHRR 248, ECHR.

be satisfied that the decision was within the range of reasonable decisions open to the secretary of state.[21]

6.16   Likewise, in *R (Mahmood) v Secretary of State for the Home Department*,[22] Laws LJ held that the appropriate intensity of review in a case involving fundamental rights was greater than that which would be applied on a conventional *Wednesbury* basis, and emphasised the objective basis of the approach to be adopted. Where a fundamental right was engaged, the court would 'insist that that fact be respected by the decision-maker, who is accordingly required to demonstrate either that his proposed action does not in truth interfere with the right, or, if it does, that there exist considerations which may reasonably be accepted as amounting to a substantial objective justification for the interference'.[23] The intensity of review in a public law case would depend on the subject matter in hand and so, in particular, any interference with a fundamental right would require a substantial objective justification. This approach and that of conventional *Wednesbury* were not, however, sealed hermetically one from the other. There was 'rather, what may be called a sliding scale of review; the graver the impact of the decision in question upon the individual affected by it, the more substantial the justification that will be required'.[24]

'Anxious scrutiny' and proportionality

6.17   Since the coming into force of the Human Rights Act (HRA) 1998, the courts have developed this approach further. The HRA 1998 itself obliges the court to have regard to the jurisprudence of the European Court of Human Rights,[25] and this has rapidly led to the development of a more intensive approach to review, founded on the principles set out in such cases as *Mahmood* but now in conjunction with the European concept of proportionality, which has become the benchmark test of intervention where fundamental rights are in play, in place of the *Wednesbury* test.

---

21   See the slightly different formulations of the approach of Simon Brown LJ at 540F and Sir Thomas Bingham MR at 554E–G. Henry LJ agreed with the Master of the Rolls (at 563A).

22   [2001] 1 WLR 840, CA.

23   [2001] 1 WLR 840 at [16].

24   [2001] 1 WLR 840 at [18]–[19]. See also the judgment of Lord Phillips of Worth Matravers MR, at [37]. The case of *R v Lord Saville of Newdigate ex p A* [2000] 1 WLR 1855, CA, per Lord Woolf MR at [37] is also instructive.

25   Human Rights Act 1998 s2(1).

6.18   The relationship, or perhaps the difference, between the traditional *Wednesbury* test and that derived from Europe, and founded on proportionality, has been explained by Laws J as follows. In *R v Ministry of Agriculture, Fisheries and Food ex p First City Trading Limited,*[26] he said:

> By our domestic law, if a public decision-maker were to treat apparently identical cases differently there would no doubt be a prima facie *Wednesbury* case against him, since on the face of it such an approach bears the hall-mark of irrationality. To that extent the rule is akin to the European principle. The Court would look for an explanation of the difference; but the justification offered would in the ordinary way only be rejected on grounds of perversity. That, I think, marks the divide. The Community rule requires the decision-maker to demonstrate a substantive justification for a discriminatory decision ... In case after case ... the Court of Justice has proceeded on the footing that the facts must be examined by the reviewing court and a view reached as to whether the decision taken measures up to the *substantive* standards which it has set ...
>
> The difference between *Wednesbury* and European review is that in the former case the legal limits lie further back. I think there are two factors. First, the limits of domestic review are not, as the law presently stands, constrained by the doctrine of proportionality. Secondly, at least as regards a requirement such as that of objective justification in an equal-treatment case, the European rule requires the decision-maker to provide a fully-reasoned case. It is not enough merely to set out the problem, and assert that within his discretion the Minister chose this or that solution, constrained only by the requirement that his decision must have been one which a reasonable Minister might make. Rather the Court will test the solution arrived at, and pass it only if substantial factual considerations are put forward in its justification: considerations which are relevant, reasonable and proportionate to the aim in view. But as I understand the jurisprudence the Court is not concerned to agree or disagree with the decision: that would be to travel beyond the boundaries of proper judicial authority, and usurp the primary decision-maker's function. Thus *Wednesbury* and European review are different models – one looser, one tighter – of the same juridical concept, which is the imposition of compulsory standards on decision-makers so as to secure the repudiation of arbitrary power.

---

26 [1997] 1 CMLR 250, QBD, at 278–9. This analysis was approved by the Court of Appeal in *R v Secretary of State for Health ex p Eastside Cheese* [1999] 3 CMLR 123, CA.

6.19   In *Daly*,[27] Lord Steyn described the application of the principle of proportionality in terms of a three-stage test.[28] The court should ask itself:

> ... whether (i) the legislative object is sufficiently important to justify limiting a fundamental right; (ii) the measures designed to meet the legislative imperative are rationally connected to it; and (iii) the means used to impair the right or freedom are no more than is necessary to accomplish the objective.

6.20   Lord Steyn recognised the overlap between the traditional grounds of review and the approach of proportionality. Most cases would be decided in the same way whichever approach was adopted. He did, however, refer to three concrete differences between proportionality and *Wednesbury*: first, proportionality may require the reviewing court to assess for itself the appropriateness of the balance between competing interests which the decision-maker has struck and not merely consider whether that balance is within the range of rational or reasonable decisions. Second, proportionality may require the attention of the court to be directed to the relative weight attached to the various relevant interests and considerations. Third, even the heightened scrutiny test developed in *Smith*[29] would not necessarily be appropriate to the protection of human rights. The European Court of Human Rights in the same case had concluded that the threshold of the test for irrationality applied by the Court of Appeal had been set so high that it effectively excluded any consideration of whether the policy under challenge met a pressing social need or was proportionate to the aims pursued.

6.21   This did not mean that there had been a shift from the court's supervisory role to a full review of the merits of the decision. It was, however, important that human rights cases be analysed in the correct way. *Mahmood* had been correct to emphasise that the appropriate intensity of review would depend on the subject matter of the case in hand, even in cases involving Convention rights. 'In law context is everything'.[30]

---

27   *R (Daly) v Secretary of State for the Home Department* [2001] UKHL 26; [2001] 2 AC 532 at [27].

28   First propounded by the Privy Council in *de Freitas v Permanent Secretary of Ministry of Agriculture, Fisheries, Lands and Housing* [1999] 1 AC 69, per Lord Clyde at 80.

29   *R v Ministry of Defence ex p Smith* [1996] QB 517, CA.

30   *R (Mahmood) v Secretary of State for the Home Department* [2001] 1 WLR 840, CA at [27]–[28].

6.22   In *Southampton Port Health Authority v Seahawk Marine Foods Ltd,*[31] the Court of Appeal expressed considerable doubt as to whether it would be wise for the court to attempt the lines of enquiry suggested by Lord Steyn in *Daly* (in particular as concerned assessing the balance struck by the decision-maker and the relative weight he or she had accorded to relevant factors)[32] in cases involving technical or professional decision-making without the benefit of evidence regarding usual practices and the practicability of the suggested alternatives. While in some cases, the court may be able to rely on common sense and its own understanding of government and administration, this would be difficult in cases involving decision-making on technical issues.

Wednesbury, proportionality and the margin of appreciation

6.23   The *Wednesbury* test affords the decision-maker a very wide margin of appreciation – any decision may validly be taken so long as no error is made and a reasonable decision-maker could have taken it. In *R v Secretary of State for the Home Department ex p Farrakhan,*[33] the Court of Appeal held that such a margin was far too wide to accommodate the requirements of the European Convention on Human Rights (the Convention). In deciding whether a restriction on a Convention right was permissible, the doctrine of proportionality must therefore be applied. The breadth of the margin of appreciation thereby accorded the decision was flexible – it would vary according to the rights in play and the facts of the case. The *Wednesbury* approach, on the other hand, was not flexible. In applying the principles of proportionality, however, it was essential to recognise and give proper respect to the margin of appreciation to which the decision-maker is entitled; only by doing so could the court avoid substituting its own decision for the decision under challenge. On the facts of that case, a very wide margin of appreciation should be accorded.

Two tests?

6.24   In *Mahmood*, Laws LJ referred to a sliding scale of review, the intensity of which would increase with the gravity of the subject matter. This does

---

31 [2002] EWCA Civ 54; [2002] ACD 35.
32 Above at paras 6.19–6.21.
33 [2002] EWCA Civ 606; [2002] QB 1391; [2002] 4 All ER 289.

not, however, entirely dispense with the difficulty that in cases where no Convention right is engaged, conventional *Wednesbury* would still appear to be the test properly applied by the courts, whereas in a Convention case, a more intense version of review, founded on the doctrine of proportionality, is likely to be undertaken by the court. While it can be argued that this is as it should be – the more serious the case, the more anxious should be the scrutiny applied to the decision under challenge – there are three difficulties with such an argument.

6.25   First, it is only persuasive if it can be demonstrated that the rights at stake in all cases involving Convention rights are more grave, or fundamental, than those at stake in every case which does not. Second, it is a little unconvincing that the availability of the doctrine of proportionality to test the legality of a decision should depend exclusively on whether or not a Convention right is at stake. That this is so results from the fact that the court historically set its face against entertaining proportionality as a distinct head of challenge or means of testing a decision.[34] It is therefore only available to the court where the Human Rights Act 1998, which requires the court to have regard to European jurisprudence, is in play. Third, it is unsatisfactory that the court should be developing and called upon to apply two increasingly distinct and divergent bodies of public law to cases brought before it under the same procedure, seeking the same remedies in respect of the same kind of (ie, public law) decision.

6.26   It is by no means clear either that all cases involving a Convention right concern more significant rights than all those which do not. This is frequently because the availability of a human rights argument does not depend on the importance of the right at stake but on whether the Human Rights Act 1998 can be said to have added anything to the protection of a particular right afforded by common law or statute. In many cases, the courts have held that a particular Convention right is in issue, or engaged,[35] but that any infringement has been lawful for reasons unrelated to the importance of the right itself, but related instead to such matters as the respect which the courts must have for the will of Parliament as expressed in legislation.[36] Such decisions

34 See, eg, *R v Secretary of State for the Home Department ex p Brind* [1991] 1 AC 696, HL.

35 But see the mild judicial disapproval of the term 'engaged' and the suggestion that 'applicable' is the more appropriate term: *Harrow LBC v Qazi* [2003] UKHL 43, per Lord Hope at [47].

36 See, eg, *Poplar HARCA v Donoghue* [2002] EWCA Civ 595; [2002] QB 48; *Begum (Runa) v Tower Hamlets LBC* [2003] UKHL 5; [2003] 2 AC 430; [2003] 1 All ER 731.

prevent reliance on the European Convention in future cases involving the same right, but does not affect the importance of the right itself.

6.27 If this is correct, then the above justifications do not provide an entirely sound basis for distinguishing between when the correct approach is that of conventional *Wednesbury* and when it is likely to require proportionality or heightened scrutiny.

6.28 The problem of two tests was considered by Lord Slynn of Hadley in *R (Alconbury) v Secretary of State for the Environment, Transport and the Regions*,[37] who stated:

> I consider that even without reference to the Human Rights Act the time has come to recognise that this principle is part of English administrative law, not only when judges are dealing with Community acts but also when they are dealing with acts subject to domestic law. Trying to keep the *Wednesbury* principle and proportionality in separate compartments seems to me to be unnecessary and confusing.

6.29 In *Daly*, Lord Cooke of Thorndon went further, suggesting that:[38]

> ... the day will come when it will be more widely recognised that *Associated Provincial Picture Houses Ltd v Wednesbury Corporation* [1948] 1 KB 223 was an unfortunately retrogressive decision in English administrative law, insofar as it suggested that there are degrees of unreasonableness and that only a very extreme degree can bring an administrative decision within the legitimate scope of judicial invalidation. The depth of judicial review and the deference due to administrative discretion vary with the subject matter. It may well be, however, that the law can never be satisfied in any administrative field merely by a finding that the decision under review is not capricious or absurd.

6.30 In *R (Association of British Civilian Internees (Far East Region)) v Secretary of State for Defence*,[39] the Court of Appeal again considered the issue, and concluded that the time had come for the *Wednesbury* approach to be dispensed with (while recognising that only the House of Lords could 'perform its burial rites'), though for rather different reasons than those put forward by Lord Cooke of Thorndon in *Daly*.[40] In the view of Lord Phillips MR, while the criteria of proportionality were

---

37 [2001] UKHL 23; [2003] 2 AC 295; [2001] 2 All ER 929 at [51].

38 [2001] UKHL 26; [2001] 2 AC 532, at [32].

39 [2003] EWCA Civ 473; [2003] 3 WLR 80, per Lord Phillips of Worth Matravers at [34]–[35].

40 *R (Daly) v Secretary of State for the Home Department* [2001] UKHL 26; [2001] 2 AC 523.

more precise and sophisticated, the strictness of the *Wednesbury* test had been relaxed in recent years so that it was, in any event, moving closer to proportionality, so much so that in some cases it was not possible to see daylight between the two tests.

Abuse of power: a doctrine of reconciliation

6.31   There has been some suggestion that a general doctrine of abuse of power may now be assuming centre stage as an all-embracing rationale for the general principles of administrative law. In *R v Department for Education and Employment ex p Begbie*,[41] Laws LJ stated that abuse of power 'has become, or is fast becoming, the root concept which governs and conditions our general principles of public law'. He described it as the rationale for the *Wednesbury* and *Padfield*[42] doctrines, for illegality as a ground of challenge, and for the requirements of proportionality, procedural fairness and legitimate expectation.

6.32   Similarly, in *R v North and East Devon Health Authority ex p Cough-lan*,[43] Lord Woolf MR stated, in the context of legitimate expectations:

> We would prefer to regard the *Wednesbury* categories themselves as the major instances (not necessarily the sole ones ...) of how public power may be misused. Once it is recognised that conduct which is an abuse of power is contrary to law its existence must be for the court to determine.[44]

6.33   Likewise, in *R (Zeqiri) v Secretary of State for the Home Department*,[45] the House of Lords referred to the denial of a legitimate expectation as but one form of the more general concept of abuse of power.

Grounds

6.34   Be all of that as it may, and in spite of the current uncertainties in this area of public law, it is still possible to discuss the general grounds for review in much the same terms, or at least under much the same rubric, as in the first edition of this book, and that is still the approach taken below. The different grounds listed below have been set out

---

41   [2001] 1 WLR 1115, CA at 1129.
42   *Padfield v Ministry of Agriculture, Fisheries and Food* [1968] AC 998, HL.
43   [2001] QB 213; [2000] 3 All ER 850; (1999) 2 CCLR 285, CA.
44   [2001] QB 213 at [81].
45   [2002] UKHL 3; [2002] All ER (D) 184.

under Lord Diplock's three headings in *CCSU*, as further explained by *Hammersmith and Fulham LBC v Secretary State for the Environment*,[46] and *Leeds CC v Spencer*.[47]

Illegality

Misdirections of law

6.35 It is plain that the decision-maker must only act within the confines of the powers which have been conferred on her or him.[48] The decision-maker must also direct her or himself properly in law, ie, understand and apply the law correctly. Thus, a decision based on a misunderstanding or misapplication of the law will not have been reached properly.[49]

Decision must be in accordance with the facts

No fundamental rights at stake

6.36 The decision must be reached on the basis of the facts of the matter in question. A decision totally at variance with the facts or for which there is no factual basis cannot be sustained. Prior to the coming into force of the Human Rights Act 1998, the courts were at pains to point out that judicial review is concerned with errors of law and not errors of fact. Thus, where no fundamental rights are at stake, to proceed (or succeed) on this basis it will be necessary to establish:

(a) that the fact in question affected the jurisdiction of the decision-maker; or

(b) if not jurisdictional, that—[50]

    (i) the decision made proceeded on an incorrect understanding of the facts, or

---

46 [1991] 1 AC 521 at 597.

47 [2000] BLGR 68 at 75.

48 See, eg, *R (Bancoult) v Secretary of State for the Foreign and Commonwealth Office* [2001] QB 1067; [2001] 2 WLR 1219. See also *Wednesbury* [1948] 1 KB 223, CA; *Anisminic v Foreign Compensation Commission* [1969] AC 426, HL; and *Council of Civil Service Unions v Ministrer of State for the Civil Service* [1985] AC 374, HL.

49 See *Wednesbury* (above); *In re Islam* [1983] 1 AC 688, HL. See also *Mercury Ltd v Director General of Telecommunications* [1996] 1 WLR 48, HL.

50 See, eg, *Edwards v Bairstow* [1956] AC 14, *Begum v Tower Hamlets LBC* [2003] UKHL 5; [2003] 2 WLR 388, HL.

(ii) there was no evidence to support the finding of fact made, or

(iii) the decision-maker took no account of them, in the sense of simply applying a pre-ordained policy, regardless of the merits,[51] or

(iv) in finding the facts, the decision-maker failed to take account of relevant matters or took account of irrelevancies, or

(v) the finding of fact was perverse or irrational.

6.37 In *Sagnata Investments v Norwich Corporation*,[52] the local authority had resolved not to permit amusement arcades in Norwich. The appellant was refused a licence and appealed. Phillimore LJ said:

> ... the Council had not exercised any form of discretion. They had simply dismissed the application after going through the necessary motions without regard to its individual merits or demerits ... the council's committee had failed to keep an open mind and had applied their policy without regard to the facts of the individual case.[53]

6.38 In *Tameside*,[54] Lord Wilberforce said:

> If a judgment requires, before it can be made, the existence of some facts, then, although the evaluation of those facts is for the Secretary of State alone, the court must enquire whether those facts exist, and have been taken into account, whether the judgment has been made on a proper self direction as to those facts, whether the judgment has not been made on other facts which ought not to have been taken into account. If these requirements are not met, then the exercise of judgment, however bona fide it may be, becomes capable of challenge: see *Secretary of State for Employment v Associated Society of Locomotive Engineers and Firemen (No 2)* [1972] 2 QB 455 at 493, per Lord Denning MR.[55]

6.39 He continued:

> ... if [the Secretary of State] had exercised his judgment on the basis of the factual situation in which this newly elected authority were placed – with a policy approved by their electorate, and massively supported by the parents – there was no ground, however much he might disagree with the new

---

51 See also 'Fettering of discretion' at paras 6.73–6.77 below.

52 [1971] 2 QB 614, CA.

53 [1971] 2 QB 614 at 639.

54 *Secretary of State for Education and Science v Tameside MBC* [1977] AC 1014, HL.

55 [1977] AC 1014 at 1047D–F.

policy ... on which he could find that the authority were acting or propos-ing to act unreasonably.[56]

6.40   See also *Hemns v Wheeler:*[57]

It is for the county court judge to find the facts and to draw the inferences from those facts, but ... it is always a question of law, which will warrant the interference of this court, whether there was any evidence to support his findings of fact and whether the inferences he has drawn are possible inferences from the facts as found.

Jurisdictional errors and precedent facts

6.41   Where the decision-maker has wrongly decided a question of fact (or of law, or a mixed question) either to deprive himself of, or confer upon himself, jurisdiction, the court can review the issue of jurisdic-tional fact or law. In such cases, the court does not approach the matter on the basis set out above, ie, by asking whether the decision-maker approached the question correctly, but will decide the jurisdictional question for itself.

6.42   This may arise, for example, where a particular status is under con-sideration. An example of this is *R v Secretary of State for the Environment ex p Davies.*[58] By Town and Country Planning Act 1990 s174, only a person with an interest in land has a right of appeal against an enforcement notice. The applicant was a traveller who claimed to have such an interest by virtue of being in adverse possession of the land in question and purported to appeal against the service of an enforce-ment notice upon her by the local authority. The secretary of state determined that she had no interest in the land and that therefore he had no jurisdiction to hear the appeal. The Court of Appeal held that it had power to determine the matter for itself. The secretary of state had conceded for the purposes of the appeal that a person in adverse pos-session could have an interest in land. On the facts, however, the court held that the applicant was not in adverse possession.[59]

---

56   [1977] AC 1014 at 1052.
57   [1948] 2 KB 61, CA, per Tucker LJ at 65–66.
58   (1990) 61 P&CR 487, CA. On the issue of adverse possession, *Davies* was held to have been wrongly decided by the House of Lords in *JA Pye (Oxford) Ltd v Graham* [2002] UKHL 30; [2002] 3 WLR 221. It was not overruled on the issue of precedent fact, however.
59   Although it has now been overruled on this point (see note 58 above). See also *R v Secretary of State for the Home Department ex p Khawaja* [1984] AC 74, HL, where the question was whether or not a person was an 'illegal entrant'.

6.43   It is not entirely clear what evidence the court will consider in such matters. In *Khawaja*,[60] the House of Lords took the view that the court could take into account any evidence before it, whether or not it had been before the secretary of state.[61] In *R v Secretary of State for the Environment ex p Powis*,[62] the Court of Appeal likewise held that where the jurisdiction of the minister depended on a question of fact, the court could entertain additional evidence for the purpose of determining the jurisdictional fact for itself. In *Davies*,[63] however, the court held that it must consider the matter solely on the basis of the evidence before the minister.[64]

6.44   Other precedent facts include whether or not a councillor has been disqualified,[65] whether a measure qualifies as state aid under the EC Treaty,[66] whether a person's detention was 'pending removal',[67] whether, in a planning context, information qualified as information relating to the environment,[68] whether a person was a deposed native chief, and thus subject to a power to be removed from an area.[69]

6.45   The following have been held not to be jurisdictional facts: whether an asylum-seeker is a refugee,[70] whether a traveller is a Gypsy,[71] whether a person has the requisite mental capacity necessary to be treated as a homeless applicant,[72] whether a fresh asylum application had been made[73].

60   See note 59 above.

61   See especially Lord Wilberforce at 105, Lord Scarman at 110, and Lord Bridge at 125. See also *R v Secretary of State for the Home Department ex p Hussain* [1978] 1 WLR 700, CA.

62   [1981] 1 WLR 584, CA.

63   (1990) 61 P&CR 487, CA.

64   There is no reference to *Khawaja* [1984] AC 74, HL or *Powis* [1981] 1 WLR 584, CA in the judgments of the court. See also *Re S (Minors)* [1995] ELR 98, in which the Court of Appeal suggested that the *Khawaja* principle was not of universal application and had only been applied where the liberty of the subject was at stake.

65   *R v Islington LBC ex p Camp* (1999) 20 July (unreported).

66   *R v Commissioners of Customs and Excise ex p Lunn Poly Ltd* [1999] EuLR 653.

67   *Tan Te Lam v Superintendent of Tai A Chau Detention Centre* [1997] AC 97.

68   *R v Secretary of State for the Environment, Transport and the Regions ex p Alliance Against the Birmingham Northern Relief Road* [1999] Env LR 447.

69   *Eshugbayi Eleko v Governor of Nigeria* [1931] AC 662, PC.

70   *R v Secretary of State for the Home Department ex p Bugdaycay* [1987] AC 514, HL.

71   *R v South Hams DC ex p Gibb* [1995] QB 158.

72   *R v Oldham MBC, ex p G* [1993] AC 509, HL.

73   *R v Secretary of State for the Home Department ex p Onibiyo* [1996] QB 768, CA; *Cakabay v Secretary of State for the Home Department (No 2)* [1999] Imm AR 176.

Fundamental rights cases

6.46 Where fundamental rights are at stake, there are now indications that a rather more interventionist approach to disputes of fact may be appropriate. In *R v Criminal Injuries Compensation Board ex p A*,[74] Lord Slynn of Hadley accepted that the court had jurisdiction to quash the decision of the Board on the ground of a material error of fact, although he did not decide the case on that basis. In *R (Alconbury Developments Ltd) v Secretary of State for the Environment, Transport and the Regions*,[75] Lord Slynn again referred to the potential ability of a judicial review court to review material errors of fact, which ability strengthened the argument that judicial review was an adequate remedy for the purposes of article 6 of the European Convention.

6.47 In *R (Wilkinson) v Broadmoor Special Hospital Authority*,[76] the claimant, who was detained under the Mental Health Act 1983, challenged the defendant's decision that he should be compulsorily treated with anti-psychotic medication (on the basis that his mental state was not such that he could validly withhold his consent). The claimant claimed interim relief in the form of an order that the doctors who had made the decision be ordered to attend court for cross-examination. The judge at first instance refused to make such an order, but the Court of Appeal allowed the claimant's appeal.

6.48 Simon Brown LJ, with whom the other members of the court agreed, stated that since the coming into force of the Human Rights Act 1998, the provisions of article 6 of the Convention required that where fundamental rights were at stake the court not only had power to, but 'must now inevitably reach its own view' on the disputed issues of fact: namely, whether the claimant was capable of consenting or refusing consent to the proposed treatment and whether the administration of the treatment would itself be contrary to the claimant's Convention rights.[77] The claimant could have litigated his claim by other means which would necessarily have entailed the adducing of oral evidence – such as an action in tort against the hospital authority for assault, or a claim under the Human Rights Act 1998 itself, for breach of Convention rights. The court would accordingly order the attendance of the

---

74 [1999] 2 AC 330, HL, at 344F–345C.
75 [2001] UKHL 23; [2003] 2 AC 295 at [53]–[54].
76 [2001] EWCA Civ 1545; [2002] 1 WLR 419; (2002) 5 CCLR 121. See generally the analysis in the judgment of Simon Brown LJ at [24]–[36], with which Brooke LJ and Hale LJ agreed.
77 [2001] EWCA Civ 1545 at para [26].

doctors for cross-examination and conduct a 'full merits' review of the propriety of the treatment proposed.[78]

6.49　　The *Wilkinson* decision was considered, albeit obiter, in *Adan v Newham LBC*.[79] In that case, it was argued, in reliance on the authorities referred to above, that on an appeal on a point of law (applying judicial review principles), the court, in the exercise of its supervisory jurisdiction, could reverse a 'material error of fact' if it considered that the fact which had been found was 'wrong'. The majority of the Court of Appeal[80] rejected this argument which was contrary to 'very powerful judicial statements throughout the common law world'.[81] The court held that it was 'quite clear ... that a court of supervisory jurisdiction does not, without more, have the power to substitute its own view of the primary facts for the view reasonably adopted by the body to whom the fact-finding power has been entrusted'.[82]

6.50　　Simon Brown LJ returned to this topic as a member of a two-judge Administrative Court in *R (Mullen) v Secretary of State for the Home Department*.[83] In that case, there was no dispute of fact at all, just a question of whether, on the true construction of Criminal Justice Act 1988 s133 (compensation for victims of miscarriages of justice) the claimant was entitled to compensation in circumstances where his conviction had been set aside by the Court of Appeal, notwithstanding that the finding of guilt was not challenged, on the basis that his trial constituted an abuse of process, due to his having been illegally returned to the United Kingdom from Zimbabwe.

6.51　　The court rejected an argument that judicial review was not an adequate remedy for the purposes of article 6 of the Convention, not only because there was no issue of fact involved but on a broader basis. The court could well envisage a case in which a factual dispute may arise, which would raise the issue of the appropriate intensity of review on a judicial review application.

> As the recent Court of Appeal decision in *R (Wilkinson) v Broadmoor Special Hospital Authority* ... amply demonstrates, the Court on judicial

78　[2001] EWCA Civ 1545 at para [36].

79　[2001] EWCA Civ 1916; [2002] 1 WLR 2120, CA.

80　The majority included Brooke LJ who had been a member of the Court of Appeal in *Wilkinson*. The dissenting judge was Hale LJ who had also been a member of the *Wilkinson* Court of Appeal.

81　[2001] EWCA Civ 1916, per Brooke LJ at [36].

82　[2001] EWCA Civ 1916 at [41].

83　[2002] EWHC 230 (Admin); [2003] 2 WLR 835.

review can and will if necessary assess any relevant facts for itself even to the extent of ordering the attendance of witnesses for cross-examination.[84]

6.52   The position, then, as to the extent of the judicial review court's power to entertain factual challenges in fundamental rights cases is not entirely clear. In *S v Airedale NHS Trust*,[85] oral expert evidence was given in a challenge to a decision to seclude a patient in a non-secure hospital. In *R (PG) v Ealing LBC*,[86] Munby J, while confirming the power of the Administrative Court to hear oral evidence, stated that *Wilkinson* plainly indicated that there would be judicial review cases in which cross-examination will be appropriate, or even essential, and cases in which compliance by the court with the Convention would demand cross-examination as part of a more intense review. Recourse to such powers would, nevertheless, be very much the exception, and the overwhelming bulk of judicial review cases would continue to be determined without oral evidence.

6.53   This has been confirmed in general terms by the House of Lords in *Begum v Tower Hamlets LBC*,[87] although neither *Wilkinson* nor *Mullen* was referred to in the speeches in that case. The judicial committee confirmed, nonetheless, that on an appeal to the county court on a point of law, in a homelessness case, where only article 6 of the Convention was in issue (ie, no other Convention rights were staked), no more intensive approach to judicial review of questions of fact was mandated, and the conventional bases of intervention in factual issues (ie, no evidence to support a finding of fact, perverse finding or finding made having regard to irrelevant factors or having no regard to relevant ones) would generally be sufficient.[88] The court could not substitute its own findings of fact for those of the decision-making authority if there was evidence to support them. Questions regarding the weight to be given to a particular piece of evidence and on the credibility of witnesses was a matter for the decision-making authority and not for the court.[89]

---

84   [2002] EWHC 230 (Admin), per Simon Brown LJ at [30].
85   [2002] EWHC 1780 (Admin), [2003] Lloyd's Rep Med 21. See also *R (N) v M* [2002] EWHC 1911 (Admin); [2003] ACD 17.
86   Also reported as *R (G) v Ealing LBC (No 2)* [2002] EWHC 250 (Admin); [2002] ACD 48.
87   [2003] UKHL 4; [2003] 2 WLR 388, HL.
88   [2003] UKHL 4, per Lord Hoffmann at [49]–[50]. See also Lord Bingham of Cornhill at [7].
89   [2003] UKHL 4, per Lord Millett at [99].

Relevant and irrelevant considerations

6.54 A decision-maker must take into account all relevant considerations before making its decision and must ignore the irrelevant.[90] Which factors are relevant and which irrelevant will, of course, depend on the facts of the individual case.

6.55 In addition, it may be unlawful for a decision-maker to pay too much regard to a relevant consideration.

6.56 In *R v Winchester CC ex p Ashton*,[91] for example, Purchas LJ held that:

> Parliament could never have intended [the prevailing housing circumstances in the local authority's area][92] to be more than something to which a local authority may have regard and I do not think Mr Stephenson would submit that it is or should be the overall determining factor. It is something that must be weighed carefully in the balance with the other factors upon which the decision under Housing Act 1996 s60(1) is reached.[14]

6.57 Similarly, in *South Oxfordshire DC v Secretary of State for the Environment*,[93] Woolf J held that while the planning history of a matter can be a material consideration, it was hard to see, in the context of the case, how it could have been, as the secretary of state contended:

> ... a vitally material consideration ... While the weight to be given to a particular consideration is for the Secretary of State, such a conclusion indicates that either the ... Secretary of State misdirected himself, or he was acting perversely.[94]

6.58 The cases referred to above could also be classified as cases involving misdirections of law: the decision-maker had fallen into legal error by misunderstanding the difference between a relevant factor to be taken into account and a factor which was conclusive to the issue under consideration. Generally, however, the weight to be given to a relevant factor is a matter for the decision-maker, with which the court cannot interfere.

---

90 *Associated Provincial Picture Houses v Wednesbury Corporation* [1948] 1 KB 223, CA; *CCSU v Minister of State for the Civil Service* [1985] AC 374, HL.

91 (1991) 24 HLR 520, CA, at 527.

92 A factor the local authority is entitled to take into account in deciding whether or not it was reasonable to expect a homeless person to have remained in accommodation for the purposes of deciding whether or not that person is homeless and/or intentionally homeless. In *Ashton*, the relevant statutory provision was Housing Act 1985 s60(4); now, see Housing Act 1996 s177(2).

93 [1981] 1 WLR 1092, QBD.

94 [1981] 1 WLR 1092 at 1099.

6.59   In *R (Daly) v Secretary of State for the Home Department*,[95] Lord Steyn suggested that the doctrine of proportionality differed from the principles of *Wednesbury* review in this regard, so that it may be appropriate and necessary for the attention of the court to be directed to the relative weight attached to the various relevant interests and considerations.[96]

What considerations?

6.60   Some considerations must be taken into account, or left out of account, because the legislation under which the decision is taken so provides, whether expressly or impliedly. Failure to take a statutorily relevant consideration into account, or leave a statutorily irrelevant one out of account, will invalidate the decision.[97]

6.61   Some examples of statutorily relevant/irrelevant matters are as follows. Housing Act 1996 ss169(1) and 182(1) require that a local authority in performing its functions under Parts VI (allocations) and VII (assistance for homeless persons) of that Act must have regard to any guidance given by the secretary of state.[98] Similar provision is made in relation to decisions as to works to remedy the contamination of land.[99] An authority proposing to approve an application for a type of housing grant must 'consider' whether the premises are fit for human habitation.[100] Local planning authorities are obliged to have regard to the applicable development plan when considering planning applications.[101] Social services authorities must have regard to the views of specified categories of person when accommodating or looking after

---

95   [2001] UKHL 26; [2001] 2 AC 532.

96   See paras 6.20 above.

97   *In re Findlay* [1985] AC 318, HL, per Lord Scarman at 333–334 approving *CREEDNZ Inc v Governor-General* [1981] NZLR 172. See also *R v Secretary of State for Transport ex p Richmond-upon-Thames LBC* [1994] 1 WLR 74.

98   And see on this point *R v Wandsworth LBC ex p Hawthorne* [1994] 1 WLR 1442.

99   Environment Act 1995 s78A.

100   Housing Grants, Construction and Regeneration Act 1996 s13(4). See generally Part I of that Act for a statutory scheme which sets out the matters to be taken into account in approving applications for grants. See also *R v Sunderland CC ex p Redezeus Ltd* (1995) 27 HLR 477, holding that the previous legislative scheme for housing grants (Local Government and Housing Act 1989 Pt VIII) set out the only factors which could be taken into account.

101   Town and Country Planning Act 1990 s70.

a child.[102] Local authorities are obliged to secure improvements in the exercise of their functions having regard to 'a combination of economy, efficiency and effectiveness'.[103]

6.62   In *R v Oadby and Wigston BC ex p Dickman*,[104] Buxton J held, construing housing benefit regulations that 'the only factors that the authority should take into consideration, are those which are specifically set out. Otherwise, the implication is that the authority is bound to take into account a factor which has been said to be not irrelevant, or at least not to be relevant. That is a conclusion I do not think is likely or even lawful.'[105] See also *R v Secretary of State for the Environment ex p Lancashire CC*,[106] in which it was held that mandatory statutory criteria could not be supplemented by guidance.[107]

6.63   By contrast, when public supply or works contracts are under consideration, a local authority is statutorily prohibited from taking account of 'non-commercial considerations'.[108]

6.64   Where statute has not intervened, the question will be for the decision-maker to decide what matters are relevant for consideration or to be left out of account as irrelevant. The court will only intervene in that decision on the ground of *Wednesbury* unreasonableness,[109] although the position may be different where fundamental rights are at stake and the court approaches the issue under the rubric of proportionality.[110]

6.65   In this situation, it is extremely difficult and almost inevitably misleading to attempt to make general propositions regarding factors which may or may not be relevant. The courts have, on occasion, suggested factors which must generally be considered. In *R v Lincolnshire*

---

102   Children Act 1989 ss20(6) and 22(4).

103   Audit Commission Act 1998 s5(1)(d); Local Government Act 1999 s3(1).

104   (1996) 28 HLR 806, QBD.

105   (1996) 28 HLR 806 at 817.

106   [1994] 4 All ER 165, QBD.

107   See also, eg, *R v Highbury Corner Metropolitan Stipendiary Magistrate ex p Di Matteo* [1991] 1 WLR 1374; *London Residuary Body v Lambeth LBC* [1990] 1 WLR 744; *Lonrho plc v Secretary of State for Trade and Industry* [1989] 1 WLR 525, HL.

108   Local Government Act 1988, Part II.

109   See, eg, *R v Secretary of State for Transport ex p Richmond upon Thames LBC* [1994] 1 WLR 74, per Laws J at 95. See also *R v Southwark LBC ex p Cordwell* (1994) 26 HLR 107, QBD. See also *South Buckinghamshire DC v Porter* [2003] UKHL 26; [2003] 2 WLR 1547.

110   See the discussion of *R (Daly) v Secretary of State for the Home Department* [2001] UKHL 26; [2001] 2 AC 532, at paras 6.17–6.23.

CC and Wealden DC ex p Atkinson,[111] for example, Sedley J stated that government guidance would be of relevance in any case, regardless of whether there was a statutory obligation to consider it, on the basis that such guidance will indicate matters which are themselves relevant. It has also been said that local authorities are, absent any statutory inhibition, entitled to act in the best interests of their inhabitants.[112] Where fundamental needs are in issue, considerations of 'common humanity' have been held to be relevant.[113]

6.66   Beyond this, however, the question of what is or is not relevant will depend on the specific decision which falls to be made and the statutory framework within which it arises. The relevance of certain considerations which decision-makers have taken into account has repeatedly come before the courts in different contexts. Even the general points made above are heavily dependent on context. Common humanity, for example, will not always be relevant. In *R v Somerset CC ex p Fewings*,[114] for example, it was held that questions of cruelty and morality were not capable of being relevant to a decision to ban fox-hunting on the authority's land in the context of an obligation to manage that land for the 'benefit, improvement or development of their area'.

Financial resources

6.67   This consideration has been held to be relevant in some contexts but not in others. In *R v Gloucestershire CC ex p Barry*,[115] the House of Lords held that an authority could take account of its limited financial resources in deciding whether a person was in need of services under Chronically Sick and Disabled Persons Act 1970 s2, and as to the services necessary to meet any identified needs. Once it had been decided that specific services were necessary, however, a lack of resources could not excuse a failure to provide them. See also *R v Sefton MBC ex p Help the Aged*,[116] holding that resources were relevant to whether a person needed services under the National Assistance Act 1948;

---

111 (1995) 8 Admin LR 529, QBD, at 535.

112 *South Hams DC v Slough* (1992) 91 LGR 202, adopted in *R v South Hams DC ex p Gibbs* [1995] 1 QB 158, CA. See now Local Government Act 2002 ss2–3.

113 *R v Lincolnshire CC and Wealden DC ex p Atkinson* (1995) 8 Admin LR 529, QBD. See also *South Buckinghamshire DC v Porter* [2003] UKHL 26; [2003] 2 WLR 1547; *R v Hillingdon LBC ex p McDonagh* [1999] LGR 459.

114 [1995] 1 WLR 1037. Simon Brown LJ dissented from this proposition, holding that such factors were necessarily relevant and could even be treated as decisive so long as other relevant matters were not left out of account.

115 [1997] AC 584, HL.

116 [1997] 4 All ER 532, CA.

R v Norfolk CC ex p Thorpe:[117] resources relevant to decision whether it was necessary or desirable to provide a pedestrian footway.

6.68   Conversely, in *R East Sussex CC ex p Tandy*,[118] the House of Lords held that the question of resources was irrelevant to the question of what constituted a suitable education for a child with special educational needs. In that case, the House of Lords held that the fact that there may have been other calls on the authority's resources did not establish that the authority enjoyed insufficient resources to comply with the statutory duty, but rather that the authority preferred to use their resources for other purposes. To permit this would be to downgrade a duty to provide a suitable education to a mere power.[119] See also *R v Birmingham CC ex p Mohammed*,[120] where resources were held to be irrelevant to the question of whether to award a disabled facilities grant; *R v Bristol CC ex p Penfold*,[121] where resources were not relevant to the issue of whether a person 'may be' in need of community care services; *R (Khan) v Newham LBC*,[122] in which the authority's resources were not relevant to the issue of whether the court should make a mandatory order that the authority must comply with its duty to secure the availability of suitable accommodation to a homeless person.

Forthcoming legislation

6.69   Future legislation which will affect the powers of a decision-maker is a factor which has been held relevant to the exercise of a current power.[123] Current powers may be used to prepare for the coming into force of new powers.[124]

Frustrating the policy of an Act

6.70   The decision-maker must act to promote, rather than to defeat the objects or policy of an Act, or other source which created the power in question.

---

117 (1998) 96 LGR 597, CA.

118 [1998] AC 714, HL.

119 [1998] AC 714, per Lord Browne Wilkinson at 891–892.

120 [1999] 1 WLR 33.

121 (1998) 1 CCLR 315.

122 [2001] EWHC Admin 589.

123 See *R v Secretary of State for the Environment ex p Birmingham CC* [1987] RVR 53, DC. Such legislation does not act as a prohibition on the use of current powers: *In re Westminster* [1986] 1 AC 668, HL.

124 *R v Secretary of State for the Environment ex p Keen* (1990) 3 Admin LR 180, QBD.

6.71   In *Padfield v Minister of Agriculture, Fisheries and Food*,[125] Lord Reid stated that the Minister:

> ... contends that his only duty ... is to consider a complaint fairly and that he is given an unfettered discretion with regard to every complaint either to refer it or not to refer it to the committee as he may think fit ... It is implicit in the argument for the Minister ... that either he must refer every complaint or he has an unfettered discretion to refuse to refer any case. I do not think that is right. Parliament must have conferred the discretion with the intention that it should be used to promote the policy and objects of the Act ... [I]f the Minister, by reason of his having misconstrued the Act or for any other reason, so uses his discretion as to thwart or run counter to the policy and objects of the Act, then our law would be very defective if persons aggrieved were not entitled to the protection of the court.[126]

6.72   This principle has been confirmed in numerous cases including *R v Secretary of State for the Home Department ex p Brind*,[127] where Lord Ackner stated that the Secretary of State's power could only be used 'to advance the purposes for which it was conferred' and 'to promote the policy and objects of the Act'.[128]

Fettering of discretion

6.73   The decision-maker must reach its own decision on each individual case. It must not fetter its discretion by approaching a decision with a pre-determined policy on how all cases falling within a particular class will be treated. This, of course, does not mean that policies are unlawful per se; very little public administration could be conducted without them.[129] It simply means that the decision-maker must approach each case on its own merits and must leave its mind 'ajar'[130] and be prepared to listen to someone with something new to say.

---

125   [1968] AC 998, HL.

126   [1968] AC 998 at 1031–1032.

127   [1991] 1 AC 696, HL.

128   [1991] 1 AC 696 at 756. See also *R v Warwickshire CC ex p Williams* [1995] ELR 326; *R v Secretary of State for the Home Department ex p Fire Brigades Union* [1995] 2 AC 513, HL; *R v Secretary of State for the Home Department ex p Yousaf* [2000] 3 All ER 649, CA.

129   A point emphasised by the House of Lords in *R v Eastleigh BC ex p Betts* [1983] 2 AC 613, HL. Indeed, see *R v Secretary of State for the Home Department ex p Hepworth* [1998] COD 146, for a policy (of incentives for prisoners) which was upheld even though it admitted of no exceptions and operated as a 'black-and-white' rule.

130   *R v Secretary of State for the Environment ex p Brent LBC* [1982] QB 593.

6.74   In *British Oxygen Co Ltd v Minister of Technology*,[131] the Board of
Trade had power to make grants towards capital expenditure for new
machinery or plant. The Board adopted a policy of refusing grants for
any item costing less than £25 each. Lord Reid stated:

> ... the general rule is that anyone who has to exercise a statutory discretion
> must not 'shut his ears to an application' ... What the authority must not
> do is to refuse to listen at all. But a Ministry or large authority may have had
> to deal already with a multitude of similar applications and then they will
> almost certainly have evolved a policy so precise that it could well be called
> a rule. There can be no objection to that, provided the authority is always
> willing to listen to anyone with something new to say. Of course I do not
> mean to say that there need be an oral hearing.[132]

6.75   In *R v Eastleigh Borough Council ex p Betts*,[133] Lord Brightman said:

> ... provided that the authority do not close their mind to the particular
> facts of the individual case ... a body which is charged with exercising an
> administrative discretion is entitled to promulgate a policy or guidelines
> as an indication of a norm which is intended to be followed ...[134]

6.76   More recently, in *R v Secretary of State for the Home Department ex p Venables*,[135] Lord Browne-Wilkinson summarised the position in similar
terms, stating that a discretionary power conferred by Parliament:

> ... must be exercised on each occasion in the light of the circumstances at
> that time. In consequence, the person on whom the power is conferred
> cannot fetter the future exercise of his discretion by committing himself
> now as to the way in which he will exercise his power in the future ... These
> considerations do not preclude the ... [decision-maker] from developing
> and applying a policy as to the approach which he will adopt in the
> generality of cases ... But the position is different if the policy which he
> has adopted is such as to preclude the ... [decision-maker] from departing
> from the policy or from taking into account circumstances which are
> relevant to the particular case ... If such an inflexible and invariable policy
> is adopted, both the policy and the decisions taken pursuant to it will be
> unlawful ...[136]

6.77   A different aspect of the possible fettering of a decision-maker's discretion was discussed, somewhat more controversially, in *Bromley*

---

131 [1971] AC 610, HL.
132 [1971] AC 610 at 625.
133 [1983] 2 AC 613, HL.
134 [1983] 2 AC 613 at 627H–628A.
135 [1998] AC 407, HL.
136 [1998] AC 407 at 496–497.

LBC v Greater London Council.[137] The Greater London Council (GLC) had introduced a scheme of subsidised fares for public transport in London, causing it to increase its precept on the London borough councils. The House of Lords held that the GLC owed a fiduciary duty to the ratepayers to have regard to their interests, and that it was in breach of that duty in failing to balance fairly the interests of the ratepayers and transport users, thus casting an inordinate burden on the ratepayers. Lord Diplock, in the course of his speech, made the following remarks:

> I see no difference between members of ... the majority party and those who are members of a minority party. In neither case, when the time comes to play their part in performing the collective duty of the GLC to make choices of policy or action on particular matters, must members treat themselves as irrevocably bound to carry out pre-announced policies contained in election manifestos even though, by that time, changes of circumstances have occurred that were unforeseen when those policies were announced and would add significantly to the disadvantages that would result from carrying them out.[138]

Unlawful delegation or dictation

6.78   The decision must be made by the decision-maker to whom it has been entrusted. Decision-makers cannot avoid their duties by allowing themselves to be dictated to by, or simply accepting the decision of, another body. Furthermore, decision-makers may not delegate their decisions to others unless they have specific power to do so and have done so properly. Where a body or official, without the power to do so, purports to reach a decision, that decision is void in law and the true decision-maker has, as a matter of law, reached no decision at all.

Delegation

6.79   In *Barnard v National Dock Labour Board,*[139] the National Dock Labour Board had delegated to the port manager its power to suspend men. Denning LJ held that:

> ... [n]o judicial tribunal can delegate its functions unless it is enabled to do so expressly or by necessary implication ... [T]here is nothing in this scheme authorising the board to delegate this function, and it cannot be

---

137   [1983] 1 AC 768, HL.
138   [1983] 1 AC 768 at 829.
139   [1953] 2 QB 18, CA.

implied ... [I]f the board have no power to delegate their functions to the port manager, they can have no power to ratify what he has done.[140]

6.80   Similarly, in *Allingham v Minister of Agriculture and Fisheries*,[141] the Minister, by regulations, delegated his powers to give directions for the use of agricultural land to a county war agricultural committee. The committee left selection of fields to its executive officer. Lord Goddard CJ stated:

> I can find no provision in any order having statutory effect or any regulation which gives the executive committee power to delegate that which the Minister has to decide and which he has power to delegate to the committee to decide for him. If he has delegated, as he has, his power of making decisions to the executive committee, it is the executive committee that must make the decision, and, on the ordinary principle of *delegatus non potest delegare*, they cannot delegate their power to some other person or body.[142]

6.81   The full rigour of this doctrine has not, however, always been applied especially in relation to central government decisions. In *Carltona Limited v Works Comissioners*,[143] the Court of Appeal accepted that it was a concomitant of the secretary of state's acceptance of responsibility for the decisions taken within his or her department that devolution to officials of decision-making powers was a practical necessity in the administration of government which did not infringe the rule against delegation.

6.82   An example of this is the case of *R v Secretary of State for the Home Department ex p Oladehinde*,[144] in which the House of Lords regarded it as 'obvious' that the secretary of state could not take all deportation decisions personally but was entitled to delegate them to suitably senior persons within his department. In *R v Southwark LBC ex p Bannerman*,[145] the court described it as commonplace in central and local government for decisions to be taken in the name of a person who had not personally taken it, and declined to investigate the internal organisation of a department but would assume in the absence of evidence to the contrary that the writer of a letter had authority to do

---

140   [1953] 2 QB 18 at 40.
141   [1948] 1 All ER 780, DC.
142   [1948] 1 All ER 780 at 781.
143   [1943] 2 All ER 560, CA.
144   [1991] 1 AC 254, HL.
145   (1990) 2 Admin LR 381.

so.[146] In *R (Chief Constable of West Midlands Police) v Birmingham Justices,*[147] the court held that a chief constable was entitled, within *Carltona* to discharge functions through another officer for whom he was responsible and answerable. The *Carltona* principle did not depend on the peculiar status of civil servants and ministers, but was a general principle predicated on the principle that the head of a department was responsible for things done under his authority.

Dictation

6.83   The case of *Lavender & Sons v Minister for Housing and Local Government*[148] illustrates the principle that a person entrusted with decision-making powers cannot allow him or herself to be dictated to. In that case, the minister had refused to grant planning permission for gravel extraction on a farm unless the Minister for Agriculture consented. Willis J held that this was unlawful, stating:

> It seems to me that he has said in language which admits of no doubt that his decision to refuse permission was solely in pursuance of a policy not to permit minerals ... to be worked unless the Minister of Agriculture was not opposed to their working ... It seems to me that by adopting and applying his stated policy he has in effect inhibited himself from exercising a proper discretion (which would of course be guided by policy considerations) in any case where the Minister of Agriculture has made and maintained an objection ... Everything else might point to the desirability of granting permission, but by applying and acting on his stated policy, I think the Minister has fettered himself in such a way that in this case it was not he who made the decision for which Parliament has made him responsible. It was the decision of the Minister of Agriculture not to waive his objection which was decisive in this case, and while that might properly prove to be the decisive factor for the Minister when taking into account all material considerations, it seems to me quite wrong for a policy to be applied which in reality eliminates all the material considerations save only the consideration, when that is the case, that the Minister of Agriculture objects. This means, as I think, that the Minister has, by his stated policy, delegated to the Minister of Agriculture the effective decision ... where the latter objects ...[149]

---

146   See also *R v Hertsmere BC ex p Woolgar* (1995) 27 HLR 703, where the court held an authority to be entitled to delegate investigative powers notwithstanding its inability to delegate the actual decision-making function.

147   [2002] EWHC 1087 (Admin); [2003] ACD 18.

148   [1970] 1 WLR 1231, DC.

149   [1970] 1 WLR 1231 at 1240–1241.

6.84 Similarly, in *R v Metropolitan Police Disciplinary Board ex p Director Complaints Bureau Metropolitan Police*,[150] it was unlawful for the Board, in deciding to dismiss a disciplinary charge brought on the same facts as a potential criminal charge, to have regarded as conclusive the decision by the Director of Public Prosecutions that there was insufficient evidence to justify a prosecution.[151]

6.85 In the same way, a decision-maker will act unlawfully if he or she simply rubber-stamps the decision of some other body or acted under the influence of or pressure from an outside agency.[152]

Secret policies

6.86 It is unlawful for a decision-maker to refrain from making a policy known to the persons to whom it applies. In *Salih v Secretary of State for the Home Department*,[153] Stanley Burnton J held that there exists a constitutional imperative that statute law be made known and that the policies of a public authority could well have an importance for an individual akin to that of a law. It was, accordingly, inconsistent with the constitutional imperative referred to above, for the secretary of state to withhold information about his policy concerning 'hard cases support' in immigration cases, which related to the exercise of statutory power.

Irrationality

Improper purposes or motives

6.87 It is a general principle of public law[154] that the decision-maker must not use the powers entrusted to him or her for purposes which fall

150 [1996] COD 324.

151 See also *Lonrho plc v Secretary of State for Trade and Industry* [1989] AC 1 WLR 525, HL, per Lord Keith of Kinkel at 538C.

152 See, eg, *R v Parole Board ex p Watson* [1996] 1 WLR 906 (the Board must exercise its own discretion and decide the matter for itself, and not simply review the reasons for revoking parole given by the secretary of state); *In re Findlay* [1985] AC 318, HL; *R v City of Sunderland ex p Baumber* [1996] COD 211 (where it was unlawful for a local authority to instruct educational psychologists not to consult other agencies for advice but to apply to the Deputy Chief Education Officer to justify why, exceptionally, access to other advice was necessary).

153 (2003) 8 October (unreported).

154 *Credit Suisse v Allerdale BC* [1997] QB 306, CA, per Neill LJ at 333, cited with approval by Lord Bingham of Cornhill in *Porter v Magill* [2001] UKHL 67; [2002] 2 WLR 37, HL.

outside the ambit of his or her authority. In *R v Tower Hamlets LBC ex p Chetnik Developments Ltd*,[155] Lord Bridge of Harwich stated:

> Statutory power conferred for public purposes is conferred as it were upon trust, not absolutely – that is to say, it can be validly used only in the right and proper way which Parliament when conferring it is presumed to have intended ...[156]

6.88   In *Congreve v Home Office*,[157] the Home Secretary announced an increase in the television licence, to take effect from 1 April. The plaintiff, along with around 24,500 other people, purchased a new licence at the old price, before 1 April. The Home Secretary threatened to revoke this licence if the plaintiff did not pay the difference between the old and new prices.

6.89   The Court of Appeal (Lord Denning MR) held that although the secretary of state had an undoubted discretion under the Act to revoke a licence, that discretion was limited to the extent that the courts would intervene if it were exercised arbitrarily or improperly. In view of the fact that the licence issued to the plaintiff on 26 March was valid on that date and the licensee had done nothing wrong at all, the Home Secretary could not lawfully revoke the licence, at any rate, not without offering the plaintiff his money back, and not even then except for good cause. It was an improper use of a minister's discretionary power to propose to revoke a licence validly obtained as a means of levying money which Parliament had given the executive no authority to demand. Accordingly, the court could and should intervene to declare that the proposed revocation of the plaintiff's licence was unlawful, invalid and of no effect.[158]

6.90   In *Westminster Corporation v London and North Western Railway Co*,[159] the Corporation had power to build public conveniences on or under any street. They built an underground convenience under the middle of Parliament Street with access from the pavement on either side of the street. The appellant alleged that the Corporation had, in

---

155   [1988] AC 858, HL, at 872.
156   [1988] AC 858 at 872. See also *R v Inland Revenue Commissioners ex p Preston* [1985] AC 35, HL (it would have been improper for the respondent to have delayed in order to render the applicant's claim time-barred); *R v St George's Healthcare NHS Trust ex p S* [1999] Fam 26 (the Mental Health Act 1983 could not properly be used to prevent a mother refusing medical intervention for an unborn child).
157   [1976] QB 629, CA.
158   [1976] QB 629, especially at 649 and 651.
159   [1905] AC 426, HL.

reality, wished to build a subway which they had no power to do. The Earl of Halsbury LC stated:[160]

> It seems to me that the ... statute itself contemplates that ... conveniences should be made beneath public roads, and if beneath public roads some access underneath the road level must be provided; and if some access must be provided, it must be a measure simply of greater or less convenience when the street is a wide one, whether an access should be provided at only one or at both sides of the street. That if the access is provided at both sides of the street, it is possible that people who have no desire or necessity to use the convenience will nevertheless pass through it to avoid the dangers of crossing the carriageway seems to me to form no objection to the provision itself ... I quite agree that if the power to make one kind of building was fraudulently used for the purpose of making another kind of building, the power given by the Legislature for one purpose could not be used for another.

6.91   More recently, in *Porter v Magill*,[161] the House of Lords held that it was an improper purpose and so unlawful for elected members of Westminster City Council to have exercised its powers to dispose of housing stock in certain wards of the borough in an attempt to secure electoral advantage (the so-called 'homes-for-votes' policy). Lord Bingham of Cornhill accepted that, in one sense, all policies are pursued for reasons of political advantage and they may properly form part of the motives for acting in a particular way, in the sense that it is not improper to hope that a properly-exercised power will be popular and earn the gratitude and support of the electorate:

> ... but a public power is not exercised lawfully if it is exercised not for a public purpose for which the power was conferred but in order to promote the advantage of a political party.[162]

6.92   This policy was a deliberate, blatant and dishonest misuse of public power; representing political corruption.[163]

---

160   [1905] AC 426 at 427–428.

161   [2001] UKHL 67; [2002] 2 WLR 37.

162   [2001] UKHL 67 at [21].

163   Per Lord Scott at [132]. In *R v Waltham Forest LBC ex p Baxter* [1988] QB 419, CA, an elected member of a local authority was entitled to take account of party loyalty in deciding to vote in favour of a rates resolution, so long as such considerations did not dominate to exclude other considerations. Conversely, however, in *R v Local Commissioner for Administration in North and North East England ex p Liverpool CC* [2001] 1 All ER 462, it was unlawful for party political considerations and influence to have been the decisive factor in the approval of a planning application for the development of part

Bad faith

6.93   The decision-maker must not act in bad faith or dishonestly. In this context, bad faith has a broader meaning than dishonesty.

6.94   In *Roberts v Hopwood*,[164] at a time when the cost of living and trade union scale wage rates had been falling for some time, Poplar Borough Council resolved not to reduce employees' wages and to pay men and women employees at the same rate. The council had power to pay 'such wages as...[it] may think fit'. Lord Sumner stated that:

> The respondents conceded that for wages fixed *mala fide* no exemption from review could be claimed and that the mere magnitude of the wages paid, relatively to the wages for which the same service was procurable, might be enough in itself to establish bad faith. This admission ... leads to two conclusions. Firstly, the final words of the section are not absolute, but are subject to an implied qualification of good faith – 'as the Board may bona fide think fit.' ... *Bona fide* here cannot simply mean that they are not making a profit out of their office or acting in it from private spite, nor is bona fide a short way of saying that the Council has acted within the ambit of its powers and therefore not contrary to law. It must mean that they are giving their minds to the comprehension and their wills to the discharge of their duty towards that public, whose money and local business they administer.[165]

6.95   In the *Westminster Corporation* case (above para 6.90) Lord MacNaghten added:

> In order to make out a case of bad faith it must be shown that the Corporation constructed this subway as a means of crossing the street under colour and pretence of providing public conveniences which were not really wanted at that particular place.[166]

6.96   In *Smith v East Elloe RDC*,[167] it was said that the meaning of bad faith had never been precisely defined as its effects had remained mainly in

---

Footnote 163 continued

> of the Anfield stadium. See also *R v Ealing LBC ex p Times Newspapers Ltd* (1986) 85 LGR 316, CA, where the authority's refusal to provide the applicant's newspapers in its public libraries was due to its political hostility to the applicant because it had dismissed workers who had taken strike action. This was not a relevant consideration to the authority's duty to provide a comprehensive and efficient library service.

164   [1925] AC 578, HL.
165   [1925] AC 578 at 603–604.
166   [1905] AC 426 at 432.
167   [1956] AC 736, HL.

the region of hypothetical cases, but that it covered fraud or corruption.[168] In *Cannock Chase DC v Kelly*,[169] it was suggested that the term should now only be used to denote dishonest misuse or abuse of power.

Imposing decision-maker's duty on a third party

6.97   Where Parliament has imposed a duty on the decision-maker, it is unlawful for the decision-maker to seek to require a third party to perform that duty instead.

6.98   In *Hall & Co v Shoreham by Sea UDC*,[170] the local authority acted unlawfully in requiring a developer to construct a road over the entire frontage of its own site at its own expense as a condition of obtaining planning permission for a development. The Court of Appeal held that this was utterly unreasonable and could not possibly have been intended by Parliament.

6.99   In *R v Hillingdon LBC ex p Royco Homes Ltd*,[171] the authority granted outline planning permission for a housing development, subject to planning conditions that the houses should be occupied by people on the authority's housing waiting list, with security of tenure for ten years. Lord Widgery CJ stated that the conditions were undoubtedly:

> ... the equivalent of requiring the applicants to take on at their own expense a significant part of the duty of the council as housing authority. However well-intentioned and however sensible such a desire on the part of the council may have been, it seems to me that it is unreasonable in the sense in which Willmer LJ was using that word in *Hall's* case.[172]

6.100   Bridge J added:[173]

> This is in my judgment as clear a case as one would expect to find of conditions being imposed which are ultra vires, because the council are seeking to impose on the citizen the performance of a duty which statute puts on them.

---

168   [1956] AC 736, per Lord Somervell at 770 (in a dissenting speech). And see
        Porter v Magill [2001] UKHL 67; [2002] 2 WLR 37.
169   [1978] 1 WLR 1, CA.
170   [1964] 1 WLR 240, CA.
171   [1974] 1 QB 720, CA.
172   [1974] 1 QB 720 at 732A–B.
173   [1974] 1 QB 720 at 732H.

6.101 In *Leeds CC v Spencer*,[174] the Court of Appeal applied this principle, holding that a local authority could not lawfully avoid performing its statutory duty under Environmental Protection Act 1990 s45, to collect household refuse by exercising its power under Prevention of Damage by Pests Act 1949 s4, to serve a notice requiring the owner of a house to clear the rubbish himself. This was to seek to place on the citizen the performance of a duty which Parliament had placed on the authority itself.

Substantive or *Wednesbury* unreasonableness

6.102 The modern approach to substantive unreasonableness as used in the *Wednesbury* sense, together with its applicability and relationship to other related doctrines such as proportionality, has been discussed above.[175] It is not proposed to repeat that discussion here. The basic principle, however, is that a decision must not be so unreasonable that no reasonable decision-maker, properly directing him or herself, could have come to it: if it is, it cannot have been taken properly. This ground is also sometimes also referred to as 'perversity' or 'irrationality'.[176] Its effect is to afford the decision-maker a range of responses within which the court will not be entitled to intervene, an effect in some ways similar to that of the European doctrine of 'margin of appreciation'.[177]

6.103 In *Re W (an infant)*,[178] Lord Hailsham of St Marylebone observed that:

> ... unreasonableness can include anything which can objectively be adjudged to be unreasonable. It is not confined to culpability or callous indifference. It can include, when carried to excess, sentimentality, romanticism, bigotry, wild prejudice, caprice, fatuousness or excessive lack of common sense.[179]

6.104 It is noteworthy that the concept of objectivity in the court's adjudication has emerged forcefully in recent times in the context of the

174 [2000] BLGR 68, CA.
175 See paras 6.6–6.33 above.
176 See Lord Greene MR in the *Associated Provincial Picture Houses v Wednesbury Corporation* [1948] 1 KB 223, CA, at 229–230 and *Lord Diplock in Council of Civil Service Unions v Minister of State for the Civil Service* [1985] AC 374, HL.
177 See chapter 1, para 1.52 and this chapter at para 6.23 above.
178 [1971] AC 682, HL.
179 [1971] AC 682 at 688.

'anxious scrutiny'/proportionality debate,[180] though it may also be observed that many of the characteristics described in the list above are primarily subjective.[181]

6.105   As has been seen above, the courts will sometimes apply a more interventionist approach to this ground, whether by means of the 'anxious scrutiny' test, or by applying the principles of proportionality instead.[182] There are other occasions, however, on which it has been held that the *Wednesbury* ground may not be available at all.

6.106   In *R v Secretary of State for the Environment ex p Nottinghamshire CC*,[183] for example, Lord Scarman, with whom the rest of the House of Lords agreed, stated that in matters of public financial administration, it was not constitutionally appropriate, save in very exceptional circumstances, for the courts to intervene on the ground of 'unreasonableness' to quash guidance which had been approved by resolution of the House of Commons. Provided that the minister did not exceed the scope of his powers, or abuse them, these were matters of political judgment for him and the House of Commons. Accordingly, an examination by the courts of the detail of the guidance or its consequences would only be justified:

> ... if a prima facie case were to be shown for holding that the secretary of state had acted in bad faith, or for an improper motive, or that the consequences of his guidance were so absurd that he must have taken leave of his senses.[184]

6.107   This statement was approved by the House of Lords in *R v Secretary of State for the Environment ex p Hammersmith and Fulham LBC*.[185] It is an approach which may be contrasted with that adopted in another House of Lords decision: *R v Greater London Council ex p Bromley LBC*,[186] in which it was held that the GLC had acted unlawfully and in breach of its fiduciary duty in implementing a policy to award a grant to the London Transport Executive so that concessionary fares may be offered on public transport in London, the grant to be paid for by the ratepayers of the London boroughs (by way of a precept issued by the GLC). While part of the decision turned on the construction of the relevant

---

180 See paras 6.17–6.30 above.
181 A comment to be found in Arden QC et al, *Local Government, Constitutional and Administrative Law* (1999, Sweet & Maxwell) p156, note 92.
182 See paras 6.14–6.30 above.
183 [1986] AC 240, HL.
184 [1986] AC 240 at 247.
185 [1991] 1 AC 521, per Lord Bridge of Harwich at 595–597.
186 [1983 1 AC 768, HL.

legislation, Lord Diplock described the policy as 'clearly' a 'thriftless use of moneys obtained by the GLC'.[187]

6.108   There are plainly both constitutional and legal differences between central and local government, in the sense that Parliament is sovereign whereas local authorities are not, and that local authorities may only act within the statutory powers which have been conferred upon them, whereas Parliament is not subject to such constraints – it may change the law. It can, nonetheless, legitimately be observed that to the extent that the courts are required to adjudicate on the legality of policy, a deference appears to extend to central government policies which is not accorded to those of local authorities, even when operating within the authority's legal powers.[188]

Proportionality

6.109   In essence, the principle of proportionality is that a measure must not be disproportionate to the mischief it is intended to address. How the principle falls to be applied in individual cases, the tests involved in its application, and the courts' apparent enthusiasm for it, have been considered above.[189] It is fair to say, however, that prior to the introduction of the Human Rights Act 1998, it had not yet found acceptance in English administrative law, although the courts had begun to indicate that it may do so in the future.

6.110   In particular, Lord Diplock in *CCSU*,[190] said:

> One can conveniently classify under three heads the grounds upon which administrative action is subject to control by judicial review. The first ground I would call 'illegality', the second 'irrationality' and the third 'procedural impropriety'. That is not to say that further development on a case-by-case basis may not in course of time add further grounds. I have in mind the possible adoption in the future of the principle of 'proportionality' which is recognised in the administrative law of several of our fellow members in the EEC.[191]

187   [1983] 1 AC 768 at 830F.

188   See also, eg, *Roberts v Hopwood* [1925] AC 578, HL, in which Lord Atkinson (at 594) referred to the authority as having failed in their duty to administer funds which did not belong to it alone, by having allowed itself 'to be guided ... by some eccentric principles of socialistic philanthropy, or by a feminist ambition to secure equality of the sexes in the matter of wages in the world of labour'. The decision in *Roberts* would almost certainly be different today (see *Pickwell v Camden LBC* [1983] 1 QB 962, CA).

189   See paras 6.17–6.30 above.

190   *Council of Civil Service Unions* (CCSU) *v Minister of State for the Civil Service* [1985] AC 374, HL.

191   [1985] AC 374 at 410.

6.111   The House of Lords in *R v Secretary of State for the Home Department ex p Brind*,[192] considered the application of this principle. Lord Templeman said:

> It seems to me that the courts cannot escape from asking themselves whether a reasonable secretary of state, on the material before him, could reasonably conclude that the interference with freedom of expression which he determined to impose was justifiable. In terms of the Convention, as construed by the European Court, the interference with freedom of expression must be necessary and proportionate to the damage which the restriction is designed to prevent.[193]

6.112   Lord Roskill added some 'observations' on the subject:

> I am clearly of the view that the present is not a case in which the first step can be taken for the reason that to apply that principle in the present case would be for the court to substitute its own judgment of what was needed to achieve a particular object for the judgment of the secretary of state on whom that duty has been laid by Parliament. But to so hold in the present case is not to exclude the possible future development of the law in this respect.[194]

6.113   In spite of such comments, however, the courts appeared to take the view that the principle added little to the *Wednesbury* doctrine in any event,[195] a view which would no longer seem tenable, in the light of recent authority.[196]

Procedural impropriety

Natural justice; duty to act fairly

6.114   In all cases, a decision-maker must act fairly, or in accordance with the principles of natural justice. The nature, content and extent of this duty will depend on the circumstances and nature of the

---

192   [1991] 1 AC 696, HL.

193   [1991] 1 AC 696 at 751.

194   [1991] 1 AC 696 at 750.

195   *R v Brent LBC ex p Assegai* (1987) 11 June (unreported), DC, per Woolf LJ: 'Where the response is out of proportion with the cause to this extent, this provides a very clear indication of unreasonableness in a *Wednesbury* sense.' See also the judgment of Lord Donaldson MR in the Court of Appeal in *ex p Brind* [1991] 1 AC 696 at 721–722.

196   See, eg, *R (Daly) v Secretary of State for the Home Department* [2001] UKHL 26; [2001] 2 AC 532, and the discussion at paras 6.17–6.30 above.

decision-maker and the decision in question. They are not 'engraved on tablets of stone'.[197] Natural justice has also been described as 'but fairness writ large and juridically. It has been described as "fair play in action"'.[198] However, the two fundamental concepts of natural justice are the rule against bias and the right to be heard.

Natural justice and article 6 of the European Convention on Human Rights

6.115 The content of the common law principles of natural justice has now been supplemented by Human Rights Act 1998 Sch 1, article 6.[199] In non-criminal matters, article 6 applies in the determination of a person's 'civil rights and obligations'.[200] Strasbourg has construed the word 'civil' to mean, in effect, 'private law'. Unfortunately, the meaning given to that term by Strasbourg, and the boundaries between private and public law are not the same as those which exist in the UK and have been described above.[201] Different states have set different boundaries between their concepts of private law and public law, and the Strasbourg court has, over time, developed its own concepts of those rights which exist in private law and those which do not, and this has been said to depend only on the 'character of the right'.[202]

6.116   In cases where it is held to apply, the scope of article 6 seems to be broader in some respects than under the common law, in terms of the rights conferred. The court has emphasised that article 6 does not control or affect the content of, or rights granted under, national law, but provides purely procedural guarantees in relation to how such rights as are accorded to an individual, under his own national law, may be determined. Moreover, in order for article 6 to apply at all, there must be a 'contestation' (ie, a dispute between the individual and a public authority as defined under the Act) as to civil rights and obligations which are (at least arguably) recognised in national law, and a decision which will be determinative of such civil rights and/or obligations.

---

197   See *Lloyd v McMahon* [1987] AC 625, HL, per Lord Bridge of Harwich at 702H.
198   *Furnell v Whangarei High Schools Board* [1973] AC 660, PC, per Lord Morris of Borth y Gest at 679G.
199   That is, article 6 of the European Convention on Human Rights.
200   Article 6(1).
201   See chapter 3.
202   *König v Federal Republic of Germany* (1978) A 27 para 90.

Civil rights and obligations

6.117   Strasbourg case-law has determined that cases concerning rights existing in contract and tort, commercial and insurance law, family law
and the law of succession, employment law (but not most public sector
employment) and the law of real property have been treated as private law rights and hence within the scope of article 6. The court has
also held that social security and welfare assistance are both private law
rights to which article 6 applies, at least to the extent that the benefit in
question is a statutory right rather than a discretionary payment.[203]
Conversely, matters concerning immigration and nationality, tax, legal
aid in civil proceedings, state education, prisoners' and tenants associations' rights, state medical treatment, elections, etc, are outside the
scope of article 6.

6.118   The UK courts are not bound to follow the Strasbourg classification
of rights, however. The Court of Appeal, for instance, has stated explicitly that, under the Human Rights Act 1998, it is for the national courts
to develop their own human rights jurisprudence rather than simply
to follow that developed in Europe.[204]

6.119   The Human Rights Act 1998 applies to all acts of courts and tribunals, however they be categorised, and there should therefore be
little or no difficulty applying article 6 in relation to litigation before
these bodies. As to the acts of those public authorities falling within
Human Rights Act 1998 s6(3)(b), however, it cannot yet be asserted
that these amount to determinations of civil rights, as is demonstrated
by the extremely cautious approach taken by the House of Lords in
Begum v Tower Hamlets LBC.[205]

6.120   The lower courts have considered whether certain types of decision have involved a determination of the claimant's civil rights and
obligations to decide the applicability of article 6: a decision about
admissions to primary school did not;[206] nor did an immigration
appeal,[207] although, whether or not this is correct, if an appellate structure is established it must comply with the essential guarantees

203   See *Schuler-Zgraggen v Switzerland* (1993) A 263, para 46.
204   See *Begum v Tower Hamlets LBC* [2002] HLR 29 and Human Rights Act
1998 s3.
205   [2003] UKHL 5; [2003] 2 WLR 388.
206   *R v Richmond upon Thames LBC ex p JC* [2001] ELR 21.
207   *MNM v Secretary of State for the Home Department* [2000] INLR 576.

provided by article 6;[208] nor did a decision to award a contract;[209] nor did a refusal of compensation under an ex gratia scheme;[210] nor did a decision to exclude a student from school.[211]

6.121　In *Begum*,[212] however, the House of Lords declined to decide this issue, by proceeding on the basis that article 6 was assumed to be applicable without deciding the point,[213] but pointed out that the original intention of the Convention's draftsman is now of no more than historical interest, and that development of the concept of 'civil rights' has been by way of gradual extensions.[214] It was, accordingly, by no means clear that a decision that duties owed to a homeless person had been discharged on the ground of a refusal of suitable accommodation would amount to a determination of the person's civil rights.[215]

Independent and impartial tribunal: 'full jurisdiction'

6.122　A person's article 6 right of access to an independent and impartial tribunal with full jurisdiction is closely related to the concept of 'civil rights'.[216] In *Begum*, Lord Bingham commented on this point, stating:

> The narrower the interpretation given to 'civil rights' the greater the need to insist on review by a judicial tribunal exercising full powers. Conversely, the more elastic the interpretation given to 'civil rights', the more flexible must be the approach to the requirement of independent and impartial review if the emasculation (by over-judicialisation) of administrative welfare schemes is to be avoided.[217]

208　*R v Secretary of State for the Home Department ex p Saleem* [2001] 1 WLR 443.

209　*R (Venture Projects Ltd) v Secretary of State for the Home Department* (2000) 20 October.

210　*R (Tawfick) v Secretary of State for the Home Department* (2000) *Times* 5 December.

211　*R (B) v Head Teacher of Alperton Community School* [2001] EWHC Admin 229; [2002] LGR 132.

212　[2003] UKHL 5; [2003] 2 WLR 388.

213　[2003] UKHL 5, per Lord Bingham of Cornhill at [6] (on the basis that a decision on the point 'would not, by any means necessarily, be favourable to [the claimant]'); Lord Hoffman at [36]; Lord Millett at [94]; Lord Walke of Gestingthorpe at [115]. See also *Adan v Newham LBC* [2001] EWCA Civ 1919, [2002] 1 WLR 2120.

214　[2003] UKHL 5 per Lord Walker at [109]–[115].

215　See the passages from *Begum* referred to above.

216　*Begum v Tower Hamlets LBC* [2003] UKHL 5; [2003] 2 WLR 388.

217　[2003] UKHL 5 at [5].

6.123   In addition, 'full jurisdiction' does not means that the tribunal must have power to reconsider every issue in dispute for itself, but only that it must have 'jurisdiction to deal with the case as the nature of the decision requires'.[218]

6.124   This issue has, in the years since the introduction of the Human Rights Act 1998, centred principally on the issue of whether judicial review is an adequate remedy for the purposes of article 6, bearing in mind that – traditionally at any rate and on whatever the appropriate approach – the judicial review court does not have power to re-examine the merits of the case before it, but only the legality of the decision and the process by which it was made.

6.125   In *Bryan v United Kingdom*,[219] the European Court of Human Rights held that the remedy of judicial review was satisfactory to meet the requirements of article 6(1) in circumstances where there was no dispute of primary fact and, therefore, the powers of the court on judicial review were sufficient to provide the safeguards guaranteed by article 6(1).

6.126   In *R (Alconbury) v Secretary of State for the Environment, Transport and the Regions*,[220] the House of Lords considered this issue for the first time after the coming into force of the Human Rights Act 1998. The judicial committee took the view that full jurisdiction did not necessarily require the availability of a full merits review of the decision under challenge. The requirement (as stated in such cases as *Albert and le Compte v Belgium*)[221] meant only that the court should have sufficient powers to deal with a case as the nature of that case demanded, as distinct from there being an entitlement to a full rehearing.[222] The statutory scheme under which the secretary of state determines planning applications is not incompatible with the right to a fair hearing guaranteed by article 6. The powers of the court when reviewing those

---

218   *R (Alconbury) v Secretary of State for the Environment, Transport and the Regions* [2001] UKHL 23; [2003] 2 AC 295; [2001] 2 WLR 1389, per Lord Hoffmann at [87]; *Begum* [2003] UKHL 5 at [33].

219   [1996] 21 EHRR 342, ECHR

220   [2001] UKHL 23; [2003] 2 AC 295.

221   (1983) 5 EHRR 533, ECHR.

222   See also *R (Kathro and others) v Rhondda Cynon Taff CBC* [2001] EWHC Admin 527; [2002] Env LR 15; QBD where the court held that the determination by the authority of their own planning decision was not a violation of article 6: *Alconbury* could not be distinguished on the basis that the planning authority's procedure contained fewer fact-finding powers. See also *Friends Provident Life and Pensions Ltd v Secretary of State for Transport, Local Government and the Regions* (2001) 19 October, (unreported) QBD: although *Holding & Barnes* was not expressly directed to the human rights

decisions were the same as those developed by the common law for the review of other administrative acts and were adequate for that purpose as they entitled the court to set aside a decision if it considered the decision to be perverse or wrong in law or procedure.

6.127   The Court of Appeal, in *R (McLellan) v Bracknell Forest DC*,[223] adopted a similar approach, holding that judicial review was an adequate remedy in relation to a statutory procedure whereby once the decision was properly taken to terminate an introductory (ie, probationary) tenancy,[224] the court could not refuse to make a possession order. The tenant, however, had the right to seek an internal review of the decision taken by a senior officer (or a panel of elected members) not involved with the taking of the original decision, followed by judicial review. The court held that there was no reason to hold that the statutory review procedure could not be operated fairly, nor that judicial review would not provide an adequate safeguard to tenants, enabling them to challenge any unfairness and/or infringement of their Convention rights. Whether or not judicial review could satisfy the requirements of 'full jurisdiction' depended on a number of factors including whether any material facts were in dispute. In the context of introductory tenancies, this was not the case:

> ... under the introductory tenancy scheme it is not a requirement that the council should be satisfied that breaches of the tenancy agreement have in fact taken place. The right question under the scheme will be whether in the context of allegation and counter-allegation it was reasonable for the council to take a decision to proceed with termination of the introductory tenancy. That is again a matter which can be dealt with under judicial review either of the traditional kind or if it is necessary so to do intensified so as to ensure that the tenant's rights are protected.[225]

Footnote 222 continued

   of a third party for planning permission, the administrative decision-making process affected a third party in a similar manner and there was therefore no reason in principle why the claimant's rights under article 6 should not be engaged. There was, however, no violation of article 6. The initial decision-making process, in which the authority were obliged to act fairly, was, when combined with the High Court's powers of review, sufficient to ensure that the procedure was compatible with article 6: applying *Bryan v United Kingdom* (1996) 21 EHRR 342, ECHR.

223   [2001] EWCA Civ 1510; [2002] 2 WLR 1448, CA.

224   Housing Act 1996 Pt V.

225   [2001] EWCA Civ 1510 at [97]. See also *R (Bewry) v Norwich CC* [2001] EWHC Admin 657; [2002] HRLR 2; *R (Bono) v Harlow DC* [2002] EWHC Admin 423; [2002] 1 WLR 2475.

6.128   A similar two-stage review process relating to decisions concerning a local authority's duties to a homeless person (stage 1: internal; stage 2: appeal on a point of law to the county court)[226] was challenged in *Begum v Tower Hamlets LBC*.[227] The Court of Appeal held that a Housing Act 1996 s202 review decision, which concerned the urgent provision (or refusal to provide) accommodation to often gravely disadvantaged people and which could lead to the grant – or the refusal to grant – a tenancy, so touched an applicant's well-being that it did amount to a determination of an applicant's civil rights and therefore engaged article 6 of the Convention. The House of Lords declined to decide this issue on appeal.[228]

6.129   Repeating the comments of Lord Hoffmann in *Alconbury*,[229] concerning the nature of full jurisdiction, Laws LJ stated that the compliance or otherwise of a statutory scheme could not vary case by case, according to the degree of factual dispute arising, as that would involve an unsustainable departure from the principle of legal certainty. Rather, compatibility was to be judged in relation to the two-stage review procedure as a whole. The fact that the first (reviewing officer) stage did not by itself comply with article 6(1) did not render its processes irrelevant for the overall judgment on compatibility. The question must be asked whether the first stage review was established and constituted in such a way that it may be expected to arrive at fair and reasonable decisions. This, in turn, could only be judged by examination of the statutory scheme as a whole. Where that scheme's subject-matter generally or systematically involved the resolution of primary fact, the conventional mechanisms for finding facts, either at first instance or on appeal would usually be required. Where not present at first instance, an appeal on judicial review grounds may be insufficient. Where, however, the scheme's subject-matter generally or systematically involved questions of discretion or judgment, or the weighing of policy issues and the rights of others not present before the decision-maker, then a form of inquisition at first instance, and judicial review on appeal, would usually suffice.[230]

---

226   Housing Act 1996 Pt VII and particularly ss202–204.

227   [2002] EWCA Civ 239; [2002] 1 WLR 2491, CA. The House of Lords decision is reported at [2003] UKHL 5; [2003] 2 AC 430. See also *Adan v Newham LBC* [2001] EWCA Civ 1919, [2002] 1 WLR 2120 (not followed in *Begum*).

228   [2003] UKHL 5; [2003] 2 AC 430, see paras 6.121–6.122 above.

229   [2001] UKHL 23; [2003] 2 AC 295, see para 6.126 above.

230   See also *R (Adlard) v Secretary of State for Environment Transport and the Regions* [2002] EWCA Civ 735; [2002] 1 WLR 2515, *R (Mohammed) v Birmingham CC* [2002] EWHC 1511 (Admin); (2002) 5 CCLR 355.

6.130   In *R (Beeson) v Secretary of State for Health*,[231] the Court of Appeal (and Laws LJ) considered this issue again, and held that the real question in two-tier cases under a statutory regime was the extent to which the matters in question had to be decided by an independent tribunal. The court must usually give respect and weight to the statutory scheme established by Parliament, and to the function of the person entrusted in administering the scheme, to exercise that statutory jurisdiction. This was particularly so in relation to public welfare schemes, given (a) that that was the will of Parliament, (b) the allocation of scarce resources was at stake and (c) such decisions would frequently affect the rights of third parties. Evaluating such matters was the function of the administrator of the scheme, which must be considered as a whole, rather than for the judge. Individual factual disputes in specific cases would not affect the legality of the statutory provisions generally. Accordingly, it would be relatively rare that a challenge to article 6 of the Convention, based on the inadequacy as a remedy of judicial review, could succeed.

6.131   The House of Lords, in *Begum*,[232] did not accept any of these formulations in their entirety, and rejected the approach of the Court of Appeal in that case on the subject-matter of the scheme in question. The officer of the authority conducting the internal review was not an independent tribunal because she was not a tribunal at all, not being part of the judicial branch of government, but an administrator.[233] In the context of the two-stage process, the second stage (in this case the county court entertaining an appeal on a point of law) did have full jurisdiction, which did not always require a complete rehearing. Accordingly, while the officer must of course act impartially and fairly, there was no need for independent findings of fact and a full appeal.

6.132   Whether an independent finder of facts would be necessary did not depend on the extent to which the particular administrative scheme was likely to involve resolution of disputes of fact. Rather, the relevant issue was whether, consistently with the rule of law and constitutional propriety, the decision-making powers in question could be entrusted to administrators. If they could, it was not relevant whether there would be many or few occasions on which findings of fact needed to be made.[234] Parliament was entitled to take the view that it was not in

---

231 [2002] EWCA Civ 1812; (2003) 6 CCLR 5.
232 *Begum v Tower Hamlets* [2003] UKHL 5; [2003] 2 AC 430.
233 [2003] UKHL 5, per Lord Hoffmann at [27].
234 [2003] UKHL 5 at [59].

the public interest that an excessive proportion of the public funds available for a welfare scheme should be consumed in administration and legal disputes.[235] Strasbourg, moreover, would accord the contracting states a margin of appreciation in this regard.[236]

6.133 Moreover, the appropriate intensity of article 6 judicial review in the context of a statutory welfare scheme, had to be consistent with that scheme. Article 6 did not provide the basis for more intensive judicial review. Where no Convention rights were engaged, other than under article 6, conventional judicial review was sufficient to comply with that article's requirements in a homelessness case.

Elements of procedural fairness

The rule against bias

6.134 The rule against bias is, in essence, that no-one may be a judge in his own cause. Of course, where actual bias can be proved, that is a plain ground for the grant of relief. In the absence of actual bias, it seems that there are two different tests, applicable to different situations.

Apparent bias

6.135 Where the judge of a cause has a direct pecuniary interest in the outcome, the court will not enquire as to the likelihood of bias, but will proceed to quash the decision. In *Dimes v Proprietors of Grand Junction Canal*,[237] the court set aside a decree of the Lord Chancellor on the basis of his interest in the canal company, notwithstanding that 'no-one can suppose that Lord Cottenham could be, in the remotest degree, influenced by' it. The court stated that this would have a 'most salutary influence' on inferior tribunals when it became known that the court was prepared to take such action.[238] See also the comments of Lord Gough of Cheively in *R v Gough*.[239]

---

235 [2003] UKHL 5 at [44]–[48].
236 [2003] UKHL 5 at [55].
237 (1852) 3 HL Gas 759, HL.
238 (1852) 3 HL Gas 759 per Lord Campbell at 793–794.
239 [1993] AC 646, HL, at 661 (though the *Gough* test itself is no longer applicable, see below).

Other cases

6.136   In all other cases, the test set out in *R v Gough*,[240] applicable in all cases where actual bias was not alleged (or not made out) has now been modified, as a result of the effect of article 6 of the Convention since the coming into force of the Human Rights Act 1998.[241] Under *Gough*, the test was whether there was a 'real danger' of bias 'on the part of a relevant member of the tribunal in question, in the sense that he might unfairly regard (or have unfairly regarded) with favour or disfavour, the case of a party to the issue under consideration by him'.

6.137   Lord Phillips MR in *Director General of Fair Trading v Proprietary Association for Great Britain*[242] suggested a 'modest adjustment' to the *Gough* test expressed in the following terms:

> When the Strasbourg jurisprudence is taken into account, we believe that a modest adjustment of the test in *R v Gough* is called for, which makes it plain that it is, in effect, no different from the test applied in most of the Commonwealth and in Scotland. The court must first ascertain all the circumstances which have a bearing on the suggestion that the judge was biased. It must then ask whether those circumstances would lead a fair-minded and informed observer to conclude that there was a real possibility, or a real danger, the two being the same, that the tribunal was biased.[243]

6.138   In other words, the test was now to be expressed in objective terms, it was a question of whether the fair-minded and informed observer would conclude that there was a real danger of bias, not whether the court considered this to be so.

6.139   In *Porter v Magill*,[244] the House of Lords approved the 'modest adjustment' to the *Gough* test with a further minor amendment. Lord Hope of Craighead stated:

> I respectfully suggest that your Lordships should now approve the modest adjustment of the test in *R v Gough* set out in [*Director General of Fair Trading*]. It expresses in clear and simple language a test which is in harmony with the objective test which the Strasbourg court applies when it is

---

240   [1993] AC 646, per Lord Goff at 670.
241   The jurisprudence of the European Court of Human Rights, to which the court must now have regard (Human Rights Act 1998 s2) was to the effect that the test should be an objective one: see, eg, *Hauschildt v Denmark* (1989) 12 EHRR 266 at 279, para 48.
242   Also known as *In re Medicaments (No 2)* [2001] 1 WLR 700, CA.
243   [2001] 1 WLR 700 at [85].
244   [2001] UKHL 67; [2002] 2 WLR 37.

considering whether the circumstances give rise to a reasonable appre-
hension of bias. It removes any possible conflict with the test which is
now applied in most Commonwealth countries and in Scotland. I would
however delete from it the reference to 'a real danger'. Those words no
longer serve a useful purpose here, and they are not used in the jurisprudence of the Strasbourg court. The question is whether the fair-minded and
informed observer, having considered the facts, would conclude that there
was a real possibility that the tribunal was biased.[245]

6.140   The current test for apparent bias is, therefore, whether a fair-minded
and informed observer, in possession of all the relevant facts, would
consider there to be a 'real possibility' of bias.

The right to be heard

6.141   The main components to this right are, briefly, as follows. A person
is entitled to have notice of details of the time and date of any oral
hearing, and of the case against him or her, which he or she will
have to meet. He or she is also entitled to have the opportunity to meet
the case.

6.142   In *Ridge v Baldwin*,[246] a chief constable was suspended for conspir-
acy to obstruct the course of justice. He was acquitted and applied to
be re-instated. The committee considering his application, however,
decided that he had been negligent and dismissed him. No specific
charge was formulated against him, but the committee considered
his statements in evidence at his trial and the judge's comments. The
House of Lords held that the decision to dismiss him was null and
void. The respondent could only dismiss the chief constable on the
grounds set out in the enabling Act and was bound to observe the
principles of natural justice, to inform him of the charges made against
him and give him an opportunity of being heard. It had failed to do so.

6.143   An alternative formulation is that of Lord Denning:

> He must know what evidence has been given and what statements have
> been made affecting him; and he must be given a fair opportunity to
> correct or contradict them.[247]

---

245   [2001] UKHL 67 at [103].

246   [1964] AC 40, HL.

247   *Kanda v Government of the Federation of Malaya* [1962] AC 322, PC, at 337,
where an application for citizenship had been refused without the grounds
being disclosed. See also *R v Chief Constable of North Wales Police ex p Evans*
[1982] 1 WLR 1155, HL, where a probationary constable who resigned to
avoid dismissal was neither told the allegations against him nor given the
chance to answer them.

6.144 Sometimes it is sufficient to inform the person of the substance of the case against him or her, without disclosing the precise evidence or sources of information. Again, this will depend on the circumstances. The requirement for natural justice must be weighed against the detriment disclosure may cause to the function of the decision-maker.[248]

6.145 A person must be given sufficient time to prepare his or her case,[249] and must have an opportunity to put that case. Usually there must be an oral hearing, though this is not always necessary. Decision-makers are, in general, masters of their own procedure. In *Lloyd v McMahon*,[250] the House of Lords held that a district auditor had acted fairly in disclosing his case to councillors and offering them only the chance to make representations in writing, when deciding whether or not to surcharge them for wilful misconduct. As a general rule, however, the more important the rights at stake, the more likely it is that fairness will require an oral hearing.

6.146 Failure to allow cross-examination may be unfair, but is more likely to be held to be so in formal as opposed to informal hearings.[251] It now seems that where it is decided to hold an oral hearing, cross-examination ought usually to be permitted, as the testing of witnesses is usually the purpose of such a hearing.[252]

6.147 There is no right to legal representation in all cases. The Court of Appeal has held that while most hearings permit representation, it was not 'self-evident that that was an advantage'. That is particularly so in relation to specialist tribunals adopting a hands-on approach. Such tribunals 'might well be able to reach the right conclusion just as often and much more cheaply and quickly, without as with such formal representation.'[253] In *R (Alliss) v Legal Services Commission*,[254] the court considered that the failure to provide a person with a lawyer may

---

248 See *R v Gaming Board for Great Britain ex p Benaim and Khaida* [1970] 2 QB 417; *R v Monopolies and Mergers Commission ex p Matthew Brown plc* [1987] 1 WLR 1235.

249 See *R v Thames Magistrates Court ex p Polemis* [1974] 1 WLR 1371.

250 [1987] AC 625, HL.

251 See *R v Hull Prison Visitors ex p St Germain (No 2)* [1979] 1 WLR 1401 (breach where cross-examination refused, but disputed evidence the applicant wished to contest was taken into account by the visitors); *Herring v Templeman* [1973] 3 All ER 569 (no necessity for witnesses).

252 *R v Army Board of the Defence Council ex p Anderson* [1992] 1 QB 169, CA, per Taylor LJ at 188.

253 *R v Secretary of State for the Home Department ex p Cheblak* [1991] 1 WLR 890, CA, per Lord Donaldson MR at 906.

254 [2003] ACD 16.

contravene the requirements of article 6 (see below) where a lawyer's assistance was indispensable to secure the right to effective access to a court or where, for reasons of fairness, the appearance of the fair administration of justice must be sustained, and to ensure that a party to civil proceedings could participate effectively. A similar conclusion was reached in relation to Convention article 2 in *R (Khan) v Secretary of State for Health*.[255]

6.148   It has been held that fairness requires that a person be given all reasonable facilities to help exercise the right to be heard. Such facilities include the help of a friend to take notes and give advice, unless the court orders otherwise in the interests of justice, maintaining order and controlling its own procedure.[256] On the other hand, the failure by a person to attend a hearing, resulting in him being unable to put his case, due to the default of his professional adviser, did not entitle him to complain of any failure by the tribunal to act fairly.[257]

Article 6 of the European Convention on Human Rights

6.149   The Human Rights Act 1998 Sch 1, article 6(1), adopts a different formulation, entitling a person, 'in the determination of his civil rights and obligations or of any criminal charge against him' a right to a 'fair and public hearing within a reasonable time by an independent and impartial tribunal established by law'.

6.150   The issue of what will amount to a determination of a person's civil rights and obligations and whether a tribunal is independent and impartial and has 'full jurisdiction' has been discussed elsewhere.[258]

Reasons

6.151   At common law, there is no general duty on decision-makers to give reasons for their decisions. However, in many cases, statute has now provided such a duty.[259]

---

255 (2003) 10 October (unreported), CA.
256 *R v Leicester City Justices ex p Barrow* [1991] 2 QB 260, CA.
257 *Al Mehdawi v Secretary of State for the Home Department* [1990] 1 AC 876, HL.
258 See paras 6.115–6.133 above.
259 See, for example, Tribunals and Inquiries Act 1992; Housing Act 1996 s184; Housing Benefit (General) Regulations 1987 SI No 1971 as amended, reg 77, etc.

A general duty?

6.152   In *R v Secretary of State for the Home Department ex p Doody*,[260] the House of Lords approached the question of whether there was a duty to give reasons by asking what fairness required, and whether the scheme operated by the secretary of state fell below the minimum standards of fairness. It was held that where, in deciding whether or not to release a life prisoner on licence, the secretary of state departed from the judicial recommendation, he was required to give reasons for so doing.

6.153   In *R v Higher Education Funding Council ex p Institute of Dental Surgery*,[261] Sedley J declined to hold that there was a general legal duty to give reasons for all administrative decisions. Instead, he held that there was a spectrum of decision-making, at one end of which the importance of the rights at stake would be such that reasons would always be required, while at the other end, reasons would not generally be necessary.

Article 6 of the European Convention on Human Rights

6.154   The right to a fair hearing guaranteed by article 6 does, so far as the European Court of Human Rights is concerned, require that the decision-maker must 'indicate with sufficient clarity the grounds on which they base their decision' in order that the individual may be in a position usefully to exercise any right of appeal.[262]

6.155   This general obligation has not, however, received unqualified acceptance by the UK courts. In *R (The Asha Foundation) v Millenium Commission*, [263] Lightman J, referring to the *Institute of Dental Surgery* case[264] and to *R v Professional Conduct Committee of the GMC ex p Salvi*,[265] stated that it was well-established that there was a category of decisions for which no reasons need be given other than those implicit in the decision itself. The Commission's decision, like academic judgments, fell into this class of case.

---

260   [1993] 3 WLR 154, HL.

261   [1994] 1 WLR 242, QBD.

262   See *Hadjianastassiou v Greece* (1992) A 252 para 33; *X v Federal Republic of Germany* (1981) 25 DR 240.

263   [2002] EWHC 916 (Admin); [2002] ACD 79 upheld on appeal to the Court of Appeal at [2003] EWCA Civ 88, (2003) *Times* 24 January.

264   [1994] 1 WLR 242, QBD.

265   (1999) 4 BMLR 167.

6.156   The judge enunciated the following principles concerning the giving of reasons:

- the requirement to give reasons was inextricably linked with the decision-making process and must be considered in that context;
- where, in the course of that process, the decision-maker was obliged to give reasons for the decision, an obligation could be imposed requiring those reasons to be disclosed to the parties affected by it;
- if there was no obligation to articulate reasons other than those implicit in the decision itself, there would be no scope to impose any further obligation to give reasons where the decision-maker did no more that he was legally bound to do;
- the obligation to give reasons was to give the actual reasons for the decision at the time and not reasons which had later been reconstructed: accordingly if no, or no fully articulated, reasons were given at the time, they could not be given later;
- if an obligation to give reasons could be identified, or had been accepted, that obligation must relate back and require reasons to be given when making the decision.[266] The Court of Appeal, in upholding Lightman J's decision, did not express a view about these principles, save to confirm that the duty to give detailed reasons will depend on the circumstances.

Content of the duty

6.157   Where a statute requires a decision-maker to give reasons, the reasons given must be 'proper, adequate and intelligible' and must deal with the substantial points which have been raised.[267] A failure to give such reasons, where there is an obligation to do so, is a sufficient ground to quash the decision.[268]

Reasons in court

6.158   In addition, it has been held that where an applicant seeks judicial review of the decision, a duty to explain it arises, in order to facilitate

---

266   See also, *R (Tucker) v Director General of the National Crime Squad* [2002] EWHC 832 (Admin); [2002] ACD 80.

267   *Westminster CC v Great Portland Estates plc* [1985] 1 AC 661, per Lord Scarman at 673, approving *In re Poyser and Mills' Arbitration* [1964] 2 QB 467, per Megaw J at 478

268   *R v Westminster CC ex p Ermakov* [1996] 2 All ER 302; (1996) 28 HLR 819.

the adjudication of the issue.[269] In *Padfield*,[270] Lord Upjohn was of the view that a:

... minister is a public officer charged ... with the discharge of a public discretion ... If he does not give any reason for his decision it may be, if circumstances warrant it, that a court may be at liberty to come to the conclusion that he had no good reason for reaching that conclusion.

6.159   In *R v Lancashire CC ex p Huddleston*,[271] the court considered that, in general, authorities should give sufficient reasons as are adequate to enable the court to ascertain whether the authority had erred in law or not. For instance, where it is alleged that irrelevant considerations were considered, this will generally entail explaining what the authority did and did not take into account.[272]

6.160   The Crown Court, sitting in its appellate capacity, must give sufficient reasons to demonstrate that it has identified the issues in contention in the case before it and how it has resolved each of those issues.[273] Where a compelling point had been raised by the defence, it was incumbent on the Crown Court to deal with the point.[274]

6.161   Where there is a statutory obligation to give reasons, the court will not entertain explanations, additional to the statutory reasons given, otherwise than by way of elucidation or correction of those statutory reasons. In particular, ex post facto explanations or rationalisations which seek to contradict the original reasons given will not be admitted. The decision of the Court of Appeal to this effect in *R v Westminster CC ex p Ermakov*,[275] was followed by Stanley Burnton J in *R (Nash) v Chelsea College of Art*.[276] In that case, the judge indicated the court would only accept later reasons in exceptional circumstances, the relevant considerations being as follows:

• whether the new reasons were consistent with those originally given;

---

269 See, eg, *Padfield v Minister for Agriculture and Fisheries* [1968] AC 998, HL, where the House of Lords commented that if the secretary of state refused to give reasons for his decision, the court may conclude that there was no good reason for it.

270 [1968] AC 998, HL.

271 [1986] 2 All ER 941, CA.

272 [1986] 2 All ER 941, per Parker LJ at 947.

273 *R v Harrow Crown Court ex p Dave* [1994] 1 WLR 98, DC.

274 *R (Taylor) v Maidstone Crown Court* (2003) 17 October (unreported), QBD.

275 See *R v Westminster CC ex p Ermakov* [1996] 2 All ER 302; (1996) 28 HLR 819. See further chapter 19 below, at paras 19.24–19.27 and the cases there cited.

276 [2001] EWHC Admin 538; (2001) *Times* 25 July.

- whether it was clear that the new reasons were the original reasons of the decision-maker;
- whether there was a real risk that the new reasons had been composed subsequently or in order to justify the decision retrospectively;
- the delay before the new reasons were advanced; and
- the circumstances in which they were advanced.

6.162   In *R (Leung) v Imperial College of Science, Technology and Medicine*,[277] Silber J suggested two additional considerations:

- whether the decision-maker would have been expected to state in the decision document the reasons that he or she later sought to advance;
- the 'over-arching factor' of whether it would be just in all the circumstances to refuse to admit the subsequent reasons.[278]

Appeals

6.163   Natural justice does not require that there should be a right of appeal.[279] An appeal may, however, sometimes cure defects in the procedure at an earlier stage.

6.164   In *Calvin v Carr*,[280] a horse-owner had been disqualified by Australian Jockey Club stewards for one year. The club committee dismissed the appeals. Lord Wilberforce held that although there is no general rule regarding whether appellate proceedings could cure a defect due to a failure of natural justice, there was a broad spectrum of domestic proceedings between those at one end where the inquiry stage could be said to have merged into the appellate stage (such as social clubs) and those where a complainant has the right to nothing less than a fair hearing at both the original and appeal stages (such as trade union membership, planning, employment, etc). Intermediate cases exist where a person who had joined in an organisation or contract was to be taken to have agreed to accept what in the end is a fair decision, reached after a consideration of the case on its merits,

---

277   [2002] EWHC 1358 (Admin); [2002] ELR 653.

278   The purpose of these additional factors was said to be that the court may be less cautious about admitting later reasons where there was no obligation to give reasons at the time. *Ermakov* and *Nash* were both cases where there was such a duty.

279   *Ward v Bradford Corporation* (1971) 70 LGR 27.

280   [1980] AC 574, PC.

notwithstanding some initial defect. In such cases, the test is whether after both original and appellate stages the complainant has had a fair deal of the kind he or she bargained for when he or she joined the organisation or entered into the contract.

6.165 In *R (AM) v Head Teacher of St George's Catholic School*,[281] the claimant was permanently excluded from school and appealed. His application for judicial review of the decision to exclude him, confirmed on appeal, was dismissed. The Court of Appeal considered the issue of the extent to which unfairness at an early stage of the three-stage appeal process could be cured by utilising the final stage of appeal.

6.166 The court held it was necessary to construe the statutory scheme as a whole, in order to ascertain the intention of Parliament concerning the effect of unfairness in an early part of the process. In this case, although Parliament did not intend any stage of the process to be unfair, nor did it intend a party aggrieved at a decision at the first stage to seek judicial review rather than appeal. Although the appeal did not give redress in respect of the earlier unfairness, the aggrieved party obtained a new, fair decision on the merits from the 'custom-built' expert and independent statutory body, following a full rehearing.

6.167 Unless the prior procedural unfairness complained of had somehow tainted the subsequent appeal, in which case the appeal decision itself would necessarily fall, the right to a fair determination of a person's case would be satisfied by the appeal hearing and decision. On a judicial review application brought instead of an appeal, the court would usually leave the claimant to his statutory remedy.

A fair hearing would have made no difference

6.168 In some circumstances, the courts have been prepared to hold that there has been no breach of natural justice where a fair hearing could have made no difference. In *Malloch v Aberdeen Corporation*,[282] Lord Wilberforce stated that the court does not act in vain. It need not determine whether a hearing was required where it could only be a useless formality because there was nothing the applicant could have said that would have affected the decision.[283] In fact, these decisions, and those concerning mixed motives and partial invalidity,[284] are closely

---

281 [2002] EWCA Civ 1822.
282 [1971] 1 WLR 1578, HL.
283 See also *Cinnamond v British Airports Authority* [1980] 1 WLR 582, CA.
284 See chapter 7.

related to those concerning the discretionary nature of the remedy in judicial review proceedings.[285]

Exclusion of natural justice

6.169 It is clear that the principles discussed above do not apply in all cases. First, there is no right to be heard before the passing of legislation, whether primary or delegated, unless statute so provides.[286] Second, it appears that the right to be heard can be excluded, for instance, in cases involving national security.[287] In addition, some classes of applicant, such as prisoners and immigrants, are similarly not always accorded the same rights as are generally applicable.

Other procedural irregularities

Legitimate expectation

6.170 The principles concerning legitimate expectations are one aspect of the duty to act fairly and are rooted in the concept of fairness.[288] Where a decision-maker has indicated that he or she will proceed in a particular manner, whether by express promise, implication or past practice, it may be unlawful to fail to do so. In order to invoke the doctrine, however, and to have an 'expectation' in the first place, the claimant must have known of the publicised procedure and relied on it. Where a promise is made by a person who has no power to make it, another decision-maker will not be bound to take it into account, even if it could amount to a legitimate expectation.[289]

---

285 See, eg, *R v Islington LBC ex p Hinds* (1995) 28 HLR 302; [1994] COD 494, QBD, where relief was refused because failure to give proper reasons had not substantially prejudiced the applicant. This case is no longer good law on the issues of reasons, however, see paras 6.161 and 6.162 above.

286 See Consultation at paras 6.184–6.185 below.

287 *Council of Civil Service Unions (CCSU) v Minister of State for the Civil Service* [1985] AC 374, HL.

288 See *R v North and East Devon Health Authority ex p Coughlan* [2001] QB 213; (1999) 2 CCLR 285, CA.

289 See *R (Bloggs 61) v Secretary of State for the Home Department* [2003] EWCA Civ 686; [2003] 33 LS Gaz R 29; (2003) *Times* 7 July, where the prison service was held not to be bound by a police promise that, in exchange for information, a prisoner would be kept in protective witness custody rather than mainstream prison. The police had no power to make the promise and the prison service did not have to take it into account in deciding to move the prisoner back to mainstream custody.

6.171 In *R v North and East Devon Health Authority ex p Coughlan*,[290] the Court of Appeal held that three categories of expectation are now recognised by law: (a) cases where the decision-maker is only obliged to bear in mind its promise, giving the promise whatever weight it considers, before deciding whether to depart from it; (b) cases where the promise induces a legitimate expectation that a certain procedure will be followed before taking a decision, such as a promise of consultation (procedural expectation); and (c) cases where the promise has induced a legitimate expectation of a substantive benefit (substantive expectation).[291]

6.172 In *Coughlan*,[292] Lord Woolf explained the courts' approach to the three types of expectation set out above, as follows:

> 57. There are at least three possible outcomes. (a) The court may decide that the public authority is only required to bear in mind its previous policy or other representation, giving it the weight it thinks right, but no more, before deciding whether to change course. Here the court is confined to reviewing the decision on *Wednesbury* grounds. This has been held to be the effect of changes of policy in cases involving the early release of prisoners (see *Re Findlay* [1985] AC 318; *R v Home Secretary ex p Hargreaves* [1997] 1 WLR 906). (b) On the other hand the court may decide that the promise or practice induces a legitimate expectation of, for example, being consulted before a particular decision is taken. Here it is uncontentious that the court itself will require the *opportunity for consultation* to be given unless there is an overriding reason to resile from it (see *A-G for Hong Kong v Ng Yuen Shiu* [1983] 2 AC 629) in which case the court will itself judge the adequacy of the reason advanced for the change of policy, taking into account what fairness requires. (c) Where the court considers that a lawful promise or practice has induced a legitimate expectation of a *benefit which is substantive*, not simply procedural, authority now establishes that here too the court will in a proper case decide whether to frustrate the expectation is so unfair that to take a new and different course will amount to an abuse of power. Here, once the legitimacy of the expectation is established, the court will have the task of weighing the requirements of fairness against any overriding interest relied upon for the change of policy.

6.173 The second and third categories differ from the first in that the court will consider the issue of fairness for itself and is not limited, as in the first class of case, to scrutiny on the basis of *Wednesbury* review. In cases falling within the third category, the court will have to decide,

---

290 Above, note 288.
291 [2001] QB 213, per Lord Woolf MR at [57].
292 [2001] QB 213; (1999) 2 CCLR 285, CA.

when necessary, whether there is a sufficient overriding interest to justify a departure from what has been previously promised.[293] Since *Coughlan*, the courts have emphasised that the categories of legitimate expectation are not closed.[294]

6.174 In *R (Zeqiri) v Secretary of State for the Home Department*,[295] the House of Lords confirmed that conduct by a public officer which was akin to breach of contract or representation could be an abuse of power for which judicial review was appropriate, the denial of a legitimate expectation being one form of the more general concept of abuse of power. A representation must be construed in the context in which it was made, and must be 'clear, unambiguous and devoid of relevant qualification'.[296] The question was not whether in private law the representation would give rise to an estoppel but whether by acting contrary to it, the decision-maker would be acting with 'conspicuous unfairness'[297] and so abusing its power.

6.175 In *R (Bibi) v Newham LBC*,[298] the Court of Appeal identified three questions which would arise in all legitimate expectation cases, whether procedural or substantive:

(1) To what has the public authority, whether by practice or by promise, committed itself?
(2) Has the authority acted or does it propose to act unlawfully in relation to its commitment?
(3) What should the court do?[299]

Procedural expectation

6.176 In *R v Attorney General of Hong Kong ex p Ng Yuen Shiu*,[300] a senior immigration officer had announced that before deporting illegal immigrants, each would be interviewed and his case 'treated on its merits'.

---

293 [2001] QB 213 at [58].
294 See paras 6.174 and 6.175 below.
295 [2002] UKHL 3.
296 See *R v Inland Revenue Commissioners ex p MFK Underwriting Agents Ltd* [1990] 1 WLR 1545, CA.
297 *R v Inland Revenue Commissioners ex p Unilever plc* [1996] STC 681, CA.
298 [2001] EWCA Civ 607; [2002] 1 WLR 237, CA. See also *R (National Association of Guardians ad Litem and Reporting Officers) v Children and Family Court Advisory and Support Service* [2001] EWHC Admin 693; [2002] 1 FLR 255; [2001] Fam Law 877; *R (Galligan) v University of Oxford* [2001] EWHC Admin 965; [2002] ACD 33.
299 *R (Bibi) v Newham LBC* [2001] EWCA Civ 607 per Schiemann LJ at [19].
300 [1983] 2 AC 629, PC.

The applicant was arrested and a removal order made against him without him having any opportunity to make representations as to why he should not be removed. The Privy Council held that the ordinary principle applied that when a public authority charged with the duty of making a decision promised to follow a certain procedure before reaching that decision, good administration required that it should act by implementing the promise provided the implementation did not conflict with the authority's statutory duty. Accordingly, assuming an alien had no general right to be heard before being deported, the making of the promise to interview each illegal immigrant and decide each case on its merits required the applicant to be given an opportunity to state his case. The failure to ask him whether he wished to make representations why he should not be removed was a sufficient ground for setting aside the decision.[301]

Substantive expectation

6.177 Traditionally, the expectation that a claimant could acquire was said to be purely procedural. A claimant could not acquire a legitimate expectation that a substantive decision would be in their favour, but only that the decision would be reached in a particular manner.

6.178 In *R v Devon CC ex p Baker*,[302] Simon Brown LJ identified two types of substantive expectation recognised by the courts:

(1) Sometimes the phrase is used to denote a substantive right: an entitlement that the claimant asserts cannot be denied him. It was used in this sense and the assertion upheld in cases such as *R v Secretary of State for the Home Department ex p Khan* [1984] 1 WLR 1337 and *R v Secretary of State for the Home Department ex p Ruddock* [1987] 1 WLR 1482 ... [T]he claimant's right will only be found established when there is a clear and unambiguous representation upon which it was reasonable for him to rely. Then the administrator or other public body will be held bound in fairness by the representation made unless only its promise or undertaking as to how its power would be exercised is inconsistent with the statutory duties imposed upon it. The doctrine employed in this sense is akin to an estoppel ...

(2) Perhaps more conventionally the concept of legitimate expectation is used to refer to the claimant's interest in some ultimate benefit which he hopes to retain (or, some would argue, attain). Here, therefore, it is the interest itself rather than the benefit that is the substance of the

301 See also *Council of Civil Service Unions v Minister of State for the Civil Service* [1985] AC 374, HL.
302 [1995] 1 All ER 73, CA.

expectation. In other words the expectation arises not because the claimant asserts any specific right to a benefit but rather because his interest in it is one that the law holds protected by the requirements of procedural fairness; the law recognises that the interest cannot properly be withdrawn (or denied) without the claimant being given an opportunity to comment and without the authority communicating rational grounds for any adverse decision. Of the various authorities drawn to our attention, *Schmidt v Secretary of State for Home Affairs* [1969] 2 Ch 149, *O'Reilly v Mackman* [1983] 2 AC 237 and the recent decision of Roch J in *R v Rochdale Metropolitan BC ex p Schemet* [1993] 1 FCR 306 are clear examples of this head of legitimate expectation.[303]

6.179   Thus where, for example, a decision-maker announces that a substantive benefit will be conferred on persons meeting certain specified criteria who apply for the benefit by a specified date, it would be an unlawful breach of the substantive expectations of those claimants who meet the published criteria and apply for the benefit for the decision-maker to change the criteria after the closing date for applications has passed, by which time it is too late to reapply.[304]

6.180   In *Coughlan*[305] the Court of Appeal reaffirmed the existence of substantive expectations, not necessarily limited in the way suggested by the court in *Baker*, but generally sustainable, as stated above, on the basis of the requirements of fairness. Lord Woolf MR stated, in this regard:

> 82. The fact that the court will only give effect to a legitimate expectation within the statutory context in which it has arisen should avoid jeopardising the important principle that the executive's policy-making powers should not be trammelled by the courts (see *Hughes v DHSS* [1985] AC 766, 788, per Lord Diplock). Policy being (within the law) for the public authority alone, both it and the reasons for adopting or changing it will be accepted by the courts as part of the factual data – in other words, as not ordinarily open to judicial review. The court's task – and this is not always understood – is then limited to asking whether the application of the policy to an individual who has been led to expect something different is a just exercise of power. In many cases the authority will already have considered this and made appropriate exceptions (as was envisaged in *British Oxygen v Board of Trade* [1971] AC 610 ...), or resolved to pay compensation where money alone will suffice. But where no such accommodation is made, it is for the court to say whether the consequent

303   [1995] 1 All ER 73, CA at 89.
304   See, eg, *R v Secretary of State for the Home Department ex p Khan* [1984] 1 WLR 1337, CA.
305   [2001] QB 213; (1999) 2 CCLR 285, CA.

frustration of the individual's expectation is so unfair as to be a misuse of the authority's power.[306]

Consistency

6.181 This is another aspect of the duty to act fairly which is akin to the principle of legitimate expectation. Decisions must not be indiscriminate and decision-makers must act consistently in their dealings with the public; reaching inconsistent or contradictory decisions on similar facts is a misuse of power.

6.182 In *HTV v Price Commission,*[307] the respondent changed its basis for calculating the percentage of HTV's profits that must be paid to the Exchequer. Denning LJ held that:

> It is ... the duty of the Price Commission to act with fairness and consistency in their dealing with manufacturers and traders ... if they regularly interpret the words of the code in a particular sense – or regularly apply the code in a particular way – they should continue to interpret it and apply it in the same way thereafter unless there is good cause for departing from it. At any rate, they should not depart from it in any case where they have, by their conduct, led the manufacturer or trader to believe that he can safely act on that interpretation of the code or on that method of applying it, and he does so act on it. It is not permissible for them to depart from their previous interpretation and application where it would not be fair or just for them to do so ... It is a misuse of power for [the Commission] to act unfairly or unjustly to a private citizen when there is no overriding public interest to warrant it.[308]

6.183 In *Inland Revenue Commissioners v Preston,*[309] however, the House of Lords held that a taxpayer could not complain of unfairness merely because the Inland Revenue Commissioners decided to perform their statutory duties, even though they had previously agreed, before receiving new information, that they would not do so. While conduct by the Commissioners equivalent to a breach of contract or representation could amount to an abuse or excess of power, it is only in exceptional circumstances that the courts could decide that something which the Commissioners had, by taking action against the taxpayer, determined to be fair, is unfair.

---

306   [2001] QB 213 at [82].
307   [1976] ICR 170, CA.
308   [1976] ICR 170 at 185.
309   [1985] AC 835, HL.

Consultation

6.184   In *Coughlan*,[310] the Court of Appeal restated the principles of consultation as follows. Where statute or previous practice establishes an obligation on a decision-maker to consult prior to making a decision, the following principles apply: the consultation must take place while the proposals are still at a formative stage (ie, when the results of the consultation may still make a difference). The consultee must be given sufficient information about, and reasons for, the proposal to be able to respond in a meaningful and intelligent way and sufficient time to be able to respond. There must then be sufficient time for the responses to be considered properly, and the responses must be considered conscientiously, in the course of taking the ultimate decision.[311]

6.185   In *R v Secretary of State for Social Security ex p AMA*,[312] the court held that a statutory exemption from the general requirement of consultation in cases of urgency could not be invoked by the secretary of state to justify his failure to consult in circumstances where he had delayed before taking action for so long that the urgency he relied on could properly be described as 'self-induced'.

Miscellaneous

Estoppel

6.186   It seems that estoppel will not lie against the Crown.[313] Moreover, a local authority cannot be estopped from performing its statutory powers or duties.[314]

6.187   An authority can, however, by its conduct or representations, waive a procedural requirement. It also seems that where power has been delegated to an officer, whom the authority has held out as having

---

310   [2001] QB 213; (1999) 2 CCLR 285, CA.

311   See also eg, *R v Brent LBC ex p Gunning* (1985) 84 LGR 168, QBD. See also *CCSU* [1985] AC 374, HL; *R v Secretary of State for Social Services ex p AMA* [1986] 1 WLR 1, QBD.

312   (1992) 25 HLR 131, QBD.

313   But see *Gowa v Attorney General* (1985) 82 LS Gaz 681, CA, which held that it could. The House of Lords in *Gowa* [1985] 1 WLR 1003 expressly left the point open.

314   *Western Fish Products Ltd v Penwith DC* (1978) 77 LGR 185, CA; *R v Lambeth LBC ex p Clayhope Properties Ltd* [1988] QB 563, CA.

delegated authority, and that officer makes a representation in reliance upon which a person acts to his or her detriment, the effect may be to bind the authority.[315] This was recently confirmed by Richards J in *Downderry Construction Ltd v Secretary of State for Transport, Local Government and the Regions.*[316]

315   See *Western Fish* (above); also *Wells v Minister for Housing and Local Government* [1967] 1 WLR 1000, CA.

316   [2002] EWHC 2 (Admin); [2002] ACD 62.

Refusal of relief, invalidity and finality

Discretionary remedy and refusal of relief

Delay

7.1 Even where one or more grounds of challenge may be made out, relief may be refused at the discretion of the court. The time limits set out in Supreme Court Act 1981 s31(6) and Civil Procedure Rules (CPR) r54.5 must be adhered to strictly, and undue delay may result in the refusal of any relief. Factors which the court must statutorily take into account in deciding whether or not to grant relief, where there has been delay, include whether the delay is such that to grant relief would cause hardship or prejudice to the respondent or would be detrimental to good administration.[1] The phrase 'detrimental to good administration' has not been defined by the courts, but the House of Lords has offered guidelines as to its meaning which are, briefly, as follows:[2]

- administrative inconvenience is not sufficient reason to deny relief: the consequence of granting it must be positive harm;
- the court can take into account the effect on other potential applicants and the effects if their applications were successful;
- there must be affirmative evidence of such detriment or at least evidence from which it can be inferred.

7.2 It was emphasised in *R v Secretary of State for Health and Elmfield Drugs Ltd ex p Furneaux, Skinner and Knox*,[3] that the causal connection must be between the grant of relief and any prejudice suffered by the respondent and not between the actual delay and the prejudice.

7.3 The Court of Appeal, in *R (Lichfield Securities Ltd) v Lichfield DC*,[4] considered this issue in the context of the new procedural regime. The court held that,[5] regardless of whether it involves repetition of the arguments about promptness canvassed at the permission stage, Supreme Court Act 1981 s31(6)(b) places the issue of undue delay on the agenda at the substantive hearing. It does not follow from this, however, that the judge at the substantive hearing should consider the matter as if the issue had never previously arisen, at least where the matter was properly argued at the permission stage. It was undesirable that one Administrative Court judge should act, in effect, as a court

---

1 Supreme Court Act 1981 s31(6).
2 *R v Dairy Produce Quota Tribunal ex p Caswell* [1989] 1 WLR 1089, HL.
3 [1994] COD 62 and 336, CA. See also *R v Swale BC ex p Royal Society for the Protection of Birds* (1990) 2 Admin LR 790.
4 [2001] EWCA Civ 304; (2001) 3 LGLR 637.
5 [2001] EWCA Civ 304 at [34].

of appeal from another or decide an issue without reference to a fellow judge's earlier decision. The matter was one of practical case-management under the CPR. In addition, the second judge must have in mind the need to prevent circumvention of CPR r54.13, which prohibits applications to set aside the grant of permission.

7.4 Accordingly, although ultimately a matter for the judge hearing the substantive application, the appropriate course in such cases would generally be that the defendant should be permitted to recanvass by way of undue delay, an issue of promptness which has been decided at the permission stage in the claimant's favour only if:

- the permission judge has expressly so indicated;
- new and relevant material is introduced on the substantive hearing;
- exceptionally, the issues have developed at the full hearing in such a way as to put a different aspect on the question of promptness; or if the first judge has plainly overlooked some relevant matter or reached a decision *per incuriam.*

7.5 Applying these principles, it would seem that it will not generally be open to the defendant at the substantive hearing to argue for the refusal of relief, under Supreme Court Act 1981 s31(6)(b), on the ground of hardship, prejudice or detriment to good administration, where these issues have been explored fully at the permission stage, even though the question at that stage was whether or not to grant permission rather than whether or not to grant relief.[6]

7.6 Having said this, although *Lichfield* considered the position under the CPR, it was a feature of that case that the permission application was adjourned into open court where it was properly argued. It must be doubted whether a permission decision taken on the papers, even with the benefit of the defendant's summary of grounds for resisting the application, should be considered to be a proper argument on the issue of delay to debar the judge hearing the substantive hearing with the benefit of detailed argument and evidence from the defendant, from considering the issue of refusal of relief.[7] Such a situation would, in any event, seem to fall within the second of the exceptions to the

---

6 See, eg, *Lichfield* [2001] EWCA Civ 304 per Sedley LJ at [37]: 'We take the same view [ie, that the claimant had acted promptly in that case], whether the question is regarded as one of promptness in applying for leave or of undue delay in seeking relief'.

7 Potential problems with the new approach have been identified by the courts: see, eg, *R v Local Commissioner ex p Field* [2000] COD 58; *R v Essex CC ex p Tarmac Roadstone Holdings Ltd* [1998] PLCR 56, QBD.

general rule enunciated in *Lichfield* – new and relevant evidence introduced at the substantive hearing.[8] This is separate from the question of whether or not the judge may re-open the question of the grant of permission to proceed, which is generally prohibited.[9]

7.7 Sometimes, notwithstanding delay, relief will be granted. The courts have held that illegality of a policy is a good reason for doing so, where otherwise the unlawful policy would continue in operation, particularly where only prospective relief is sought. In *R v Rochdale BC ex p Schemet*,[10] Roch J cited the comments of Nicholls LJ in *R v Westminster CC ex p Hilditch*[11] that:

> ... if a policy is unlawful, prima facie it should be discontinued. The mere fact that the policy has been in place for nearly three years is not a sufficient reason for the court countenancing its continuing implementation for the indefinite future. There is here good reason for extending time for the making of an application for judicial review, at any rate so far as the relief sought is directed at retraining the further implementation of the allegedly unlawful policy.

7.8 In *Schemet* itself, the court refused mandatory relief which would have affected the budget of the respondent education authority for the previous two years, granting only declarations on the illegality of the impugned decisions.[12] In *R v East Sussex CC ex p Ward*,[13] permission was granted on the express basis that no relief would be granted in respect of any period prior to six months before the grant of permission itself (in fact only declaratory relief was granted for various reasons).[14]

Alternative remedies

7.9 In addition, the court may refuse relief on the basis that the claimant has not used an alternative remedy (such as an internal or statutory appeal) which would be more convenient for the disposal of the issue in question. Judicial review is often referred to as a remedy of last resort, and the court will usually be extremely reluctant to embark upon enquiries into disputes of fact, especially where an alternative

8 *Lichfield* [2001] EWCA Civ 304 at [34].
9 *R v Criminal Injuries Compensation Board ex p A* [1999] 2 AC 330, HL.
10 [1994] ELR 89, QBD, at 100–101.
11 (1990) 14 June (unreported), transcript p17.
12 See also *R v Warwickshire CC ex p Collymore* [1995] ELR 217.
13 (2000) 3 CCLR 132, QBD.
14 (2000) 3 CCLR 132 at 140A–C.

forum, better equipped to do so, exists. In *R v Secretary of State for the Home Department ex p Swati*,[15] Sir John Donaldson MR said:

> In giving or refusing leave to apply for judicial review, account must be taken of alternative remedies available to the applicant … [T]he jurisdiction [will] not be exercised where there [is] an alternative remedy by way of appeal, save in exceptional circumstances. By definition, exceptional circumstances defy definition, but where Parliament provides an appeal procedure, judicial review will have no place, unless the applicant can distinguish his case from the type of case for which the appeal procedure was provided.[16]

7.10   Where, however, proceeding by way of judicial review is genuinely more appropriate, this will be permitted, even where an alternative remedy is available. Examples of valid reasons for using judicial review have been:

- where the applicant seeks not to challenge the individual decision so much as the underlying legality of some determination of which the instant decision is just one manifestation;[17]
- where the decision in question was, on its face, made without jurisdiction or contained an error of law;[18] and
- where costs were available on judicial review but would not be on appeal.[19]

7.11   Generally, however, a right of appeal must be exhausted before resort may be had to judicial review. In *R v Birmingham CC ex p Ferrero*,[20] Taylor LJ emphasised that it would be exceptional to permit judicial review in such cases and stated that it would therefore be necessary, where the exception was sought to be invoked, to look carefully at the suitability of the statutory appeal in the context of the particular case.

7.12   More recently, in *R (Sivasubramaniam) v Wandsworth County Court*,[21] the appellant sought to challenge by way of judicial review decisions of the circuit judge, refusing permission to appeal from a decision of the district judge and refusing to set aside the district judge's order.

---

15 [1986] 1 WLR 477, CA.
16 [1986] 1 WLR 477 at 485. See also *R v Chief Constable of Merseyside Police ex p Calveley* [1986] QB 424, CA, to the same effect.
17 See *R v Paddington Valuation Officer ex p Peachey Property Corporation Ltd* [1966] 1 QB 380, CA.
18 *R v Hillingdon LBC ex p Royco Homes Ltd* [1974] QB 720, DC.
19 *R v Inspector of Taxes ex p Kissane* [1986] 2 All ER 37, QBD.
20 [1993] 1 All ER 530.
21 [2002] EWCA Civ 1738; [2003] 2 All ER 160.

The Court of Appeal dismissed the appeals. The only exception to the general rule that judicial review of a discretionary decision would not be permitted where there was an alternative remedy, was where the alternative remedy was less satisfactory than judicial review.[22] Litigants should not be permitted to circumvent the sensible and proportionate statutory scheme of appeals under the Access to Justice Act 1999, and thereby defeat the objects of the Act, save in truly exceptional cases. Refusals of permission to appeal were not susceptible to judicial review save in exceptional cases where the challenge to the decision was founded on a claim of jurisdictional error or procedural irregularity. This did not affect the susceptibility to judicial review of refusals of permission to appeal by the Immigration Appeal Tribunal, which was based on matters peculiar to immigration appeals.[23]

7.13   In some circumstances, the secretary of state has power under statute to make an order declaring a local authority to be in breach of its statutory duties and to give directions to ensure that the duties are properly carried out.[24] It appears that whether or not such powers amount to an alternative remedy sufficient to preclude judicial review until they have been exhausted, will, like so much else in this area of the law, depend on the circumstances. In *R v Durham CC ex p Curtis*,[25] the Court of Appeal held that the power under Local Authority Social Services Act 1970 s7D did constitute an alternative remedy which must be exhausted, save where what was required was an authoritative resolution of a legal issue, in which case judicial review would be appropriate.

7.14   However, that decision should be contrasted with *R v Brent LBC ex p Sawyers*,[26] in which a differently constituted Court of Appeal dealt

---

22   This is a less restrictive formulation of the test than in the other cases referred to above. The judgment does not indicate that the court was seeking to relax the test. This would be unlikely, given the court's other comments, and given other recent decisions which have clearly sought to reinforce the strictness of the test: see, eg, *R (Cowl) v Plymouth CC* [2001] EWCA Civ 1935; [2002] 1 WLR 803; (2002) 5 CCLR 42.

23   But see now CPR Part 54 section II – considered in more detail below, at chapter 8.

24   See, eg, Children Act 1989 s84; Education Act 1944 s68; Local Authority Social Services Act 1970 s7D (inserted by National Health Service and Community Care Act 1990).

25   [1993] 11 BMLR 141, CA, (heard with and reported under *R v Devon CC ex p Baker*), per Simon Brown LJ at 160.

26   [1994] 1 FLR 203, CA. But see *R v Kingston-upon-Thames RLBC ex p T* [1994] FLR 798, DC, in relation to the Children Act 1989 s26 complaints procedure as an alternative remedy. See also paras 15.33–15.36 below.

with Children Act 1989 s84, which was identical in all material respects to Local Authority Social Services Act 1970 s7D. It held that although the existence of the default power could properly be taken into account as an avenue of redress alternative to judicial review, it did not amount to a right of appeal. Therefore, in the circumstances of that case, it was wrong to treat it as a more suitable remedy than judicial review.[27]

The modern approach – ADR and alternative remedies

7.15   Cases such as *Sawyers*[28] now do need to be treated with caution. The modern approach is to require claimants to make use of any alternative remedy, even if it would not afford all the relief that the claimant seeks and could not even consider all the issues. The reasons for this relate to the requirement to attempt alternative dispute resolution, and are considered in more detail elsewhere.[29] There are, accordingly, numerous recent examples of the courts refusing relief on the basis that an alternative remedy, especially a right of appeal, ought to have been used in preference to judicial review.

7.16   In *Falmouth and Truro Port Health Authority v South West Water*,[30] the Court of Appeal re-emphasised the court's distaste, in general terms, for permitting judicial review to be a means of circumventing the usual, and statutorily prescribed procedures. The court rejected an argument that judicial review was appropriate because the statutory procedures, by way of appeal to the magistrates' court, were so protracted and subject to delay that they were not a realistic alternative remedy, especially given that the abatement notice which was challenged would have remained in operation pending an appeal to the magistrates. The court stated that the aim must be to make the statutory remedy effective rather than 'to surmise that it is so ineffective that judicial review is permitted'. There was no reason why the procedure laid down by Parliament should not be made an effective procedure. It was the duty of the courts to ensure that it was. Cases where judicial review was appropriate would be rare.

7.17   Similarly, in *M v Bromley LBC*,[31] the Court of Appeal upheld the refusal of relief on judicial review, on the ground of a more suitable

27 [1994] 1 FLR 203, per Peter Gibson LJ at 214.

28 [1994] 1 FLR 203.

29 See *R (Cowl) v Plymouth CC* [2001] EWCA Civ 1935 and chapter 17 at paras 17.9–17.21.

30 [2001] QB 445, CA.

31 [2002] EWCA Civ 1113; [2002] 2 FLR 802, CA.

alternative remedy. M challenged a finding of an investigation by the authority that he had abused children in his care while employed by the authority as a care-worker, alleging procedural impropriety. The court held that an appeal to the Care Standards Tribunal was the more appropriate course because it would enable the merits of the finding – which was the most important aspect – and not just the legality, to be examined in the round.

7.18   In *R (AM) v Head Teacher of St George's Catholic School*,[32] the claimant was permanently excluded from school, and appealed in accordance with a statutory right of appeal which had three stages. Before reaching the final stage, he sought judicial review of the decision to exclude him. The application was dismissed as was an appeal to the Court of Appeal.

7.19   The Court of Appeal considered the issue of the extent to which unfairness at an early stage of the three-stage appeal process could be cured by utilising the final stage of appeal, and held that it was necessary to construe the statutory scheme as a whole, in order to ascertain the intention of Parliament regarding the effect of unfairness in an early part of the process. In this case, although Parliament did not intend any stage of the process to be unfair, nor did it intend a party aggrieved at a decision at the first stage to seek judicial review rather than appeal. Although the appeal did not give redress in respect of the earlier unfairness, the aggrieved party obtained a new, fair decision on the merits from the 'custom-built' expert and independent statutory body, following a rehearing. Unless, therefore, the prior procedural unfairness complained of had somehow tainted the subsequent appeal, in which case the appeal decision itself would necessarily fall, the right to a fair determination of a person's case would be satisfied by the appeal hearing and decision. On a judicial review application brought instead of an appeal, the court would usually leave the claimant to his statutory remedy.[33]

7.20   On a procedural note, in *R (Wilkinson) v Chief Constable of West Yorkshire*,[34] the question of whether an alternative remedy was more appropriate than judicial review had been fully argued at the permission stage. The judge, in granting permission, had indicated that the point was arguable and the trial judge would have regard to his observations. The court at the substantive hearing could not, therefore,

32 [2002] EWCA Civ 1822.
33 See also *R (Sivasubramaniam) v Wandsworth County Court* [2002] EWCA Civ 1738; [2003] 2 All ER 160.
34 [2002] EWHC 2353 (Admin).

decline jurisdiction to entertain the claim and consider the issue. Conversely, however, the grant of permission in an alternative remedy case was not an inviolate ruling. Alternative remedy arguments could still be considered in relation to the grant of relief.[35]

Other factors

7.21 Other factors the court will consider are whether the grant of a remedy appears futile, academic or otherwise unnecessary, whether the claimant has waived any breach, and the nature of the matter challenged.

7.22 In *R v Secretary of State for Social Services ex p Association of Metropolitan Authorities*,[36] the court refused to quash Housing Benefit Regulations on various grounds, primarily related to the general administrative inconvenience and, in the particular circumstances of the case, the futility of so doing. This was also associated with the facts that the challenge was against delegated legislation, that the principal complaint was not over the substance of the instrument but the non-compliance with a mandatory duty of consultation, and that the secretary of state had, by the time of the hearing, issued further regulations which were accepted by the claimant to be lawful and which superseded the challenged instrument. Accordingly, only a declaration that the secretary of state had acted unlawfully in failing to consult was granted.

7.23 In another case involving the Secretary of State for Social Services and the Association of Metropolitan Authorities,[37] the court again granted only a declaration for similar reasons. In this case, however, the effect was that the regulations remained in force in spite of the unlawful manner of their implementation.

7.24 In *Chief Constable for the North Wales Police ex p Evans*,[38] the House of Lords refused the applicant, a probationary constable who had been dismissed in breach of his right to a fair hearing, an order of mandamus even though the judicial committee accepted that that would have been the only satisfactory remedy to obtain his reinstatement to

---

35 Compare the position concerning delay and refusal of relief considered in *R (Lichfield Securities Ltd) v Lichfield DC* [2001] EWCA Civ 304; (2001) 3 LGLR 637.

36 [1986] 1 WLR 1, QBD.

37 *R v Secretary of State for Social Security ex p Association of Metropolitan Authorities* (1993) 25 HLR 131, QBD.

38 [1982] 1 WLR 1155, HL.

the constabulary. To grant such an order, however, was impractical and would border upon usurpation of the Chief Constable's role.[39]

7.25   Objections to the grant of relief may be raised by the court or by the respondent, either at the permission stage or on the full application. If there is to be an argument at the full hearing over whether it is appropriate to grant relief and, if so, the form it should take, it is not uncommon for the court to adjourn such argument until after judgment has been given.

Invalidity

7.26   One of the most difficult issues in judicial review is that of the status of an unlawful decision. On the one hand, ultra vires decisions and acts are frequently said to be void and of no effect, or described as nullities. On the other hand, as Hobhouse LJ observed in *Credit Suisse v Allerdale BC*,[40] even unlawful decisions plainly do have effects until they are quashed and even afterwards.[41] The court, may in its discretion refuse any mandatory relief, or any relief at all, for a variety of reasons which will almost inevitably have little or nothing do with the legality of the decision itself, as the issue of relief only arises if a decision has been found to be unlawful.[42] In addition, the presumption of regularity is sometimes invoked to the effect that a decision will be presumed lawful until proved to be invalid.

7.27   In *London & Clydeside Estates v Aberdeen DC*,[43] Lord Hailsham referred to a spectrum of unlawful decisions, some being so obviously unlawful that the citizen may take no action to challenge them until

---

39   See also *R v Islington LBC ex p Hinds* [1994] COD 494, QBD, where relief was refused on a reasons challenge because the failure to give reasons did not substantially prejudice the applicant (although this decision could not survive the Court of Appeal's decision in *R v Westminster CC ex p Ermakov* [1996] 2 All ER 302, CA; and *R v CICB ex p Aston* [1994] COD 500, QBD, where relief was refused because no other decision could have been reached.

40   [1997] QB 306, CA at 352B–355H.

41   See, eg, the cases where relief has been granted only prospectively, explicitly on the basis that the court was not prepared to undo the prior effects of the impugned act or decision: *R v Rochdale BC v Schemet* [1994] ELR 89, QBD; *R v Westminster CC ex p Hilditch* (1990) 14 June (unreported).

42   See, eg, *R v Secretary of State for Social Security ex p AMA* (1993) 25 HLR 131, QBD, where a declaration that the secretary of state had unlawfully introduced housing benefit regulations by reason of a failure to comply with the mandatory duty of consultation deliberately left the regulations themselves in force. See also the cases on refusal of relief referred to above at paras 7.1–7.25.

43   [1981] 1 WLR 182, HL, at 189–190: see para 7.33 below.

action is taken by the decision-maker to seek to enforce them; others defective in such trivial respects that the decision-maker can safely rely on them nonetheless, in the knowledge that the court would reject any challenge. In between, there will be cases where the citizen needs to take action to protect her or his rights and the decision-maker will need to attempt to remedy the fault. Hobhouse LJ, in *Credit Suisse* resolved the problems he had identified by reference to this passage from Lord Hailsham's speech in *London & Clydeside Estates*, concluding that terms such as 'ultra vires', 'void' and 'nullity' bore different meanings in public and private law: 'It is not correct to take terminology from administrative law and apply it without the necessary adjustment and refinement of meaning to private law.'[44]

7.28 In *Boddington v British Transport Police*,[45] the House of Lords considered the issue in the context of a challenge by a defendant in criminal proceedings to the validity of the byelaw for breach of which the prosecution had been brought. Lord Irvine LC stated that it was permissible to challenge the validity of the byelaw in this manner and considered some of the issues discussed above. He said:[46]

> Subordinate legislation, or an administrative act, is sometimes said to be presumed lawful until it has been pronounced to be unlawful. This does not, however, entail that such legislation or act is valid until quashed prospectively. That would be a conclusion inconsistent with the authorities ... In my judgment, the true effect of the presumption is that the legislation or act which is impugned is presumed to be good until pronounced to be unlawful, but is then recognised as never having had any legal effect at all.

7.29 This was a consequence of the judiciary's place in the legal system, as Lord Diplock had recognised in *Hoffmann La Roche & Co v Secretary of State for Trade and Industry*,[47] stating:

> Under our legal system, however, the courts as the judicial arm of government do not act on their own initiative. Their jurisdiction to determine that a statutory instrument is ultra vires does not arise until its validity is challenged in proceedings ... Unless there is such a challenge and, if there is, until it has been upheld by a judgment of the court, the validity of the statutory instrument and the legality of acts done pursuant to the law declared by it are presumed. It would, however, be inconsistent with

---

44 [1997] QB 306, CA, at 355H.
45 [1999] 2 AC 143, HL.
46 [1999] 2 AC 143 at 155B–D.
47 [1975] AC 295, HL, at 365.

the doctrine of ultra vires ... if the judgment of a court ... that a statutory instrument was ultra vires were to have any lesser consequence in law than to render the instrument incapable of ever having had any legal effect.

7.30   Thus, said Lord Irvine in *Boddington*,[48] Lord Hailsham in *London & Clydeside Estates*,[49] was simply observing how the parties may feel it safe and/or prudent to react to differing degrees of unlawful action. That was a matter for the putative parties to decide.

> Subject, however, to any statutory qualification upon his right to do so, the citizen could ... choose to accept the risk of uncertainty, take no action at all, wait to be sued or prosecuted by the public body and then put forward his arguments on validity and have them determined by the court hearing the case against him. That is a matter of right in a case of ultra vires action by the public authority, and would not be subject to the discretion of the court ... [A]ny other interpretation of Lord Hailsham LC's speech could not be reconciled with the decision of this House in the *Anisminic* case ...[50]

7.31   In the context of a challenge in criminal proceedings to the validity of the measure in reliance on which the prosecution was brought, this reasoning is wholly convincing and constitutes a welcome and long overdue clarification of the applicable principles. It does not, however, address all of difficulties referred to by Hobhouse LJ in *Credit Suisse*.[51] In particular, even the quashing of a decision does not in many cases result in the removal of all the effects of that decision prior to its being stuck down. A tenancy, for example, granted pursuant to an illegal housing allocations policy does not become 'ungranted' or otherwise liable to be set aside when the policy itself is quashed.

Mandatory and directory requirements

7.32   This is one aspect of the topic of validity and effect of a decision taken unlawfully.[52] Failure to comply with the procedures laid down by Parliament will not always have as its corollary that the resulting decision or act will be void and of no effect. Where Parliament does not specify the result of such a failure, it will be for the courts to determine what that result should be. The mechanism the courts have

48   [1999] 2 AC 143, HL.
49   [1981] 1 WLR 182, HL.
50   [1999] 2 AC 143 at 157H–158D.
51   [1997] QB 306, CA.
52   See also 'Severability', at paras 7.38–7.43 below.

evolved for doing this is to decide whether or not compliance with the provision in question is mandatory. If it is mandatory the failure will result in the decision being rendered void: if it is simply directory, then it will not be rendered void. At one level, it might seem surprising that the courts are in a position to hold that compliance with some of Parliament's requirements is not mandatory. On the other hand, this doctrine may be seen as necessary to avoid the administrative chaos that could ensue if decisions were struck down for the most technical, minor or immaterial of failures of compliance.

7.33   There is a danger of over-simplification in this matter. The courts have warned against attempting to fit the facts of any case into fixed categories labelled 'mandatory' and 'directory'. In *London and Clydeside Estates v Aberdeen DC*,[53] Lord Hailsham LC said:

> When Parliament lays down a statutory requirement for the exercise of legal authority it expects its authority to be obeyed down to the minutest detail. But what the courts have to decide in a particular case is the legal consequence of non-compliance on the rights of the subject viewed in the light of a concrete state of facts and a continuing chain of events. It may be that what the courts are faced with is not so much a stark choice of alternatives but a spectrum of possibilities in which one compartment or description fades gradually into another. At one end of this spectrum there may be cases in which a fundamental obligation has been so outrageously or flagrantly ignored or defied that the subject can safely ignore what has been done and treat it as having no legal consequences upon himself ... At the other end of the spectrum the defect in procedure may be so trivial and nugatory that the authority can safely proceed without remedial action, confident that if the subject is so misguided as to rely on the fault, the court will decline to listen to his complaint. But in a very great number of cases ... it may be necessary for a subject, in order to safeguard himself, to go to court for a declaration of his rights, the grant of which may well be discretionary, and ... it may be wise for the authority ... to do everything in its power to remedy the fault in its procedure so as not to deprive the subject of his due or themselves of their power to act.[54]

7.34   In deciding whether a particular duty is mandatory or directory, the courts have held that the following matters should be considered:

(a) the nature and purpose of the legislation;
(b) the importance of the provision breached;

---

53   [1981] 1 WLR 182, HL.
54   [1981] 1 WLR 182 at 189–190.

(c) the relationship between the provision and the purpose of the legislation; and

(d) the prejudice suffered by the applicant.[55]

7.35 More recently, in *Haringey LBC v Awaratife*,[56] the Court of Appeal held that a failure to include statutorily prescribed information in a housing benefit notification did not invalidate the benefit authority's determination or render it unenforceable. The issue was whether the recipient landlord had suffered substantial harm as a result of the breach. On the facts, the breaches of the regulations had not caused such harm; were directory rather than mandatory and so the authority were entitled to claim they had substantially complied with the regulations and the landlord had not been deprived of a right of appeal.[57]

7.36 Conversely, in *R v Thanet DC ex p Warren Court Hotels Ltd*,[58] the judge held that a housing benefit notification relating to the recovery of overpaid benefit was invalid for failure to include required information, namely the recipient's right to request a statement of reasons, and the reasons for recovery of the overpayment. Substantial prejudice had been caused in this case by increasing the administrative burden on the claimant's staff. The defects were not cured by the service of a later invoice which did state the reasons for recovery of the overpayment, as this invoice still did not inform the landlord of the right to request reasons, and it was in any event extremely inconvenient for the company to have the reasons set out on a separate sheet of paper sent some time after the determination.

7.37 Where Parliament has provided for consultation before legislation, the courts have held such a requirement to be mandatory.[59] Duties to give notice are usually mandatory, although in *Langridge*,[60] the particular duty was held to be directory only. A requirement to inform a person of a right of appeal is mandatory.[61]

55 *Secretary of State for Trade and Industry v Langridge* [1991] 3 All ER 591, CA.

56 (1999) 32 HLR 517, CA.

57 (1999) 32 HLR 517 at 526–527 and 529.

58 (2001) 33 HLR 32, QBD.

59 *R v Secretary of State for Social Services ex p Association of Metropolitan Authorities* [1986] 1 WLR 1; *R v Secretary of State for Social Security ex p Association of Metropolitan Authorities* (1993) 25 HLR 131, DC.

60 *Secretary of State for Trade and Industry v Langridge* [1991] 3 All ER 591, CA.

61 *London and Clydeside Estates v Aberdeen DC* [1981] 1 WLR 182, HL.

Severability

7.38 Where a decision-maker has acted partly lawfully and partly unlawfully, eg, has made an order partly within jurisdiction and partly in excess of it, or partly for lawful purposes and partly for unlawful ones, or in breach of some procedural rules, the court may decide not to quash the decision if the lawful part, purpose, etc, is the dominant one and the unlawful one is cleanly severable.

7.39 The following have been severed:

- planning conditions;[62]
- an order of a disciplinary board;[63]
- an order of a licensing authority.[64]

7.40 Where a training board was under a duty to consult trade unions before making an order, the order was declared to be valid against those that had been consulted but invalid against those that had not.[65]

7.41 Similarly, where a statutory body gives reasons for a decision which may be clearly disentangled, and where the court is satisfied that although one reason may be bad in law, the body would have reached precisely the same decision for the remaining, valid reasons, the court may well refuse to intervene.[66]

7.42 Where, however, the good and the bad, or the motives, etc, overlap, the power has not been properly exercised and the decision must be quashed.[67]

7.43 In relation to instruments and, in particular, delegated legislation, the test now appears to be one of substantial severability rather than the old blue pencil test. Where the bad words can be severed from the good and still leave a valid text unaffected by the presence of the invalid,

---

62 *Hartnell v Minister of Housing and Local Government* [1965] AC 1134, HL.

63 *Bowman v State and State Services Commission* [1972] NZLR 78.

64 *R v Bournemouth Justices ex p Maggs* [1963] 1 WLR 320.

65 *Agricultural, Forestry and Horticultural Industry Training Board v Aylesbury Mushrooms Ltd* [1972] 1 WLR 190.

66 See *R v Broadcasting Complaints Commission ex p Owen* [1985] QB 1153, DC; *R v Rochdale MBC ex p Cromer King Mill* [1982] 3 All ER 761, QBD.

67 See *Westminster Corporation v London and North Western Railway Company* [1905] AC 426, HL; *R v Brighton Corporation ex p Shoosmith* (1907) LT 762; *Webb v Minister of Housing and Local Government* [1964] 1 WLR 1295, QBD. See also *London and Clydeside Estates v Aberdeen DC* [1982] 1 WLR 182, HL, where the House of Lords held that a planning certificate which did not include notice of a right of appeal was not severable, because of the mandatory nature of the duty to give the applicant this information.

the court may sever the good from the bad, and leave the valid part of the text to take effect. Where this is not possible, the court may apparently 'modify the text' and grant a declaration that the instrument shall not take effect to the extent that the maker of it exceeded his or her powers. This can only be done, however, if the court is satisfied that in so doing it is effecting no change to the substance and purpose of the impugned provision.[68]

Ouster and finality clauses

7.44   This is an extremely complex topic, to which much space could be devoted. In brief, however, provisions may be included in statutes which purport to exclude the court's supervisory jurisdiction by means of a variety of phrases. Such examples include statements that a decision shall be 'final', that a delegated decision 'shall take effect as if enacted' in the Act, that certiorari[69] 'shall not issue' in respect of particular decisions, or that they 'shall not be questioned in any proceedings whatever'.

7.45   In general, the courts have accepted that such clauses prevent any appeal, but do not exclude the operation of judicial review where a decision-maker has acted in excess of jurisdiction. It has been held, for instance, that the so-called 'no certiorari' clause does not prevent the court from quashing the act or decision where it was made in excess of jurisdiction (though it may prevent quashing for mere error on the face of the record).[70] Similarly, the 'as if enacted' formula only protects decisions in conformity with the Act (ie, lawful decisions), since these were the only ones contemplated by the Act, and does not impede judicial control of irregular decisions.[71]

7.46   In particular, the *House of Lords in Anisminic Ltd v Foreign Compensation Commission,*[72] held that the provision which stated that a

---

68   See *DPP v Hutchinson* [1990] 2 AC 783, HL, per Lord Bridge of Harwich at 811; *R v Inland Revenue Commissioners ex p Woolwich Equitable Building Society* [1990] 1 WLR 1400, HL, per Lord Goff of Chievely at 1418. See also *Credit Suisse v Allerdale BC* [1997] QB 306 (contract); *R v Southwark LBC ex p Dagou* (1996) 28 HLR 72 (decision letter).

69   That is, a quashing order.

70   See *R v Medical Appeal Tribunal ex p Gilmore* [1957] 1 QB 574, CA, and the cases there referred to by Denning LJ.

71   *Minister of Health v Yaffé* [1931] AC 494, HL.

72   [1969] 2 AC 147, HL.

'determination ... shall not be questioned in any court of law', the most common form of the modern ouster clause, was subject to the same doctrine as 'no certiorari' clauses: it did not exclude judicial control in cases of excess of jurisdiction.

> It is a well established principle that a provision ousting the ordinary juris-diction of the court must be construed strictly – meaning, I think, that, if such a provision is reasonably capable of having two meanings, that mean-ing shall be taken which preserves the ordinary jurisdiction of the court.[73]

7.47　The House of Lords also held that no tribunal has jurisdiction to make an error of law.

> Lack of jurisdiction may arise in various ways ... [W]hile engaged on a proper inquiry, the tribunal may depart from the rules of natural justice; or it may ask itself the wrong questions; or it may take into account mat-ters which it was not directed to take into account. Thereby it would step outside its jurisdiction. It would turn its inquiry to something not directed by Parliament and fail to make the inquiry which Parliament did direct. Any of these things would cause its purported decisions to be a nullity ...[74]

7.48　This decision therefore renders all errors of law, jurisdictional errors. It was held that the term 'determination' did not include everything which purported to be a determination but which was in fact not one at all because of an error of law.

7.49　In *R v Secretary of State for the Home Department ex p Fayed*,[75] the Court of Appeal held that a provision that a decision 'shall not be sub-ject to appeal to, or review in, any court' did not preclude judicial review on traditional grounds. In *R v Bradford MBC ex p Sikander Ali*,[76] the court suggested that judicial review proceedings were not civil proceedings, in circumstances where challenge to a decision was pro-hibited in 'civil or criminal' proceedings. In *Sivasubramaniam*,[77] the Court of Appeal declined to hold that the Civil Procedure Rules and in particular Part 52 (appeals) had ousted the supervisory juris-diction of the Administrative Court. The court held that such an ouster would require the clearest of words and could not be achieved by implication.

73　[1969] 2 AC 147 per Lord Reid at 170.
74　[1969] 2 AC 147 per Lord Pearce at 195.
75　[1998] 1 WLR 763, CA.
76　[1994] ELR 299.
77　*R (Sivasubramaniam) v Wandsworth County Court* [2002] EWCA Civ 1738; [2003] All ER 160.

7.50   Partial ouster clauses, such as those contained in the Town and
           Country Planning Act 1990 ss285 and 286 onwards, to the effect that
           a decision shall not be questioned in any proceedings whatsoever
           except by way of the appeal mechanism provided by the Act itself, are
           enforced by the courts without resistance.

7.51   Moreover, in *R v Acting Returning Officer for Devon and East
           Plymouth European Constituency ex p Sanders*,[78] the court declined juris-
           diction to review a decision of the respondent that a candidate's elec-
           tion nomination paper was valid, on the basis that the Parliamentary
           Election Rules provided that such a decision was 'final and shall not be
           questioned in any proceeding whatsoever'. The court held that, unlike
           Anisminic, this was only a partial ouster clause since it did not apply to
           decisions that a nomination paper was invalid. Furthermore, once the
           result of the voting was known, there was a right of appeal by elec-
           toral petition, and so recourse to law was only postponed by the rules
           and not precluded. The intention was to protect the integrity of the
           electoral process so that it could only be undone by objection brought
           once voting was over.

78 [1994] COD 497, QBD.

CHAPTER 8

Judicial review and immigration and asylum law

Introduction

8.1 Non-British citizens are subject to immigration control. Generally, they will require leave to enter, and/or to remain, in the United Kingdom (unless they possess a right of abode).[1] Leave may be granted for a limited or an indefinite period. The relevant legislation creates separate procedures for asylum and non-asylum applications and provides for appeals from decisions made in respect of such applications. Together with the 'Immigration Rules', they are intended to form a comprehensive code for immigration control.[2]

8.2 The Immigration and Asylum Act 1999[3] introduced a comprehensive, new appeals structure which has diminished the role of judicial review.[4] Immigration law is, however, complex, controversial and continually changing. More relevantly, there is a significant degree of discretion inherent in any scheme for determining entitlements to enter, undertake activities and/or reside in the United Kingdom. Of itself, such discretion provides scope for judicial review.

Principal Acts and the Immigration Rules

8.3 The structure of immigration control, including the duties and powers of immigration officers and system of appeals, is set out in a number of different statutes, as supplemented by regulations and orders made under their authority. The principal Acts currently governing immigration and asylum law are:[5]

---

1 Citizens of the Republic of Ireland are not subject to British immigration controls as the Republic of Ireland is located with the Common Travel Area. Although immigration controls do apply to European Union (EU) nationals, they are subject to the freedom of movement and the freedom to supply services provisions of the Treaty of Rome; in relation to immigration control, these freedoms have been transposed into domestic law by the Immigration Act 1988 and the Immigration (European Economic Area) Regulations 2000 (SI No 2326, as amended), the effect of which is to exempt EU citizens (in so far as such a concept exists) from the requirement of leave to enter the UK.

2 Although the secretary of state does retain a residual discretion outside the Immigration Rules. The Rules are published as a House of Commons Paper. See further at para 8.5 below.

3 As amended by the Nationality, Immigration and Asylum Act 2002.

4 In addition, judicial review of refusals of leave to appeal by the Immigration Appeals Tribunal has now been replaced with a much more restrictive form of statutory review: see CPR Part 54 Section II, and generally, chapter 18 below at paras 18.148–18.154.

5 Note that some of the provisions in these Acts have been repealed and/or amended by subsequent legislation.

- Immigration Act 1971
- British Nationality Act 1981
- Asylum and Immigration Appeals Act 1993
- Asylum and Immigration Act 1996
- Immigration and Asylum Act 1999
- Nationality, Immigration and Asylum Act 2002.

8.4 Reference should also be made to the National Assistance Act 1948, as this may still – in certain circumstances – impose duties to provide assistance to asylum-seekers.[6]

8.5 The Immigration Rules are published by the secretary of state under powers conferred by the Immigration Act 1971.[7] The Rules are not a statutory instrument, but simply the secretary of state's published statement[8] of the manner in which he or she will consider applications falling within their ambit. Accordingly, the secretary of state retains a residual discretion to deal with applications in a different manner, and may do so in exceptional or compassionate circumstances. It has been held by the Court of Appeal that – although the Rules do not have the force of statute or of a statutory instrument – they do have the force of law for the adjudicators who deal with and administer the immigration process.[9]

General scheme of the legislation

8.6 Immigration law confers decision-making functions on a variety of individuals and bodies: immigration officers at the point of entry deal with leave to enter the UK; the secretary of state deals with leave to remain, and questions arising from those who overstay their leave to remain in the UK.[10] It has been held by the Court of Appeal that the

---

6 This is considered in more detail in the context of housing (chapter 9, below at paras 9.27–9.32). See also, paras 8.29–8.31 below.

7 Immigration Act 1971 ss1(4),(5) and 3(2).

8 The Rules must be laid before and approved by Parliament. The current Rules are published as HC 395.

9 *Pearson v Immigration Appeal Process* [1978] Imm AR 212, CA.

10 The actual administration of support for persons entering the UK – as distinct from the control of immigration and asylum – is similarly apportioned between distinct bodies, although with less clarity than the control over entry. The issue is particularly acute with regard to asylum-seekers, the support of which is principally the duty of the National Asylum Support Service but duties also fall on local authorities (see *R (Westminster CC) v Secretary of State for the Home Department* [2002] UKHL 38; [2002] HLR 58; (2002) 5 CCLR 511).

secretary of state is entitled to delegate such matters to immigration officers, in accordance with the *Carltona* principle.[11]

8.7 The precise details of the law relating to permission to enter the UK and control over those who are granted such permission is beyond the scope of this work.[12] If, however, a person requires leave to enter the UK (and, where necessary, entry clearance),[13] such leave may be granted for limited or an indefinite period. Limited leave to remain may – and often is – subject to conditions such as that the recipient may not have recourse to public funds or restrictions, and/or may not take up employment.[14] An application for leave to enter is determined in accordance with the Immigration Rules, which prescribe circumstances in which it is to be refused and those in which it may be granted.[15] There is a right of appeal against a refusal of leave to enter, although this is only available if certain conditions are satisfied.[16]

8.8 Once leave to enter has been granted, it may be extended, revoked or amended.[17] A person subject to immigration control may apply to have her or his leave varied, usually to extend it or to have conditions (such as those prohibiting employment) removed.[18] Such an application must be made on a prescribed form and must conform with the Rules.[19] There are circumstances where statute provides for an extension of leave,[20] but most applications are determined by the secretary of state

11 See *R v Secretary of State for the Home Department ex p Oladehinde* [1991] AC 254, HL, per Lord Griffiths at 300. The *Carltona* principle is explained above at paras 6.81–6.82.

12 Reference should be had to the major works on this area, including Macdonald and Webber, *Macdonald's Immigration Law and Practice* (5th edn, Butterworths, 2001); and Supperstone and O'Dempsey, *Supperstone and O'Dempsey on Immigration and Asylum* (4th edn, FT Law & Tax, 1996 (now Sweet & Maxwell)).

13 Leave to enter is – in most instances – granted or refused in the country of departure: Immigration (Leave to Enter and Remain) Order 2000 SI No 1161. Note that entry clearance is also required for a wider class of persons.

14 Immigration Act 1971 s3(1).

15 Immigration Rules (IR), HC 395, para 320. Mandatory grounds for refusal of leave include where a person is subject to a deportation order or has no passport.

16 Immigration and Asylum Act 1999 s60.

17 Indefinite leave to remain cannot be amended or varied.

18 Immigration Act 1971 s3.

19 See *R v Secretary of State for the Home Department ex p Immigration Law Practitioners' Association* [1997] Imm AR 189, where a claim for judicial review to challenge the vires of the rigid rules governing the completion of an application to vary leave was dismissed.

20 Immigration Act 1971 s3C and Immigration and Asylum Act 1999 Sch 4. An example is the automatic extension of leave to remain if an application to vary is submitted but not determined by the time the original leave expires.

in accordance with the Immigration Rules. An application will be refused where the variation or extension of leave is sought for a purpose not covered by the Rules. In prescribed circumstances, an extension of leave will usually be refused.[21] A refusal of an extension or variation of leave to remain, may have the effect that the applicant must leave the UK.

Asylum-seekers

8.9   Asylum-seekers are considered under an analogous but distinct scheme. Under the Geneva Convention 1951 relating to the Status of Refugees, host states owe certain duties to refugees, as defined in the Convention. Under UK law, an application for asylum is an application a refusal to accept which would be contrary to the UK's obligations under the Convention.[22] An asylum-seeker who applies for asylum on arrival in the UK will either be detained[23] or granted temporary leave to enter, pending determination of the application.

8.10   The asylum-seeker must claim asylum as soon as reasonably practicable following arrival in the UK. New penalties for those who failed to do so were introduced by the Nationality, Immigration and Asylum Act (NIAA) 2002, including the withdrawal of any support.[24] It is then the responsibility of the secretary of state – through the Immigration and Nationality Directorate – to investigate and determine the asylum claims.[25] A determination that an applicant is not an asylum-seeker should be accompanied by full reasons for rejecting the claim, but such reasons are not mandatory.[26]

---

21 IR para 322. An example of circumstances that may lead to a refusal of an extension of leave is where the applicant has failed properly or at all to comply with conditions attached to the original grant of leave.

22 Immigration and Asylum Act 1999 s69(6); IR para 327.

23 Immigration Act 1971 Sch 2, para 16; Nationality, Immigration and Asylum Act (NIAA) 2002 s62.

24 NIAA 2002 ss54–55, the Witholding and Withdrawal of Support (Travel Assistance and Temporary Accommodation) Regulations 2002 SI No 3078. See also *R (Q) v Secretary of State for the Home Department* [2003] EWCA Civ 364; [2003] 2 All ER 905.

25 IR para 328.

26 See *R v Secretary of State for the Home Department ex p Gurmeet Singh* [1987] Imm AR 489, DC, and, generally in relation to the need to give reasons for administrative decisions, *R v Secretary of State for the Home Department ex p Doody* [1994] 1 AC 531 and *R v Higher Education Funding Council ex p Institute of Dental Surgery* [1994] 1 WLR 242, QBD. See generally, chapter 6 at paras 6.151–6.16 above.

The appeals structure

8.11   The statutory provisions relating to appeals to adjudicators and then to the Immigration Appeal Tribunal are now contained in NIAA 2002 Part V which came into force on 1 April 2003. The rules of procedure for appeals are set out in the Immigration and Asylum Appeals (Procedure) Rules 2003[27] (the 'Procedure Rules'), the Immigration and Asylum Appeals (One-Stop Procedure) Regulations 2002,[28] (the 'One-Stop Rules') and the Immigration and Asylum Appeals (Fast Track Procedure) Rules 2003[29] (the 'Fast Track Rules').

8.12   Appeals against decisions made on the basis that the exclusion, departure, deportation, etc, of the appellant is conducive to the public good or in the interests of national security are made to the Special Immigration Appeals Commission, a body set up specifically for this purpose, the membership of which is determined by the Lord Chancellor.[30] Appeals made under this Act are subject to their own procedure rules: the Special Immigration Appeals Commission (Procedure) Rules 2003.[31]

NIAA 2002 and Procedure Rules

8.13   There is a two-tier system of appeals:[32] initially to an adjudicator (sitting at one of the regional centres located throughout the country);[33] and thereafter on a point of law to the Immigration Appeal Tribunal

---

27   SI No 652.

28   SI No 2244.

29   SI No 801. Under these rules, applicable to decisions made on or after 10 April 2003, if the appellant has been detained, and such detention continues after service of the decision notice, any appeal he or she may bring must be processed more quickly than usual.

30   Special Immigration Appeals Commission Act 1997 s2 and Sch 1. The Commission is made up of at least one judge or former judge who has held 'high judicial office' within the meaning of the Appellate Jurisdiction Act 1876 (ie, High Court or above); and at least one former or current chief adjudicator or member of the Immigration Appeal Tribunal. Customarily, there is a third member of any panel who is usually a high-ranking (or former) civil servant. The Lord Chancellor is now the Secretary of State for Constitutional Affairs.

31   SI No 1034.

32   This structure is not applicable in national security or public good cases, see above, n 30.

33   NIAA 2002 ss82–83. Note that by s81 of this Act, a new role of Deputy Regional Adjudicator is added to the existing roles of Chief Adjudicator, Deputy Chief Adjudicator and Regional Adjudicators within the Immigration Appellate Authority.

(consisting of a panel of up to three members).[34] Permission to appeal to the tribunal is required and is considered by the tribunal itself.[35] Until recently, judicial review was available where the tribunal refused permission, but the NIAA 2002 provides a more limited remedy of 'statutory review': such applications are heard by a single Administrative Court judge, on written submissions; the judge may affirm or reverse the decision of the tribunal not to grant permission and may, if the application had no merit, issue a certificate to that effect.[36]

8.14   The right to utilise these routes of appeal may not be available to an appellant who remains in the United Kingdom.[37] Generally, this will be so if the secretary of state removes, or proposes to remove, the appellant to a country which he has certified to be safe,[38] or has certified that the appellant's proposed human rights challenge is clearly unfounded.[39]

8.15   Following a final determination by the tribunal, there is a right of appeal to the Court of Appeal on a point of law.[40]

Appeals process

8.16   Nationality, Immigration and Asylum Act 2002 s82(1) confers a general right to appeal to an adjudicator against an 'immigration decision' which has been made against her or him. An 'immigration decision' is one of the following decisions:[41]

- refusal of leave to enter the United Kingdom;
- refusal of entry clearance;
- refusal of a certificate of entitlement under NIAA 2002 s10 (ie, right of abode);
- refusal to vary a person's leave to enter or remain in the United Kingdom if the result of the refusal is that the person has no leave to enter or remain;

---

34   See NIAA 2002 s101.
35   NIAA 2002 s101.
36   NIAA 2002 s101(3).
37   NIAA 2002 s93.
38   Immigration and Asylum Act 1999 ss11–12 and the Asylum (Designated Safe Third Countries) Order 2000 SI No 2245.
39   NIAA 2002 s93(2).
40   NIAA 2002 s103(1)(b).
41   NIAA 2002 s82(2).

- variation of a person's leave to enter or remain in the United Kingdom if when the variation takes effect the person has no leave to enter or remain;
- revocation, under NIAA 2002 s76, of indefinite leave to enter or remain in the United Kingdom;
- a decision that a person is to be removed from the United Kingdom by way of directions under Immigration and Asylum Act 1999 s10(1)(a), (b) or (c) (removal of a person unlawfully in the United Kingdom);
- a decision that an illegal entrant is to be removed from the United Kingdom by way of directions under Immigration Act 1971 Sch 2 paras 8–10;
- a decision that a person is to be removed from the United Kingdom by way of directions given by virtue of Immigration Act 1971 Sch 2 para 10A (family);
- a decision to make a deportation order under Immigration Act 1971 s5(1); and
- a refusal to revoke a deportation order under Immigration Act 1971 s5(2).

8.17 Where a person has made an asylum claim and his claim has been rejected by the secretary of state but he or she has been granted leave to enter or remain in the UK for a period of more than one year, he or she may appeal to the adjudicator against the rejection of his or her asylum claim.[42]

8.18 An appeal to the adjudicator must be brought on one or more of the statutory grounds and on a 'point of law',[43] although where the applicant appeals from outside the UK against her or his removal from the UK, he or she has restricted grounds for doing so.[44] The general (ie, not restricted) grounds for appeal are as follows:[45]

- that the decision is not in accordance with immigration rules;
- that the decision is unlawful by virtue of Race Relations Act 1976 s19B (discrimination by public authorities);

---

42 NIAA 2002 s83.
43 NIAA 2002 s101.
44 NIAA 2002 s95, which removes the right to appeal under s82(1) on the ground provided by s84(1)(g), except in cases to which s94(9) applies (removals to a country, of which the person removed is not a national, certified by the secretary of state (NIAA 2002 s94(7)) as a country where there is no reason to suspect that the person's Convention rights will not be respected.
45 NIAA 2002 s84.

- that the decision is unlawful under Human Rights Act 1998 s6 as being incompatible with the appellant's Convention rights;
- that the appellant is a European Economic Area national or a member of the family of an EEA national and the decision breaches the appellant's rights under the Community Treaties in respect of entry to or residence in the United Kingdom;
- that the decision is otherwise not in accordance with the law;
- that the person taking the decision should have exercised differently a discretion conferred by immigration rules;
- that removal of the appellant from the United Kingdom in consequence of the immigration decision would breach the United Kingdom's obligations under the Refugee Convention or would be unlawful under Human Rights Act 1998 s6 as being incompatible with the appellant's Convention rights.

8.19 On an appeal, the adjudicator must treat the appeal against a decision 'as including an appeal against any decision in respect of which an appellant has a right of appeal'.[46] The adjudicator may, therefore, have to consider the legality of a different decision (or a number of different decisions) other than that against which the appeal on its face is brought.[47] Moreover, 'an adjudicator may consider evidence about any matter which he thinks relevant to the substance of the decision, including evidence which concerns a matter arising after the date of the decision'.[48]

8.20 The secretary of state can grant a certificate that a particular appeal is finally determined.[49] The effect of such a certificate is to prevent any further appeal proceedings.[50] Similarly, the secretary of state has wide powers to prevent appeals being heard where the asylum claim is certified as 'clearly unfounded',[51] or where he considers that an applicant could – or should – have dealt with the issue in an earlier appeal.[52]

---

46 NIAA 2002 s85(1).
47 Though it must still, of course, be an immigration decision within NIAA 2002 s82(2).
48 NIAA 2002 s85(4). This provision overturns the principle set out in *R v Immigration Appeal Tribunal ex p Kotecha* [1983] 1 WLR 487, under which an appeal was not considered an extension of the original decision-making process but rather a method for enabling the original decision to be reviewed.
49 Immigration and Asylum Act 1999 s73.
50 Immigration and Asylum Act 1999 s58(6) and (7).
51 Nationality, Immigration and Asylum Act (NIAA) 2002 s94.
52 NIAA 2002 s96.

Judicial review and immigration and asylum law

Appeal or judicial review

8.21   Decisions of the secretary of state, immigration officers, and the Immigration Appeal Tribunal[53] may be subject to judicial review in the High Court on the usual principles of administrative law. In general, however, judicial review will not be an appropriate remedy where a statutory right of appeal exists,[54] and therefore – save in exceptional circumstances – the courts will require the statutory appeal to be pursued and will not entertain a judicial review claim.

8.22   It is to be noted that the right of appeal to the tribunal (and thence to the Court of Appeal) may be limited by the scope of the provision under which the appeal is brought. In other words, if the tribunal is limited by statute to considering the effect of a power rather than its exercise, any challenge to the exercise of the power will only be justiciable by way of judicial review.[55] Similarly, where the basis of challenge is alleged procedural impropriety or unfairness the most appropriate forum for the determination of such allegations will be judicial review.[56]

8.23   An appeal to the Court of Appeal from the tribunal is only available, and so only operates as an alternative remedy preventing recourse to judicial review, where the tribunal has made a final determination, thus it would seem that, for example, a ruling on a preliminary matter may be challenged by way of judicial review. More significantly, where a person is removed from the UK, other than to a country certified as 'safe' by the secretary of state – with the result that the right of appeal is circumscribed – judicial review may provide the only remedy.[57] For the same essential reason, a decision by the secretary of state to remove an asylum-seeker to a third country pending determination of his application may also be justiciable by way of judicial review.[58]

---

53   But not, now, refusing permission to appeal, where the only remedy is 'statutory review' under CPR Part 54 section II.

54   *R v Secretary of State for the Home Department ex p Swati* [1986] 1 WLR 477, CA.

55   See *R v Secretary of State for the Home Department ex p Oladehinde* [1991] 1 AC 254; *R v Secretary of State for the Home Department ex p Malhi* [1992] 2 All ER 357.

56   *Macharia v Immigration Appeal Tribunal* [2000] INLR 156.

57   See Nationality, Immigration and Asylum Act 2002 ss95, and note 44 above.

58   See NIAA 2002 ss93–94.

8.24   Judicial review of immigration and asylum decisions can arise in the following situations:

- where there is no statutory right of appeal;
- where leave to appeal is not granted (but this is now a restricted 'statutory review');[59]
- where the applicant has not exhausted his statutory rights of appeal but 'exceptional circumstances' exist to justify granting permission to apply for judicial review;[60]
- to challenge the Immigration Rules themselves.[61]

8.25   In *Doorga v Secretary of State for the Home Department*,[62] the court held, following *Swati*, that the proper remedy was to exercise the statutory right of appeal even if this caused hardship for the appellant. In *Grazales v Secretary of State for the Home Department*,[63] the Court of Appeal held that to take a case out of the usual rule laid down in *Swati* and *Doorga*, required 'exceptional circumstances' the alleged nature of which would be germane to the decision whether or not the applicant ought to be required to utilise the statutory right of appeal. The applicant, in *Grazales*, had not shown any danger or practical obstacle to pursuing his appeal in the usual way (out-of-country) and, accordingly, no exceptional circumstances were shown.[64]

8.26   It seems that political pressures preventing an effective out-of-country right of appeal would constitute exceptional circumstances. In *R v Chief Immigration Officer, Gatwick Airport ex p Kharrazi*,[65] the applicant was a student from Iran who contended successfully that the war in Iran would, as a matter of practicality, prevent him from appealing (out-of-country) under Immigration Act 1971 s13. Personal and professional inconvenience will not, however, constitute exceptional circumstances: *R v Secretary of State for the Home Department ex p Salamat*.[66]

---

59 See paras 18.148–18.154 below.
60 Judicial review of extra-statutory functions of the secretary of state in considering requests to apply a discretion outside the Immigration Rules is rare: Supperstone and O'Dempsey, *Halsbury's Laws of England* (Vol 4(2), para 140).
61 *R v Immigration Appeal Tribunal ex p Manshoora Begum* [1986] Imm AR 385.
62 [1990] Imm AR 98.
63 [1990] Imm AR 505, CA.
64 The court distinguished *R v Chief Immigration Officer ex p Kharrazi* [1980] 3 All ER 573.
65 [1980] 3 All ER 573.
66 [1993] Imm AR 239.

Even if the Immigration Officer has erred in not considering all the relevant rules, the proper course following *Swati* is to appeal: *R v Secretary of State for the Home Department ex p Abeywickrema*.[67]

8.27   Exceptional circumstances will rarely be established. In *R v Secretary of State for the Home Department ex p Pulgarin*,[68] for example, it was argued that it would be exceedingly inconvenient for the applicant (a Columbian student) to return to Columbia to exercise his right of appeal as this would interrupt his academic career and would create great difficulties with his children. The court, however, held that no exceptional circumstances justifying an application for judicial review had been shown.

8.28   In *Ryoo v Secretary of State for the Home Department*,[69] the Court of Appeal held that there was no authority for the proposition that an alternative remedy had to be shown to be as convenient and effective as judicial review for permission to be refused. Russell LJ stated:[70]

> For my part I see no support for this proposition in principle or upon authority. Of course it would not be convenient for this applicant to pursue her remedy before an adjudicator outside the United Kingdom, and of course it would be more convenient for her to remain in the United Kingdom should she be permitted to do so to pursue an application for judicial review. But to permit her to take this course would, in my judgment, fly in the face of section 13(3) of the Immigration Act and all that has been said in *Swati* and other cases.

Support

8.29   Judicial review retains a major role in settling disputes as to the support to be afforded to those subject to immigration control. Most significantly, there is a significant degree of friction between the provision of support to asylum-seekers through the National Asylum Support Service and the duties imposed on local authorities to provide assistance to the destitute.[71]

8.30   The issue of support is likely to continue to develop as a source for judicial review following the introduction of new powers to withdraw

---

67   [1991] Imm AR 535, DC.
68   [1992] Imm AR 96, QBD.
69   [1992] Imm AR 59, CA.
70   [1992] Imm AR 59 at 66–67.
71   See *R (Westminster CC) v Secretary of State for the Home Department* [2002] UKHL 38; [2002] HLR 58; (2002) 5 CCLR 511, HL; *R (Mani) v Lambeth LBC* [2003] EWCA Civ 836; (2003) 6 CCLR 376.

support from certain classes of person.[72] The categories of person exempt from support are defined in complex terms and subject to exceptions, both prescribed in the Nationality, Immigration and Asylum Act 2002 itself and to be prescribed by the secretary of state in regulations. Such regulations 'may confer a discretion on the secretary of state'.[73] The introduction of a discretion concerning the exemption from withdrawal of support may well give rise to claims for judicial review on the grounds of reasonableness and rationality. Statutory exemptions exist where the provision of support is necessary to avoid a breach of either European Convention rights or EU rights.[74] This may lead to challenges regarding the circumstances in which such rights are breached[75] and the balance to be struck between those rights and the rights of the state.

8.31 Where an unaccompanied child enters the UK and claims asylum, local social services authorities will fall under a duty to provide for her or him as a child in need in their area.[76] Should the child turn 18 years old prior to a decision on the asylum claim, he or she would usually fall under the remit of the National Asylum Support Scheme (NASS). The Secretary of State for Health has, however, issued mandatory guidance[77] under Local Authority Social Services Act 1970 s7 requiring local authorities to continue to provide services, including accommodation,[78] for most children who had been 'looked after' prior to their eighteenth birthday, on the basis that dispersal of such children should

---

72 Nationality, Immigration and Asylum Act 2002 ss54–55 and Sch 3.

73 NIAA 2002 Sch 3, para 2(2).

74 NIAA 2002 Sch 3, para 2(3).

75 The question as to whether failure to support an asylum-seeker amounted to a violation of art 3 was considered in *R (Q) v Secretary of State for the Home Department* [2003] EWCA Civ 364; [2003] 2 All ER 905. Similarly, the lack of a concept of European Citizenship in the EU Treaties means that the fundamental freedoms on which the EU is built – notably in this context free movement of workers – remains (at least technically) parasitic on the concept of work, rather than being a free-standing right to move within the EU (see, Case C–184/99 *Grzelczyk* [2001] ECR I–6193; Case 48/75 *Royer* [1976] ECR 497; Case 413/99 *Bambast v Secretary of State for the Home Department* (2002) 17 September (unreported); Case 109/01 *Secretary of State for the Home Department v Akrich* (2003) 23 September (unreported)).

76 Children Act 1989 Part III.

77 Children (Leaving Care) Act 2000 Regulations and Guidance.

78 Under Children Act 1989 ss23C and 24, and Sch 2 para 19B as amended by the Children (Leaving Care) Act 2000. See also the Children (Leaving Care) (England) Regulations 2000 SI No 2878, especially reg 3. Further, see *R (Berhe) v Hillingdon LBC* [2003] EWHC 2075 Admin; (2003) *Times* 22 September.

not take place. Where possible, the accommodation provided should be the same accommodation that the child was living in prior to her or his eighteenth birthday. NASS are expected to pay for the accommodation identified by the local authority.[79]

---

79 Secretary of State for Health's Guidance, chapter 2, paras 2–11, see n 77 above.

Judicial review and housing law

continued overleaf

9.43   **Impermissible challenges**

9.43   Secure, introductory and demoted tenancies

9.45   Houses in multiple occupation

Introduction

9.1 The duty to provide public housing has historically fallen principally on local authorities. Although there is now a range of social landlords providing such accommodation, local authorities still have a central role to play in this area, whether by exercising specific housing functions (eg, those contained in the Housing Acts 1985 and 1996) or housing-related social services functions (eg, under the Children Act 1989 and the National Assistance Act 1948).[1]

9.2 The scope for judicial review of decisions made in exercise of these functions has been significantly reduced by the introduction of a more extensive system of reviews and appeals (although the introduction of the Human Rights Act 1998 led to a considerable number of claims on the basis of alleged breaches of the right, under article 8 of the European Convention on Human Rights (the Convention), to respect for the home, and/or the right, under article 6 of the Convention, to a fair hearing.)[2]

Homelessness

9.3 One of the principal housing duties imposed upon local authorities is the duty to provide assistance to homeless people.[3] In essence, where a person applies to an authority as homeless, the authority is under a duty to conduct inquiries into whether he or she is eligible for assistance, homeless or threatened with homelessness, in priority need and not homeless intentionally. If, following inquiries, the authority is satisfied that the applicant fulfils those requirements, it comes under

---

1 For a general overview of housing law, reference should be made to Arden and Hunter, *Manual of Housing Law* (7th edn, Sweet & Maxwell, 2003).

2 Notable in this regard was *R v Bracknell Forest BC ex p McLellan* [2001] EWCA Civ 1510; (2001) 33 HLR 86, where the claimant sought judicial review on the ground that the introductory tenancy scheme established under Housing Act 1996 Part V (which permits an authority to regain possession of a property without the need to prove grounds for possession) deprived her of the right to a fair trial. The Court of Appeal dismissed the claim on the ground that a decision to evict was susceptible to judicial review on public law grounds and that the availability of judicial review provided an adequate remedy to ensure compliance with article 6 of the Convention.

3 Housing Act 1996 Part VII (as amended). It is not possible in this work to give a detailed explanation of the law governing homeless applications or homelessness in general – a detailed and complex area of law. Reference should be made in particular to Arden and Hunter, *Homelessness and Allocations* (Revised 6th edn, Legal Action Group, 2003).

a duty to secure that accommodation becomes available for the applicant and anyone who might reasonably be expected to live with her or him.

9.4   The role of judicial review in the context of homelessness decision-making has been reduced significantly by the introduction of a procedure for the review of and appeal against such decisions.[4] A housing applicant may seek an internal review of most decisions, including those regarding what, if any, duty is owed and/or the suitability of accommodation offered[5] and, thereafter, may appeal to the county court on a point of law.[6] The existence of this alternative remedy in relation to most homelessness decisions renders judicial review as a means of challenging an authority's actions, available only in very limited situations.

Provision for accepting applications

9.5   Authorities must make reasonable provision for receiving applications from the homeless (although they may not require an application to take any particular form)[7] and failure to do so may give rise to a claim for judicial review on the ground that the arrangements are not reasonable.[8] Moreover, an authority cannot refuse to consider an application simply on the basis that the claimant does not live in its area or have a local connection with that area – such considerations can only be taken into account in the course of determining the application.[9] A refusal to consider an application, or an abnormal delay in considering an application is an issue that may be resolved on judicial review.

9.6   A frequent reason for judicial review claims to be brought in relation to homelessness functions relates to the material submitted in support of the application; although there is no duty on the local authority to reconsider in the light of additional information in support

---

4 Housing Act 1996 ss202–204A.

5 Housing Act 1996 s202.

6 Housing Act 1996 s204 – the county court's jurisdiction in this regard is akin to the High Court's jurisdiction on judicial review and therefore a 'point of law' includes not only matters of legal interpretation but also the full range of issues akin to those which would otherwise be the subject of judicial review: *Nipa Begum v Tower Hamlets LBC* [2000] 1 WLR 361; (2000) 32 HLR 445, CA.

7 *R v Chiltern DC ex p Roberts* (1991) 23 HLR 387, QBD; see also *R v Northavon DC ex p Palmer* (1994) 26 HLR 572, QBD.

8 *R v Camden LBC ex p Gillan* (1988) 21 HLR 114, QBD.

9 Although it is best practice for a claimant to apply to the local authority in which he or she lives – see *Hackney LBC v Sareen* [2003] HLR 54, CA.

of an application, where that information amounts to a material change in circumstances such a duty does arise.[10] Similarly, if the authority determines the application, there is no duty to reconsider the decision on the basis of fresh information, save where that information amounts to a material change in circumstances since the original application.[11]

Enquiries

9.7　There are certain procedural rules and principles that must be followed when making enquiries; these broadly reflect the principles of procedural fairness that must be adopted by any person or body exercising statutory decision-making powers.[12] Accordingly, an authority is obliged to make the necessary enquiries and to pursue them rigorously and fairly;[13] an applicant is entitled to an opportunity to explain those matters which the authority considers to be adverse to his or her case;[14] where there is uncertainty the issue must be resolved in the applicant's favour;[15] and, inquiries must be current – and relate to the facts – as at the date of the decision.[16] Although failure to comply with these principles has previously given rise to grounds for judicial review,[17] such matters are more likely now to lead to a request for a review, and thereafter an appeal to the county court. This is not to exclude the possibility of judicial review where the authority fundamentally fails to conduct sufficient inquiries, to the point where they can be said to have failed to complete a lawful assessment.[18]

10　*R v Tower Hamlets LBC ex p Nadia Saber* (1992) 24 HLR 611, QBD.

11　*R v Southwark LBC ex p Campisi* (1998) 31 HLR 560, CA. There may, of course, be a requirement to review the decision (Housing Act 1996 s202).

12　See *Ridge v Baldwin* [1964] AC 40, HL.

13　Although, there is no duty to conduct 'CID type' inquiries: *Lally v Kensington and Chelsea RLBC* (1980) *Times* 27 March, ChD.

14　*R v Hackney LBC ex p Decordova* (1994) 27 HLR 108, QBD; *R (Begum) v Tower Hamlets LBC* [2002] EWHC 633 (Admin), [2003] HLR 8, QBD.

15　*R v Thurrock BC ex p Williams* (1981) 1 HLR 129, QBD.

16　*Mohammed v Hammersmith and Fulham LBC* [2001] UKHL 57; [2002] 1 AC 547.

17　See, for example, *R v Tynedale DC ex p McCabe* (1991) 24 HLR 385, QBD (decision quashed because the authority failed to direct their attention to the correct inquiries); *R v Brent LBC ex p Babalola* (1995) 28 HLR 196, QBD (decision quashed because the authority required the applicant to substantiate her allegations of neighbour nuisance, rather than investigating the matter themselves).

18　*R (Begum) v Tower Hamlets LBC* [2002] EWHC 633 (Admin); [2002] HLR 8, QBD.

Interim accommodation

9.8 Pending determination of the inquiries necessary to determine what, if any, duty is owed, an authority must – if it believes or has reason to believe that the applicant may be homeless, eligible for assistance and in priority need – secure that accommodation is made available for her or his occupation.[19] Such accommodation must be suitable.[20] In securing accommodation for the applicant, the authority must therefore have regard to what is suitable and not simply what is available.[21] The suitability of accommodation is a matter that used frequently to be considered in judicial review proceedings but is now a matter for review and appeal to the county court. Whatever the forum, a wide discretion as to suitability is afforded to authorities.[22]

Decision on application

9.9 Similarly, the decision made by the authority is properly challenged by way of a request for a review under Housing Act 1996 s202, whether the challenge concerns the substance of the decision (ie, whether the applicant was eligible, homeless, in priority need and not intentionally homeless) or the procedure followed in making it (including claims that the authority gave insufficient reasons for their decision or that the decision-making process was flawed and/or unfair).[23] Where an authority receives a request for a review but fails to make a decision on review within the statutory time-frame[24] the appeal may be brought against the original decision: judicial review therefore is still inappropriate.[25]

---

19 Housing Act 1996 s188(1).

20 Housing Act 1996 ss205 and 206(1). See also *R v Ealing LBC ex p Surdonja* (1998) 31 HLR 686, QBD.

21 *R v Newham LBC ex p Ojuri (No 3)* (1998) 31 HLR 452, QBD.

22 But see, eg, *R v Brent LBC ex p Omar* (1991) 23 HLR 446, QBD for a suitable challenge that succeeded.

23 *R v Merton LBC ex p Sembi* (1999) 32 HLR 439, QBD.

24 The decision must be made within eight weeks of receipt of the request – see Housing Act 1996 s203(1) and (7) and the Allocation of Housing and Homelessness (Review Procedures) Regulations 1999 SI No 71.

25 Similarly, an authority's refusal to exercise its discretion to undertake a further, non-statutory review, is a matter for challenge by way of appeal to the county court and not on judicial review: *R v Westminster CC ex p Ellioua* (1998) 31 HLR 440, CA.

The 'full' housing duty: suitability

9.10 Where an authority is under a duty to secure that accommodation becomes available for the applicant, that accommodation must be 'suitable'. The authority is therefore required to have regard to the applicant's circumstances and those of her or his family,[26] including their needs with regard to work, education and health.[27] Although accommodation outside of an authority's area may be suitable[28] the decision to offer such accommodation must be made rationally and with regard to all the circumstances: in *R (Yumsak) v Enfield LBC*[29] the claimant successfully argued that the decision to place her in bed and breakfast accommodation outside the authority's area was irrational because the authority knew the social, medical and educational needs of her and her family would best be met in their area and because the authority had failed to demonstrate that there was no suitable accommodation available in their area.

9.11 Compliance with a full housing duty may not be deferred.[30] Accordingly, where a duty has been accepted but no progress made towards its fulfilment, (ie, no accommodation identified or offered) it may be possible to bring judicial review proceedings to compel the performance of the duty, although the court will take account of the realities of the situation, including the length of time that has elapsed since the acceptance of the duty, and will not order a local authority to do the impossible.[31]

9.12 Local authorities with limited housing stock may continue to accommodate successful applicants in interim bed and breakfast accommodation, pending the availability of temporary or permanent accommodation.[32] As noted above, there are various considerations to which an authority must have regard when determining suitability and it is for the authority to determine – on the date on which the offer is made[33] – what is suitable for the applicant, having regard to all

---

26 *R v Haringey LBC ex p Karaman* (1996) 29 HLR 366, QBD.

27 *R v Newham LBC ex p Sacupima* (2000) 33 HLR 1, QBD; *R v Newham LBC ex p Ojuri (No 3)* (1998) 31 HLR 452, QBD.

28 *R v Newham LBC ex p Sacupima* (2000) 33 HLR 2, CA.

29 [2002] EWHC 280; [2003] HLR 1.

30 *R v Newham LBC ex p Begum* (1999) 32 HLR 808, QBD.

31 (1999) 32 HLR 808 at 815–816 per Collins J.

32 They are, however, only permitted to do so for a limited period and must look for alternative ways to discharge their duties: *R (Khan) v Newham LBC* [2001] EWHC Admin 589.

33 *R v Lambeth LBC ex p Ekpo-Wedderman* (1998) 31 HLR 498, QBD.

of the applicant's circumstances.[34] An applicant who is dissatisfied with the suitability of accommodation may appeal against the suitability of an offer, whether or not he or she accepts the offer.[35]

Review and appeal

9.13   Following the introduction of the Human Rights Act 1998, questions arose as to whether the review and appeals procedure contained in the Housing Act 1996 was sufficient to afford an applicant adequate access to an independent and impartial tribunal in order to comply with the requirements of article 6 of the Convention. In *Adan v Newham LBC*,[36] the Court of Appeal commented (obiter) that the procedure may not be article 6 compliant, on the basis that the appeal to the county court under Housing Act 1996 s204 is, in effect, equivalent to a claim for judicial review in that the county court may only interfere with the local authority's decision on judicial review principles and may not conduct a full merits appeal.[37] This view was, however, subsequently rejected in *Begum v Tower Hamlets LBC*.[38] The House of Lords held that, although the review process was not a review by an

---

34   *R v Wycombe DC ex p Hazeltine* (1992) 25 HLR 68, CA. There is guidance on what amounts to suitable accommodation – Homelessness (Suitability of Accommodation) Order 1996 SI No 3204 – but the final decision is a composite assessment of all relevant factors: *R v Lewisham LBC ex p Dolan* (1992) 25 HLR 68, QBD.

35   See Housing Act 1996 s202 as amended by Homelessness Act 2002 s8(2). For examples of such challenges (brought under the old procedure by way of judicial review) see *R v Tower Hamlets LBC ex p Subhan* (1992) 24 HLR 541, QBD – authority failing to consider racial harassment problems on the estate in which the applicant was to be housed; *R v Haringey LBC ex p Karaman* (1996) 29 HLR 366, QBD – failure to consider the proximity of the accommodation to the applicant's estranged husband, who had previously been violent towards her; *R v Tower Hamlets LBC ex p Kaur, Ali et al* (1994) 26 HLR 597, QBD – affordability of accommodation.

36   [2001] EWCA Civ 1916; [2002] 1 WLR 2120; [2002] HLR 28.

37   *Nipa Begum v Tower Hamlets LBC* [2000] 1 WLR 306, CA. This reflects the issue in *Runa Begum v Tower Hamlets LBC* [2003] UKHL 5; [2003] 2 AC 430, ie, whether a court exercising a supervisory jurisdiction could constitute a court of full jurisdiction to provide the necessary safeguards to comply with article 6 of the Convention – compare *R (Alconbury Developments Ltd) v Secretary of State for the Environment, Transport and the Regions* [2001] UKHL 23; [2003] 2 AC 295, which raised similar issues in the planning context and was applied in *Runa Begum*.

38   [2003] UKHL 5; [2003] 2 AC 430.

independent and impartial person, the right of appeal to the county court was an appeal to a court of full jurisdiction.[39]

Accommodation pending review or appeal

9.14   An issue which has frequently given rise to judicial review is the provision of accommodation pending review and/or appeal.[40] The local authority has a discretion to provide such accommodation and so must consider whether to exercise that discretion. When considering this issue, the authority must take account of three matters which will always be relevant: the merits of the applicant's case that the decision under review/on appeal was flawed; whether there exists any new material that might well have affected the decision; and the applicant's personal circumstances.[41]

9.15   There is now a distinction to be drawn between the appropriate methods of challenging decisions not to provide interim accommodation pending a review under Housing Act 1996 s202, and decisions not to do so pending appeal under Housing Act 1996 s204. Where the decision has been taken pending an appeal, there is now a statutory right of appeal to the county court, introduced by the Homelessness Act 2002.[42] The existence of this right will preclude the availability of judicial review to require accommodation pending an appeal.[43] There is still no right of appeal, however, in relation to refusals of accommodation pending a section 202 review, and any challenge can only be brought by way of judicial review.[44]

---

39   The requirements of article 6 are discussed further in chapter 6 at paras 6.115–6.133 above.

40   The statutory duty to provide accommodation pending inquiries ends when the applicant is notified of the outcome of her or his decision – Housing Act 1996 s188(3).

41   *R v Camden LBC ex p Mohammed* (1997) 30 HLR 315, QBD; *R v Newham LBC ex p Lumley* (2000) 33 HLR 11. In *R v Brighton and Hove Council ex p Nacion* (1999) 31 HLR 1095, CA, the Court of Appeal expressly approved the application of this test in relation to accommodation pending appeal.

42   Inserting a new section 204A into the Housing Act 1996.

43   The same approach as was identified in *Mohammed* (1997) 30 HLR 315; *Lumley* (2000) 33 HLR 11; and *Nacion* (1999) 31 HLR 1095, will be applied on a statutory appeal: *Francis v Kensington and Chelsea RLBC* [2003] 2 All ER 1052.

44   See the cases referred to at notes 41 and 43 above.

Allocations

9.16   The allocation of housing accommodation is governed by Housing Act 1996 Part VI.[45] An authority must have a scheme for determining priorities in the allocation of their housing stock and may not allocate other than in accordance with that scheme.[46] Although the scheme must be framed to secure that a reasonable preference is given to persons with specified housing needs (eg, those with a medical or a welfare need for accommodation),[47] authorities have a wide discretion regarding the rules and priorities that may be included within their scheme.[48] An authority is obliged, however, to make a composite assessment where an applicant falls within more than one category of need.[49]

9.17   Accommodation may only be allocated, however, to 'eligible persons' as defined in Housing Act 1996 Part VI – eligibility may depend on immigration status and may be determined by reference to any applicant's behaviour: an authority may decide to treat someone as ineligible if he or she, or a member of his or her household, has been guilty of unacceptable behaviour.[50]

9.18   The scope for judicial review in relation to the allocation of accommodation extends, primarily, to the legality of the allocation scheme adopted by the authority, the application of the scheme to the claimant's particular circumstances and the assessment of the claimant's housing needs carried out by the authority. In *R (A) v Lambeth LBC; R (Lindsay) v Lambeth LBC*,[51] the Court of Appeal upheld a finding by the High Court that the authority's allocation scheme was unlawful as its structure failed to afford applicants the proper preferences required by statute.[52] In *R (Giles) v Fareham BC*,[53] the claimant sought to challenge

---

45   As amended by the Homelessness Act 2002.

46   Housing Act 1996 s167(1).

47   Housing Act 1996 s167(2). Though the authority is entitled to depress the preference that would otherwise have been given by reference to factors such as previous rent arrears: *R v Wolverhampton MBC ex p Watters* (1997) 29 HLR 931, CA.

48   Housing Act 1996 s167(5) and (6) and see *R (Giles) v Fareham BC* [2002] EWHC 2951 (Admin); [2003] HLR 36.

49   *R v Islington LBC ex p Reilly and Mannix* (1998) 31 HLR 651, QBD; *R v Westminster CC ex p Al-Khorsan* [2001] HLR 6, QBD; *R v Tower Hamlets LBC ex p Uddin* (1999) 32 HLR 391, QBD.

50   That is behaviour that would entitle an authority to possession under Housing Act 1985 grounds 1 to 7: Housing Act 1996 s160A.

51   [2002] EWCA Civ 1084; [2002] HLR 57.

52   [2002] EWCA Civ 1084.

53   [2002] EWHC 2951 (Admin); [2003] HLR 36.

a rule within the authority's allocation scheme, by which the authority could defer allocations of accommodation if the applicant had committed acts of anti-social behaviour in previous accommodation. The court held that authorities had a wide discretion in framing their allocation schemes, which discretion extended to deferring offers of accommodation where the applicant had previously committed acts of anti-social behaviour.[54]

9.19   In *R (Begum) v Tower Hamlets LBC*,[55] the claimant sought a declaration compelling the authority to allocate her a specific property. The court held that an allocation scheme must be applied at the date on which accommodation is allocated and that therefore it was only in exceptional circumstances, if at all, that a property may be highlighted or ear-marked for a particular applicant in advance.

9.20   The introduction of the concept of eligibility, and the power to find applicants ineligible on the basis of anti-social behaviour, are likely to lead to challenges to decisions about eligibility. In that regard, authorities will need to ensure that the rules contained with their scheme are lawful and sufficiently flexible to permit a reasonable degree of discretion in the manner in which they are applied. The procedure to be followed in making findings that affect eligibility, moreover, must conform with the general public law concepts of rationality, reasonableness and fairness.

Other duties to provide housing

Children Act 1989

9.21   Local authorities' social services departments are under a duty to provide services, which can include accommodation, to children in need in their area.[56]

9.22   The principal duties are contained in Children Act (CA) 1989 s17 – which confers a general duty to safeguard and promote the welfare of children in their area – and section 20 – which imposes a specific duty to accommodate a child who appears to require accommodation for certain specified reasons, including that her or his carer has been

---

54   It should be noted, however, that authorities may not adopt rigid policies or rules that have the effect of excluding an applicant's individual circumstances from consideration: *R v Canterbury CC ex p Gillespie* (1986) 19 HLR 7, QBD.

55   [2002] EWHC 633 (Admin); [2003] HLR 8.

56   Children Act 1989 s20.

prevented from providing her or him with suitable accommodation. A failure to comply with these provisions – or to exercise the powers and duties contained within them – may give rise to a claim for a judicial review.[57]

9.23   There has been a number of recent judicial review claims focusing on the scope of the duties imposed by the CA 1989. In *R (G) v Barnet LBC*,[58] the claimant sought judicial review of the authority's decision to discharge their duty under CA 1989 s17 by funding the costs of returning the claimant and her son to their country of origin. The Court of Appeal held that while the duty imposed by CA 1989 s17 included a power to accommodate the family of a child in need, nevertheless it could properly be discharged by providing financial assistance to return the child and her or his family to their country of origin, rather than through the provision of accommodation.

9.24   In *R (A) v Lambeth LBC*,[59] the authority assessed the needs of the claimant's children under CA 1989 s17 and concluded that they had a need for accommodation. The claimant sought judicial review to compel the authority to discharge their duty under section 17 and provide accommodation for her and her children. At first instance, the judge held that section 17(1) created only a target duty, not giving rise to any specific rights owed to or enforceable by individual children. Accordingly, a refusal by an authority to provide accommodation was not reviewable on the basis of a failure to comply with the section 17 duty, but only potentially on a *Wednesbury* basis.[60]

9.25   The Court of Appeal's decision in that case, holding that the section 17 duties were not directed towards – and did not permit – the provision of accommodation,[61] was subsequently held to be per incuriam by a differently constituted Court of Appeal in *R (W) v Lambeth LBC*.[62] The Court of Appeal's decision, as refined by *W* was upheld in the House of Lords at [2003] UKHL 57. In *W*, the Court of Appeal held that CA 1989 s17 did confer a power to provide a child and his or her family with accommodation, but that the exercise of that power could lawfully be

---

57   This appears to be so notwithstanding the right under CA 1989 s84 to apply to the secretary of state to exercise his or her default powers under the Act: *R v Brent LBC ex p Sawyers* [1994] 1 FLR 203, CA.

58   [2001] EWCA Civ 540; (2001) 33 HLR 59; (2001) 4 CCLR 128.

59   (2001) 33 HLR 60, QBD; [2001] EWCA Civ 1624; [2002] HLR 13; (2001) 4 CCLR 486.

60   [2001] EWCA Civ 486 at [43].

61   See *R (J) v Enfield LBC* [2002] EWHC 432 (Admin); [2002] HLR 38; (2002) 5 CCLR 434.

62   [2002] EWCA Civ 613; [2002] HLR 41; (2002) 5 CCLR 203.

reserved for extreme cases. This raises the issue of what constitutes an extreme case and little guidance is to be derived from *W* itself save that, in that case, the court placed emphasis on the 'intelligible and adequate reasons' given by the authority for refusing to exercise the power. It would appear, therefore, and as suggested in *A* at first instance, that challenges to the exercise of the section 17 discretions will focus on established public law principles concerning the adequacy and lawfulness of public law decision-making.

9.26   Children Act 1989 s17 has now been amended to confirm that the powers it confers are wide enough to encompass the provision of accommodation.[63]

National Assistance Act 1948

9.27   National Assistance Act 1948 s21 provides a 'last resort' for those in need of accommodation.[64] It confers a duty on local authorities to provide assistance to those 'in need of care and attention' that is not otherwise available to them.[65]

9.28   Section 21 may therefore be used to provide accommodation for elderly persons, either in local authority owned or private care homes.[66] Judicial review in respect of the exercise of this power may be either to the results of an assessment as to what, if any, needs the elderly person has[67] or to the continued discharge of the duty. In *R v Servite Houses and Wandsworth LBC ex p Goldsmith and Chatting,*[68] the claimants had been placed by the authority in a care home. The owners of the care home intended to close the home and relocate the residents. The claimants sought judicial review on the ground that the decision to close the home breached their legitimate expectation of a home for life. The judgment focused on whether the care-home owner – as a private landlord – was a public body and therefore susceptible to judicial

---

63   See Adoption and Children Act 2002 s16(1), which has amended Children Act 1989 s17(6).

64   *R v Wandsworth LBC ex p O, R v Leicester CC ex p Bhikha* [2000] 1 WLR 2539; (2000) 33 HLR 39; (2000) 3 CCLR 237,CA.

65   See Department of Health Circular: LAC (93)10, App 1.

66   In *R v Wandsworth LBC ex p Beckwith (No 1)* [1996] 1 WLR 60, HL, it was held that the duty imposed by National Assistance Act 1948 s21 could be discharged by entering into arrangements with other bodies.

67   Such assessments are conducted under the National Health Service and Community Care Act 1990 s47(1).

68   (2000) 33 HLR 35; (2000) 3 CCLR 325, QBD.

review: the court held that it was not.[69] This conclusion was reinforced by the Court of Appeal decision in R *(Heather) v Leonard Cheshire Foundation*,[70] although the court confirmed in the latter case that it was not inappropriate to have pursued the action by means of a judicial review claim.[71]

9.29   Persons not entitled to receive certain state benefits[72] are expressly excluded from the ambit of the duty under National Assistance Act 1948 s21. The purpose of this exclusion is to prevent persons subject to immigration control, those who overstay in the UK after the expiration of their leave to remain here, and asylum-seekers[73] from obtaining assistance under the provision. Where an applicant is caught by the exclusion, he or she will only qualify for assistance under section 21 if her or his need for care and attention arises for some reason other than solely destitution: National Assistance Act 1948 s21(1A).[74]

9.30   Whether a local authority is obliged to discharge their duty under section 21 in such circumstances is largely a matter of fact and degree, regard being had to the situation of the applicant and whether his need for care and attention arises solely from destitution.[75] Where a local authority receives an application for assistance under section 21, it is a matter for it to conduct the necessary assessments and to determine – in the circumstances – whether the applicant's destitution is made more acute by some other factor. Such a decision will be susceptible to judicial review.

---

69 See also R v North and East Devon Health Authority ex p Coughlan [2001] QB 213; (1999) 2 CCLR 285, CA, and contrast R *(Heather and others) v Leonard Cheshire Foundation* [2002] EWCA Civ 366; [2002] 2 All ER 936; [2002] HLR 49; (2002) 5 CCLR 317.

70 [2002] EWCA Civ 366; [2002] 2 All ER 936; [2002] HLR 49; (2002) 5 CCLR 317.

71 See paras 3.18–3.30 above for further consideration of this issue.

72 The prohibition applies to 'a person to whom section 115 of the Immigration and Asylum Act 1999 apples' – in essence this excludes asylum-seekers and those subject to immigration control.

73 Support for asylum-seekers is provided by the National Asylum Support Service: Immigration and Asylum Act 1999, see further chapter 8, paras 8.9–8.20.

74 See R v Wandsworth LBC ex p O, R v Leicester CC ex p Bhikha [2000] 1 WLR 2539 (2000) 33 HLR 39; (2000) 4 CCLR 237, CA.

75 'Destitution' is defined in Immigration and Asylum Act 1999 s95(3). The circumstances that will engage the duty under National Assistance Act 1948 s21 occur where destitution is made more acute by reason of age, illness or disability: Bhikha (above).

9.31 Accordingly, judicial review is often used as a remedy for those who are prima facie excluded from assistance under National Assistance Act 1948 s21 but seek to claim that their need for care and attention, although primarily arising from destitution, is made more acute by some other factor such as age, illness or disability. In *R v Wandsworth LBC ex p O, R v Leicester CC ex p Bhikha*,[76] both claimants had overstayed their leave to remain in the UK and sought to challenge the respective authorities' refusals to provide them with assistance under section 21 on the ground that they suffered from health problems. Allowing the appeal, Simon Brown LJ said:[77]

> Assistance under the 1948 Act is, it need hardly be emphasised, the last refuge for the destitute. If there are to be immigrant beggars on our streets, then let them at least not be old, ill or disabled.

9.32 Given that section 21 does not, therefore, completely exclude the provision of accommodation to those who prima facie are excluded, claims are often brought by asylum-seekers – or by local authorities – for a declaration on whether the local authority or the National Asylum Support Service (NASS) falls under a duty to provide accommodation and/or assistance.[78]

Grants

General

9.33 Local housing authorities have powers and duties to provide grants for home improvements. The award of these grants is now discretionary, save for disabled facilities grants which are mandatory where certain, prescribed conditions are met.[79] Authorities are required to prepare a grants policy – which must be prepared in accordance with guidance issued by the secretary of state – and are only able to award grants in accordance with that policy.[80] This is conceptually similar to

76 [2000] 1 WLR 2539; (2000) 33 HLR 39; (2000) 3 CLR 237, CA.
77 [2000] 1 WLR 2539 at [36].
78 *R (Westminster CC) v National Asylum Support Service* [2002] UKHL 38; [2002] HLR 58; (2002) 5 CCLR 511; *R (Mani) v Lambeth LBC* [2003] EWCA Civ 836; (2003) 6 CCLR 376.
79 The grants regime is now contained in the Regulatory Reform (Housing Assistance) (England and Wales) Order 2002 SI No 1860, which repealed and replaced the former regime contained in the Housing Grants, Construction and Regeneration Act 1996.
80 2002 SI No 1860 arts 3(1) and 4.

the housing allocation scheme which must be adopted and complied with under Housing Act 1996 Part VI.[81] Accordingly, judicial review is likely to arise in similar situations, ie, to challenge the vires of the policy itself or to the application of that policy in specific cases. The award of a grant may be made subject to conditions,[82] which may, of themselves, give rise to a challenge on the grounds of irrationality and/or unreasonableness.

9.34   Local authority grants are funded by central government, which enjoys considerable discretion in respect of the award of funding to, and its recovery from, local authorities.[83] As with any public discretion, these ministerial powers must be exercised in accordance with the general principles of administrative law.

Disabled facilities grants

9.35   Disabled facilities grants present a different form of potential challenge. The local authority has no discretion over the award of a grant – the award of grant is mandatory if the prescribed conditions are met – and so judicial review may be used to ensure the proper discharge of the duty. In *R v Greenwich LBC ex p Glen International,*[84] the application for a (then) mandatory renovation grant was not accompanied by the two estimates required by the legislation.[85] Accordingly, the authority refused to award a grant. The claimants successfully sought judicial review of that decision on the basis that the grant sought was a mandatory grant and the authority were therefore obliged to exercise their discretion to dispense with the need for two estimates.

Defective housing

9.36   Defective housing grants may also be available from local authorities.[86] Such grants are only payable where the secretary of state

---

81   See paras 9.16–9.20 above.
82   Regulatory Reform (Housing Assistance) (England and Wales) Order 2002 SI No 1860 art 3(4).
83   2002 SI No 1860 arts 7 and 8.
84   (2001) 33 HLR 87, CA. The legislation under which this decision was reached was repealed by the Housing Grants, Construction and Regeneration Act 1996, which in turn was replaced by SI 2002 No 1860 (note 82), but the principles remain relevant – in particular with regard to disabled facilities grants.
85   Local Government and Housing Act 1989 s102(2)(b).
86   Housing Act 1985 Part XVI.

has designated a dwelling – or class(es) of dwelling – as defective. In addition, only those people who have purchased such a dwelling from a local authority may claim the grant.[87] There is some scope for judicial review as a remedy in relation to the operation of the regime governing the award of these grants,[88] although provision is made for appeals which militate against the use of judicial review as a remedy.[89]

Other housing functions

9.37　The significance of housing law, in its widest sense, as a local authority function should not be underestimated. A detailed analysis of all of the applicable powers and duties is beyond the scope of this work.

9.38　It should not be forgotten, however, in the context of judicial review, that local authorities have complex financial obligations in respect of their housing stock. Authorities are, for example, obliged to keep a ring-fenced housing revenue account[90] relating to all sums falling to be credited or debited in respect of, among other things, properties provided in discharge of their functions under the Housing Acts 1985 and 1996. The account must be kept, broadly, in balance and may not be subsidised from other funds.

9.39　This financial mechanism provides scope for judicial review in respect of those items that may be credited or debited to the account. Thus, in *R v Ealing LBC ex p Lewis*,[91] the applicant successfully challenged the authority's attempt to debit from the account various items relating to the salaries of staff employed by them. Although such claims are rare, they do demonstrate the potential breadth of housing law as a source of judicial review claims.

Statutory nuisance

9.40　Although not solely related to housing law, the provisions of Environmental Protection Act 1990 Part III are a useful means of

---

87　That is, people who have exercised the right to buy or who have otherwise purchased from an authority's housing stock.

88　See, for example, *R v Thurrock BC ex p Welham* (1991) 23 HLR 434, QBD.

89　See *R v Sandwell MBC ex p Cashmore* (1993) 25 HLR 544, QBD.

90　See Local Government and Housing Act 1989 s75 and Sch 4, as substantially amended by the Local Government Act 2003.

91　(1992) 24 HLR 484, CA.

enforcing housing conditions, where the problem does not constitute disrepair for the purposes of Landlord and Tenant Act 1985 s11. Because a statutory nuisance claim under section 82 of the 1990 Act is, in law, a criminal prosecution before the magistrates, the remedy of judicial review to challenge a decision of the magistrates will apply as it does to any other case heard by the magistrates' court. The courts have, however, indicated that an appeal by way of case-stated is likely to be more appropriate, unless the claimant's grounds include a breach of natural justice.[92]

9.41   Similarly, if a local authority serves an abatement notice under Environmental Protection Act 1990 s80, the court will generally expect the recipient to challenge the notice by way of the statutory appeal route under the Act, and there will only be very limited room for judicial review claims. The fact that the appeal route is not generally considered effective (due primarily to the delay in obtaining a hearing) will not be a reason for permitting claimants to seek judicial review instead.[93]

Housing benefit

9.42   This topic is dealt with elsewhere.[94]

Impermissible challenges

Secure, introductory and demoted tenancies

9.43   Questions arising under Housing Act 1985 Part IV, relating to secure tenancies, or Housing Act 1996 (concerning demoted tenancies)[95] may all be determined by the county court.[96] The use of judicial review is firmly discouraged by the provisions that any person commencing proceedings in the High Court which could have been commenced in the county court is not entitled to any costs at all.[97]

---

92   See *R (Clark-Darby) v Highbury Magistrates' Court* [2001] EWHC Admin 959.
93   See *R v Falmouth and Truro Port Health Authority ex p South West Water* [2001] QB 445, CA.
94   See chapter 11 below at paras 11.32–11.35.
95   Inserted by the Anti-social Behaviour Act 2003 Part II and Sch 1.
96   See Housing Act 1985 s110 and Housing Act 1996 ss138 and 143N.
97   See Housing Act 1985 s110(3); Housing Act 1996 ss138(3) and 143N(4).

9.44   Introductory tenancies, however, are treated differently. Because the county court has no jurisdiction to refuse to grant a possession order where the notice given to the tenant that proceedings are to be commenced is valid, any challenge to the merits of the decision to evict or to the conduct of the statutory review to which the tenant is entitled can only be brought by way of judicial review, and cannot be relied on as a defence to the possession proceedings themselves.[98]

Houses in multiple occupation

9.45   Where the validity of a notice served by a local authority on a person in control of a house in multiple occupation is challenged on the basis that the house is not in multiple occupation, it is not necessary to use judicial review proceedings. The county court has jurisdiction to determine that question.[99] This is not to say that judicial review may not be used in appropriate circumstances.[100]

---

98   See *Manchester CC v Cochrane* [1999] 1 WLR 89; (1999) 31 HLR 810, CA.

99   *Nolan v Leeds CC* (1991) 23 HLR 135.

100 See, eg, *R v Lambeth LBC ex p Clayhope Properties Ltd* [1988] 1 QB 563, CA (judicial review granted of refusal to pay mandatory repair grant).

CHAPTER 10

Judicial review and education law

continued overleaf

10.79   **Judicial review, appeals and default powers**

10.88   Who should be the claimant?

10.91   **Higher education**

10.1 Judicial review has become an increasingly important method of challenging decisions relating to education and there is now a considerable body of case-law in this area.

Legislation

10.2 The law on education is complex, with a sizeable number of statutes and regulations governing the area. However, the Education Act (EA) 2002 marks a shift away from exhaustive legislation, in accordance with new central government policy to introduce 'a lighter touch schools framework, with more devolution and more decision-making at school level'.[1]

10.3 Prior to the EA 2002, the statutory framework of education was set out in the Education Act 1996 as amended by the Education Act 1997 and the School Standards and Framework Act 1998. The EA 1996 consolidated, with amendments, the Education Act 1944 and certain other enactments.[2] The School Standards and Framework Act 1998 made significant changes, however, including the introduction of a new framework for schools and the re-categorisation of all existing maintained schools.[3] The EA 2002 makes further significant changes to both of the principal Acts.

10.4 The Education Reform Act 1988[4] and the Further and Higher Education Act 1992 govern the provision of higher education within a single framework, removing the distinction between universities, polytechnics and higher education colleges.

10.5 The Special Educational Needs and Disability Act 2001 amends the Education Act 1996 and, significantly, extends the provisions of the Disability Discrimination Act 1995 to schools.

Education Act 2002

10.6 The EA 2002 was intended to bring about significant change to education legislation. One of its stated purposes is to 'facilitate the

---

1 David Miliband, Minister for School Standards: *Hansard*, HC Vol 389, col 73, 15 July 2002.
2 Including the Education Act 1980 (in part), Education (No 2) Act 1986 (in part), Education Reform Act 1988 (in part) and the Education Act 1993. See also the Learning and Skills Act 2000 with regard to the 16–19 age group.
3 The new categories of school are outlined below at paras 10.15–10.17.
4 Part II. See also the Learning and Skills Act 2000.

implementation by qualifying bodies of innovative projects that may ... contribute to the raising of educational standards ...'[5] In order to achieve this, qualifying schools can opt out of certain legislative requirements relating to the curriculum, pay and conditions.[6]

10.7   Other changes brought about by the EA 2002 include the enabling of school governing bodies to form or invest in companies,[7] and the replacement for maintained schools of much of the governance provisions of the School Standards and Framework Act 1998 with more relaxed regulatory powers. Changes have also been made to the law on admissions and exclusions.

General duties of local education authorities

10.8   The general functions of local education authorities are now contained in the Education Act 1996.[8] Section 14 of that Act requires such authorities to secure that sufficient primary and secondary schools are available for their area, which must be sufficient in number, character and equipment to provide all pupils with the opportunity of an appropriate education.[9] They must also contribute towards the spiritual, moral, mental and physical development of the community, by securing that efficient primary, secondary and further education are available to meet the needs of the population of their area.[10]

Human rights[11]

10.9   Under article 2 of protocol 1 of the European Convention on Human Rights (the Convention), no-one may be denied the right to education. There are, in addition, a number of rights arising from other articles of the Convention which are important in the education context, such as:

5   Education Act 2002 s1(1).
6   Education Act 2002 ss6–10.
7   Education Act 2002 ss11–12.
8   Education Act 1996 ss12–19 and Sch 1.
9   This term is defined by Education Act 1996 s14(3).
10   Education Act 1996 s13(1).
11   But see *Hounslow LBC v School Admission Appeals Panel for Hounslow LBC* [2002] EWCA Civ 900; [2002] 3 FCR 142 at [62], in which the Court of Appeal, in the context of an admissions case, held that while human rights considerations are not entirely irrelevant, extended reference to them 'would not advance matters'.

- article 9 – the right to freedom of thought, conscience and religion (ie, in the exercise of its functions, the state must respect the rights of parents to ensure that education conforms with their own religious and philosophical convictions);[12]
- article 10 – the right to freedom of expression;
- article 8 – respect for private and family life (the courts have ruled that article 8 cannot be relied upon in cases concerning corporal punishment, sex education, choice of school, exclusion from a particular school or language of instruction in the classroom);[13]
- article 14 – the right to freedom from discrimination.

Judicial review

10.10 Where an education body, such as a local education authority (LEA) or board of governors, or a head teacher, is alleged to have acted beyond its powers or contrary to the principles of natural justice, it is susceptible to judicial review. In addition to such bodies, funding authorities are also susceptible to judicial review.

10.11 City technology colleges may also be amenable to review. In *R v Governors of Haberdashers' Aske's Hatcham College Trust ex p T,*[14] Dyson J granted an application for judicial review against a charitable company which was operating a city technology college.

10.12 The decisions of independent schools are not generally subject to judicial review, except in extremely limited circumstances, because their authority derives from either contract or the consent of parents. As such, any remedy must be sought in contract. Where, however, an independent school was participating in an assisted places scheme, judicial review was held to be available. In *R v Cobham Hall School ex p G,*[15] Dyson J applied *ex p T,*[16] granting an application for judicial review against the decision of an independent school to withdraw an assisted place.

10.13 Universities may also be amenable to review but, again, in limited circumstances. Chartered universities are private bodies, but may be susceptible to judicial review in relation to their statutory functions.

---

12 See further paras 10.37–10.40 below.
13 See further paras 10.18–10.40 and 10.51–10.55.
14 [1995] ELR 356, QBD.
15 [1998] ELR 389, QBD.
16 [1995] ELR 356, QBD.

Where a university has a 'visitor', however, claimants will be expected to make use of that procedure before coming to court.[17]

10.14 The following areas of decision-making can give rise to applications for judicial review:

- admission and re-admission of pupils to maintained schools;
- exclusion of pupils;
- admission, re-admission and exclusion appeals;
- special education needs;
- reorganisation of schools, including school closures, the establishment of new schools, amalgamations and changes in the 'character' of schools;[18]
- the school curriculum;
- school transport;
- financial and other support for pupils;
- grants and awards for pupils.

Categories of maintained schools

School Standards and Framework Act 1998

10.15 Schools maintained by local education authorities on or after 1 September 1999 fall into 5 categories:[19]

- community schools;[20]
- foundation schools;[21]
- voluntary schools (voluntary-aided and voluntary-controlled);[22]

---

17 *R v Lord President of the Privy Council ex p Page* [1993] AC 682, HL. See also *Clark v University of Lincolnshire and Humberside* [2000] 1 WLR 1988, CA.

18 Richard Gordon, *Judicial Review; law and procedure* (2nd edn, Sweet & Maxwell, 1996) pp274–278. See also Richard McManus, *Education and the Courts* (Sweet & Maxwell, 1998).

19 School Standards and Framework Act 1998 s20(1) as amended by Education Act 2002 Sch 21, para 95.

20 County schools will become community schools.

21 Grant-maintained schools which were formerly county schools or were established by the Funding Agency for Schools will become foundation schools.

22 Controlled schools will become voluntary-controlled schools. Aided and special agreement schools will become voluntary-aided schools. Grant-maintained schools which were formerly aided or special agreement schools or were established by promoters will also become voluntary-aided schools.

- community special schools; [23] and
- foundation special schools. [24]

10.16   In addition, there will still be nursery schools and pupil referral units.

10.17   Grant-maintained status for schools (which was introduced under the Education Reform Act 1988) will be abolished. Grant-maintained schools will become either foundation or voluntary-aided schools.

Admissions

Parental preference: Education Act 1996 s9[25]

10.18   In carrying out their powers and duties, local education authorities should take account, so far as may be compatible with the provision of efficient education, of the wishes of parents of the pupils. Education Act 1996 s9[26] provides:

> In exercising or performing all their respective powers and duties under the Education Acts, the secretary of state, local education authorities and the funding authorities shall have regard to the general principle that pupils are to be educated in accordance with the wishes of their parents, so far as that is compatible with the provision of efficient instruction and training and the avoidance of unreasonable public expenditure.

10.19   The Education Act (EA) 2002[27] provides for regulations to be made requiring local education authorities to formulate a 'qualifying scheme' regarding admissions in their area. Under such a scheme, parents are to be given application forms for all schools in that area, which they can then rank in order of preference.

10.20   The general duty under EA 2002 s9, to educate in accordance with parents' wishes, can be fairly easily defeated, however. Parental wishes have been held to be merely one factor which the authority should take into account. It is free to take into account and give greater priority to other factors. [28]

---

23   Maintained special schools will become community special schools.

24   Grant-maintained special schools will become foundation special schools.

25   See further *Halsbury's Laws of England*, 4th edn, Vol 15(1) at para 3, note 5 regarding the first protocol to the European Convention on Human Rights.

26   As amended by School Standards and Framework Act 1998 s140(1) and Sch 30, paras 57 and 61.

27   Inserting a new section 89B into the School Standards and Framework Act 1998.

28   *Watt v Kesteven CC* [1955] 1 QB 408.

10.21   In *Watt v Kesteven CC,*[29] a Roman Catholic father declined, on religious grounds, to send his children to an independent secondary
grammar school which was in the local education authority's area and
at which the authority had agreed to pay their tuition fees. Instead,
he sent his children to a Roman Catholic boarding school that was
located elsewhere and applied to the authority to pay the tuition fees –
which were, in fact, less than at the school proposed by the authority.
The authority refused and the father sought a declaration that this
refusal constituted a breach of statutory duty to provide secondary
school education for his children at a school to which he had chosen to
send them.

10.22   The Court of Appeal held that the duty of the local education authority to secure that there are sufficient schools available for their area[30]
only required that schools be made available in the authority's area. If
a parent wished to send his child to a school of his own choice, with
which the education authority had no arrangement, he could not claim
as of right that the authority should pay the fees. Denning LJ said:[31]

> [The section] does not say that pupils must in all cases be educated in
> accordance with the wishes of their parents. It only lays down a general
> principle to which the county council must have regard. This leaves it
> open to the county council to have regard to other things as well, and also
> to make exceptions to the general principles if it thinks fit to do so. It
> cannot therefore be said that a county council is at fault simply because it
> does not see fit to comply with the parent's wishes.

10.23   In *Cummings v Birkenhead Corporation,*[32] Lord Denning MR said:

> There are many other things to which the education authority may have
> regard and which may outweigh the wishes of the parents. They must
> have regard, for instance, not only to the wishes of the parents of one par-
> ticular child, but also to the wishes of the parents of other children and of
> other groups of children.

10.24   In this case, a parent unsuccessfully challenged a local education
authority's admission policy. The local authority had sent a circular
letter to parents stating that, save in exceptional circumstances, children
from Roman Catholic primary schools would only be considered for

29   [1955] 1 QB 408.
30   Then Education Act 1944 s8; now Education Act 1996 s14.
31   [1955] 1 QB 408 at 424.
32   [1972] Ch 12 at 36.

Roman Catholic secondary schools. The reason behind the policy was that the authority only expected to have enough spaces in non-Roman Catholic schools for pupils from county and Church of England schools.

10.25   The difficulty in challenging a decision that does not accord with a parent's wishes was explained by Lord Keith of Kinkel in a Scottish case:[33]

> In order to succeed in securing judicial review, the applicant must show either that the respondents paid no regard at all to the general principle embodied in section 28(1), or that they paid to it a degree of regard lesser than any reasonable education authority would have paid.

10.26   In *R v Birmingham CC ex p Youngson*,[34] where the parents of an aspiring ballet dancer wanted their local education authority to pay for him to attend a private ballet school outside the authority's area, the court upheld the principle that the concept of parental preference as expressed by Education Act 1996 s9 is qualified by the avoidance of unreasonable expenditure. The court also found that the Human Rights Act 1998 Sch 1, article 2 of protocol 1 is qualified in the same way.[35]

10.27   The court referred to a comment of Slade LJ in *R v Surrey County Council Education Committee ex p H*,[36] to the effect that Parliament has not placed local authorities under an obligation to provide a child with the best possible education. There is no duty on an authority to provide such a utopian system or to educate her or him to her or his maximum potential.

10.28   Recently, in *R (K) v Newham LBC*,[37] Collins J said:

> ... the religious conviction of a parent is something to which due weight must be given in considering admission to a particular school.

10.29 On the fact of that case, therefore, the local education authority was obliged to give due weight to the parents' religious convictions, namely that their child should be educated in a single-sex school.

---

33 *Harvey v Strathclyde Regional Council* [1989] SLT 612 at 615. This case concerned the Education (Scotland) Act 1980 s28(1) – a provision almost identical to Education Act 1996 s9.

34 [2001] LGR 18, QBD.

35 See Human Rights Act 1998 Sch 3, Part II for the UK's qualified acceptance.

36 (1984) 83 LGR 219 at 235.

37 [2002] EWHC 405 (Admin); [2002] ELR 390, QBD, at [29].

Admission to maintained schools

10.30   The law in this area is governed by School Standards and Framework
Act 1998 Part III, although the Education Act 2002 has brought about
a number of changes concerning admissions. In particular, admission and exclusion appeals will now be governed by regulations rather
than primary legislation.[38] The secretary of state is under a duty to
issue a Code of Practice on admissions, to be laid before Parliament,
and local education authorities and governing bodies will be under a
duty to have regard to the provisions of the code. In fact, the Department for Education and Skills has issued Codes of Practice on School
Admissions and Schools Admission Appeals.

10.31   Parents have increasingly been seeking to challenge, by way of
judicial review, decisions taken by schools or local education authorities refusing to admit pupils to a particular school.[39]

10.32   In the event of over-subscription, a school is entitled to have a policy
on admissions, in order to determine which applications will be successful. A policy cannot discriminate between those children within the
LEA area and those outside the area,[40] but can discriminate between religious persuasions in order to preserve the character of a church school.[41]
A policy which considers applications from Roman Catholic children
for places at non-denominational schools only *after* all other applicants have been placed has also been held to be lawful where the
school is oversubscribed: *R v Lancashire CC ex p Foster.*[42]

10.33   In *R v Brighouse School Appeal Committee ex p G and B,*[43] the court
rejected a school appeals committee's argument that a child could not
be admitted to the school because it had already admitted the maximum
number of pupils under its admissions policy and to allow more children to enter the school would prejudice the provision of efficient education and/or the use of resources. The court held that the committee
had improperly restricted its consideration to the policy and numbers
and had thereby fettered its discretion when reaching its decision.

10.34   In *Hounslow LBC v School Admission Appeals Panel for Hounslow
LBC,*[44] the issue of admissions to maintained schools was considered.

---

38   EA 2002 ss50–52.
39   See Parental preference, paras 10.18–10.29 above.
40   See para 10.36 below.
41   See paras 10.37–10.38 below.
42   [1995] 1 FCR 212; [1995] COD 45, DC.
43   [1997] ELR 39, QBD.
44   [2002] EWCA Civ 900; [2002] 1 WLR 3147, CA.

The Court of Appeal held that each case must be considered on its individual facts and that there was 'nothing intrinsically unlawful about admission arrangements which favour on the one hand children who have a brother or sister at the school, or on the other hand those who live close to it. But inflexible application of either criterion – or, in another case, of other criteria – may produce a perverse decision in an individual case.'[45]

10.35   Significantly, the Court of Appeal commented that the circumstance would need to be 'quite exceptional' for the courts to interfere with a decision on an admissions appeal.

10.36   In *R v Greenwich LBC ex p Governors of John Ball Primary School*,[46] the governing body of a primary school in Lewisham sought judicial review of a policy adopted by the neighbouring borough of Greenwich – to give first preference to children resident in Greenwich together with residents in other areas with a sibling connection to the school applied for. The Court of Appeal held that local education authorities were under a duty, subject to the statutory exceptions, to comply with the expressed preference of parents as to the school at which they wished their children to be educated, without distinction between children resident within and outside an authority's area. The borough's decision to adopt a school admissions policy giving priority to children within their own area was, therefore, ultra vires. Lloyd LJ said:[47]

> I do not regard efficient education or the efficient use of resources as being the sole source of lawful policy ... In my judgment a local education authority can have any reasonable policy they think fit, provided it does not conflict with their duties under [section 9] or any other enactment ... Sibling priority and the proximity rule are sound and lawful policies whether or not they promote efficient education ... It may well be understandable for Greenwich to give their own residents priority over all other areas in Greenwich schools. But it conflicts with the clear provisions of [the Act].

10.37   In *Choudhury v Governors of Bishop Challoner Roman Catholic Comprehensive School*,[48] the applicants (parents of a Hindu child and parents of a Muslim child) sought judicial of the Governors' and Appeal Committee's decisions to refuse admission to the applicants' daughters to an oversubscribed (voluntary-aided) Roman Catholic girls' school.

---

45   [2002] EWCA Civ 900, per May LJ at [60].
46   (1990) 88 LGR 589, CA.
47   (1990) 88 LGR 589 at 599.
48   [1992] 2 AC 182, HL.

Admission was refused on the basis that it would prejudice the provision of efficient education and that the girls did not meet the admission criteria, which gave priority to Roman Catholics and other Christians. The issue to be decided was whether the governors of an oversubscribed voluntary-aided school were entitled to operate an admissions policy which gave preference to children of a particular religious persuasion notwithstanding the preference expressed by the parent.

10.38   The House of Lords held that where a school was oversubscribed, compliance with the preference of all the applicants would necessarily prejudice efficient education and, in such circumstances, the school had to have an admissions policy, which would – whatever the criteria adopted – inevitably result in defeating the preference of some applicants. Since the school was oversubscribed there was, therefore, no duty on the governors to give effect to the applicants' preferences. Lord Browne-Wilkinson, delivering the only speech,[49] adopted the following passage from the judgment of Taylor LJ in the Court of Appeal:

> ... if compliance with all parental preferences would result in overcrowding then the governors may apply any reasonable criteria to make the necessary reduction in numbers. Those criteria include sibling priority and geographical proximity. Likewise, in a church school, priorities such as those stated in the admissions policy here can properly be applied.

10.39   Other admissions policies which are prima facie lawful include catchment areas and feeder primary or nursery schools. It has, however, been held to be unlawful for a local education authority to fail to ascertain parental preferences at the beginning of the process of placing a child, before addressing the question of the catchment area into which the child might fall.[50]

10.40   In *R v Cleveland CC ex p Commission for Racial Equality*,[51] the Commission failed to obtain judicial review of the council's decision under the Education Act 1980 to allow, in accordance with parental preference, the transfer of a pupil from a racially-mixed school. The Court of Appeal held, upholding the decision of Macpherson J,[52] that as the minister's decision did not contravene the power granted by the Act, his decision was not based on an error of law. The transfer of the child in this case, moreover, from a predominantly Asian school to a

49   [1992] 2 AC 182 at 191–192.
50   *R v Rotherham MBC ex p Clark* [1998] 1 FCR 509; [1998] ELR 152, QBD.
51   (1993) 91 LGR 139, CA.
52   In the same case (1992) 4 Admin LR 417, QBD.

predominantly white school, did not amount to an act of segregation on racial grounds and so the council had not committed an act of discrimination contrary to the Race Relations Act 1976.

Admissions appeals

10.41　School Standards and Framework Act (SSFA) 1998 s94(1) confers upon parents a right of appeal against:

- any decision made by or on behalf of an authority as to the school at which education is to be provided for a child; and
- any decision made by or on behalf of the governors of a county or controlled school maintained by an authority, refusing a child admission to such a school.

10.42　SSFA 1998 s94(2) provides a right of appeal for parents against any decision made by or on behalf of the governors of any aided or special agreement (now voluntary-aided) school refusing admission to the child.

10.43　SSFA 1998 s95 removes the right of appeal by a parent against a refusal to admit a child to a school, if that child has been permanently excluded from two or more schools, the last exclusion being within the previous two years. Instead, the governing body of a school now has a right of appeal against a decision by the local education authority to admit such a child.[53]

10.44　Appeals are heard by education appeal committees.[54] Decisions of an education appeal committee are susceptible to judicial review on normal administrative law principles. Judicial review is the only route for challenging such decisions.[55]

Exclusions

10.45　Exclusions are now governed by Education Act 2002 s52. The head teacher and the pupil's teacher have the power to exclude a pupil, either for a fixed period or permanently.[56]

53　School Standards and Framework Act 1998 s95(2).
54　School Standards and Framework Act 1998 Sch 24.
55　The appeal routes provided by Education Act 1996 ss496 and 497 (as amended by the SSFA 1998) do not apply. See also Oliver Hyams, *The Law of Education* (Sweet & Maxwell, 1998), para.6–283.
56　Education Act 2002 s52(1)–(2).

.46   The section also makes provision for regulations to govern appeal procedures. The Education (Pupil Exclusions and Appeals) (Maintained Schools) (England) Regulations 2002,[57] and Education (Pupil Exclusions and Appeals) (Pupil Referral Units) (England) Regulations 2002[58] came into force on 20 January 2003.[59] Generally, these regulations reflect the law as it previously existed under the regime of the School Standards and Framework Act 1998, although some changes have been made.

10.47   New guidance has also been published in the form of *Improving Behaviour and Attendance: guidance on exclusions from schools and pupil referral units* which also came into force on 20 January 2003 and which applies to any exclusion on or after this date.

10.48   Parents cannot challenge the decision of an independent school to expel a pupil by way of judicial review,[60] because such a school is not a public body and, while it operates within a statutory framework of control, the relationship between private schools and their pupils is founded on the contract made between the schools and those paying for the education of the pupils (ie, a private law contract with no statutory underpinning).

Appeals against permanent exclusions

10.49   The School Standards and Framework Act 1998 simplified the procedure for excluding pupils from maintained schools. There is still a right of appeal, however, to an education appeal committee.

10.50   Education Act (EA) 1996 s159(1), provides a right of appeal for parents against any decision not to reinstate a registered pupil who has been permanently excluded from a county, controlled or special school maintained by the authority. The governing body of a school also have a right of appeal against any direction for the reinstatement of such a pupil, which has been given by the local education authority to the head teacher of the school. EA 1996 s156(2) confers a similar right of appeal against any decision not to reinstate such a pupil to any aided or special agreement school.[61] Appeals are heard by education appeal committees and must be in accordance with Education Act 1996 Sch 16.

---

57   SI No 3178.
58   SI No 3179.
59   Transitional arrangements apply to pupils excluded before 20 January 2003.
60   *R v Fernhill Manor School ex p A* [1994] ELR 67.
61   Now voluntary-aided schools: Education Act 2002, see note 22 above.

10.51   A right of appeal against permanent exclusions is provided for in School Standards and Framework Act 1998 s67 and Sch 18. In the past, the courts could be sympathetic to judicial review applications made without first having exhausted the appeal procedure. In *R v Governing Body of the Rectory School and Richmond LBC ex p WK (a minor),*[62] where significant procedural unfairness was alleged, the court held that the appeal procedure was not appropriate for dealing adequately with such issues.

10.52   More recently, however, in *R (AM) v Head Teacher of St George's Catholic School,*[63] the claimant was permanently excluded from school, and appealed in accordance with the statutory right of appeal. Before reaching the final stage of the appeal process, however, he sought judicial review, alleging procedural unfairness. The application was dismissed as was an appeal to the Court of Appeal.

10.53   The Court of Appeal considered the issue of the extent to which unfairness at an early stage of the three-stage appeal process could be cured by utilising the final stage of appeal, and held that it was necessary to construe the statutory scheme as a whole, in order to ascertain the intention of Parliament regarding the effect of unfairness in an early part of the process. In this case, although Parliament did not intend any stage of the process to be unfair, neither did it intend a party aggrieved at a decision at the first stage to seek judicial review rather than appeal.

10.54   Although the appeal did not give redress in respect of the earlier unfairness, the aggrieved party obtained a new, fair decision on the merits from the 'custom-built' expert and independent statutory body, following a rehearing. Unless, therefore, the prior procedural unfairness complained of had somehow tainted the subsequent appeal, in which case the appeal decision itself would necessarily fall, the right to a fair determination of a person's case would be satisfied by the appeal hearing and decision. On a judicial review application brought instead of an appeal, the court would usually leave the claimant to his or her statutory remedy.[64]

10.55   In *R v Governors of B School ex p C,*[65] the court held that reinstatement does not necessarily entail full integration into the classroom, even when that was the previous state of affairs. Other matters that

---

62   [1997] ELR 484.
63   [2002] EWCA Civ 1822.
64   See also *R (Sivasubramaniam) v Wandsworth County Court* [2002] EWCA Civ 1738; [2003] 2 All ER 160.
65   [2001] ELR 285.

may be taken into account are, for example, threatened strike action by members of staff if full reinstatement were to occur.

Special educational needs

10.56 The application of the Disability Discrimination Act 1995 to schools is highly significant and has brought about fundamental changes in this area concerning discrimination by bodies responsible for schools on the basis of disability.

10.57 Local education authorities have various duties to identify, assess and provide for the special educational needs of children with learning difficulties, for whom they are responsible.[66] By Education Act 1996 s321, authorities are also obliged to identify those children with special educational needs where it is necessary for the authority to determine the special educational provision required by any learning difficulty the child may have. Once the authority has identified a child with special educational needs, it must assess that child's needs,[67] which may lead to a statement of special educational needs.[68] The authority also has a duty to assess a child's needs at the request of the parents.[69]

Special educational needs appeals

10.58 The availability of judicial review in this field has been limited by the introduction of the Special Educational Needs Tribunals (SENTs) in 1993.[70] Appeals were formerly heard by an appeal committee of the local education authority or the secretary of state. As from September 2002, the Special Educational Needs Tribunal became the SENDIST (Special Educational Needs and Disability Tribunal).[71]

10.59 The Special Educational Needs Tribunal Regulations 2001,[72] apply to appeals, as do the Special Educational Needs and Disability Tribunals (General Provisions and Disability Claims Procedure)

---

66 'Learning difficulties' is defined in Education Act 1996 s312(2).

67 Education Act 1996 s323.

68 Education Act 1996 s324 and Sch 27.

69 Education Act 1996 s329.

70 Education Act 1993 s177, now Education Act 1996 Part IV, especially ss326 and 333.

71 Special Educational Needs and Disability Act 2001 s17 (inserting a new section 28H into the Disability Discrimination Act 1995).

72 SI No 600.

Regulations 2002.[73] All claims must be brought within six months. The tribunal is able to make declarations of unlawful discrimination (but cannot award compensation). A parent has a right of appeal to a SENDIST against the following:

- admissions appeals regarding independent and all other schools, except maintained schools;
- fixed-term exclusions for maintained schools; and
- permanent exclusions for independent and non-maintained schools.

10.60 Decisions of the SENT/SENDIST may be challenged by way of statutory appeal to the High Court under Tribunals and Inquiries Act 1992 s11.[74] A further appeal (with permission) may be brought to the Court of Appeal.[75]

10.61 In *R v Special Educational Need Tribunal ex p South Glamorgan CC*,[76] the Court of Appeal held that judicial review is not the correct forum in which to challenge a SENT decision because of the availability of an alternative route of appeal. Reference was made to *R v Inland Revenue Commissioners ex p Preston*,[77] and *R v Secretary of State for the Home Department ex p Swati*,[78] as authority for the proposition that statutory rights of appeal must be exhausted before judicial review is sought.[79]

10.62 Judicial review is still a possible route, however, for challenging decisions which fall outside the jurisdiction of the SENT, such as those relating to the funding obligations of local education authorities.[80]

Reorganisation of schools

10.63 The School Standards and Framework Act 1998 also made new provision for the establishment, alteration and discontinuance of schools.[81]

73 SI No 1985.
74 As amended by Education Act 1996 Sch 37, para 118.
75 Tribunals and Inquiries Act 1992. See further paras 10.78–10.86 below.
76 [1996] ELR 326.
77 [1985] AC 835, HL.
78 [1986] 1 WLR 477, CA.
79 See also *Re M (a minor)* [1996] ELR 135, CA, which reaffirmed this principle.
80 *White v Ealing LBC* (1998) LGR 829, CA. Similarly, a measure taken by a tribunal which does not directly relate to the child's learning difficulties falls outside the meaning of 'special educational provision' and is therefore not subject to appeal to a SENT under Education Act 1996 s326; *R v Wakefield MBC ex p G* [1998] 2 FCR 597.
81 School Standards and Framework Act 1998 ss28–35, as amended by Education Act 2002 ss24 and 70–71.

The provisions deal with the procedure for the establishment or alteration by a local education authority of community, foundation or voluntary schools,[82] and also for their closure or discontinuance, and that of maintained nursery schools.[83]

10.64   The procedure involves a process of publication of proposals,[84] together with consultation.[85] Local education authorities and other bodies will also need to have regard to any guidance issued by the secretary of state before publishing their proposals and a copy of the published proposals must be sent to the relevant school organisation committee (or, in Wales, the secretary of state), who will be required to approve, reject or modify any proposals in certain circumstances.[86]

10.65   One of the most important issues in the context of school closure is the manner in which the required consultation is undertaken. All interested parties should be consulted and full and proper information provided.[87]

10.66   Although challenges to grant-maintained status by way of judicial review were relatively frequent, the School Standards and Framework Act 1998 has now abolished the grant-maintained status.

School transport

10.67 Local education authorities are under a mandatory duty to consider whether transport arrangements are necessary to secure a child's attendance at school and to provide that transport free of charge or fund the child's travel arrangements.[88] If no such provision is made, the parent of the child cannot be prosecuted for failing to secure the attendance of the child at school under Education Act 1996 s444.[89] It will be necessary to provide free transport where a child is registered at a school that is not within 'walking distance' (by the shortest 'available route')

---

82 School Standards and Framework Act 1998 s28.

83 School Standards and Framework Act 1998 s29 and Sch 6.

84 School Standards and Framework Act 1998 s28(1).

85 School Standards and Framework Act 1998 s28(5).

86 School Standards and Framework Act 1998 Sch 6.

87 See, eg, *R v Brent LBC ex p Gunning* (1985) 84 LGR 168, where judicial review was granted on the ground of inadequate consultation. See also, generally paras 6.184–6.185 above.

88 Education Act 1996 s509, as amended by Education Act 2002 Schs 21 and 22. This provision was previously contained in Education Act 1944 s55.

89 Previously Education Act 1944 s39.

from her or his home and the authority does not enable the child to be registered at a school closer to home, although there appears to be some uncertainty as to the application of the law in this area.[90]

10.68　It should be noted that the possibility of judicial review is limited by the availability of an alternative means of redress under the Education Act (EA) 1996.[91] EA 1996 ss496 and 497 (secretary of state's powers to prevent unreasonable exercise of functions by a local education authority, governing body of a county, voluntary or maintained special school, or governing body of any grant-maintained school, and his general default powers).

10.69　Under EA 1996 s509(1), the secretary of state is given a wide discretion to direct a local education authority to provide school transport. These alternative remedies must be exhausted before making an application for permission to apply for judicial review: *R v Essex CC ex p EB.*[92]

Discrimination

10.70　Local education authorities and bodies responsible for educational establishments in the public sector are under a general duty to secure that facilities for education and any ancillary benefits or services are provided without sex or racial discrimination.[93]

10.71　In addition to the general duty not to discriminate, Sex Discrimination Act 1975 s22 and Race Relations Act 1976 s17 specify kinds of discrimination in the field of education that are unlawful. The provisions apply to local education authorities and other responsible bodies. Accordingly, discrimination is unlawful:

- in the terms of an offer of admission;
- by refusal or deliberate omission of acceptance of an application for admission;
- in the way in which access is afforded to any benefits, facilities or services;
- where such access is refused or deliberately omitted;

90　See *R (H) v Brent LBC* [2002] EWHC 1105; [2002] ELR 509 in which the basis of the claim was unclear.

91　Education Act 1996 ss496–497 and 509(1).

92　[1997] ELR 327. See also para 10.85 below.

93　See Sex Discrimination Act 1975 s25; Race Relations (Amendment) Act 2000 ss1, 46–51 and Sch 1 (repealing and replacing Race Relations Act 1976 s19).

- by exclusion from an establishment; or
- by subjecting a person to any other detriment.

10.72   It is also unlawful for a local education authority or other responsible body to discriminate in the performance of any of their other functions under the Education Acts, although exceptions are made[94] permitting single-sex educational establishments and for giving particular racial groups access to educational facilities to meet their special needs.

10.73   Any contravention of the discrimination provisions referred to above can be remedied by the secretary of state under his default powers.[95] This will limit the availability of any challenge by way of judicial review. The Equal Opportunities Commission and Commission for Racial Equality may also make formal investigations into any alleged contravention, and will give notice to the secretary of state so that he may exercise his default powers.

Discriminatory selection procedures

10.74   In *R v Birmingham CC ex p Equal Opportunities Commission,*[96] the Equal Opportunities Commission challenged a local authority's selection procedure for the provision of secondary education in its area. The Commission alleged that in carrying out its duties under the legislation, the authority was discriminating against girls (female pupils required higher marks in the entrance examination to enter grammar schools as fewer places were available for them) and was therefore in breach of the relevant statutory provisions. The House of Lords confirmed that this procedure was discriminatory and unlawful.

10.75   Further proceedings were brought against the authority as a result of its failure adequately to comply with the House of Lords ruling: see *R v Birmingham CC ex p Equal Opportunities Commission (No 2).*[97] The authority had attempted to remedy the illegality found by the House of Lords by changing the status of one of the boys' schools from grammar school to grant-maintained school, which meant that the school was no longer maintained by the authority and had the effect, by leaving it out of account, that the number of grammar school places available to boys and girls became broadly similar.

---

94   Sex Discrimination Act 1975 s26; Race Relations Act 1976 s35.
95   Education Act 1996 ss496–497.
96   [1989] 1 AC 1155, HL.
97   [1994] ELR 282, CA.

10.76   The Court of Appeal held that in complying with its duty to secure sufficient places in its area for secondary education, the authority could not ignore a school which had obtained grant-maintained status and offered places only to boys, but must have regard to all schools in the area, whether or not maintained by the authority itself. The fact that the number of places available to boys and girls was broadly the same, leaving that school out of account, was therefore irrelevant.

10.77   Neill LJ said:[98]

> It seems to us ... in considering whether sufficient schools are available, the local education authority has to take account, and only take account, of places which are available free. The relevant 'pool', as we would term it, is the pool of free places in single-sex schools providing a grammar school education. The pool may include assisted places at independent schools, but in our judgment it certainly includes grant-maintained schools.
>
> The duty of securing that sufficient schools are available for providing secondary education of a suitable kind is a different duty to provide such schools.

10.78   The court did recognise, however, the difficulties faced by the authority and stated that the relevant civil liberties legislation was in need of reform:[99]

> [The Sex Discrimination Act 1975], and comparable legislation in the field of race relations, requires close examination when the duties and obligations of bodies responsible for the provision of public sector education are being formulated. It seems to us that if and when further legislation in the field of education is being considered it is important that account should be taken of:
> (a) the fact that both the secretary of state and the local education authority retain under the present legislation some overall responsibilities for public sector education as a whole;
> (b) the fact that the discrimination with which a court would be likely to be primarily concerned would be discrimination against an individual boy or girl or groups of boys or girls.
>
> In these circumstances we consider that amendments should be introduced to enable the elimination of discrimination to take place in accordance with a sensible and suitable time-scale.

---

98   [1994] ELR 282 at 297.
99   [1994] ELR 282 per Neill LJ at 297–298.

Judicial review, appeals and default powers

10.79   As stated above,[100] the secretary of state has default powers under Education Act 1996 ss496 and 497.[101] He or she also has a general reserve power to secure proper performance.[102]

10.80   When considering whether the powers of the Secretary of State preclude resort to the courts, the older cases demonstrate a distinction between unlawful acts and omissions to exercise functions. In *Cummings v Birkenhead Corporation*,[103] for example, it was held that what is now the s496 power excludes the jurisdiction of the courts except where an ultra vires act, such as a breach of the principles of natural justice, is alleged. Similarly, in *Herring v Templeman*,[104] the court held that although what is now the s496 power precluded resort to the courts where a mere wrong exercise of discretion was alleged (in that case a failure to hold an oral hearing), it did not prohibit such resort where ultra vires was alleged.

10.81   The modern approach of the courts, however, appears to be not to regard the default power as automatically ousting an application for judicial review. In *R v Inner London Education Authority ex p Ali*,[105] the applicant alleged that the authority had breached its duty under what was then Education Act 1944 s8 to secure provision of sufficient schools in the area. The applicant complained to the secretary of state, who declined to exercise his default power. As a preliminary point, the court considered the nature of the duty imposed by s8 and the relevance of the existence of the Secretary of State's default power.

10.82   The Court of Appeal held that the existence of the default power did not preclude an application for judicial review. Where the secretary of state had decided not to exercise his default power in a particular case, moreover, and then an application was made for judicial review, the court would not be bound by the secretary of state's decision, although it would be a factor to be taken into account when considering whether or not to grant relief.

---

100   At paras 10.68.
101   Formerly Education Act 1944 ss68 and 99.
102   Education Act 1996 s497A, inserted by School Standards and Framework Act 1998 s8.
103   [1972] Ch 12, CA.
104   [1973] 2 All ER 581.
105   (1990) 2 Admin LR 822.

10.83   Woolf LJ said that he:[106]

> ... would not accept that the language of the default powers contained in sections 68 and 99 of [the Education Act 1944, now sections 496–497 of the Education Act 1996] indicate that Parliament intended the jurisdiction of the courts to be ousted from considering the issues which can be considered by the secretary of state under those sections.

10.84   In *R v Newham LBC ex p R*,[107] however, the applicants were parents of a child with special educational needs. They appealed against a statement of special educational needs, which was then remitted back to the local education authority for reconsideration. The parents then sought judicial review of the second statement. One question for the court was whether the applicants had an alternative remedy by way of appeal to the secretary of state. The Divisional Court held that it was not the court's function to redraft the statement and that the secretary of state was better placed than the court to form a view as to what should be in the statement and thus dispose of the outstanding issues.

10.85   Schiemann J stated:[108]

> The law as to the circumstances in which the court will refuse relief by way of judicial review on the ground that an alternative remedy is available is now well settled. However, I think the following may be regarded as uncontroversial. Judicial review is a discretionary remedy and relevant factors in deciding whether to exercise the discretion to grant leave to move for judicial review or to grant particular relief include a consideration of:
> (1) whether a refusal to quash will be to leave the applicant without remedy; and, in particular,
> (2) whether there is available an alternative forum in front of which the applicant can argue his substantive and legal points and which can dispose of them;
> (3) whether the court's judgment will dispose of the outstanding issues;
> (4) the chance of a point of law sought to be raised in the judicial review proceedings surfacing again in any alternative forum;
> (5) the time implications of allowing the judicial review procedure to start or continue.
>
> Where the matter justifies the making of a general declaration, then the appropriate way of proceeding, if the declaration would be of value to the applicant, would be to go by way of judicial review. That is because this court is the only one having power to make such a declaration. Insofar as the

---

106   (1990) 2 Admin LR 822 at 831B–C.
107   [1995] ELR 156.
108   (1990) 2 Admin LR 822 at 165.

complaint is that a particular child has been the subject of a mistaken value judgment by the local education authority then the appropriate way of proceeding is by way of appeal to the secretary of state. Even if the complaint is that the mistaken value judgment by the local education authority was arrived at in part by reason of mistakes of law, it is in general appropriate to proceed by way of appeal rather than by judicial review unless the alleged mistakes of law are likely to be repeated by the secretary of state.

10.86   In *R v Essex CC ex p EB*,[109] the Divisional Court refused permission to apply for judicial review of a local education authority's decision regarding whether school transport was 'necessary', as the secretary of state was best placed to determine the question under Education Act 1996 ss496–497. McCullough J said:[110]

> It is not for the court to judge safety. The court could not go to the route and look at it itself. The secretary of state, on the other hand, through his officials, could do exactly that and, if need be, on different occasions. He is in a far better position to assess safety by watching the traffic, considering visibility, taking into account width, and perhaps the absence of verges and so on – all matters more suitable for decision by the secretary of state.

10.87   In *R v Brent LBC ex p F*,[111] the Divisional Court held that where the issues were really educational ones, the best person to resolve them was the secretary of state, using his far-reaching powers under EA 1996 s497.

Who should be the claimant?

10.88   A final point to consider in judicial review applications in the field of education is who should bring the claim. Either the parents or the child could be the claimant. There are important ramifications, however, regarding funding where the claimant is a child.

10.89   In the context of school admissions cases, it has been held that while the child may well have a sufficient interest to mount a challenge, nevertheless the parent(s) should usually be named as the claimant(s), as the only reason for bringing a challenge in the name of the child is usually to be able to obtain public funding for the challenge and to protect the parents in costs should the challenge fail.

---

109   [1997] ELR 327, DC.
110   [1997] ELR 327 at 329.
111   [1999] ELR 32.

This was an abuse and a device and a reason for refusing permission to apply for judicial review.[112]

10.90   In relation to school closure, however, the position appears to be somewhat different. In *R (WB and KA) v Leeds School Organisation Committee*,[113] Scott Baker J held that that issue was relevant not to standing but to abuse and therefore the court's discretion. Both parents and children had a sufficient interest to bring judicial review proceedings in school closure or re-organisation cases, and while in many cases it may be the parents who had the real interest and while it may be an abuse of process to name the child as the claimant for the purposes of obtaining funding and protection against a possible costs order, clear evidence would be needed to establish such an abuse. The school admissions cases, referred to above, were distinguished on the basis that the appellate regime there under consideration made it clear that the right of appeal was that of the parent and not the child. There was no indication that the court's decisions in those cases were intended for any wider application.[114]

Higher education

10.91   For the purposes of judicial review, distinctions are drawn between the different origins in law of the various universities and colleges. There are three different types of legal origin.[115] Many universities are chartered bodies created by Royal Charter issued pursuant to the royal prerogative. Traditionally, a chartered body was not subject to the ultra vires rule, as the charter simply grants corporate capacity to the body, not statutory power, and so they have been treated as domestic institutions. The internal affairs of these universities are regulated by a 'visitor', who is appointed in accordance with the statutes and other instruments which govern the university's constitution. As the visitor has sole and exclusive jurisdiction over internal matters, the courts will usually lack the jurisdiction to intervene: *Thomas v University of Bradford*.[116] The remedy of appeal to the visitor will, in any event, constitute an alternative remedy, precluding judicial review.

112   *R v Richmond LBC ex p JC* [2001] ELR 13, and *B v Head Teacher of Alperton Community School* [2001] ELR 359.

113   [2002] EWHC 1927 (Admin); [2003] ACD 5.

114   Ibid, at [32]–[37].

115   See Richard McManus, *Education and the Courts* (Sweet & Maxwell, 1998), chapter 9.

116   [1987] 1 AC 795, HL.

10.92   In *R v Lord President of the Privy Council ex p Page*,[117] a majority of the House of Lords held, on the facts, that the visitor of Hull University was not susceptible to judicial review, as he had been acting within his jurisdiction. Judicial review would lie, however, if he had acted outside his jurisdiction in the sense that he had no power under the regulating documents to adjudicate on the dispute or, more importantly, if he had abused his power or acted in breach of the rules of natural justice.

10.93   It has also been stated by the House of Lords, albeit by way of obiter dicta and in another context, that relief by way of judicial review is available to restrain a chartered corporation – in that case a local authority – from carrying out unauthorised acts,[118] that is, acts inconsistent with the charter. However, universities will not automatically be considered public bodies as the powers derived from their charter are not derived from the prerogative, even though the charter itself is. Moreover, there has never been any doubt that a local authority is susceptible to review. In practice, the courts will rarely intervene in the exercise of the visitor's discretion or judgment unless it is satisfied that it is wrong in law: *R v University of London ex p Vijayatanga*.[119]

10.94   The second way in which a university may originate is that of an Act of Parliament, such as the Universities of Oxford and Cambridge Act 1571. Universities created by statute can be the subject of judicial review.

10.95   Finally, modern institutions of higher education are usually higher education corporations, which are conducted in accordance with the instruments and articles of government. Some are companies, usually limited by guarantee.[120] Judicial review may lie where a university fails to act in accordance with its own regulations.[121]

117   [1993] AC 682, HL.
118   *Hazell v Hammersmith and Fulham LBC* [1992] 2 AC 1, HL.
119   [1988] QB 322
120   Education Reform Act 1988 ss121, 124 and 129.
121   See, eg, *R v Board of Governors of Sheffield Hallam University ex p R* [1995] ELR 267; *R v Manchester Metropolitan University ex p Nolan* [1994] ELR 38.

CHAPTER 11

Judicial review and social security law

Introduction

11.1 Judicial review has less importance than might be expected in the field of social security law. This is due to the comprehensive appeals system which exists in relation to decisions concerning most benefits. The Social Security Act 1998 introduced a number of reforms intended to modernise the social security decision-making and appeals system by streamlining the procedures for applications, reviews and appeals. More recently, and as a result of the coming into force of the Human Rights Act 1998, the Child Support, Pensions and Social Security Act 2000 has brought the review and appeals structure for Housing Benefit and Council Tax Benefit in line with the regime for most other benefits.

The legislation

Primary legislation

11.2 The principal Acts concerning the social security system are the Social Security Contributions and Benefits Act 1992 and the Social Security Administration Act 1992. Together, these Acts consolidated the bulk of previously existing legislation.

11.3 Subsequent statutory provisions which amend and/or supplement the principal Acts include:

- Social Security (Mortgage Interest Payments) Act 1992 s2;
- Social Security (Contributions) Act 1994 ss1 and 3;
- Statutory Sick Pay Act 1994;
- Social Security (Incapacity for Work) Act 1994;
- Jobseekers Act 1995;
- Pensions Act 1995 ss126–129, 131–134, 148, 177, Sch 4 and Sch 7 Pt11;
- Social Security Act 1998;
- Welfare Reform and Pensions Act 1999;
- Immigration and Asylum Act 1999 ss115 and 123;
- Child Support, Pensions and Social Security Act 2000;
- Tax Credits Acts 1999 and 2002.

Delegated legislation

11.4 The Social Security and Child Support (Decisions and Appeals) Regulations 1999[1] provide for new procedural rules and other requirements of the new unified appeals system introduced by the Social Security Act 1998 concerning social security, contracting out of pensions, child support and vaccine damage decisions. These regulations revoke, among other things, the Social Security (Adjudication) Regulations 1995,[2] Adjudication Amendment Regulations 1996 and Adjudication Amendment (No 2) Regulations 1996.

Decision-making structure (not social fund)

11.5 The Social Security Act 1998 made considerable changes to the previous structure of determinations, reviews and appeals, amending both the Social Security Contributions and Benefits Act (SSCBA) 1992 and the Social Security Administration Act 1992.[3]

11.6 Key changes included:

- Decision-making functions previously exercised by independent Adjudication Officers, social fund officers and child support officers became the responsibility of the secretary of state.[4]
- A unified appeals tribunal replaced all the tribunals previously in existence under the umbrella of the Independent Tribunal Service.[5] The new tribunal is a one- or two-person tribunal (not a three-person tribunal as previously existed).[6]
- Provision is made for automated decision-making by computers.[7] Assurances have been given by the government that decisions which require the exercise of discretion or the exercise of judgment will continue to be reserved for staff. Rights of appeal will not be affected.

---

1 SI No 991.
2 SI No 1801.
3 Transitional provisions are contained in Social Security Act (SSA) 1998 s83 and Sch 6.
4 SSA 1998 s1.
5 Social Security Appeals Tribunal, Disability Appeals Tribunal, Medical Appeals Tribunal, Child Support Appeals Tribunal and Vaccine Damage Tribunal.
6 SSA 1998 s4.
7 SSA 1998 s2.

Determinations

11.7   These are now made by the secretary of state in relation to most claims for benefit and any claim for Social Fund payments.[8] This will include determinations relating to:

- Benefits paid under SSCBA 1992 Parts II to V;
- Jobseekers Allowance;
- Income Support;
- Disability Working Allowance;
- Social Fund payments (SSCBA 1992 ss138(1)(a), (b) and (2);
- Child Benefit;
- Such other benefits as may be prescribed.

Reviews, revisions and supersessions

11.8   The terminology of 'review' has been replaced with that of 'revision' and 'supersessions' (ie, the superseding of a decision with another decision). The secretary of state may revise a decision[9] made under Social Security Act (SSA) 1998 s8 (initial determinations) or SSA 1998 s10 (superseded decisions) either on application or his own initiative.[10] Claimants have one month to seek a revision (on any ground) and a further month in which to appeal. The secretary of state may supersede a decision[11] either on application or his own initiative.

11.9   The grounds for the revision and supersession of decisions are set out in the Social Security and Child Support (Decisions and Appeals) Regulations 1999.[12] In summary, a decision may be revised on any ground within the 'dispute' period of one month. Once the dispute period has expired, however, a decision may only be revised on prescribed grounds, including: (a) that the decision arose out of an official error, or (b) that the decision was made in ignorance of, or based on a mistake of material fact and as a result was more advantageous to the claimant than it would otherwise have been.

11.10   Grounds for supersession include the following: (a) relevant changes (or anticipated changes) of circumstances since the decision was made; (b) that the decision was wrong in law or made in ignorance of, or

---

8   SSA 1998 s8.
9   Other than discretionary social fund decisions: see SSA 1998 s36.
10   SSA 1998 s9.
11   SSA 1998 s10. He or she may not 'supersede' discretionary social fund decisions. See SSA 1998 s36.
12   SI No 991. Regs 3 and 6.

based on a mistake of, material fact and an application for supersession was made (or the secretary of state acted on his own initiative) outside the dispute period (ie, after a month from notification of the decision); (c) the decision of an appeal tribunal or commissioner was made in ignorance of, or based on a mistake of, material fact.

Appeal to the Appeal Tribunal

11.11   Some decisions of the secretary of state may be appealed to a single (ie, unified) Appeal Tribunal.[13] This provision effectively re-enacts Social Security Administration Act 1992 s22, with some amendments. Under the new provision, the Appeal Tribunal may only consider the matter in review and not the whole application. The SSA1998 sets out those matters which carry a right of appeal[14] and those which do not.[15] The position in this regard is not much changed. The Appeal Tribunal has power to rehear a case, without the need for a further appeal to the Commissioner, where it has made an error of law.[16]

Appeal to the Commissioner

11.12   There continues to be provision for appeal to a Commissioner on a point of law.[17]

Appeal to the Court of Appeal

11.13   Likewise, there continues to be provision for appeal to the Court of Appeal, with permission of the Commissioner or the court.[18]

The Social Fund decision-making structure

11.14   Discretionary social fund decisions are made by appropriate officers (formerly known as social fund officers) of the secretary of state.[19] This

13   SSA 1998 s12.
14   SSA 1998 Sch 2.
15   SSA 1998 Sch 3.
16   SSA 1998 s13.
17   SSA 1998 s14 which, in effect, re-enacts Social Security Administration Act 1992 s23 with minor drafting amendments.
18   SSA 1998 s15, which re-enacts Social Security Administration Act 1992 s24.
19   SSA 1998 s36, replacing (with modifications) Social Security Administration Act 1992 s64.

represents very little change to the pre-1998 position in relation to the discretionary social fund. The system of revisions and supersessions described above is disapplied in relation to discretionary social fund decisions.[20] Instead, application may be made for the review of such decisions by an appropriate officer and thereafter by a social fund inspector.[21]

Transfer of administration of some benefits to Inland Revenue

11.15   The principal purpose of the Social Security Contributions (Transfer) Act 1999 was to transfer from the Secretary of State for Social Security to the Inland Revenue certain functions in relation to National Insurance contributions, statutory sick pay, statutory maternity/paternity pay, statutory adoption pay and contracting out of the state earnings related pension scheme.[22] These are the benefits which arise primarily out of employment relationships, or at least a presumption of employment.

11.16   The decisions and appeals procedure for contributory benefits is similar in form and structure to that described above in relation to benefits administered by the Secretary of State for Work and Pensions under the Social Security Act 1998.[23]

11.17   Taking statutory sick pay as an example, an employee who is incapable of working for at least four or more consecutive days may, subject to certain procedural restrictions,[24] claim statutory sick pay from his employer.[25] Where an employer refuses or stops payment of statutory sick pay, an employee may, within six weeks of that decision, request an officer of the Inland Revenue to make a decision on that entitlement.[26]

---

20   SSA 1998 s36(3).
21   SSA 1998 s38.
22   Social Security Contributions (Transfer) Act 1999 s1.
23   Detailed provision in relation to the decision-making and appeals process under the 1999 Act is contained in the Social Security Contributions (Decisions and Appeals) Regulations 1999 SI No 1027.
24   Social Security Contributions and Benefits Act 1992 ss150–152.
25   Detailed provision is contained in the Statutory Sick Pay (General) Regulations 1982 SI No 894.
26   Social Security Contributions (Transfer) Act 1999 s8. These functions were previously exercised by the secretary of state under Social Security Administration Act 1992 s17(1).

11.18   There is a right of review and appeal against the decision of the Inland Revenue. There is a similar regime to that described above, under the Social Security Act 1998, for the Inland Revenue to vary a decision if it considers the decision to have been wrong or to supersede the decision if it is no longer correct for any reason.[27]

11.19   Both employee and employer have a right of appeal to the Tax Appeal Commissioners.[28] If dissatisfied with the decision of the Commissioners, an appeal lies to the High Court on a point of law.[29] Where the Commissioners or the court order an employer to pay a contributory benefit but he fails to do so, the Inland Revenue should pay the benefit.[30]

The Tax Credits Acts 1999 and 2002

11.20   The introduction of tax credits by the Tax Credits Act 1999 marked a further attempt to modernise the social security system and a further movement away from the traditional use of the Department of Social Security, now the Department for Work and Pensions, to administer all state benefits. The Tax Credits Act 2002 repealed and replaced the 1999 Act.

11.21   Tax credits are aimed at encouraging benefit claimants into work (and thus away from reliance on Jobseeker's Allowance) and rewarding those who continue in full-time work.

11.22   From 6 April, 2003, there are two tax credits: child tax credit and working tax credit.[31] Child tax credit replaces several previous forms of benefit in respect of children such as the child element in income

---

27 Social Security Contributions (Transfer) Act 1999 s10. See also Social Security Contributions (Decisions and Appeals) Regulations 1999 SI No 1027, regs 5 and 6.

28 Social Security Contributions (Transfer) Act 1999 s11. Such appeals are usually heard by the General Commissioners (appointed under Taxes Management Act 1970 s2) but may also be heard by the Special Commissioners (appointed under Taxes Management Act 1970 s4). The Special Commissioners may be more appropriate where an appeal concerns complex issues as they are legally qualified adjudicators whereas the General Commissioners are lay representatives assisted by a legal clerk.

29 Social Security Contributions (Decisions and Appeals) Regulations 1999 SI No 1027, reg 12.

30 Social Security Contributions and Benefits Act 1992 s151(6), as amended by Social Security Contributions (Transfer) Act 1999 Sch 7.

31 Tax Credits Act 2002 ss1, 8 and 10.

support and income-based jobseeker's allowance. Working tax credit replaces working families tax credit, disabled persons tax credit and the New Deal 50 plus.

Initial decisions

11.23   Tax credits are administered by the Inland Revenue and, accordingly, the initial decision as to the entitlement to and amount of any award are made by Inland Revenue officers.[32] Once an initial decision has been made, a notice is served on the applicant requiring a declaration to be made that there has been no relevant change in circumstances and that the applicant is accordingly entitled to the tax credit at the rate assessed.[33]

Revised decisions

11.24   Once that declaration has been received, the Inland Revenue must make a decision as to whether the applicant was entitled to tax credit at the rate assessed[34] and may – within the specified time limit – institute an enquiry to satisfy themselves that the applicant was so entitled.[35] Where that time limit has expired, but the applicant's tax liability is revised or the Inland Revenue has reasonable grounds for believing that a decision regarding entitlement was wrong, due to fraud or neglect, it may make a 'decision on discovery' – a decision to revise that decision.[36]

11.25   If notified of a change in the applicant's circumstances, the Inland Revenue are under a duty to make a revised decision as to the rate of the award.[37] Similarly, where, during the period for which an award is made, the Inland Revenue has reasonable grounds for believing that an applicant is receiving a tax credit to which he or she is not

---

32 Tax Credits Act 2002 s14. Detailed provision in relation to entitlement to the two benefits is to be found in the Child Tax Credit Regulations 2002 SI No 2007 and the Working Tax Credit (Entitlement and Maximum Rate) Regulations 2002 SI No 2005.

33 Tax Credits Act 2002 s17(2).

34 Tax Credits Act 2002 s18.

35 Tax Credits Act 2002 s19. Inherent in this power of enquiry are the general powers of the Inland Revenue, among other things, to demand a personal tax return under Taxes and Management Act 1970.

36 Tax Credits Act 2002 s20. This power is subject to a long-stop time-limit of five years after the end of the tax year to which the decision relates.

37 Tax Credits Act 2002 s15.

entitled or at a rate to which he or she is not entitled, it may, of its own motion, amend or terminate the award.[38] Where there are not reasonable grounds for that belief, but the Inland Revenue holds the belief nonetheless, it may serve the applicant with notice requiring such information or evidence as it considers necessary.[39]

Appeals

11.26 The applicant must be notified of any revised decision and of her or his right to appeal.[40] The right of appeal relates to initial decisions, revised decisions, a decision following enquiry or on discovery, a decision imposing a penalty and a decision to charge interest on an overpayment of tax credit.[41] Appeals are currently dealt with by the Appeals Tribunal Service in the same way as are appeals concerning other forms of welfare benefits.[42] This is, however, a temporary measure and it is intended that – as with other benefits transferred to the Inland Revenue – appeals will, eventually, be dealt with by the Tax Commissioners.[43]

11.27 Accordingly, as with a majority of social security benefits, there is little scope for judicial review in relation to tax credits as the legislation provides a comprehensive appeals system. There may, however, be scope for a challenge on general public law grounds in relation to the extensive powers of the Inland Revenue to conduct enquiries, further enquiries and discovery into the validity of entitlement. It is also to be noted that there is no right of appeal against a decision to recover overpayments of tax credits.

---

38 Tax Credits Act 2002 s16.

39 Tax Credits Act 2002 s16(2).

40 Tax Credits Act 2002 s23. See also the Tax Credits (Claims and Notifications) Regulations 2002 SI No 2014.

41 Tax Credits Act 2002 s38. Note that there is no right of appeal against a decision to recover an overpayment. Detailed provision in relation to appeals is contained in the Tax Credits (Appeals) Regulations 2002 SI No 2926, the Tax Credits (Appeals) (No 2) Regulations 2002 SI No 3196 and the Tax Credits (Claims and Notifications) Regulations 2002 SI No 2014.

42 Tax Credits Act 2002 ss39 and 63 – ie, an appeal is made to an Appeal Tribunal, then to the Commissioner and, thereafter, with permission, to the Court of Appeal.

43 Tax Credits Act 2002 s39. See also notes to Sweet & Maxwell's *Current Law Annotated Statutes 2002* Vol 1 and Child Poverty Action Group's *Welfare Benefits and Tax Credits Handbook 2003/04*, p1362.

The Child Support, Pensions and Social Security Act 2000

11.28   The most significant aspect of this Act for the purposes of this book is its introduction of a new system of reviews and appeals in relation to housing benefit and council tax benefit, aligning those schemes with the appeals procedure prescribed by the Social Security Act 1998.[44] The detail of this scheme in relation to housing benefit is dealt with below.

11.29   The Act also introduced 'discretionary housing payments'. These payments are – unusually in the field of social security – wholly discretionary and are paid by local authorities from a cash-limited budget[45] in order to assist an applicant to meet her or his rent or council tax liability. Eligibility for discretionary payments is restricted to those in receipt of housing and/or council tax benefit and who appear to an authority to require some further financial assistance.[46] Payments are made on a claim to the authority and may continue for so long as the authority consider the recipient to be eligible. The maximum amount payable is a sum equal to the applicant's rent or council tax liability.[47] There is no right of appeal against a refusal to award a discretionary payment, but authorities are required to operate a review procedure and to give written notice with reasons for any decision on review.[48]

11.30   The absence of a defined appeal structure leaves open the possibility of judicial review in respect of any failure to award a discretionary payment, on usual administrative law principles, although the wide discretion conferred on authorities will make it more difficult to succeed on a challenge to a decision under this scheme unless the authority has made a clear legal error in its decision-making process.

11.31   The Act also makes provision for the loss of certain benefits (Income Support, Jobseeker's Allowance and such other benefits as may be prescribed) where the applicant has failed to comply with the terms of

44   Child Support, Pensions and Social Security Act 2000 Sch 7.
45   Funds for such payments are available in the form of a grant from the secretary of state; an authority may only award payments equal in amount to the amount of the grant: Child Support, Pensions and Social Security Act 2000 s70.
46   Child Support, Pensions and Social Security Act 2000 s69(1).
47   Discretionary Financial Assistance Regulations 2001 SI No 1167 reg 4.
48   Child Support, Pensions and Social Security Act 2000 regs 6(3) and 8.

a community order.[49] This provision is currently being piloted. An appeal in respect of withdrawal of benefit under this provision follows the same procedure as other social security appeals.[50] These penal provisions form part of the current policy trend of 'tightening up' the social security system and restricting the rights of those who are deemed to have abused the system.[51] It would appear that the availability of a system for appeals will militate against the use of judicial review in relation to these penalties.

Housing Benefit and Council Tax Benefit

11.32 Decisions relating to housing benefit and council tax benefit continue to be made by local authorities, but the system for review and further review has been altered.

11.33 Prior to 1 July 2001, the Housing Benefit (General) Regulations[52] and the Council Tax Benefit (General) Regulations 1992[53] made provision for the applicant to make written representations for the original decision to be reviewed, and thereafter to seek a further review by a Housing Benefit Review Board, comprising at least three elected members of the authority. There was no right of appeal to a judicial body such as the Social Security Commissioner or the court and, accordingly, the only means of challenging a decision of a review board was judicial review.

11.34 This system became the subject of judicial criticism following the commencement of the Human Rights Act 1998. In R (Bewry) v Norwich CC,[54] Moses J held that an authority's Housing Benefit Review Board was not independent and impartial for the purposes of article 6 of the European Convention on Human Rights, or indeed the common law, because it was made up of councillors of the authority. That lack of

---

49 Child Support, Pensions and Social Security Act 2000 s62. The term 'community order' is defined as a community service order, a probation order (now a community rehabilitation order) and a community punishment order (Powers of the Criminal Courts (Sentencing) Act 2000) a combination order or any other such order as may be prescribed. See also, for further detail, the Social Security (Breach of Community Order) Regulations 2001 SI No 1395.

50 See paras 11.8–11.13 above.

51 See also Social Security Fraud Act 2001 at paras 11.36–11.38 below.

52 SI No 1971 as amended, regs 79(2) and 81–84.

53 SI No 1814, as amended, regs 68–76.

54 [2001] EWHC Admin 657; [2002] HRLR 2.

impartiality could not be remedied by the availability of judicial review because the High Court had limited jurisdiction to determine findings of fact. In *R (Bibi) v Rochdale MBC Housing Benefit Review Board*,[55] however, Newman J held that, although such boards were not independent and impartial, their decisions were not necessarily tainted to the point of being incompatible with article 6 of the Convention.[56]

11.35   This debate was, however, almost entirely academic as Child Support, Pensions and Social Security Act 2000 Sch 7 made fundamental changes to the system for the review of and appeal from decisions relating to housing benefit and council tax benefit. With effect from 1 July 2001, a new appeal structure has been put in place, similar to that used in relation to other social security benefits, of revisions, superseding decisions and appeal to an independent tribunal under the auspices of the Appeals Service.[57] The scope for judicial review has therefore reduced accordingly.

Social Security Fraud Act 2001

11.36   The Social Security Administration Act 1992 has long provided local authorities, the Department of Work and Pensions,[58] and the Inland Revenue with powers to investigate benefit fraud and, in certain circumstances, to prosecute applicants who have provided false or dishonest information or otherwise obtained benefit through fraudulent means.[59] The possible sanctions were, however, extended by the Social Security Fraud Act (SSFA) 2001.

---

55 [2002] EWHC 967 (Admin).
56 See also *R (Kershaw) v Rochdale MBC Housing Benefit Review Board* [2002] EWHC 2385 (Admin) and *R (Bono) v Harlow DC* [2002] EWHC 423; [2002] 1 WLR 2475.
57 Housing Benefit and Council Tax Benefit (Decisions and Appeals) Regulations 2001 SI No 1002.
58 Formerly the Department of Health and Social Security, then the Department of Social Security.
59 Social Security Administration Act 1992 Part VII, as amended by the Social Security Administration (Fraud) Act 1997 governs the gathering of information, Part VI is concerned with enforcement. These sanctions do not preclude the possibility of criminal prosecutions under the Theft Act 1968: *Osinunga v DPP* (1997) *Times* 26 November.

11.37 Under the SSFA 2001, a person who is convicted of one or more benefit offences[60] in two separate sets of proceedings may, subject to certain qualifying conditions, be disqualified from receiving any social security benefit, other than certain specified benefits.[61]

11.38 There is no formal appeal structure concerning a decision to disqualify a person from receipt of benefit under the SSFA 2001. Nor is there any clear procedure for obliging an administering body to continue to award a benefit during a fraud investigation or to require the swift conduct of such an investigation. Recourse to judicial review may be possible, and indeed necessary, to compel the Department of Work and Pensions, Inland Revenue or local authority to conclude an investigation and make a decision regarding its outcome. Similarly, judicial review may be the only remedy available where, following a previous finding of fraud, an administering body refuses to provide support during extended enquiries into an application.[62]

Relationship between the appeal structure and judicial review

11.39 While, as stated above, the role of judicial review is plainly limited in the field of social security, it is not ousted altogether. It could be used, for instance, to challenge the validity of regulations. In cases where there is an effective remedy, however, by virtue of the statutory routes

60 That is, any offence in connection with a claim for Jobseeker's Allowance, or any social security benefit other than tax credits, statutory sick pay, paternity or maternity pay or any war pension – referred to as disqualifying benefits: Social Security Fraud Act 2001 s7(8).

61 The benefits from which a person may be disqualified are called 'sanctionable benefits' and are defined in the Social Security Fraud Act 2001 s7(8) and include all disqualifying benefits other than retirement pensions, disability living allowance, attendance allowance, social fund payments. Where the sanctioned benefit is housing benefit, council tax benefit, Income Support or Jobseeker's Allowance, those benefits are not excluded altogether but are awarded at a reduced rate throughout the disqualification period: Social Security Fraud Act 2001 s7(4) and the Social Security (Loss of Benefit) Regulations 2001 SI No 4022. These relate, in particular to benefits that include provision for children, though whether the scope of these provisions will now be extended once financial support for children is moved entirely to tax credits rather than being included in general benefits, remains to be seen.

62 See the notes at p1113 of Child Poverty Action Group's *Welfare Benefits and Tax Credits Handbook 2003/04*, which contend that there is a distinction between the role of fraud officer and the role of an officer determining an application for benefit and that the two roles are to be treated separately.

of appeal, the claimant would need to persuade the court that there is a good reason why he or she should be permitted to bring a judicial review claim instead of an appeal. It is likely to be difficult to do so in the majority of cases, given the principle that a claimant must exercise all alternative remedies available to her or him before bringing judicial review proceedings. A right of appeal, in particular, will usually preclude judicial review.

11.40   It is not only the validity of legislation that may continue to be challenged by judicial review but also its extent. In *R (National Association of Colliery Overman Deputies and Shot-firers) v Secretary of State for Work and Pensions*,[63] the claimant sought and was granted judicial review of the secretary of state's failure to reconsider whether to include a certain type of test for diagnosing vibration-induced white finger.

11.41   It has also been held that judicial review may be available if, for example, an authority promises to carry out a review but fails to do so. In *R v Lambeth LBC ex p Ogunmuyiwa*,[64] no formal application for a review had been made, but the authority had raised an expectation that a review would be carried out. Poppelwell J stated[65] that 'although it does not strictly come within the statutory framework of the regulations, it seems to me that that is a particular reason why the ordinary rule of exploring every other avenue should in the instant case be rejected.'

11.42   Another potential area in which judicial review may be appropriate is in respect of refusals by the Social Security Commissioner to grant leave to appeal from the decision of an appeal tribunal.[66] The standard of proof in such a case, however, will be high:

> A claimant has to show that the reasons which caused the commissioner to refuse leave were improper or insufficient, or that there were no good grounds on which leave would have been refused in the proper exercise of the commissioner's discretion. Even if the claimant manages to establish such grounds, judicial review will nonetheless be refused, if it can be seen that there are still good grounds on which the commissioner would have been entitled to refuse leave in the proper exercise of his discretion.[67]

---

63   [2003] EWHC 607 (Admin).
64   (1997) 29 HLR 950, DC.
65   (1997) 29 HLR 950.
66   *Bland v Chief Supplementary Benefit Officer* [1983] 1 All ER 537.
67   Per Maurice Kay J in *R (Latif) v Social Security Commissioners* [2002] EWHC 2355 (Admin) at [6], applying *R v Secretary of State for Social Services ex p Connolly* [1986] 1 All ER 998.

11.43 This has not inhibited several attempts to challenge refusals of leave,[68] which are often made on a variety of grounds.[69]

11.44 Where the complaint is, in essence, one of maladministration rather than procedural impropriety, the proper course is to lodge a complaint with a Commissioner for Local Administration (the Local Government Ombudsman) under the Local Government Act 1974. In *R v Lambeth LBC ex p Crookes*,[70] the claimant was the owner of a bed and breakfast hotel. His main complaints related to failures by the local authority to process properly, or within the statutory time limits, the claims of many of his residents, or their requests for reviews of determinations or for further reviews to be conducted by the Housing Benefit Review Board. In giving judgment, Sir Louis Blom-Cooper stated:[71]

> Whenever a challenge in this court is made to the decision of a local authority under housing or allied legislation, which is exclusively or mainly on the grounds of procedural irregularity, the question instinctively arises whether, in essence, the challenger's claim is that he or she, to use the language of ombudsmanry, sustained injustice as a consequence of maladministration on the part of the local authority. In short, therefore, should not the complaint more appropriately be directed to the Commissioner for Local Adminstration (the local government ombudsman) for investigation, rather than be subjected to the process of judicial review?
>
> ... It should be noted that any denial of relief in the context of the local authority's duties under housing or allied legislation must be limited to the judicial review equivalent of maladministration ... The question of alternative remedies arises when there is an overlap between cases clearly within the jurisdiction of the local government ombudsman and those with which the courts can deal. Housing is a prime example of an area of local administration which may give rise to complaints of either injustice flowing from maladministration or procedural irregularity. Every procedural irregularity is likely to exhibit maladministration. But not every maladministration will be encompassed by procedural irregularity.

---

68 See, eg, *R (Begum) v Social Security Commissioners* [2002] EWHC 401 (Admin); *R (Percy-Pole) v Social Security Commissioners* [2002] EWCA Civ 1684; *R (Hoare) v Social Security Commissioners* [2001] EWHC Admin 32.

69 In *R (Nahar) v Social Security Commissioners* [2002] EWCA Civ 859; (2002) ACD 105, the claimant sought judicial review on the grounds of legitimate expectation, unfairness, abuse of process, human rights abuse, inconsistency and issue estoppel.

70 (1997) 29 HLR 28.

71 (1997) 29 HLR 28 at 29–30 and 35–36.

Judicial review and police powers

General

12.1 It has been held by the courts that judicial review is available to supervise the statutory and non-statutory duties and discretionary powers of the police. For example, in *D'Souza v DPP*,[1] (actually an appeal by case stated, but on which the court in effect applied judicial review principles), which concerned police powers of entry under the Police and Criminal Evidence Act 1984, the appeal was allowed since the purpose for which the police were in fact exercising their powers of entry was not one within the Act; hence they were not exercising any valid power at all. In *R v Commissioner of the Police of the Metropolis ex p Blackburn*,[2] judicial review was granted of a decision by the Commissioner not to enforce certain laws, contrary to the general duty on chief constables to enforce the law; in *R v Chief Constable of Kent County Constabulary ex p L*,[3] the discretion to prosecute rather than caution was held to be reviewable.

12.2 It has also been held that the statutory powers of arrest which confer executive discretion are subject to judicial review.[4] If this is so, it may be that, similarly, the common law power of arrest should be subject to the supervisory jurisdiction; it is difficult to determine any reason in principle why the availability of judicial review should be limited to the statutory power. What is clear, however, is that operational decisions will not usually be susceptible to judicial review.

Circumstances where judicial review may arise

12.3 Judicial review most frequently arises in relation to two areas of decision-making:

- internal disciplinary proceedings; and
- the exercise of police powers, such as the power to caution; arrest; execute a search warrant; and exercise other powers under statute, eg, under the Public Order Act 1986 and the Police and Criminal Evidence Act 1984.

---

1 [1992] 1 WLR 1073.
2 [1968] 2 QB 118.
3 [1993] 1 All ER 756.
4 See *Mohammed-Holgate v Duke* [1984] AC 437, HL.

12.4 A challenge by way of judicial review may be brought where the police have taken a decision not to act,[5] where there is a clear duty to act, or where they have acted but have done so unreasonably.[6] Judicial review may also be sought in respect of a general policy decision, where there has been improper exercise of discretion, or in relation to a specific police decision made by an individual officer.[7] In practice, however, the courts are generally reluctant to interfere where the police have a discretion.

12.5 A police authority may bring a claim for judicial review against an executive order of central government.[8]

Internal disciplinary proceedings

12.6 In *R v Chief Constable of Merseyside Police ex p Calveley*,[9] complaints were made against five police officers. The officers concerned did not receive formal notice of the complaints, under the Police (Discipline) Regulations 1977,[10] until some two years later. The Chief Constable proceeded with disciplinary hearings and the officers were found guilty and dismissed or required to retire. The officers enjoyed a right of

---

5 For example, in *R v Chief Constable of Devon and Cornwall ex p Central Electricity Generating Board* (1981) 3 All ER 826, CA, the applicant applied for judicial review seeking an order to compel the chief constable to remove or assist in the removal of protesters who were obstructing a survey being conducted by the applicant. The court refused to make the order, on the ground that although the police had powers to intervene in the removal of persons who resisted removal by CEGB and were under a duty to uphold the law, they could not be compelled to remove all persons interfering with CEGB's work.

6 In this respect, judicial review may also lie against a court's decision to compel an individual to comply with police powers – see *R v Bristol Crown Court ex p Bristol Press and Picture Agency Ltd* (1986) *Times* 11 November, CA, where the claimant sought judicial review of an order made under Police and Criminal Evidence Act (PACE) 1984 s9, compelling them to produce photographs taken during a public order offence (see also *R v Central Criminal Court ex p Adegbesan* (1986) 1 WLR 1292, DC).

7 *R v Cambridge Chief Constable ex p Michel* (1991) 91 Crim App Rep 325, for example, concerned the decision of a custody officer to detain a juvenile under Police and Criminal Evidence Act 1984 s38. Leave to move for judicial review was refused.

8 See *R v Secretary of State for the Home Department ex p Northumbria Police Authority* [1987] 1 All ER 556, CA, concerning the Home Secretary's decision to issue certain riot equipment against the wishes of the police authority.

9 [1986] QB 424, CA.

10 SI No 508.

appeal against the Chief Constable's decision under Police Act 1964 s37, which they proceeded to exercise. Before the appeal was heard, however, the officers sought judicial review of the decision.

12.7　　The Court of Appeal held that judicial review should not be attempted where there was an alternative remedy, save in exceptional circumstances. In considering exceptional circumstances, the court would have regard to the speed of the alternative procedure, whether it was convenient and whether the matter depended on particular technical knowledge available to the appellate body. The delay of two years in the instant case was a serious departure from the disciplinary procedure which amounted to an abuse of process. The five officers had been prejudiced and, consequently, judicial review in these circumstances was justified.

12.8　　In *R v Chief Constable of Merseyside Police ex p Merrill*,[11] the court quashed disciplinary proceedings against a detective constable where the Chief Constable had erroneously concluded that the service of a complaint notice on him under the disciplinary rules could be deferred until after his criminal trial (at which he was acquitted). The court held that prima facie delay caused prejudice and the greater the delay (in this case 18 months), the greater the prejudice.

12.9　　A right of appeal against dismissal is now contained in Police Act 1996 s85, as amended. Appeals, which were previously heard by the Home Secretary, are now heard by a tribunal.[12] There is no further right of appeal from the tribunal's decision.

Complaints

12.10　The Police Reform Act 2002 introduced the Independent Police Complaints Commission (IPCC), which will replace the Police Complaints Authority in April 2004. The IPCC is headed by a chairman and must investigate complaints and 'conduct matters'.[13] Although there is, to date, no case law on point, decisions of the IPCC are likely – as are those of other statutory decision-makers – to be subject to challenges by way of judicial review (either by the police authority or officer affected or by a complainant) on public law grounds.

11　[1989] 1 WLR 1077.
12　Police Act 1997 ss38 and 82.
13　Police Reform Act 2002 s13 and Sch 3.

Police powers[14]

Cautions and decisions to prosecute

12.11 In *R v Chief Constable of Kent ex p L,*[15] the applicant, a juvenile, sought judicial review of a decision to prosecute rather than caution him, contrary to the police's general policy of cautioning instead of prosecuting juveniles in circumstances which pertained in his case. It was held that the discretion whether to prosecute was reviewable, but would only be interfered with if the decision to prosecute was clearly contrary to the settled policy of the Director of Public Prosecutions.

12.12 In *R v Commissioner of Police of the Metropolis ex p P,*[16] a 12-year-old boy of good character sought judicial review of a decision to caution him, contrary to Home Office guidance. The Divisional Court held that where a formal caution was administered in clear breach of Home Office guidelines, the court could properly exercise its jurisdiction to review the legality of the caution. In that case, the caution was quashed as there was a clear breach of the condition that an offender had to admit the offence before a caution could be appropriately administered. The police had failed to apply the further condition that where the suspect was under 14 years of age, it was necessary to establish whether he knew that what he was doing was seriously wrong.

12.13 In *ex p P,*[17] the court cited *ex p L.* Watkins LJ said:[18]

> I have come to the conclusion that if judicial review lies in relation to current criminal proceedings, in contrast to a failure to take any action against a person suspected of a criminal offence, it lies against the body which has the last and decisive word, the CPS [Crown Prosecution Service]. A refusal to prosecute or even possibly to caution by the police is another matter. In that event the police may be vulnerable to judicial review, but only upon a basis which, the cases show, is rather severely circumscribed.

12.14 The case of *R v DPP ex p C,*[19] was also referred to. That case had similarly involved a decision not to prosecute, contrary to guidelines.

---

14 The powers of police officers and of police authorities are principally contained in the Police and Criminal Evidence Act 1984, the Police Acts 1996 and 1997 and the Police Reform Act 2002.

15 [1993] 1 All ER 756.

16 (1996) 8 Admin LR 6; (1995) *Times* 24 May, QBD.

17 (1996) 8 Admin LR 6.

18 [1993] 1 All ER 756 at 767.

19 [1995] 1 Crim App Rep 136; (1994) *Times* 7 March.

The Divisional Court held that it had power to review a decision not to prosecute, but the power to review should be used sparingly.

12.15   Where the discretion to prosecute is concerned, it can therefore be seen that the court will be reluctant to intervene unless there has been a clear breach of settled policy.

Search warrants

12.16   In *R v Chief Constable of Lancashire ex p Parker*,[20] the Divisional Court reviewed the execution of a search warrant, granting leave (now permission) to move for judicial review, on the basis that the police had failed to produce or supply a copy of the warrant to the person whose premises were being searched. The search was therefore declared unlawful, as consequently was the seizure and retention of materials taken during the search.

12.17   In *R v Chief Constable of Warwickshire ex p Fitzpatrick*,[21] the Divisional Court held that judicial review was not an appropriate remedy where an individual complained of excessive seizure of material pursuant to a search warrant. Jowett J emphasised that judicial review was not a fact-finding exercise and was an extremely unsatisfactory tool by which to determine, in any but the clearest cases, whether there had been a seizure of material not permitted by a search warrant. He stated:[22]

> In my judgment a person who complains of excessive seizure ... should not, save in such cases, seek his remedy by way of judicial review but should rely on his private law remedy when he will have a tribunal which will be able to hear evidence and make findings of fact unfettered by *Wednesbury* principles. In an appropriate case the court in a private law action is able to grant interlocutory relief on a speedy basis on well recognised principles so that in all but the clearest cases ... judicial review has only disadvantages and no advantages when compared with the private law remedy.

12.18   In *R (Rottman) v Commissioner of Police for the Metropolis*,[23] the police arrested the claimant, on the driveway outside his house, under a magistrates' warrant issued under the Extradition Act 1989. The police went with the claimant into his house and, on doing so, searched the house and seized certain computer equipment. The claimant sought

---

20 [1993] QB 577, DC.
21 [1999] 1 WLR 564, DC.
22 [1999] 1 WLR 564 at 579.
23 [2002] UKHL 20; [2002] 2 AC 692.

judicial review on the ground that the search had been illegal as there had been no warrant permitting the police to search the property or seize goods.

12.19 The Divisional Court held that an officer only had power to enter and search a property for the purposes of executing a warrant of arrest and that there was no common law power entitling him or her to conduct the search. The House of Lords allowed an appeal by the police,[24] on the ground that the power to search an arrested person logically and as a matter of common sense also permitted the police officer to search the premises in which he was arrested. It was further held that there was a common law power to search and seize property after the execution of a warrant of arrest. The contention that the seizure of goods amounted to a violation of the claimant's rights under article 8 (right to respect for the home and family life) of the European Convention on Human Rights (the Convention) was also rejected on the basis that the seizure had been in accordance with the law and was justified, proportionate and necessary to promote the legitimate aim of preventing crime.

Persons in custody

12.20 In *R v Chief Constable of Avon and Somerset ex p Robinson*,[25] the Divisional Court rejected a challenge by way of judicial review to the refusal of the police to afford access to police stations to unqualified legal clerks so that they might interview clients.

12.21 In *R v Chief Constable of South Wales ex p Merrick*,[26] the Divisional Court granted judicial review of the police's refusal to permit an applicant to consult a solicitor after 10 am while on remand in custody at a magistrates' court. It was held that, although the right to consult a solicitor under Police and Criminal Evidence Act (PACE) 1984 s58(1) did not extend to a person on remand in custody, there was a common law right to consult a solicitor which was in no way abrogated by PACE 1984. The right was on request, to see a solicitor as soon as reasonably practicable. The police policy to refuse such a request on the sole ground that the request was made after 10 am was unlawful.

---

24 Lord Hope of Craighead dissented on the basis that the common law powers of search and seizure following execution of a warrant did not extend to warrants issued under the Extradition Act 1989.

25 (1991) 90 Cr App Reps 27, DC.

26 [1994] 1 WLR 663, DC.

12.22   In *R (Bloggs 61) v Secretary of State for the Home Department,*[27] a prisoner sought judicial review of the Home Secretary's decision to move him from a protected witness unit and place him in mainstream prison, on the ground that – following his arrest – the police had promised that he could remain in protected witness custody for the duration of his sentence if he provided them with information, which promise amounted to a legitimate expectation. The court dismissed the application on the ground that the police had no power to make such a promise and that the prison service were not, therefore, obliged to take that promise into account, even if it did amount to a legitimate expectation.

Duty to enforce the law

12.23   In *R v Commissioner of Police for the Metropolis ex p Blackburn,*[28] the Commissioner made a policy decision, circulated to senior officers in a confidential instruction, not to take proceedings against gaming clubs unless there were complaints of cheating or they had become the haunts of criminals. On a challenge to the policy, the Court of Appeal held that the police owed the public a duty to enforce the law and that the court could, if necessary, compel performance of that duty. While the Commissioner had a discretion not to prosecute, his discretion to make policy was not absolute.

12.24   Lord Denning MR stated:[29]

> I hold it to be the duty of ... every Chief Constable, to enforce the law of the land. He must take steps so to post his men that crime may be detected; and that honest citizens may go about their affairs in peace. He must decide whether or no suspected persons are to be prosecuted; and, if need be, bring the prosecution or see that it is brought ...

12.25   He continued:[30]

> Although ... chief officers of police are answerable to the law, there are many fields in which they have a discretion with which the law will not interfere. For instance, it is for the Commissioner ... to decide in any particular case whether inquiries should be pursued, or whether an arrest should be made, or a prosecution brought. It must be for him to decide on the disposition of his force and the concentration of his resources on any

---

27 [2003] EWCA Civ 686; [2003] 33 LS Gaz R 29; (2003) *Times* 7 July.
28 [1968] 2 QB 118, CA.
29 [1968] 2 QB 118 at 136.
30 [1968] 2 QB 118.

particular crime or area. No court can or should give him direction on such a matter. He can also make policy decisions and give effect to them, as, for instance, was often done when prosecutions were not brought for attempted suicide. But there are some policy decisions with which I think, the courts can, if necessary, interfere. Suppose a chief constable were to issue a directive to his men that no persons should be prosecuted for stealing any goods less than £100 in value. I should have thought that the court could countermand it. He would be failing in his duty to enforce the law ...

12.26 In *R v Oxford ex p Levey*,[31] however, the Court of Appeal dismissed an appeal against the judge at first instance's refusal to quash a decision of the Chief Constable of Merseyside not to pursue a suspect into the Toxteth area of Liverpool. The claimant had been robbed in Liverpool, and a police car gave chase but withdrew when the suspect entered Toxteth. The court held that there was no evidence of any breach or failure of duty by the chief constable in policing the Toxteth area and the application failed on its merits. Sir John Donaldson MR stated that it was not for the courts to review the chief constable's choice of methods provided that he did not exceed the limits of his discretion.

12.27 *Blackburn*,[32] was also distinguished by the Court of Appeal in *R v Chief Constable of Sussex ex p International Trader's Ferry Ltd*.[33] Live animal exporters were afforded police protection against demonstrators at a port. The ferry company sought judicial review of the chief constable's decision to reduce the level of protection afforded. The court held that the chief constable was entitled to conclude that he could not provide effective policing throughout his police area and maintain the level of policing at the port without significant extra resources which he had no realistic prospect of obtaining. Accordingly, he had to decide how best to deploy his limited resources in order to keep the peace and enforce the law and, in the circumstances, his decision to reduce policing at the port was not unreasonable.

12.28 Kennedy LJ, delivering the judgment of the court, said:[34]

> The situation cannot be compared with that which was considered by this Court in ... *ex p Blackburn* ... where as a result of a policy decision, the police did not attempt to enforce one section of the Betting, Gaming and Lotteries Act 1963.

31 (1987) 151 LG Rev 371, CA *affirming* (1985) *Times* 18 December, QBD.
32 [1968] 2 QB 118, CA.
33 [1998] QB 477, CA.
34 [1998] QB 477 at 492.

12.29   Applying the dicta of Neill LJ in *Harris v Sheffield United Football Club Ltd,*[35] Kennedy LJ continued:

> I see the force of the argument that the court must be very slow before it interferes in any way with a decision of a chief constable about the deposition of his forces ...

12.30   In *R v Greater Manchester Police Authority and Chief Constable of Police for Greater Manchester ex p Central Motors (Farnworth) Ltd,*[36] the police authority had, historically, discharged its duty to remove vehicles from the road by an informal agreement with local contractors including the claimant. In 1994, that agreement was varied and the police entered into a contract with the third defendant for the removal of vehicles. The claimant brought judicial review proceedings on the ground that this contract was unlawful as the police authority and/or the chief constable were acting ultra vires when they entered it.

12.31   The Court of Appeal dismissed the claim on the basis that statute permitted a police authority to delegate certain functions[37] and that they were therefore entitled to enter into a contract with a private company in order to discharge their statutory duty to remove vehicles from the road.[38]

Operational decisions: disclosure of information

12.32   The courts are reluctant to interfere with an operational decision. In *R v Chief Constable of North Wales ex p AB,*[39] the police had adopted a policy of disclosing information about paedophiles to people in the locality where it was in the public interest to do so and necessary for the protection of persons who might otherwise become the victims of crime. In pursuance of this policy, the police informed a caravan site owner that two convicted paedophiles were staying at the caravan site.

---

35   [1988] QB 77, CA, at 91. That case concerned the legality of the police charging for their services at a football ground.

36   (1998) 3 March (unreported), CA.

37   Local Government Act 1972 ss101 and 111. See also *R v South Yorkshire Police ex p Chief Constable of South Yorkshire* [2000] 1 WLR 55, CA, where s111 was said to provide the power for the police authority to fund individual officers' criminal defences to private prosecutions brought against them in respect of the Hillsborough disaster.

38   As to the power to delegate functions relating to the detention or transfer of prisoners, see Police Reform Act 2002 Part IV.

39   [1999] QB 396, CA.

The owner required the paedophiles to leave. They sought judicial review of the police policy.

12.33   The Court of Appeal held that the decision to disclose the names was not irrational, nor was the original policy or its implementation unlawful. Lord Woolf MR stated:[40]

> ... the court would be slow to characterise as irrational an operational decision such as the NWP [North Wales Police] made here to disclose information about sex offenders where their motive was to protect children.

12.34   Similarly, in *Woolgar v Chief Constable of Sussex Police*,[41] the Court of Appeal held that the police were entitled to release details of an interview with a registered nurse who had been arrested but against whom no charges had been brought. The claimant sought an injunction to prevent the details being disclosed to the UK Central Council for Nursing who were conducting their own investigation. Where a regulatory body operating in the field of public health and safety sought access to confidential material in the possession of the police, the police were entitled to release the information if they were reasonably persuaded that it was of some relevance to the subject matter of the enquiry being conducted by the regulatory body.

12.35   By contrast, however, in *R v A Local Authority in the Midlands and A Police Authority in the Midlands ex p LM*,[42] the claimant had entered into a contract with an education authority, subject to submitting to a police check, to provide school bus services. He sought judicial review and an injunction to prohibit the police, on the check, from disclosing information that allegations of child abuse had been made against him ten years previously in respect of which no further action had been taken. Dyson J allowed the claim, holding that even though the claimant had agreed to submit to a police check, it could not be said that he had no grounds of complaint. Disclosure of such allegations should only be made where there was a pressing need for it; it should be the exception and not the rule because the consequences of disclosure could be very damaging for the subject of the allegations. Article 8 of the Convention was relevant because one of the consequences of disclosure would be to interfere with the claimant's private life. The decision in this case to disclose was irrational, as nothing in the information suggested that the claimant posed any risk to children on school buses.

---

40   [1999] QB 396, CA, at 430A.
41   [2000] 1 WLR 25, CA.
42   (1999) 2 LGLR 1043, QBD.

12.36 Authorities must examine the facts and balance the public interest in the need to protect children against the need to safeguard the individual's right to a private life. In particular, they must consider their belief in the truth of the allegations (the greater the conviction that an allegation was true, the more pressing would be the need to disclose it); the interest of the third party in obtaining the information (the greater the legitimacy of that interest, the more pressing would be the need for disclosure); and the degree of risk posed by the person if disclosure was not made.

Operational decisions: other decisions

12.37 In *R v Chief Constable of Devon and Cornwall ex p Central Electricity Generating Board*,[43] the Court of Appeal refused to intervene in a decision not to assist the applicant by removing protesters from land on which they were obstructing the claimant's officers. The applicant was considering possible sites for a nuclear power station – one such site being in Cornwall. Protesters on the land prevented the claimant's officers from carrying out its statutory duties to investigate and survey the land. Accordingly, the claimant wrote to the chief constable asking for assistance. The chief constable declined to assist on the basis that there had been no actual or apprehended breach of the peace or unlawful assembly and that he therefore enjoyed no power to arrest the protestors. The claimant sought an order of mandamus.

12.38 Lord Denning MR, in the Court of Appeal declined to interfere with the chief constable's decision. He said:[44]

> I would not give any orders to the Chief Constable or his men. It is of the first importance that the police should decide on their own responsibility what action should be taken in any particular situation ... the decision of the Chief Constable not to intervene in this case was a policy decision with which I think the courts should not intervene.

43 [1982] 1 QB 458, CA.
44 [1982] 1 QB 458 at 472. And compare his judgment in *R v Commissioner of Police for the Metropolis ex p Blackburn* [1968] 2 QB 118, CA, discussed above at paras 12.23–12.25.

Judicial review and planning law

Introduction

13.1 Planning law covers a range of matters, from development control to compulsory purchase to decisions concerning the environment. Accordingly, it is an area of law that affects society as a whole, in one form or another, and decisions must, naturally, be subject to a system of review. Most planning decisions, in common with some other areas of public law decision-making, are subject to a statutory system of appeals which has thereby relegated judicial review proceedings to a subordinate role.

13.2 A right of appeal, however, is not conferred on every party who may be affected by a planning decision, given the nature of the planning process as a matter between an applicant (the developer) and decision-maker (the local authority). In particular, where a proposed development is granted permission, there are likely to be many people, and/or groups of people, who objected to the grant of permission and who may wish seek to challenge the decision. The statutory rights of appeal do not, however, apply to challenge the grant of planning permission; only its refusal. Accordingly, judicial review remains of relevance in this situation, the supervisory jurisdiction exerting some control over the exercise of planning functions.

13.3 Equally importantly, judicial review can provide a second stage of review, where an appeal lies to a body that is not, in all the circumstances, independent or impartial for the purposes of article 6 of the European Convention on Human Rights (Human Rights Act 1998 Sch 1, art 6).

Legislation

Town and Country Planning Act 1990

13.4 The principal legislation governing the planning process is contained in the Town and Country Planning Act (TCPA) 1990 and in secondary legislation made under its authority.[1] The TCPA 1990 confers the initial decision-making powers in relation to planning control on local planning authorities – which, in most instances – will be the local

---

1 Reference should also be had to the Planning (Listed Buildings and Conservation Areas) Act 1990, which makes special provision for buildings listed by the secretary of state and for conservation areas.

district (or unitary) authority in whose area the development is proposed.[2] Part II of the Act creates the duty to compile development
plans; Part III makes provision for the control of development, including applications for planning permission,[3] the determination of applications by planning authorities,[4] the secretary of state's powers to call
applications,[5] and the right to appeal to the secretary of state against a
refusal of planning permission.[6]

13.5   The enforcement of planning control is governed by Part VII. Part
XII of the TCPA 1990 makes provision, among other things, for a
statutory right of appeal, on a point of law to the High Court,[7] against
a decision by the secretary of state. The TCPA 1990 is supplemented
by secondary legislation and by Regional Planning Guidance and Plan-
ing Policy Guidance notes, issued by the government department with
responsibility for planning.[8]

Planning and Compulsory Purchase Bill

13.6   There are proposals currently before parliament for new planning legislation: the Planning and Compulsory Purchase Bill. The bill will
make various amendments to the TCPA 1990, the principal intention
being to speed up the planning process and limit the scope for long
planning inquiries, particularly in relation to proposed developments
of regional or national significance.

Decision-making and the role of judicial review

13.7   In most cases, applications for planning permission are determined
by the local planning authority. The secretary of state has a discretion, however, to call in applications and determine them himself,
following a public inquiry, if so requested by the applicant or the planning authority.[9] Where planning permission is granted, it may be

---

2 The definition of 'local planning authority' is contained in Town and Country
   Planning Act 1990 s1.
3 Town and Country Planning Act 1990 ss62–64.
4 Town and Country Planning Act 1990 ss70–76.
5 Town and Country Planning Act 1990 ss77–81.
6 Town and Country Planning Act 1990 s78.
7 Such statutory appeals are dealt with by the Administrative Court.
8 Currently, the Office of the Deputy Prime Minister.
9 Town and Country Planning Act 1990 s77. See also Planning Policy Guidance
   PPG–1, Annex Dm para D7.

granted unconditionally, as outline permission or with conditions attached.[10]

13.8   Where the local planning authority refuses permission, grants conditional permission or does not determine an application within the applicable time limits, the applicant may appeal to the secretary of state. An appeal to the secretary of state is, in the majority of cases, determined by a planning inspector, appointed by the secretary of state following an inquiry, although the secretary of state may decide to take the decision her or himself, following the inquiry.[11] Where the appeal is dismissed by the secretary of state – or where the secretary of state determines a called-in application adversely to the applicant – there is a statutory right of appeal on a point of law to the High Court.[12]

13.9   Judicial review has no role in this process, save in the sense that an appeal on a point of law is conducted on judicial review principles. There is, however, no right of appeal against the grant of permission and therefore an objector has no remedy other than to seek judicial review of the decision to grant permission.

13.10   Such claims frequently concentrate on an alleged failure by the decision-maker to have regard to relevant considerations, or to give a consideration sufficient weight.[13] It is for the court to decide whether a consideration is material but usually a matter for the

10   Some applications do not require formal planning consent, such as a change of use of land that is governed by the Town and Country Planning (Use Classes) Order 1987 SI No 764 (as amended) or where an applicant applies simply for a certificate of lawful use (Town and Country Planning Act 1990 s192).

11   The procedure of inquiries conducted by an inspector is governed by the Town and Country Planning (Determination by Inspectors) (Inquiries Procedure) (England) Rules 2000 SI No1625. See, eg, *R (Alconbury) v Secretary of State for the Environment, Transport and the Regions* [2001] UKHL 23; [2003] 2 AC 295 for an example of an appeal decided by the secretary of state rather than an inspector.

12   Town and Country Planning Act 1990 s289.

13   Town and Country Planning Act s70(2) provides that, in determining a planning application, the authority must have regard to (a) the local development plan and (b) any other material consideration. Decision-makers must have regard to any relevant EU provisions that impact on the decision to grant or refuse permission, including the impact the development would have on the environment – Town and Country Planning (Environmental Impact Assessment) (England and Wales) Regulations 1999 SI No 293; the protection of natural habitats – Conservation (Natural Habitats, etc) Regulations 1994 SI No 2716; and, waste management – Waste Licensing Regulations 1994 SI No 1056.

decision-maker to determine what weight is to be afforded to relevant considerations.[14]

13.11   In *R (Jones) v Mansfield DC*,[15] the claimant sought to challenge the grant of planning permission on the ground that the authority had failed properly to consider the environmental impact of their decision to grant permission.[16] The court held that it was a matter for the planning authority, in the circumstances of each case, to decide whether a development was likely to have significant environmental effects. While the authority must have regard to any uncertainties and the impact they may have on its ability to reach a reasonable conclusion, the local authority had been entitled in that case to consider that the large body of information available to it, even though incomplete, was nevertheless sufficient for it to make a decision about the likelihood of significant environmental effects.[17]

13.12   A claim for judicial review may also be brought to challenge an authority's decision to grant a certificate of lawful proposed use under Town and Country Planning Act 1990 s192.[18]

13.13   Similarly, where a developer successfully applies to have the grant of permission varied[19] – eg, by the removal of a condition originally attached to the permission – it is open to an interested party to seek to challenge that decision by way of judicial review.[20] In *R (Barker) v Waverley BC*,[21] the claimant sought judicial review of the authority's

14   *Bolton MBC v Secretary of State for the Environment* [1991] JPL 241. But see *R v South Oxfordshire DC ex p Secretary of State for the Environment* [1981] 1 WLR 1092, QBD, where a decision was quashed for giving conclusive weight to a relevant consideration.

15   [2003] EWHC 7 (Admin); [2003] 1 P&CR 31.

16   See also *R (Barker) v Bromley LBC* [2002] P&CR 8; *R (Lebus) v South Cambridgeshire DC* [2003] 2 P&CR 5.

17   See *British Telecommunications plc v Gloucester City Council* [2001] EWHC Admin 1001; [2002] 2 P&CR 33.

18   See *R v Thanet DC ex p Tapp* [2001] EWCA Civ 559; [2002] 1 P&CR 7.

19   The power to make such an application is conferred by Town and Country Planning Act 1990 s73.

20   The legality and rationality of conditions is a matter that may be challenged by way of judicial review. See *Newbury DC v Secretary of State for the Environment* [1981] AC 578, HL, for guidance as to the legal validity of planning conditions. Conditions must fulfil a planning purpose (*R v Hillingdon LBC ex p Royco Homes Ltd* [1974] 1 QB 720); should fairly and reasonably relate to the permitted development; and, should not be manifestly unreasonable. See also, generally, *R (Ayers) v Secretary of State for the Environment, Transport and the Regions* [2002] EWHC 295 (Admin) and DoE Circular 11/95, The Use of Conditions in Planning Permissions.

21   [2001] EWCA Civ 566; [2002] 1 P&CR 6.

decision to remove a condition as to future use attached to planning consent on the grounds, among other things, that he had a legitimate expectation that the land would be restored to its original use and that the authority's decision was therefore *Wednesbury* unreasonable. The Administrative Court allowed the claim, but an appeal to the Court of Appeal by the authority was allowed: the applicant's legitimate expectation did not have legal primacy over the authority's need to have regard to all material considerations and their decision to remove the condition was not, therefore, unreasonable.

13.14   Judicial review is also the appropriate forum for challenging the validity of planning legislation. It is open to a local planning authority to challenge secondary legislation made by the secretary of state[22] as well as to an individual affected by a decision flowing from the legislation. In *R (Alconbury) v Secretary of State for the Environment, Transport and the Regions,*[23] the claimants applied for judicial review of the secretary of state's decision to call in a planning application, on the grounds that the power to do so was contrary to article 6 of the European Convention on Human Rights as the secretary of state was not an independent and impartial tribunal.[24]

13.15   The Divisional Court found that the legislation was incompatible with article 6 and made a declaration of incompatibility under Human Rights Act 1998 s4. The House of Lords allowed an appeal, stating that, although the secretary of state was not an independent and impartial tribunal, any decisions made by the secretary of state were reviewable on a statutory appeal to the High Court, which was a court of full jurisdiction.

Time limits

13.16   Until recently, a judicial doctrine was applied that an application for judicial review of a grant of planning permission must be brought within six weeks of the substantive decision (probably the resolution to grant permission rather than the formal grant itself) on the basis that

22   See *R (Spelthorne BC) v Secretary of State for the Environment Transport and the Regions* (2000) 82 P&CR 10.

23   [2001] UKHL 23; [2000] 2 AC 295.

24   Conjoined applications related to the secretary of state's power to recover appeals for consideration by himself (under Town and Country Planning Act 1990 Sch 6, para 3) and to the secretary of state's powers of compulsory purchase, on the basis that appeals against both types of decision would be contrary to article 6 of the Convention as they would lie to the secretary of state, who was not an independent or impartial tribunal.

the time limit for a developer to bring a statutory appeal to the High Court was six weeks and objectors should not be afforded any more generous time limit.[25]

13.17   In *R (Burkett) v Hammersmith and Fulham LBC*, however, the House of Lords decided that the courts had been wrong to adopt the principles described above. In particular, it was a misconception that the three-month period was in fact shortened to six weeks by the planning cases referred to above, as a statutory time limit could not be 'counteracted by a judicial policy decision'.[26]

Planning enforcement decisions

13.18   Judicial review may also be available against a local authority's decision to – or not to – enforce planning control on a developer. In *R (Prokopp) v London Underground Ltd and others*,[27] the claimant sought to prevent the first defendant from undertaking demolition works in connection with a proposed extension of one of its railway lines. He sought judicial review against them, and against the two relevant local authorities, whose decisions not to take enforcement action against the railway company he challenged on the basis that the railway company did not have planning permission for the demolition. (The permission which had been granted had expired because, due to a mistake in its implementation rendering that implementation unlawful, it had not been *lawfully* implemented within the requisite five-year period). The claimant obtained an interim injunction against the railway company prohibiting them from commencing work, notwithstanding concerns about his standing as a private individual to seek to enforce breaches of planning control in circumstances where the authorities charged with doing so had decided not to take action.

13.19   The court held that it could be appropriate to grant interim relief to a private individual against a developer, to prevent the taking of irrevocable steps which the claimant contended to be unlawful but which were not being enforced by the local planning authority. In such a

---

25 See *R v Secretary of State for Trade and Industry ex p Greenpeace* [1998] ELR 41 LR 684, CA; *R (Burkett) v Hammersmith and Fulham LBC* [2001] Env LR 684 at [12]; *Ex p Garnett* [1997] JPL 1015; *R v Ceredigion CC ex p McKeown* [1998] 2 PLR 1 at 2.

26 [2001] Env LR 684, per Lord Steyn at [53]. See, generally, as to time limits, chapter 18, below at paras 18.17–18.56.

27 [2003] EWHC 960 (Admin), [2003] 19 EGCS 119. Hackney LBC and Tower Hamlets LBC were the second and third defendants.

case, while the claim would initially be brought against the developer, the local authority must be added as a defendant and the claim would proceed against the authority with the developer taking part as an interested party. A private individual could not, however, obtain a permanent injunction in a public law claim, which would, in effect, amount to an enforcement action, which was the responsibility of the local authority and which carried with it procedural safeguards for the developer such as a right of appeal.

13.20   The Court of Appeal reversed the judge's decision on other grounds but did not comment on these issues.[28]

28   [2003] EWCA Civ 961; (2003) *Times* 28 August.

Judicial review and access to information

Introduction

14.1   The Freedom of Information Act 2000 has created a limited general right of access to information held by public bodies. The coming into force of this Act has, however, been significantly delayed – the relevant provisions will not come into force until 30 November 2005[1]. Until that date, rights of access to information held by public bodies are limited to such rights as are available under the Data Protection Act 1998, concerning personal files and medical records, and any non-statutory rights to certain information under the *Code of Practice on Access to Government Information.*

Data Protection Act 1998

14.2   The Data Protection Act (DPA) 1998[2] makes new provision for regulating the processing of information relating to individuals. This includes the obtaining, holding, use or disclosure of such information. The Act also creates new rights of access to processed personal information. It repeals the Data Protection Act 1984 and Access to Personal Files Act 1987. Royal Assent was given in July 1998 and the Act came into force in March 2000.[3]

14.3   In essence, the rights created by the DPA 1998 entitle an individual, on request, to be informed[4] by a data controller if any personal data

1   Freedom of Information Act 2000 s87(3) provides that the Lord Chancellor (which would presumably include the Secretary of State for Constitutional Affairs) may prescribe an earlier commencement date.

2   The Act gives effect to the requirements of EU Council Directive 95/46 EC on the protection of individuals with regard to the processing of personal data, and on the free movement of such data. The directive required implementation within three years of its adoption (ie, by 24 October 1998); processing 'already underway' must be brought into compliance within a further three years (ie, 2001); and (although at the discretion of member states) information already held in manual files must be brought into compliance within 12 years of the directive's adoption (ie, 2007), except for subject access which applies from 2001.

3   Minor provisions came into force on Royal Assent; commencement of the remainder of the Act was on 1 March 2000: Data Protection Act 1998 (Commencement) Order 2000 SI No 183.

4   The data controller may charge a reasonable fee for supplying any information in response to a request (see Data Protection (Subject Access) (Fees and Miscellaneous Provisions) Regulations 2000 SI No 191, as amended by 2001 SI No 3223) and is under no obligation to disclose any information until the fee is paid or until he has verified the identity of the individual by requesting such information as he considers necessary: Data Protection Act 1998 s7(2)(b), (3).

relating to her or him is being processed and, if it is, to be provided with a description of the data, the purpose for which it is being processed and the person(s) to whom it may be disclosed.[5] The individual is also entitled to be provided with the information held by the data controller and to be informed of the source of that data.[6]

Terminology

14.4 'Data' means information which:

- is being processed[7] by means of equipment operating automatically in response to instructions for that purpose (ie, data held on computers);
- is recorded with the intention that it should be processed by means of such equipment;
- is recorded as part of a relevant filing system or with the intention that it should form part of a relevant filing system (ie, data which is manually filed in a filing system and is easily accessible);
- does not fall within any of the above but forms part of an 'accessible record'.

14.5 'Relevant filing system' means any set of information relating to individuals to the extent that, even if the information is not processed by means of computer equipment, the set is structured, either by reference to individuals or by reference to criteria relating to individuals, in such a way that specific information relating to a particular individual is readily accessible.[8]

14.6 The scope of the DPA 1998 is considerably wider than that of the DPA 1994, which only applied to data stored electronically, whereas the DPA 1998 includes manual records. Indeed, the Information Commissioner[9] has contended for an extremely wide application of the Act, on the basis of this definition of 'relevant filing system':

> It is our view that on the above definition manual files held by a Local Authority Housing Department which relate to individual tenants, manual files held by the Home Office which relate to immigration applications, and personnel files held by employers would be covered. All the above will

---

5 Data Protection Act 1998 s7(1)(a) and (b).
6 Data Protection Act 1998 s7(1)(c).
7 Data Protection Act 1998 s1(1), for the definition of 'processed'.
8 Data Protection Act 1998 s1(1).
9 Currently, Elizabeth France, formerly the Data Protection Registrar.

comprise of sets of information relating to, and structured by reference to, individuals. Certainly an efficient manual filing system, conventionally arranged alphabetically, should ensure that information relating to a particular individual would be accessible.[10]

14.7 'Accessible record' means:[11]

- a health record;[12]
- an educational record;[13]
- an accessible public record.[14] This term refers to information held by a local housing authority for the purposes of any of the authority's functions, as well as to information held by a local social services authority for any purpose relating to that authority's functions.

14.8 'Personal data' means data which relate to individuals who can be identified from that data. That individual is referred to as the 'data subject'.

Rights of access

14.9 The Act confers on data subjects the following rights:[15]

- the right to be informed by any data controller (ie, the person who holds the data) whether personal data of which he or she is the data subject are being processed by or on behalf of the data controller;
- if so, the right to be given a description, by the data controller, of the personal data concerned, the purposes for which they are being processed and the recipients or classes of recipients to whom they are disclosed or may be disclosed;
- the right to be told in an intelligible form the information constituting the personal data, and any information available to the data controller as to the source of the data; and
- where data relating to the data subject is processed by automatic means for the purpose of evaluating matters relating to the data

---

10 See House of Commons Library Research Paper 98/48 (available online at www.parliament.uk).
11 Data Protection Act 1998 s68.
12 As defined by Data Protection Act 1998 s68(2).
13 As defined by Data Protection Act 1998 Sch 11.
14 As defined by Data Protection Act 1998 Sch 12. See also Data Protection Act 1998 Sch 12, para 3 which provides that accessible records are governed by separate rules.
15 Data Protection Act 1998 s7(1).

subject, such as her or his performance at work, creditworthiness, reliability or conduct, and that processing was or is likely to be the sole basis for the taking of a decision significantly affecting the data subject, he or she has a right to be informed by the data controller of the 'logic involved in that decision-taking'.[16]

Exclusions from the right of access

14.10 There are a number of exclusions from the right of access.[17] These include:

- national security;[18]
- crime and taxation;[19]
- health, education and social work;[20]
- regulatory activity;[21]
- journalism, literature and art;[22]
- research, history and statistics;[23]
- information made available to the public by or under another enactment;[24]
- disclosures required by law;[25]
- confidential references given by the data controller;[26]
- armed forces;[27]
- judicial appointments and honours;[28]

16 Data Protection Act 1998 s12.
17 Data Protection Act 1998 Part IV.
18 Data Protection Act 1998 s28. A ministerial certificate will be conclusive of the fact it asserts that the information is excluded by reason of national security (although there is a right of appeal against a certificate: see Data Protection Act 1998 Sch 6).
19 Data Protection Act 1998 s29.
20 Data Protection Act 1998 s30, which does not itself provide this exemption but instead permits the secretary of state to make such exemptions by order. See Data Protection (Subject Access Modification) (Health) Order 2000 SI No 413; Data Protection (Subject Access Modification) (Education) Order 2000 SI No 414; Data Protection Act (Subject Access Modification) (Social Work) Order SI No 415.
21 Data Protection Act 1998 s31.
22 Data Protection Act 1998 s32.
23 Data Protection Act 1998 s33.
24 Data Protection Act 1998 s34.
25 Data Protection Act 1998 s35.
26 Data Protection Act 1998 Sch 7, para 1.
27 Data Protection Act 1998 Sch 7, para 2.
28 Data Protection Act 1998 Sch 7, para 3.

- Crown employment and Crown or Ministerial appointments;[29]
- management forecasts;[30]
- corporate finance;[31]
- negotiations with the data subject;[32]
- examination marks and/or scripts;[33]
- legal professional privilege;[34]
- self-incrimination.[35]

14.11 A request for information need only be complied with where the individual makes the request in writing; pays any applicable fee (which must not exceed the prescribed maximum)[36] and gives the data controller such information as he or she reasonably requires in order to identify the person making the request and locate the information requested.[37] The Act prescribes time limits for complying with requests – generally 40 days, provided that all of the information referred to above has been supplied to the data controller.[38]

14.12 There is no obligation to disclose information requested if to do so would also necessitate disclosure of information relating to another individual, unless that individual consents or it is reasonable in all the circumstances to comply with the request without her or his consent.[39] In determining the reasonableness of disclosing information without consent, the data controller must have regard to any duty of confidentiality, any steps taken to obtain consent, any express refusal of consent and the question whether the individual is capable of giving consent.[40]

---

29 Data Protection Act 1998 Sch 7, para 4.
30 Data Protection Act 1998 Sch 7, para 5.
31 Data Protection Act 1998 Sch 7, para 6.
32 Data Protection Act 1998 Sch 7, para 7.
33 Data Protection Act 1998 Sch 7, paras 8 and 9.
34 Data Protection Act 1998 Sch 7, para 10.
35 Data Protection Act 1998 Sch 7, para 11.
36 Currently £10: Data Protection (Subject Access) (Fees and Miscellaneous Provisions) Regulations 2000 SI No 191, reg 3 (these regulations have been amended by 2001 SI No 3223).
37 Data Protection Act 1998 s7.
38 Data Protection Act 1998 s7.
39 Data Protection Act 1998 s7(4). Information relating to another individual includes a reference to information that would identify the individual as the source of the information: Data Protection Act 1998 s7(5).
40 Data Protection Act 1998 s7(6).

Unstructured data

14.13 There is no general right of access to unstructured data, ie, any recorded information held by a data controller that is not structured by reference to individuals or criteria relating to individuals. The Freedom of Information Act 2000 will introduce a limited right of access to such information, held by public authorities, with effect from the commencement date of 30 November 2005,[41] but only if the request contains a description of such data. Public authorities will not be obliged to disclose unstructured data, in any event, if they estimate that the cost of doing so would exceed a prescribed limit.[42]

Right to prevent processing

14.14 A data subject may require a data controller not to process information, or to stop processing it, on the ground that its being processed would – or would be likely to – cause substantial and unwarranted distress to him or to another person.[43] The data controller may decline to comply with such a request if the data subject has previously given consent, or if the processing is necessary for the performance of a contract, compliance with a legal obligation or the protection of the vital interests of the data subject.[44] The data subject also has the right to restrict processing of personal data for the purposes of direct marketing[45] and to require the data controller not to make any decision affecting the data subject based solely on automatic processing of personal data.[46]

Remedies and enforcement

14.15 Where a data controller refuses to comply with a data subject's request for information, or has refused, on request, to stop processing data for marketing purposes or otherwise, or has, in spite of a request not to do so, taken a decision against the data subject solely on the basis of automatically processed data, the data subject may apply to the county court or High Court for an order that the data controller must comply with the request.[47]

41 Data Protection Act 1998 s9A, which was inserted by the Freedom of Information Act 2000 and will not come into force until 30 November 2005.
42 Data Protection Act 1998. No limit has yet been prescribed.
43 Data Protection Act 1998 s10.
44 Data Protection Act 1998 s10(2) and Sch 2, paras 1–4.
45 Data Protection Act 1998 s11.
46 Data Protection Act 1998 s12.
47 Data Protection Act 1998 ss7(9), 10(4), 11(2), 12(8) and 15(1).

14.16   Other enforcement provisions, contained in the DPA 1998 include the power of the Information Commissioner to issue an enforcement notice where he or she considers that a data controller is acting in breach of one of the data protection principles.[48] A data subject, moreover, has the right to request the Information Commissioner to assess whether or not personal data is being processed in accordance with provisions of the Act.[49] If the Information Commissioner decides that data is being processed otherwise than in accordance with the DPA 1998, he or she may serve a variety of notices requiring compliance or further information.[50] The recipient of such a notice has a right to appeal to the Information Tribunal and, thereafter, to the High Court.[51]

14.17   There is no right of appeal, however, from a decision of the Information Commissioner not to serve a notice or take any other enforcement action. Accordingly, the only means of challenging such a decision is likely to be by way of judicial review.

Access to information from local authorities

14.18   The Local Government Act 1972 provides for access to meetings and certain information of a local authority.[52] The general principle is that meetings must be open to the general public, but authorities are entitled to exclude them from all or part of a meeting, in specific

---

48   Data Protection Act 1998 s40. The data protection principles are contained in Data Protection Act 1998 Sch 1. They are, in summary, that: 1) personal data must be processed fairly and lawfully; 2) personal data must only be obtained for specified and lawful purposes; 3) personal data must be adequate, relevant and not excessive in relation to the purpose for which it is processed; 4) personal data must be accurate and kept up to date; 5) personal data must not be kept for longer than is necessary; 6) personal data must be processed in accordance with the DPA 1998; 7) adequate technical and organisational measures must be taken to protect against unlawful or unauthorised processing, and accidental loss or destruction, of personal data; and 8) personal data must not be transferred to a non-EEA country, unless that country ensures an adequate level of protection for the rights and freedoms of data subjects.

49   Data Protection Act 1998 s42.

50   Data Protection Act 1998 ss40, 43 and 44.

51   Data Protection Act 1998 ss48–49. The appellate procedure is governed by Data Protection Act 1998 Sch 6. Further rights of appeal lie where data is not disclosed on the ground of national security.

52   See Local Government Act 1972 Part VA, inserted by the Local Government (Access to Meetings) Act 1985.

circumstances.[53] If a meeting is being held in public, members of the public may not be excluded, except to prevent disorderly conduct or other misbehaviour. Accredited newspaper representatives must also be afforded reasonable facilities for reporting and for making telephone calls at their own expense.

14.19 The Local Government Act 1972 does not, however, require or authorise the disclosure of confidential information in breach of confidence. The public must be excluded from meetings during items of business where it is likely that their presence, would result in such disclosure to them. They may also be excluded during items of business where it is likely that their presence would result in the disclosure to them of 'exempt' information.

Agendas and reports

14.20 Copies of the agenda for a meeting must be open to public inspection, generally at least three clear days before the meeting, at the authority's offices. This also applies to copies of any report for the meeting except parts of a report relating to items to be discussed in private, which may be excluded. Where a meeting must be held in public, a reasonable number of copies of agendas and reports must be made available for members of the public present at the meeting. After a meeting, a copy of the minutes of – and reports relating to – the public parts of the meeting and of the agenda, must be open to inspection by the public for six years.

14.21 Documents must be open to inspection at all reasonable hours and free of charge, although a fee may be charged for copying them. It is a criminal offence to refuse to provide copies to a person entitled to them or intentionally to obstruct a person exercising his rights to inspect or copy documents.

14.22 The Freedom of Information Act 2000 makes further provision for rights of access to information held by public bodies, which will include local authorities but, as noted above, it will not come into effect until 30 November 2005.

---

53 Local Government Act 1972 s101A(1). See also the Public Bodies (Admission to Meetings) Act 1960.

Housing and social services data

14.23 As noted above, the Data Protection Act 1998 gives a data subject the right of access to information (ie, personal files) held by a local housing authority for the purposes of any of the authority's functions and, likewise, to information held by a local social services authority for any purpose relating to the authority's social services functions.[54]

14.24 The procedure for gaining access to such information is still governed by the Access to Personal Files (Housing) Regulations 1989[55] and the Access to Personal Files (Social Services) Regulations 1989,[56] both made under the Access to Personal Files Act 1987, neither of which has been revoked by the Data Protection Act 1998. The procedure is very similar to that set out above in relation to general requests under the DPA 1998.[57]

14.25 In relation to social services records, the regulations exempt from the general right of access, personal health information from a health professional[58] and certain other information.[59] Certain exemptions are also provided in the case of housing records.[60]

Education records

14.26 The Education (School Records) Regulations 1989[61] relate to access to educational records. These regulations provide for disclosure, free of charge, of a pupil's educational record to an 'entitled' person on receipt of a written request, and for the supply of a copy of the record to that

---

54 Data Protection Act 1998 s68 and Sch 12.

55 SI No 503.

56 SI No 206.

57 See paras 14.9–14.14 above.

58 Access to Personal Files (Social Services) Regulations 1989 SI No 206, reg 8.

59 1989 SI No 206, reg 9. The exemptions relate to disclosure which would identify a third party who has not consented or which would cause serious harm to physical or mental or emotional health; legally-privileged information; information held for the purposes of detecting or preventing crime or dealing with offenders; information contained in a report prepared for a court; certain information relating to adoptions.

60 Access to Personal Files (Housing) Regulations 1989, reg 4. Exemptions relate principally to disclosure which would identify a third party who has not consented or which would cause serious harm to physical or mental health; legally-privileged information; information held for the purposes of detecting or preventing crime.

61 SI No 1261.

person on payment of a fee. There are, however, certain restrictions on disclosure.[62]

Health

14.27 Access to medical and health records is still governed by the Access to Medical Reports Act 1988 (which permits an individual to see medical reports prepared about her or him for employment or insurance purposes, subject to certain exclusions) and the Access to Health Records Act 1990[63] (which gives a general right of access to health records, again, subject to exclusions). There is also a non-statutory code of practice: *Code of Practice on Openness in the NHS*.

Access to information concerning the environment

14.28 Access to environmental information may be obtained under the Environmental Information Regulations 1992.[64] These regulations make provision for access to any information relating to the environment (as defined) that is held by a relevant person in an accessible form, and otherwise than for the purposes of any judicial or legal functions. The regulations apply to any information not already required to be disclosed under any other enactment.

The code of practice on access to government information

14.29 The code of practice is a non-statutory code introduced by the Conservative government in April 1994 (and revised in January 1997) as part of its Open Government initiative. The code does not require a government department to acquire information not already in its possession, nor to provide information which it does not consider to be

---

62 See SI No 1261, regs 9 and 10. The principal exemptions relate to information supplied by persons not employed by the local education authority in circumstances where disclosure would be likely to identify the informant; and information provided, eg, by way of references.

63 As amended by the Data Protection Act 1998.

64 SI No 3240 (as amended by 1998 SI No 1447). This implements EC Council Directive 90/313 on Freedom of Access to information on the Environment.

reliable, regardless of whether such information has been relied upon by the government. There is no obligation to release under the code information which is already made available via another route and for which a charge is made.

14.30 The code only applies to government departments and other bodies falling within the jurisdiction of the Parliamentary Ombudsman under the terms of the Parliamentary Commissioner Act 1967. It does not therefore apply to local authorities.

14.31 The overriding principle of the code is that '[t]he approach to release of information should in all cases be based on the assumption that information should be released except where disclosure would not be in the public interest, as specified in Part II of this code'.[65]

14.32 Paragraph 3 of the code outlines the information which the government will release:

> Subject to the exemptions in Part II, the code commits departments and public bodies under the jurisdiction of the Parliamentary Commissioner for Administration (the Ombudsman):
> (i) to publish the facts and analysis of the facts which the government considers relevant and important in framing major policy proposals and decisions ...
> (ii) to publish or otherwise make available, as soon as practicable after the code becomes operational, explanatory material on departments' dealings with the public (including such rules, procedures, internal guidance to officials and similar administrative manuals as will assist better understanding of departmental action in dealing with the public) except where publication could prejudice any matter which should properly be kept confidential under Part II of the code;
> (iii) to give reasons for administrative decisions to those affected;
> (iv) to publish, in accordance with the Citizen's Charter:
> • full information about how public services are run, how much they cost, who is in charge, and what complaints and redress procedures are available;
> • full and, where possible, comparable information about what services are being provided, what targets are set, what standards of service are expected and the results achieved;
> (v) to release, in response to specific requests, information relating to their policies, actions, decisions and other matters related to their areas of responsibility.

14.33 Part II of the code sets out a long list of exemptions (15 headings in total) comprising: (i) defence, security and international relations; (ii)

---

65 Code, Part I para 1.

internal discussion and advice; (iii) communications with the Royal Household; (iv) law enforcement and legal proceedings; (v) immigration and nationality; (vi) effective management of the economy and collection of tax; (vii) effective management and operations of the public service; (viii) public employment, public appointments and honours; (ix) voluminous or vexatious requests; (x) publication and prematurity in relation to publication; (xi) research, statistics and analysis; (xii) privacy of an individual; (xiii) third parties' commercial confidences; (xiv) information given in confidence; and (xv) statutory and other restrictions. Many of these exemptions are subject to a 'public interest' test.

14.34   The code, as a non-legal instrument, is not enforceable through the courts, but it may give rise to a legitimate expectation that an authority subject to it will provide the requested data in accordance with the published principles of disclosure. If a body, moreover, refuses to comply with a request or imposes an unreasonable charge, the applicant may request a review of the decision and, thereafter, complain to the Parliamentary Ombudsman.

The Freedom of Information Act 2000

14.35   The Freedom of Information Act 2000 makes provision for a general right of access to information held by public authorities in the course of carrying out their public functions, subject to certain conditions and exemptions.[66]

14.36   The term 'public authority',[67] includes government departments and executive agencies, nationalised industries, public corporations, local authorities and other public bodies, bodies performing public functions and privatised utilities, etc. The scope of the Act is therefore wider than that of the code of practice, and it puts on a statutory footing the rights of access to information from such bodies. The main provisions of the Act, however, will not, as noted above, come into force until 30 November 2005.

---

66 The Act has been criticised as a substantial retreat from the government White Paper *Your Right to Know* Cm 3818 (December 1997). Critics highlight the broad categories of exemptions covering, for example, policy advice and decision-making, and the heavy reliance on discretionary disclosure. Further criticism concerns the failure to adopt an overriding 'public interest' test for the disclosure of information.

67 Defined in Freedom of Information Act 2000 s10.

14.37   The purposes of the Act include:

- to extend progressively the right the public have to access official information held by public authorities and to have that information communicated to them;[68]
- to require each authority to prepare, adopt and publish a publication scheme which specifies the classes of information which the authority intends to publish, the manner in which that information will be published and whether the authority will charge for the provision of the information;[69]
- to ensure that reasons are given for decisions taken by public authorities to the people affected by them; and
- to ensure that guidelines used by public authorities in making decisions affecting people are publicly available.

Limitations and exclusions

14.38   The Act applies similar limitations to the right to information to those applicable under the Data Protection Act 1998. A public authority is, accordingly, not obliged to provide information unless it has been given sufficient details to identify the information requested[70] and is not obliged to provide information where it estimates that the cost of doing so will exceed a prescribed limit.[71] Nor is an authority required to comply with a vexatious request.[72]

14.39   There are also numerous exclusions to the right to information.[73] Aside from the familiar exemptions relating to such matters as national security, defence, international relations, etc, an authority is not required to provide information that is accessible by other means[74] or that relates to any investigation into the possibility of prosecution for an offence[75] or to any documents that are in the authority's possession as a

---

68   The duty imposed by the Act is to provide an applicant with information promptly and, in any event, within 20 working days following receipt of a request for the information: Freedom of Information Act 2000 s10(1).
69   Freedom of Information Act 2000 s19. Such schemes must be approved by the Information Commissioner.
70   Freedom of Information Act 2000 s1(3).
71   Freedom of Information Act 2000 s12.
72   Freedom of Information Act 2000 s13.
73   The exclusions are set out at Freedom of Information Act 2000 Part II.
74   Freedom of Information Act 2000 s21.
75   Freedom of Information Act 2000 s30.

consequence of court proceedings.[76] There is no right to information that contains personal data of which the person requesting disclosure is not the subject.[77]

Codes of practice

14.40 The Freedom of Information Act 2000 requires the secretary of state[78] to produce a code of practice providing guidance on the practices that public authorities should adopt in connection with the discharge of their functions under the Act. In particular, the code of practice must include guidance about: procedures for giving advice and assistance to people who have made or propose to make requests for information; transferring a request to another authority which holds the information requested; consulting with people to whom the information requested relates or who are likely to be affected by its disclosure; inserting terms into contracts concerning the disclosure of information; and the introduction by public authorities of complaints procedures relating to their compliance with their obligations under the Act.[79]

14.41 The Lord Chancellor (now the Secretary of State for Constitutional Affairs) must also produce a code of practice, offering guidance to relevant authorities[80] on the practice that would be desirable for them to follow in respect of the keeping, management and destruction of their records.[81]

14.42 A further obligation is placed on the Information Commissioner to promote good practice and, in particular, the observance by public authorities with the requirements of the Act and the codes of practice laid down under it.[82]

Enforcement and appeals

14.43 Provision is also made for enforcing the obligations of public authorities under the Act. Where a person (the 'complainant') has requested

---

76 Freedom of Information Act 2000 s32.
77 Freedom of Information Act 2000 s40.
78 Secretary of state is the Secretary of State for the Home Department.
79 Freedom of Information Act 2000 s45.
80 A 'relevant authority' means a public authority or any other office or body, not a public authority, whose administrative and departmental records are public records for the purposes of the Public Records Act 1958 or the Public Records (Northern Ireland) Act 1923: Freedom of Information Act 2000 s46(7).
81 Freedom of Information Act 2000 s46.
82 Freedom of Information Act 2000 s47.

information from a public authority, he or she may apply to the Information Commissioner for a decision on whether, in any specified respect, the request has been dealt with in accordance with the Act.[83] The commissioner must make a decision on the application unless it appears to her or him that the complainant has not exhausted any complaints procedure operated by the authority under the secretary of state's code of practice, or has delayed unduly, or that the application is frivolous or vexatious (or has been abandoned or withdrawn).[84]

14.44   If the Information Commissioner considers that the complaint is made out, he or she must serve on the complainant and the public authority a 'decision notice', specifying steps that should be taken and the time limit within which they must be taken.[85] Where the commissioner does not make a decision on the application, he or she must notify the complainant of this and of his or her grounds for not doing so.[86]

14.45   If, independently of any application from a complainant, the commissioner is satisfied that a public authority has failed to comply with any of the requirements of the Act, he or she has power to issue an 'enforcement notice', which specifies the provision(s) of the Act that have not been complied with, and the steps that must be taken to remedy that non-compliance.[87] If the authority fails to comply with the requirements of the Information Commissioner, the commissioner may certify that non-compliance, which may then be dealt with by the court as if it were a contempt of court,[88] although the court enquires into the matter for itself, including hearing evidence and reading statements, and does not merely accept the commissioner's decision in that regard.[89] The Act creates no right of action in civil proceedings, however, for a failure to comply with any duty it imposes.[90]

---

83 Freedom of Information Act 2000 s50.
84 Freedom of Information Act 2000 s50(2). The Information Commissioner also has power to request information from a public authority, by means of serving an 'information notice', before reaching a decision on the application: Freedom of Information Act 2000 s51.
85 Freedom of Information Act 2000 s50(3)(b).
86 Freedom of Information Act 2000 s50(3)(a).
87 Freedom of Information Act 2000 s52.
88 Freedom of Information Act 2000 s54.
89 Freedom of Information Act 2000 s54.
90 Freedom of Information Act 2000 s56.

14.46   In certain circumstances, particular public authorities[91] are not required to comply with either a decision notice or an enforcement notice. Where a notice is served on such an authority, in relation to a failure to confirm or deny the existence of information (falling within the exclusions contained in Part II of the Freedom of Information Act 2000), or failing to disclose information (which is exempt), the 'accountable person'[92] within that authority may give the commissioner a certificate signed by him or her stating that on reasonable grounds he or she has formed the opinion that there was no failure to comply with the Act.[93] Such certificate, if given, causes the notice to cease to have effect.[94]

14.47   The complainant or the public authority has a right of appeal against a decision notice to the Information Tribunal. A public authority may also appeal to the tribunal against an information or enforcement notice.[95] The tribunal has power to allow or dismiss an appeal and to substitute an alternative notice where appropriate. In reaching its decision on appeal, the tribunal can review any finding of fact made by the commissioner on which the notice appealed against was based.[96] An appeal lies from the tribunal to the High Court, on a point of law.[97]

14.48   There is no right of appeal against a certificate issued by the 'accountable person', and it therefore seems that the only method of challenging such a certificate will be judicial review. Given the narrow

---

91 Namely, any central government department, the National Assembly for Wales or any other public body so designated by an order of the secretary of state: Freedom of Information Act 2000 s53(1)(a).

92 The 'accountable person' is the First Secretary of the National Assembly for Wales (in relation to the Assembly), the First Minister and Deputy First Minister in Northern Ireland acting jointly (in relation to a Northern Ireland public authority), or (in relation to any other public authority) a minister of the Crown who is also a member of the cabinet, or the Attorney-General or Advocate-General in Scotland or Attorney-General for Northern Ireland: Freedom of Information Act 2000 s53(8).

93 Freedom of Information Act 2000 s53. Such a certificate should not be confused with a certificate under Freedom of Information Act 2000 s23 or s24 stating that information cannot be disclosed on the ground of national security. An appeal against the latter type of certificate lies to the Information Tribunal.

94 Freedom of Information Act 2000 s53(2).

95 Freedom of Information Act 2000 s57. Appeals are governed by the procedure set down in Data Protection Act 1998 Sch 6.

96 Freedom of Information Act 2000 s58.

97 Freedom of Information Act 2000 s59.

scope of the discretion and the fact that it relates to exempt information, challenges are likely to be rare and difficult to establish. Moreover, the comprehensiveness of the appeals structure set up by the Act, to a specialist statutory tribunal and thereafter to the High Court, will rule out judicial review save in the exceptional case.

CHAPTER 15

Judicial review and children

The legislation

15.1   The law relating to the care and upbringing of children is contained within the Children Act (CA) 1989 (as amended).

15.2   Children Act 1989 Part III obliges local authorities to assist with the care of children of those people who have parental responsibility for them. This includes the responsibility to provide services for families within the area and can include power to provide accommodation for children of those families.

Duties to children in need

15.3   Section 17(1) of the 1989 Act creates a duty to 'safeguard and promote the welfare' of children who are in need and promote the upbringing of such children by their parents by providing a range and level of services 'appropriate to those children's needs'.

15.4   This is a general duty imposed on local authorities, the performance of which is facilitated by the more specific duties and powers conferred by CA 1989 Part III.[1] This includes, for example, the duty to identify children in need in their area;[2] to assess those needs;[3] to maintain a register of disabled children;[4] and to provide accommodation where necessary to protect the child.[5] Local authorities must provide services for children living with their families 'as they consider appropriate', including advice, counselling and guidance, home help and assistance to enable such children to have a holiday.[6]

15.5   A child is defined as 'in need' if:

- he is unlikely to achieve or maintain, or have the opportunity of achieving or maintaining, a reasonable standard of health or development without provision for him of services by a local authority under the Act; or
- if his health or development is likely to be significantly impaired, or further impaired without the provision of such services; or
- he is disabled.[7]

1   Children Act 1989 s17(2) and Sch 2, Part I.
2   Children Act 1989 Sch 2, para 1.
3   Children Act 1989 Sch 2, para 3.
4   Children Act 1989 Sch 2, para 2.
5   Children Act 1989 Sch 2, para 5.
6   Children Act 1989 Sch 2, para 8.
7   Children Act 1989 s17(10). 'Disabled' is defined in Children Act 1989 s17(11).

15.6 The duty under Children Act 1989 s17 has been described as a 'target' duty.[8] In *R (G) v Barnet LBC*,[9] the Court of Appeal held that s17 imposes a general duty on a local authority, in addition to other duties imposed upon them, to safeguard and promote the welfare of children in their area. In *R (A) v Lambeth LBC*,[10] at first instance, Scott Baker J held that:

> ... the duty owed under section 17 of the Children Act 1989 is a target duty owed to children in general and is not justiciable by judicial review. It is to be distinguished from a specific duty such as that in section 20 to provide accommodation for the whole family.[11]

Duties to children 'looked after' by an authority

15.7 Local authorities are under certain, specific, duties to children who are looked after by them. 'Looked after' means in their care or accommodated by them (for a period longer than 24 hours) in the exercise of any social services functions.[12]

15.8 Authorities must safeguard and promote the welfare of such children and provide such services for children cared for by their parents as appears reasonable.[13] Other duties imposed include those to

---

8 *R (A) v Lambeth LBC* [2003] UKHL 57; (2003) 6 CCLR December; [2001] EWCA Civ 1624; [2002] HLR 13; (2002) 4 CCLR 486; *R v Bexley LBC, ex p B* (2000) 3 CCLR 15; *X (Minors) v Bedfordshire CC* [1995] 2 AC 633. As to target duties generally, see *R v Inner London Education Authority ex p Ali* (1990) 2 Admin LR 822, QBD where Woolf LJ described the duty imposed on local education authorities by Education Act 1944 s8 (to secure the provision of sufficient schools in their area) as a target duty. See also generally, chapter 3 above, paras 3.46–3.48.

9 [2001] EWCA Civ 540; (2001) 33 HLR 59; (2001) 4 CCLR 128.

10 [2001] EWHC Admin 376; (2001) 33 HLR 60.

11 [2001] EWHC Admin 376. The House of Lords ([2003] UKHL 57) agreed with this analysis: see para 3.48 and note 70 above, in *R (W) v Lambeth LBC* [2002] EWCA Civ 613; [2002] HLR 41; (2002) 5 CCLR 203, the court did not reject the finding as to the generality of the duty imposed by s17; indeed, given the finding that s17 was only to be used for accommodating children in extreme cases, it could be argued that the court impliedly accepted the generality of the duty. The specific principles involved in *A* and *W* (the provision of accommodation) are considered elsewhere (see chapter 9 above at paras 9.21–9.26) above in the context of housing and judicial review.

12 Children Act 1989 s22(1).

13 Children Act 1989 s22(3).

accommodate and maintain children by, among other things, placing them with foster parents.[14]

15.9   There are continuing duties to children looked after by local authorities.[15] Children Act 1989 s24 includes children looked after by local authorities within the definition of 'persons qualifying for advice and assistance' – accordingly a person between the age of 16 and 21, who was being looked after when he or she became 16 and who needs help, must be advised and befriended by the authority as if he or she were being looked after by them.[16] There is also a duty to provide financial assistance to persons qualifying for advice and assistance in seeking employment and in attending higher or further education.[17]

15.10   Given the various duties that are owed to children – depending, among other things, on whether they are children in need, relevant children,[18] looked after children[19] or eligible children[20] – disputes may arise as to what, if any, definition a child falls within and therefore what, if any, duties may be owed. Thus, in *R (Berhe) v Hillingdon LBC*,[21] the authority provided social services assistance under Children Act 1989 s17 (including accommodation) to an unaccompanied asylum-seeker child. On reaching 18, the claimant requested assistance as a person formerly 'looked after' by the authority, and thereby falling within the scope of assistance owed to formerly looked after 18 to 21-year-olds (ie, as a 'former relevant child').[22]

15.11   The authority refused such assistance on the ground that the claimant was not a former relevant child, having been provided not with accommodation under Children Act 1989 s20 but merely with services (including accommodation) under s17. The claimant had therefore not, it was contended, been looked after, and so was not now a 'former relevant' child. On the claimant's application for judicial review of that decision, the Administrative Court held that there was no

14 Children Act 1989 s23.
15 A looked after child may become an 'eligible child': see Children Act 1989 Sch 2, para 19B. Local authorities must assess the needs of an eligible child and prepare a pathway plan for him, which must be kept under review: Children Act 1989 Sch 2, para 19B(4) and (5).
16 Children Act 1989 s24A(3).
17 Children Act 1989 s24B.
18 Children Act 1989 s23A.
19 Children Act 1989 s23.
20 Children Act 1989 Sch 2, para 19B.
21 [2003] EWHC 2075 Admin; [2003] 39 LS Gaz R 38.
22 Children Act 1989 s23C.

distinction between providing housing by way of a service and accommodating a child and that therefore the claimant had been looked after by the authority.

Duties to all children

15.12 Local authorities have a duty to provide some services where appropriate – and a power to provide others – to all children and their families, whether or not they are 'in need'. They must, for example, provide family centres,[23] and may provide day care and/or supervised activities,[24] financial help[25] and recreational facilities.[26] Certain services must be provided for children under the age of five, whether or not they are in need. An example is such day care as is appropriate for children who are not yet attending school.[27] This provision may also be extended to other children. Local authorities must also take reasonable steps to prevent neglect and abuse[28] and to reduce the need for legal proceedings in respect of children in their area.[29]

Duty to provide accommodation

15.13 A local authority must comply with specific duties in relation to the provision of accommodation and placements. In particular, Children Act 1989 s20 provides that authorities 'shall' provide accommodation for any child in need in their area who 'appears to them to require accommodation' as a result of specified situations,[30] and for any child aged 16 or above whose welfare the authority 'considers is likely to be seriously prejudiced' if accommodation is not provided.[31] The Children Act 1989 does not provide the courts with a power of reviewing the local authority's decision in relation to the placement of a child. Judicial review, or a complaint to the secretary of state, would therefore be the only available remedy.

23 Children Act 1989 Sch 2, para 9.
24 Children Act 1989 s18.
25 Children Act 1989 s17(6).
26 Local Government (Miscellaneous Provisions) Act 1976 s19(1).
27 Children Act 1989 s18.
28 Children Act 1989 Sch 2, para 4.
29 Children Act 1989 Sch 2, para 7.
30 Children Act 1989 s20(1)(a)–(c).
31 Children Act 1989 s20(3).

15.14   The position is different, however, in relation to the use of the authority's Children Act 1989 s17 powers. *R (A) v Lambeth LBC*[32] is authority for the proposition that local authorities may use their powers under section 17 to provide accommodation. Section 17, however, provides only a general or 'target' duty (supported by a range of powers) that is, by definition, not justiciable or enforceable by way of a claim for judicial review.[33]

15.15   It is suggested, however, that while this may prevent a judicial review claim seeking to enforce a section 17 duty, it does not preclude a challenge to a decision of an authority as to what powers to use (or, more usually in this situation, what powers not to use) on the basis that the authority's decision was tainted with illegality, irrationality or procedural impropriety on traditional *Wednesbury* principles.[34] Nor does the reasoning of the court in *A* regarding the section 17 duty, preclude the enforcement of the duties imposed by other parts of the CA 1989, notably section 20,[35] and failure to comply with which may also be enforced by way of judicial review.

Other duties

15.16   Local authorities also have responsibilities, outside the Children Act 1989, which may give rise to judicial review claims. Such duties include the duty to maintain the Child Protection Register,[36] to convene case conferences,[37] to maintain Area Child Protection Committees,[38] and to provide access to social services files.[39]

---

32 [2003] UKHL 57; (2003) 6 CCLR December.

33 See the discussion of *R (A) v Lambeth LBC*, at paras 9.21–9.26 above.

34 See *A*, (above) per Lord Hope of Craighead at [91].

35 *R (A) v Lambeth LBC* per Lord Scott at [137].

36 See note 40 below.

37 'A case conference is a multi-disciplinary meeting to discuss the case of a particular child, convened at the request of either the local authority or any other agency involved, but chaired by a local authority officer. The decision of the case conference is not binding upon the local authority, but is a recommendation to a particular agency for action.' Hershman and McFarlane, *Children Law and Practice* (Jordans, Looseleaf), para B[7]. In practice, however, a case conference's recommendation is usually followed.

38 See note below.

39 Access to Personal Files (Social Services) Regulations 1989 SI No 206. See also paras 14.23–14.25 above.

15.17   The duty to maintain a Child Protection Register[40] has given rise to challenge by way of judicial review in *R v Norfolk CC ex p M*,[41] *R v Harrow LBC ex p D*,[42] and *R v Hampshire CC ex p H*.[43] In all of these cases, however, the courts have been reluctant to interfere with the discretion of the local authority, unless there has been a clear breach of the principles of natural justice or the decision is plainly irrational. In *D*, the Court of Appeal suggested that challenges to entries on the register are special cases in which the welfare of the child should be a paramount consideration.

15.18   In *M*,[44] the applicant sought to challenge the local authority's decision to follow a recommendation of a case conference and place his name on the child abuse register. The applicant was a married man of good character against whom no charges had been brought following a police investigation into the allegation of abuse. The applicant complained that he had enjoyed no opportunity to refute the allegations and that his employers had wrongly been informed. The Divisional Court held that the consequences of registration were sufficiently serious to impose a duty on the council to act fairly. Waite J said:[45]

> It has to be remembered ... that Parliament has entrusted virtual autonomy to local authorities in the discharge of their statutory duties of child care, and the powers of judicial intervention have to be made to fit into that framework. I have held that it is the duty of a case conference (or other agency of local government) exercising a discretion whether or not to enter the name of an alleged child abuser on the child abuse register to act fairly ... It is not the function of the courts – vigilant though they will always be to restrain an oppressive use of these registers – to substitute their own view as to how such a balance is to be resolved for that of the informed and specialist authorities who have been charged by statute with the duty of resolving it. If, therefore, it can be demonstrated in future cases that the particular procedure or range of inquiry followed by a local authority in the course of registering the name of an alleged abuser had represented a genuine attempt, reasonable in all the circumstances, to reconcile the duty of child protection on the one hand and the duty of fairness to the

---

40 Local authorities should maintain a central register of all children in their area who are considered to be suffering from or likely to suffer from significant harm and for whom there is a child protection plan; *Working Together to Safeguard Children* (HMSO 1999), para 5.99. This is binding guidance issued by the Secretary of State under Local Authority Social Services Act 1970 s7.
41 [1989] QB 619, DC.
42 [1990] 1 FLR 79; [1990] 3 All ER 12, CA.
43 [1999] 2 FLR 359, CA.
44 [1989] QB 619, DC.
45 [1989] QB 619 at 629–630.

alleged abuser on the other, it is unlikely that the courts will intervene through judicial review to strike the registration down.

15.19 In *R v Harrow LBC ex p D*, a local authority decided to place the names of a mother and her children on the 'at risk' register, following the recommendation of a case conference. The mother had not been permitted to attend the case conference but had been able to submit written representations. She sought to challenge the decision by way of judicial review. The authority contended that judicial review would not lie in relation to a decision to place a name on the register.

15.20 The Court of Appeal rejected the submission of the local authority and held that if it could be shown that the decision was utterly unreasonable (which had not been shown in the instant case), judicial review would lie. The court emphasised, however, that recourse to judicial review should be rare and, furthermore, that in proceedings involving children, the welfare of that child was a paramount consideration over and above the interests of any individual who might have been prejudiced or any decision-maker which might be criticised. Butler-Sloss LJ said:[46]

> Unless there are exceptional features leading to a conclusion, such as in the *Norfolk* case, I for myself would hesitate long before encouraging a review of the way in which a particular case conference arrived at the recommendation required before the register entry is made ... It would also seem that recourse to judicial review is likely to be, and undoubtedly ought to be rare. Local authorities have laid on them by Parliament the specific duty of protection of children in their area. The case conference has a duty to make an assessment as to abuse and the abuser, if sufficient information is available. Of its nature, the mechanism of the case conference leading to the decision to place names on the register, and the decision-making process is unstructured and informal ... it is not a judicial process. It is part of a protection package for a child believed to have been the victim of abuse. Unlike other areas of judicial review, the considerations are not limited to the individual who may have been prejudiced and the tribunal or organisation being criticised. In this field, unusually, there is a third component of enormous importance: the welfare of the child who is the purpose of the entry on the register. In proceedings in which the child is subject, his or her welfare is paramount.

15.21 In the most recent case of *R v Hampshire CC ex p H*,[47] the court adopted a very similar line to that in *D*.[48] In *H*, however, the application for judicial review – which concerned the decision to place a child's name

46 [1990] 1 FLR 79 at 85.
47 [1999] 2 FLR 359, CA.
48 [1990] 1 FLR 79, CA.

on the child protection register and the decision, following a recommendation of a case conference, to continue that registration – was granted on the basis that there was insufficient material to justify the registration. The court, however, reiterated the principle that recourse to judicial review should be rare in the field of child protection.

Reviews, complaints and appeals

Reviews of cases

15.22 The secretary of state may make regulations requiring the case of each child who is being looked after by a local authority to be reviewed in accordance with the provisions of regulations which he is empowered to make.[49]

15.23 The regulations[50] may, make provision for a number of matters, including:[51]

- the manner in which each case is to be reviewed;
- the considerations to which the local authority are to have regard in reviewing each case;
- the time when each case is to be first reviewed and the frequency of subsequent reviews;
- the people whose views the authority must seek, before conducting any review (including the child, persons with parental responsibility and other persons whose views the authority consider relevant).

Complaints procedures

15.24 Various persons[52] may complain to the local authority, under Children Act 1989 s26,[53] in relation to the authority's powers and duties to provide support for families and children under Part III[54] of that Act.

---

49 Children Act 1989 s26(1).
50 The Review of Children's Cases Regulations 1991 SI No 895, as amended.
51 Children Act 1989 s26(2).
52 See paras 15.25–15.26 below.
53 Note that various substantive and procedural amendments will be made to this by Adoption and Children Act 2002 s26.
54 And such of its functions under Parts IV and V as the secretary of state may specify in regulations made under Children Act 1989 s26(3A), inserted by Adoption and Children Act 2002 s117.

15.25   By CA 1989 s26(3), local authorities are obliged to establish a procedure for considering any representations, including complaints, made by the following persons:

- a child in need or a child being looked after by the local authority;
- a person who qualifies for advice and assistance under CA 1989 s24;
- a parent or other person with parental responsibility;
- any foster parent; or
- any other person as the authority or voluntary organisation consider has a sufficient interest in the child's welfare to warrant representations being considered by them concerning the discharge by them of any of their functions under CA 1989 Part III.[55]

15.26   This complaints procedure is clearly intended to deal with a wide range of issues which may be raised by a wide range of persons. Children other than those in need or those being looked after, however, are not specified as potential complainants.

15.27   The complaints procedure must have an independent element,[56] and the local authority must have due regard to the findings of those who have considered the representations and must notify the child, the person making the representations and other affected persons of their decision, their reasons and of any action taken or to be taken.[57] The procedure to be followed is set out in the Representations Procedure (Children) Regulations 1991.[58]

15.28   In addition to the s26 complaints procedure, there are two further avenues of complaint:

- a complaint in relation to children's homes or voluntary organisations may be made within their own procedures; and
- a complaint in relation to all matters not within the scope of the CA 1989 s26(3) may be made to the local authority under Local Authority Social Services Act 1970 s7B.

55 Children Act 1989 s26(3B), inserted by Adoption and Children Act 2002 s117, specifies two additional categories of potential complainant: (a) a person mentioned in s3(1) of the 2002 Act (person for whose needs provision is made by the Adoption Service) and any other person to whom arrangements for the provision for adoption support services extends; and (b) any other person as the authority consider has sufficient interest in a child who has been or may be adopted to warrant his representations being considered.

56 Children Act 1989 s26(4). The requirement for an independent element will be circumscribed in cases prescribed by the secretary of state in regulations made under Children Act 1989 s26(4A), inserted by Adoption and Children Act 2002 s117.

57 Children Act 1989 s26(7).

58 SI No 894.

Default powers of the secretary of state

15.29 Under Children Act 1989 s84, the secretary of state may declare a local authority to be in default, where he or she is satisfied that they have, without reasonable cause, failed to comply with a duty under the CA 1989. The secretary of state then has power to issue directions to compel the local authority to comply with the duty and may enforce these directions by a mandatory order.[59]

Appeals

15.30 A right of appeal lies to the High Court against the making by a magistrates' court of any order under the CA 1989 or the refusal to make such an order. This includes care and supervision orders (including an interim order).[60]

Judicial review and the appeal structure

Judicial review of Children Act 1989 duties

15.31 The Children Act 1989 has conferred wide discretionary powers on local authorities and social workers, and has thereby increased the possibilities for using judicial review in child cases, particularly in relation to authorities' duties under Part III of the Act (local authority support for children and their families). The other parts of the CA 1989 are less significant in the field of administrative law and are, consequently, not dealt with in this chapter.

15.32 The use of judicial review is, however, limited by the availability of the case review and complaints procedure under CA 1989 s26, and by the secretary of state's default powers under s84.[61] Each of these procedures will usually provide an alternative remedy. The wide discretion conferred on local authorities in performance of many of their duties under the Act often makes it difficult to bring a successful challenge by way of judicial review. There remains, obviously, the ability to

---

59 This power is similar to that conferred by Education Act 1996 s497 (as amended).
60 Children Act 1989 s94(1) as amended.
61 See paras 7.9–7.20.

challenge the vires of any subordinate legislation, and/or the failure of an authority to acknowledge that any duty is owed to a child.[62]

Children Act 1989 s26 as an alternative remedy

15.33　It has been held that the complaints procedure under Children Act 1989 s26 is an appropriate alternative remedy which ought to be exhausted before any application for judicial review is made. In *R v Kingston upon Thames RLBC ex p T*,[63] the Divisional Court refused permission to apply for judicial review of a local authority's decision regarding the placement of the applicant's daughter as a child in need, stating that the complaints procedure under s26 offered an appropriate alternative remedy.

15.34　Ward J held that the s26 procedure was quicker and cheaper than judicial review, no specialist knowledge was required and the members of the panel would consider the matter anew, exercising their own independent judgment of the facts on the merits, including any new facts placed before them. The panel was not confined to finding *Wednesbury* unreasonableness or that the decision was plainly wrong. There was little difference between the effectiveness of judicial review to bring about change, and the due regard to the recommendations of the panel which the Act and the regulations required the local authority to have. If the local authority failed to heed the panel's recommendations, judicial review could then be invoked. He continued:[64]

> By far the most compelling argument for first requiring these panel procedures to be enforced before intervening by way of judicial review is that such an order of priority would seem to me to fall within the broad legislative purpose of the Act. Parliament has quite clearly assigned certain functions in controlling the lives of our children to the local authorities. Parliament has most definitely denied the court power to intervene. That is quite clear from the whittling down of the inherent jurisdiction of wardship. It is quite clear from the provisions of section 37 of the Act, which gives the court no other power than to invite the local authority to intervene in a case where the court wishes there to be consideration of care or supervision. Part III is intended to operate in a new climate of partnership between the local authorities and the family. It is part of the philosophy of

62　An interesting example of the latter is *R (B) v Merton LBC* [2003] EWHC 1689 (Admin), in which the local authority refused to accept a duty to the claimant on the basis that they were not satisfied that he was a child at all, as he could not prove his age.

63　[1994] 1 FLR 798, DC.

64　[1994] 1 FLR 798 at 815.

sitting down and trying to work things out together. It is better than adversarial contest in the courts. The door of the court is the last door that should be opened.

15.35 In *R v Birmingham CC ex p A*,[65] Sir Stephen Brown held that judicial review was not the appropriate remedy for a complaint of unreasonable delay in placing a child in appropriate accommodation. This was not a case which sought to clarify the law, but rather a case which sought to find the local authority in breach of Children Act 1989 s20 in failing to act with reasonable diligence and expedition. The more appropriate remedy was the complaints procedure under s26, which provided for a wide-ranging procedure to investigate cases where there was an allegation of culpable neglect on the part of the local authority.

15.36 The cases that have been decided concerning the compliance of review processes with article 6 of the European Convention on Human Rights have indicated, however, that judicial review provides an important procedural safeguard, given that review procedures cannot, in their nature, comprise independent tribunals and exceptional cases may exist where a person will not be obliged to use them before resorting to the Administrative Court.[66] Judicial review may, therefore, continue to have a relevance in Children Act 1989 proceedings, notwithstanding the availability of a complaints process.

Children Act 1989 s84 as an alternative remedy

15.37 In *R v Brent LBC ex p Sawyers*,[67] the Court of Appeal held that an alleged breach of an authority's duty under Children Act 1989 s23(8) – the duty, where an authority provides accommodation for a child it is looking after, to secure, so far as is reasonably practicable, that the accommodation is not unsuitable for the child's needs – was properly litigated by way of judicial review, notwithstanding the secretary of state's default powers under CA 1989 s84. The court, overruling Owen J at first instance, held that these default powers did not provide an alternative remedy to deprive the applicant of the right to apply to the High Court.

15.38 The Court of Appeal in *Sawyers* nevertheless did consider that the procedure under CA 1989 s26, where available, did provide an alternative remedy. CA 1989 s84, by contrast, did not confer either

65 [1997] 2 FLR 841, DC.
66 See *R (Alconbury Developments Ltd) v Secertary of State for the Environment, Transport and the Regions* [2001] UKHL 23; [2003] 2 AC 295.
67 [1994] 1 FLR 203, CA.

an express or implied right of 'appeal' from a decision by a local
authority by which a person was aggrieved.

15.39   Peter Gibson LJ stated:[68]

> In my judgment it is manifest from those provisions [sections 26(3) and
> 84] that Parliament intended that a person aggrieved by the way a local
> authority exercised its functions (including powers as well as duties) would
> have a remedy by making a representation to the authority and so setting
> in train the representations procedure. That remedy is available to a person
> ... as of right, and it is to be contrasted with the absence of a corresponding
> right under section 84.

15.40   Although relating to local authorities' social services functions and
the secretary of state's default power under Local Authority Social Services Act 1970 s7D, *R v Devon CC ex p Baker*,[69] is another example of a
case in which the Court of Appeal held that a statutory default power
was not an adequate alternative remedy so as to preclude the use of
judicial review.

15.41   The Court of Appeal held that it was not clear whether or not the
default power was available because it was not clear whether the subject-matter of the claim – an alleged failure to consult properly prior to
the decision to close a residential home – was a social services function.
Given this, and that the essence of the complaint was a matter of law
in a developing field, it was particularly appropriate for decision by
the court.

15.42   This does not mean, however, that the existence of a default power
will always be disregarded by the court on the question of alternative
remedies, particularly in the current judicial climate of insistence that
alternative methods of dispute resolution be attempted, even where
those methods will be unlikely to resolve all the issues between
the parties.[70]

---

68 [1994] 1 FLR 203 at 212.
69 [1995] 1 All ER 73, CA.
70 See, eg, *Cowl v Plymouth CC* [2001] EWCA Civ 1935; [2002] 1 WLR 803; (2002)
    5 CCLR 42.

CHAPTER 16

Judicial review and Legal Services Commission funding

Structure

16.1   The Access to Justice Act 1999, created the Legal Services Commission (LSC), which – in relation to the administration of public funds for
litigation – replaced the Legal Aid Board. The new arrangements for the
administration of public funding are considerably altered from the
arrangements which they replaced.[1]

16.2   The administration of public funding (formerly 'legal aid') is
separated into two branches, both controlled by the Commission:

- the Community Legal Service, which is concerned with funding
  for civil actions; and
- the Criminal Defence Service, dealing with criminal cases.

Community Legal Service

16.3   The essential features of the Community Legal Service (CLS) system
are as follows:[2]

(a) public funding will only be available to approved contractors who
meet certain, specified quality control standards;[3]

(b) the CLS is obliged to follow 'priorities' established by the Commission in relation to the funding of legal services;[4]

(c) the CLS may fund any services which it considers appropriate,[5]
save for certain services which are specifically excluded;[6]

---

1   See, generally, *Legal Services Commission Manual* (Sweet & Maxwell) – this
work contains all the relevant legislation, guidance and directions relating to
Legal Services Commission (LSC) funding. In relation to funding for civil
proceedings, the relevant guidance is the Funding Code Part 1 (criteria) and
Part 2 (procedures) – the set of rules used to decide which individual cases are
to be funded by the LSC as part of the CLS, replacing the 'merits test' for civil
legal aid – and the decision-making guidance. Although copies of these
documents are contained in the manual, they are frequently amended; up-to-
date copies can be obtained from the Legal Services Commission website:
www.legalservices.gov.uk.

2   The precise detail relating to LSC funding is complex and beyond the scope of
this chapter, which is intended only to provide an overview of the aspects
which may effect judicial review. For detailed analysis, see the LSC manual
and, in particular, the Funding Code Procedures and the Narrative and
Guidance sections.

3   Access to Justice Act 1999 ss4(8) and 12(4).

4   Access to Justice Act 1999 s6(1)(a).

5   Access to Justice Act 1999 s6(2).

6   Listed in Access to Justice Act 1999 Sch 2, see also s6(6).

(d) The Lord Chancellor (or Secretary of State for Constitutional Affairs) has power to require the CLS to fund any of the excluded services in such circumstances as he may direct and may authorise the funding of services in specified circumstances or, at the request of the LSC, in individual cases;[7]

(e) The allocation of CLS funding automatically places a statutory charge, equal to the amount spent by the CLS on funding services, over any property recovered in the course of the proceedings,[8] although there are exceptions to this general rule and some property is excluded.[9] There is an exception where the CLS funds services which it considers have a wider public interest (ie, test cases).[10]

Criminal Defence Service

16.4   In relation to the Criminal Defence Service (CDS), similar provisions apply. Services may only be provided by accredited bodies; the CDS must provide such advice and assistance as it considers necessary to any individual who has been arrested or who is held in custody;[11] representation in court must also be funded[12] and the individual may choose which representative he wishes to represent her or him.[13]

16.5   In relation to both the CLS and CDS, detailed provision relating to the administration of funding is contained in the Funding Code.[14]

---

7   Access to Justice Act 1999 s6(8). See the *Lord Chancellor's Direction: Scope of the CLS Fund Exceptions to the Exclusions*, 2 April 2001.

8   Access to Justice Act 1999 s10(7) – this may include circumstances where a person recovers possession of a property as a result of the proceedings: *Parkes v Legal Aid Board* [1994] 2 FLR 850 confirmed on appeal [1997] 1 WLR 1547. As to the maximum amount of this charge, see LSC Manual Vol 2.

9   See Community Legal Service (Financial) Regulations 2000 SI No 516, reg 44.

10 Community Legal Service (Financial) Regulations 2000 SI No 516, reg 47.

11 Access to Justice Act 1999 s13.

12 Access to Justice Act 1999 s14 and Sch 3.

13 Access to Justice Act 1999 s15.

14 The Funding Code is reproduced in the LSC Manual and is made under Access to Justice Act 1999 s8. The code must be approved by a resolution of both Houses of Parliament.

Funding assessments and appeals

16.6   Where costs are subject to assessment by the court, the provisions of Civil Procedure Rules (CPR) Part 47 apply. A person dissatisfied with the assessment may apply for permission to appeal.[15]

16.7   Where either the CLS or CDS awards funding, the LSC is obliged to pay any remuneration properly due.[16] Public funding is, however, subject to assessment by a costs committee, the procedure for which varies depending on the nature of the action. A client who has a financial interest in his solicitor's costs has a right of review or appeal against remuneration decisions, at which he or she can make representations to a costs committee.[17]

16.8   Similarly, solicitors or counsel may appeal against the assessment of their costs.[18] In the first instance, such an appeal is by way of a request for a review to a Funding Review Committee, which may vary or confirm the original assessment. Thereafter, if there is a point of principle or of general importance that needs to be considered, there is a right of appeal to a freshly constituted costs committee. A final right of appeal lies to the Costs Appeal Committee. Thereafter challenge is by way of judicial review.[19]

Applications, reviews and appeals

16.9   The LSC must appoint a regional director to consider applications for funding and make the initial determination on whether funding

15   Civil Legal Aid (General) Regulations 1989 SI No 339, reg 113.
16   See Community Legal Service (Funding) Order 2000 SI No 627, the Community Legal Service (Financial) Regulations 2000 SI No 516, the Civil Legal Aid (General) Regulations 1989 SI No 339, as amended by the Civil Legal Aid (General) (Amendment) Regulations 2000 SI No 451 and the Community Legal Service (Financial) Regulations 2000 SI No 516; Community Legal Service (Funding) Order 2000 SI No 627; Criminal Defence Service (Funding) Order 2001 SI No 855; Community Legal Service (Funding) (Counsel in Family Proceedings) Order 2001 SI No 1077; Criminal Defence Service (General) (No 2) Regulations 2001 SI No 1437.
17   Civil Legal Aid (General) Regulations 1989 reg 105A. See also *R (Wulfsohn) v Legal Services Commission* [2002] EWCA Civ 250; [2002] CP Rep 34 where a litigant-in-person successfully appealed against the High Court's refusal to order the defendant to pay him his costs for research involved in a claim for judicial review against a decision of the LSC to refuse him funding.
18   Civil Legal Aid (General) Regulations 1989 SI No 339 reg 105.
19   As to which see paras 16.16–16.21. It is also open to the Legal Services Commission to challenge an award of costs made against them: *R (Gunn) v Secretary of State for the Home Department (recovery of costs)* [2001] EWCA Civ 891; [2001] 1 WLR 1634.

should be granted, having regard to the Funding Code of Guidance.[20] Where the regional director is satisfied that all relevant criteria and procedures have been complied with,[21] and that the applicant is financially eligible, he or she must issue a certificate to that effect,[22] unless the actual or likely costs of the case exceed a defined threshold, in which case he must refer the matter to the Special Cases Unit.[23] Where the director considers that the applicant is not eligible, he or she must notify the applicant (and his solicitor) and provide a brief statement of his reasons.[24]

16.10   The director also has power to amend or withdraw a certificate,[25] the latter may take place if the applicant enters into a conditional fee arrangement, if his or her conduct justifies withdrawal, or if he or she is no longer eligible financially.[26]

16.11   Where an application is refused, or a certificate withdrawn or amended, the applicant may ask the director to review the decision.[27] The director must consider any representations made on the review and may decide to affirm, amend or reverse his or her earlier decision.

16.12   An applicant who is dissatisfied with the decision on review or with the decision of a Special Cases Unit, may ask for the decision to be referred to the Funding Review Committee.[28] This committee may:

(a) determine certain issues of fact, such as the prospects of success and the cost/benefit analysis;

(b) consider whether the decision under review was improper or unreasonable in the sense that it was a decision no reasonable

---

20 In some circumstances, an authorised solicitor may grant funding under devolved powers. Where this is the case, the same appeal process arises against a decision to refuse funding. Provision is also made for emergency representation and emergency certificates, which may be granted subject to conditions regarding a substantive application being made: Funding Code: Procedures, r11.

21 The criteria and procedures are set out, respectively, in the Funding Code: Criteria and the Funding Code: Procedures, which should be read together with the Guidance.

22 Funding Code Procedures, r14.

23 Funding Code Procedures, r23.

24 Funding Code Procedures, r19.

25 Funding Code Procedures, r36.

26 Funding Code Procedures, r55. It would appear that it is not open to a director to place an embargo on funding, pending the outcome of enquiries into the applicant's continued eligibility – *R (Machi) v Legal Services Commission* [2001] EWCA Civ 2010; [2002] 1 WLR 983.

27 Funding Code Procedures, r21.

28 Funding Code Procedures, r59.

decision-maker could have made or whether the decision-maker failed to act in accordance with the code;

(c) confirm the decision on review; or

(d) refer the matter back to the decision-maker for a further review, the decision on which is final.[29]

Commission funding for judicial review proceedings[30]

16.13 Judicial review proceedings may themselves attract CLS funding.[31] The Code of Guidance issued by the LSC states, however, that an application for CLS funding in relation to investigative help (as distinct from assistance by way of representation) may be refused if the act under challenge does not appear to be amenable to judicial review.[32]

16.14 When determining whether CLS funding is available for a judicial review claim, different considerations apply depending on whether permission has been granted. If permission has not been granted, then the CLS must consider: (i) whether judicial review is available; (ii) whether all other appeals or other procedures have been exhausted; (iii) if the respondent public authority has been given a reasonable opportunity to respond to the challenge and deal with the complaint; (iv) the prospects of success;[33] and, (v) whether the likely benefits of the proceedings justify the likely costs.[34]

16.15 Where permission has been granted, and the claim has a wider public interest or is of overwhelming importance to the client or raises human rights issues, there is a presumption that funding will be granted unless, in all the circumstances, it appears unreasonable for representation to be granted. If none of those factors is present then funding will be refused if the prospects are poor or borderline or the likely benefits of the proceedings do not justify the likely costs.[35]

---

29 Funding Code Procedures, r65.5.

30 The funding of judicial review claims, including standard limitations, is considered in more detail in chapter 8.

31 Considerable guidance is offered in the LSC Manual, Part C – The Funding Code: Decision Making Guidance, section 16.

32 Code of Guidance, para 7.2.2.

33 Funding will be refused if the prospects are unclear, borderline (save if the case raises an important point of wider public interest) or poor.

34 Funding Code of Guidance, para 7.4.

35 Funding Code of Guidance, para 7.5.

Challenging funding decisions

16.16 Clearly, given the relatively comprehensive nature of the appeals and review system, the scope for judicial review of a decision by the LSC is restricted and, in any event, such a claim could only exist after the appeals system had been exhausted. There remains, however, the possibility of challenging a refusal to award funding on public law grounds.[36]

16.17 Challenges to the legality or rationality of the LSC's decisions (or the decisions of Funding Review Committees on appeal) are not limited to decisions to refuse funding; judicial review may equally be sought of a decision to discharge a certificate before the proceedings have reached a conclusion, or on a matter of statutory interpretation.

16.18 In *R (Machi) v Legal Services Commission,*[37] the LSC informed the claimant on the day before the hearing that his entitlement to funding was being reviewed and that, until a decision had been made, no further work could be done under the certificate unless expressly approved by the LSC itself. The result was that the claimant was unrepresented at the hearing. He applied for judicial review of the LSC's decision on the ground that they had acted unfairly or irrationally by effectively discontinuing his funding on the day before the hearing and, in any event, that they did not have power to withdraw funding pending a review of entitlement.[38]

16.19 The court held that a funding certificate was valid until it was discharged and that there was no statutory power to embargo the use of

---

36 In *R (Bateman) v Legal Services Commission* [2001] EWHC Admin 797; [2002] ACD 29, the court held that the LSC's decision to withdraw the claimants' funding certificates on the ground that the claimants had failed to disclose material facts was irrational because the facts that had not been disclosed would not have affected the claimants' eligibility for funding. The claimants' costs awards, however, were significantly reduced as they had pursued 'hopeless', 'futile' and 'untenable' arguments. Errors of law, in this context, may include the giving of inadequate reasons, or an alleged failure to consider the effect of other statutory provisions (*R v Legal Aid Board ex p W (Children)* [2000] 1 WLR 2502, CA).

37 [2001] EWCA Civ 2010; [2002] 1 WLR 983.

38 The relevant legal power derived from the Civil Legal Aid (General) Regulations 1989 SI No 339, and the Legal Aid Act 1988.

the certificate pending review of eligibility. Accordingly, the claim was allowed.[39]

16.20 In *R (Toth) v Legal Services Commission*,[40] Hooper J dismissed an argument that the cost/benefit analysis used when determining whether the claimant's funding certificate should be discharged was ultra vires.

16.21 Claims relating to the construction and/or legality of legislation may also involve arguments relating to human rights – in *R (Alliss) v Legal Services Commission*,[41] the claimant successfully sought judicial review of the withdrawal of his funding on the ground, among other things, that this deprived him of effective access to a court and thus the right to a fair hearing for the purposes of Human Rights Act 1998 Sch 1, article 6(1). It should be noted, however, that applicants involved in civil proceedings which will determine their civil rights have no automatic Convention right to public funding.[42] In *X v United Kingdom*,[43] it was held that 'only in exceptional circumstances, namely where withholding of legal aid would make the assertion of a civil claim practically impossible, or where it would lead to an obvious unfairness of the proceedings, can ... article 6(1) of the Convention [be invoked].[44]

---

39 As to statutory interpretation, see also *R v Legal Services Commission ex p Burrows (t/a David Burrows (a firm))* [2001] EWCA Civ 205; [2001] 2 FLR 998, where the claimant sought to challenge the LSC's decision to limit the amount of costs payable to him (as a legal representative) on the basis that the word 'limitations' in Legal Aid Act 1988 s15(4) did not include financial limitations but extended only to limitations on the scope of assistance. See also *R (Pearson) v Legal Services Commission* [2001] EWHC Admin 1048, which concerned the interpretation of Civil Legal Aid (General) Regulations 1989 SI No 339 reg 46(3) and was brought after a review by a funding review committee.

40 [2002] EWHC 5 (Admin).

41 [2002] EWHC 2079 (Admin).

42 *P, C and S v United Kingdom*, ECHR, July 16, 2002. See also *Airey v Ireland* (1979) 2 EHRR 305, ECHR.

43 (1984) 6 EHRR 136.

44 It should also be noted that, in applying the test laid down in *X v United Kingdom*, the LSC must act reasonably – *R (Jarrett) v Legal Services Commission and others* [2001] EWHC Admin 389.

Pre-application procedure

Introduction

17.1   Since the introduction of the Civil Procedure Rules (and due as much to the philosophy which led to their introduction as to the provisions of the rules themselves), the courts have begun to place much greater emphasis on requiring litigants to follow procedures and take all possible alternative measures to resolve their dispute prior to having to resort to legal proceedings.[1] Despite the very strict time limits involved,[2] this is no less true of judicial review claims than of any other type of civil action. Nor is it simply a matter of following the judicial review pre-action protocol. Although compliance with the protocol is plainly important, the courts' requirements go much further, including that at the very least active consideration is given to attempting alternative dispute resolution,[3] and the use of any available alternative remedies,[4] before a claim is brought in the Administrative Court.

17.2   Where proceedings are necessary, the court may take a pro-active stance in relation to the issues which it will permit to be raised.[5] Alternatively, it may adjudicate on all the issues and then penalise the parties afterwards for raising those it considers to have been unreasonably litigated.[6]

17.3   Much may ultimately depend, including the grant or refusal of permission, the availability of public funding and the costs orders made at the end of proceedings, on the attention which the parties, particularly the claimant, have paid to these matters before the commencement of proceedings. These issues do not, however, concern only the claimants' advisers. There is now a clear, and openly expressed,[7] judicial agenda that all parties must recognise and take account of the cost

---

1   See, eg, Civil Procedure Rules (CPR) r1.4(2)(e) and (f).

2   See chapter 18 below at paras 18.17–18.57.

3   CPR r1.4(2)(e) provides that the court's duty to manage cases includes 'encouraging the parties to use an alternative dispute resolution procedure if the court considers that appropriate and facilitating the use of such procedure'.

4   See chapter 7 above at paras 7.9–7.20.

5   See, eg, CPR rr1.4(2)(c) and 54.12(b). See also *R (Opoku) v Southwark College Principal* [2002] EWHC 2092 (Admin); [2003] 1 WLR 234, and now *R (Smith) v Parole Board* [2003] EWCA Civ 1014; [2003] 1 WLR 2548, where an attempt to raise grounds at the full hearing for which permission to apply had been refused.

6   See, eg, *R (Bateman) v Legal Services Commission* [2001] EWHC Admin 797; [2002] ACD 29.

7   See, eg, *Bateman* [2001] EWHC Admin 797; *R (Cowl) v Plymouth CC* [2001] EWCA Civ 1935; [2002] 1 WLR 803; (2002) 5 CCLR 42; *Dunnett v Railtrack plc* [2002] EWCA Civ 303; [2002] 1 WLR 2434.

of and time taken by judicial proceedings (especially in terms of the public money which is involved in every case – even if the claimant is not publicly funded, the defendant as a public body is extremely likely to be; even if neither party is publicly funded, the court itself is funded by public taxation) and consider these matters in relation to what is likely to be achieved by litigation as compared with other, cheaper means of resolving disputes.

17.4   This, together with other requirements (such as, for the defendant, the requirement of a pleaded summary of the ground of defence in the acknowledgement of service)[8] is likely to make it imperative that both parties have properly considered the strengths and weaknesses of their own case, and indeed what they hope to achieve by litigation (and what possible opportunities there may be for avoiding proceedings) at a far earlier stage than was formerly (or traditionally) the case.

17.5   One, perhaps ironic, effect of this is likely to be that both claimants and defendants will be involved in the expenditure of not inconsiderable sums of money at a much earlier stage in a dispute, which costs are likely to be wholly irrecoverable if proceedings do not result. This may affect defendants disproportionately, given that it will be a dangerous, not to say reckless, response to first notification of a potential claim simply to deny the legitimacy of the claim and wait and see if proceedings develop. Defendants as well as claimants run the risk of adverse costs orders, even if they ultimately succeed in the proceedings where, for instance, the court does not consider that they have engaged sufficiently with the possibility of alternative dispute resolution at a sufficiently early stage.[9]

17.6   In many cases, it will be essential for the claimant's adviser to obtain as much information as possible about the circumstances of the decision, and the facts about the claimant known to the decision-maker when the decision was taken. This will often involve requesting to see the information held about the claimant in the decision-maker's files.[10]

---

8 CPR r54.8(4)(a)(i).

9 See, eg, *Dunnett v Railtrack plc* [2002] EWCA Civ 303; [2002] 1 WLR 2434. This has, in fact, been a risk for defendants for many years. In *R v Kensington and Chelsea RLBC ex p Ghebregiogis* (1995) 27 HLR 602, QBD, where costs were awarded against a local authority defendant which had conceded the claim prior to the permission hearing, as their failure to consider the merits of the claim properly on receipt of the letter before action caused the necessity for proceedings to be issued.

10 See Pre-action disclosure at paras 17.22–17.25 below. See also paras 5.55–5.59 and chapter 14 generally.

17.7   Equally, it can be difficult to gauge the correct balance to strike between seeking to resolve the dispute in ways that do not involve resort to the judicial review court and seeking to follow the requirements of the pre-action protocol on the one hand, and acting promptly so as not to fall foul of the time limits on the other.

17.8   This chapter explores these issues.

Alternative dispute resolution

17.9   In spite of the necessity to act promptly to challenge a public law decision, and the greater need to do so where third party rights may be affected by any challenge,[11] nevertheless judicial review may be refused if the court considers that some form of alternative dispute resolution (ADR) ought to have been attempted before proceedings were commenced, and would have been a satisfactory alternative remedy.

17.10   In R (Cowl) v Plymouth CC,[12] the Court of Appeal (Lord Woolf CJ) upheld the dismissal of a judicial review application concerning the closure of two residential homes, where the defendant authority had offered to treat the application as a complaint under the applicable statutory complaints procedure, to convene a panel with an independent chair to consider the complaint as soon as reasonably practicable and, while the conclusions of the panel would not be binding, to give them adequate weight. The offer had been contained in an open letter sent by the defendant to the claimants prior to the permission application having been dealt with.[13]

17.11   The claimants rejected the offer, on the basis that the complaints procedure was not a true alternative remedy in that it would not resolve all the issues that could be dealt with on judicial review, in particular the issues of law. Although permission was granted, the substantive claim was dismissed and the claimants appealed.

17.12   The Court of Appeal considered that the offer of the complaints procedure was 'very sensible' and could and should have formed the basis for negotiations, rather than being rejected.[14] The court stated that both parties had been wrong to believe that the claimants were entitled to proceed with their judicial review claim unless either the parties agreed otherwise or the offer of a complaints procedure constituted an

---

11 See chapter 18 below at para 18.25.

12 [2001] EWCA Civ 1935; [2002] 1 WLR 803; (2002) 5 CCLR 42.

13 R (Cowl) v Plymouth CC [2001] EWCA Civ 1935, per Lord Woolf CJ at [7]–[10].

14 [2001] EWCA Civ 1935 at [11].

alternative remedy which would fulfil all the functions of judicial review. This was too narrow an approach. Under the CPR, parties do not have a right to the resolution of their respective contentions by way of judicial review in the absence of an entirely equivalent alternative remedy. If the alternative procedure can resolve a significant part of the issues, the court should not permit judicial review proceedings to proceed, except for good reason. If a legal issue subsequently calls for resolution by the court, it can be examined at that stage and the court may be considerably assisted by the findings made in the course of the alternative procedure.[15]

17.13   The court went further. Lord Woolf CJ stated:

> [25] ... What followed was due to the unfortunate culture in litigation of this nature of over-judicialising the processes which are involved ... Without the need for the vast costs which must have been incurred in this case already being incurred, the parties should have been able to come to a sensible conclusion as to how to dispose of the issues which divided them. If they could not do this without help, then an independent mediator should have been recruited to assist. That would have been a far cheaper course to adopt. Today, sufficient should be known about ADR to make the failure to adopt it, in particular when public money is involved, indefensible.

17.14   Accordingly:

> [2] ... the courts should scrutinise extremely carefully applications for judicial review in the case of applications of the class with which this appeal is concerned. The courts should then make appropriate use of their ample powers under the CPR to ensure that the parties try to resolve the dispute with the minimum involvement of the courts. The legal aid authorities should co-operate in support of this approach.
> [3] To achieve this objective the court may have to hold, on its own initiative, an inter partes hearing at which the parties can explain what steps they have taken to resolve the dispute without the involvement of the courts. In particular the parties should be asked why a complaints procedure or some other form of ADR has not been used or adapted to resolve or reduce the issues which are in dispute. If litigation is necessary the courts should deter the parties from adopting an unnecessarily confrontational approach to the litigation.

17.15   It is a little difficult to know how far-reaching these last comments are intended to be, as *Cowl* contains no indication of what was meant by 'applications of the class' with which it was concerned. It seems unlikely that it refers solely to cases involving the closure of residential homes (ie, the specific subject-matter of *Cowl* itself). If, on the other hand, it refers to applications which could reasonably and sensibly be

15 [2001] EWCA Civ 1935 at [14].

dealt with by means other than litigation, then there can be little quarrel with the – on the face of it – somewhat extreme suggestion that the courts should ensure their involvement is minimal.

17.16   The funding authorities (at least in a number of areas) do now apply a requirement that alternative means of resolving a dispute must generally be attempted before recourse is had to the courts, refusing funding for judicial review cases for this reason, even potentially in cases where there is no available alternative course of action which would necessarily amount to an alternative remedy.[16]

17.17   In *Dunnett v Railtrack plc,*[17] the Court of Appeal adopted the same approach by reference, in part, to CPR r1.4(2)(e), obliging the court to manage cases actively, including 'encouraging the parties to use an alternative dispute resolution procedure if the court considers that appropriate and facilitating the use of such procedure'.

17.18   In that case, the court refused to make any order for costs in favour of the respondent, even though it had successfully resisted the appeal, because the respondent had rebuffed an advance from the appellant to consider ADR before expending costs on the appeal. Brooke LJ stated that it was to be hoped that any publicity given to this part of the court's judgment would draw the attention of lawyers to their duties to further the overriding objective in the way that is set out in CPR Part 1 and to the possibility that, if they turn down out of hand the chance of alternative dispute resolution when suggested by the court, as had happened on this occasion, they may have to face uncomfortable costs consequences.

17.19   The only safe conclusion to draw from these cases is that ADR is firmly on the agenda in judicial review cases, and cannot be ignored. It will not always be appropriate or possible to engage in an ADR process (not least where there is a fundamental dispute on a point of law on which the defendant cannot compromise) but the parties must be in a position to demonstrate both to funding authorities and to the courts the consideration that has been given to the possibility of resolving the dispute without court proceedings and the reasons why this has not been successful or not even attempted.

16   See paras 17.20–17.21 below and see *Funding Code*, April 2000, paras 7.2.3 and 7.4.3, and especially *Funding Code Decision-making Guidance*, Release 9, April 2003, para 16.5, where specific reference to *Cowl* is made and confirmation given of the funding authorities' support for that approach.

17   [2002] EWCA Civ 303; [2002] 1 WLR 2434. But see also, as examples of cases where the court accepted that ADR would have made a difference, and so did not hold a refusal to undertake it against the party concerned: *R (Rodriguez-Bannister) v Somerset Partnership NHS and Social Care Trust* [2003] EWHC 2184 (Admin); *Valentine v Nash* [2003] EWCA Civ 1274.

Alternative remedies

17.20   That alternative remedies must generally be used in preference to judicial review has long been the position – judicial review is often referred to as a remedy of last resort.[18] It is therefore unsurprising that the Court of Appeal considered this issue as an integral part of its reasoning in *Cowl* (above). A full discussion of alternative remedies, their use and the potential consequences of failure to use them, appears elsewhere in this book.[19] Nevertheless, the availability of any such remedy, even if not wholly satisfactory from the claimant's point of view must form part of the consideration of the possible alternative means of resolving the dispute.

17.21   This is, conceptually, different from the question of whether judicial review or private law proceedings are appropriate. Different principles apply, and the court's reaction has tended to be different, at least in recent times.[20] That issue is considered elsewhere in this book.[21]

Pre-action disclosure

17.22   Claimants can now generally obtain information about themselves, held by public bodies (as data controllers) under the Data Protection Act 1998 s7. (A specific right relating to information held by public bodies is created by the Freedom of Information Act 2000, but this is not expected to come into force until 30 November 2005.)

17.23   By Data Protection Act 1998 s7, a person is entitled to be informed whether any personal data is held by a data controller and to have that information communicated to him in an intelligible form (ie, he can have copies). Information can be withheld if its disclosure would involve disclosing personal data about a third party who has not consented to the release of that information about him.[22] The data controller

---

18   See the statements to this effect in numerous cases, including *R v Secretary of State for the Home Department ex p Swati* [1986] 1 WLR 477; *R v Chief Constable of Merseyside Police ex p Calveley* [1989] AC 1228, HL, and the cases referred to above at paras 7.9–7.21.

19   See chapter 7 above at paras 7.9–7.21.

20   See, eg, *R (Heather) v Leonard Cheshire Foundation* [2002] EWCA Civ 366; [2002] 2 All ER 936; (2002) 5 CCLR 317; *R (Clark-Darby) v Highbury Magistrates' Court* [2001] EWHC Admin 959; [2002] RVR 35; *Trustees of the Dennis Rye Pension Fund v Sheffield CC* [1998] 1 WLR 840.

21   See chapter 3 above at paras 3.18–3.30.

22   Data Protection Act 1998 s7(4). See generally chapter 14.

can refuse to provide copies if to do so would involve disproportionate effort.[23] The data controller is entitled to charge a fee not exceeding a prescribed maximum, for the communication of the information.[24]

17.24   This right can and ought to be exercised by claimants prior to the commencement of proceedings. It is noteworthy that the standard form pre-claim letter annexed to the pre-action protocol provides for a request for information, while providing that the protocol itself confers no obligation on public bodies to provide information additional to their pre-existing obligations.[25] In many cases, it may be necessary to have sight of this information in order properly to formulate the grounds of challenge to be included in the pre-claim letter.

17.25   For this reason combined with the length of time it can take actually to receive the information requested, and in the context of the strict judicial review time limits, the obligation to consider alternatives to litigation, and the duty of full and frank disclosure,[26] it will usually be sensible for advisers to request all relevant information as early as possible and prior to sending the pre-claim letter. Where time is pressing, however, the letter before claim can include the request for information.

Pre-action protocol

17.26   The judicial review pre-action protocol has been in force since 4 March 2002. In substance, it imposes a requirement in most cases that the claimant should send a detailed letter before claim to the defendant and give the defendant time to respond before proceedings are lodged. Fourteen days is usually sufficient time to respond. If the defendant does not consider that time to be sufficient, it should send an interim reply and propose a reasonable extension.

Contents of the letter before claim

17.27   The purpose of the letter before claim is expressed to be to identify the issues in dispute and establish whether litigation can be avoided. A pro-forma letter is annexed to the protocol itself (see appendix A, p445, below).[27] In essence, the matters with which the letter must deal

23 Data Protection Act 1998 s8(2).
24 Data Protection Act 1998 s7(2).
25 See para 17.30 below.
26 See chapter 18 below at paras 18.99–18.106.
27 Protocol, Annex A.

are no more extensive than those which would usually be covered in a letter before action, namely:

- a clear summary of the facts on which the claim is based;
- the date and details of the decision or act or omission under challenge;
- the reason that decision is said to be wrong;
- the action that the defendant is expected to take (and the timescale for the taking of such action);
- the details of any information sought (including a more detailed explanation of the decision under challenge);
- the claimants' details and those of his or her legal advisers;
- the address for reply and service of court documents;
- the details of any interested parties known to the claimant;
- the defendant's reference details; and
- the proposed reply date.

The defendant's response

17.28 A standard format letter of response is also appended to the protocol (see appendix A, p450).[28] Defendants should usually respond within 14 days and a failure to do so will be taken into account by the court in the absence of good reasons.[29] Where it is not possible to respond within this time limit, an interim reply and request for a reasonable extension of time should be sent, giving reasons for the need for an extension and, where necessary, any additional information requested. The claimant will not be bound to grant the extension, particularly given the time limits for applying for judicial review, but if the court considers that the claimant has brought proceedings prematurely (ie, in this instance because the extension ought to have been granted) it may impose sanctions.[30]

17.29 If the claim is being conceded in full, the response should say so 'in clear and unambiguous terms'.[31] If the claim is not being conceded at all, or only in part, the response should set this out clearly and:

- where appropriate, contain a new decision clearly identifying which aspects of the claim are, and which are not, conceded, or give a clear timescale within which a new decision will be issued;

28 Protocol, Annex B.
29 Protocol, Annex B, para 13 and note 5, referring to CPR Pre-Action Protocol Practice Direction, paras 2–3.
30 Protocol, Annex B, para 14.
31 Protocol, Annex B, para 15.

- give a more detailed explanation of the original decision, if appropriate;
- address any points of dispute or explain why they cannot be addressed;
- enclose any relevant documentation requested by the claimant or explain why they are not enclosed; and
- where relevant state whether or not any application for interim relief will be opposed.[32]

17.30   As to the provision of information or documentation requested by the claimant, the protocol states that it does not impose any greater obligation upon public bodies to disclose documents or give reasons for decisions than that already provided for in statute or at common law. Where, however, the court considers that the body ought to have provided a relevant document and/or information, it may impose sanctions, especially where the failure amounts to a breach of such statutory or common law obligations.[33]

17.31   The response should be sent to all interested parties identified by the claimant, and give details of any other parties the defendant considers to have an interest.[34]

Applying the protocol

17.32   The protocol describes itself as a 'code of good practice' which 'contains the steps which parties should generally follow before making a claim for judicial review'.[35] In reality, as noted above, it is far more than that – many of its provisions, while stating that they do not impose obligations as such, warn of sanctions if the court considers that the parties should have behaved differently in applying those provisions.[36] Worthy of note is the warning that the judge may refuse to hear the case where alternative procedures have not been used, though all the circumstances, including the nature of the alternative remedy, will be

---

32 Protocol, Annex B, para 16.
33 Protocol, Annex B, para 6.
34 Protocol, Annex B, para 17.
35 Protocol, para 5.
36 See Protocol, eg, paras 3, 6, 7, 13, 14.

taken into account.[37] Claimants are strongly advised to seek appropriate legal advice.[38]

17.33 The protocol is expressed not to be appropriate in two classes of case.[39] First, where the defendant does not have the legal power to alter the decision under challenge, such as a tribunal which having exercised its powers no longer enjoys any jurisdiction in relation to the case which was before it (the protocol cites the immigration appeal authorities as an example of this, but most tribunals will fall into the same category).

17.34 Second, the protocol will not be appropriate in urgent cases and/or where emergency interim relief is sought, such as where a person is to be removed from the United Kingdom, or where a homeless applicant has been refused – or is about to lose – temporary accommodation. Even in urgent cases, however, the claimant must fax a copy of the claim form to the defendant prior to issue of the proceedings.[40]

17.35 In other cases, however, it is left to claimants to 'satisfy themselves' whether or not they should follow the protocol, 'depending on the circumstances of the case'.[41] Where the court considers that the protocol ought to have been used, it will take account of compliance or non-compliance in making case management directions and/or when making costs orders. This will apply both to claimants who do not send a letter before claim and defendants who do not respond.[42] It should be noted, in addition, that the Legal Commission Service (LSC) expects all funded judicial review claims to be conducted in accordance with the protocol.[43]

17.36 Accordingly, wherever it is even conceivable that use of the protocol would be considered appropriate by the court, it would seem sensible to follow the procedure it sets out, particularly given that that procedure involves nothing more than the sending of a letter before claim or, for defendants, a response to that letter. If strict compliance

37 Protocol, para 3. See also *R (Wilkinson) v Chief Constable of West Yorkshire* [2002] EWHC 2353 (Admin), where it was held that the court at the substantive hearing could not decline jurisdiction on the ground of an unused alternative remedy (where the permission judge had considered the point arguable), but that the issue would be relevant to relief.

38 Protocol, para 4.

39 Protocol, para 6.

40 See Protocol, para 7 and Form N463, the 'urgency' form. See also chapter 18 below at paras 18.82–18.86.

41 Pre-action Protocol, para 7.

42 Pre-action Protocol, para 7.

43 See Funding Code Decision-making Guidance, Release 9, April 2003, para 16.3.7.

is not possible it is still preferable for claimants to comply as closely as possible (for example, by giving the defendant a shorter time to respond to the letter before claim, where 14 days is not available), rather than to send no letter at all.

The protocol and time limits

17.37 The protocol makes it clear that compliance with its terms will not of itself affect the application of the time limits for judicial review[44] (ie, that claims must be made promptly and in any event within three months of the grounds for challenge first arising and that undue delay may lead to a refusal of permission or of any remedy). The introductory paragraph specifically states that the protocol 'does not affect the time limit specified by' the rules. It is also stated that while the court has a discretion under CPR r3.1(2)(a) to extend time to permit a late claim to be brought, this will only be used in 'exceptional circumstances' and that 'compliance with the protocol alone is unlikely to be sufficient to persuade the court to allow a late claim', though it is doubtful that 'exceptional circumstances' is in fact the correct test.[45]

17.38 Likewise, as noted above, the fact that the time limits are unaffected by the protocol is reflected in the statement that a defendant's request for an extension of time to serve a response may not be agreed by the claimant as it will not affect the time limits for making a claim for judicial review.[46]

17.39 It is difficult to know where this leaves claimants' advisers. In particular, this is likely to arise where a client only seeks legal advice for the first time well after the decision was made, so that there may be only a few days remaining before the claim would go outside the three-month stop-period for commencing proceedings. Accordingly, using the protocol procedure and allowing 14 days for a response to the letter before claim would take the commencement of proceedings beyond the relevant time limits.

---

44 Supreme Court Act 1981 s31(6) and CPR r54.5. See also chapter 18 below at paras 18.17–18.57.

45 Protocol, note 1. The reference to 'exceptional circumstances' is not found in CPR r3.1(2)(a) itself, nor in rr3.9 or 3.10, which also confer power on the court to relieve a party from a sanction for failure to comply with a rule. Under RSC Ord 53 r4(1), the test was whether the court considered there to be 'good reason' to extend time.

46 Protocol, para 14.

17.40 Lateness of this sort would not seem to bring the case within the urgency exception to the use of the protocol in that it would appear to be properly classified as delay rather than urgency: the need for permission or relief is not urgent, there is simply very little time left before the expiry of the time for bringing the claim. Indeed, the protocol makes it clear that it cannot be used as a means of extending time and thereby avoiding the application of the usual time limits, and warns that if those time limits are not observed, time will only be extended in exceptional cases.

17.41 On the other hand, the rules, the courts and the protocol itself insist that the parties must not commence proceedings prematurely or without exploring alternative methods of resolving the dispute, on pain of sanctions in costs or in the refusal of permission or relief or even funding. Yet CPR 54.5(2) states that time cannot be extended by agreement between the parties.

17.42 In such cases, the following course would seem to be appropriate, and difficult for the courts to criticise. If there is any time left before the expiry of three months since the decision under challenge was made, a letter before claim in the form appended to the pre-action protocol should be sent to the defendant giving a time for a response shortened so that it will expire prior to the expiry of the three-month time limit. Proceedings should be issued within the three-month period in order to protect the claimant's position (though this will not protect the claimant from the possible consequences of having delayed, it will at least not be necessary to seek a formal extension of time beyond the three-month back stop).

17.43 The defendant should be informed that proceedings are being issued for this reason but that the claimant will seek a stay of those proceedings from the court,[47] in order that the protocol procedure can be worked through and it can be established whether the proceedings need to be fully (or at all) contested.

17.44 In fact, there is no reason why a request for an extension of time by a defendant cannot be dealt with on a similar basis in appropriate

---

47 By CPR r1.4(1), the court is under a duty to further the overriding objective by actively managing cases. CPR r1.4(2)(e) and (f) provide that active case management includes: encouraging the parties to use alternative dispute resolution if the court considers it appropriate and facilitating the use of such procedure; and helping the parties to settle the whole or part of the case. Thus, while CPR r26.4 does not apply (application for a stay for the purpose of ADR on the filing of allocation questionnaires), the court has ample power under its case management functions to grant a stay for the purposes of ADR. The procedure for applying for a stay is set out above, and should generally comply with CPR Practice Direction 24, para 3.1(a).

cases: rather than simply refuse an extension, it may be more sensible to agree to it on the basis that proceedings will be issued but a stay sought for the period of the extension. The question of which party should bear the costs of issuing, in the event that the claim is ultimately conceded can be agreed or resolved by the court.

17.45   In many ways, the pre-action protocol simply reflects pre-existing best practice in the manner in which judicial review claims are prepared. The court has, for many years made plain its disapproval of claimants who sought permission to apply for judicial review without first serving a proper letter before action on the defendant. More than ten years ago, in *R v Horsham DC and another ex p Wenman*,[48] Brooke J, describing the following propositions as 'elementary', held that judicial review proceedings should not be embarked upon before the decision-maker has received a complaint and been given an opportunity to say whether or not that complaint was accepted and, if not, to give its reasons. Judicial review proceedings were wholly inappropriate as the forum for the resolution of issues of disputed fact, and that all material matters, including the existence of an alternative, statutory remedy, had to be placed before the judge invited to grant permission. Wasted costs orders may be made against legal representatives who failed to comply with these elementary propositions.

17.46   The same difficulties as those suggested above, particularly in relation to time limits, has therefore arisen for a considerable time and the pre-action protocol only exacerbates them in the sense that the sanctions imposed retrospectively for what the court considers to have been an inappropriate exercise of judgment are potentially more far reaching. While it is perhaps disappointing that the protocol has not provided any solutions to these difficulties, it is likely that the court will not penalise parties who have acted sensibly and reasonably in all the circumstances.

Time limits and other letters

17.47   Sometimes before a decision is reached, a decision-maker will indicate his or her current view of the claimant's case, and give the claimant a chance to make comments on that view, in time to influence the decision. This is usual, for example, in immigration cases, for example, where the Home Secretary will usually send a 'minded to refuse' letter,

---

48 (1992) 24 HLR 669, QBD, and [1994] 4 All ER 681, QBD (not an alternative report of the same decision but a report of a subsequent decision in the same case).

briefly setting out the reasons why the application as it stands is not accepted.

17.48　This is another occasion on which carefully worded representations are important, not only because such representations may change the decision-maker's view. It may be that the decision-maker's approach, as set out in its own letter, can be shown to be legally defective, so that even if that approach is persisted in, the groundwork for a challenge has been laid.

Where delay has occurred

17.49　Where it is thought that the claimant may have been guilty of some delay or, after the decision has been taken, more material is obtained which an claimant wishes to put before the decision-maker, it should be remembered that a person is always entitled to ask the decision-maker to reconsider his or her decision in the light of the new evidence or even just further representations. Any refusal to reconsider may become challengeable in the same way as a reconsideration which results in another refusal. Where a later decision is under challenge, it may be possible to include in that challenge the original decision, even though the claimant's delay might otherwise have led to the refusal of leave or relief. Accordingly, advisers should generally challenge all the decisions complained of in relation to the application, and not merely the latest in time.

Drafting the letter before claim

17.50　The letter before claim is an important document, not only in that it is likely to be the first explicit statement of the errors which the decision-maker is alleged to have made, but also because the response it elicits from the defendant may amplify and further explain the reasons already given for the decision. This may help the claimant and his or her adviser to understand better the approach and procedure which the decision-maker adopted.

17.51　Any failure by the claimant without good reason to include an issue which is later included in the claim itself, may lead to unnecessary costs arguments, particularly if the issue proves to be important or decisive, and the defendant can establish that the inclusion of that issue in the letter before claim would have led it to adopt a different approach to the litigation. Accordingly, letters before claim should generally be fully argued, setting out all the claimant's main contentions.

Responding to the letter before claim

17.52   As stated above, the defendant receiving a letter before claim ignores it, or pays it only cursory attention at her or his peril. The formal letter before claim may not be the first intimation of a possible claim, as correspondence often precedes such a letter, and so the defendant may have had some prior opportunity to investigate matters and reach a view on both the merits of the claim and the appropriate way of dealing with it.

17.53   The defendant's response should be as full as possible and should, even if not raised by the claimant, draw attention to any issues which the defendant may wish to raise in the summary grounds of defence, should proceedings be issued, including such matters as delay, the availability of alternative remedies, etc. The response should also propose any possible methods of resolving or narrowing the issues between the parties (again, whether or not mentioned by the claimant) that would be acceptable to the defendant, aside from litigation.

17.54   The defendant may quite properly also suggest that, even if any such proposals are not acceptable to the claimant, the claimant should make her or his own proposals and the issue of proceedings should be held back for a period of time, while discussions about alternative means of resolving the dispute are explored.

Pre-emptive costs orders

17.55   This issue is dealt with in chapter 18 below.[49] Consideration of whether an application may properly be made, however, will generally be necessary prior to the issue of proceedings. Indeed, if an application is contemplated, the defendant should be alerted to this as early as possible. A reference to such an application is not out of place in the letter before claim.[50]

Costs-only proceedings

17.56   Civil Procedure Rules (CPR) r44.12A provides for an unusual procedure whereby a party to a dispute which has been settled on all issues apart

---

49   See paras 18.143–18.147.

50   *R (Campaign for Nuclear Disarmament) v The Prime Minister (Costs)* [2002] EWHC 2712 (Admin); (2002) *Times* 27 December, per Maurice Kay J at [7].

from that of costs (which settlement is confirmed in writing), and where no proceedings have yet been commenced, may start proceedings in accordance with CPR Part 8.[51]

17.57 The court must dismiss the claim, however, if it is opposed by the other party to the dispute.[52] Accordingly, it would seem that the procedure may only be invoked where all parties desire the court to resolve the costs position. It is also highly unlikely that the Legal Services Commission would grant funding for such a claim.

Funding

17.58 The funding criteria for judicial review proceedings are contained in s7 of the Funding Code[53] and s16 of the Guidance.[54] The criteria for both investigative help and full representation are different from those applicable to other types of civil claim.

Investigative help

17.59 As to investigative help, the general criteria concerning the availability of a conditional fee agreement and minimum damages levels are disapplied,[55] and two additional criteria specified. These are (a) the availability of 'administrative appeals or other procedures which should be pursued before proceedings are considered', and (b) whether the decision under challenge does not appear to be susceptible to judicial review.[56] Either of these additional criteria will be a basis for the refusal of investigative help, although it will not be refused on the basis that the decision is not judicially reviewable if there is 'at least a good argument' that the decision is susceptible to challenge.[57]

17.60 If an alternative remedy or other procedure is, in principle, available, it is for the legal representative completing the application form to explain why it has not been followed in the particular case. If there is a good reason for proceeding to judicial review straight away,

---

51 CPR r44.12A(1)–(2).
52 CPR r44.12A(4)(b).
53 April 2000 edition.
54 *Funding Code Decision-making Guidance*, Release 9, April 2003.
55 *Funding Code*, para 7.2.1.
56 *Funding Code*, paras 7.2.2–7.2.3.57.
57 *Funding Code Decision-making Guidance*, R9 April 2003, para 16.4.3.

funding will not be refused.[58] The LSC will support the approach set out by the Court of Appeal in *Cowl*,[59] however, and will apply the test of whether the reasonable privately-paying client would go to court rather than pursuing an alternative, taking account of the likely effectiveness of the available alternatives compared with what might be obtained on judicial review, the urgency of the case, the attitude of the opponent and all the other circumstances.[60]

17.61   Other matters which may lead to the refusal of investigative help are the decisions: (a) in straightforward cases, that Legal Help is a more appropriate basis for funding,[61] or (b) that a person other than the applicant ought to bring the claim.[62]

17.62   Investigative help will usually be limited to making further enquiries, writing a full letter before claim and seeking counsel's opinion on the merits. It will not usually cover the making of the permission application, except in urgent cases.[63]

Full representation

17.63   The criteria for full representation vary depending on whether the funding application is made before or after permission has been granted.[64] Before the grant of permission, funding may be refused, as above, if the decision does not appear susceptible to judicial review or if alternative remedies (or procedures) have not been pursued appropriately.[65] In addition, full representation will be refused if the proposed respondent has not been given 'a reasonable opportunity to respond to the challenge or deal with the applicant's complaint, save where this is impracticable in the circumstances'.[66]

17.64   Regard is also had to the prospects of success and cost benefit considerations. The prospects of success are defined as the 'prospects of obtaining the substantive order sought in the proceedings',[67] in assessing which the LSC will consider the primary relief sought and the

---

58 *Funding Code*, para 16.5.3.
59 [2001] EWCA Civ 1935; [2002] 1 WLR 803; (2002) 5 CCLR 42.
60 *Funding Code Decision-making Guidance*, R9 April 2003, paras 16.5.4–16.5.5.
61 *Funding Code*, para 16.3.2 and 10.3
62 *Funding Code*, para 16.3.5.
63 *Funding Code*, para 16.8.1.
64 *Funding Code*, para 7.3.
65 *Funding Code*, paras 7.4.2–7.4.3.
66 *Funding Code*, para 7.4.4.
67 *Funding Code*, para 7.4.5.

prospect of obtaining it, including consideration of whether relief – and indeed permission – may be refused.[68] Funding will be refused where prospects are unclear[69] or poor, or where they are borderline and there is no significant wider public interest oroverwhelming importance to the client or significant human rights issues raised.[70]

17.65 Funding may also be refused unless, having regard to the prospects of success and all the other circumstances, the likely benefits justify the likely costs.[71] This involves consideration of more than just the 'private client test' (ie, would a reasonable privately-paying client bring or continue the proceedings in the same circumstances and with the same prospects of success), though if the private client test is satisfied, so will be the cost benefit criteria.[72] Where the private client test is not satisfied, wider questions, such as the importance of the issues, the seriousness of the alleged wrongdoing and the degree to which the case did not meet the private client test, should be considered.[73]

17.66 The LSC may also consider under this rubric the likelihood of the public body changing its mind if the decision is quashed, but will usually only do so where it is otherwise doubtful about granting funding, and is most likely to do so in challenges based on procedural irregularity rather than illegality or irrationality.[74]

17.67 Once permission has been granted, there is what is described as a presumption of funding, which operates as follows. If the case has a significant wider public interest, is of overwhelming importance to the client or raises significant human rights issues, then so long as the standard criteria set out in s4 of the Funding Code[75] are satisfied, funding will be granted unless it appears unreasonable to do so in the light of information (a) which was not before the court which granted permission or (b) which has subsequently come to light.[76] This will include reconsideration of funding at the stage where the defendant submits its evidence and detailed grounds of defence.[77]

68 *Funding Code Decision-making Guidance*, R9 April 2003, para 16.6.3.
69 Investigative help may be available where prospects are unclear.
70 *Funding Code*, para 7.4.5.
71 *Funding Code*, para 7.4.6.
72 *Funding Code Decision-making Guidance*, Release 9 April 2003, para 4.9.3(c).
73 *Funding Code Decision-making Guidance*, para 4.9.3(d).
74 *Funding Code Decision-making Guidance*, para 16.6.6.
75 That is, the general eligibility criteria.
76 *Funding Code*, para 7.5.2.
77 *Funding Code Decision-making Guidance*, Release 9 April 2003, para 16.7.2.

17.68   Where there is no significant wider public importance, overwhelming importance to the client or significant human rights issue,
the LSC will exercise a more general discretion on whether to fund
the case. While 'due weight' will be given to the judicial decision granting permission, legal representation will be refused if the prospects of
success are borderline or poor, or the likely benefits of the proceedings do not justify the likely costs, having regard to prospects of success
and all the other circumstances.[78] This is most likely to arise where
new information comes to light (whether or not on filing of the defendant's evidence and detailed grounds of defence) which 'seriously and
adversely affects the assessment of prospects of success' or where the
case is not considered to be cost effective.[79]

Standard limitations

17.69   Certificates are usually limited to the application for permission on
the papers and, if permission is granted, all steps up to the receipt of
the defendant's evidence and detailed grounds of defence and counsel's
opinion thereafter.[80] If permission is refused on the papers, the certificate will not usually permit an oral renewal of the application,
but will require amendment for the oral hearing.[81] The same will
apply if permission is refused after an oral hearing and an appeal to
the Court of Appeal is sought.[82] Given the short (seven day) time limits
for both renewal and appeal, the regional offices will deal urgently
with applications to extend certificates and will accept such applications
by fax.[83]

17.70   The application should include counsel's opinion or solicitor's
report as to why, in the light of the judge's reasons for refusing permission, the permission application should be renewed orally. In addition, the application for an extension must be accompanied by a copy
of the claim form, any acknowledgement of service, and the order
refusing permission with the judge's reasons. Applications for an

---

78 *Funding Code,* para 7.5.3.
79 *Funding Code Decision-making Guidance,* Release 9 April 2003, paras 16.7.3 and
4.9, and see the discussion of cost benefit criteria at paras 17.65–17.66 above.
80 Standard limitation JR004.
81 If granted, the extension will cover the oral application only (standard
limitation JR006) but not a subsequent appeal.
82 Standard limitation JR007.
83 *Funding Code Decision-making Guidance,* Release 9 April 2003, paras 16.8.2,
16.8.3 and 16.8.6–16.8.7.

extension to appeal to the Court of Appeal must similarly set out the reasons why the client should be permitted to appeal and be accompanied by the documents referred to above together with a transcript of the judgment following the oral hearing or, if not available, a detailed note by counsel or solicitor.[84]

17.71 Firms exercising devolved powers to extend an emergency certificate must include the same information when notifying the regional office of their decision to extend the certificate (though if a substantive certificate is in force, there is no devolved power to extend it).[85]

17.72 Where an urgent application includes a claim for interim relief, and the court decides to deal with the question of relief at an oral hearing, the work will be covered under the standard limitation applicable to the initial grant of funding (ie, covering the paper application for permission).[86]

84 *Funding Code Decision-making Guidance*, paras 16.8.2–16.8.6.
85 *Funding Code Decision-making Guidance*, para 16.8.4.
86 *Funding Code Decision-making Guidance*, para 16.8.5.

CHAPTER 18

The permission application

continued overleaf

New procedural regime

18.1   An application for permission to apply for judicial review is made to a High Court judge, usually one of the Queen's Bench Division who has been assigned to hear matters listed in the Administrative Court List (formerly the 'Crown Office list').

18.2   Applications for judicial review are now governed by the Civil Procedure Rules (CPR) Part 54 (together with a Practice Direction) which have made significant alterations to the judicial review procedure and which replace the old Rules of the Supreme Court (RSC) Ord 53. The majority of the substantive changes affect the initial stages of an application for judicial review. In particular, there is a new claim form for applications, new requirements for notifying other parties that an application is to be made, and new provisions relating to the leave, now 'permission', hearing.

18.3   Much of the language of judicial review has also changed, many of which changes have been brought about by the *Practice Direction: the Administrative Court:*[1] eg, the parties are now referred to as 'claimant' and 'defendant', not 'applicant' and 'respondent'; the leave stage has become the 'permission' stage; the Crown Office List is now the 'Administrative Court' (the Crown Office has become the 'Administrative Court Office'); the prerogative orders – *certiorari, mandamus* and *prohibition* – are now known as 'quashing orders', 'mandatory orders' and 'prohibiting orders';[2] and the familiar title: 'R v [Respondent], ex p [Applicant]' has become 'The Queen on the application of [Claimant] v [Defendant].[3]

Requirement for permission

18.4   By CPR r54.4, the court's permission to proceed is required in a claim for judicial review, whether or not the claim has been commenced under the Part 54 procedure.

---

1   [2000] 1 WLR 1654.

2   CPR r54.1(b)–(d) and see *Practice Direction: the Administrative Court* (note 1 above). A slight peculiarity of these provisions is that the remedies of *certiorari, mandamus* and *prohibition* have not as such been replaced, they are just 'called' by the new names for the purposes of the Practice Direction and CPR Part 54. This may be because Supreme Court Act 1981 s31(1)(a), which refers to *certiorari, mandamus* and *prohibition* has not been amended and so the traditional names continue to have a residual existence.

3   See *Practice Direction: the Administrative Court* [2000] 1 WLR 1654. This title is regularly abbreviated to: R (Claimant) v Defendant.

When to use the CPR Part 54 procedure

18.5 The question of whether the subject matter of a case is suitable to be litigated in judicial review proceedings (eg, whether the claim involves private or public law rights; whether the decision-maker is susceptible to judicial review) is considered elsewhere.[4] There is also, however, a procedural aspect to the issue of whether a claim may, or indeed must, be brought by way of judicial review, which is considered here.

18.6 In procedural terms, the CPR Part 54 procedure must be used where the claimant is seeking a quashing order, a mandatory order, a prohibiting order or an injunction under Supreme Court Act 1981 s30 (ie, to restrain a person from acting in an office in which he is not entitled to act).[5]

18.7 A claimant seeking a declaration or injunction in combination with a quashing, mandatory and/or prohibiting order must also use the judicial review procedure; where the only relief claimed is a declaration and/or injunction, the procedure may be used but is not mandatory.[6] The court has power to grant a declaration and/or injunction where it considers that it would be just and convenient to do so having regard to the nature of the matters in respect of which relief could be granted by a quashing, mandatory or prohibiting order, the nature of the persons/bodies against whom relief is sought and all the circumstances of the case.[7]

18.8 A judicial review claim may include a claim for damages, but the procedure may not be used if damages are all that is claimed.[8] A claim for damages will only be possible, moreover, if the claimant already enjoys a right to damages in private law or, now, under the Human Right Act 1998:[9] the judicial review procedure itself creates no free-standing right to damages.[10]

Transfer to and from the Administrative Court

18.9 Civil Procedure Rules r54.20 confers power on the court to transfer proceedings out of the Administrative Court. The rule itself is in

---

4 See chapters 2 and 3.
5 CPR r54.2, and see generally chapter 5.
6 CPR r54.3(1), and see generally chapter 5.
7 Supreme Court Act 1981 s31(2).
8 CPR r54.3(2), and see generally chapter 5.
9 Human Rights Act 1998 s8.
10 Supreme Court Act 1981 s31(4)(b) and see generally chapter 5 above.

unlimited terms – that the court may order a claim brought under Part 54 to continue as if it had not been commenced under that Part, ie, as an ordinary claim under CPR Part 7 or Part 8, and, where it does so, may give directions about the future management of the claim. This contrasts with the equivalent power contained in the old rules,[11] under which the court could only order that a judicial review application continue as an ordinary action where the relief claimed was a declaration, injunction or damages. Accordingly, the restrictive construction that the courts gave to this former power may no longer be wholly applicable, although the principle that at least some viable private law claim must already be discernible in the proceedings as drafted would seem to remain relevant.[12]

18.10   In addition to the power referred to above, the provisions of the CPR[13] concerning transferring cases, among other things, into and out of specialist lists, are also expressly applied to the Administrative Court.[14] The effect of this is not entirely clear. CPR r30.5(2) provides simply that the High Court may 'order proceedings to be transferred to or from a specialist list'. On a broad construction, this could permit the court to transfer a claim commenced as an ordinary civil action into the Administrative Court. A narrow construction, however, would only entitle the court to transfer in what was in effect already a judicial review application which for some reason was not commenced in the Administrative Court.

18.11   This issue is likely to arise particularly in judicial review proceedings; the specialist proceedings referred to in CPR r49.2 (which do not include Administrative Court proceedings) do not contain the same procedural safeguards for defendants as apply to judicial review proceedings.[15]

18.12   An indication of the probable answer may be found in the combination of CPR rr30.5(3), 54.4 and Practice Direction (PD) 54 para 14.2. The first of these provides that an application to transfer proceedings

---

11 RSC Ord 53 r9(5).

12 See *R v East Berkshire Health Authority ex p Walsh* [1985] QB 152, CA, per Sir John Donaldson at 166. For a fuller discussion of this issue, see chapter 3 above at paras 3.18–3.30 and chapter 5 at paras 5.36–5.39.

13 CPR rr30.5 and 49.1(2).

14 CPR r54.20, which applies the provisions of CPR Part 30.

15 For example, the three-month time limit for commencing proceedings, the requirement for permission, the usual absence of disclosure and cross-examination: see above, chapter 17.

to or from a specialist list must be made to a judge dealing with claims in that list. CPR r54.4 states that permission to proceed is required in a claim for judicial review whether started under Part 54 or transferred to the Administrative Court. Paragraph 14.2 of PD 54 states that in deciding whether a claim is suitable for transfer to the Administrative Court, the court will consider whether it raises issues of public law to which Part 54 should apply. It would seem, then, that the broader construction referred to above is that intended by the Civil Procedure Rules. This construction also accords with the statements about the flexibility of the CPR, in the context of transfer made in the cases referred to at paras 3.22–3.30.

18.13   In addition to consideration of the issue referred to in the Practice Direction, the court will take account of whether a transfer would circumvent the procedural safeguards for defendants which are implicit in the Part 54 procedure, to the prejudice of the defendant (especially delay), particularly bearing in mind that the use of the Part 54 procedure is mandatory where a quashing, mandatory and/or prohibition order are sought.[16] As stated above, it is also made explicit by CPR r54.4 that a transfer of proceedings to the Administrative Court cannot be effected in such a way as would enable the claimant to avoid the permission stage.

18.14   For these reasons, if a significant amount of re-drafting would be necessary, the court may be cautious about transferring a case into the Administrative Court. This was certainly the general approach adopted by the court in relation to the power under RSC Ord 53 r9(5) (power to permit certain judicial review applications to continue as if commenced by writ).[17]

18.15   The court is likely to be sympathetic, however, to an application to transfer into the Administrative Court where, for example, the question of whether judicial review proceedings were appropriate is unclear,[18] the ordinary proceedings have been commenced promptly (in public law terms)[19] and the issues are already clearly defined in the claim form. In *R (Heather) v Leonard Cheshire Foundation*,[20] Lord Woolf CJ emphasised that the courts do not have an appetite, under the new rules, to

---

16   CPR r54.2.
17   See above, chapter 3 at paras 3.22–3.30.
18   See the discussion of public and private law in chapter 3 at paras 3.1–3.6.
19   See Supreme Court Act 1981 s31(6) and CPR r54.5.
20   [2002] EWCA Civ 366; [2002] 2 All ER 936; (2002) 5 CCLR 317.

embark on the kinds of dispute about forum, which took up so much judicial time under the old procedure:

> 38. ... there was ... reflected in the decision of the court below ... an idea that if LCF [Leonard Cheshire Foundation] was not forming a public function, proceedings by way of judicial review were wrong. This is an echo of the old demarcation disputes as to when judicial review was or was not appropriate under Order 53. Part 54 CPR is intended to avoid any such disputes which are wholly unproductive ...
>
> 39. We wish to make clear that the CPR provides a framework which is sufficiently flexible to enable all the issues between the parties to be determined ... In view of a possibility of a misunderstanding as to the scope of judicial review we draw attention to this and the powers of transfer under Part 54.[21]

18.16 It therefore appears likely that claimants should no longer be vulnerable to the kind of procedural dispute regarding the appropriateness of the procedure adopted, which occupied so much of the courts' time in the 1980s and 1990s, so long as they have behaved reasonably. In such cases, where there is genuine difficulty as to the correct procedure, strike-out applications based on the use of the wrong procedure will not be viewed sympathetically by the courts, but instead the power to transfer in and out of the Administrative Court will be used to ensure that valid claims are able to proceed in the most appropriate way.

Time limits

18.17 Strict time limits are imposed on the making of applications, and they must be adhered to. By CPR r54.5(1), the claim form must be filed promptly and, in any event, not later than three months after the grounds for making the claim first arose (generally the date of the decision). This rule does not apply where any other enactment specifies a shorter time limit for bringing the claim.[22]

18.18 Civil Procedure Rules r54.5(2) states that the time limit in rule 54.5(1) may not be extended by agreement between the parties. This is a new provision, not contained in the previous rule,[23] but it does not mark any major substantive change. Under the old rules, a party could agree not to take a point on delay, but the court could – and did – still

---

21 See also the discussion at chapter 3 above.
22 CPR r54.5(3).
23 RSC Ord 53 r4(1).

raise the matter itself. This new rule appears simply to formalise that position; the question of extending time is one for the court and not for the parties. It is also important to note that compliance with the pre-action protocol does not absolve the claimant from the requirement to bring the application within the time limits set out in rule 54.5(1).[24]

18.19   As mentioned below,[25] if there has been delay, even within the three-month period, then the reasons for that delay should be set out on the claim form.

18.20   Rule 54.5 must be read in conjunction with Supreme Court Act 1981 s31(6) and (7).

18.21   Supreme Court Act 1981 s31(6) provides:

Where the High Court considers that there has been undue delay in making an application for judicial review, the court may refuse to grant–
(a) leave for the making of the application; or
(b) any relief sought on the application, if it considers that the granting of the relief sought would be likely to cause substantial hardship to, or substantially prejudice the rights of, any person or would be detrimental to good administration.

18.22   This section is 'without prejudice to any enactment or rule of court which has the effect of limiting the time within which an application of judicial review may be made'.[26]

18.23   It is clear, then, that the question of delay arises in two contexts. The first relates to whether or not permission should be granted; the second to whether or not relief should be granted even if the decision under challenge is found to have been unlawful.

The permission decision

18.24   The effect of the provisions described above is not that an applicant has three months within which to make an application, as is the case, for instance, in an employment tribunal. The requirement is that an application be made promptly. The three-month period referred to is simply a long-stop. In *R v Lichfield DC ex p Lichfield Securities Ltd*,[27] the Court

---

24 See above, chapter 17 at paras 17.37–17.46.
25 This is part of the duty to give full and frank disclosurre, see paras 18.74, 18.99–18.106.
26 Supreme Court Act 1981 s31(7).
27 [2001] EWCA Civ 304; (2001) 3 LGLR 637.

of Appeal stated that 'promptness' is 'simply a function of the factors, ranging from the systemic to the idiosyncratic, which affect the fairness of letting a particular application proceed in a particular situation after a particular lapse of time; and these will ordinarily be the same factors as determine whether there has been undue delay.'[28] The question has been raised whether the requirement for promptness coupled with the three-month long stop is sufficiently certain to comply with the EC law and the European Convention on Human Rights.[29]

18.25   Accordingly, permission (or relief) can be refused even where the application has been made within the three-month limit.[30] In *R v Independent Television Commission ex p TV NI Ltd and another*,[31] the Court of Appeal refused permission on the ground of delay to two television companies which had not been awarded licences, even though the applications were made only two months after the decision complained of. Permission was refused on the ground that by the time the applications were made, those companies who had been awarded licences had acquired firm rights with which they could deal and on the strength of which they could spend money. Conversely, in *R v Birmingham CC ex p Dredger and Paget*,[32] the applicants' delay in applying for permission until six weeks after the date of the decision relating to the rent to be charged to market traders, and two weeks after the decision was implemented, did not count against them.

18.26   In this regard, it is noteworthy that the specific reference in the old rules to the three-month long-stop being subject to the power of the court to extend time where it considered that 'there is good reason for extending the period',[33] is not reproduced in CPR Part 54. This does not, however, mean that the court no longer enjoys any power to extend the period. CPR r3.1(2)(a), for example, confers express power to extend the time for compliance with any rule.[34] Indeed, in *Lichfield*,[35] the

---

28 [2001] EWCA Civ 304, per Sedley LJ at [33].
29 See *R (Burkett) v Hammersmith and Fulham LBC* [2002] UKHL 23; [2002] 1 WLR 1593, at [6], [53] and [59]–[66].
30 See, eg, *R v Dairy Produce Quota Tribunal ex p Caswell* [1990] 2 AC 738, HL.
31 (1991) *Times* 30 December; see also *R v Secretary of State for Health ex p Alcohol Recovery Project* [1993] COD 344, DC.
32 [1993] 91 LGR 532; [1993] COD 340, QBD.
33 [1993] 91 LGR 532.
34 And see CPR rr3.9 and 3.10 regarding relief from sanctions for failure to comply with a rule.
35 [2001] EWCA Civ 304; (2001) 3 LGLR 637.

Court of Appeal indicated that the formal enlargement of time can, in practice, be restricted to applications made outside the three-month time limit.[36]

18.27   While it does not necessarily follow that the discretion under the new rules will be exercised identically with that under the old rules, as the express requirement for 'good reason' no longer exists, it appears that the court will continue to apply substantially the same criteria, and follow its previous decisions, under the new rules. Indeed, the *Notes for Guidance* state that the court will only extend (or abridge) time for 'very good reasons'.[37] The pre-action protocol suggests that time will only be extended 'in exceptional circumstances', though it is submitted that this is not the appropriate test and is not a test suggested by Supreme Court Act 1981 s31(6) or the rules themselves.[38] The onus for demonstrating good reason falls on the claimant.[39]

18.28   Delay caused by the necessity for obtaining legal aid can amount to good reason for extending time,[40] or at least go 'a very long way down that road',[41] but will not automatically do so, especially where the court is not satisfied as to the efforts made in that regard.[42]

18.29   Where an applicant has tried to obtain a remedy by other means, such as by pursuing an alternative remedy, it is suggested that this may also constitute good reason for delay.[43] Communications with the

---

36   [2001] EWCA Civ 304, per Sedley LJ at para [33].

37   N461A, para 4.

38   See Pre-action Protocol, note 1. There is no reference to a requirement of exceptional circumstances for an extension of time to be granted in provisions of CPR r3.1(2)(a) – the rule referred to in the note itself – or rr3.9 and 3.10 (relief from sanctions), nor was that the test under RSC Ord 53 r4(1) ('good reason'). See also the comments of Lord Steyn in *R (Burkett) v Hammersmith and Fulham LBC* [2002] UKHL 23; [2002] 1 WLR 1593 at [53], concerning the counteracting of statutory time limits by judicial policy decision.

39   See, eg, *R v Warwickshire CC ex p Collymore* [1995] ELR 217, at 228F.

40   See *In re Wilson* [1985] AC 750, HL, at 755B; *R v Stratford on Avon DC ex p Jackson* [1985] 1 WLR 1319; *R v Surrey Coroner ex p Wright* [1997] QB 786.

41   *R v Governors of La Sainte Union Convent School ex p T* [1996] ELR 98.

42   See *R v University of Portsmouth ex p Lakareber* [1999] ELR 135. In *R v Sandwell MBC ex p Cashmore* (1993) 25 HLR 544 Owen J was of the view that delay in obtaining legal aid cannot usually be a good reason for extending time, although if the applicant would be left with no other remedy, the two features, taken together, might constitute good reason.

43   See, eg, *R v Chief Constable of North Wales Police ex p Evans* [1982] 1 WLR 1155, where the applicant had first taken his case to the industrial tribunal; *R v Secretary of State for the Home Department ex p Oladehinde* [1991] 1 AC 254, where the applicant had utilised his statutory right of appeal; *R (Javed) v Secretary of State for the Home Department* [2001] EWCA Civ 789; [2002] QB 129.

proposed defendant may be a good reason.[44] It appears that the 'general importance of the issues' and the public interest in the application can afford good reason, notwithstanding that the delay has not been satisfactorily explained.[45] Lack of knowledge of a reviewable decision can amount to a good reason,[46] as can the strength of the challenge,[47] the absence of prejudice,[48] and the importance of the rights at stake.[49] The default of a professional, non-legal adviser has been held not to constitute good reason.[50] Nor was good reason shown where a local authority had agreed to a deferment of proceedings, but the other defendant, a government department who funded the function in question and whose regulations were challenged, had not been approached to agree.[50a]

18.30   It cannot be asserted that a particular factor will always amount to a good reason for extending time. For almost any case in which the court has extended time on the basis of a specific matter, another can be found in which the same matter has been held not to amount to good reason for doing so. The most important consideration, in any given case, is likely to be the court's view of the overall reasonableness of the claimant's conduct causing the delay, judged in the context of the length of the delay, the explanation for it, and any hardship/prejudice or detriment to good administration relied on by the defendant or third parties.[51]

---

44   *R v Harrow LBC ex p Carter* (1994) 26 HLR 32, QBD; *R v Greenwich LBC ex p Patterson* (1994) 26 HLR 159.

45   *R v Secretary of State for the Home Department ex p Ruddock* [1987] 1 WLR 1482, DC. *R v Secretary of State for Trade and Industry ex p Greenpeace* [2000] Env LR 221, QBD. See also, eg, *R v Essex CC ex p Jackson Projects Ltd* [1995] COD 155, where one of the factors for refusing an extension of time was the absence of any point of general importance.

46   See *R v Secretary of State for the Home Department ex p Ruddock* [1987] 1 WLR 1482; *R v Licensing Authority ex p Novartis Pharmaceuticals Ltd* [2000] COD 232.

47   See, eg, *R v Warwickshire CC ex p Collymore* [1995] ELR 217.

48   See, eg, *R (Burkett) v Hammersmith and Fulham LBC* [2002] UKHL 23; [2002] 1 WLR 1593.

49   *Ahmad v Secretary of State for the Home Department* [1999] Imm AR 356, CA.

50   *R v Tavistock General Commissioners ex p Worth* [1985] STC 564.

50a *R (Camacho) v Haringey LBC* [2003] EWHC 1497 (Admin).

51   See, eg, *R v Commissioner for Local Administration ex p Croydon LBC* [1989] 1 All ER 1033, CA; *R v Durham CC ex p Huddleston* [2000] 1 WLR 1484; [2000] 2 CMLR 229; [2000] Env LR D20.

Delay at the substantive hearing: the Supreme Court Act 1981 and the Civil Procedure Rules

18.31   The courts have explored, in a number of decisions,[52] the relationship between the role of the court in relation to delay at the permission stage and that at the substantive hearing and, indeed, the somewhat obscure relationship between Supreme Court Act 1981 s31(6) and the relevant rules of court. In *R v Dairy Produce Quota Tribunal ex p Caswell.*[53] In that case, Lord Goff of Chievely stated:

> Even if the Court thinks there was a good reason for the delay, it may still refuse leave or, if leave has been granted, refuse substantive relief, where in the Court's opinion the granting of such relief is likely to cause hardship or prejudice or would be detrimental to good administration independently of hardship or prejudice.

18.32   The House of Lords and the Court of Appeal have both considered the issue again more recently. What emerges from these decisions, in summary, is that if the question of delay is fully considered at the per-mission stage, and permission is granted, the court may only reconsider the issue at the substantive hearing in limited circumstances. The House of Lords set out the following principles in *R v Criminal Injuries Compensation Board ex p A:*[54]

• on a permission application, permission to apply for judicial review out-of-time may be granted, refused or deferred to the substantive hearing;

• permission may be given if the court considers that good reason for extending the period has been shown. The good reason is generally to be seen from the standpoint of the claimant;

• it is possible, though unusual on a without notice application, that if the court considers that hardship, prejudice or detriment to good administration has been shown, permission may be refused even if good reason for extending time has been made out;

• if permission is given, an application to set it aside may be made, though this is not to be encouraged. Under the new rules, an appli-cation to set aside permission may not be made,[55] though the court

---

52   In *R (Burkett) v Hammersmith and Fulham LBC* [2002] UKHL 23 at [23], the dovetailing of s31(6) with the rules was described as 'inept'; in *R v Criminal Injuries Compensation Board ex p A* [1999] 2 AC 330, HL, per Lord Slynn of Hadley at 340, as 'perhaps curious'.

53   [1990] 2 AC 738, HL.

54   [1999] 2 AC 330, HL.

55   CPR r54.13.

retains an inherent jurisdiction in some circumstances to set aside permission;[56]

- if permission is given then, unless set aside, it does not fall to be reopened at the substantive hearing on the basis that there is no ground for extending time. At the substantive hearing there is no application for permission to apply for judicial review, permission having already been given;

- the court is probably unable to refuse to 'grant ... leave' – ie, apply Supreme Court Act 1981 s31(6)(a) – at the substantive hearing on the grounds of hardship, prejudice or detriment to good administration; by that stage it is too late to refuse leave unless it sets aside the original grant without a separate application having been made for that to be done;

- if the application is adjourned to the full hearing, the questions of good reason for extending time and of hardship, prejudice or detriment to good administration justifying a refusal of permission may both fall for determination.[57]

18.33　The Court of Appeal, in *Lichfield*,[58] considered this issue in the context of the new procedural regime. The court held that,[59] regardless of whether it involves repetition of the arguments about promptness canvassed at the permission stage, Supreme Court Act 1981 s31(6)(b) places the issue of undue delay on the agenda at the substantive hearing. It does not follow from this, however, that the judge at the substantive hearing should consider the matter as if the issue had never previously arisen, at least where the matter was properly argued at the permission stage. It was undesirable that one Administrative Court judge should act, in effect, as a court of appeal from another or decide an issue without reference to a fellow judge's earlier decision. The matter was one of practical case management under the CPR. In addition, the second judge must have in mind the need to prevent circumvention of CPR r54.13, which prohibits applications to set aside the grant of permission.

18.34　Accordingly, although ultimately a matter for the judge hearing the substantive application, the appropriate course in such cases would generally be that the defendant should be permitted to recanvass by way

56　*R (Webb) v Bristol CC* [2001] EWHC Admin 696.

57　*R v Criminal Injuries Compensation Board ex p A* [1999] 2 AC 330, HL, per Lord Slynn at 341B–F.

58　*R V Lichfield DC ex p Lichfield Securities Ltd* [2001] EWCA Civ 304; (2001) 3 LGLR 637.

59　[2001] EWCA Civ 304 at [34].

of undue delay, an issue of promptness which has been decided at the permission stage in the claimant's favour only if:

- the permission judge has expressly so indicated;
- new and relevant material is introduced on the substantive hearing;
- exceptionally, the issues have developed at the full hearing in such a way as to put a different aspect on the question of promptness; or
- if the first judge has plainly overlooked some relevant matter or reached a decision per incuriam.

18.35   Applying these principles, it would seem that it will not generally be open to the defendant at the substantive hearing to argue for the refusal of relief, under Supreme Court Act 1981 s31(6)(b), on the ground of hardship, prejudice or detriment to good administration, where these issues have been explored fully at the permission stage, even though the question at that stage was whether or not to grant permission rather than whether or not to grant relief.[60]

18.36   Having said this, although *Lichfield* considered the position under the CPR, Part 54 was not yet in force, and it was a feature of that case that the permission application was adjourned into open court where it was properly argued. It must be doubted whether a permission decision taken on the papers, even with the benefit of the defendant's summary of grounds for resisting the application, should be considered to be a proper argument on the issue of delay to debar the judge at the substantive hearing, with the benefit of detailed argument and evidence from the defendant, from considering the issue of refusal of relief.[61] Such a situation would, in any event, seem to fall within the second of the exceptions to the general rule enunciated in *Lichfield* – new and relevant evidence introduced at the substantive hearing.[62] This is separate from the question of whether or not the judge may re-open the question of the grant of permission to proceed, which is generally prohibited.[63]

---

60   See, eg, *Lichfield* [2001] EWCA Civ 304 per Sedley LJ at [37]: 'We take the same view [ie, that the claimant had acted promptly in that case], whether the question is regarded as one of promptness in applying for leave or of undue delay in seeking relief'.

61   Potential problems with the new approach have been identified by the courts: see, eg, *R v Local Commissioner ex p Field* [2000] COD 58; *R v Essex CC ex p Tarmac Roadstone Holdings Ltd* [1998] PLCR 56.

62   *Lichfield* [2001] EWCA Civ 304 at [34].

63   *R v Criminal Injuries Compensation Board ex parte A* [1999] 2 AC 330, HL.

Refusal of relief

18.37 The considerations relating to refusal of relief on the grounds of hardship, prejudice or detriment to good administration are considered in chapter 7 at paras 7.1–7.8.

When time starts to run .

18.38 The House of Lords has now considered this issue, which has vexed the lower courts for a number of years. In *R (Burkett) v Hammersmith and Fulham LBC*,[64] the judicial committee decided that the claimants had not been guilty of delay by reason of their not having challenged the local authority planning committee's resolution to grant planning permission but instead having waited until the formal grant of planning permission.

The former position

18.39 The claimants, in that case, had been refused permission to apply for judicial review of the grant of planning permission on the ground that they had delayed too long before commencing proceedings. There had grown up a body of case-law to the effect that time would generally start to run from the date of the substantive decision of which they complained and that it would not necessarily be safe to wait until the formal manifestation of that decision.

18.40 In *R v Secretary of State for Trade and Industry ex p Greenpeace*,[65] for example, Laws J stated:

> A judicial review applicant must move against the substantive act or decision which is the real basis of his complaint. If, after that act has been done, he takes no steps but merely waits until something consequential and dependent upon it takes place and then challenges that, he runs the risk of being put out of court for being too late …

18.41 Thus, in planning cases, permission had been refused where the claimant challenged the formal grant of planning consent, rather than challenging the resolution to grant it.[66]

18.42 In addition, in certain types of case, the court had begun to impose particularly strict time limits for commencing judicial review

---

64 [2002] UKHL 23; [2002] 1 WLR 1593.
65 [1998] ELR 415.
66 See *R (Burkett) v Hammersmith and Fulham LBC* [2001] Env LR 684, CA, at [12]; see also, eg, *R v North Somerset DC ex p Garnett* [1997] JPL 1015, QBD.

challenges.[67] Where, for example, a related statutory scheme prescribes time limits shorter than three months for bringing a statutory appeal, such as Town and Country Planning Act 1990 s289 (six-week time limit for a statutory appeal to the High Court against a refusal of planning permission), the Administrative Court repeatedly refused permission where the claimant challenging the grant of planning permission (who enjoyed no statutory appeal rights) had waited more than six weeks before commencing the challenge.

18.43   In *R v Ceredigion CC ex p McKeown*,[68] Laws J stated that he found it 'nearly impossible to conceive of a case' in which permission to apply for judicial review would be granted where the application was lodged more than six weeks after the grant of the planning permission. This was because:

> I can see no rhyme or reason in permitting the common law remedy of judicial review to be enjoyed upon a timescale in principle more generous to an applicant than Parliament has seen fit to fix in relation to those who desire to challenge a refusal of [planning] permission or its grant subject to conditions. I do not say that there cannot be such a case, but in my judgment it would be a wholly exceptional one.

18.44   The Court of Appeal, in *Burkett*,[69] while disapproving the 'somewhat mathematical emphasis' which had sometimes been placed on Laws J's dictum, stated that the time set by Town and Country Planning Act 1990 s288 'should be kept in mind as a touchstone of varying usefulness'.

The law after Burkett

18.45   The House of Lords decided that the courts had been wrong to adopt the principles described above. In particular, it was a misconception that the three-month period was in fact shortened to six weeks by the planning cases referred to above, as a statutory time limit could not be 'counteracted by a judicial policy decision'.[70] As Lord Steyn pointed out, moreover, the importance of this issue is not limited to an obscure area of planning law but potentially applies across the board, whenever a decision-maker informs the citizen that he or she is minded to reach a decision adverse to that citizen. For time to run from the expression of that provisional view would 'plainly not be sensible and would

---

67   See also CPR r54.5(3).
68   [1998] 2 PLR 1 at 2.
69   [2001] Env LR 684 at [20].
70   *Burkett* [2002] UKHL 23, per Lord Steyn at [53].

involve waste of time and money'. It would also be contrary to principle to require the citizen to take such premature legal action.[71]

18.46   Lord Steyn stated[72] referring to the requirement of the rules that a claim must be brought not later than three months 'from the date when the grounds for the application first arose',[73] stated that the natural and obvious meaning was that the grounds for an application first arose when the decision was made. The fact that the illegality in a decision was foreseeable at some point before the decision was actually made did not detract from this meaning.

18.47   The contrary argument, that it was disruptive of good administration to permit a citizen to delay his or her challenge until the actual formal decision was made, could not prevail. While the court would have jurisdiction to entertain a challenge to a resolution to grant planning consent both before and after that decision was made formal by the actual grant, it was a 'jump in legal logic' to say that a person must challenge the resolution on pain of losing the right to bring a challenge to the actual grant which gives effect to the resolution and so is the decision which actually affects that person's rights.[74]

18.48   There were a number of policy considerations which militated in favour of time starting to run only when a formal decision had been made:

- the context of the issue about when time began to run was a rule of court which, by imposing a time limit, may deprive the citizen of the right to challenge abuses of power not necessarily involving only individual rights but also potentially community interests. That context weighed heavily in favour of a clear and straightforward interpretation of the rule which would lead to a readily ascertainable start date. Allowing the courts to ascertain the start date retrospectively was antithetical to the context of a time limit barring proceedings;
- legal policy favours simplicity and certainty rather than complexity and uncertainty. In the absence of indications to the contrary, the legislature must be presumed to have intended to create a certain and predictable regime. The citizen and the decision-maker – and

---

71   [2002] UKHL 23 at [43].
72   [2002] UKHL 23 at [39].
73   This was the language of RSC Ord 53 r4(1), but CPR r54.5(1)(b), the equivalent current procedural rule, is almost identical referring to the requirement that a claim be made not later than three months ('after the grounds to make the claim first arose').
74   *Burkett* [2002] UKHL 23, per Lord Steyn at [42].

indeed an interested third party such as the developer – must know where they stand, particularly where the effect of the rule to be interpreted may result in the loss of the right to challenge an unlawful exercise of power. For the court retrospectively to assess the appropriate date by which proceedings ought reasonably to have been commenced, with the attendant lack of certainty, would be 'a recipe for sterile procedural disputes and unjust results';

• the preparation of judicial review cases was a burdensome task. Lord Steyn referred, in particular, to the duty of full and frank disclosure, and the obligation to present to the court a detailed statement of grounds, evidence, supporting documents in a paginated and indexed bundle, a list of essential reading with the relevant passages sidelined and legislative sources in a paginated indexed bundle. This was a heavy burden on individuals and (for funded claimants) the Legal Services Commission. A claimant is also at risk of having to pay substantial costs. All of these factors reinforced the view that it is unreasonable to require the citizen to challenge a decision that may never take effect and unfair to subject him or her to a retrospective decision by the court as to the date when the time limit for commencing proceedings was triggered.

Continuing illegality

18.49 An issue not dealt with in *Burkett* is when time begins to run, and indeed how the rules relating to delay apply generally, where what is challenged is a continuing failure to act lawfully. Examples of this may be a continuing failure to make a lawful decision in relation to an application for accommodation under Housing Act 1996 Part VI; or a continuing failure to conduct an assessment of need under the community care legislation, or to make a statement of special educational need.

18.50 Frequently, the allegation of a continuing failure to make a lawful decision is not based on a failure to make any decision at all. Instead, the illegality may arise from the making of a decision which is unlawful (hence the continuing failure to make a *lawful* one). It may be insufficient for the decision-maker simply to make a new decision, for example, where the illegality of the decision stems from its having been taken in accordance with, or having regard to, an unlawful policy which is still in place and which would therefore continue to inform and so invalidate any new decision.

18.51 The unlawful decision may have been taken, and indeed the policy is likely to have been adopted, some time – possibly years – prior to the challenge being brought. In the case of a policy, there would be no reason for the claimant ever to consider its legality until it was actually applied to his or her case.

18.52 The questions therefore arise when time starts to run in such cases. Are decisions and policies rendered immune from challenge, on the basis that they were implemented more than three months prior to the commencement of proceedings?

18.53 The courts have, in general, declined to accept this as the position, by adopting a variety of different responses. In principle, the continued failure to make a lawful decision over time can be analysed as a new failure arising each day, starting the running of time again.[75] Even so, this does not render it irrelevant to have regard, in considering delay, to the date when the breach began.[76] In other cases, the courts have simply stated that delay does not absolve a public authority from performing its duty.[77]

18.54 Similarly, the courts have held that illegality of a policy is a good reason for extending time, where otherwise the unlawful policy would continue in operation, particularly where only prospective relief is sought. In *R v Rochdale BC ex p Schemet*,[78] Roch J cited the comments of Nicholls LJ in *R v Westminster CC ex p Hilditch*[79] that:

> ... if a policy is unlawful, prima facie it should be discontinued. The mere fact that the policy has been in place for nearly three years is not a sufficient reason for the court countenancing its continuing implementation for the indefinite future. There is here good reason for extending time for the making of an application for judicial review, at any rate so far as the relief sought is directed at retraining the further implementation of the allegedly unlawful policy.

18.55 In *Schemet* itself, the court refused mandatory relief which would have affected the budget of the respondent education authority for the previous two years, granting only declarations as to the illegality of the

---

75 See, eg, *R v Islington LBC ex p Camp* (transcript TLQ/99/0996) July 20, 1999.
76 See *R v Essex CC ex p C* [1994] ELR 54, QBD.
77 See, eg, *London and Clydeside Estates v Aberdeen DC* [1980] 1 WLR 182. See also the cases on the importance of the issues at stake constituting good reason for extending time, eg, *R v Secretary of State for the Home Department ex p Ruddock* [1987] 1 WLR 1482; *R v Secretary of State for Foreign and Commonwealth Affairs ex p World Development Movement* [1995] 1 WLR 386.
78 [1994] ELR 89, QBD, at 100–101.
79 (1990) 14 June (unreported), transcript p17.

impugned decisions.[80] In *R v East Sussex CC ex p Ward*,[81] permission was granted on the express basis that no relief would be granted in respect of any period prior to six months before the grant of permission itself (in fact only declaratory relief was granted for various reasons).[82]

Dealing with time limits

18.56   *R (Burkett) v Hammersmith and Fulham LBC*[83] clearly eases the burden on claimants by clarifying the position in relation to the start of the running of time. It has no easing effect, however, on the obligation to act promptly once the final decision to be challenged has been made. Having said this, advisers should remember that decision-makers may frequently communicate more than one reviewable decision, in any particular case, and where a reconsideration has been undertaken but has confirmed the original decision, the later decision can – and generally should – be challenged especially where it replaces or supersedes the original decision. This may well assist the claimant, even if he or she has been guilty of delay in relation to the initial decision.

18.57   If a request for a reconsideration has been refused, that decision may in itself be reviewable, although the court is more likely in such a case to take the view that the substance of the claimant's complaint is the original adverse decision rather than the refusal on the part of the decision-maker to reconsider. In such cases, all decisions of the decision-maker should be included on the claim form. Apart from other considerations, it may be more difficult for a decision-maker to claim hardship, prejudice or detriment to good administration in relation to a challenge to his or her initial decision, if a reconsideration has recently been undertaken.

Commencement of proceedings

18.58   Judicial review cases are dealt with by the Administrative Court in London except, potentially, in two situations. The first is where the claim or any remedy sought involves a devolution issue[84] arising out of

---

80   See also *R v Warwickshire CC ex p Collymore* [1995] ELR 217.
81   (2000) 3 CCLR 132, QBD.
82   (2000) 3 CCLR 132 at 140A–C.
83   [2002] UKHL 23; [2002] 1 WLR 1593.
84   See para 18.69–18.71 below.

the Government of Wales Act 1998, or an issue concerning the National Assembly for Wales, the Welsh executive or any Welsh public body including a Welsh local authority (whether or not a devolution issue is involved).[85] In such a case, the proceedings may be brought in the Administrative Court in Wales, or in London.[86]

18.59　The second is where urgency makes it necessary for the claim to be made outside London or Cardiff. In such cases, the Administrative Court Office in London should be consulted, if necessary by telephone, prior to the filing of the claim form.[87]

18.60　The judicial review application is a species of a CPR Part 8 claim, though Part 54 modifies the Part 8 procedure,[88] and therefore the general provisions of Part 8 will apply to the proceedings, save where Part 54 makes other provision.

18.61　An application is commenced by filing with the Administrative Court Office[89] two copies of a paginated and indexed bundle[90] containing a completed claim form (N461 – see appendix A, p454)[91] together with the mandatory accompanying documents.[92] The full address is: Administrative Court Office, Royal Courts of Justice, Strand, London WC2A 2LL. In Wales, the address is the Law Courts, Cathays Park, Cardiff, CF10 3PG.[93]

Court fees

18.62　The fee, payable on the commencement of the judicial review procedure, ie, on filing the documents mentioned above, is currently £30.[94] If permission is granted, an additional fee of £120 becomes payable

85　CPR Practice Direction 54, para 3.1.
86　CPR Practice Direction 54 paras 3.1–3.2.
87　CPR Practice Direction 54 para 2.4.
88　CPR r54.1(2)(e).
89　CPR Practice Direction 54 para 2.1–2.2.
90　CPR Practice Direction 54 para 5.9. There appears to be an error in this paragraph, as it refers to the requirements of paragraphs 4.6 and 4.7. Given that the Practice Direction contains no such paragraphs, it is assumed that the reference was intended to be to paragraphs 5.6 and 5.7.
91　Available in a downloadable format from www.courtservice.gov.uk – follow the link to 'Forms & Guidance'.
92　See further below and, generally, CPR r54.6 and CPR Practice Direction 54 paras 5.1–5.8 together with the various other provisions of the CPR there referred to.
93　CPR Practice Direction 54 paras 2.2–2.3.
94　Supreme Court Fees Order 1999 SI No 687 (as amended), Sch 1, para 1.6(a).

within seven days of the service on the claimant of the order granting permission.[95]

Formal requirements of the claim form

18.63   The formal requirements of the claim form are set out in CPR rr8.2; 54.6 and the Practice Direction. The matters which must be specified by virtue of Rule 8.2 are as follows:

- that Part 8 applies to the claim,[96] although there appears to be no reference to this point in the claim form N461;
- the question which the court is asked to decide:[97] this appears to be dealt with at s3 (details of the decision to be judicially reviewed) and s6 (detailed statement of grounds) of the claim form;
- the remedy sought (including any interim remedy) and the legal basis, or grounds, for the claim to that remedy:[98] again, see s6 of the claim form as regards the grounds (note that the Practice Direction – reflected at s6 – permits the grounds to be drafted as a document accompanying the claim form),[99] and s7 on the remedy sought;
- the enactment, if any, under which the claim is made;[100]
- if the claimant is claiming in a representative capacity, what that capacity is;[101]
- if the defendant is being sued in a representative capacity, what that capacity is: these last three requirements, to the extent that they are applicable to a judicial review claim, would also, in practice, be dealt with by including the relevant information in the grounds;[102]

---

95   Supreme Court Fees Order 1999 para 1.6(b). By para 1.6(c), if the claim was commenced otherwise than by using the judicial review procedure, the additional fee payable within seven days of service of the order granting permission is £30. At first sight, it is not entirely clear when this provision may apply, although it could refer to the power of the court, pursuant to CPR r54.20, applying CPR r30.5, to transfer cases begun by ordinary civil process to the Administrative Court. As to this power, see further above at paras 18.9–18.16.

96   CPR r8.2(a).

97   CPR r8.2(b).

98   CPR r8.2(b). The requirement that any remedy claimed (including any interim remedy) and the grounds for the claim be included is repeated by CPR r54.6(1)(c) and CPR Practice Direction 54 para 5.6(1).

99   CPR Practice Direction 54 para 5.6(1), and see further below.

100   CPR r8.2(c).

101   CPR r8.2(d).

102   CPR r8.2(e).

- that the claimant is requesting permission to apply for judicial review: see s4 of the claim form;[103]
- the name and address of any person considered to be an interested party:[104] this is dealt with at s2 of the claim form. Where the claim relates to proceedings before a court or tribunal, any other parties to those proceedings must be named as interested parties;[105]
- a statement of truth:[106] the statement of truth contained in the claim form, under its s9, confirms the truth of the facts stated in s8 (statement of facts relied on) of the form.[107] Accordingly, where the statement of facts relied on (see below) is drafted as separate documents accompanying the claim form, it is probably unnecessary that it should include an additional statement of truth, as the facts stated in the separate document would still fall within s8 of the form. The position concerning the grounds for review is not so clear. If it is drafted as a separate document and contains facts, as is likely, then these ought to be verified by a statement of truth,[108] though the form makes no provision for this. For this reason, the safest course would be to add a statement of truth where the grounds are drafted as a separate document attached to the claim form. Verification by a statement of truth is essential where the claimant wishes to rely on the contents of the claim form as evidence in the claim, whether in relation to a claim for interim relief or generally.[109]

18.64 The claim form must also include or be accompanied by the following information:

- a detailed statement of the grounds for seeking review.[110] Given their probable length, it is likely to be more practical to draft the statement of grounds as a separate document accompanying the

---

103 CPR r54.6(1)(b).
104 CPR r54.6(1)(a).
105 CPR Practice Direction 54 paras 5.1–5.2.
106 CPR rr8.2 and 22.1.
107 The previous version of the form (as reproduced in the White and Green Books, Sweet & Maxwell) referred to the facts stated in s9 of the form: this was presumably an error.
108 CPR rr8.2 and 22.1.
109 CPR r8.5(7) states that the matters set out in the claim form may be relied on as evidence if the claim form is verified by a statement of truth. In relation to claims for interim relief, an analogous provision is contained in CPR r32.6(2) and Practice Direction 32 paras 1.3 and 26.1. As to interim injunctions, see CPR Practice Direction 25A para 3.2.
110 CPR Practice Direction 54 para 5.6(1).

claim form, as is permitted by the Practice Direction, rather than to include the grounds at s6 of the claim form itself. As stated above, where this practice is adopted, the grounds should probably contain their own statement of truth;

- a statement of the facts relied on:[111] s8 of the claim form. Where the statement is contained in a separate document accompanying the claim form, it is probably not necessary to include an additional statement of truth, though no criticism would attach to including one;
- any application to extend the time limit for filing the claim form:[112] this would, in practice generally be included at s9 of the claim form. Likewise, if the contents of any application pleaded under s9 of the claim form are to be used as evidence in the application, a statement of truth must be included in s9;[113]
- any application for directions:[114] also included at s9;
- a time estimate for the substantive (ie, not the permission) hearing:[115] see s5 of the claim form.

Additional requirements in human rights cases

18.65   In any case where the claimant seeks to raise any issue under the Human Rights Act 1998, or seeks a remedy available under that Act, the claim form must also:[116]

- state that fact;[117]
- give precise details of the right under the European Convention on Human Rights (the Convention) which is alleged to have been infringed and details of the alleged infringement;[118]
- specify the relief sought;[119]
- state if the relief sought includes a declaration of incompatibility under Human Rights Act 1998 s4 or damages in respect of a judicial act to which s9(3) of that Act applies (ie, damages for an arrest or for detention in breach of article 5 of the Convention;[120]

---

111   CPR Practice Direction 54 para 5.6(2).
112   CPR Practice Direction 54 para 5.6(3).
113   See note 109 above.
114   CPR Practice Direction 54 para 5.6(4).
115   CPR Practice Direction 54 para 5.6(5).
116   CPR Practice Direction 54 para 5.3.
117   CPR Practice Direction 16 para 16.1(1).
118   CPR Practice Direction 16 para 16.1(2)(a).
119   CPR Practice Direction 16 para 16.1(2)(b).
120   CPR Practice Direction 16 para 16.1(2)(c).

- where the relief sought does include a declaration of incompatibility, give precise details of the legislative provision alleged to be incompatible and details of the alleged incompatibility;[121]
- where the claim is founded on a finding of unlawfulness made by another court or tribunal, give details of that finding;[122]
- where the claim is founded on a judicial act alleged to have infringed a Convention right as provided by Human Rights Act 1998 s9, state the judicial act complained of and the court or tribunal alleged to have so acted.[123]

18.66 The discussion, above,[124] concerning statements of truth would appear also to apply to these requirements.

18.67 In cases where the claimant seeks damages for a judicial act and/or a declaration of incompatibility, the relevant secretary of state (or, in the case of a judicial act, the Lord Chancellor – now the Secretary of State for Constitutional Affairs)[125] should be listed in the claim form as an interested party.[126] In either case, CPR Part 19 requires notice of such a claim to be given to the Crown and entitles a minister, or person nominated by him, to be joined as a party to the proceedings. Indeed, no award of damages for a judicial act may be made unless the minister responsible for the court concerned or a person or government department nominated by him has been joined.[127]

---

121 CPR Practice Direction 16 para 16.1(2)(d).
122 CPR Practice Direction 16 para 16.1(2)(e).
123 CPR Practice Direction 16 para 16.1(2)(f).
124 At paras 18.63–18.64.
125 Or, in the case of courts martial, the Secretary of State for Defence: CPR Practice Direction 19A para 6.6(2).
126 See the list of authorised government departments annexed to CPR Practice Direction 19A.
127 Human Rights Act 1998 s9(4). CPR r19.4A (3) provides that where a claim is made for damages in respect of a judicial act and no application to be joined is made by the minister or person nominated by him within 21 days, or such other period as the court directs, of notice having been served, the court may join the minister or other person as a party. CPR r19.4A(1)–(2) provides that a court may not make a declaration of incompatibility unless 21 days' notice, or such other period as the court directs has been given to the Crown, and that where notice has been given, a minister or other person nominated by him must be joined as a party to the proceedings on giving notice to the court. For the detailed provisions concerning these matters and, in particular, how notification to the Crown should be made in such cases, see: Human Rights Act 1998 ss4 and 9; CPR r19(4A); and CPR Practice Direction 19A paras 6.1–6.6.

18.68   In *Poplar Housing and Regeneration Community Association Ltd v Donoghue*,[128] the Court of Appeal set out the procedure to be adopted for notifying the Crown in cases where the possibility of a declaration of incompatibility arises:[129]

(i) the formal notice which the Human Rights Act and the CPR require should always be given by the court. This is because the court will be in the best position to assess whether there is a likelihood of a declaration of incompatibility being made.

(ii) So as to give the Crown as much notice as possible, whenever a party is seeking a declaration of incompatibility or acknowledges that a declaration of incompatibility may be made, it should give as much informal notice to the Crown as practical of the proceedings and the issues that are involved.

(iii) The formal and informal notice to the Crown should be given to a person named in the list published under s17 of the Crown Proceedings Act 1947.

(iv) At the same time as the party gives notice informally to the Crown, it should send a copy of such notice to the court so that the court is alerted to the fact that it will have to consider whether a formal notice should be given. It should also send a copy of the notice to the other parties.

(v) In these circumstances, we are referring to the court that will hear the proceedings. That is a trial court at the level of the High Court or, in the case of appeals, the Court of Appeal or the High Court (in the case of appeals to the High Court). The county court cannot make a declaration of incompatibility (Human Rights Act 1998 s4(5)).

Additional requirements in cases raising devolution issues

18.69   A devolution issue, in essence, is an issue concerning whether an act of the Scottish Parliament; the National Assembly for Wales; or the Northern Ireland Assembly; or the exercise of a function by the Scottish Executive or any minister is within the devolved powers conferred by the relevant Acts of Parliament or breaches a Convention right or EU law.[130]

128 [2001] EWCA Civ 595; [2001] 3 WLR 183; (2001) 33 HLR 73.
129 [2001] 3 WLR 183, per Lord Woolf CJ at 191A–E.
130 See Scotland Act 1998 s98 and Sch 6; Government of Wales Act 1998 s109 and Sch 8; Northern Ireland Act 1998 s79 and Sch 10.

18.70   Where a devolution issue is raised, the claim form must:[131]

- specify that such an issue is being raised and identify the relevant provisions of the relevant Act;[132]
- contain a summary of the facts, circumstances and points of law on the basis of which a devolution issue is alleged to arise.

18.71   The discussion above,[133] concerning the need for statements of truth would appear also to apply to these requirements.

Documents to be filed with the claim form

18.72   The claim form must be accompanied by the following additional documents:

- any written evidence in support of the claim or application to extend time;[134]
- a copy of any order that the claimant seeks to have quashed;[135]
- where the judicial review claim relates to a decision of a court or tribunal, an approved copy of the court or tribunal's reasons for reaching the decision challenged;[136]
- copies of any documents on which the claimant proposes to rely;[137]
- copies of any relevant statutory material;[138]
- a list of essential documents for advance reading by the court with page references to the passages relied on.[139]

18.73   If it is not possible to file all of these documents with the claim form, the claimant must indicate the documents which have not been filed, and the reasons why they are not currently available. Section 10 of the claim form contains a checklist with boxes which may be ticked to indicate whether a document is included in the body of the form, attached to it or will be filed later. Section 10 of the form requires not only a statement of the reasons why a document not available at the time of filing the claim form has not been supplied, but also the date when it is expected to be available.

131   CPR Practice Direction 54 para 5.4.
132   That is, the Scotland Act 1998, the Government of Wales Act 1998 or the Northern Ireland Act 1998.
133   At paras 18.63–18.64.
134   CPR Practice Direction 54 para 5.7(1) and CPR r8.5(1).
135   CPR Practice Direction 54 para 5.7(2).
136   CPR Practice Direction 54 para 5.7(3).
137   CPR Practice Direction 54 para 5.7(4).
138   CPR Practice Direction 54 para 5.7(5).
139   CPR Practice Direction 54 para 5.7(6).

Drafting the grounds or statement of facts

18.74   Many aspects of the old practice relating to the drafting of the grounds for seeking review remain valid under the new procedural code. The grounds should be fully pleaded and include the reasons for any delay, even if an extension of time is not required because the three-month back-stop period for making the claim has not expired.[140] In practice, there would seem to be no reason why the grounds and statement of facts[141] relied on should not be incorporated into one document containing appropriate subheadings.[142] As regards the statement of facts, it is worth bearing in mind that as there is no longer any formal[143] requirement for an affidavit or witness statement in support of the claim form, the statement of facts must include a full statement of all those facts relied on.

18.75   The grounds should include any authorities to which the claimant intends to refer at the hearing. In citing authorities, however, it is necessary to comply with the *Practice Direction (Citation of Authorities)*[144] which prohibits the citing of certain types of authority (subject to exceptions)[145] and imposes new requirements concerning the methods of citing authorities,[146] and the use of authorities from other

140   See under 'Delay' above at paras 18.17–18.57.
141   CPR Practice Direction 54 para 5.6(2).
142   For a precedent of such a document, see appendix A at p459.
143   See under 'Evidence in support' below at paras 18.89–18.93.
144   [2001] 1 WLR 1001 (Sup Ct).
145   The following categories of judgment may not be cited before any court unless it clearly indicates that it purports to establish a new principle of law or to extend the law: Practice Direction para 6.1. Those categories are: applications attended by one party only; applications for permission to appeal; decisions on applications that only decide that the application is arguable; county court cases unless (a) cited to illustrate the measure of damages in personal injury cases (and presumably, by analogy, housing disrepair cases) or (b) cited in a county court on an issue in respect of which no authority of a higher court is available: Practice Direction para 6.2. In addition, advocates will be required to justify a decision to cite a judgment in which it is indicated that it only applied decided law to the facts of the particular case; or that it does not extend or add to the existing law: Practice Direction para 7.1–7.2.
146   It is necessary to state, in respect of each authority cited, the proposition of law demonstrated by the authority, the parts of the judgment that support the proposition and, if more than one authority is cited for the same proposition, the reason for doing so: Practice Direction para 8.1. Any list of authorities must bear a certification by the advocate responsible that these requirements have been complied with: Practice Direction para 8.3.

jurisdictions.[147] The *Practice Direction (Supreme Court: Judgments: Neutral Citations)*,[147a] must also be complied with.

18.76 It has been held, under the old rules, that authorities which are unfavourable to the claimant's case should be mentioned and where possible distinguished in the grounds.[148] Statutory provisions ousting the jurisdiction of the court should also be mentioned in the grounds which should explain why it is claimed such clauses do not apply to the application in question.[149]

18.77 If damages are claimed, the usual rules of pleading apply and full particulars should be given.[150]

18.78 The claim form, as a statement of case, must, if drafted by a legal representative, be signed by him or her. If drafted by a legal representative as a member or employee of a firm, it must be signed in the name of the firm.[151]

18.79 In drafting the grounds, it should be borne in mind that they will form the basis not only of the argument on the permission application, but also of the full application if permission is granted. It is essential to set out precisely what is complained of in an intelligible manner. Although such matters always entail questions of individual style, it is probably better to draft the grounds more in the style, and with the detail, of a short skeleton argument rather than that of a civil pleading. Although they may be amended, with permission,[152] at a later stage, it is worth spending time (where this is available) formulating the grounds properly, not least so as to increase the chances of permission being granted.

Interim relief

18.80 Any claim for interim relief must be included in the claim form together with the substantive relief sought.[153] Details of all remedies

---

147 See Practice Direction paras 9.1–9.2 (though they do not apply to decisions of the European Court of Justice or organs of the European Convention on Human Rights which are governed by the previous paragraphs: Practice Direction para 9.3).

147a [2002] 1 WLR 346.

148 *R v Crown Prosecution Service ex p Hogg* [1994] COD 237, QBD.

149 *R v Cornwall CC ex p Huntingdon and another* [1992] 3 All ER 566, DC, at 576.

150 Formerly RSC Ord 53 r7(2) applying RSC Ord 18 r12. No specific reference to this appears in CPR Part 54, but it remains good practice.

151 CPR Practice Direction 5 para 2.1. See also para 2.2 for the general requirements as to the form of all court documents.

152 CPR r54.15.

153 CPR r54.6(1)(c).

being sought, including interim remedies, are in practice, set out at s7 of the claim form. By CPR r25.3(2), an application for interim relief must be supported by evidence unless the court orders otherwise. In general, evidence at hearings other than the trial is given by witness statement unless the court, a practice direction or an enactment requires otherwise,[154] although a party may if he or she wishes rely solely on the contents of his or her statement of case or application provided that they have been verified by a statement of truth.[155] The evidence must set out the facts on which the claimant relies for the claim for interim relief, including all facts of which the court should be aware.[156] If an application for interim relief is made without notice to the defendant, the evidence in support must state the reasons why notice was not given.[157]

18.81   In practice, the application will be made using ss7 and 9 of the claim form, supported by evidence. This may be the evidence contained in the statement of facts (s8) and/or that contained in a witness statement.[158] As stated above,[159] if the statement of facts is drafted to contain the evidence required to support the claim for interim relief, it is probably unnecessary for it to contain a separate statement of truth (though there is nothing to be lost by including one).

Urgent cases and interim injunctions

18.82   Even in urgent cases, and those in which interim injunctions are sought, the court will generally initially consider the matter on the papers. The Administrative Court has now issued guidance on the procedure to be followed in all cases where the application for permission is urgent and/or where an interim injunction is sought.[160] Although stated to be guidance, it is the duty of the advocate for the claimant to comply with the procedure it sets out, and

154   CPR r32.6(1).
155   CPR r32.6(2), and see CPR 22.1(1) and (3), and see the discussion at paras 18.63–18.64 above.
156   CPR Practice Direction 25A para 3.3.
157   CPR r25.3(3) and Practice Direction 25A para 3.4 (see also Practice Direction 25A paras 4.1–4.5).
157   See 'Evidence in support' at paras 18.89–18.93.
159   See paras 18.63–18.64.
160   *Practice Statement (Administrative Court: Administration of Justice)* [2002] 1 WLR 810 Scott Baker J, 1 February 2002.

where a 'manifestly inappropriate' application is made, consideration will be given to the making of a wasted costs order.[161]

18.83 The procedure is as follows. Where an application is made for the permission application to be heard as a matter of urgency, and/or where an interim injunction is sought, the prescribed form attached to the guidance (see appendix A, p475), must be completed, which states:

- the need for urgency;
- the timescale within which consideration of the permission application is sought (eg, 72 hours or sooner if necessary); and
- the date by which the substantive hearing should take place.[162]

18.84 Where an interim injunction is sought, the claimant must also provide:

- a draft order; and
- the grounds for seeking the injunction.[163]

18.85 The claimant must serve, by e-mail or fax, and post, the claim form and the application for urgency on the defendant and interested parties, advising them of the application and of their right to make representations.[164] Where an interim injunction is sought, the claimant must also serve, by e-mail or fax, and post, the draft order and grounds for the application, again advising the defendant and interested parties of the application and of their right to make representations.[165]

18.86 The Administrative Court currently allocates paper applications for permission on a daily basis, and one judge acts as the 'Urgent Judge'. The application will be considered within the timescale requested, and the judge may make such order as he or she considers appropriate. If an oral hearing within a specified time is directed, the Administrative Court will liaise with the representatives of the parties to fix a permission hearing within the time period directed.[166] Where the matter is so urgent that the urgency procedure cannot be complied with because there is no time to issue proceedings, the claimant can still apply orally for permission and/or interim relief to the duty judge in court 37 at the Royal Courts of Justice. Alternatively, CPR PD 25 para 4.5 indicates that, where interim relief is urgently sought, the claimant's representative can telephone the Royal Courts of Justice on 020 7947 6000, between 10.00 am and 5.00 pm and ask to be put through to a

161 [2002] 1 WLR 810 para 2.
162 [2002] 1 WLR 810 para 4.
163 [2002] 1 WLR 810 para 5.
164 [2002] 1 WLR 810 para 6.
165 [2002] 1 WLR 810 para 7.
166 [2002] 1 WLR 810 paras 2, 8 and 9.

Judge available to deal with an emergency application in a judicial review matter (though in practice, this can be a difficult procedure to invoke). Urgent telephone applications out of hours may be made by telephoning the Royal Courts of Justice and asking security to be put through to the Duty Judge's clerk, who will contact the Duty Judge if the matter is sufficiently urgent. In any of these circumstances, the claimant will need to undertake to issue the claim and the injunction application with evidence in support in accordance with the judge's direction; the claim form should normally be served on the defendant with the sealed copy of the injunction order.

Other matters

18.87   As stated above, the practice of the Administrative Court is that all applications will initially be considered by a judge on the papers, unless the court directs otherwise, to deal with permission applications more speedily and avoid unnecessary cost.[167] An application for interim relief may well be a reason why the court would direct an oral hearing. The previous practice that claimants should request an oral hearing if they are seeking interim relief,[168] therefore, no longer seems applicable, particularly in the light of the guidance on urgent cases.[169] There is no provision in the rules, however, to prevent the claimant requesting an oral hearing in appropriate circumstances: if such an application is to be made, it should be set out in ss7 and 9 of the claim form.

18.88   Under the old provisions, the court indicated that where judicial review is sought in a matrimonial or family context, it is desirable for the claimant to request on the claim form that the matter be heard by a judge of the Family Division.[170] This would seem still to be good practice, and such a request may be included at ss 7 and 9 of the claim form. Even if no such request is included, it has been suggested that in sensitive family matters, the Administrative Court Office should always seek to put the claim before a judge with both Administrative Court and Family Division experience, or before the President of the Family Division.[171]

---

167   See Practice Statement para 6(7) and form N461A para 9(ii).
168   See eg, *R v Kensington and Chelsea RLBC ex p Hammell* [1989] QB 518, per Parker LJ at 539.
169   See paras 18.82–18.86 above.
170   *R v Dover Magistrates Court ex p Kidner* [1983] 1 All ER 475, QBD.
171   See *R (X and Y) v Gloucestershire CC* [2003] EWHC 850 (Admin); [2003] FLR 171, per Munby J at [42].

Evidence in support

18.89 Under the former provisions, it was a requirement that a statement be made by or on behalf of the applicant, verifying the facts relied on in the application.[172] This is not a requirement of the new rules. Instead, a statement of facts relied on must be included in or attached to the claim form, which must be verified by a statement of truth in any event.[173] The claimant may rely on the contents of the statement of case as evidence, provided the contents of the form have been verified by a statement of truth.[174] If written evidence is to be used on behalf of the claimant, however, it must be filed with the claim form.[175]

18.90 In spite of the relaxation of the formal requirement for evidence, in practice, it will frequently be advisable to file evidence in support, not least in order to exhibit other documents required by the practice direction.[176]

18.91 The importance of a witness statement in support of the claim, made by the claimant, should not be underestimated. Even though the claim form will contain a statement of the relevant facts, a witness statement will still enable the claimant to raise matters which are more appropriately dealt with in evidence (such as statements of belief, feelings, etc) and indeed to emphasise matters which although dealt with in the statement of facts, will probably carry more weight if the claimant is willing to attest to them personally (such as denying allegations made against him or making allegations against the decision-maker).

18.92 The general position is that no written evidence may be relied on unless it has been served in accordance with any rule under CPR Part 54 or a direction of the court[177] (the provisions of CPR r8.6(1) are disapplied)[178] or unless the court gives permission.[179] Accordingly, the court has power to allow statements to be used by the claimant, even if none has been filed with the claim form. It may be, however, that this power would not be exercised in the case of a party who for no good reason has failed to file evidence at the proper time, unless there were strong reasons for doing so.

172 RSC Ord 53 r3(2)(b).
173 See paras 18.63–18.64 above.
174 CPR r8.5(7).
175 CPR Practice Direction 54 para 5.7.1. See also CPR r8.5(1) and (2).
176 Especially that referred to at CPR Practice Direction 54 para 5.7.2–5.7.4.
177 CPR r54.16(2)(a).
178 By CPR r54.16(1).
179 CPR r54.16(2)(b): see further below.

Formal requirements of written evidence

18.93   The majority of the formal requirements regarding the content of written evidence are contained in CPR Part 32[180] and Practice Direction 32. In brief, the statement must include the heading of the case and,[181] in the top right-hand corner, must appear: the party on whose behalf the statement is made; the initials and surname of the witness; the number of the statement in relation to that witness; the identifying initials and number of each exhibit; and the date on which the statement was made.[182]

18.94   The statement must, if practicable, be in the witness's own words and should be expressed in the first person.[183] It must also state:

- the full name of the witness;
- the address at which he lives or, if the statement is made in his professional or business capacity, the address at which he works, the position he holds and the name of his firm or employer;
- his or her occupation or, if none, description;
- if it is the case, the fact that he or she is a party or the employee of a party to the proceedings;[184]
- which of the statements are made from the witness' own knowledge and which are matters of information and belief;
- the source of any matters of information or belief.[185]

18.95   Exhibits should be verified and identified by the witness, and remain separate from the statement itself.[186] References in the statement to an exhibit should use the words 'I refer to the [description of exhibit] marked "...".'[187] Where more than one statement to which there are exhibits is made by a witness in the proceedings, the exhibits should be numbered consecutively throughout the statements and not start again with each statement.[188]

18.96   Provision is also made for the format of the statement, the exhibits, and the statement of truth[189] and other ancillary matters.[190]

180   See, in particular, CPR r32.8.
181   Practice Direction 32 para 17.1.
182   Practice Direction 32 para 17.2.
183   Practice Direction 32 para 18.1.
184   Practice Direction 32 para 18.1(1)–(4).
185   Practice Direction 32 para 18.2(1)–(2).
186   Practice Direction 32 para 18.3.
187   Practice Direction 32 para 18.4.
188   Practice Direction 32 para 18.6.
189   Practice Direction 32 paras 11.3–15.4; 19.1–20.3.
190   See generally Practice Directions 22 and 32.

18.97   Hearsay evidence is now generally admissible in civil proceedings, the quality of the evidence going to its weight rather than its admissibility.[191] This is subject to two qualifications: first, the power of the court to exclude evidence which would otherwise be admissible,[192] and second, the fact that hearsay evidence may remain inadmissible on other grounds, such as its relevance. In judicial review proceedings, hearsay evidence is commonly used in the form of information derived from the files and records of the decision-maker. The use of such evidence is usually uncontroversial.

18.98   Cases in judicial review, and particularly permission hearings, are won and lost on the quality of the claimant's paperwork: judicial review cases are very different from other civil cases, where deficiencies in the papers can frequently be overcome by oral evidence and submission. The foregoing applies, of course, with particular force where, as is now the general practice,[193] permission is considered on the papers alone.

Full and frank disclosure

18.99   Under the former rules,[194] the permission application was formally made without notice to the defendant. At least in the later years of those rules, however, the application had in reality become, in most cases, a hybrid type of application in relation to which the court generally disapproved of claimants coming to court without – at the very least – notifying defendants of their intention to do so by a full letter before action, and at which defendants frequently submitted short written evidence and were represented.

18.100   Nevertheless, formerly, even applications at which both parties were present were made 'ex parte on notice' rather than inter partes. This had implications for the contents of the documents, especially the witness statement, in that the claimant was under a duty to give full and frank disclosure of all relevant matters, even if unfavourable to

---

191 Civil Evidence Act 1995, especially s2, and see the notice requirements contained in CPR Part 33. It had previously been held that statements of information and belief were only admissible at the permission stage but not, without leave, at the substantive hearing: *R v Sandhutton Parish Council ex p Todd and Fox* [1992] COD 409, QBD. However, this would not seem to survive the Civil Evidence Act 1995.

192 CPR r32.1.

193 See N461A, *Notes for Guidance on Applying for Judicial Review*, para 9(i).

194 RSC Ord 53.

his or her case. Failure to give such disclosure could constitute grounds for setting leave aside, or for refusing the relief sought at the full hearing. This duty extended not simply to matters of fact,[195] but also to the existence of alternative remedies, ouster clauses and other points of law, including case-law, which were adverse to the claim.[196]

18.101 The position under the CPR Part 54 appears to remain the same, notwithstanding the new requirement of service of the documents filed at court on the defendant, and the opportunity for the defendant to file an acknowledgement of service setting out the grounds for contesting the claim.[197] The essential nature and purpose of the permission hearing, as a mechanism for filtering out unarguable or otherwise improper claims, remains the same and defendants are not intended, in the acknowledgement of service, to file lengthy, fully argued, defences nor to file detailed evidence in reply. Accordingly, the court will still view with disapproval a judicial review claim which does not set out all the material facts known to the claimant whether or not they support the claimant's case.[198]

18.102 In any event, in urgent cases where permission is sought without any acknowledgement of service having been filed, the requirements of full and frank disclosure are plainly still applicable.[199]

Content of the duty to give full and frank disclosure

18.103 The courts have indicated that, particularly where the case is to be considered on the papers, claimants should draw the attention of the judge to a body of authority which is against the claimant's case and state why it is distinguishable.[200] This obligation is generally applicable to matters which may affect the outcome of the application, or affect any

---

195 As to which, see, eg, *R v Secretary of State for the Home Department ex p Comfort Henry* [1995] Imm AR 42; *R v Secretary of State for the Home Office ex p Shahina Begum* [1995] COD 176.

196 See, eg, *R v Crown Prosecution Service ex p Hogg* [1994] COD 237, QBD; *R v Cornwall CC ex p Huntingdon and another* [1992] 3 All ER 566, DC, at 576; *R v Secretary of State for the Home Department ex p Li Bin Shi* [1995] COD 135.

197 CPR rr54.7 and 54.8, and see further at paras 18.108–18.112 below.

198 A failure to give full and frank disclosure can lead to permission being set aside: see *R (Webb) v Bristol CC* [2001] EWHC Admin 696.

199 See, eg, CPR Practice Direction 25A para 3.3 in relation to the duty to disclose all material facts on applications for interim injunctions, and see further paras 18.103–18.106 below. As to the procedure for making urgent applications, see paras 18.82–18.86 above.

200 *R v Crown Prosecution Service ex p Hogg* [1994] COD 237, QBD; *R v Secretary of State for the Home Department ex p Li Bin Shi* [1995] COD 135.

remedy granted, such as the existence of ouster clauses,[201] alternative remedies,[202] and delay. In *R v Bromley LBC ex p Barker*,[203] the judge set aside permission on the basis that the claimant's application notice had not dealt adequately with the question of delay, and had failed to request an extension of time or give reasons why such an extension should be granted. It has also been held that the duty extends to disclosure of any defence the claimant has reason to anticipate may be advanced.[204] In practice, this last aspect of the duty is likely to be satisfied by explaining the defendant's position as it has been explained to the claimant.

18.104   This is one aspect of the duty laid on the claimant to make full and frank disclosure to the court on the application for permission. In *R v Jockey Club Licensing Committee ex p Wright (Barrie John)*,[205] Potts J considered the full extent of that duty on a paper application. He held that the applicant must show utmost good faith and make full and frank disclosure of the material facts; the material facts are those it is material for the judge to know, and materiality is to be decided by the court and not by the applicant's advisers. The applicant must make proper enquiries before applying for leave, and the duty of disclosure includes a duty to disclose such facts as would have been known to the applicant had he or she made such enquiries. The extent of the enquiries which would constitute 'proper' enquiries would depend on all the circumstances of the case, including the nature of the case and the relief sought, the degree of urgency and the amount of time available for such enquiries to be made.

18.105   Where it transpires that there has been a material non-disclosure, the court should be astute to ensure that the applicant is deprived of any advantage derived by obtaining permission, in breach of the duty of disclosure. Whether or not the fact which had not been disclosed warranted immediate and automatic discharge of the leave, without consideration of the merits, may depend on the importance of the fact to the issues involved in the application. The court has discretion in the matter and will not automatically discharge the leave for every

---

201   *R v Cornwall CC ex p Huntington* [1992] 3 All ER 566, DC.
202   For example, *R v Horsham DC ex p Wenman* [1995] 1 WLR 680.
203   [2001] Env LR 1, QBD.
204   *Lloyds Bowmaker Ltd v Britannia Arrow Holdings* [1988] 1 WLR 1337.
205   [1991] COD 306, QBD, and see *Brink's-MAT Ltd v Elcombe* [1988] 1 WLR 1350, CA.

omission.[206] Nevertheless, it has recently been held that if a person does not comply with the obligation to make full and frank disclosure, he or she will be deprived of the fruits of his or her order whether or not had the disclosure been made he or she would still have obtained the order and whether or not the omission was deliberate or innocent, some limited latitude being allowed for a slip, though even then only where the party concerned had corrected it quickly.[207]

18.106   The duty to keep the court informed does not cease once the application has been filed or even when permission has been granted. It continues for so long as the proceedings continue without notice to the other side.[208] In this respect, the new rules on notification of the defendant and other interested parties[209] will render it unlikely that many claims will reach the permission stage on a 'without notice' basis.

Service on the defendant and interested parties

18.107   This series of new provisions, concerning service of the claim form and acknowledgement of service by the defendant comprises one of the more important procedural changes effected by CPR Part 54. By CPR r54.7, the claim form must be served on the defendant and, unless the court directs otherwise, any person the claimant considers to be an interested party (ie, any person other than the claimant and the defendant who is directly affected by the claim)[210] within seven days after the date of issue. The court will not serve these documents.[211] Although the rule not does explicitly require service of the documents to be filed with the claim form (including any evidence in support), these documents should also be served, and failure to do so would be very likely to have costs consequences.

206   See *R v Secretary of State for the Home Department ex p Beecham (Grazyna)* [1996] Imm AR 87, QBD, and *R v Jockey Club Licensing Committee ex p Wright* [1991] COD 306, QBD.

207   *R (Tshikangu) v Newham LBC* [2001] EWHC Admin 118; [2001] NPC 33. In this case, permission was set aside on the basis that, among other things, the claimant's solicitors had failed to inform the court that judicial review was no longer required by the claimant, and had not sent a letter before action to the defendant. See also, eg, *Fitzgerald v Williams* [1996] QB 657, CA; *Network Telecom (Europe) Ltd v Telephone Systems International Inc* [2003] EWHC 2890 (QB).

208   *Tshikangu* [2001] EWHC Admin 118.

209   See paras 18.107–18.112 below.

210   CPR r54.1(2)(f).

211   See Practice Direction 54 para 6.1.

Acknowledgement of service

18.108 A person who has been served with the claim form and who wishes to take part in the judicial review proceedings must file and serve an acknowledgement of service.[212] Practice form N462 should be used for this purpose.[213] The acknowledgement must be filed not more than 21 days after the service of the claim form[214] and served on the claimant and, unless the court directs otherwise, any other person named in the claim form not later than seven days after it is filed.[215] These time limits may not be extended by agreement between the parties[216] but, presumably, may be extended by the court pursuant to its general powers.[217]

18.109 The acknowledgement must state whether the person filing it contests the claim[218] and, if this is the case, must contain a summary of the grounds for doing so.[219] It must also state whether the person filing it (who may be an interested party wishing to support the claim) seeks a different remedy from that set out in the claim form and, if so, what remedy is sought.[220]

18.110 In all cases, the filing party's name should be set out in full. Where that party has been set out incorrectly in the claim form, it should be correctly set out in the acknowledgement, followed by the words 'described as' and the incorrect name.[221] It must be signed by the party or its legal representative and include an address for service.[222] The acknowledgement must also state the name and address of any person

---

212 CPR r54.8(1).
213 It appears that acknowledgement can be given by an informal document such as a letter, provided it contains all the requisite information: see CPR Practice Direction 8 para 3.2. See also appendix A, p478.
214 CPR r54.8(2)(a).
215 CPR r54.8(2)(b) and see CPR r54.7(b).
216 CPR r54.8(3).
217 See, eg, CPR r3.1(2)(a). See also CPR rr3.8–3.10 for the general power to relieve a party in default from the sanctions for failure to comply with the rules, and to rectify errors of procedure. See also CPR r6.9 for the power to dispense with service of a document.
218 CPR r8.3(2)(a).
219 CPR r54.8(4)(a)(i).
220 CPR r8.3(2)(b).
221 CPR Practice Direction 10 paras 5.1–5.2.
222 CPR r10.5.

the party filing it considers to be an interested party,[223] and may include or be accompanied by an application for directions.[224]

18.111   Other general provisions concerning acknowledgements of service are as follows:

- If two or more parties acknowledge service through the same legal representative at the same time, only one acknowledgement of service is necessary.[225]
- An acknowledgement may be withdrawn or amended only with the permission of the court: an application for this purpose must be made in accordance with the CPR Part 23 procedure and supported by evidence.[226]

18.112 Although the wording of CPR r54.8(1) would suggest that failure to file and serve an acknowledgement of service within the specified time limits precludes a person from taking any part in the judicial review claim, this is not the effect of the sanction provisions of CPR r54.9, which are far less draconian. A failure to file and serve an acknowledgement of service in time will, however, preclude a person served with the claim form from taking part in a permission hearing, unless the court allows him or her to do so.[227] Such a person will be able to take part at the substantive hearing, so long as he or she complies with the rules,[228] or any direction of the court, for filing and serving detailed grounds for resisting (or supporting) the claim and written evidence.[229] The failure to acknowledge service of the claim form may, however, be taken into account by the court in relation to costs.[230] The general rule, contained in CPR r8.4, concerning failure to file and serve an acknowledgement in time is disapplied.[231]

---

223 CPR r54.8(4)(a)(ii), and see CPR r54.1(2)(f) for the definition of 'interested party'.
224 CPR r54.8(4)(b). CPR r54.8(5) disapplies r10.3(2), which subjects the general provisions of the CPR r10.3(1) concerning the time for filing acknowledgement of service to two other rules: CPR r6.22 (period for acknowledgement where claim form served out of the jurisdiction) and CPR r6.16(4) (period for responding to claim for served on agent of overseas principal).
225 CPR Practice Direction 10 para 5.3.
226 CPR Practice Direction paras 5.4–5.5.
227 CPR r54.9(1)(a).
228 CPR r54.14.
229 CPR r54.9(1)(b).
230 CPR r54.9(2).
231 CPR r54.9(3).

Evidence in reply

18.113 There is nothing in the rules preventing the defendant from filing evidence in reply at the permission stage. Indeed, there is something to be said for doing so where it would assist the court to make a decision on permission and perhaps prevent the pointless incurring of additional costs. Such evidence should be submitted sufficiently long before the permission decision for the claimant to be able to file further evidence, should this be necessary. The court is unlikely to be sympathetic to defendants bombarding it with material prior to the permission decision, or to the late filing of evidence causing delay in the making of the decision or necessitating a hearing which would otherwise have been unnecessary.

The test for permission

18.114 At the permission stage, the court must, in principle, be satisfied that there is an arguable case for review, and that the claimant has sufficient interest in the subject matter of the claim, or standing. The court may also consider questions of delay.[232] A favourable finding on matters of standing is no guarantee that the court at the full hearing will not take a different view of those matters. The court should generally not reconsider the issue of delay if it has been resolved in the claimant's favour at the permission stage.[233]

18.115   Consideration of the application for permission should be relatively brief, as its stated purpose is only to sift out the hopeless or frivolous cases. The Notes for Guidance[234] state that permission hearings are listed on the assumption that they will last no more than 20 minutes. If counsel considers that more time will be required, then a time estimate must be provided so that a special fixture can be arranged. In practice, even where a special fixture is requested, applications will often be listed in the general permission list. Administrative Court judges frequently call all the cases in the list into court at the start of the morning's business and decide the running order by reference to the probable length of time each case is likely to take to be heard.

---

232   See paras 18.17–18.57 above.
233   See paras 18.32–18.36 above.
234   N461A, para 9(ii). Previously, this was contained in the *Practice Direction* reported at [1987] 1 All ER 1184.

18.116   In practice, it not unusual for the court to go into the matter in some depth at the permission stage. Hearings can last considerably longer than the allotted time, particularly where the defendant attends. On occasion, oral applications for permission can last several hours, especially where (for instance, in deportation cases when a time for removal has been set) the issues involved are extremely important, and the permission hearing will effectively dispose of the matter.

The permission decision

18.117   The court will consider the permission application on the papers.[235] Where permission is granted, the court may also give directions, including ordering a stay of the proceedings to which the claim relates (ie, the decision-making process challenged, not the judicial review proceedings themselves).[236] The orders which may be made on the grant of permission are discussed elsewhere.[237]

18.118   On granting or refusing permission, whether on the papers alone or following an oral hearing, the court will serve its order to that effect, including any directions given, on the claimant, the defendant and any other person who filed an acknowledgement of service.[238] Where the court decides on the papers to refuse permission, or to grant it subject to conditions or on certain grounds only, it will also serve its reasons for that decision at the same time as serving the order.[239]

Adjourning into open court

18.119   If the court is not sure whether permission should be granted on the papers, it has power to adjourn the permission application into open court for a hearing at which the defendant and other interested parties may – or must – attend.[240] This power is most likely to be used where the defendant is in possession of important information which will

---

235   CPR Practice Direction 54, para 8.4.
236   CPR r54.10(1)–(2).
237   Above at paras 5.42–5.51 and below at paras 18.136–18.139.
238   CPR r54.11.
239   CPR r54.12(1)–(2).
240   There is nothing in CPR Part 54 requiring the court to consider the application on the papers. This is referred to in the Practice Direction (paras 8.4–8.6) as a general rule but it is no more than that.

have a material influence on whether permission should or should not be granted, where the judge requires clarification of the defendant's position, or where issues of delay arise for consideration.[241]

18.120   An application for interim relief may, additionally, render an oral hearing appropriate, though this will no longer inevitably be the case, given the defendant's opportunity to state its case in the acknowledgement of service. Under the old rules, the court indicated that where a claimant sought interim relief, it should be the practice to seek an oral hearing to which the defendant should be invited to make representations.[242]

Sensitive applications concerning children

18.121   In *R (X and Y) v Gloucestershire CC*,[243] the following guidance was suggested for dealing with cases (which were much to be deprecated) where judicial review claims were brought seeking to restrain the institution of care or other proceedings for the protection of a child, or otherwise to raise matters that were properly raised in such proceedings as were already on foot. To avoid delay, in such a situation, which could be extremely damaging to a child who may be urgently in need of the court's protection:

- the Administrative Court Office should upon receipt of the papers immediately issue the proceedings and then immediately place the file before an Administrative Court judge who is also a judge of the Family Division. If no such judge is immediately available, the file should be put before the President of the Family Division;
- the judge before whom the file is placed should give immediate directions, with a view, where appropriate, to the case being 'fast-tracked' and disposed of as quickly as possible. It may be appropriate to dispense both with the acknowledgement of service and with any preliminary decision by the judge on the papers, and to proceed immediately to an oral hearing before a judge (who should always be an Administrative Court and Family Division judge).

---

241   See paras 18.27–18.30 above.
242   *R v Kensington and Chelsea RLBC ex p Hammell* [1989] QB 518 per Parker LJ at 539.
243   [2003] EWHC 850 (Admin), per Munby J at [42].

Renewal of applications

18.122 There is no right of appeal against a paper refusal or conditional grant of permission, or a grant on restricted grounds only, but the claimant may request that it be reconsidered at an oral hearing. Such a request must be filed within seven days of the service of the reasons.[244] No indication is given in the Civil Procedure Rules, the Part 54 Practice Direction or the Notes for Guidance as to how the request is made. A Practice Statement[245] has been issued, however, which requires claimants, when completing the form used for renewing permission applications, to set out the grounds for renewal in the light of the reasons given by the single judge when refusing permission on the papers. The Practice Statement makes reference to the existence of a revised form for this purpose.[246]

18.123 In practice, the Administrative Court Office will serve, with the order and reasons for refusal/conditional/limited permission, a form to be completed and filed requesting an oral hearing.

18.124 At least two days' notice of the hearing date will be given to the claimant, defendant and any other person who filed an acknowledgement of service.[247] This provision formalises what was generally the position under the old rules, namely that oral permission hearings (particularly those following the refusal of permission on the papers) will be on notice to the defendant and all interested parties. The Practice Direction makes clear, however, that notification of a hearing does not oblige the defendant or other interested party to attend, unless the court directs otherwise, and that attendance will not generally lead to a costs order being made against the claimant.[248]

18.125 The oral hearing is treated as a new application. There is no additional burden on the claimant to demonstrate that the judge refusing, or granting conditional permission was wrong to have done so. The test is the same as that applied on the paper application: whether the claimant can demonstrate an arguable case. Where an application is renewed, however, it is usually sensible to prepare a skeleton argument for the hearing, although this is not required by the rules or

---

244 CPR r54.12(3)–(4). Under the old rules, the claimant had ten days to renew the application: RSC Ord 53 r3(5).

245 *Practice Statement*, Scott Baker J, 1 February 2002, [2002] 1 All ER 633 at 636.

246 [2002] 1 All ER 633 at 636d. This states that the revised form is annexed to the *Practice Statement* at Annex C, but this is not the case.

247 CPR r54.12(5).

248 CPR Practice Direction 54 paras 8.5–8.6.

practice directions. The advantage of so doing is to deal with the reasons given for the first decision and to put before the second judge points and arguments which have not already been rejected by the judge who considered the matter on the papers. It also offers the chance to set out the claimant's contentions more clearly or more persuasively.

18.126   In addition, where permission has been refused on a specific factual basis, such as that of undue delay, it will generally be necessary for further evidence to be submitted, in addition to any skeleton argument, dealing with the points of fact arising, eg, explaining the reasons for the delay.

Appeals against the refusal of permission

Non-criminal applications

18.127 Where permission is refused following an oral hearing, in a non-criminal judicial review application, the claimant may apply to the Court of Appeal for permission to appeal against the refusal.[249] This is a change from the procedure under the old rules, where the claimant did not appeal the refusal of permission but renewed the permission application to the Court of Appeal.[250] Perhaps more importantly, it is to be noted that the right of appeal to the Court of Appeal may be narrower than the right to request an oral hearing in the Administrative Court,[251] in that it appears to apply only to a refusal of permission, and not to a conditional grant.

18.128   The application for permission to appeal must be made within seven – not the usual 14 – days of the judge's refusal of permission to apply for judicial review.[252] Permission to appeal is sought by completing an appellant's notice[253] in the usual way, but different

249 CPR r52.15(1).
250 RSC Ord 59 r14.
251 See paras 18.122–18.125 above, and CPR r54.12(3). CPR r52.15 states that it applies where permission has been refused at an oral hearing in the High Court. See further paras 19.33–19.35.
252 CPR r52.15(2). The general power to extend time applies to appeals, and an application to extend time should be made in the usual way.
253 Form N161 – see generally CPR Part 52.

provisions are made regarding the documents which must be filed with the appellant's notice.[254] The documents to be filed are:

- one additional copy of the appellant's notice for the Court of Appeal;[255]
- one copy of the appellant's notice for each respondent, to be sealed and returned;[256]
- the order refusing permission to apply for judicial review;[257]
- the Form N461 and statement of facts;[258]
- a copy of the original decision which is the subject of the judicial review application;[259]
- any witness statements or affidavits in support of any application included in the appellant's notice;[260]
- a copy of the bundle of documents used in the High Court;[261]
- the skeleton argument relied on in the High Court;[262]
- a transcript of the judgment.[263]

18.129 Where it is not possible to file all the above documents, the appellant must indicate which documents have not yet been filed and the reasons why they are not currently available.[264]

18.130 Unless the Court of Appeal orders otherwise, a sealed copy of the appellant's notice, including any skeleton argument, must be served on all respondents to the application for permission to appeal as soon as practicable and, in any event, not later than seven days after it is filed.[265] Where it is impracticable for the appellant's skeleton argument to accompany the appellant's notice, it must be lodged and served on all respondents within 14 days of filing the notice.[266] An unrepresented

---

254 CPR Practice Direction 52 para 15.4.
255 CPR Practice Direction 52 para 15.4(1).
256 CPR Practice Direction 52 para 15.4(2).
257 CPR Practice Direction 52 para 15.4(3).
258 CPR Practice Direction 52 para 15.4(4). This paragraph actually requires the filing of Form 86A, the claim form under the old rules, but this requirement must now be read as referring to the current claim form.
259 CPR Practice Direction 52 para 15.4(5).
260 CPR Practice Direction 52 para 15.4(6).
261 CPR Practice Direction 52 para 15.4(7).
262 CPR Practice Direction 52 para 15.4(8).
263 CPR Practice Direction 52 para 15.4(9).
264 CPR Practice Direction 52 para 15.6. The general provisions for documents which must be filed, and those for service of the appellant's notice, contained respectively in paras 5.6 and 5.19 of the Practice Direction, are disapplied.
265 CPR r52.4(3) and Practice Direction 52 paras 15.5 and 5.21.
266 CPR Practice Direction 52 paras 15.5, 5.21 and 5.9(2).

appellant is not obliged to lodge a skeleton argument, but is encouraged to do so to assist the court.[267]

18.131 On an application for permission to appeal against the refusal of permission, the Court of Appeal may, instead of giving permission to appeal, grant permission to apply for judicial review. Where it does so, the case will proceed in the High Court unless the Court of Appeal orders otherwise.[268] The Practice Direction indicates that, where permission to apply for judicial review is granted by the Court of Appeal, it will be rare for the Court of Appeal to hear the substantive application. This may be appropriate, however, where,eg, the Administrative Court would be bound by authority or an appeal to the Court of Appeal would be inevitable for some other reason.[269]

18.132 The power to grant permission to apply for judicial review rather than permission to appeal against the refusal of permission is akin to the procedure under the old rules. It will generally be more appropriate for the Court of Appeal to adopt this course than to grant permission to appeal which would then require a further full appeal hearing on the issue of whether permission to apply for judicial review ought to have been refused. Such a course would incur additional costs and may be thought inappropriate bearing in mind that if the test for permission to appeal is satisfied – that the judge below was arguably wrong to refuse permission to apply – it is likely to follow that the judicial review claim was itself arguable and that no purpose would be served by a full appeal on this issue.[270] This may not be the course adopted however; in *Burkett* the Court of Appeal granted permission to appeal but dismissed the full appeal on the issue of delay.

Criminal applications

18.133 In criminal applications, there is no right to appeal to the Court of Appeal against the refusal of permission.[271]

---

267 CPR Practice Direction 52 paras 15.5, 5.21 and 5.9(3).

268 CPR r52.15(3)–(4).

269 CPR Practice Direction 52 para 15.3.

270 See the notes to the *White Book* (Autumn 2003, Sweet & Maxwell) Vol 1 p1281, para 52.15.3.

271 Supreme Court Act 1981 s18(1)(a) and see *R v Tottenham Justices ex p Ewing* (1986) 30 July (unreported).

Further appeal

18.134   It used to be thought that there was no right of appeal to the House of Lords against a refusal of permission to appeal or to apply for judicial review. In *R (Burkett) v Hammersmith and Fulham LBC,*[272] however, the House of Lords held that it did indeed have jurisdiction to entertain an appeal from the Court of Appeal, where the Court of Appeal had granted permission to appeal against the refusal of permission to apply for judicial review, but had then dismissed the appeal on the merits after a full hearing.

18.135   In other cases, it appears that the formerly understood position still holds good: there is no right of appeal to the House of Lords,[273] nor any right to appeal against the refusal of permission to apply for judicial review itself on a renewed application to the Court of Appeal.[274] The rationale for this is that the only application before the Court of Appeal is for permission to appeal, which cannot be the subject of further appeal; nor can the House of Lords entertain an appeal from a renewed application for permission to apply for judicial review which had been rejected by the Court of Appeal.[275]

Directions and orders on the grant of leave

18.136   The court hearing the permission application has power to allow the applicant to amend his or her claim form.[276] Where permission is granted, the court has power to give directions, including imposing a stay on the decision-making process which is the subject matter of the application.[277] The position under the old rules, under which interim relief could only be granted where such relief would have been available in an action commenced by writ,[278] is not continued by CPR Part 54.

---

272   [2002] UKHL 23; [2002] 1 WLR 1593.
273   See *R v Secretary of State for Trade and Industry ex p Eastaway* [2000] 1 WLR 2222, HL.
274   *Re Poh* [1983] 1 WLR 2, HL. Though this decision was doubted in *Kemper Reinsurance Co v Minister of Finance* [2000] 1 AC 1, PC, it was confirmed in *Eastaway* [2000] 1 WLR 2222.
275   See *R v Secretary of State for Trade and Industry ex p Eastaway* [2000] 1 WLR 2222, HL.
276   CPR r17.1(2).
277   CPR r54.10(1)–(2).
278   RSC Ord 53 r3(6).

18.137   The court may order that the hearing of the substantive application be expedited and abridge the defendant's time for filing evidence in reply.[279] These powers may be of particular importance, for example, in homelessness cases if an injunction is refused.[280] In deciding whether to seek expedition, it should be remembered that in 2001, the average waiting time for non-expedited cases, from lodging to final decision, was 20 weeks. Expedited cases were listed in a matter of weeks. In 2002/03, the average waiting time was 28 weeks.[281]

18.138   The court may otherwise grant permission on terms.[282] In *R v Westminster CC ex p Residents' Association of Mayfair*,[283] an order for security for costs was made. The court also has inherent jurisdiction to grant bail where permission is granted (or even pending the permission application), but not if permission is refused.[284]

18.139   More detailed consideration of the powers of the court to grant interim relief may be found in chapter 5.[285]

Costs

18.140   Civil Procedure Rules Part 54 makes no specific provision regarding costs. Ordinarily, if permission is granted, costs will be reserved to the full application, or will be ordered to be in the cause. The court may well consider the issue of costs, even on granting permission, if it is considered that the matter is likely to be resolved without the need for a full hearing. In particular, in these circumstances, it is likely to be worthwhile obtaining an order for a detailed assessment of a claimant's publicly funded costs.

---

279 CPR r3.1(2)(a) and (b).

280 Although see *R v Cardiff CC ex p Barry* (1990) 22 HLR 261, where it was held that, where necessary, an injunction ought ordinarily to follow from the grant of leave in homelessness cases.

281 *Practice Statement* [2002] 1 All ER 633 at 634F. According to the Administrative Court Annual Statement 2002–2003, p3, average waiting times for permission decisions is now eight weeks; for a substantive determination 28 weeks (including the eight weeks referred to above). See www.courtservice.gov.uk/cms/media/admin-crt-stmnt-2003.pdf.

282 CPR r54.12(b)(i).

283 [1991] COD 182, QBD.

284 See *R v Secretary of State for the Home Department ex p Turkoglu* [1988] QB 398.

285 See paras 5.42–5.74 above.

18.141   If the defendant concedes, or the application is not pursued for other reasons, before the permission hearing, it is still unusual for the claimant to be awarded the costs even of issuing the application.[286] For a full discussion of the issue of costs, see chapter 20 below.[287]

18.142   Even if the defendant appears and permission is refused, the court will be unlikely to make a costs order against the claimant,[288] though the court will take account of the claimant's compliance or otherwise with the pre-action protocol, and the conduct of the parties generally.[289]

Pre-emptive costs orders

18.143   The principle of the pre-emptive costs order[290] was established under the old Rules of the Supreme Court in *R v Lord Chancellor ex p Child Poverty Action Group*[291] and has been affirmed under the CPR by *R v Hammersmith and Fulham LBC ex p CPRE London Branch*[292] and, most recently by a two-judge Administrative Court in *R (Campaign for Nuclear Disarmament) v The Prime Minister and others (Costs)*.[293] This enables a claimant to obtain a protective order, in advance of the determination of the substantive issues in the case and so in advance of any costs order being made against him, limiting the amount of costs he or she would be obliged to pay should the claim fail and a costs order be made against him or her.

---

286   See *R (Boxall) v Waltham Forest LBC* [2000] All ER (D) 2445 and see *R v Kensington and Chelsea RLBC ex p Ghebregiogis* (1994) 27 HLR 602; [1994] COD 502, QBD for an exception; costs were awarded against a respondent who conceded before the leave hearing.

287   See paras 20.34–20.57.

288   CPR Practice Direction 54 para 8.6. Under the old rules, costs were frequently awarded on the usual inter partes principles, especially where the defendant had been required by the court to attend: see, eg, *R v Committee of Advertising Practice ex p Bradford Exchange Ltd* [1991] COD 43, QBD, (although the applicant made no submissions to the contrary and had sought interim relief). See also *R v Commissioners of Inland Revenue ex p Mead and Cook* [1993] COD 324 (where costs were not awarded).

289   See paras 17.32–17.46 above at chapter 17, and see also CPR r44.3(4)(a).

290   The jurisdiction for which appears to arise from the general provisions of CPR r44.3.

291   [1999] 1 WLR 347, QBD. See also *Hodgson v Imperial Tobacco* [1998] 1 WLR 1056 at 1068A,

292   (1999) 26 October (unreported).

293   [2002] EWHC 2712 (Admin); (2002) *Times* 27 December.

18.144   Generally, such an order will only be made in exceptional circumstances.[294] The following criteria must also be made out. First, the court must be satisfied that the application raises issues of general importance, and that it has a sufficient appreciation of the merits to decide whether it is in the public interest to make such an order. Second, the court will have regard to the financial resources of each party and the amount of the costs likely to be in issue. It will be more likely to make an order if the defendant 'has a superior capacity to bear the costs of proceedings than the applicant, and where it is satisfied that unless the order is made the applicant would probably discontinue the proceedings and will be acting reasonably in so doing.'[295]

18.145   In the *Campaign for Nuclear Disarmament* case,[296] apparently the first case in which the court's jurisdiction has ever been exercised, the claimant applied for a pre-emptive costs order limiting the costs it would be obliged to pay if unsuccessful in its judicial review proceedings to £25,000. The application was made prior to consideration of the permission application in a claim for an advisory declaration that UN Resolution 1441 did not authorise the use of military force against the regime of Saddam Hussein in Iraq.

18.146   The claimant contended that the circumstances were exceptional: it was a private company limited by guarantee, it had only modest resources and had not been able to raise money to finance the claim, given the short timescale within which the application had to be made. In the event of a large, adverse costs order, it would run the risk of either being forced into liquidation or at least severely having to curtail its activities. The issues were of undoubted public importance but it would be unable to proceed with the application in the absence of a limitation on its prospective costs liability. £25,000 was an appropriate limit, as that sum would be sufficient to cover its own costs and, if – as the defendant asserted – the claim was found to be without merit and so permission were refused, that sum would surely meet the defendant's entitlement in costs. In any event, if no order was made and the challenge foundered, an alternative claimant would be available, possibly with public funding, in which case the defendant could not hope even to recover £25,000 in costs.

294   See *Campaign for Nuclear Disarmament* [2002] EWHC 2712 (Admin), per Simon Brown LJ at [3].
295   See *ex p CPRE* (1999) 26 October (unreported), per Richards J.
296   [2002] EWHC (Admin); (2002) *Times* 27 December.

18.147   The court made the order sought, remarking that these arguments were compelling, particularly given that most claimants could usually hope to obtain the court's decision on permission without any adverse costs order at all, and that if permission were refused, the defendant would be unlikely to have incurred more by way of costs than the £25,000 suggested. It was undoubtedly appropriate to make the order sought, which kind of order would be particularly appropriate where such a course would ensure a quick ruling against the claimants if the case were unfounded.[297] Notice of this type of application should be given by the claimant at an early stage, preferably by including it in the claim form.[298]

Statutory review of Immigration Appeal Tribunal decisions

18.148   Nationality, Immigration and Asylum Act 2002 s101(2) provides a new means of challenging a decision of the Immigration Appeal Tribunal to grant or refuse permission to appeal against a decision of an adjudicator. This remedy is intended to replace the previous remedy of seeking judicial review of such decisions.[299]

18.149   Civil Procedure Rules Part 54 section II, in force from 1 April 2003, governs applications for statutory review. Applications are made by filing an application notice accompanied by submissions setting out the grounds on which it is contended that the tribunal made an error of law and reasons in support of those grounds,[300] together with the following documents:

- the decision to which the application relates (ie, the Home Office decision)[301] and any document giving reasons for the decision;
- the grounds of appeal to the adjudicator;
- the adjudicator's determination;
- the grounds of appeal to the Immigration Appeal Tribunal together with any documents sent with them to the tribunal;

297   [2002] EWHC (Admin) per Simon Brown LJ at [4]–[6].
298   [2002] EWHC (Admin) per Maurice Kay J at [7].
299   The availability of judicial review, exceptionally, to challenge refusals of permission to appeal was said to turn on matters 'peculiar' to immigration appeals in *R v (Sivasubramaniam) v Wandsworth County Court* [2002] EWCA Civ 1738; [2003] 1 WLR 475.
300   CPR r54.22(4).
301   See the definition of 'decision' at CPR r54.22(5).

- the tribunal's determination on the application for permission to appeal;
- any other documents material to the application which were before the adjudicator.[302]

18.150 The time limit for the application is 14 days from the date on which the applicant is deemed to have received notice of the tribunal's decision.[303] The court may only extend this time limit in 'exceptional circumstances', and any application to extend time must be made in the application notice and supported by written evidence verified by a statement of truth.[304]

18.151 As soon as practicable after filing the application notice and written submissions, they must be served on the tribunal. In addition, if the application is for review of a decision to grant permission to appeal (ie, a challenge brought by the government), the other party to the appeal to the tribunal must be served with the application notice, written submissions and all the accompanying documents, save where those documents have already been served on or have come from that party.[305]

18.152 The application itself is determined by a single judge on the papers – there is no right to renew the application at an oral hearing nor any right of appeal[306] – and by reference only to the written submissions and the documents filed with them. Any evidence sought to be relied on by the applicant which was not before the adjudicator or tribunal may not be taken into account by the judge unless he or she is satisfied that there were good reasons why it was not before them.[307]

18.153 If the tribunal refused permission to appeal, the court may only reverse that decision if satisfied that the tribunal may have made an error of law and either the appeal would have a real prospect of success ore there is some other compelling reason why the appeal should be heard. Where the tribunal granted permission to appeal, the court may only intervene if satisfied that the appeal would have no real prospect of success *and* there is no other compelling reason why it should be heard. If the court reverses a refusal of permission by the tribunal, the court's order itself amounts to a grant of permission to

---

302 CPR r54.22(3).
303 CPR r54.23(1) and see Nationality, Immigration and Asylum Act 2002 s106.
304 CPR r54.23(2) and (3).
305 CPR r54.24.
306 CPR r54.25(7).
307 CPR r54.25(1) and (2).

the tribunal and the court may limit the grant of permission to specific grounds.[308]

18.154   The court will serve a copy of its decision on the applicant,[309] the secretary of state and the tribunal.[310] If the court decides to issue a certificate, under Nationality, Immigration and Asylum Act 2002 s101(3)(d), certifying that the application had no merit, it will send a copy of the certificate together with the order to the parties on whom it serves the order, with the addition of the Legal Services Commission if the applicant is in receipt of public funding.[311] The court may reserve the costs of an application to be dealt with by the tribunal.[312]

308   CPR r54.25(4)–(6).
309   Except where the application relates to an asylum claim, the tribunal has refused permission to appeal and the court upholds that refusal, in which case, the court serves the secretary of state and the secretary of state must serve the applicant, and notify the court that he or she has done so and the method and date of such service: CPR r54.26(2) and (3).
310   CPR r54.26(1).
311   CPR r54.26(4).
312   CPR r54.27.

The post-permission procedure

No further requirement of service

19.1   There is no longer any requirement on claimants who have been granted permission to serve a notice of motion on the defendant and interested parties. Service now takes place prior to the application for permission.[1] Even where the urgency procedure for seeking permission is invoked, it is still necessary to send the claim form by e-mail or fax to the defendant and interested parties prior to issuing the proceedings, and the urgency form (N463) requires the claimant's advocate personally to confirm the date and time that this was done (see appendix A p474).[2]

19.2   Accordingly, the time for the respondent's response, following the grant of permission, no longer starts to run from the date of service of a notice of motion by the claimant (as it used to under the old rules),[3] but instead from the date of service by the court of the order granting permission.[4]

Fees

19.3   On the grant of permission, an additional fee of £120 becomes payable. The fee must be paid within seven days of service on the claimant of the order granting permission.[5] If the proceedings were commenced otherwise than by the judicial review procedure, the additional fee on the grant of permission is only £30.[6] This would presumably apply where an ordinary claim had been brought (and the £120 issue fee paid) but was then transferred into the Administrative Court under Civil Procedure Rules (CPR) r54.20,[7] so that the claimant would not be obliged to pay double fees.

19.4   A failure to pay the fees referred to above gives rise to the sanctions provided by CPR r3.7.[8] If the fee has not been paid within the seven-day period referred to above, and no application for exemption or remission has been made, the court will initially serve a notice on the claimant requiring payment of the fee by a date specified in the notice.[9]

1   CPR r54.7.
2   See paras 18.82–18.86 above.
3   RSC Ord 53 r14(1).
4   CPR r54.14.
5   Supreme Court Fees Order 1999 SI No 687 as amended, Sch 1, para 1.6(b).
6   Supreme Court Fees Order 1999 Sch 1, para 1.6(c).
7   See chapter 18 above at paras 18.62 (and note 95).
8   See CPR r3.7(1)(d).
9   CPR r3.7(2) and (3). The notice is in form N173.

If the fee is not paid by that date (and no application for exemption from or remission of the fee has been made) the claim will be struck out and the claimant will become liable for any costs incurred by the defendant, unless the court orders otherwise.[10]

19.5   If the claimant applies to be relieved from this sanction,[11] and to have the claim reinstated, any such reinstatement will be conditional on the claimant either paying the fee or filing evidence of exemption from or remission of the fee within two days of the date of the order reinstating the claim.[12]

Setting aside permission

Civil Procedure Rules rule 54.13

19.6   Civil Procedure Rules r54.13 provides that 'neither the defendant nor any other person served with the claim form may apply to set aside an order giving permission to proceed'. This is the logical consequence of service of the proceedings on the defendant and all interested parties taking place prior to the permission application being dealt with, enabling those parties to put their arguments before the judge considering the permission application by means of the acknowledgement of service and, if there is an oral hearing, by attending that hearing. This procedure is designed to ensure that all relevant information from all parties is before the judge when the permission decision is made, rendering it unnecessary – and indeed undesirable – for defendants to have a second chance to prevent the application proceeding to a full hearing under the guise of a set-aside application.

Inherent jurisdiction

19.7   In *R (Webb) v Bristol CC*,[13] however, the Administrative Court held that, notwithstanding CPR r54.13, it retains an inherent jurisdiction to set aside an order granting permission. In *Webb*, permission had been

---

10 CPR r3.7(4). CPR r3.7(5) and (6) deal with the effect of an application for an exemption from or remission of the fee. If the application is refused, the court will serve a notice requiring payment by a specified date. If payment is not made by that date, the claim will be struck out and the claimant become liable for the defendant's costs unless the court orders otherwise.

11 Under CPR r3.9.

12 CPR r3.7(7).

13 [2001] EWHC Admin 696.

granted on a paper application prior to the expiry of the time for filing the defendants' acknowledgement of service. Accordingly, the defendants had not had an opportunity to put their case to the judge granting permission. There was no suggestion of bad faith on the part of the claimant's advisers, who had genuinely considered the case to be urgent.

19.8   Turner J held that the power to set aside an order made where one party had not had the opportunity to put its case why the order should not be made was part of the court's inherent jurisdiction which had been expressly preserved by Supreme Court Act 1981 s19(2). There was no satisfactory juridical basis for such a power, expressly preserved by statute, being removed by delegated legislation such as the CPR, notwithstanding the apparently express terms of CPR r54.13.

19.9   CPR Part 54 contemplated that the consideration of an application for permission would not take place prior to the filing of the defendant's acknowledgement of service, including its arguments why permission should not be granted, save in 'circumstances of high exception'.[14] Accordingly, CPR r54.13 had to be read down 'in the context of the pre-existing power of this court to exercise its inherent jurisdiction'[15] and *Webb* was one of the rare cases in which it was appropriate to exercise that power to set the grant of permission aside.

Principles applicable under the old rules

19.10   The power to set aside not having been abolished altogether by CPR Part 54, the case-law under the old rules may still be instructive on the making of such applications.

19.11   Rules of the Supreme Court (RSC) Ord 32 r6 was generally considered to be the basis for set-aside applications under the old rules (general power to set side orders made without notice). There was no power contained within RSC Ord 53 itself. The application to set aside had to be made promptly and, if possible, to the same judge who granted permission. Moreover, the court indicated on numerous occasions that set-aside applications should only be made in exceptional circumstances.

19.12   The court did not approve of applications to set aside based on objections that could more properly be dealt with at the substantive hearing. Those based, for instance, on contentions which were in reality no more than a substantive defence to the claimant's allegations would

14 [2001] EWHC Admin 696 at [13].
15 [2001] EWHC Admin 696 at [15].

be regarded by the court as an unacceptable attempt to 'jump the queue' of cases waiting to be heard. Accordingly, permission would be set aside only 'where the respondent can show that the substantive application will clearly fail.'[16]

19.13   Grounds upon which it had been held proper to apply to set aside included those where the application was fundamentally misconceived, where the applicant had failed to identify a proper point of law for review or where there had been fraud or material non-disclosure in obtaining permission.[17]

19.14   The grounds upon which it is sought to set aside permission must be specified with particularity.[18] Any prejudice which may be suffered by the defendant should the matter proceed to the full hearing should be set out in the application (although such an argument should generally be accompanied by an application, in the alternative, for expedition).

19.15   The test on an application to set aside is the same as that on an application for permission: does the applicant have an arguable case, or a case fit for further consideration?[19] The court should be wary of going too deeply into the substance of the matter, although in some cases it has been prepared to do so.[20]

Appeals from decision to set aside

19.16   If permission is set aside, there seems to be no reason why the claimant may not appeal, with permission,[21] or renew his or her application to the Court of Appeal (see above). In *R v Secretary of State for the Home Department ex p Rukshanda Begum*,[22] the Court of Appeal inclined to the

---

16   This statement was contained in *Supreme Court Practice* 1993 Vol 1 p841 53/1–14/1 para 3.

17   *R v Secretary of State for the Home Department ex p Chinoy* [1991] COD 381, QBD; *R v Secretary of State for the Home Department ex p Sholola* [1992] COD 226, QBD; *R v Bromsgrove DC ex p Kennedy* [1992] COD 129; *R v Social Security Commissioner ex p Pattni* [1993] Fam Law 213.

18   *R v Lloyd's of London ex p Briggs and others* [1992] COD 456, DC.

19   *R v Secretary of State for the Home Department ex p Rukshanda Begum* [1990] COD 109, CA.

20   See also *R v Darlington BC ex p Association of Darlington Taxi Owners* [1994] COD 424, QBD (see para 4.9 above): permission set aside because of lack of capacity.

21   CPR r52.3

22   [1990] COD 109, CA.

view that either course was appropriate, however this indication must now be viewed in the light of the provisions of CPR r52.15(1), under which the correct procedure for challenging a refusal of permission is to appeal – and no longer to renew the application – to the Court of Appeal. It would seem logical to assume that the same procedure (ie, appeal) is to be followed where the claimant wishes the Court of Appeal to consider whether permission ought to have been set aside.

19.17   Where the court refuses to set aside permission, the defendant may appeal, again with permission, to the Court of Appeal.[23] The court has indicated, however, that where a judge has been satisfied, after hearing argument from both parties, that there is a case meriting further consideration, only rarely would an appeal be likely to succeed, and it would be necessary to establish that the judge's decision had been plainly wrong.[24]

The defendant's response

19.18   The requirements imposed on a defendant, or interested party who wishes either to contest or support the claim, have been made more onerous by CPR Part 54 in two respects. First, while under the old rules, all that was required to be served was evidence, now detailed grounds for defending (or supporting) the claim must be filed and served, along with any written evidence. Second, the time limit for filing and serving these documents is 35 days from service of the order containing the grant of permission[25] (under the old rules it was 56 days, though under Part 54, the defendant will already have had 21 days prior to the permission decision in which to summarise the grounds of defence).[26]

19.19   The requirement for giving detailed grounds for contesting or supporting the claim is new. It is not entirely clear what it adds, given the requirement of skeleton arguments,[27] but would seem, consistent with the new approach to judicial review discernible from the provisions of CPR Part 54 as a whole, that the intention is to inform all parties, as

---

23 See para 19.41 below.
24 *R v Secretary of State for the Home Department ex p Rukshanda Begum* [1990] COD 109, CA.
25 CPR r54.14.
26 CPR r54.8(2)(a).
27 CPR Practice Direction 54 para 15.

early in the proceedings as possible, of the detail of each party's contentions, in order to facilitate the more efficient dealing with the proceedings.

19.20 This is not to say that the proliferation of documentation for the hearing is desirable for its own sake. If the defendant has filed a full statement of defence in the acknowledgement of service[28] and genuinely has nothing additional to say, it may be that there is nothing to be gained by filing and serving a repetitious document and that the preferable course would be simply to prepare a document making it clear that the summary grounds contained in the acknowledgement of service will be relied upon. Of course, defendants should be very careful to ensure, if adopting such an approach, that the contents of the summary grounds does in fact cover all the arguments to be raised at the hearing in sufficient detail to comply with the requirements of CPR r41.14(1)(a).

19.21 Written evidence may not be relied on unless it has been served in accordance with the provisions of CPR Part 54, or the court directs or permits otherwise.[29]

19.22 The contents of the defendant's detailed grounds and witness statements are as important as the grounds and evidence of the claimant, since this is the defendant's only opportunity to explain his or her decision, how and why it was reached and its legality and reasonableness. Much of the hearing may turn on the defendant's explanations as set out in these documents,[30] and so it is worthwhile to devote careful attention to their drafting.

19.23 The witness statement is also the appropriate means by which the defendant can take issue with the claimant's version of events. The witness statement, rather than the detailed grounds, is the more appropriate vehicle to raise such disputes. Issues such as delay and the failure to exhaust other remedies, together with the prejudice/hardship/detriment to good administration that such matters will cause should also be addressed in the documentation. Likewise, factual matters would generally be more suitable for inclusion in the witness statement and matters of law in the detailed grounds.

---

28 See paras 18.108–18.112 above.
29 CPR r54.16.
30 But see below regarding supplementing statutorily-required reasons, paras 19.25–19.27.

Supplementary reasons

19.24   In some cases, the defendant is entitled to amplify the reasons for his or her decision in the affidavit.[31] In *Re C and P*,[32] Simon Brown J set out the types of case in which this was possible. No evidence, even to supplement and explain the reasons, would be admitted in relation to arbitrators' awards and the decisions of statutory medical boards, decisions of certain tribunals, such as employment tribunals, or where the decision can be set aside for mere inadequacy of reasoning, such as planning cases and cases where the reasoning is made fundamental to the decision.

19.25   In *R v Westminster CC ex p Ermakov*,[33] the Court of Appeal stated that in the context of a statutory requirement for reasons to be given for decisions, deficiencies in the decision letter cannot be rectified by evidence to explain the 'real' basis for the decision given in the course of proceedings. The court would permit evidence to elucidate or, exceptionally, correct or add to the reasons already given, such as where a word was inadvertently omitted in the original decision, or there was a mistake in transcription, but would be very cautious about doing so and would not generally allow written evidence the purpose of which was to show that the reasons previously stated were not in fact the true basis of the decision, or to provide some 'ex post facto rationalisation'.[34]

19.26   In other cases, particularly where reasons were not given at the time, it has been held that it is the duty of the defendant to give sufficient explanation of the decision taken that the court can properly adjudicate on the claim. It was also held that in the absence of an explanation for a decision, the court may have to conclude that there was no good reason for having taken it.[35] These cases predated the coming into force of the Human Rights Act 1998, and the more general acceptance of the need to explain decisions. (Schedule 1 article 6 of that Act).

---

31 See chapter 6 above.

32 [1992] COD 29, QBD.

33 [1996] 2 All ER 302; (1996) 28 HLR 819. See also *R v Secretary of State for the Home Department ex p Lillycrop* (1996) *Times* 13 December; *R (on the application of McGowan) v Brent Justices* [2001] EWHC Admin 814; [2002] HLR 55.

34 *R v Westminster CC ev p Ermakov* [1996] 2 All ER 302, per Hutchison LJ at 315F–317C. See also the later cases discussed at paras 6.161–6.162.

35 See *R v Lancashire CC ex p Huddleston* [1986] 2 All ER 941, CA. See also *Padfield v Minister of Agriculture, Fisheries and Food* [1968] AC 997, HL.

19.27   While, therefore, the content of the defendant's evidence and detailed grounds is a matter to be decided in each individual case, and such evidence/grounds should plainly deal fully with all matters to be advanced at the hearing, and which may assist the court, *Ermakov* will serve to limit the propriety of extensive restatements of the decision and/or the reasons for it, whether in a witness statement or in the detailed grounds of defence, where reasons were given at the time.

Receipt of defendant's response

19.28   On receipt of the defendant's evidence and detailed grounds, the claimant's legal representatives are under a professional obligation to reconsider the merits of the application and to withdraw it if it appears that there are no longer reasonable prospects of success. This obligation arises in all cases, regardless of whether or not the applicant is publicly funded. It is separate from any duty to report to the Legal Services Commission, which, of course, only arises in funded applications.

19.29   If the court takes the view at the full hearing that the application should not have been continued, there may be costs consequences, whether for the applicant or even for the legal representative(s) concerned.[36]

Additional grounds or evidence

19.30   If either party wishes to rely on evidence which has not been served in accordance with the provisions of CPR Part 54, the permission of the court will be required.[37] Thus, a claimant may wish to reply to the evidence filed by the defendant, or simply to update the court as to his or her current circumstances, exhibit a new document or report, etc. Permission to rely on such evidence can be granted at any stage, either on an interim application or at the full hearing.

19.31   If it is intended to seek to rely on additional evidence, a copy of the evidence should be sent to the other parties with a request that they consent. If consent is not received, an application should be made to the court in the normal way. It will usually be sensible for such an

36 See Supreme Court Act 1981 s51(6), CPR Part 43, and *R v Horsham DC and another ex p Wenman* (1992) 24 HLR 669, and [1994] 4 All ER 681, QBD.

37 CPR r54.16(2)(b).

application to be made returnable at the substantive hearing, unless the party wishing to rely on the evidence will wish to take some other action if permission is not granted. Generally, so long as the other parties have sufficient time to deal with the new evidence before the hearing (including filing fresh evidence themselves) permission will be granted.

19.32   A claimant will also require permission to rely on any grounds at the substantive hearing other than those for which he or she was given permission at the permission stage.[38] The procedure for obtaining permission is generally the same as that referred to above in relation to additional evidence, save that notice must be given to the court and the other parties served with the claim form no later than seven clear days before the date of the hearing (or the warned date, where appropriate).[39]

19.33   The position is different where an additional ground sought to be relied on was included in the claim form, but permission on that ground was refused (though granted on other grounds). In R (Opoku) v Southwark College Principal,[40] where permission had been granted but not on all the pleaded grounds, the claimant sought to rely at the substantive hearing on the ground for which permission had been refused. It would have been open to him to have appealed the refusal of permission in relation to that ground, but no such appeal had been brought.

19.34   The court held that the appropriate procedure would have been to have brought such an appeal, but that the failure to have done so did not deprive the court of its powers to permit the additional ground to be raised. In such a situation, however, the court should only exercise its powers in limited circumstances, namely: where the claimant established a significant change of circumstances since the permission decision; where there were significant new facts; or where a proposition of law, not available at the time permission was considered, was now available.[41]

19.35   In R (Smith) v Parole Board,[42] the Court of Appeal, however, held that this approach was too restrictive. Although the judge at the full hearing would require justification before taking a different view from that

38   CPR r54.15.
39   CPR Practice Direction 54 para 11.1.
40   [2002] EWHC 2092 (Admin); [2003] 1 WLR 234.
41   [2002] EWHC 2092 (Admin) at [16].
42   [2003] EWCA Civ 1014; [2003] 1 WLR 2548.

of a permission judge who had heard full argument at that stage, if the judge concluded that there was good reason – and there would need to be a real justification – to allow argument on an additional ground, permission should be granted. Each case should be considered in relation to its own circumstances, but the judge should bear in mind that if permission to rely on an additional ground was refused, the Court of Appeal would be prevented from considering it should there be an appeal from the first instance decision.

Other interim applications

19.36   The Administrative Court has power to grant broadly the same forms of interim relief as any other court.[43] Abridgement of time for the defendant to file and serve its response, and expedition of the substantive hearing are commonly granted, even though the time allowed by the rules has itself been reduced by 21 days. Injunctions and stays are equally common.

19.37   Disclosure is not required unless ordered by the court,[44] and is not generally ordered, unless there is a specific reason for so doing.[45] In many cases, however, claimants will have the right to see information held by the defendant concerning their case.[46]

19.38   Oral evidence and cross-examination may still be ordered by the court, in appropriate cases. The Administrative Court so held in *R (PG) v Ealing LBC (No 2)*,[47] in spite of the indication to the contrary contained in CPR r54.16(1) as originally enacted. It was argued that the disapplication of CPR r8.6, by rule 54.16 (including the power contained in CPR r8.6(2) to call oral evidence) had effect to exclude the court's power to order oral cross-examination. This argument was rejected. CPR r54.16 has now been amended so that the disapplication now applies to CPR r8.6(1) alone.[48]

19.39   The courts have shown themselves to be far more willing to order oral evidence and cross-examination in claims involving fundamental

43 See 'Directions and orders on the grant of permission' at paras 18.136–18.139 above. See also 'Remedies' at chapter 5 above.

44 CPR Practice Direction 54 para 12.1.

45 See 'Interim Remedies' at paras 5.55–5.59 above.

46 Data Protection Act 1998 s7. See 'Pre-application procedure' at paras 17.22–17.25 above, but see also, generally chapter 14.

47 [2002] EWHC 250 (Admin); (2002) *Times* 18 March 18.

48 Civil Procedure (Amendment) Rules 2002 SI No 2058 (in force from 2 December 2002).

rights than in other cases,[49] and have indicated that a similar approach may be adopted in relation to disclosure.[50] Nevertheless, the scope for these forms of interim relief is more limited in a public law context than in private law actions. As regards cross-examination, this is because, ordinarily, there has already been a determination of fact with which the court will interfere only reluctantly. In *O'Reilly v Mackman*,[51] Lord Diplock expressed the fear that hearing oral evidence may present the court with a temptation, not always easily resisted, to substitute its own view of the facts.

Making interim applications

19.40　Under the Civil Procedure Rules, applications following the permission stage (which can be included in the claim form) are made in the same way as in any other civil litigation, namely by means of an application notice and evidence, whether contained in a separate witness statement or in the application form itself.[52] In relation to many types of applications, however, the Administrative Court's practice is to require only a letter setting out the basis of the application. The Administrative Court's *Guidance Notes* however, indicate that the CPR Part 23 procedure should be used, once the permission decision has been made.[53] If in doubt, advisers should contact the Administrative Court Office.

49　See, eg, *R (Wilkinson) v Broadmoor Special Hospital Authority* [2001] EWCA Civ 1545; [2002] 1 WLR 419; (2002) 5 CCLR 121; *S v Airedale NHS Trust* [2002] EWHC Admin 1780; (2002) *Times* 5 September; *R (PG) v Ealing LBC* [2002] EWHC 250 (Admin); *R (Mullen) v Secretary of State for the Home Department* [2002] EWHC Admin 230; [2002] 1 WLR 1857.

50　See, eg, *R v Ministry of Defence ex p Smith* [1996] QB 517, CA, per Henry LJ at 543.

51　[1983] 2 AC 237, HL.

52　See CPR Parts 23 and 25; Form N244.

53　*Administrative Court Notes for Guidance on Applying for Judicial Review*, February 2002, para 19.

Appeals from interim orders

19.41   In non-criminal cases, there is a right of appeal to the Court of Appeal, but permission is required.[54] In criminal cases, it appears that interim judgments may only be appealed to the House of Lords, by virtue of the Administration of Justice Act 1960.[55]

---

54   CPR r52.3(1). In relation to an appeal concerning a case management decision (including decisions concerning disclosure, filing statements, timetable, etc), the court considering the application for permission to appeal may take into account whether the issues are of sufficient importance to justify an appeal; whether the procedural consequences of an appeal (eg, loss of trial date) outweigh the significance of the decision appealed; and whether it would be more convenient to determine the issue at or after trial: CPR Practice Direction 52 paras 4.4–4.5.

55   See Supreme Court Act 1981 s18(1)(a).

CHAPTER 20

The hearing

continued overleaf

Discontinuance and settlement

Discontinuance

20.1   The rules on discontinuance are generally governed by Civil Procedure Rules (CPR) Part 38. Discontinuance has a special significance in judicial review proceedings given the obligation on the claimant to reconsider the merits of the claim on receipt of the evidence and detailed grounds for contesting the claim by the defendant (and any interested party). On the other hand, given the unfavourable costs consequences of discontinuance (and limitations on its availability where interim relief has been granted) claimants may find it preferable to seek to negotiate the consensual withdrawal or dismissal of the claim, in circumstances where they consider it inappropriate, for whatever reason, to continue to the full hearing.

20.2   The claimant has a right to discontinue the claim at any time,[1] save in certain circumstances, which include the situations where an interim injunction has been granted (or an undertaking to the court given) and where there is more than one claimant. In the first of these situations, the permission of the court will be required. In the second, either every other claimant must consent or the permission of the court must be obtained.[2]

20.3   Subject to the points noted above, the procedure for discontinuing a claim is, in summary, as follows. The claimant must file a notice of discontinuance at the Administrative Court Office, and serve a copy of the notice on every other party.[3] The defendant may apply to have the notice of discontinuance set aside, provided such an application is made not more than 28 days after the notice of discontinuance was served on him or her.[4]

20.4   Discontinuance takes effect on the date of the service of the notice and the proceedings come to an end on that date, subject to any application to set aside the notice, though proceedings to deal with any question of costs may still continue.[5]

---

1 CPR r38.2(1).
2 CPR r38.2(2).
3 CPR r38.3(1).
4 CPR r38.4. This provision appears to be aimed at the prevention of the abuse of the discontinuance procedure, its use for the purpose of gaining some tactical or other advantage. The court may impose conditions for the discontinuance of the proceedings.
5 CPR r38.5.

20.5   The claimant who discontinues proceedings is liable for the costs of the defendant up to the date of the discontinuance.[6] The permission of the court will be required to bring a further claim against the same defendant based on substantially the same facts if the claim was discontinued after a defence was filed.[7] In relation to judicial review proceedings, it is not entirely clear what is the equivalent stage to the filing of a defence, though the nearest equivalent would seem to be the lodging of the acknowledgement of service.[8] Given that permission would in any event be required for any future claim brought by the claimant, this provision is probably of less significance in the context of the CPR Part 54 procedure, however, than it is in the context of civil proceedings generally.

Settlement and consent orders

20.6   If the parties agree on the final order that should be made, they must submit a draft of terms of the proposed agreed order (with two copies), signed by all the parties, together with a short statement of the reasons justifying the proposed agreed order and copies of any authorities or statutory provisions relied on.[9] If the proposed order only relates to the question of costs, however, it is not necessary to include a statement of reasons or to attach any documents.[10]

20.7   The court will consider the reasons and documents, if any, and decide whether to grant the agreed order or whether, if it is not satisfied that the order should be made, to list the matter for hearing.[11]

20.8   It appears that even if the defendant capitulates before the full hearing, the claimant may be entitled to proceed in order to obtain a declaration, if it is necessary to do so in order to proceed with a claim for damages which has been pursued in the application. Without a determination of the applicant's rights, it may be that no claim for damages could be brought, and where this is so, it seems that a declaration may be awarded.[12]

---

6   CPR r38.6(1).
7   CPR r38.7.
8   CPR r54.8.
9   Practice Direction 54 para 17.1.
10   Practice Direction 54 para 17.4.
11   Practice Direction 54 paras 17.2–17.3.
12   *R v Northavon District Council ex p Palmer* (1993) 25 HLR 674, QBD.

Decision without a hearing

20.9 The court may decide the claim without a hearing where all the parties agree.[13] This is most likely to happen where the parties are agreed as to the final order, having compromised the action, but the rules do not so limit the ability of the parties to consent. It is now becoming common for questions of costs to be dealt with in this manner where the claim has not been contested. The parties put in written representations on costs, following which a decision is made.

Listing

20.10 Assuming a hearing is to take place, the Administrative Court's listing policy is summarised in the *Notes for Guidance on Applying for Judicial Review*[14] and set out in more detail in an Annex to the February 2002 Practice Statement.[15] Once the case is ready for a substantive hearing (ie, once the defendant and any interested party has filed its evidence and detailed grounds of defence, or the time for doing so has elapsed), it will enter the warned list and all parties will be informed of this.

Expedited warned list

20.11 There are, in effect, three parts to the warned list. The first is the 'expedited warned list'. This contains cases where an expedited, or early, hearing has been ordered. Cases in this list take priority over others waiting to be fixed.

Short warned list

20.12 Secondly, there is the 'short warned list'. This contains cases that may come on at any time during a specified period. Parties will be informed that their case may be listed from a certain date on less than a day's notice. Around six cases will be warned for any particular week. The reason for short warning is stated to be the need to provide cover for the large number of settlements that occur in the Administrative Court.

---

13 CPR r54.18.
14 February 2002, at paragraph 15.
15 Annex C to *Practice Statement,* Scott Baker J, 1 February 2002, [2002] 1 All ER 633.

In other words, if some cases could not be called on at very short notice, Administrative Court judges may be left with no cases to hear.

20.13 The Practice Statement does not state the criteria which will be applied in deciding which cases to short warn, but the general philosophy of short warned lists is that they should be the more straightforward cases, given that they are listed without consultation with the parties and so a new advocate may be required to pick them up at, by definition, less than a day's notice if the advocate previously instructed is not available.

20.14 If the case does not come into the list in the period during which it is short warned, the parties will be consulted on the listing, which will be as soon as possible after the short warned period.

Warned list

20.15 The rest of the cases in the warned list are listed by consultation with the parties. A range of dates is offered to the advocates whose names appear on the court record, and they are given 48 hours to accept one of them. If the list office is not contacted within that 48-hour period, it will fix the case for hearing on one of the offered dates, without further consultation with the parties, who will be informed of the hearing date by letter.

20.16 Where listing occurs in this fashion, the Administrative Court Office will only vacate the hearing date by the consent of both parties. If consent cannot be achieved, a formal application for an adjournment must be made to the court on notice to all parties.[16]

Vacating hearings

20.16 The court may vacate hearings at very short notice. The Practice Statement confirms that this may occur as late as 4.30 pm on the day before the hearing, suggesting that this may be necessary for example where a case overruns or a judge becomes unavailable. It may also occur where a very urgent case comes into the list and must be heard immediately.

20.17 If a hearing has to be vacated, the List Office will consider the cases listed for the following day and will decide which hearing to vacate using the following criteria, specified in the Practice Statement:

- the removal of which case(s) will cause the least disruption to the list (the aim being to adjourn as few cases as possible, ideally one);

16 The same procedure applies where the claimant is in person.

- how many cases need to be adjourned, given the reduced listing time available;
- whether any cases have previously been adjourned by the court;
- the urgency and age of the cases listed;
- where the parties and/or their representatives are based (this is considered relevant as in some cases the parties and representatives travel to London the day before the hearing);
- whether a case can be 'floated' in the event that another case goes short (cases are only floated with the consent of the parties);
- the likelihood of a judge becoming available to hear a floated case.

20.18   Once a decision has been taken, the parties concerned will be informed that their case will have to be refixed. It will be noted on the case record that it is not to be adjourned again by the court. The court will then endeavour to refix the case at the next available date convenient to the parties.

Documentation for the hearing

20.19   The claimant must file and serve a skeleton argument and a bundle of documents for the hearing not less than 21 working days (ie, just over four weeks) prior to the date of the hearing, or the warned date.[17] Defendants and other persons wishing to make representations at the hearing must file and serve a skeleton argument not less than 14 working days before the hearing date (or warned date).[18]

The skeleton argument

20.20   The skeleton argument must contain:
- the time estimate for the complete hearing (including judgment);
- a list of issues;
- a list of the propositions of law to be advanced at the hearing;
- the authorities relied on in support of each such proposition of law, with page references to passages relied on;
- a chronology of events (with page references to the paginated bundle);
- a list of the essential documents for advance reading by the court, with page references to the passages relied on (if different from

17   CPR Practice Direction 54 paras 15.1 and 16.1.
18   CPR Practice Direction 54 para. 15.2.

those included in the claim form) and *a time estimate for that advance reading;* and

• a list of persons referred to.[19]

The bundle

20.21   One copy of the bundle must be filed, unless the matter is to be heard by a Divisional Court,[20] instead of the single judge, in which case two copies will be required.[21]

20.22   The bundle must be paginated and indexed, and must contain all relevant documents required for the hearing, including those documents required by the defendant(s) and any other party taking part in the hearing.[22] It is clear, therefore, that the compiling of the bundle is intended to be a matter of co-operation between the parties. In the light of the time limits, consideration of the contents of the bundle may need to begin early where it appears that there may be disagreement.

20.23   This could be important as, given the requirement to give a time estimate for the court's pre-reading of the bundle, it is necessary to be able to assess accurately what the court does need to have read before the hearing and, given that if a large number of documents are included (particularly if listed as essential pre-reading) that the court considers irrelevant, there may be costs consequences for the party which required their inclusion.

20.24   Civil Procedure Rules r39.5 and Practice Direction 39A contain more detailed provisions regarding the contents of bundles and the manner in which they should be compiled (although these general requirements will give way to the provisions of CPR Part 54 itself where there is any conflict.[23]

20.25   The preparation and production of the bundle is the responsibility of the legal representative who has conduct of the case for the claimant, even where the work is delegated to another person.[24] A copy of the

---

19   CPR Practice Direction 54 para 15.3.
20   A Divisional Court now appears to comprise only two judges – see the *Administrative Court Guidance Notes on Applying for Judicial Review,* February 2002, para 16. Formerly, a Divisional Court could comprise two or three judges, depending on the importance of the case.
21   See the *Administrative Court Guidance Notes on Applying for Judicial Review* February 2002, para 18.
22   *Guidance Notes* paras 16.1–16.2.
23   See CPR Practice Direction 39A paras 3.1–3.2.
24   CPR Practice Direction 39A para 3.4.

bundle, identical with that which has been filed, should be supplied to each of the parties, including any interested parties.[25]

20.26   The parties should agree the bundle where possible (as stated above) and also agree that the documents it contains are authentic (whether or not they have been disclosed under CPR Part 31) and that they may be taken as evidence of the facts stated in them (whether or not a notice under the Civil Evidence Act 1995 has been served). If such agreement is not possible, a summary of the points in dispute should be included.[26]

20.27   Where a document included in a bundle is illegible, a typescript of it should be included, next to it in the bundle, with appropriate cross-referencing.[27] The originals of documents included in the bundle should be available at the hearing.[28] If applicable, experts' reports may be contained in a separate bundle with cross-references to them included in the main bundle.[29]

20.28   In general, bundles must be paginated continuously throughout. If they contain more than 100 pages, numbered page-dividers should be placed at intervals between groups of documents. The bundle must also be indexed with the index including a description of each document and giving its page number.[30]

20.29   The bundle should usually be contained in a ring binder or lever-arch file. If it is in more than one volume, each volume must be clearly distinguishable, for example, by the use of numbers or letters (or colours). If there are numerous volumes, a core bundle should be prepared including only the essential documents, with references to the supplementary documents in the other volumes.[31]

20.30   In *R v Humberside CC ex p Bogdal*,[32] it was held that the claimant could not pick and choose among issues raised in the claim. Accordingly, an attempt to strike out certain documents included by the defendant in its bundle was unsuccessful. Once the claimant sought to quash a decision, the court should not be excluded from having before it the relevant background documents. All documents before the court, however, must be relevant, on the ordinary principles of litigation.

---

25 CPR Practice Direction 39A para 3.10.
26 CPR Practice Direction 39A para 3.9.
27 CPR Practice Direction 39A para 3.7.
28 CPR Practice Direction 39A para 3.3.
29 CPR Practice Direction 39A para 3.7.
30 CPR Practice Direction 39A para 3.5.
31 CPR Practice Direction 39A para 3.6.
32 [1991] COD 66, QBD.

Power to hear any person

20.31   Even if not served as an interested party, any person may apply for permission to file evidence and/or be heard at the full hearing. Such an application must be made promptly.[33] Where the court gives permission, it may do so on conditions and may give case management directions.

The hearing

20.32   The hearing is generally before a single judge assigned to the Administrative Court, although the court may direct that a Divisional Court should hear the claim. The hearing will generally take place at the Royal Courts of Justice in London, although claims against the National Assembly for Wales are now heard in Cardiff. In urgent cases, it may be possible for a hearing to be arranged in other locations.[34]

Remedies

20.33   The grant of relief is at the discretion of the court. The principles on which such discretion will be exercised and the types of remedy available are discussed elsewhere.[35]

Costs

General principles

20.34   The general costs provisions of CPR Part 44 are applicable to judicial review proceedings. Accordingly, the court will be obliged, in exercising its discretion regarding the award of costs, to take account of the factors in CPR r44.3.[36]

20.35   Costs will generally follow the event,[37] but the court may make a different order, and will be likely to do so in the following situations.

33   CPR r54.17.
34   See chapter 18 above at para 18.59.
35   Remedies are dealt with in chapter 5 at paras 5.1–5.41; the principles of discretion are dealt with in chapter 7 at paras 7.1–7.25.
36   See, in particular, CPR r44.3(2)–(7).
37   See CPR r44.3(2)(a).

20.36   If the decision-maker does not appear, it is unusual for costs to be awarded against him or her. The situation may be different if the court considers that the decision-maker's error calls for the court's disapproval (eg, bad faith).[38] In *R v Huntingdon Magistrates' Court ex p Percy*,[39] the court, exceptionally, ordered the justices to pay the applicant's costs of the judicial review proceedings where they had refused to state a case on the ground that the application for them to do so was 'frivolous'. Their refusal was maintained even after they were informed that leave to move for judicial review of their decision had been granted, a stance which the Divisional Court found 'surprising, to put it mildly'.[40]

20.37   Where a person who has not been served has been heard by virtue of CPR r54.17, it is rare for that person to be awarded costs. The same appears to be the case where a party who has been served has appeared in support of the application. For instance, in *R v Secretary of State for Social Security ex p Association of Metropolitan Authorities*,[41] Hackney LBC appeared but was not awarded costs, even though the claim succeeded. This may be an application of the principle that two or more parties with the same interest will not each be granted their costs. The court is reluctant to award more than one set of costs.[42] However, there is no inflexible rule to this effect.[43]

20.38   More significantly, however, is the willingness of the courts to take into account the conduct of the parties in such a way as to deprive successful claimants of their costs, or part of them, on the basis that their conduct of proceedings prolonged them unreasonably, thereby causing the unnecessary or unreasonable incurring of additional costs. The availability of this reason for refusing a costs order in favour of successful parties is founded on the provisions of CPR r44.3(4), (5) and (6).

20.39   CPR r44.3(4)(a) requires the court to have regard, when making a costs decision, to the conduct of the parties, which includes the question of conduct before as well as during proceedings, including compliance with the pre-action protocol; whether it was reasonable to raise,

---

38 *R v West Yorkshire Coroner* (1984) *Times* 11 April.

39 [1994] COD 323, DC.

40 See also *R v Maidstone Coroner ex p Johnstone* (1994) *Times* 19 October, DC, where the coroner was ordered to pay the applicant's costs even though no strong disapproval was shown.

41 (1993) 25 HLR 131, QBD.

42 See *R v Industrial Disputes Tribunal ex p American Express Co Ltd* [1954] 1 WLR 1118.

43 *R v Registrar of Companies ex p Central Bank of India* [1986] QB 1114 at 1162; *R v HM Inspectorate of Pollution and the Ministry of Agriculture, Fisheries and Food ex p Greenpeace Ltd* [1994] COD 116, QBD.

pursue or contest a particular allegation or issue; the manner in which a party has pursued or defended his case or a particular allegation or issue; and whether a successful (whether wholly or in part) claimant has exaggerated the claim.[44] CPR r44.3(4)(b) requires the court to take account of whether a party has succeeded on part of his case, even if not wholly successful. Offers of settlement also fall to be considered.[45]

20.40   The court may make costs orders, among others, that require a party to pay a proportion only of another party's costs or which relate only to a distinct part of the proceedings.[46]

20.41   The courts generally have used their powers under these rules to make orders for costs, in some cases, based on success or failure on individual issues rather than overall success or failure, particularly where the winning party raised an issue or issues on which he or she was unsuccessful and which took up a significant part of the hearing.

20.42   In *AEI Rediffusion Music v Phonographic Performance Ltd*,[47] for example, Lord Woolf MR described the 'costs follow the event' principle as a 'starting point from which a court can readily depart'. In numerous subsequent cases, the courts have made costs orders that do not follow the event where they considered it appropriate to do so. The Master of the Rolls continued that '... it is no longer necessary for a party to have acted *unreasonably* or *improperly* to be deprived of his costs of a particular issue on which he has failed'.[48]

20.43   Specifically, in relation to judicial review proceedings, attention must be drawn to the decision of Munby J in *R (Bateman) v Legal Services Commission*.[49] In that case, the claimants, though successful in their challenge to the LSC's decision to revoke their funding certificates, were deprived of a proportion of their costs on the basis of their conduct of the proceedings; in particular, their persisting in a number of grounds of challenge which the court considered to have been always doomed to failure. It is noteworthy that the fact that permission had been granted to pursue these grounds did not dissuade the judge from

44 CPR r44.3(5)(a)–(d).
45 CPR r44.3(4)(c).
46 CPR r44.3(6).
47 [1999] 1 WLR 1507, CA, at 1523H.
48 See also, eg, *Summit Property Ltd v Pitmans* [2001] EWCA Civ 2020; *Kastor Navigation Ltd v AGF MAT* [2003] EWHC 472 (Comm); and *Stena Rederi Aktiebolag v Irish Ferries Ltd* [2003] EWCA Civ 214. In *Kastor*, at [18], the rejection of a CPR Part 36 payment did not prevent the court from departing from the usual rules relating to the rejection of a payment by a party who then failed to beat it.
49 [2001] EWHC Admin 797; [2002] ACD 29.

penalising the claimants in costs for arguing them, for two related reasons. The first was that:

> ... it is only comparatively infrequently that the judge who grants permission will be in any effective position to limit the ambit of the subsequent application for which he has granted permission.[50]

and that:

> ... [t]he fact that the judge who grants permission has not made adverse comment on some part of the claimant's case is not, in my judgment, to be taken as any judicial acknowledgment of the appropriateness of pursuing that particular point further.[51]

20.44 The second reason was that the claimants' legal advisers were under a duty to consider with care, even where permission had been granted, which arguments should and which should not be pursued at the full hearing. This is why the form used by the court on the grant of permission includes the words:

> Where permission to apply has been granted, claimants and their legal advisers are reminded of their obligation to reconsider the merits of their application in the light of the defendant's evidence.

20.45 Munby J went on to say:

> The need for conscientious performance of this obligation has been pointed out on previous occasions: see for example Brooke J in *R v Horsham D ex p Wenman* [1995] 1 WLR 680 at p 701A referring to what Hodgson J had earlier said in *R v Secretary of State for the Home Department ex p Brown* (1984) *Times* 6 February. People must appreciate that failure in this regard may be visited with adverse costs orders.[52]

20.46 In reducing the costs awarded to Mrs Bateman and Mr Bateman, who had claimed separately, by 15 per cent and 25 per cent respectively, the court took account of the following factors:

- that the case was one of the utmost gravity to both claimants;
- that the penalty which had been inflicted on them by the Legal Services Commission and which they sought to challenge was a draconian one;
- that no allegation of dishonesty or deliberate concealment had been made against Mrs Bateman and that the allegation which had been made against Mr Bateman had been introduced in a profoundly unsatisfactory manner;

50 [2001] EWHC Admin 797 at [19].
51 [2001] EWHC Admin 797 at [20].
52 [2001] EWHC Admin 797 at [21].

- that the judge had granted permission and had expressly regarded as arguable one of the points on which the claimants ultimately lost;
- that the defendant had rejected an offer of settlement made by Mrs Bateman; and
- that the claimants had succeeded in overturning the defendant's decision not just on one but on a number of grounds.

> But the stark fact nevertheless remains that both claimants, and Mr Bateman to a greater extent than Mrs Bateman, pursued, at no little expenditure of time and money, a great number of points on which they ultimately failed, many of them, I have to say, in circumstances where the prospects of success were from the outset exiguous or worse ... Mrs Bateman showed somewhat more restraint, but Mr Bateman, in effect, took virtually every point that could possibly have been taken without going beyond the limits of what is proper.[53]

20.47   At one level, the *Bateman* decision is simply a decision on its own facts which states no more than that where 'unmeritorious points [are] vigorously pursued ... [t]hat, in my judgment, is something which ought fairly to be reflected in my order as to costs'.[54]

20.48   It is, however, suggested that decisions of this sort leave the parties, and particularly those advising claimants, in an unfortunately difficult and uncertain position. This was recognised by the judge, who referred to the tension, which had existed for as long as there had been professional advocates, between the pursuit of forensic brevity and the fear of betraying the client's interests by not raising every possible point.[55]

20.49   Nevertheless, if even an express ruling at the permission stage that a ground is arguable, and an express ruling in the judgment following the full hearing that it was entirely proper to raise it, does not necessarily protect the party advancing that ground from a retrospective judicial re-evaluation of its arguability for the purposes of a costs decision, then it is difficult to know by what yardstick legal representatives are meant to comply with their obligation to reconsider the merits of their case on receipt of the defendant's grounds for contesting it, or to consider which grounds ought to be pursued and which abandoned.

20.50   If it is correct that in judicial review cases the judge is not in an effective position to limit the ambit of the case as it proceeds to the

---

53 [2001] EWHC Admin 797 at [25].
54 [2001] EWHC Admin 797 at [26].
55 [2001] EWHC Admin 797 at [17] referring to an exchange between Pliny and Regulus, later recounted by Pliny in a letter to Tacitus (Ep I, xx, 14).

substantive hearing, that would appear to entail the proposition that the judges are not in a position at the permission stage to decide which grounds are arguable and which are not, which calls into question the purpose of (and the reliability of decision-making at) the permission stage, and the purpose of the rule permitting the court to refuse permission on some grounds while granting it on others.

Failure to withdraw applications

20.51   If the claimant ought to have withdrawn his or her application because of the defendant's conduct (such as offering a reconsideration upon the grant of permission) or for any other reason (such as a decision of the court in another matter which effectively decides the issue in the case, or the defendant's evidence disclosing that the decision complained of was lawful), then the defendant may recover his or her costs from the date on which the claimant ought to have withdrawn.[56] There is also the danger of a wasted costs order against the claimant's legal representative(s) being considered.[57]

20.52   There is another possible danger, where claimants proceed with cases which ought to have been withdrawn. In the case of funded parties, the defendant may object to the claimant being granted a detailed assessment of his or her publicly funded costs (see below), rather than applying for a personal costs order against the claimant's legal representative.

20.53   Alternatively, the court may order that, on a detailed assessment of publicly funded costs, the costs of certain matters or procedural steps, etc, should be disallowed. Either course, from the defendant's point of view, has a severe deterrent effect upon the bringing of applications while not involving the time and expense of the kind occasioned by an application for a personal costs order, where notice to show cause must be given and the matter further investigated by the court at a further hearing.[58]

---

56   See *R v Warley Justices ex p Callis* [1994] COD 240, QBD. See also *R v Liverpool CC ex p Newman* [1993] COD 65, QBD.

57   *R v Horsham DC and another ex p Wenman* (1992) 24 HLR 669 and [1994] 4 All ER 681, QBD.

58   See Supreme Court Act 1981 s51; CPR r48.7.

Costs following settlement

20.54   In R (Boxall) v Waltham Forest LBC,[59] Scott-Baker J suggested that the following principles apply where the dispute has been settled but no agreement has been reached about costs:

(i)   the court has power to make a costs order when the substantive proceedings have been resolved without a trial but the parties have not agreed about costs;

(ii) it will ordinarily be irrelevant that the claimant is legally aided;

(iii) the overriding objective is to do justice between the parties without incurring unnecessary court time and consequently additional cost;

(iv) at each end of the spectrum there will be cases where it is obvious which side would have won had the substantive issues been fought to a conclusion. In between, the position will, in differing degrees, be less clear. How far the court will be prepared to look into the previously unresolved substantive issues will depend on the circumstances of the particular case, not least the amount of costs at stake and the conduct of the parties;

(v)   in the absence of a good reason to make any other order the fall back is to make no order as to costs;

(vi) the court should take care to ensure that it does not discourage parties from settling judicial review proceedings, for example, by a local authority making a concession at an early stage.

20.55   *Boxall* was approved by the Court of Appeal, albeit in a different context in *Brawley v Marczynski and Business Lines Ltd.*[60]

Central funds

20.56   In criminal cases, there is power to award costs (either in whole or in such part as is just and reasonable) to any party to be paid out of central funds, except for a prosecutor who is also, or is appointed by or acting on behalf of, a public authority.[61]

---

59   (2001) 4 CCLR 258 at [22]. See also *R v Liverpool CC ex p Newman* [1993] COD 65, QBD.

60   [2002] EWCA Civ 756; [2002] 4 All ER 1060.

61   Prosecution of Offences Act 1985 ss16 and 17.

Publicly funded cases

20.57 Funded parties should remember to request a detailed assessment of their publicly funded costs.

Appeal to the Court of Appeal

20.58 In civil matters, an appeal to the Court of Appeal lies, with permission, from the refusal of an application for judicial review, or from the refusal of relief. Permission, if not obtained from the Administrative Court judge at the conclusion of the case, must be sought from the Court of Appeal within 14 days of judgment.[62]

Appeal to the House of Lords

Civil matters

20.59 A further appeal, from an order of the Court of Appeal, lies to the House of Lords on a point of general public importance. This requires the leave of the Court of Appeal, or of the Appellate Committee itself.[63]

Criminal matters

20.60 There is no appeal to the Court of Appeal in criminal matters.[64] Instead, an appeal from the Divisional Court lies direct to the House of Lords. Leave is required, and may be granted by the Divisional Court certifying a point of general public importance and considering the matter suitable for consideration by the Appellate Committee. If refused by the Divisional Court, leave may be granted by the Appellate Committee itself.[65]

---

62 See generally, CPR r52.3 and Practice Direction 52 para 4.
63 The procedure for obtaining leave to appeal from the House of Lords is set out at *Civil Procedure* (the *White Book* 2003), Sweet & Maxwell, Vol 2, pp 1155–1252.
64 Supreme Court Act 1981 s18(1)(a).
65 Administration of Justice Act 1960 s1.

Fresh evidence

First instance

20.61   The single judge or Divisional Court will admit fresh evidence, which was not before the decision-maker, in certain situations. It may receive such evidence to show what materials were before the decision-maker. In addition, where the question before the court is one of jurisdictional fact or whether essential procedural requirements were observed, the court may consider additional evidence to determine that jurisdictional fact or procedural error.[66]

20.62   Further, evidence is admissible, where the decision-maker or another party has been guilty of misconduct, to prove the misconduct alleged (eg, bias, perjury, fraud, etc).[67]

On appeal

20.63   The principles of *Ladd v Marshall*,[68] which usually govern the admissibility of fresh evidence on appeal, do not strictly apply. They are: (a) that the evidence could not have been obtained with reasonable diligence for use at the trial; (b) that the evidence would have an important influence on the result of the case; and (c) that the evidence is apparently credible, though it need not be incontrovertible. The Court of Appeal, in judicial review proceedings, appears to have a wider discretion to receive fresh evidence. However, in the interests of finality of litigation, the court will generally adopt a similar approach to that set out in *Ladd v Marshall*, but has discretion to depart from it if the wider interests of justice so require.[69]

---

66   *R v Secretary of State for the Home Department ex p Khawaja* [1984] AC 74, HL.
67   See *R v Secretary of State for the Environment ex p Powis* [1981] 1 WLR 584.
68   [1954] 1 WLR 1489.
69   See *Momin Ali v Secretary of State for the Home Department* [1984] 1 WLR 663, CA.

APPENDICES

Precedents

LETTER BEFORE CLAIM

[Dee Pechmoad Solicitors]
[12 High Street]

12 August 2003

[Paula Fastwun]
[Style Council]

Dear [Ms Fastwun]

Our client: [Bea Steabois, 6 Acacia Avenue]

Proposed claim for judicial review

We are instructed by [Ms Steabois] who yesterday received notice from the County Court Bailiffs, dated 10 August 2003, that a warrant for possession of her home at [6 Acacia Avenue] (the 'house') will be executed on 21 August 2003.

Briefly, the background to this matter is as follows. On 16 October 2002, [Ms Steabois] was granted by your authority an introductory tenancy of the house. On 21 May 2003, you served a notice of proceedings on her under section 128 of the Housing Act 1996 (the '1996 Act'), stating that you intended to bring possession proceedings against her on the basis that she was in arrears with her rent in the sum of £1,560.36. Our client requested a review of the decision pursuant to section 129 of the 1996 Act by letter of 23 May 2003. The grounds for the review were that the rent arrears were caused entirely by failures on the part of your authority's housing benefit department. The review was unsuccessful and proceedings were issued on 24 June 2003. Our client attended the hearing on 29 June, but the judge informed her that he had no power to refuse your authority a possession order.

On 15 July 2003, housing benefit was finally paid into our client's rent account, paying off the arrears in full. By letter of yesterday's date, we requested that the authority reconsider the decision to evict in the light of the payment of the arrears, the medical evidence concerning 445 our client's mental health and vulnerability which we enclosed with the letter and the effect of the decision on our client's three children who are currently looked after by your authority's social services department but who had been expected to return to live with our client in a few weeks' time. We asked you to agree to withdraw the warrant in order to facilitate your reconsideration.

In response, we were telephoned this morning by a [Hugh Manleeg], who we understand is your authority's Housing Department Evictions Team Leader. He informed me that in spite of the fact that our client's rent account is now clear, and in spite of the effect on her health and her children which would be caused by an eviction, he intended to evict our client in any event, on the basis that she is not suitable to be a council tenant, and that she has already had her 'day in court' before the review panel and in the court proceedings, and that the law was 'on the council's side'. He stated that he would not reconsider this decision and would not withdraw the warrant. He confirmed this to us in writing in a letter he faxed to our offices this afternoon.

We are writing to inform you that we believe the above decisions to be unlawful for the reasons set out below. [Ms Steabois] has instructed us, and we have public funding, to commence judicial review proceedings against you, including a claim for interim relief to stay the warrant, unless by 10.00 am on 18 August 2003, we have received your agreement to the proposals which we set out below.

For your convenience, we enclose with this letter a copy of the warrant for possession referred to above, together with a copy of our letter of yesterday's date and the medical evidence included with it, and a copy of [Mr Manleeg's] reply.

Judicial Review Pre-action Protocol

The remainder of this letter will follow the format set out at Annex A to the Judicial Review Pre-action Protocol. In accordance with that protocol, a copy of this letter has been sent to [Mr Manleeg].

The claimant

[Ms Bea Steabois, 6 Acacia Avenue]

Reference details

Ours: [details]
Yours: [details].

Details of the matter being challenged

The decisions of your authority:

(a)   to issue proceedings against her on 24 June 2003, culminating in a possession order being made against her;

(b) notified to our client only by way of the notice of eviction referred to above, to evict her from the house in spite of the fact that the only reason for her rent arrears was a failure by your authority to pay her housing benefit to which she was entitled and which has now been paid;

(c) notified to us by a letter from [Mr Manleeg] of today's date, refusing to reconsider the decision to evict; and

(d) also notified to us by the letter of today's date, to refuse to withdraw the warrant.

The issues

We believe these decisions to be unlawful for the following, principal reasons:

1. You have failed to take account of relevant considerations, in relation to the original decision to issue proceedings, namely:

    (a) the cause of the arrears being entirely due to your housing benefit department's unlawful refusal of benefit, our client's request for a revision of which decision was still under consideration at the date proceedings were issued;

    (b) the effect of the Disability Discrimination Act 1995 (see *Devon Homes Ltd v Brazier* [2003] EWHC 574 (QB); (2003) 22 EG 141);

    (c) the effect on our client's children of their mother being evicted;

    (d) the authority's awareness at all times of our client's health problems, difficulties with her children, and housing benefit problems; and

    (e) the authority's failure to offer our client any support for her tenancy at any time prior to the service of the section 128 notice.

2. You have failed to take account of relevant considerations in taking the decision to evict, to refuse to reconsider and to refuse to withdraw the current warrant, namely:

    (a) the factors set out at paragraph 1(a) to (e) above;

    (b) the fundamental change in our client's circumstances arising from the payment of all the arrears;

    (c) the fact that the grant of full benefit on revision by your authority indicates that benefit ought not to have been refused – and so the arrears ought not to have arisen – in the first place, and that our client was not at fault in relation to her rent arrears;

    (d) that in the light of these factors, your conclusion that our client is 'an unsuitable tenant' is clearly unsubstantiated and wrong; and

    (e) the medical evidence concerning our client's mental health and vulnerability which you now have.

3. If you did have regard to the above considerations in reaching the decisions challenged, those decisions were perverse in the *Wednesbury* sense and unfair.

4.   You had regard, in refusing to reconsider the decision to evict, to irrelevant matters, and erred in law, namely: (a) that our client had already had her 'day in court'; (b) that our client was an 'unsuitable tenant'; and (c) that the authority had the law on its side.

5.   The decision to evict in these circumstances breached our client's rights under article 8 of Schedule 1 to the Human Rights Act 1998. We rely on the comments of Laws LJ in *Sheffield CC v Smart* [2002] EWCA Civ 4; [2002] HLR 34, at para [40]. It is accepted that in *Harrow LBC v Qazi* [2003] UKHL 43, the speeches of Lords Millett and Scott of Foscote were inconsistent with the passage from *Smart* referred to above, but Lord Hope expressly reserved his position on that passage (at [79]) and Lords Bingham of Cornhill and Steyn disagreed with Lords Millett and Scott.

In any event, the principles of administrative law form part of the relevant domestic law in relation to consideration of whether or not the proposed eviction of an introductory tenant is lawful (see *Manchester CC v Cochrane* [1999] 1 WLR 809, CA). While, therefore, the county court, on a claim for possession of an introductory tenancy, has no power to consider human rights issues, the defendant cannot lawfully simply give them no weight and/or pay them no regard at all.

6.   The decision to evict was contrary to the Disability Discrimination Act 1995. None of the conditions set out at section 24(3) of that Act are made out in our client's case.

7.   The decision to evict is disproportionate and perverse (see *R (Daly) v Secretary of State for the Home Department* [2001] UKHL 26; [2001] 2 AC 532, per Lord Steyn at [27]–[28]; and Lord Cooke of Thorndon at [32]) bearing in mind that our client's rent account is no longer in arrears, the reasons why the arrears arose and the consequences of eviction for her and her children.

Action to be taken

We shall issue an application for judicial review without further notice to you unless, by 10.00 am on 18 August 2003, you have confirmed to us that you will reconsider your decision refusing to withdraw the current warrant (and so the urgency of the threat of eviction) in order that we may negotiate further. It is the imminent threat of eviction which causes us to threaten judicial review at this stage.

We are mindful of our obligations to attempt to resolve this dispute without the need to involve the court (see *R (Cowl) v Plymouth CC* [2001] EWCA Civ 1935; [2002] 1 WLR 803). Accordingly, if you will withdraw the warrant, we are willing to discuss with you ways in which this matter may be resolved.

To that end, we would inform you that the substance of our client's case is that the possession proceedings were unlawfully brought, and that the possession order itself ought to be set aside and our client's introductory tenancy revived. At the very least, however, it is quite clear to us that your decision to execute the possession order and refusal to reconsider that decision need to be reconsidered. We are willing to hold off issuing proceedings for a reasonable time in order to discuss these issues with you in more detail but, as stated above, we cannot hold off while our client is due to be evicted in nine days' time.

Claimant's legal advisers

The solicitor with conduct of this case on behalf of the claimant is [name of adviser] who can be contacted using the details at the head of this letter. Please use our ref: [details].

Interested parties

If proceedings are issued, we shall seek a direction, should permission be granted, as to whether it is necessary to join [Name County Court] to these proceedings for the purpose of seeking to quash the possession order.

Information sought

Please supply, pursuant to section 7 of the Data Protection Act 1998, a copy of our client's housing file. We enclose a signed permission from our client for this purpose, and enclose a cheque to cover your fee.

Necessary documents

See above under information sought.

Address for reply and service of court documents

Please use the address at the head of this letter.

Proposed reply date

10.00 am on 18 August 2003.

Yours sincerely,

[Dee Pechmoad Solicitors]

cc [Mr Hugh Manleeg]
Housing Department Evictions Team Leader

RESPONSE TO LETTER BEFORE CLAIM

[Paula Fastwun (Director)]
[Style Council]

17 August 2003

[Dee Pechmoad Solicitors, 12 High Street]

Dear ...,

[Bea Steabois]

Thank you for your letter of 12 August 2003. It seemed to raise very serious issues for this Authority with its commitment to renewal and best value, and I called in [Mr Manleeg] to discuss its contents with me. This we did at some considerable length, and I am now in a position to reply to the detailed points you raise. As did your letter, this reply will follow the suggested format of Annex B to the Judicial Review Pre-Action Protocol, albeit that this is somewhat cumbersome.

Claimant
[Bea Steabois, 6 Acacia Avenue]

Response from
[Paula Fastwun (Director)]
[Style Council]

Reference Details
Yours: [Details]
Ours: [Details]

I have been handling this matter personally with [Mr Hugh Manleeg], the Authority's Housing Evictions Team Leader.

Details of challenge
I have considered the proposed grounds of challenge set out in your letter before claim. I should like to make the following preliminary comments. I must admit that I was initially troubled by your claim, in particular the grounds concerning relevant and irrelevant considerations and perversity. If it were the case that the Authority had failed in the manner you allege, I should be able to see the force of your arguments. [Mr Manleeg], however, has assured me that all

relevant matters known to the Authority were taken into account at the appropriate stages to which you refer. He has also persuaded me that there is no merit in your arguments for the following main reasons (in no particular order):

(i)   it does not follow from the award of housing benefit on revision that the initial refusal was wrong. Your client gave information to the benefits department on the revision that was absent from her original claim;

(ii)   it is the tenant's responsibility to pay the rent;

(iii) no rent was paid for the first six months of the tenancy;

(iv)   it is not this authority's responsibility to 'support' your client in the sense of giving her benefit to which she was not entitled on the basis of the claim form she submitted;

(v)   contrary to your assertions, we did not know about your client's ill health or her children until your letter before claim. We therefore could not have taken them into account when issuing proceedings. By the time of the letter before claim, other factors were considered to outweigh them;

(vi)   although [Mr Manleeg's] reasons may have been expressed in a less than sophisticated way, in essence he was right – your client has already had two bites at the cherry of retaining her tenancy: in the review of the decision to serve the section 128 notice and at court on the possession proceeding when she could have applied for an adjournment to seek judicial review but did not (for whatever reason);

(viii) your client is an unsuitable tenant because she did not pay her rent, did not efficiently process her benefit claim so that her rent was not paid for her; and has been guilty of anti-social behaviour through her children while they were being looked after by this authority;

(ix)   the fact that the arrears have now been paid is not the only issue; we are entitled to consider your client unsuitable taking account of her history of persistent non-payment and her children's bad behaviour while in our care;

(x)   your human rights and disability discrimination claims are unarguable and nonsensical. *Qazi* plainly rules out a human rights challenge and *Brazier* does not apply because your client is, since the possession order expired, an unlawful occupier. I do not understand what *Daly* has to do with it;

(xi)   in summary, then, although perhaps inelegantly expressed, [Mr Manleeg] seems to me to have been quite right in substance to the effect that the authority has the law on its side.

Response to the proposed claim

I have made this Authority's position clear above. I am not prepared to stay the eviction currently planned for 21 August. That eviction will go ahead.

In addition, I would point out that you are guilty of delay in challenging the decision to institute proceedings against your client. Although that decision was made less than three months ago, you will be aware that your obligation under CPR Rule 54.5 is to act 'promptly' and that a claimant can be guilty of delay within the long-stop period of three months. What your client should have done was apply for an adjournment to the possession proceedings and seek judicial review at that stage. There is no basis for seeking to challenge that decision now. Once the challenge to that decision is gone, the rest of your claim is flimsy in the extreme.

Leaving aside, however, the Authority's formal position as a matter of law, I would make you the following proposal in the hope of being able to short-circuit this dispute, especially given that public funds on both sides will bear the costs of any legal proceedings.

Although I am not prepared to stay the eviction, I am prepared to treat your letter before claim as a complaint within the authority's corporate complaints service. The complaint would be dealt with by our dedicated Complaints Service and not by [Mr Manleeg] or myself. The procedure is in four stages, ultimately being dealt with by the Chief Executive personally. If your client's case is accepted, we would be willing to arrange bed and breakfast accommodation for your client until she finds somewhere for herself to live in the private sector. Seeing as she now understands the benefit system, this should not take her too long. The average length of time it takes a complaint to complete the four stages of our procedure is two years, but this is only because or our commitment to considering complaints carefully and thoroughly.

If you can demonstrate exceptional hardship on the part of your client, I would be prepared to recommend to the Complaints Service that such accommodation be made available pending the outcome of the complaint. Your client may even be able to have her children live with her, although not if they continue to behave badly.

This seems to me to be by far the most sensible way forward for your client, and I would remind you that if you do issue judicial review proceedings, you must include a copy of this letter in the bundle placed before the court.

Other interested parties

None, but I note your comments about the County Court.

Address for correspondence/service of documents

Please use the address at the head of this letter, quoting our reference. We do not accept service by fax, e-mail or on our e-community notice board.

Yours sincerely,

[Paula Fastwun (Director)]
[Style Council]

cc [Mr Hugh Manleeg]
Housing Evictions Team Leader

JUDICIAL REVIEW CLAIM FORM N461

Judicial Review Claim Form	In the High Court of Justice Administrative Court

Notes for guidance are available which explain how to complete the judicial review claim form. Please read them carefully before you complete the form.

For Court use only	
Administrative Court Reference No.	
Date filed	

Seal

SECTION 1   Details of the claimant(s) and defendant(s)

Claimant(s) name and address(es)

name
Ms Bea Steabois

address
6 Acacia Avenue

Telephone no.

Fax no.

E-mail address

Claimant's or claimant's solicitors' address to which documents should be sent.

name
Dee Pechmoad Solicitors

address
12 High Street

Telephone no.
0101 123 456

Fax no.
0101 123 789

E-mail address
deepechmoad@deepechmoad.co.uk

Claimant's Counsel's details

name
Thear Tofnoys

address
New Chambers

Telephone no.
0101 123 321

Fax no.
0101 123 654

E-mail address
ttofnoys@newchambers.co.uk

1st Defendant

name
Style Council

Defendant's or (where known) Defendant's solicitors' address to which documents should be sent.

name
Paula Fastwun

address
Style Council
Council Chambers

Telephone no.
0101 123 987

Fax no.
0101 123 963

E-mail address
paulafastwun@stylecouncil.gov.uk

2nd Defendant

name

Defendant's or (where known) Defendant's solicitors' address to which documents should be sent.

name

address

Telephone no.

Fax no.

E-mail address

SECTION 2 Details of other interested parties

Include name and address and, if appropriate, details of DX, telephone or fax numbers and e-mail

name | name

address | address

Telephone no. | Fax no. | Telephone no. | Fax no.

E-mail address | E-mail address

SECTION 3 Details of the decision to be judicially reviewed

Decision:
(1) to issue proceedings against the claimant on 24 June 2003; (2) to apply for a warrant of possession to evict the claimant; (3) to refuse to reconsider (2) above; and (4) to refuse to withdraw the warrant referred to in (2) above.

Date of decision:
(1) Not known, but about 24 June 2003; (2) Not known, notified on 11 August 2003; (3) and (4) 12 August 2003.

Name and address of the court, tribunal, person or body who made the decision to be reviewed.

name
Hugh Manleeg

address
Housing Evictions Team Leader
Style Council
Council Chambers

SECTION 4 Permission to proceed with a claim for judicial review

I am seeking permission to proceed with my claim for Judicial Review.

Are you making any other applications? If Yes, complete Section 7. ☑ Yes ☐ No

Is the claimant in receipt of a Community Legal Service Fund (CLSF) certificate? ☑ Yes ☐ No

Are you claiming exceptional urgency, or do you need this application determined within a certain time scale? If Yes, complete Form N463 and file this with your application. ☑ Yes ☐ No

Have you complied with the pre-action protocol? If No, give reasons for non-compliance in the space below. ☐ Yes ☑ No

A letter before claim was sent to the defendant's Director of Legal Services dated 12 August 2003. The defendant was only given until 10.00am on 18 August to respond (ie, less than the suggested period of 14 days) due to the urgency of the case. A fully considered response was given by the defendant, however, within the timescale referred to ablve.

Does the claim include any issues arising from the Human Rights Act 1998? If Yes, state the articles which you contend have been breached in the space below. ☑ Yes ☐ No

SECTION 5 Detailed statement of grounds

☐ set out below   ☑ attached

See attached

SECTION 6 Details of remedy (including any interim remedy) being sought

(1) A quashing order, quashing the decisions referred to in Section 3 above.

(2) Further, or alternatively, a quashing order quashing the possession order granted by Style County Court on 29 June 2003.

(3) Further, or alternatively, a mandatory order requiring the defendant to reconsider its decision to apply for a warrant for possession to evict the claimant.

(4) Further, or alternatively, a declaration that the said decisions were unlawful and must be reconsidered.

(5) Interim relief in the form of a stay on the warrant for possession due to be executed on 21 August 2003.

(6) An order that this claim is suitable to be expedited and abridging the time for the filing and service of the defendant's evidence and detailed grounds of resisting this claim to 21 days.

(7) Further or other relief.

SECTION 7 Other applications

I wish to make an application for:-
(1) An order, should permission be granted, that the hearing of this application be expedited and that the time for filing and service of the defendant's evidence and detailed grounds of resisting this claim be abridged to 21 days.

(2) A direction whether it is necessary to the the Style County Court, which made the possession order the claimant seeks to quash, as an interested party, or to join it as a defendant.

SECTION 8 Statement of facts relied on

See attached.

Statement of Truth

I believe (The claimant believes) that the facts stated in this claim form are true.

Full name_____

Name of claimant's solicitor's firm _____

Signed_____ Position or office held_____

       Claimant ('s solicitor)   (if signing on behalf of firm or company)

SECTION 9 Supporting documents

If you do not have a document that you intend to use to support your claim, identify it, give the date when you expect it to be available and give reasons why it is not currently available in the box below.

Please tick the papers you are filing with this claim form and any you will be filing later.

☑ Statement of grounds   ☐ included   ☑ attached

☑ Statement of the facts relied on   ☐ included   ☑ attached

☐ Application to extended the time limit for filing the claim form   ☐ included   ☐ attached

☐ Application for directions   ☑ included   ☐ attached

☑ Any written evidence in support of the claim or application to extend time

☐ Where the claim for judicial review relates to a decision of a court or tribunal, an approved copy of the reasons
     for reaching that decision

☑ Copies of any documents on which the claimant proposes to rely

☑ A copy of the legal aid or CSLF certificate *(if legally represented)*

☑ Copies of any relevant statutory material

☑ A list of essential documents for advance reading by the court *(with page references to the passages relied upon)*

Reasons why you have not supplied a document and date when you expect it to be available:-

Signed _____ Claimant ('s Solicitor)_____

ATTACHED STATEMENT OF FACTS AND GROUNDS FOR REVIEW

R (Steabois) v Style Council

Claim Form sections 5 and 8

STATEMENT OF FACTS AND GROUNDS FOR REVIEW

FACTS

Introduction

1. The claimant is a single woman with three daughters: Terri (d.o.b: 12 November 1991); Jerri (d.o.b: 23 July 1993); and Kerri (d.o.b: 4 June 1995). She has a history of mental health problems including severe depression and has suffered repeated breakdowns.

2. On 16 October 2002, after a period of homelessness during which she suffered a breakdown, the claimant was granted by the defendant an introductory tenancy of a house at 6 Acacia Avenue. On the same date she made an application for housing benefit.

3. The claimant's benefit application was not processed. The claimant chased up the defendant's housing benefit department as best she could but given her state of health, she was not able to do so as proactively as she would have liked. In January 2003, the defendant's social services department agreed to look after the claimant's children for a short period while the claimant attempted to recover her health.

The benefit application

4. By letter of 16 January 2003 [(bundle pXX)], the defendant's housing benefit department demanded, pursuant to regulation 73 of the Housing Benefit (General) Regulations 1987 SI No 1971, as amended, (the 'Benefit Regulations') that the claimant produce details of her bank account and two recent utility bills to establish her residence at the premises. The claimant provided her most recent water and gas bills but informed the benefit office that she did not have a bank account. Instead, she provided a copy of her building society passbook [(bundle ppXX-XX)].

5. By letter of 23 March 2003 [(bundle ppXX-XX)], the benefits department informed her that her claim for benefit was refused as she had failed to comply with their reasonable request for information. Although two utility bills had been provided, one of these was a water bill which was not satisfactory and no bank statements had been provided. The building society passbook was

'insufficient' to award benefit because there was less than £25 in the account, which was 'not enough to live on', and it was 'not considered credible' that the claimant did not have a bank account.

6.   The claimant requested a revision of this decision (under regulation 4 of the Housing Benefit and Council Tax Benefit (Decisions and Appeals) Regulations 2001 SI No 1002) by letter of 28 February 2003 [(bundle pXX)].

The decision to evict the claimant

7.   On 21 May 2003, the defendant served a notice on the claimant under section 128 of the Housing Act 1996 (the '1996 Act'), informing her that they intended to issue proceedings to recover possession of her home. The reason given for this decision was that she was in arrears with her rent in the sum of £1,560.36. The letter informed her that proceedings would not be commenced before 24 June, 2003 and of her right to request a review of the decision to take proceedings under section 129 of the 1996 Act [(bundle ppXX-XX)].

8.   The claimant, without seeking legal advice, did request a review of the decision by letter of 23 May 2003. The grounds for the review were that the rent arrears were caused entirely by failures on the part of the defendant's housing benefit department, in that they had wrongly refused her benefit, which decision she had sought to get revised, a decision on which was still outstanding. She told them that she felt very low and was recovering from a breakdown. She also told them that her children were currently being looked after by the defendant's social services department but that it had been suggested to her that they ought to return to her within the following eight weeks. She requested the defendant to decide not to take any steps to evict her until their own benefit department had completed the revision process. [(bundle ppXX-XX)].

9.   The decision on review, given on 14 June 2003 was to confirm the original decision to recover possession of the claimant's home. The reasons given for this was that the rent arrears, now £1,665.49, were significant, there had been a long history of non-payment, and the tenant was 'deemed responsible' for either paying the rent personally or else arranging for housing benefit. The claimant had done neither and so was not 'deemed suitable to be a council tenant' [(bundle pXX)].

10   Possession proceedings were issued on 24 June 2003. At the first hearing on 29 June, 2003, the claimant attended in person – still without the benefit of legal advice – and asked the judge to allow her to defend the proceedings on the basis of her still outstanding request for a revision of the original refusal of housing benefit. The judge informed her, correctly, that under the scheme of Part V of the 1996 Act for the recovery of possession of premises let under introductory tenancies, so long as he was satisfied that the section 128 notice was valid and complied with the relevant statutory requirements, which

he was, he had no discretion to do anything other than make an order for possession. The judge ordered that the claimant must give up possession by 10 August, ie, six weeks from the date of the hearing (Housing Act 1989 s89) [(bundle pXX)].

11. By a letter of 15 July 2003, the claimant was informed that her request for a revision of the refusal of housing benefit had succeeded and that the benefit had been credited to her rent account [(bundle pXX)]. This had the effect of paying off her arrears of rent in full, as she had been paying the water rates element personally since the beginning of the tenancy.

12. On 11 August 2003, the defendant applied for a warrant for possession of the claimant's home. The warrant was issued the same day and notification was delivered by hand to the claimant informing her that a date for eviction of 21 August had been set [(bundle pXX)]. At this point, the claimant sought legal advice for the first time, from the solicitors she has now instructed in this claim.

13. By letter of 11 August 2003, the claimant's solicitor requested the defendant to reconsider the decision to evict in the light of the payment of the arrears. She enclosed medical evidence which the claimant had obtained via social services setting out the claimant's history of mental health problems and continuing vulnerabilities. She further informed the defendant of the effect of the decision to evict the claimant on her three children who had been expected to return to live with the claimant within a very few weeks' time. The claimant's solicitor's letter requested the defendant at the very least to agree to withdraw the warrant in order to facilitate a proper reconsideration of the position [(bundle ppXX-XX)].

14. In response to this letter, the claimant's solicitor was telephoned on 12 August 2003, by the defendant's Housing Department Evictions Team Leader, Mr Hugh Manleeg. Mr Manleeg informed the claimant's solicitor that despite the fact that the claimant's rent account was now clear, and in spite of the effect on her health and her children which would be caused by an eviction, he intended to evict the claimant in any event, on the basis that she was not suitable to be a council tenant, and that she had already had her 'day in court' before the review panel and in the court proceedings, and that the law was 'on the council's side'. He stated that he would not reconsider this decision and would not withdraw the warrant. He confirmed this decision in a letter of 12 August, faxed to the solicitor's offices that same day [(bundle ppXX-XX)].

15. The material part of the letter states:

As far as I am concerned, your client has already had her chance to be a council tenant but she blew it big time by not paying any rent (until the 11 hour before eviction). She has also already had her 'day in court' both at the review stage and in the county court but the fact remains that the law is on the council's side. I have no cause to reconsider the fair and reasonable position which this Authority has adopted in relation to your client. A person who does not pay the rent and does not arrange for housing benefit in due time is not suitable to be a council tenant, certainly not of this authority. The order will be executed as planned. She will be evicted. I trust this answers your query.

16.   By letter before claim of 12 August 2003, the claimant's solicitor informed the defendant that these proceedings would be issued unless the defendant agreed to withdraw the current warrant by 10.00am on 18 August 2003, in order to remove the imminent threat of eviction and facilitate further discussion [(bundle ppXX-XX)].

17.   The defendant responded by letter of 17 August 2003 [(bundle ppXX-XX)], refusing to withdraw the warrant or postpone the eviction, and raising for the very first time an allegation that the claimant had been 'guilty of anti-social behaviour' through her children 'while they were being looked after' by the defendant.

18.   The letter offered, purportedly as a means of resolving the dispute without recourse to the courts, to treat the claimant's letter before claim as a complaint, to be referred to the defendant's four-stage corporate complaints service. The average time it took for a complaint to complete all four stages was two years. In the interim, the eviction would go ahead so that the claimant would lose her home even if her complaint succeeded. She would only be accommodated while the complaint was pending if she could demonstrate 'exceptional hardship' and even then only in bed and breakfast accommodation where it was far from clear whether her children would be able to join her. If the complaint did succeed, it would only result in the defendant making bed and breakfast accommodation available until the claimant could make her own arrangements. This is no better than the claimant could achieve if she presented herself to the defendant as homeless (1996 Act, Part VII), as she is entitled to do, and was found to be intentionally homeless. It would be wholly unreasonable to expect the claimant to accept this offer.

19.   The claimant's eviction is still scheduled for 21 August 2003.

LEGAL FRAMEWORK

20.   Part V of the 1996 Act governs introductory tenancies. By section 125, where a local authority elect to operate an introductory tenancy regime, a tenancy granted by the authority will take effect as an introductory tenancy (with certain exceptions not here relevant), and therefore without security of tenure, for the first twelve months of its existence.

21.   By section 127 of the 1996 Act:

(1)   The landlord may only bring an introductory tenancy to an end by obtaining an order of the court for the possession of the dwelling-house.

(2)   The court shall make such an order unless the provisions of section 128 apply.

(3)   Where the court makes such an order, the tenancy comes to an end on the date on which the tenant is to give up possession in pursuance of the order.

22.   By section 128, of the 1996 Act:

(1)   The court shall not entertain proceedings for the possession of a dwelling-house let under an introductory tenancy unless the landlord has served on the tenant a notice of proceedings complying with this section.

(2)   The notice shall state that the court will be asked to make an order for the possession of the dwelling-house.

(3)   The notice shall set out the reasons for the landlord's decision to apply for such an order.

(4)   The notice shall specify a date after which proceedings for the possession of the dwelling-house may be begun.

The date so specified must not be earlier than the date on which the tenancy could, apart from this Chapter, be brought to an end by notice to quit given by the landlord on the same date as the notice of proceedings.

(5)   The court shall not entertain any proceedings for possession of the dwelling-house unless they are begun after the date specified in the notice of proceedings.

(6)   The notice shall inform the tenant of his right to request a review of the landlord's decision to seek an order for possession and of the time within which such a request must be made.

(7)   The notice shall also inform the tenant that if he needs help or advice about the notice, and what to do about it, he should take it immediately to a Citizens' Advice Bureau, a housing aid centre, a law centre or a solicitor.

23.   Section 129 of the 1996 Act makes provision for the conduct of the review referred to in section 128(6):

129(1)   A request for review of the landlord's decision to seek an order for possession of a dwelling-house let under an introductory tenancy must be made before the end of the period of 14 days beginning with the day on which the notice of proceedings is served.

(2)   On a request being duly made to it, the landlord shall review its decision.

(3)   The Secretary of State may make provision by regulations as to the procedure to be followed in connection with a review under this section.

Nothing in the following provisions affects the generality of this power.

(4)   Provision may be made by regulations–

(a) requiring the decision on review to be made by a person of appropriate seniority who was not involved in the original decision, and

        (b) as to the circumstances in which the person concerned is entitled to an oral hearing, and whether and by whom he may be represented at such a hearing.

(5)   The landlord shall notify the person concerned of the decision on the review.

        If the decision is to confirm the original decision, the landlord shall also notify him of the reasons for the decision.

(6)   The review shall be carried out and the tenant notified before the date specified in the notice of proceedings as the date after which proceedings for the possession of the dwelling-house may be begun.

24. The Introductory Tenants (Review) Regulations 1997 SI No 72 makes detailed provision for the conduct of reviews under section 129 of the 1996 Act.

25. In addition, the Secretary of State has given guidance to local authorities as to the operation of introductory tenancies and decisions to evict introductory tenants (Department of the Environment Circular 2/97).

GROUNDS FOR SEEKING JUDICIAL REVIEW

Ground 1

26. The defendant's decision to proceed with possession proceedings against the claimant was perverse and/or failed to take account of relevant considerations:

27. In the light of the following relevant factors, namely:

(a) the fact that the claimant's rent arrears, said to form the basis for the decision to recover possession, were caused entirely by the wrong and unlawful refusal of housing benefit to the claimant by defendant's own housing benefit department. The claimant's request for a revision of that refusal was still being considered by the defendant's housing benefit department at the date proceedings were issued;

(b) the effect of the Disability Discrimination Act 1995 (see *Devon Homes Ltd v Brazier* [2003] EWHC 574 (QB); (2003) 22 EG 141);

(c) the effect on the claimant's children of the claimant being evicted;

(d) the fact that the defendant was fully aware at all times of the claimant's health problems, difficulties with her children, and housing benefit problems;

(e) the defendant's failure to offer the claimant any assistance or support for her tenancy at any time prior to the decision to commence proceedings against the claimant; and

(f) the Secretary of State's guidance (circular 2/97), in particular paragraphs 11.1-11.9;

the decision to take possession proceedings pending the outcome of the housing benefit revision decision was perverse. It was not necessary for the defendant to commence such proceedings in order to preserve its position in the event that the housing benefit decision was adverse to the claimant, because the claimant's introductory tenancy 'trial period' (ie, 12 months after it was first granted) will not expire until 15 October 2003.

28. Further or alternatively, the said decision was reached without any or any proper account having been taken of the factors set out at paragraph 27 above.

Ground 2

29. The defendant has perversely refused:

(a) to reconsider, properly or at all, its decision to evict the claimant from her home in the light of the fundamental change in the claimant's circumstances, brought about by her repayment of all of her rent arrears; and

(b) to withdraw the warrant to evict the claimant, due to be executed on 21 August 2003, pending further negotiations or pending the outcome of these proceedings.

30. The repayment of the rent arrears in full, following the defendant's housing benefit department's decision to accede to the claimant's request for a revision of their original decision, taken into account with:

(a) the claimant's medical and family problems, of which the defendant is now aware, including the medical evidence submitted;

(b) the severely detrimental effect of losing her accommodation, given the likelihood of her not being able to have her children returned to her without accommodation;

(c) the fact that the defendant's own housing benefit department has, by revising its decision to refuse benefit to the claimant and paying all benefit due to her since the commencement of the tenancy, accepted that the claimant was not responsible for or at fault in relation to her rent arrears;

(d) the defendant's awareness of the claimant's personal and health problems when the tenancy was granted;

(e) the matters referred to at paragraph 27 above;

(f) the fact that the claimant's rent account is no longer in arrears; and

(g) the representations made by the claimant's solicitor concerning the case of *Devon Homes Ltd v Brazier* and the Disability Discrimination Act 1995, and the fact that the failure to have considered these issues prior to the decision to terminate the tenancy taken in March 2003, was likely to have rendered that decision unlawful;

render it perverse, and wrong in law, for the defendant to have refused to reconsider their position concerning the claimant's eviction or to withdraw the warrant referred to above.

31.   The only written response to the claimant's solicitor's letters, explaining this decision, has been the letter of 12 August 2003 set out at paragraph 15 above, which did not deal with these points, and the response to the claimant's letter before claim, which confirmed that the defendant considered that it had the law on its side, while denying knowledge of the claimant's personal problems (of which it was clearly aware, see, eg, bundle ppXX-XX; XX-XX and XX – extracts from the claimant's housing file case record); made new, unsubstantiated and wholly irrelevant allegations of anti-social behaviour against the claimant's children while being looked after by the defendant itself, and held against the claimant that fact that her rent had not been paid notwithstanding the matters referred to at paragraphs 27 and 30 above, concluding that she was not a 'suitable tenant'.

32.   This does not amount to any proper reconsideration, nor to any evidence of such a reconsideration having taken place.

33.   In the premises, the defendant's decision not to carry out any or any proper reconsideration of the claimant's case is irrational and unfair. In the alternative, any reconsideration which has taken place is irrational for the reasons set out above, has failed to take account of relevant considerations (as set out above) and has considered an irrelevant matter (the alleged anti-social behaviour – see ground 3 below).

Ground 3

34.   The defendant has taken account of an irrelevant consideration, namely the allegations of anti-social behaviour made against the claimant's children. This factor could have no possible relevance to the issues before the defendant for the following reasons:

(a)   they are wholly unparticularised, unsubstantiated and raised for the first time in the response to the claimant's pre-claim letter;

(b)   the allegations concern the behaviour of the children while they have been looked after by, and living in accommodation provided by, the defendant. Even if true, therefore, the behaviour was accordingly entirely outside the control of the claimant – and within the control of the defendant, wholly unrelated to her occupation of her home (having occurred nowhere near it), and cannot have any relevance to the question of whether she has acted in such a way as to render it lawful for the defendant to conclude that she should not be entitled to remain as a tenant of her home.

Ground 4

35. The defendant has failed to have regard to relevant considerations (see paragraphs 27 and 30 above) and has unlawfully discriminated against the claimant on the grounds of her disability.

36. In the taking of the original decision to take proceedings and, if any reconsideration of that decision has been carried out, in such reconsideration, there does not appear to have been any consideration of the effect of the Disability Discrimination Act 1995 or the *Brazier* case. None of the conditions in section 24(3) of the Disability Discrimination Act 1995 are made out in relation to the claimant's case. The defendant is on notice of the claimant's disabilities, but any reconsideration which has taken place has failed to have regard to this issue. Indeed, the initial decision to evict, taken in March 2003, was unlawful for this very reason.

Ground 5

37. The defendant has, in addition, acted incompatibly with the claimant's rights under article 8 of the Human Rights Act 1998, Schedule 1. In the alternative, the defendant has failed to have regard to such rights and accordingly failed to have regard to a relevant consideration and has misdirected itself in law.

38. In *Sheffield CC v Smart* [2002] EWCA Civ 4; [2002] HLR 34, Laws LJ, at para [40] stated:

> I can see that if a tenant sought a judicial review upon being served with a notice to quit, the Administrative Court might now look at the case more closely than upon the conventional *Wednesbury* approach, not least given the recent decision of their Lordships' House in *Daly* [2001] 2 WLR 1389, and especially the observations of Lord Cooke of Thorndon. I can see also that at the stage of the trial of the possession proceedings, there might be the rare case where something wholly exceptional has happened since service of the notice to quit, which fundamentally alters the rights and wrongs of the proposed eviction; and the county judge might be obliged to address it in deciding whether or not to make an order for possession. What I am clear the court cannot do is to take a position which disrupts the day-to-day operation of the scheme provided by Parliament in Part VII of Housing Act 1996; and in my judgment, not least given the particular matters relied on by Mr Underwood which I have set out at paragraph 23, that entails the conclusion that the balance of interests arising under Article 8(2) has in all its essentials been struck by the legislature.

39. It is accepted that in *Harrow LBC v Qazi* [2003] UKHL 43, Lords Scott and Millett gave speeches which are inconsistent with the above citation from the judgment of Laws LJ, holding that if an eviction is in accordance with domestic law, article 8 cannot provide a defence.

40. Nevertheless, Lord Hope expressly reserved his position on this issue at paragraph [79]:

> I wish to reserve my opinion as to whether it would be open to the tenant, in a wholly exceptional case, to raise these issues in the county court where proceedings for possession were being taken following the service of a notice to quit by the housing authority, bearing in mind as Lord Millett points out that its decision to serve the notice to quit would be judicially reviewable in the High Court so long as the application was made within the relevant time limit. The situation in the present case is different, as it was a notice to quit served by one of the joint tenants that terminated the tenancy.

41. Lords Bingham and Steyn did not agree with the speeches of Lords Scott and Millett, and dissented from the result of the appeal.

42. Moreover, the principles of administrative law form part of the relevant domestic law in relation to consideration of whether or not the proposed eviction of an introductory tenant is lawful (see *Manchester CC v Cochrane* [1999] 1 WLR 809, CA).

43. While, therefore, the county court, on a claim for possession of an introductory tenancy, has no power to consider human rights issues, the defendant cannot lawfully simply give them no weight and/or pay them no regard at all.

Ground 6

44. Further, or in the further alternative, if the defendant has reconsidered the matters referred to above, which is not accepted, its decision is disproportionate and perverse (see *R (Daly) v Secretary of State for the Home Department* [2001] UKHL 26; [2001] 2 AC 532, per Lord Steyn at [27]–[28]; and Lord Cooke of Thorndon at [32].

45. The consequences for the claimant of being evicted are so severe that, when considered alongside the basis for the eviction and the mischief which that eviction seeks to remedy (namely the non-payment of charges), the refusal to delay the eviction on the basis of an agreement to repay the amounts outstanding is perverse and disproportionate.

Signed [Dee Pechmoad]

CLAIMANT'S WITNESS STATEMENT (OPTIONAL)

Claimant
1st statement
B Steabois
Date: 19.08.03
Filed: 19.08.03
Exhibits: 'BS-1' – 'BS-2'

CO/............./2003

IN THE HIGH COURT OF JUSTICE
QUEEN'S BENCH DIVISION
ADMINISTRATIVE COURT

THE QUEEN

on the application of BEA STEABOIS

Claimant

and

STYLE COUNCIL

Defendant

WITNESS STATEMENT OF THE CLAIMANT

I, BEA STEABOIS, of 6 Acacia Avenue (the 'property'), visitation adviser, WILL SAY as follows:

INTRODUCTION

1. I am the claimant, and I make this statement in support of my claim for judicial review of the decisions of Style Council referred to in my Claim Form. I have read the statement of facts attached to the Claim Form and so far as they are within my knowledge, they are true. The purpose of this statement is not to repeat what has been said there but to give the court some further information about the events which caused me to be unable to pay my rent and about the course of the possession proceedings which were taken against me.

2. The facts contained in this statement are either within my own knowledge, in which case they are true, or I have obtained them from an outside source, in which case the source is indicated and they are true to the best of my knowledge and belief.

3.   I have suffered from depression and other mental health problems since I was a child. I now produce, marked 'BS-1', a copy of the latest medical report which I have recently obtained and which my solicitor tells me she sent to the defendant on 11 August 2003. This explains my problems in detail.

MY BENEFIT CLAIM

4.   I was granted an introductory tenancy of the property on 16 October 2002, and I applied for housing benefit by filling in a claim at the defendant's housing benefit office on the same day. I did not keep a copy of the claim form because the officer who I gave it to said that the department's copiers could not be used by members of the public and, as she put it, did I want to make my claim or didn't I?

5.   On the claim form, however, I put the property down as my home address and that of my children.

6.   I did not hear anything. I would normally have been far more proactive in chasing it up, because I have been a tenant all my adult life and I am aware of the importance of paying my rent on time. I was, however, very unwell at the time. I had split with my partner as a result of domestic violence and was homeless for about 6 months, during which time everything became too much for me and I suffered a breakdown.

7.   In November, 2002, I went into my local housing office to explain to them that I had applied for benefit but had not heard anything back, and that I was worried about my rent. No-one seemed very interested and they just told me I had to wait till the benefit came through. I asked if they could ring the benefit office for me, but they said the Benefit Office were having their Christmas party that day and I would not get any sense out of them.

8.   I telephoned the benefit office in early January about 10 times, but I just got an answerphone message which said that they could not come to the phone because they were training staff and I could not leave a message because the mailbox was full.

9.   Then I got a letter from the benefit office dated 16 January 2003 demanding that I provide evidence that I lived at the property. They said I had to give them copies of my bank statements and two recent utility bills to provide that I lived there. They did not explain why they thought I might not live there.

10.   I took in to the benefit office a copy of my most recent water and gas bills. Because I had only moved in to the property so recently, they were the first bills I had received. I also told the receptionist that I did not have any bank statements because I do not have a bank account. I showed her my building society pass book, which is the only account I have. She took a copy of it but said it would be no good because it was not a bank statement.

11.   Again, I heard nothing. Then, I got a letter dated 23 March 2003 in which the benefits manager stated that my benefit claim had been

refused because I had not provided the information they had reasonably requested. Although two utility bills had been provided, one of these was a water bill which was not satisfactory and no bank statements had been provided. The letter went on that the building society passbook was 'insufficient' to award benefit because there was less than £25 in the account, which was 'not enough to live on', and it was 'not considered credible' that I did not have a bank account in the twenty-first century.

12. I was so cross that I wrote back stating that I did not consider it credible that the benefits office could employ such an idiot in the twenty-first century, but I then regretted having been so rude and I wrote a letter of apology.

13. I should say that all this time, I had been paying £5 a week in cash at the housing office which was what I was told I would have to pay for my water rates.

14. I went to my local CAB and they told me that I had the right to ask for a 'revision' of the decision, and they explained how I could do this and helped me to write my request, which I sent off on. I requested a revision of this decision (under Regulation 4 of the Housing Benefit and Council Tax Benefit (Decisions and Appeals) Regulations 2001 SI No 1002) by letter of 28 March 2003.

15. Eventually, after all the possession proceedings had taken place, I heard from the benefit office on 15 July 2003 saying that they had decided to accept my case and that they had paid all the outstanding benefit into my rent account. The letter said that they would agree to work on the basis of the information that I had provided, given that they were not actually disputing that I lived at the property but were just saying that they needed evidence of it for their records.

16. I could not understand why this issue had caused so much fuss at all, but I was relieved, because I thought that at least now the defendant would not evict me from the property.

SOCIAL SERVICES

17. Going back to January, when I could not get any answer from the benefit office everything started getting too much for me again and so I asked the defendant's social services department to look after my children for me for a little while so that I could try and sort things out.

18. I was just worried and depressed for most of this year, about my benefit and not having the children, and breaking up with my partner. Then the possession notice came through the door in May and that just made everything worse. I asked for a review of that decision, and I told them that the benefit office's decision was wrong and that I had asked them to review it. I told them about my depression and my children, but I was not surprised that it went against me. The social worker had started saying that I must start thinking about having my children back because she thought that they were suffering from

being away from their mother and that I was suffering too, but I did not feel able to cope. Anyway, it looked like I was going to be evicted so there did not seem any point in trying to make arrangements for their return.

19.   Winning my benefit was such a relief, that I started to believe I could cope looking after my children – and I thought that the eviction was all behind me now that the rent had been paid off. I agreed with social services that my children would come and stay the weekend with me to start with so we could all get used to each other again.

20.   They did come home on the first weekend in August and it went so well that the social worker said that they should come back to me permanently really soon. I was so excited about the thought of them coming home, and I was just about to sort out the arrangements for this when I got the eviction notice from the court. I was devastated.

21.   I had not sought legal advice before (other than going to the CAB about my benefit) because I was told by the housing officer that I did not have a leg to stand on and that the defendant 'had the law on their side'. The housing officers all kept saying this whenever I saw them at court or when I went to the housing office or pay my water rates and asked them about what was going on.

22.   I was so devastated at the thought that my children might not come home to me after all that I went to see my solicitor, and she got in touch with the defendant and wrote to them and advised me that I had a good case for judicial review.

23.   I now produce a bundle of documents containing all the correspondence I have referred to in this statement, marked 'BS-2'.

CONCLUSION

24.   I do not understand why the defendant still wants to evict me. All the rent has been paid off and it is their fault that it wasn't paid in the first place because of the stance they took about the information I had provided. The fact that it was their fault is confirmed by the fact that on review, the review officer said that he agreed with me that the information I had provided was adequate for the purpose.

25.   If I lose my home now I will not be able to have my children live with me, which will devastate me and them, and for no good reason. I will also be homeless and I am afraid that because the possession order was made because the rent did not get paid, the homelessness department might say that I am intentionally homeless and refuse to find me anywhere to go. I have no deposit for a private sector tenancy and no confidence in the benefit office to pay me benefit in time to stop me being evicted again even if I did find somewhere to go.

26.   Even if an intentional homeless decision would be challengeable, I am advised by my solicitor that the council do not have to provide me with accommodation while I challenge it. I do not know where I could go if I were evicted from the property. I have no family or

friends I could stay with. I would have to sleep on the street or try to go back to live with my ex-partner, but I do not feel I can do that bearing in mind the violence I suffered from him, which caused me to leave in the first place.

27. There are no rent arrears, the benefit is now being paid, and it was entirely the defendant's fault that the benefit and so the rent were not paid to start with. There is therefore no prejudice to the defendant in letting me stay in the property, at least on a temporary basis while this claim is being dealt with. For all of these reasons, I would respectfully request the court to allow my claim for judicial review and grant me the interim relief I seek.

STATEMENT OF TRUTH

I believe that the facts stated in this witness statement are true

Signed: Bea Steabois
          (Claimant)
Date: 19/8/03

URGENCY FORM N463

Judicial Review
Application for urgent consideration

This form must be completed by the Claimant or the Claimant's advocate if exceptional urgency is being claimed and the application needs to be determined within a certain time scale.

The claimant, or the claimant's solicitors must serve this form on the defendant(s) and any interested parties with the N461 Judicial review claim form.

To the Defendant(s) and Interested party(ies) Representations as to the urgency of the claim may be made by defendants or interested parties to the Administrative Court Office by fax - 020 7947 6802

In the High Court of Justice	
Administrative Court	
Claim No.	CO/1828/2003
Claimant(s) *(including ref.)*	Bea Steabois
Defendant(s)	Style Council
Interested Parties	None

SECTION 1 Reasons for urgency

1. This challenge concerns the defendant's decision to evict the claimant from her home.

2. The urgency arises from the fact that the eviction is currently scheduled to take place on 21 August 2003. The defendant has refused to postpone it pending the resolution of these proceedings. Accordingly, the claimant requires interim relief to stay the eviction on that date, pending the outcome of these proceddings.

SECTION 2 Proposed timetable *(tick the boxes and complete the following statements that apply)*

☑ a) The N461 application for permission should be considered within by 4.00pm today ___ hours/days

☑ b) Abridgement of time is sought for the lodging of acknowledgements of service

☐ c) If permission for judicial review is granted, a substantive hearing is sought by _____ (date)

SECTION 3 Interim relief *(state what interim relief is sought and why in the box below)*

A draft order must be attached.

1. The claimant seeks an interim order staying thr proposed eviction of the claimant from her home to 21 August 2003. and forbidding the defendant from executing the possession order it obtained against her dated 29 June 2003.

2. The claimant is an introductory tenant against whom an order for possession has been made. The claimant challenges the defendant's decision to commence the proceedings leading to the order for possession and also decisions to apply for a warrant for possession. If interim relief is not granted, the warrant will be executed before this claim has been resolved, leaving the claimant homeless and rending the claim academic, even if well founded.

3. Accordingly, the claimant seeks the orders referred to at paragraph 1 above, in order to preserve her position pending the resolution of these proceedings.

SECTION 4 Service

A copy of this form of application was served on the defendant(s) and interested parties as follows:

Defendant

☑ by fax machine to   time sent
┌─Fax no.──────────┐ ┌─time────┐
│ 0101 123 987   │ │ 9.28am │
└──────────────────┘ └─────────┘

☐ by handing it to or leaving it with
┌─name─────────────────────────┐
│   │
└──────────────────────────────┘

☐ by e-mail to
┌─e-mail address───────────────┐
│   │
└──────────────────────────────┘

Date served
┌─Date─────────────┐
│ 19/08/2003   │
└──────────────────┘

Interested party

☐ by fax machine to   time sent
┌─Fax no.──────────┐ ┌─time────┐
│   │ │   │
└──────────────────┘ └─────────┘

☐ by handing it to or leaving it with
┌─name─────────────────────────┐
│   │
└──────────────────────────────┘

☐ by e-mail to
┌─e-mail address───────────────┐
│   │
└──────────────────────────────┘

Date served
┌─Date─────────────┐
│   │
└──────────────────┘

Name of claimant's advocate
┌─name─────────────────────────┐
│ Dee Pechmoad .   │
└──────────────────────────────┘

Claimant (claimant's advocate)
┌─Signed───────────────────────┐
│   │
└──────────────────────────────┘

DRAFT ORDER

CO/1823/2003

IN THE HIGH COURT OF JUSTICE
QUEEN'S BENCH DIVISION
ADMINISTRATIVE COURT

THE QUEEN

on the application of BEA STEABOIS

Claimant

and

STYLE COUNCIL

Defendant

---

draft/ORDER

ON reading the claimant's Claim Form, Application for Urgent Consideration and Witness Statement, all dated 19 August 2003.

IT IS ORDERED

1. that the warrant for possession of 6 Acacia Avenue, (the 'property'), due to be executed on 21 August 2003, be stayed until the final resolution of these proceedings or further order of this Court;

2   that the defendant be prohibited from executing the order for possession of the property, dated 29 June 2003, until the final resolution of these proceedings or the further order of this Court;

3. that the defendant do have permission to apply to the court for the variation or discharge of this order on 48 hours written notice to the claimant's solicitor.

ACKNOWLEDGEMENT OF SERVICE N462

Judicial Review
Acknowledgment of Service

Name and address of person to be served

name
Bea Steabois

address
c/o Dee Pechmoad
12 High Street

In the High Court of Justice	
Administrative Court	
Claim No.	CO/1823/2003
Claimant(s) *(including ref.)*	BEA STEABOIS
Defendant(s)	STYLE COUNCIL
Interested Parties	

SECTION A
Tick the appropriate box

1. I intend to contest all of the claim ☑

   }   complete sections B, C, D and E

2. I intend to contest part of the claim ☐

3. I do not intend to contest the claim ☐   complete section E

4. The defendant (interested party) is a court or tribunal and **intends** to make a submission. ☐   complete sections B, C and E

5. The defendant (interested party) is a court or tribunal and **does not intend** to make a submission. ☐   complete sections B and E

Note: If the application seeks to judicially review the decision of a court or tribunal, the court or tribunal need only provide the Administrative Court with as much evidence as it can about the decision to help the Administrative Court perform its judicial function.

SECTION B
Insert the name and address of any person you consider should be added as an interested party.

name

address

Telephone no.   **Fax no.**

E-mail address

name

address

Telephone no.   **Fax no.**

E-mail address

SECTION C

Summary of grounds for contesting the claim. If you are contesting only part of the claim, set out which part before you give your grounds for contesting it. If you are a court or tribunal filing a submission, please indicate that this is the case.

1. The claimant's grounds are hopeless, for the following reasons.

2. The defendant was entitled to conclude that the claimant was not a suitable tenant, to issue proceedings against her and to enforce the posession order obtained (including to refuse to stay the execution of the warrant pending the outcome of these proceedings, on the basis that for a period of more than seven months, she did not pay any rent due on her introductory tenancy.

3. The fact that the claimant was eventually awarded housing benefit does not affect this. It does not follow from the award of housing benefit on revision that the initial refusal of benefit was wrong, because the claimant gave additional information to the benefits department on her request for the revision that she had not given when making her original claim.

4. In any event:
  (i) it is the tenant's responsibility to pay the rent;
  (ii) it is not the defendant's responsibility to 'support' the claimant in her tenancy in the sense of awarding her benefit to which she was not entitled on the basis of the claim form she submitted or applying for housing benefit for her.

5. At no time prior to the letter before claim did the claimant inform the defendant of her ill-health or of her children being looked after by the defendant. The defendant could not, therefore, have taken such considerations into account when issuing proceedings. By the time of the letter before claim, other factors outweighed them, including:
  (i) the claimant's failure to mention them until the eleventh hour before her eviction;
  (ii) the claimant's failure to challenge the decisions at the time of the possession hearing (by seeking an adjournment of that hearing in order to seek judicial review then. It is an abuse of the process of the court for the claimant to seek to delay her eviction by bringing proceedings at the last minuute which should have been brought months earlier.

6. The claimant's human rights and disability discrimination claims are unarguable and nonsensical. The decision of the majority of the House of Lords in Harrow LBC v Qazi [2003] UKHL 43 plainly rules out a human rights challenge on the basis that Human Rights Act 1998 Sch 1, article 8 cannot confer any right to remain in occupation of the premises additional to those which exist as a matter of property law. The comments of the Court of Appeal in Sheffield CC v Smart [2002] EWCA Civ 4; [2002] HLR 34 cannot withstand the Qazi decsion.

7. North Devon Homes Ltd v Brazier [2003] EWHC 574 (QB); (2003) 6 CCLR 245 has no relevance to this case because the claimant is, since the possession order expired, an unlawful occupier. Her disability has nothing to do with her eviction. R (Daly) v Secretary of State for the Home Department [2001]21 WLR 1389, HL, is wholly irrelevant to this claim.

8. The purpose of the introductory tenancy regime was to permit local authorities to evict unsuitable tenants without the need for lengthy and expensive legal procedures. The judicial review court should not be used as a substitute for the county court in this type of case, where Parliament has expressly legislated to the contrary.

9. The defendant was entitled to make the decisions it did and permission to proceed with this claim should be refused.

[SOLICITOR/COUNSEL TO THE COUNCIL]

SECTION D

Give details of any directions you will be asking the court to make, or tick the box to indicate that a separate application notice is attached.

SECTION E

*delete as appropriate

*(I believe)(The defendant believes) that the facts stated in this form are true.

*I am duly authorised by the defendant to sign this statement.

(if signing on behalf of firm or company, court or tribunal)

Position or office held

(To be signed by you or by your solicitor or litigation friend)

Signed

Date

Give an address to which notices about this case can be sent to you

name

address

Telephone no.

Fax no.

E-mail address

If you have instructed counsel, please give their name address and contact details below.

name

address

Telephone no.

Fax no.

E-mail address

Completed forms, together with a copy, should be lodged with the Administrative Court Office, Room C315, Royal Courts of Justice, Strand, London, WC2A 2LL, within 21 days of service of the claim upon you, and further copies should be served on the Claimant(s), any other Defendant(s) and any interested parties within 7 days of lodgement with the Court.

RENEWAL OF CLAIM (FORM 86B)

IN THE HIGH COURT OF JUSTICE   CO Ref No: CO/1354/2003
QUEEN'S BENCH DIVISION
ADMINISTRATIVE COURT

In the matter of a claim for Judicial Review

The Queen on the application of
BEA STEABOIS

versus

STYLE COUNCIL

Notice of RENEWAL of claim for permission to apply for Judicial Review (CPR 54.12).

1.   *This notice must be lodged in the Administrative Court Office and served upon the defendant (and interested parties who were served with the claim form) within 7 days of the service on the claimant or his solicitor of the notice that the claim for permission has been refused.*

2.   *If this form has not been lodged within 7 days of service (para 1 above) please set out the* **reasons for delay:**

3.   *Set out below the grounds for renewing the application:*

1.   The learned judge wrongly concluded that the claimant's claim was wholly misconceived. The claimant repeats her pleaded grounds for review and the matters and her witness statement.

2.   The learned judge was also wrong to state that the claimant had delayed because she had not sought an adjournment of her possession proceedings in order to challenge the defendant's decision at that time. At the date of the hearing of the possession claim, on 29 June 2003, the claimant was in an entirely different situation:

   (a)   she had no legal advice or representation;

   (b)   and her housing benefit was still in dispute, with the defendant asserting that she was not entitled to any housing benefit, and her rent account was therefore considerably in arrears (see bundle ppXX-XX).

3.   In any event, it is not suggested that the rights of any third parties are in any way affected by these proceedings, so as to call for particular or unusual promptness in bringing a claim. The claimant is aware of the primary obligation to act promptly, but she is still within the backstop period of three months for an application and the facts of this matter are such that she should be considered to have acted promptly.

4. *Please supply:*
COUNSEL'S NAME: THEAR TOFNOYS
COUNSEL'S TELEPHONE NUMBER: 0101 123 321

Signed:
Dated:
Claimant's Ref No.
Tel No. 0101 123 321
Fax No. 0101 123 654

To the Master of the Crown Office, Royal Courts of Justice, Strand, London, WC2A 2LL

DETAILED GROUNDS FOR DEFENDING CLAIM

CO/1823/2003

IN THE HIGH COURT OF JUSTICE
QUEEN'S BENCH DIVISION
ADMINISTRATIVE COURT

THE QUEEN

On the application of BEA STEABOIS

Claimant

and

STYLE COUNCIL

Defendant

DETAILED GROUNDS FOR DEFENDING THE CLAIM

HOUSING BENEFIT
1. The claimant's case depends on the twin propositions that the payment of her housing benefit on review, reducing her arrears to nothing:

(a) must necessarily mean that the defendant was wrong to have refused it initially; and

(b)   must necessarily render it now unreasonable to continue with her eviction.

2.   Neither of these propositions is correct. The mere fact that, on review the defendant's housing benefit review officer was prepared to waive the requirements originally imposed by the benefits manager in no way indicates that those original requirements were unreasonable or impossible for the claimant to have complied with. It simply means that the reviews officer considered it appropriate to waive them in the circumstances of this particular review.

PUBLIC LAW CHALLENGE

3.   Nor is the decision whether or not to evict limited to consideration of only the identical circumstances to those which formed the subject of the housing benefit review. The introductory tenancy regime left it to the landlord to decide whether or not it wished to continue with a person as its tenant. There is no right for the county court to interfere with that decision, given that there is no defence to possession proceedings other than the invalidity of the section 128 notice which is not even alleged here.

4.   While it is not suggested that this excludes the jurisdiction of the court on judicial review, it is not for this court to second guess the decision of the local authority on the merits. Indeed, it is suggested that the court should only interfere with such decisions sparingly, by analogy with the well-known passage of Lord Brightman in *R v Hillingdon LBC ex p Puhlhofer* [1986] AC 484.

Relevant considerations

5.   As can be seen from the witness statement of Hugh Manleeg, the defendant took account only of relevant matters and considered all relevant matters known to them at the time. The claimant can hardly claim, in a public law challenge, that the defendant was somehow obliged to take account of matters she never put before them. It can be seen from the tenancy file exhibited to Mr Manleeg's statement that none of the matters now complained of relating to the claimant's mental health and her children were before the defendant at the relevant time. When they were put before Mr Friedman at the eleventh hour, he was entitled to refuse to change his mind.

DECISION TO ISSUE PROCEEDINGS

6.   It is the tenant's responsibility to ensure the rent is paid, and properly to process any benefit claim she may make. The claimant did not do so. Nor did she persuade a review panel that she should not be evicted. Critically, she is not seeking to challenge the panel's decision. Once it is accepted that the panel was entitled to reach the decision it did (as the claimant must be taken to accept in the absence of challenge), the decision to issue proceedings resultant on the decision of the review panel must be unchallengeable.

7.   Parliament did not set up a review procedure only to require officers to reconsider the review which had just happened before proceedings could be validly brought. To impute such an intention to Parliament is absurd.

HUMAN RIGHTS/DISABILITY DISCRIMINATION

8.   The claimant's human rights point is unarguable following *Harrow LBC v Qazi* [2003] UKHL 43, in which the House of Lords rejected an almost identical argument to that now raised by the claimant. That argument should be dismissed.

9.   If the claimant did not alert the defendant to her disability, it can hardly be said as a matter of logical possibility, that the defendant discriminated against her on the grounds of it. The point of *Brazier* was that the disability was the reason for the conduct which led to the eviction. Here, the reason for the eviction is that the claimant is an unlawful occupier, a possession order having been made against her. The two situations are entirely different.

RELIEF

10.   In any event, the Court should in its discretion refuse any relief to the claimant on the grounds of her delay. The correct time for her to have challenged the decisions of which she now complains was at the time of the possession order being made. She could and should have sought an adjournment of the proceedings in order to bring this claim *Manchester CC v Cochrane* [1999] 1 WLR 825, CA.

11.   No reason whatsoever has been advanced to explain why this was not done, other than a bald assertion that the claimant was not legally represented. That was the claimant's choice. It did not prevent her from challenging the defendant at the appropriate time and she should not now be permitted to do so some two months later, given the prejudice and detriment to good administration it will cause: namely the defendant will lose this unit of accommodation which it could otherwise have offered to one of the 312 families waiting for accommodation of this sort on its waiting list.

12   For these reasons, this claim must be rejected.

Signed

[SOLICITOR/COUNSEL TO THE COINCIL]
18 October 2003

DEFENDANT'S EVIDENCE

Defendant
1st statement
H Manleeg
Date: 15.10.03
Filed: 15.10.03
Exhibit 'HM-1'

CO/1823/2003

IN THE HIGH COURT OF JUSTICE
QUEEN'S BENCH DIVISION
ADMINISTRATIVE COURT

THE QUEEN

On the application of BEA STEABOIS

Claimant

and

STYLE COUNCIL

Defendant

WITNESS STATEMENT OF HUGH MANLEEG

I, HUGH MANLEEG, of Style Council, Council Chambers, Local Government Officer, WILL SAY as follows:

1.   I am the defendant's Housing Department Evictions Team Leader and I am authorised to make this witness statement on behalf of the defendant, resisting this application for judicial review. I have been employed in my current post for five years, before which I was the manager of the Anytown Civic Amenity Tip for seven years.

2.   I made all the decisions challenged in this case, and so the facts stated in this witness statement are within my own knowledge and are true. I now produce, marked 'HM-1' a true copy of the claimant's tenancy file.

DECISION TO TAKE PROCEEDINGS

3. I took the decision in May 2003 to issue proceedings for possession against the claimant, she having already been served with a notice of proceedings under section 128 of the Housing Act 1996, and having fought and lost a review under section 129 if the same Act. I took no part in the review, but a panel of elected members decided to uphold the section 128 notice.

4. I have to say that this was one of the factors I took into account when deciding to issue proceedings. It seemed to me that, Parliament having provided for a review procedure under section 129 which must be completed before the date specified in the section 128 notice as the date after which possession proceedings may be begun (section 129(6)), it must have been Parliament's intention that the decision on the review will be influential in the decision whether or not to issue proceedings. I am no saying it is the only relevant factor, but it was a strong indication to me that proceedings should be issued.

5. What was there to set against that? Not very much. The claimant was more than £1,600 in arrears with her rent; she had been refused housing benefit on the basis of her own default in supplying information requested by the housing benefits department. The only matter to counter all of that was the fact that she had put in a request for a revision of the refusal of her housing benefit. I did not know about her children, nor about her depression because she had never put this information before the defendant.

6. Such requests are extremely common, however, and do not indicate without more that the request has any merit. I thought this request stood very little chance of success. Although with hindsight, that turned out not to be so, and the revision was made, I cannot be criticised for not being able to foresee that happening. It had not happened when I made my decision so I could not have considered it. Weighing up all these factors, I decided that we should issue proceedings. There was no material before me to indicate the contrary.

DECISION TO ISSUE WARRANT/REFUSAL TO WITHDRAW WARRANT

7. I now turn to explain the decision to request the warrant and my refusal to withdraw it. Style Council obtained a possession order from the judge. There was no reason why I should not enforce it. The fact that the housing benefit had finally been paid did not alter the fact that the defendant had been kept out its money for some 9 months by the time of that payment. The defendant is a local authority not a bank giving interest-free loans. Paying the rent in full and on time is the tenant's responsibility. I am of course sympathetic to anyone who has difficulties claiming housing benefit, but the fact remains that if the claimant had produced the information requested in January 2003, when it was requested, none of this would ever have happened.

8. It does not follow, moreover, from the award of housing benefit on revision that the initial refusal was wrong. The decision on revision was, as I read it, made as a concession to the claimant, not by way of a strict application of the Housing Benefit Regulations. In any event, I cannot be bound by a decision of a housing benefit officer. Our roles are entirely different, as are the considerations to be taken into account.

9. The claimant, by this time, had already had two bites at the cherry of retaining her tenancy: in the review of the decision to serve the section 128 notice and at court on the possession proceeding when she could have applied for an adjournment to seek judicial review but did not (for whatever reason).

10. For all these reasons, I took the view, as I believe I was entitled to, that the claimant was an unsuitable tenant. because persistently she did not pay her rent, did not organise her housing benefit, and did not, therefore, behave in a tenant-like manner. Nor did she challenge the making of a possession order at the appropriate time. In fact she did nothing at all until the eleventh hour, at which point she suddenly announced a number of additional problems never previously raised.

11. I do not believe, in the circumstances, that those matters – at this stage – oblige me to change my mind. Style Council does not want the claimant as their tenant. That decision is reasonable and supportable. The implementation of it is the very purpose of the introductory tenancy regime.

12. For these reasons, I would ask the court to refuse this application.

STATEMENT OF TRUTH

I believe the facts contained in this witness statement to be true

Signed: Hugh Manleeg
Date: 15/10/03

Dated this 15th day of October 2003.

CONSENT ORDER

C0/1823/2003

IN THE HIGH COURT OF JUSTICE
QUEEN'S BENCH DIVISION
ADMINISTRATIVE COURT

THE QUEEN

On the application of BEA STEABOIS

Claimant

and

STYLE COUNCIL

Defendant

CONSENT ORDER

ON the parties coming to terms in this application

BY CONSENT, it is ORDERED:

1. that the claimant's application for judicial review be dismissed;
2. that the defendant shall pay the claimant's costs of and incidental to this application, to be subject to detailed assessment if not agreed.
3. that there be a detailed assessment of the claimant's publicly funded costs.

The reason for the making of this order is that the defendant has agreed that the possession order obtained by the defendant from the Style County Court on 29 June 2003 (copy attached) be set aside and that the possession proceedings within which they were made should be dismissed by consent. Accordingly, this claim is now rendered academic, and there is no need for the court to adjudicate on it.

Signed   Signed
Thear Tofnoys   Paula Fastwun
Counsel for the claimant   Counsel for the defendant
4 November, 2003.   4 November 2003.

Supreme Court Act 1981 ss29–31 and 43

SUPREME COURT ACT 1981

Orders of mandamus, prohibition and certiorari

29(1)   [Subject to subsection (3A),][1] the High Court shall have jurisdiction to make orders of mandamus, prohibition and certiorari in those classes of cases in which it had power to do so immediately before the commencement of this Act.

(2)   Every such order shall be final, subject to any right of appeal therefrom.

(3)   In relation to the jurisdiction of the Crown Court, other than its jurisdiction in matters relating to trial on indictment, the High Court shall have all such jurisdiction to make orders of mandamus, prohibition or certiorari as the High Court possesses in relation to the jurisdiction of an inferior court.

(3A)   The High Court shall have no jurisdiction to make orders of mandamus, prohibition or certiorari in relation to the jurisdiction of a court-martial in matters relating to–

(a)   trial by court-martial for an offence, or

(b)   appeals from a Standing Civilian Court;

and in this subsection 'court-martial' means a court-martial under the Army Act 1955, the Air Force Act 1955 or the Naval Discipline Act 1957.[2]

(4)   The power of the High Court under any enactment to require justices of the peace or a judge or officer of a county court to do any act relating to the duties of their respective offices, or to require a magistrates' court to state a case for the opinion of the High Court, in any case where the High Court formerly had by virtue of any enactment jurisdiction to make a rule absolute, or an order, for any of those purposes, shall be exercisable by order of mandamus.

(5)   In any enactment–

(a)   references to a writ of mandamus, of prohibition or of certiorari shall be read as references to the corresponding order; and

(b)   references to the issue or award of any such writ shall be read as references to the making of the corresponding order.

(6)   In subsection (3) the reference to the Crown Court's jurisdiction in

---

1   Words in square brackets inserted by Armed Forces Act 2001 s23(1) and (2).

2   Subsection 3A inserted by Armed Forces Act 2001 s23(1) and (3).

matters relating to trial on indictment does not include its jurisdiction relating to orders under section 17 of the Access to Justice Act 1999.[3]

Injunctions to restrain persons from acting in offices in which they are not entitled to act

30(1) Where a person not entitled to do so acts in an office to which this section applies, the High Court may–

(a) grant an injunction restraining him from so acting; and

(b) if the case so requires, declare the office to be vacant.

(2) This section applies to any substantive office of a public nature and permanent character which is held under the Crown or which has been created by any statutory provision or royal charter.

Application for judicial review

31(1) An application to the High Court for one or more of the following forms of relief, namely–

(a) an order of mandamus, prohibition or certiorari;

(b) a declaration or injunction under subsection (2); or

(c) an injunction under section 30 restraining a person not entitled to do so from acting in an office to which that section applies,

shall be made in accordance with rules of court by a procedure to be known as an application for judicial review.

(2) A declaration may be made or an injunction granted under this subsection in any case where an application for judicial review, seeking that relief, has been made and the High Court considers that, having regard to–

(a) the nature of the matters in respect of which relief may be granted by orders of mandamus, prohibition or certiorari;

(b) the nature of the persons and bodies against whom relief may be granted by such orders; and

(c) all the circumstances of the case,

it would be just and convenient for the declaration to be made or of the injunction to be granted, as the case may be.

(3) No application for judicial review shall be made unless the leave of the High Court has been obtained in accordance with rules of court; and the court shall not grant leave to make such an application unless it considers that the applicant has a sufficient interest in the matter to which the application relates.

(4) On an application for judicial review the High Court may award damages to the applicant if–

(a) he has joined with his application a claim for damages arising from any matter to which the application relates; and

3   Subsection 6 inserted by Access to Justice Act 1999 s24, Sch 4 paras 21 and 23.

(b)   the court is satisfied that, if the claim had been made in an action begun by the applicant at the time of making his application, he would have been awarded damages.

(5)   If, on an application for judicial review seeking an order of certiorari, the High Court quashes the decision to which the application relates, the High Court may remit the matter to the court, tribunal or authority concerned, with a direction to reconsider it and reach a decision in accordance with the findings of the High Court.

(6)   Where the High Court considers that there has been undue delay in making an application for judicial review, the court may refuse to grant–

(a)   leave for the making of the application; or

(b)   any relief sought on the application,

if it considers that the granting of the relief sought would be likely to cause substantial hardship to, or substantially prejudice the rights of, any person or would be detrimental to good administration.

(7)   Subsection (6) is without prejudice to any enactment or rule of court which has the effect of limiting the time within which an application for judicial review may be made.

Power of High Court to vary sentence on certiorari

43(1)   Where a person who has been sentenced for an offence–

(a)   by a magistrates' court; or

(b)   by the Crown Court after being convicted of the offence by a magistrates' court and committed to the Crown Court for sentence; or

(c)   by the Crown Court on appeal against conviction or sentence,

applies to the High Court in accordance with section 31 for an order of certiorari to remove the proceedings of the magistrates' court or the Crown Court into the High Court, then, if the High Court determines that the magistrates' court or the Crown Court had no power to pass the sentence, the High Court may, instead of quashing the conviction, amend it by substituting for the sentence passed any sentence which the magistrates' court or, in a case within paragraph (b), the Crown Court had power to impose.

(2)   Any sentence passed by the High Court by virtue of this section in substitution for the sentence passed in the proceedings of the magistrates' court or the Crown Court shall, unless the High Court otherwise directs, begin to run from the time when it would have begun to run if passed in those proceedings; but in computing the term of the sentence, any time during which the offender was released on bail in pursuance of section 37(1)(d) of the Criminal Justice Act 1948 shall be disregarded.

(3)   Subsections (1) and (2) shall, with the necessary modifications, apply in relation to any order of a magistrates' court or the Crown Court which is made on, but does not form part of, the conviction of an offender as they apply in relation to a conviction and sentence.

Civil Procedure Rules (extracts)

PART 8

ALTERNATIVE PROCEDURE FOR CLAIMS

Contents of this part

Types of claim in which part 8 procedure may be followed

8.1(1) The Part 8 procedure is the procedure set out in this Part.

(2) A claimant may use the Part 8 procedure where–

    (a) he seeks the court's decision on a question which is unlikely to involve a substantial dispute of fact; or

    (b) paragraph (6) applies.

(3) The court may at any stage order the claim to continue as if the claimant had not used the Part 8 procedure and, if it does so, the court may give any directions it considers appropriate.

(4) Paragraph (2) does not apply if a practice direction provides that the Part 8 procedure may not be used in relation to the type of claim in question.

(5) Where the claimant uses the Part 8 procedure he may not obtain default judgment under Part 12.

(6)   A rule or practice direction may, in relation to a specified type of proceedings–

(a)   require or permit the use of the Part 8 procedure; and

(b)   disapply or modify any of the rules set out in this Part as they apply to those proceedings.

(Rule 8.9 provides for other modifications to the general rules where the Part 8 procedure is being used)

Contents of the claim form

8.2   Where the claimant uses the Part 8 procedure the claim form must state –

(a)   that this Part applies;

(b)   (i)   the question which the claimant wants the court to decide; or

(ii)   the remedy which the claimant is seeking and the legal basis for the claim to that remedy;

(c)   if the claim is being made under an enactment, what that enactment is;

(d)   if the claimant is claiming in a representative capacity, what that capacity is; and

(e)   if the defendant is sued in a representative capacity, what that capacity is.

(Part 22 provides for the claim form to be verified by a statement of truth)

(Rule 7.5 provides for service of the claim form)

(The costs practice direction sets out the information about a funding arrangement to be provided with the claim form where the claimant intends to seek to recover an additional liability)

('Funding arrangement' and 'additional liability' are defined in rule 43.2)

Issue of claim form without naming defendants

8.2A(1) A practice direction may set out circumstances in which a claim form may be issued under this Part without naming a defendant.

(2)   The practice direction may set out those cases in which an application for permission must be made by application notice before the claim form is issued.

(3)   The application notice for permission–

(a)   need not be served on any other person; and

(b)   must be accompanied by a copy of the claim form that the applicant proposes to issue.

(4)   Where the court gives permission it will give directions about the future management of the claim.

Acknowledgment of service

8.3(1) The defendant must–

    (a) file an acknowledgment of service in the relevant practice form not more than 14 days after service of the claim form; and

    (b) serve the acknowledgment of service on the claimant and any other party.

(2) The acknowledgment of service must state–

    (a) whether the defendant contests the claim; and

    (b) if the defendant seeks a different remedy from that set out in the claim form, what that remedy is.

(3) The following rules of Part 10 (acknowledgment of service) apply–

    (a) rule 10.3(2) (exceptions to the period for filing an acknowledgment of service); and

    (b) rule 10.5 (contents of acknowledgment of service).

(4) Revoked

(The costs practice direction sets out the information about a funding arrangement to be provided with the acknowledgment of service where the defendant intends to seek to recover an additional liability) ('Funding arrangement' and 'additional liability' are defined in rule 43.2)

Consequence of not filing an acknowledgment of service

8.4(1) This rule applies where–

    (a) the defendant has failed to file an acknowledgment of service; and

    (b) the time period for doing so has expired.

(2) The defendant may attend the hearing of the claim but may not take part in the hearing unless the court gives permission.

Filing and serving written evidence

8.5(1) The claimant must file any written evidence on which he intends to rely when he files his claim form.

(2) The claimant's evidence must be served on the defendant with the claim form.

(3) A defendant who wishes to rely on written evidence must file it when he files his acknowledgment of service.

(4) If he does so, he must also, at the same time, serve a copy of his evidence on the other parties.

(5) The claimant may, within 14 days of service of the defendant's evidence on him, file further written evidence in reply.

(6) If he does so, he must also, within the same time limit, serve a copy of his evidence on the other parties.

(7) The claimant may rely on the matters set out in his claim form as evidence under this rule if the claim form is verified by a statement of truth.

Evidence – general

8.6(1) No written evidence may be relied on at the hearing of the claim unless–

   (a)   it has been served in accordance with rule 8.5; or

   (b)   the court gives permission.

(2)   The court may require or permit a party to give oral evidence at the hearing.

(3)   The court may give directions requiring the attendance for cross-examination(GL) of a witness who has given written evidence.

   (Rule 32.1 contains a general power for the court to control evidence)

Part 20 claims

8.7   Where the Part 8 procedure is used, Part 20 (counterclaims and other additional claims) applies except that a party may not make a Part 20 claim (as defined by rule 20.2) without the court's permission.

Procedure where defendant objects to use of the part 8 procedure

8.8(1)   Where the defendant contends that the Part 8 procedure should not be used because–

   (a)   there is a substantial dispute of fact; and

   (b)   the use of the Part 8 procedure is not required or permitted by a rule or practice direction,

he must state his reasons when he files his acknowledgment of service.

   (Rule 8.5 requires a defendant who wishes to rely on written evidence to file it when he files his acknowledgment of service)

(2)   When the court receives the acknowledgment of service and any written evidence it will give directions as to the future management of the case.

   (Rule 8.1(3) allows the court to make an order that the claim continue as if the claimant had not used the Part 8 procedure)

Modifications to the general rules

8.9   Where the Part 8 procedure is followed–

   (a)   provision is made in this Part for the matters which must be stated in the claim form and the defendant is not required to file a defence and therefore–

      (i)   Part 16 (statements of case) does not apply;

      (ii)   Part 15 (defence and reply) does not apply;

      (iii) any time limit in these Rules which prevents the parties from taking a step before a defence is filed does not apply;

      (iv)   the requirement under rule 7.8 to serve on the defendant a form for defending the claim does not apply;

(b) the claimant may not obtain judgment by request on an admission and therefore–

    (i) rules 14.4 to 14.7 do not apply; and

    (ii) the requirement under rule 7.8 to serve on the defendant a form for admitting the claim does not apply; and

(c) the claim shall be treated as allocated to the multi-track and therefore Part 26 does not apply.

PART 8 PRACTICE DIRECTION – ALTERNATIVE PROCEDURE FOR CLAIMS

THIS PRACTICE DIRECTION SUPPLEMENTS CPR PART 8

TYPES OF CLAIM IN WHICH PART 8 PROCEDURE MAY BE USED

1.1 A claimant may use the Part 8 procedure where he seeks the court's decision on a question which is unlikely to involve a substantial dispute of fact.

1.2 A claimant may also use the Part 8 procedure if a practice direction permits or requires its use for the type of proceedings in question.

1.3 The practice directions referred to in paragraph 1.2 above may in some respects modify or disapply the Part 8 procedure and, where that is so, it is those practice directions that must be complied with.

1.4 The types of claim for which the Part 8 procedure may be used include:

    (1) a claim by or against a child or patient which has been settled before the commencement of proceedings and the sole purpose of the claim is to obtain the approval of the court to the settlement,

    (2) a claim for provisional damages which has been settled before the commencement of proceedings and the sole purpose of the claim is to obtain a consent judgment, and

    (3) provided there is unlikely to be a substantial dispute of fact, a claim for a summary order for possession against named or unnamed defendants occupying land or premises without the licence or consent of the person claiming possession.

1.5 Where it appears to a court officer that a claimant is using the Part 8 procedure inappropriately, he may refer the claim to a judge for the judge to consider the point.

1.6 The court may at any stage order the claim to continue as if the claimant had not used the Part 8 procedure and, if it does so, the court will allocate the claim to a track and give such directions as it considers appropriate.[1]

---

1 Rule 8.1(3).

ISSUING THE CLAIM

2.1 Part 7 and the practice direction which supplements it contain a number of rules and directions applicable to all claims, including those to which Part 8 applies. Those rules and directions should be applied where appropriate.

2.2 Where a claimant uses the Part 8 procedure, the claim form (practice form N208) should be used and must state the matters set out in rule 8.2 and, if paragraphs 1.2 or 1.3 apply, must comply with the requirements of the practice direction in question. In particular, the claim form must state that Part 8 applies; a Part 8 claim form means a claim form which so states.

(The Costs Practice Direction supplementing Parts 43 to 48 contains details of the information required to be filed with a claim form to comply with rule 44.15 (providing information about funding arrangements))

RESPONDING TO THE CLAIM

3.1 The provisions of Part 15 (defence and reply) do not apply where the claim form is a Part 8 claim form.

3.2 Where a defendant who wishes to respond to a Part 8 claim form is required to file an acknowledgment of service, that acknowledgment of service should be in practice form N210[2] but can, alternatively, be given in an informal document such as a letter.

3.3 Rule 8.3 sets out provisions relating to an acknowledgment of service of a Part 8 claim form.

3.4 Rule 8.4 sets out the consequence of failing to file an acknowledgment of service.

3.5 The provisions of Part 12 (obtaining default judgment) do not apply where the claim form is a Part 8 claim form.

3.6 Where a defendant believes that the Part 8 procedure should not be used because there is a substantial dispute of fact or, as the case may be, because its use is not authorised by any rule or practice direction, he must state his reasons in writing when he files his acknowledgment of service.[3] If the statement of reasons includes matters of evidence it should be verified by a statement of truth.

MANAGING THE CLAIM

4.1 The court may give directions immediately a Part 8 claim form is issued either on the application of a party or on its own initiative. The directions may include fixing a hearing date where:

(1) there is no dispute, such as in child and patient settlements, or

---

2 Rule 8.3(1)(a).

3 Rule 8.8(1).

(2)   where there may be a dispute, such as in claims for mortgage possession or appointment of trustees, but a hearing date could conveniently be given.

4.2   Where the court does not fix a hearing date when the claim form is issued, it will give directions for the disposal of the claim as soon as practicable after the defendant has acknowledged service of the claim form or, as the case may be, after the period for acknowledging service has expired.

4.3   Certain applications, such as a consent application under section 38 of the Landlord and Tenant Act 1954, may not require a hearing.

4.4   The court may convene a directions hearing before giving directions.

EVIDENCE

5.1   A claimant wishing to rely on written evidence should file it when his Part 8 claim form is issued[4] (unless the evidence is contained in the claim form itself).

5.2   Evidence will normally be in the form of a witness statement or an affidavit but a claimant may rely on the matters set out in his claim form provided that it has been verified by a statement of truth.

(For information about (1) statements of truth see Part 22 and the practice direction that supplements it, and (2) written evidence see Part 32 and the practice direction that supplements it.)

5.3   A defendant wishing to rely on written evidence, should file it with his acknowledgment of service.[5]

5.4   Rule 8.5 sets out the times and provisions for filing and serving written evidence.

5.5   A party may apply to the court for an extension of time to serve and file evidence under Rule 8.5 or for permission to serve and file additional evidence under Rule 8.6(1).

(For information about applications see Part 23 and the practice direction that supplements it)

5.6(1)   The parties may, subject to the following provisions, agree in writing on an extension of time for serving and filing evidence under Rule 8.5(3) or Rule 8.5(5).

(2)   An agreement extending time for a defendant to file evidence under Rule 8.5(3)–

(a)   must be filed by the defendant at the same time as he files his acknowledgement of service; and

(b)   must not extend time by more than 14 days after the defendant files his acknowledgement of service.

---

4   Rule 8.5.

5   Rule 8.5(3).

(3)   An agreement extending time for a claimant to file evidence in reply under Rule 8.5(5) must not extend time to more than 28 days after service of the defendant's evidence on the claimant.

PART 8 PRACTICE DIRECTION

THIS PRACTICE DIRECTION SUPPLEMENTS CPR PART 8, AND SCHEDULE 1 AND SCHEDULE 2 TO THE CPR

TERMINOLOGY

1.1   In this practice direction 'Schedule rules' means provisions contained in the Schedules to the CPR, which were previously contained in the Rules of the Supreme Court (1965) or the County Court Rules (1981).

CONTENTS OF THIS PRACTICE DIRECTION

2.1   This practice direction explains–
(1)   how to start the claims referred to in Sections A and B;
(2)   which form to use as the claim form; and
(3)   the procedure which those claims will follow.
(Further guidance about Forms other than claim forms can be found in the practice direction supplementing Part 4.)
(Form 87 (modified as necessary) should be used when making an application for a writ of habeas corpus under RSC Order 54 (Schedule 1). Attention is drawn to the relevant existing Administrative Court practice directions for further guidance)

HOW TO USE THIS PRACTICE DIRECTION

3.1   This Practice direction is divided into Sections A and B. Only one section will be relevant to how to make a particular claim.
3.2   If the claim is described in paragraph A.1 – use section A.
3.3   If the claim is described in paragraph B.1 – use section B.

SECTION A

Application

A.1   Section A applies if–
(1)   the claim is listed in Table 1 below;
(2)   an Act provides that a claim or application in the High Court is to be brought by originating summons; or
(3)   before 26 April 1999, a claim or application in the High Court would have been brought by originating summons, and no other

method for bringing the claim or application on and after 26 April 1999 is specified in a rule or practice direction.

A.2   (1)   The claimant must use the Part 8 procedure unless an Act, rule, or practice direction, makes any additional or contrary provision.

(2)   Where such additional or contrary provision is made the claimant must comply with it and modify the Part 8 procedure accordingly.

Claim form

A.3   The claimant must use the Part 8 claim form.

Table 1

RSC Ord 17 r3(1)	Interpleader (Mode of application)
RSC Ord 77 r11	Proceedings by and against the Crown (Interpleader: Application for order against Crown)
RSC Ord 77 r16(2)	Proceedings by and against the Crown (Attachment of debts, etc.)
RSC Ord 77 r17(1)	Proceedings by and against the Crown (Proceedings relating to postal packets)
RSC Ord 77 r18(1)	Proceedings by and against the Crown (Applications under sections 17 and 29 of Crown Proceedings Act)
RSC Ord 79 r 8(2)	Criminal Proceedings (Estreat of recognizances)
RSC Ord 79 r 9(2)	Criminal Proceedings (Bail)
RSC Ord 81 r10(1)	Partners (Applications for orders charging partner's interest in partnership property)
RSC Ord 93 r5(2)	Applications and Appeals to High Court under Various Acts: Chancery Division (Applications under section 2(3) of the Public Order Act 1936)
RSC Ord 93 r18(2)	Applications and Appeals to High Court under Various Acts: Chancery Division (Proceedings under section 86 of the Civil Aviation Act 1982)
RSC Ord 94 r5	Applications and Appeals to High Court under Various Acts: Queen's Bench Division (Exercise of jurisdiction under Representation of the People Acts)
RSC Ord 95 r2(1)	Bills of Sale Acts 1878 and 1882 and the Industrial and Provident Societies Act 1967 (Entry of satisfaction)
RSC Ord 95 r3	Bills of Sale Acts 1878 and 1882 and the Industrial and Provident Societies Act 1967 (Restraining removal on sale of goods seized)

RSC Ord 96 r1	The Mines (Working Facilities and Support) Act 1966 etc. (Assignment to Chancery Division)
RSC Ord 96 r 3	The Mines (Working Facilities and Support) Act 1966 etc. (Issue of claim form)
RSC Ord 106 r3(2)	Proceedings Relating to Solicitors: The Solicitors Act 1974 (Power to order solicitor to deliver cash account etc.)
RSC Ord 106 r6(2)	Proceedings Relating to Solicitors: The Solicitors Act 1974 (Applications under schedule 1 to the Act)
RSC Ord 106 r8	Proceedings Relating to Solicitors: The Solicitors Act 1974 (Interim order restricting payment out of banking account)
RSC Ord 109 r1(3)	Administration Act 1960 (Applications under Act)

SECTION B

Application

B.1 Section B applies if the claim–

(1) is listed in Table 2;

(2) in the county court is for, or includes a claim for damages for harassment under Section 3 of the protection from Harassment Act 1997; or

(3) would have been brought before 26 April 1999–

    (a) in the High Court, by originating motion;

    (b) in the county court–

        (i) by originating application; or

        (ii) by petition, and

no other procedure is prescribed in an Act, a rule or a practice direction.

Table 2

Schedule Rule	Claim Form
RSC Ord 77 r8(2)[6]	Proceedings by and against the Crown (Summary applications to the court in certain revenue matters)
RSC Ord 93 r19(1)	Applications and Appeals to High Court under Various Acts: (Proceedings under section 85(7) of the Fair Trading Act 1973 and the Control of Misleading Advertisements Regulations 1988)

6 This type of claim may also be brought by the Part 8 procedure.

RSC Ord 93 r22(3) Applications and Appeals to High Court under Various Acts: Chancery Division (Proceedings under the Financial Services and Markets Act 2000)

RSC Ord 94 r1(2) Applications and Appeals to High Court under Various Acts: Queens Bench Division (Jurisdiction of High Court to Quash Certain Orders, Schemes etc.)

RSC Ord 94 r7(2) Applications and Appeals to High Court under Various Acts: Queens Bench Division (Reference of Question of Law by Agricultural Land Tribunal)

RSC Ord 94 r11(4) Applications and Appeals to High Court under Various Acts: Queens Bench Division (Case stated by Mental Health Review Tribunal)

RSC Ord 94 r12(5)(c) Applications and Appeals to High Court under Various Acts: Queens Bench Division Applications for permission under section 289(6) of the Town and Country Planning Act 1990 and section 65(5) of the Planning (Listed Buildings and Conservation Areas) Act 1990

RSC Ord 94 r13(5) Applications and Appeals to High Court under Various Acts: Queens Bench Division Proceedings under sections 289 and 290 of the Town and Country Planning Act 1990 and under section 65 of the Planning (Listed Buildings and Conservation Areas) Act 1990

RSC Ord 94 r14(2) Applications and Appeals to High Court under Various Acts: Queens Bench Division Applications under section 13 of the Coroners Act 1988

RSC Ord 94 r15(2) Applications and Appeals to High Court under Various Acts: Queens Bench Division Applications under section 42 of the Supreme Court Act 1981

RSC Ord 98 r2(1) Local Government Finance Act 1982, Part III (Application by auditor for declaration)

RSC Ord 109 r2(4) Administration of Justice Act 1960 (Appeals under section 13 of Act)

RSC Ord 115 r2B(1) Confiscation and Forfeiture in Connection with Criminal Proceedings (I. Drug Trafficking Act 1994 and Criminal Justice (International Co-operation) Act 1990 – Application for confiscation Order)

RSC Ord 115 r3(1) Confiscation and Forfeiture in Connection with Criminal Proceedings (I. Drug Trafficking Act 1994 and Criminal Justice

	(International Co-operation) Act 1990 – Application for restraint order or charging order)
RSC Ord 115 r7(1)	Confiscation and Forfeiture in Connection with Criminal Proceedings (I. Drug Trafficking Act 1994 and Criminal Justice (International Co-operation) Act 1990 – Realisation of property)
RSC Ord 115 r26(1)	Confiscation and Forfeiture in Connection with Criminal Proceedings (III. Terrorism Act 2000 – Application for restraint order)
RSC Ord 116 r5(1)	The Criminal Procedure and Investigations Act 1996 (Application under section 54(3)).
CCR Ord 44 r1(1)	The Agricultural Holdings Act 1986 (Special case stated by arbitrator)
CCR Ord 44 r3(1)	The Agricultural Holdings Act 1986 (Removal of arbitrator or setting aside award)
CCR Ord 45 r1(1)	The Representation of the People Act 1983 (Application for detailed assessment of returning officer's account) N408
CCR Ord 46 r1(1)	The Legitimacy Act 1976 (Manner of application)
CCR Ord 49 r5(1)	Miscellaneous Statutes: Fair Trading Act 1973 (Proceedings under section 35, 38 or 40)
CCR Ord 49 r6B(1)	Miscellaneous Statutes: Housing Act 1996: Injunctions and Powers of Arrest (Application for injunction under section 152) N16A
CCR Ord 49 r7(2)	Miscellaneous Statutes: Injunctions to Prevent Environmental Harm: Town and Country Planning Act 1990 etc. (Application for injunction)
CCR Ord 49 r10(3)	Miscellaneous Statutes: Local Government Finance Act 1982
CCR Ord 49 r12(2)	Miscellaneous Statutes: Mental Health Act 1983 (Application)
CCR Ord 49 r15(1)	Miscellaneous Statutes: Postal Services Act 2000 (Application under section 92)

The Local Government Act 1972 (claims under section 92 – proceedings for disqualification)

Special provisions take precedence

B.2 The claimant must first comply with any special provision set out in the Schedule rules, practice direction or any Act relating to the claim. (In Schedule 2, CCR O.6 makes special provisions about particulars of claim for certain types of claim.)

B.3 Special provisions contained in Schedule rules or an Act may set out–

(1) where the claim may be started;

(2) the contents of the claim form;

(3) whether a hearing is required;

(4) the nature of evidence required in support of the claim, and when it must be filed or served;

(5) the method of service of the claim form and evidence;

(6) persons on whom service must or may be effected;

(7) the form and content of Notices, and when they must or may be filed, and on whom served;

(8) the form and content of any affidavit, answer, or reply and when they must or may be filed or served;

(9) persons who may apply to be joined as parties to the claim;

(10) minimum periods of notice before the hearing date.

B.4 Where a Schedule rule makes special provision for the contents of particulars of claim, those particulars must be attached to the claim form and served with it.

B.5 Subject to any special or contrary provision in an Act or Schedule rule, the claimant must use the procedure set out in the remainder of this section.

Restrictions on where to start the claim

B.6 Where the claimant is bringing a claim in a county court that claim may only be started–

(1) in the county court for the district in which

    (a) the defendants or one of the defendants lives or carries on business; or

    (b) the subject matter of the claim is situated; or

(2) if there is no defendant named in the claim form, in the county court for the district in which the claimant or one of the claimants lives or carries on business.

B.7 Where the claimant is making a claim in the county court for–

(1) enforcing any charge or lien on land;

(2) the recovery of moneys secured by a mortgage or charge on land, the claim must be started in the court for the district in which the land, or any part of it, is situated.

Claim form

B.8 This paragraph sets out which Form is to be used as the claim form–

(1) where a claim form number is listed against a particular claim in Table 2, the claimant must use that numbered form as the claim form;

(2) in every other claim, the claimant must use the Part 8 claim form.

Court will fix a date

B.9   When the court issues the claim form it will–
(1)   fix a date for the hearing; and
(2)   prepare a notice of the hearing date for each party.

Service of the claim form

B.10   The claim form must be served not less than 21 days before the hearing date.

B.11   Where the claimant serves the claim form, he must serve notice of the hearing date at the same time, unless the hearing date is specified in the claim form. (CPR Rule 3.1(2) (a) and (b) provide for the court to extend or shorten the time for compliance with any rule or practice direction, and to adjourn or bring forward a hearing)

Defendant is not required to respond

B.12   The defendant is not required to serve an acknowledgment of service.

At the hearing

B.13   The court may on the hearing date–
(1)   proceed to hear the case and dispose of the claim; or
(2)   give case management directions.

B.14   Case management directions given under paragraph B.13 will, if the defendant has filed a defence, include the allocation of a case to a track, or directions to enable the case to be allocated.

B.15   CPR rule 26.5(3) to (5) and CPR rules 26.6 to 26.10 apply to the allocation of a claim under paragraph B.14.

PART 19

Rule 19.4A

HUMAN RIGHTS

19.4A   Section 4 of the Human Rights Act 1998
(1)   The court may not make a declaration of incompatibility in accordance with section 4 of the Human Rights Act 1998 unless 21 days' notice, or such other period of notice as the court directs,has been given to the Crown.
(2)   Where notice has been given to the Crown a Minister, or other person permitted by that Act, shall be joined as a party on giving notice to the court.

(Only courts specified in section 4 of the Human Rights Act 1998 can make a declaration of incompatibility)

Section 9 of the Human Rights Act 1998

(3) Where a claim is made under that Act for damages in respect of a judicial act–

    (a) that claim must be set out in the statement of case or the appeal notice; and

    (b) notice must be given to the Crown.

(4) Where paragraph (3) applies and the appropriate person has not applied to be joined as a party within 21 days, or such other period as the court directs, after the notice is served, the court may join the appropriate person as a party.

(A practice direction makes provision for these notices).

PART 19 PRACTICE DIRECTION – ADDITION AND SUBSTITUTION OF PARTIES

THIS PRACTICE DIRECTION SUPPLEMENTS CPR PART 19

A party applying for an amendment will usually be responsible for the costs of and arising from the amendment.

CHANGES OF PARTIES

General

1.1 Parties may be removed, added or substituted in existing proceedings either on the court's own initiative or on the application of either an existing party or a person who wishes to become a party.

1.2 The application may be dealt with without a hearing where all the existing parties and the proposed new party are in agreement.

1.3 The application to add or substitute a new party should be supported by evidence setting out the proposed new party's interest in or connection with the claim.

1.4 The application notice should be filed in accordance with rule 23.3 and, unless the application is made under rule 19.2(4),[7] be served in accordance with rule 23.4.

1.5 An order giving permission to amend will, unless the court orders otherwise, be drawn up. It will be served by the court unless the parties wish to serve it or the court orders them to do so.

7 See rule 19.4(3)(a).

Addition or substitution of claimant

2.1 Where an application is made to the court to add or to substitute a new party to the proceedings as claimant, the party applying must file:

(1) the application notice,

(2) the proposed amended claim form and particulars of claim, and

(3) the signed, written consent of the new claimant to be so added or substituted.

2.2 Where the court makes an order adding or substituting a party as claimant but the signed, written consent of the new claimant has not been filed:

(1) the order, and

(2) the addition or substitution of the new party as claimant,

will not take effect until the signed, written consent of the new claimant is filed.

2.3 Where the court has made an order adding or substituting a new claimant, the court may direct:

(1) a copy of the order to be served on every party to the proceedings and any other person affected by the order,

(2) copies of the statements of case and of documents referred to in any statement of case to be served on the new party,

(3) the party who made the application to file within 14 days an amended claim form and particulars of claim.

Addition or substitution of defendant

3.1 The Civil Procedure Rules apply to a new defendant who has been added or substituted as they apply to any other defendant (see in particular the provisions of Parts 9, 10, 11 and 15).

3.2 Where the court has made an order adding or substituting a defendant whether on its own initiative or on an application, the court may direct:

(1) the claimant to file with the court within 14 days (or as ordered) an amended claim form and particulars of claim for the court file,

(2) a copy of the order to be served on all parties to the proceedings and any other person affected by it,

(3) the amended claim form and particulars of claim, forms for admitting, defending and acknowledging the claim and copies of the statements of case and any other documents referred to in any statement of case to be served on the new defendant.

(4) unless the court orders otherwise, the amended claim form and particulars of claim to be served on any other defendants.

3.3 A new defendant does not become a party to the proceedings until the amended claim form has been served on him.[8]

8 *Kettleman v Hansel Properties Ltd* (1987) AC 189, HL.

Removal of party

4 Where the court makes an order for the removal of a party from the proceedings:

(1) the claimant must file with the court an amended claim form and particulars of claim, and

(2) a copy of the order must be served on every party to the proceedings and on any other person affected by the order.

Transfer of interest or liability

5.1 Where the interest or liability of an existing party has passed to some other person, application should be made to the court to add or substitute that person.[9]

5.2 The application must be supported by evidence showing the stage the proceedings have reached and what change has occurred to cause the transfer of interest or liability.

(For information about making amendments generally, see the practice direction supplementing Part 17.)

HUMAN RIGHTS, JOINING THE CROWN

Section 4 of the Human Rights Act 1998

6.1 Where a party has included in his statement of case–

(1) a claim for a declaration of incompatibility in accordance with section 4 of the Human Rights Act 1998, or

(2) an issue for the court to decide which may lead to the court considering making a declaration,

then the court may at any time consider whether notice should be given to the Crown as required by that Act and give directions for the content and service of the notice. The rule allows a period of 21 days before the court will make the declaration but the court may vary this period of time.

6.2 The court will normally consider the issues and give the directions referred to in paragraph 6.1 at the case management conference.

6.3 Where a party amends his statement of case to include any matter referred to in paragraph 6.1, then the court will consider whether notice should be given to the Crown and give directions for the content and service of the notice.

(The practice direction to CPR Part 16 requires a party to include issues under the Human Rights Act 1998 in his statement of case)

6.4 (1) The notice given under rule 19.4A must be served on the person named in the list published under section 17 of the Crown Proceedings Act 1947.

9 See rule 19.2(4).

(The list, made by the Minister for the Civil Service, is annexed to this practice direction)

(2)   The notice will be in the form directed by the court but will normally include the directions given by the court and all the statements of case in the claim. The notice will also be served on all the parties.

(3)   The court may require the parties to assist in the preparation of the notice.

(4)   In the circumstances described in the National Assembly for Wales (Transfer of Functions)(No 2) Order 2000 the notice must also be served on the National Assembly for Wales.

(Section 5(3) of the Human Rights Act 1998 provides that the Crown may give notice that it intends to become a party at any stage in the proceedings once notice has been given)

6.5   Unless the court orders otherwise, the Minister or other person permitted by the Human Rights Act 1998 to be joined as a party must, if he wishes to be joined, give notice of his intention to be joined as a party to the court and every other party. Where the Minister has nominated a person to be joined as a party the notice must be accompanied by the written nomination.

(Section 5(2)(a) of the Human Rights Act 1998 permits a person nominated by a Minister of the Crown to be joined as a party. The nomination may be signed on behalf of the Minister)

Section 9 of the Human Rights Act 1998

6.6   (1)   The procedure in paragraphs 6.1 to 6.5 also applies where a claim is made under sections 7(1)(a) and 9(3) of the Human Rights Act 1998 for damages in respect of a judicial act.

(2)   Notice must be given to the Lord Chancellor and should be served on the Treasury Solicitor on his behalf, except where the judicial act is of a Court-Martial when the appropriate person is the Secretary of State for Defence and the notice must be served on the Treasury Solicitor on his behalf.

(3)   The notice will also give details of the judicial act, which is the subject of the claim for damages, and of the court or tribunal that made it.

(Section 9(4) of the Human Rights Act 1998 provides that no award of damages may be made against the Crown as provided for in section 9(3) unless the appropriate person is joined in the proceedings. The appropriate person is the Minister responsible for the court concerned or a person or department nominated by him (section 9(5) of the Act))

ANNEX

CABINET OFFICE
CROWN PROCEEDINGS ACT
1947

List of Authorised Government Departments and the names and addresses for service of the person who is, or is acting for the purposes of the Act as, Solicitor for such Departments, published by the Minister for the Civil Service in pursuance of Section 17 of the Crown Proceedings Act 1947.

This list supersedes the list published on 10 July 1998

AUTHORISED GOVERNMENT DEPARTMENTS	SOLICITOR AND ADDRESSES FOR SERVICE
Advisory, Conciliation and Arbitration Service Board of Trade Building Societies Commission Cabinet Office Crown Prosecution Service Ministry of Defence Department for Education and Employment Director General of Electricity Supply Director General of Electricity Supply for Northern Ireland Department of the Environment, Transport and the Regions Export Credits Guarantee Department Director General of Fair Trading Department for International Development Friendly Societies Commission Director General of Gas for Northern Ireland Director General of Gas Supply Health and Safety Executive Her Majesty's Chief Inspector of Schools in England	The Treasury Solicitor Queen Anne's Chambers 28 Broadway Westminster London SW1H 9JS (see notes (1) and (2)

AUTHORISED GOVERNMENT DEPARTMENTS	SOLICITOR AND ADDRESSES FOR SERVICE
Her Majesty's Chief Inspector of Schools in Wales Home Office Lord Chancellor's Department Department for Culture, Media and Sport National Savings Office for National Statistics Ordnance Survey Northern Ireland Office Director of Passenger Rail Franchising Public Works Loan Board The Rail Regulator The International Rail Regulator Serious Fraud Office Director General of Telecommunications Department of Trade and Industry Her Majesty's Treasury Wales Office (Office of the Secretary of State for Wales) (see Note (3)	The Treasury Solicitor Queen Anne's Chambers 28 Broadway Westminster London SW1H 9JS (see notes (1) and (2)
Ministry of Agriculture, Fisheries and Food (see note (3))	The Solicitor to the Ministry of Agriculture Fisheries and Food 55 Whitehall London SW1A 2EY
Commissioners of Customs and Excise	The Solicitor for the Customs and Excise New King's Beam House 22 Upper Ground London SE1 9PJ

AUTHORISED GOVERNMENT DEPARTMENTS	SOLICITOR AND ADDRESSES FOR SERVICE
Intervention Board for Agricultural Produce	The Solicitor to the Intervention Board for Agricultural Produce Kings House Kings Road Reading, Berks RG1 3BH
Commissioner of Inland Revenue	The Solicitor of Inland Revenue Somerset House The Strand London WC2R 1LB
Crown Estate Commissioners	The Solicitor to the Crown Estate Commissioners Crown Estate Office 16 Carlton House Terrace London SW1Y 5AH
Department of Health Department of Social Security Food Standards Agency	The Solicitor to the Departments of Health and Social Security New Court 48 Carey Street London WC2A 2LS
Director General of Water Services	The Solicitor to the Director General of Water Services Centre City Tower 7 Hill Street Birmingham B5 4UA
National Assembly of Wales	The Counsel General to the National Assembly for Wales Cathays Park Cardiff CF10 3NQ

NOTES

(1) Section 17(3) and section 18 of the Crown Proceedings Act 1947 provide as follows–

17(3) Civil proceedings against the Crown shall be instituted against the appropriate authorised Government department, or, if none of the authorised

Government departments is appropriate or the person instituting the proceedings has any reasonable doubt whether any and if so which of those departments is appropriate, against the Attorney General.

18   All documents required to be served on the Crown for the purpose of or in connection with any civil proceedings by or against the Crown shall, if those proceedings are by or against an authorised Government department, be served on the solicitor, if any, for that department, or the person, if any, acting for the purposes of this Act as solicitor for that department, or if there is no such solicitor and no person so acting, or if the proceedings are brought by or against the Attorney General, on the Solicitor for the affairs of His Majesty's Treasury.

(2)   The above-mentioned provisions do not apply to Scotland, where in accordance with the Crown Suits (Scotland) Act 1857, as amended by the Scotland Act 1998, civil proceedings against the Crown (other than the Scottish Administration) or any Government Department (other than the Scottish Executive) may be directed against the Advocate General for Scotland. The Advocate General's address for service is the Office of the Solicitor to the Advocate General for Scotland, Victoria Quay, Edinburgh EH6 6QQ. Civil proceedings against the Scottish Administration may be directed against the Scottish Ministers at St. Andrew's House, Edinburgh EH1 3DG, or against the Lord Advocate for and on behalf of the Scottish Executive. The Lord Advocate's address for service is 25 Chambers Street, Edinburgh, EH1 1LA.

(3)   The Solicitor and address for service for the purpose of or in connection with any civil proceedings brought by or against the Crown which relate to those matters for which the Secretary of State for Wales is responsible in Wales and for which the Minister for Agriculture, Fisheries and Food is responsible in England is the Solicitor to the Ministry of Agriculture, Fisheries and Food, 55 Whitehall, London, SW1A 2EY.

The Treasury Solicitor is the Solicitor acting for the Wales Office (Office of the Secretary of State for Wales) in all other civil proceedings affecting that Office.

CABINET OFFICE
WHITEHALL
LONDON SW1

SIR RICHARD WILSON
2000

PART 23

GENERAL RULES ABOUT APPLICATIONS FOR COURT ORDERS

Contents of this part

Meaning of 'application notice' and 'respondent'

23.1 In this Part–

'application notice' means a document in which the applicant states his intention to seek a court order; and

'respondent' means–

(a) the person against whom the order is sought; and

(b) such other person as the court may direct.

Where to make an application

23.2 (1) The general rule is that an application must be made to the court where the claim was started.

(2) If a claim has been transferred to another court since it was started, an application must be made to the court to which the claim has been transferred.

(3) If the parties have been notified of a fixed date for the trial, an application must be made to the court where the trial is to take place.

(4) If an application is made before a claim has been started, it must be made to the court where it is likely that the claim to which the application relates will be started unless there is good reason to make the application to a different court.

(5) If an application is made after proceedings to enforce judgment

have begun, it must be made to any court which is dealing with the enforcement of the judgment unless any rule or practice direction provides otherwise.

Application notice to be filed

23.3 (1) The general rule is that an applicant must file an application notice.

(2) An applicant may make an application without filing an application notice if—

(a) this is permitted by a rule or practice direction; or

(b) the court dispenses with the requirement for an application notice.

Notice of an application

23.4 (1) The general rule is that a copy of the application notice must be served on each respondent.

(2) An application may be made without serving a copy of the application notice if this is permitted by—

(a) a rule;

(b) a practice direction; or

(c) a court order.

(Rule 23.7 deals with service of a copy of the application notice)

Time when an application is made

23.5 Where an application must be made within a specified time, it is so made if the application notice is received by the court within that time.

What an application notice must include

23.6 An application notice must state—

(a) what order the applicant is seeking; and

(b) briefly, why the applicant is seeking the order.

(Part 22 requires an application notice to be verified by a statement of truth if the applicant wishes to rely on matters set out in his application notice as evidence)

Service of a copy of an application notice

23.7 (1) A copy of the application notice—

(a) must be served as soon as practicable after it is filed; and

(b) except where another time limit is specified in these Rules or a practice direction, must in any event be served at least 3 days before the court is to deal with the application.

(2) If a copy of the application notice is to be served by the court, the

applicant must, when he files the application notice, file a copy of any written evidence in support.

(3) When a copy of an application notice is served it must be accompanied by–

(a) a copy of any written evidence in support; and

(b) a copy of any draft order which the applicant has attached to his application.

(4) If–

(a) an application notice is served; but

(b) the period of notice is shorter than the period required by these Rules or a practice direction,

the court may direct that, in the circumstances of the case, sufficient notice has been given and hear the application.

(5) This rule does not require written evidence–

(a) to be filed if it has already been filed; or

(b) to be served on a party on whom it has already been served.

(Part 6 contains the general rules about service of documents including who must serve a copy of the application notice)

Applications which may be dealt with without a hearing

23.8 The court may deal with an application without a hearing if–

(a) the parties agree as to the terms of the order sought;

(b) the parties agree that the court should dispose of the application without a hearing, or

(c) the court does not consider that a hearing would be appropriate.

Service of application where application made without notice

23.9 (1) This rule applies where the court has disposed of an application which it permitted to be made without service of a copy of the application notice.

(2) Where the court makes an order, whether granting or dismissing the application, a copy of the application notice and any evidence in support must, unless the court orders otherwise, be served with the order on any party or other person–

(a) against whom the order was made; and

(b) against whom the order was sought.

(3) The order must contain a statement of the right to make an application to set aside$^{(GL)}$ or vary the order under rule 23.10.

Application to set aside or vary order made without notice

23.10 (1) A person who was not served with a copy of the application notice before an order was made under rule 23.9, may apply to have the order set aside$^{(GL)}$ or varied.

(2)   An application under this rule must be made within 7 days after the date on which the order was served on the person making the application.

Power of the court to proceed in the absence of a party

23.11 (1)   Where the applicant or any respondent fails to attend the hearing of an application, the court may proceed in his absence.

(2)   Where–

(a)   the applicant or any respondent fails to attend the hearing of an application; and

(b)   the court makes an order at the hearing,

the court may, on application or of its own initiative, re-list the application.

(Part 40 deals with service of orders)

PART 23 PRACTICE DIRECTION – APPLICATIONS

THIS PRACTICE DIRECTION SUPPLEMENTS CPR PART 23

Reference to a judge

1   A Master or district judge may refer to a judge any matter which he thinks should properly be decided by a judge, and the judge may either dispose of the matter or refer it back to the Master or district judge.

Application notices

2.1   An application notice must, in addition to the matters set out in rule 23.6, be signed and include:

(1)   the title of the claim,

(2)   the reference number of the claim,

(3)   the full name of the applicant,

(4)   where the applicant is not already a party, his address for service, and

(5)   either a request for a hearing or a request that the application be dealt with without a hearing.

(Practice Form N244 may be used.)

2.2   On receipt of an application notice containing a request for a hearing the court will notify the applicant of the time and date for the hearing of the application.

2.3   On receipt of an application notice containing a request that the application be dealt with without a hearing, the application notice will be sent to a Master or district judge so that he may decide whether the application is suitable for consideration without a hearing.

2.4 Where the Master or district judge agrees that the application is suitable for consideration without a hearing, the court will so inform the applicant and the respondent and may give directions for the filing of evidence. (Rules 23.9 and 23.10 enable a party to apply for an order made without a hearing to be set aside or varied.)

2.5 Where the Master or district judge does not agree that the application is suitable for consideration without a hearing, the court will notify the applicant and the respondent of the time, date and place for the hearing of the application and may at the same time give directions as to the filing of evidence.

2.6 If the application is intended to be made to a judge, the application notice should so state. In that case, paragraphs 2.3, 2.4 and 2.5 will apply as though references to the Master or district judge were references to a judge.

2.7 Every application should be made as soon as it becomes apparent that it is necessary or desirable to make it.

2.8 Applications should wherever possible be made so that they can be considered at any other hearing for which a date has already been fixed or for which a date is about to be fixed. This is particularly so in relation to case management conferences, allocation and listing hearings and pre-trial reviews fixed by the court.

2.9 The parties must anticipate that at any hearing the court may wish to review the conduct of the case as a whole and give any necessary case management directions. They should be ready to assist the court in doing so and to answer questions the court may ask for this purpose.

2.10 Where a date for a hearing has been fixed and a party wishes to make an application at that hearing but he does not have sufficient time to serve an application notice he should inform the other party and the court (if possible in writing) as soon as he can of the nature of the application and the reason for it. He should then make the application orally at the hearing.

Applications without service of application notice

3 An application may be made without serving an application notice only:
(1) where there is exceptional urgency,
(2) where the overriding objective is best furthered by doing so,
(3) by consent of all parties,
(4) with the permission of the court,
(5) where paragraph 2.10 above applies, or
(6) where a court order, rule or practice direction permits.

Giving notice of an application

4.1 Unless the court otherwise directs or paragraph 3 of this practice direction applies the application notice must be served as soon as practicable after it has been issued and, if there is to be a hearing, at least 3 clear days before the hearing date (rule 23.7(1)(b)).

4.2 Where an application notice should be served but there is not sufficient time to do so, informal notification of the application should be given unless the circumstances of the application require secrecy.

Pre-action applications

5 All applications made before a claim is commenced should be made under Part 23 of the Civil Procedure Rules. Attention is drawn in particular to rule 23.2(4).

Telephone hearings

6.1 The court may order than an application or part of an application be dealt with by a telephone hearing.

6.1A The applicant should indicate on his application notice if he seeks a court order under paragraph 6.1. Where he has not done so but nevertheless wishes to seek an order the request should be made as early as possible.

6.2 An order under 6.1 will not normally be made unless every party entitled to be given notice of the application and to be heard at the hearing has consented to the order.

6.3 (1) Where a party entitled to be heard at the hearing of the application is acting in person, the court–

    (a) may not make an order under 6.1 except on condition that arrangements will be made for the party acting in person to be attended at the telephone hearing by a responsible person to whom the party acting in person is known and who can confirm to the court the identity of the party; and

    (b) may not give effect to an order under 6.1 unless the party acting in person is accompanied by a responsible person who at the commencement of the hearing confirms to the court the identity of the party.

    (2) The 'responsible person' may be a barrister, solicitor, legal executive, doctor, clergyman, police officer, prison officer or other person of comparable status.

    (3) If the court makes an order under 6.1 it will give any directions necessary for the telephone hearing.

6.4 No representative of a party to an application being heard by telephone may attend the judge in person while the application is being heard unless the other party to the application has agreed that he may do so.

6.5 If an application is to be heard by telephone the following directions will apply, subject to any direction to the contrary:

    (1) The applicant's legal representative must arrange the telephone conference for precisely the time fixed by the court. The

telecommunications provider must be capable of connecting the parties and the court.

(2) He must tell the operator the telephone numbers of all those participating in the conference call and the sequence in which they are to be called.

(3) It is the responsibility of the applicant's legal representative to ascertain from all the other parties whether they have instructed counsel and, if so the identity of counsel, and whether the legal representative and counsel will be on the same or different telephone numbers.

(4) The sequence in which they are to be called will be:

(a) the applicant's legal representative and (if on a different number) his counsel,

(b) the legal representative (and counsel) for all other parties, and

(c) the judge.

(5) The applicant's legal representative must arrange for the conference to be recorded on tape by the telecommunications provider whose system is being used and must send the tape to the court.

(6) Each speaker is to remain on the line after being called by the operator setting up the conference call. The call may be 2 or 3 minutes before the time fixed for the application.

(7) When the judge has been connected the applicant's legal representative (or his counsel) will introduce the parties in the usual way.

(8) If the use of a 'speakerphone' by any party causes the judge or any other party any difficulty in hearing what is said the judge may require that party to use a hand held telephone.

(9) The telephone charges debited to the account of the party initiating the conference call will be treated as part of the costs of the application.

Video conferencing

7 Where the parties to a matter wish to use video conferencing facilities, and those facilities are available in the relevant court, they should apply to the Master or district judge for directions.

Note of proceedings

8 The procedural judge should keep, either by way of a note or a tape recording, brief details of all proceedings before him, including the dates of the proceedings and a short statement of the decision taken at each hearing.

EVIDENCE

9.1 The requirement for evidence in certain types of applications is set out in some of the rules and practice directions. Where there is no specific requirement to provide evidence it should be borne in mind that, as a practical matter, the court will often need to be satisfied by evidence of the facts that are relied on in support of or for opposing the application.

9.2 The court may give directions for the filing of evidence in support of or opposing a particular application. The court may also give directions for the filing of evidence in relation to any hearing that it fixes on its own initiative. The directions may specify the form that evidence is to take and when it is to be served.

9.3 Where it is intended to rely on evidence which is not contained in the application itself, the evidence, if it has not already been served, should be served with the application.

9.4 Where a respondent to an application wishes to rely on evidence which has not yet been served he should serve it as soon as possible and in any event in accordance with any directions the court may have given.

9.5 If it is necessary for the applicant to serve any evidence in reply it should be served as soon as possible and in any event in accordance with any directions the court may have given.

9.6 Evidence must be filed with the court as well as served on the parties. Exhibits should not be filed unless the court otherwise directs.

9.7 The contents of an application notice may be used as evidence (otherwise than at trial) provided the contents have been verified by a statement of truth.[10]

Consent orders

10.1 Rule 40.6 sets out the circumstances where an agreed judgment or order may be entered and sealed.

10.2 Where all parties affected by an order have written to the court consenting to the making of the order a draft of which has been filed with the court, the court will treat the draft as having been signed in accordance with rule 40.6(7).

10.3 Where a consent order must be made by a judge (i.e. rule 40.6(2) does not apply) the order must be drawn so that the judge's name and judicial title can be inserted.

10.4 The parties to an application for a consent order must ensure that they provide the court with any material it needs to be satisfied that it is appropriate to make the order. Subject to any rule or practice direction a letter will generally be acceptable for this purpose.

10.5 Where a judgment or order has been agreed in respect of an application or claim where a hearing date has been fixed, the parties

---

10 See Part 22.

must inform the court immediately. (note that parties are reminded that under rules 28.4 and 29.5 the case management timetable cannot be varied by written agreement of the parties.)

Other applications considered without a hearing

11.1 Where rule 23.8(b) applies the parties should so inform the court in writing and each should confirm that all evidence and other material on which he relies has been disclosed to the other parties to the application.

11.2 Where rule 23.8(c) applies the court will treat the application as if it were proposing to make an order on its own initiative.

Applications to stay claim where related criminal proceedings

11A.1 An application for the stay of civil proceedings pending the determination of related criminal proceedings may be made by any party to the civil proceedings or by the prosecutor or any defendant in the criminal proceedings.

11A.2 Every party to the civil proceedings must, unless he is the applicant, be made a respondent to the application.

11A.3 The evidence in support of the application must contain an estimate of the expected duration of the stay and must identify the respects in which the continuance of the civil proceedings may prejudice the criminal trial.

11A.4 In order to make an application under paragraph 11A.1, it is not necessary for the prosecutor or defendant in the criminal proceedings to be joined as a party to the civil proceedings.

Miscellaneous

12.1 Except in the most simple application the applicant should bring to any hearing a draft of the order sought. If the case is proceeding in the Royal Courts of Justice and the order is unusually long or complex it should also be supplied on disk for use by the court office.

12.2 Where rule 23.11 applies, the power to re-list the application in rule 23.11(2) is in addition to any other powers of the court with regard to the order (for example to set aside, vary, discharge or suspend the order).

Costs

13.1 Attention is drawn to the costs practice direction and, in particular, to the court's power to make a summary assessment of costs.

13.2 Attention is also drawn to rule 44.13(i) which provides that if an order makes no mention of costs, none are payable in respect of the proceedings to which it relates.

PART 30

Rule 30.5

Transfer between divisions and to and from a specialist list

30.5 (1) The High Court may order proceedings in any Division of the High Court to be transferred to another Division.

(2) The court may order proceedings to be transferred to or from a specialist list.

(3) An application for the transfer of proceedings to or from a specialist list.

PART 32

EVIDENCE

Contents of this part

Power of court to control evidence

32.1 (1) The court may control the evidence by giving directions as to–

(a) the issues on which it requires evidence;

(b) the nature of the evidence which it requires to decide those issues; and

    (c) the way in which the evidence is to be placed before the court.

(2) The court may use its power under this rule to exclude evidence that would otherwise be admissible.

(3) The court may limit cross-examination.[GL]

Evidence of witnesses – general rule

32.2 (1) The general rule is that any fact which needs to be proved by the evidence of witnesses is to be proved–

    (a) at trial, by their oral evidence given in public; and

    (b) at any other hearing, by their evidence in writing.

(2) This is subject–

    (a) to any provision to the contrary contained in these Rules or elsewhere; or

    (b) to any order of the court.

Evidence by video link or other means

32.3 The court may allow a witness to give evidence through a video link or by other means.

Requirement to serve witness statements for use at trial

32.4 (1) A witness statement is a written statement signed by a person which contains the evidence which that person would be allowed to give orally.

(2) The court will order a party to serve on the other parties any witness statement of the oral evidence which the party serving the statement intends to rely on in relation to any issues of fact to be decided at the trial.

(3) The court may give directions as to–

    (a) the order in which witness statements are to be served; and

    (b) whether or not the witness statements are to be filed.

Use at trial of witness statements which have been served

32.5 (1) If–

    (a) a party has served a witness statement; and

    (b) he wishes to rely at trial on the evidence of the witness who made the statement,

he must call the witness to give oral evidence unless the court orders otherwise or he puts the statement in as hearsay evidence.

(Part 33 contains provisions about hearsay evidence)

(2) Where a witness is called to give oral evidence under paragraph (1), his witness statement shall stand as his evidence in chief[GL] unless the court orders otherwise.

(3) A witness giving oral evidence at trial may with the permission of the court–

    (a) amplify his witness statement; and

    (b) give evidence in relation to new matters which have arisen since the witness statement was served on the other parties.

(4) The court will give permission under paragraph (3) only if it considers that there is good reason not to confine the evidence of the witness to the contents of his witness statement.

(5) If a party who has served a witness statement does not–

    (a) call the witness to give evidence at trial; or

    (b) put the witness statement in as hearsay evidence, any other party may put the witness statement in as hearsay evidence.

Evidence in proceedings other than at trial

32.6 (1) Subject to paragraph (2), the general rule is that evidence at hearings other than the trial is to be by witness statement unless the court, a practice direction or any other enactment requires otherwise.

(2) At hearings other than the trial, a party may, rely on the matters set out in–

    (a) his statement of case; or

    (b) his application notice, if the statement of case or application notice is verified by a statement of truth.

Order for cross-examination

32.7 (1) Where, at a hearing other than the trial, evidence is given in writing, any party may apply to the court for permission to cross-examine the person giving the evidence.

(2) If the court gives permission under paragraph (1) but the person in question does not attend as required by the order, his evidence may not be used unless the court gives permission.

Form of witness statement

32.8 A witness statement must comply with the requirements set out in the relevant practice direction.

(Part 22 requires a witness statement to be verified by a statement of truth)

Witness summaries

32.9 (1) A party who–

    (a) is required to serve a witness statement for use at trial; but

    (b) is unable to obtain one, may apply, without notice, for permission to serve a witness summary instead.

(2)   A witness summary is a summary of–
- (a)   the evidence, if known, which would otherwise be included in a witness statement; or
- (b)   if the evidence is not known, the matters about which the party serving the witness summary proposes to question the witness.

(3)   Unless the court orders otherwise, a witness summary must include the name and address of the intended witness.

(4)   Unless the court orders otherwise, a witness summary must be served within the period in which a witness statement would have had to be served.

(5)   Where a party serves a witness summary, so far as practicable rules 32.4 (requirement to serve witness statements for use at trial), 32.5(3) (amplifying witness statements), and 32.8 (form of witness statement) shall apply to the summary.

Consequence of failure to serve witness statement or summary

32.10   If a witness statement or a witness summary for use at trial is not served in respect of an intended witness within the time specified by the court, then the witness may not be called to give oral evidence unless the court gives permission.

Cross-examination on a witness statement

32.11   Where a witness is called to give evidence at trial, he may be cross-examined on his witness statement whether or not the statement or any part of it was referred to during the witness's evidence in chief.[GL]

Use of witness statements for other purposes

32.12   (1)   Except as provided by this rule, a witness statement may be used only for the purpose of the proceedings in which it is served.

(2)   Paragraph (1) does not apply if and to the extent that–
- (a)   he witness gives consent in writing to some other use of it;
- (b)   the court gives permission for some other use; or
- (c)   the witness statement has been put in evidence at a hearing held in public.

Availability of witness statements for inspection

32.13   (1)   A witness statement which stands as evidence in chief[GL] is open to inspection during the course of the trial unless the court otherwise directs.

(2)   Any person may ask for a direction that a witness statement is not open to inspection.

(3)   The court will not make a direction under paragraph (2) unless

it is satisfied that a witness statement should not be open to inspection because of–

(a)   the interests of justice;

(b)   the public interest;

(c)   the nature of any expert medical evidence in the statement;

(d)   the nature of any confidential information (including information relating to personal financial matters) in the statement; or

(e)   the need to protect the interests of any child or patient.

(4)   The court may exclude from inspection words or passages in the statement.

False statements

32.14   (1)   Proceedings for contempt of court may be brought against a person if he makes, or causes to be made, a false statement in a document verified by a statement of truth without an honest belief in its truth.

(Part 22 makes provision for a statement of truth)

(2)   Proceedings under this rule may be brought only–

(a)   by the Attorney General; or

(b)   with the permission of the court.

Affidavit evidence

32.15   (1)   Evidence must be given by affidavit$^{(GL)}$ instead of or in addition to a witness statement if this is required by the court, a provision contained in any other rule, a practice direction or any other enactment.

(2)   Nothing in these Rules prevents a witness giving evidence by affidavit$^{(GL)}$ at a hearing other than the trial if he chooses to do so in a case where paragraph (1) does not apply, but the party putting forward the affidavit$^{(GL)}$ may not recover the additional cost of making it from any other party unless the court orders otherwise.

Form of affidavit

32.16   An affidavit$^{(GL)}$ must comply with the requirements set out in the relevant practice direction.

Evidence affidavit made outside the jurisdiction

32.17   A person may make an affidavit$^{(GL)}$ outside the jurisdiction in accordance with–

(a)   this Part; or

(b)   the law of the place where he makes the affidavit.$^{(GL)}$

Notice to admit facts

32.18 (1) A party may serve notice on another party requiring him to admit the facts, or the part of the case of the serving party, specified in the notice.

(2) A notice to admit facts must be served no later than 21 days before the trial.

(3) Where the other party makes any admission in response to the notice, the admission may be used against him only–

(a) in the proceedings in which the notice to admit is served; and

(b) by the party who served the notice.

(4) The court may allow a party to amend or withdraw any admission made by him on such terms as it thinks just.

Notice to admit or produce documents

32.19 (1) A party shall be deemed to admit the authenticity of a document disclosed to him under Part 31 (disclosure and inspection of documents) unless he serves notice that he wishes the document to be proved at trial.

(2) A notice to prove a document must be served–

(a) by the latest date for serving witness statements; or

(b) within 7 days of disclosure of the document, whichever is later.

PART 32 PRACTICE DIRECTION – WRITTEN EVIDENCE

THIS PRACTICE DIRECTION SUPPLEMENTS CPR PART 32

EVIDENCE IN GENERAL

1.1 Rule 32.2 sets out how evidence is to be given and facts are to be proved.

1.2 Evidence at a hearing other than the trial should normally be given by witness statement[11] (see paragraph 17 onwards). However a witness may give evidence by affidavit if he wishes to do so[12] (and see paragraph 1.4 below).

1.3 Statements of case (see paragraph 26 onwards) and application notices[13] may also be used as evidence provided that their contents have been verified by a statement of truth.[14]

---

11 See rule 35.6(1).

12 See rule 32.15(2).

13 See Part 23 for information about making an application.

14 Rule 32.6(2) and see Part 22 for information about the statement of truth.

(For information regarding evidence by deposition see Part 34 and the practice direction which supplements it.)

1.4   Affidavits must be used as evidence in the following instances:

(1)   where sworn evidence is required by an enactment;[15] rule, order or practice direction,

(2)   in any application for a search order, a freezing injunction, or an order requiring an occupier to permit another to enter his land, and

(3)   in any application for an order against anyone for alleged contempt of court.

1.5   If a party believes that sworn evidence is required by a court in another jurisdiction for any purpose connected with the proceedings, he may apply to the court for a direction that evidence shall be given only by affidavit on any pre-trial applications.

1.6   The court may give a direction under rule 32.15 that evidence shall be given by affidavit instead of or in addition to a witness statement or statement of case:

(1)   on its own initiative, or

(2)   after any party has applied to the court for such a direction.

1.7   An affidavit, where referred to in the Civil Procedure Rules or a practice direction, also means an affirmation unless the context requires otherwise.

AFFIDAVITS

Deponent

2   A deponent is a person who gives evidence by affidavit or affirmation.

Heading

3.1   The affidavit should be headed with the title of the proceedings (see paragraph 4 of the practice direction supplementing Part 7 and paragraph 7 of the practice direction supplementing Part 20); where the proceedings are between several parties with the same status it is sufficient to identify the parties as follows:

	Number:
A.B. (and others)	Claimants/Applicants
C.D. (and others)	Defendants/Respondents
(as appropriate)	

3.2   At the top right hand corner of the first page (and on the backsheet) there should be clearly written:

(1)   the party on whose behalf it is made,

---

15   See, eg, Protection from Harassment Act 1997 s3(5)(a).

(2)   the initials and surname of the deponent,

(3)   the number of the affidavit in relation to that deponent,

(4)   the identifying initials and number of each exhibit referred to, and

(5)   the date sworn.

Body of affidavit

4.1   The affidavit must, if practicable, be in the deponent's own words, the affidavit should be expressed in the first person and the deponent should:

(1)   commence 'I (*full name*)of (*address*) state on oath ... ',

(2)   if giving evidence in his professional, business or other occupational capacity, give the address at which he works in (1) above, the position he holds and the name of his firm or employer,

(3)   give his occupation or, if he has none, his description, and

(4)   state if he is a party to the proceedings or employed by a party to the proceedings, if it be the case.

4.2   An affidavit must indicate:

(1)   which of the statements in it are made from the deponent's own knowledge and which are matters of information or belief, and

(2)   the source for any matters of information or belief.

4.3   Where a deponent:

(1)   refers to an exhibit or exhibits, he should state 'there is now shown to me marked ' ... ' the (*description of exhibit*)', and

(2)   makes more than one affidavit (to which there are exhibits) in the same proceedings, the numbering of the exhibits should run consecutively throughout and not start again with each affidavit.

Jurat

5.1   The jurat of an affidavit is a statement set out at the end of the document which authenticates the affidavit.

5.2   It must:

(1)   be signed by all deponents,

(2)   be completed and signed by the person before whom the affidavit was sworn whose name and qualification must be printed beneath his signature,

(3)   contain the full address of the person before whom the affidavit was sworn, and

(4)   follow immediately on from the text and not be put on a separate page.

Format of affidavits

6.1 An affidavit should:

(1) be produced on durable quality A4 paper with a 3.5cm margin,

(2) be fully legible and should normally be typed on one side of the paper only,

(3) where possible, be bound securely in a manner which would not hamper filing, or otherwise each page should be endorsed with the case number and should bear the initials of the deponent and of the person before whom it was sworn,

(4) have the pages numbered consecutively as a separate document (or as one of several documents contained in a file),

(5) be divided into numbered paragraphs,

(6) have all numbers, including dates, expressed in figures, and

(7) give the reference to any document or documents mentioned either in the margin or in bold text in the body of the affidavit.

6.2 It is usually convenient for an affidavit to follow the chronological sequence of events or matters dealt with; each paragraph of an affidavit should as far as possible be confined to a distinct portion of the subject.

Inability of deponent to read or sign affidavit

7.1 Where an affidavit is sworn by a person who is unable to read or sign it, the person before whom the affidavit is sworn must certify in the jurat that:

(1) he read the affidavit to the deponent,

(2) the deponent appeared to understand it, and

(3) the deponent signed or made his mark, in his presence.

7.2 If that certificate is not included in the jurat, the affidavit may not be used in evidence unless the court is satisfied that it was read to the deponent and that he appeared to understand it. Two versions of the form of jurat with the certificate are set out at Annex 1 to this practice direction.

Alterations to affidavits

8.1 Any alteration to an affidavit must be initialled by both the deponent and the person before whom the affidavit was sworn.

8.2 An affidavit which contains an alteration that has not been initialled may be filed or used in evidence only with the permission of the court.

Who may administer oaths and take affidavits

9.1 Only the following may administer oaths and take affidavits:

(1) Commissioners for oaths,[16]

16 Commissioner for Oaths 1889 an 1891.

(2) Practising solicitors,[17]

(3) other persons specified by statute,[18]

(4) certain officials of the Supreme Court,[19]

(5) a circuit judge or district judge,[20]

(6) any justice of the peace,[21] and

(7) certain officials of any county court appointed by the judge of that court for the purpose.[22]

9.2 An affidavit must be sworn before a person independent of the parties or their representatives.

Filing of affidavits

10.1 If the court directs that an affidavit is to be filed,[23] it must be filed in the court or Division, or Office or Registry of the court or Division where the action in which it was or is to be used, is proceeding or will proceed.

10.2 Where an affidavit is in a foreign language:

(1) the party wishing to rely on it–

    (a) must have it translated, and

    (b) must file the foreign language affidavit with the court, and

(2) the translator must make and file with the court an affidavit verifying the translation and exhibiting both the translation and a copy of the foreign language affidavit.

EXHIBITS

Manner of exhibiting documents

11.1 A document used in conjunction with an affidavit should be:

(1) produced to and verified by the deponent, and remain separate from the affidavit, and

(2) identified by a declaration of the person before whom the affidavit was sworn.

11.2 The declaration should be headed with the name of the proceedings in the same way as the affidavit.

---

17 Solicitors Act 1974 s81.

18 Administration of Justice Act 1985 s65; Courts and Legal Services Act 1990 s113 and Commissioners for Oaths (Prescribed Bodies) Regulations 1994 and 1995.

19 Commissioners for Oaths Act 1889 s2.

20 County Courts Act 1984 s58.

21 County Courts Act 1984 s58.

22 County Courts Act 1984 s58.

23 Rules 32.1(3) and 32.4(3)(b).

11.3   The first page of each exhibit should be marked:
(1)   as in paragraph 3.2 above, and
(2)   with the exhibit mark referred to in the affidavit.

Letters

12.1   Copies of individual letters should be collected together and exhibited in a bundle or bundles. They should be arranged in chronological order with the earliest at the top, and firmly secured.

12.2   When a bundle of correspondence is exhibited, the exhibit should have a front page attached stating that the bundle consists of original letters and copies. They should be arranged and secured as above and numbered consecutively.

Other documents

13.1   Photocopies instead of original documents may be exhibited provided the originals are made available for inspection by the other parties before the hearing and by the judge at the hearing.

13.2   Court documents must not be exhibited (official copies of such documents prove themselves).

13.3   Where an exhibit contains more than one document, a front page should be attached setting out a list of the documents contained in the exhibit; the list should contain the dates of the documents.

Exhibits other than documents

14.1   Items other than documents should be clearly marked with an exhibit number or letter in such a manner that the mark cannot become detached from the exhibit.

14.2   Small items may be placed in a container and the container appropriately marked.

General provisions

15.1   Where an exhibit contains more than one document:
(1)   the bundle should not be stapled but should be securely fastened in a way that does not hinder the reading of the documents, and
(2)   the pages should be numbered consecutively at bottom centre.

15.2   Every page of an exhibit should be clearly legible; typed copies of illegible documents should be included, paginated with 'a' numbers.

15.3   Where affidavits and exhibits have become numerous, they should be put into separate bundles and the pages numbered consecutively throughout.

15.4   Where on account of their bulk the service of exhibits or copies of exhibits on the other parties would be difficult or impracticable, the directions of the court should be sought as to arrangements for bringing the exhibits to the attention of the other parties and as to their custody pending trial.

Affirmations

16 All provisions in this or any other practice direction relating to affidavits apply to affirmations with the following exceptions:

(1) the deponent should commence 'I (*name*) of (*address*) do solemnly and sincerely affirm ...', and

(2) in the jurat the word 'sworn' is replaced by the word 'affirmed'.

WITNESS STATEMENTS

Heading

17.1 The witness statement should be headed with the title of the proceedings (see paragraph 4 of the practice direction supplementing Part 7 and paragraph 7 of the practice direction supplementing Part 20); where the proceedings are between several parties with the same status it is sufficient to identify the parties as follows:

	Number:
A.B. (and others)	Claimants/Applicants
C.D. (and others)	Defendants/Respondents
	(as appropriate)

17.2 At the top right hand corner of the first page there should be clearly written:

(1) the party on whose behalf it is made,

(2) the initials and surname of the witness,

(3) the number of the statement in relation to that witness,

(4) the identifying initials and number of each exhibit referred to, and

(5) the date the statement was made.

Body of witness statement

18.1 The witness statement must, if practicable, be in the intended witness's own words, the statement should be expressed in the first person and should also state:

(1) the full name of the witness,

(2) his place of residence or, if he is making the statement in his professional, business or other occupational capacity, the address at which he works, the position he holds and the name of his firm or employer,

(3) his occupation, or if he has none, his description, and

(4) the fact that he is a party to the proceedings or is the employee of such a party if it be the case.

18.2 A witness statement must indicate:

(1) which of the statements in it are made from the witness's own knowledge and which are matters of information or belief, and

(2)   the source for any matters of information or belief.

18.3   An exhibit used in conjunction with a witness statement should be verified and identified by the witness and remain separate from the witness statement.

18.4   Where a witness refers to an exhibit or exhibits, he should state 'I refer to the (description of exhibit) marked ' ... ''.

18.5   The provisions of paragraphs 11.3 to 15.4 (exhibits) apply similarly to witness statements as they do to affidavits.

18.6   Where a witness makes more than one witness statement to which there are exhibits, in the same proceedings, the numbering of the exhibits should run consecutively throughout and not start again with each witness statement.

Format of witness statement

19.1   A witness statement should:

(1)   be produced on durable quality A4 paper with a 3.5cm margin,

(2)   be fully legible and should normally be typed on one side of the paper only,

(3)   where possible, be bound securely in a manner which would not hamper filing, or otherwise each page should be endorsed with the case number and should bear the initials of the witness,

(4)   have the pages numbered consecutively as a separate statement (or as one of several statements contained in a file),

(5)   be divided into numbered paragraphs,

(6)   have all numbers, including dates, expressed in figures, and

(7)   give the reference to any document or documents mentioned either in the margin or in bold text in the body of the statement.

19.2   It is usually convenient for a witness statement to follow the chronological sequence of the events or matters dealt with, each paragraph of a witness statement should as far as possible be confined to a distinct portion of the subject.

Statement of truth

20.1   A witness statement is the equivalent of the oral evidence which that witness would, if called, give in evidence; it must include a statement by the intended witness that he believes the facts in it are true.[24]

20.2   To verify a witness statement the statement of truth is as follows:

'I believe that the facts stated in this witness statement are true'

20.3   Attention is drawn to rule 32.14 which sets out the consequences of verifying a witness statement containing a false statement without an honest belief in its truth.

---

24 See Part 22 for information about the statement of truth.

Inability of witness to read or sign statement

21.1 Where a witness statement is made by a person who is unable to read or sign the witness statement, it must contain a certificate made by an authorised person.

21.2 An authorised person is a person able to administer oaths and take affidavits but need not be independent of the parties or their representatives.

21.3 The authorised person must certify:

(1) that the witness statement has been read to the witness,

(2) that the witness appeared to understand it and approved its content as accurate,

(3) that the declaration of truth has been read to the witness,

(4) that the witness appeared to understand the declaration and the consequences of making a false witness statement, and

(5) that the witness signed or made his mark in the presence of the authorised person.

21.4 The form of the certificate is set out at Annex 2 to this practice direction.

Alterations to witness statements

22.1 Any alteration to a witness statement must be initialled by the person making the statement or by the authorised person where appropriate (see paragraph 21).

22.2 A witness statement which contains an alteration that has not been initialled may be used in evidence only with the permission of the court.

Filing of witness statements

23.1 If the court directs that a witness statement is to be filed,[25] it must be filed in the court or Division, or Office or Registry of the court or Division where the action in which it was or is to be used, is proceeding or will proceed.

23.2 Where the court has directed that a witness statement in a foreign language is to be filed:

(1) the party wishing to rely on it must–

(a) have it translated, and

(b) file the foreign language witness statement with the court, and

(2) the translator must make and file with the court an affidavit verifying the translation and exhibiting both the translation and a copy of the foreign language witness statement.

25   Rule 32.4(3)(b).

Certificate of court officer

24.1 Where the court has ordered that a witness statement is not to be open to inspection by the public[26] or that words or passages in the statement are not to be open to inspection[27] the court officer will so certify on the statement and make any deletions directed by the court under rule 32.13(4).

Defects in affidavits, witness statements and exhibits

25.1 Where:

(1) an affidavit,

(2) a witness statement, or

(3) an exhibit to either an affidavit or a witness statement,

does not comply with Part 32 or this practice direction in relation to its form, the court may refuse to admit it as evidence and may refuse to allow the costs arising from its preparation.

25.2 Permission to file a defective affidavit or witness statement or to use a defective exhibit may be obtained from a judge[28] in the court where the case is proceeding.

STATEMENTS OF CASE

26.1 A statement of case may be used as evidence in an interim application provided it is verified by a statement of truth.[29]

26.2 To verify a statement of case the statement of truth should be set out as follows:

> '[I believe][the (*party on whose behalf the statement of case is being signed*) believes] that the facts stated in the statement of case are true'.

26.3 Attention is drawn to rule 32.14 which sets out the consequences of verifying a witness statement containing a false statement without an honest belief in its truth.

(For information regarding statements of truth see Part 22 and the practice direction which supplements it.)

(Practice directions supplementing Parts 7, 9 and 17 provide further information concerning statements of case.)

AGREED BUNDLES FOR HEARINGS

27.1 The court may give directions requiring the parties to use their best endeavours to agree a bundle or bundles of documents for use at any hearing.

---

26 Rule 32.13(2).

27 Rule 32.13(4).

28 Rule 2.3(1); definition of judge.

29 See rule 32.6(2)(a).

27.2   All documents contained in bundles which have been agreed for use at a hearing shall be admissible at that hearing as evidence of their contents, unless–

(1)   the court orders otherwise; or

(2)   a party gives written notice of objection to the admissibility of particular documents.

PENALTY

28.1   (1)   Where a party alleges that a statement of truth or a disclosure statement is false the party shall refer that allegation to the court dealing with the claim in which the statement of truth or disclosure statement has been made.

(2)   the court may–

(a)   excercise any of its powers under the rules;

(b)   initiate steps to consider if there is a contempt of court and, where there is, to punish it;

(The practice direction to RSC Order 52 (Schedule 1) and CCR Order 29 (Schedule 2) makes provision where committal to prison is a possibility if contempt is proved)

(c)   direct the party making the allegation to refer the matter to the Attorney General with a request to him to consider whether he wishes to bring proceedings for contempt of court.

28.2   (1)   An application to the Attorney General should be made to his chambers at 9 Buckingham Gate London SW1E 6JP in writing. The Attorney General will initially require a copy of the order recording the direction of the judge referring the matter to him and information which–

(a)   identifies the statement said to be false; and

(b)   explains–

(i) why it is false, and

(ii) why the maker knew it to be false at the time he made it;

and

(c)   explains why contempt proceedings would be appropriate in the light of the overriding objective in Part 1 of the Civil Procedure Rules.

(2)   The practice of the Attorney General is to prefer an application that comes from the court, and so has received preliminary consideration by a judge, to one made direct to him by a party to the claim in which the alleged contempt occurred without prior consideration by the court. An application to the Attorney General is not a way of appealing against, or reviewing, the decision of the judge.

28.3   Where a party makes an application to the court for permission for that party to commence proceedings for contempt of court, it must be supported by written evidence containing the information specified in paragraph 27.2(1) and the result of the application to the Attorney General made by the applicant.

28.4 The rules do not change the law of contempt or introduce new categories of contempt. A person applying to commence such proceedings should consider whether the incident complained of does amount to contempt of court and whether such proceedings would further the overriding objective in Part 1 of the Civil Procedure Rules.

VIDEO CONFERENCING

29.1 Guidance on the use of video conferencing in the civil courts is set out at Annex 3 to this practice direction.

ANNEX 1

CERTIFICATE TO BE USED WHERE A DEPONENT TO AN AFFIDAVIT IS UNABLE TO READ OR SIGN IT

Sworn at . . . . this . . . . . . day of . . . . Before me, I having first read over the contents of this affidavit to the deponent [*if there are exhibits, add* 'and explained the nature and effect of the exhibits referred to in it'] who appeared to understand it and approved its content as accurate, and made his mark on the affidavit in my presence.

Or; (after, Before me) the witness to the mark of the deponent having been first sworn that he had read over etc. (*as above*) and that he saw him make his mark on the affidavit. (*Witness must sign*).

CERTIFICATE TO BE USED WHERE A DEPONENT TO AN AFFIRMATION IS UNABLE TO READ OR SIGN IT

Affirmed at . . . . this . . . . . . day of . . . . Before me, I having first read over the contents of this affirmation to the deponent [*if there are exhibits, add* 'and explained the nature and effect of the exhibits referred to in it'] who appeared to understand it and approved its content as accurate, and made his mark on the affirmation in my presence.

Or, (after, Before me) the witness to the mark of the deponent having been first sworn that he had read over etc. (as above) and that he saw him make his mark on the affirmation. (*Witness must sign*).

ANNEX 2

CERTIFICATE TO BE USED WHERE A WITNESS IS UNABLE TO READ OR SIGN A WITNESS STATEMENT

I certify that I [*name and address of authorised person*] have read over the contents of this witness statement and the declaration of truth to the witness [*if there are exhibits, add* 'and explained the nature and effect of the exhibits referred to in it'] who appeared to understand (a) the statement and approved its content as accurate and (b) the declaration of truth and the consequences of making a false witness statement, and made his mark in my presence.

ANNEX 3

VIDEO CONFERENCING GUIDANCE

This guidance is for the use of video conferencing (VCF) in civil proceedings. It is in part based, with permission, upon the protocol of the Federal Court of Australia. It is intended to provide a guide to all persons involved in the use of VCF, although it does not attempt to cover all the practical questions which might arise.

Video conferencing generally

1. The guidance covers the use of VCF equipment both (a) in a courtroom, whether via equipment which is permanently placed there or via a mobile unit, and (b) in a separate studio or conference room. In either case, the location at which the judge sits is referred to as the 'local site'. The other site or sites to and from which transmission is made are referred to as 'the remote site' and in any particular case any such site may be another courtroom. The guidance applies to cases where VCF is used for the taking of evidence and also to its use for other parts of any legal proceedings (for example, interim applications, case management conferences, pre-trial reviews).

2. VCF may be a convenient way of dealing with any part of proceedings: it can involve considerable savings in time and cost. Its use for the taking of evidence from overseas witnesses will, in particular, be likely to achieve a material saving of costs, and such savings may also be achieved by its use for taking domestic evidence. It is, however, inevitably not as ideal as having the witness physically present in court. Its convenience should not therefore be allowed to dictate its use. A judgment must be made in every case in which the use of VCF is being considered not only as to whether it will achieve an overall cost saving but as to whether its use will be likely to be

beneficial to the efficient, fair and economic disposal of the litigation. In particular, it needs to be recognised that the degree of control a court can exercise over a witness at the remote site is or may be more limited than it can exercise over a witness physically before it.

3. When used for the taking of evidence, the objective should be to make the VCF session as close as possible to the usual practice in a trial court where evidence is taken in open court. To gain the maximum benefit, several differences have to be taken into account. Some matters, which are taken or granted when evidence is taken in the conventional way, take on a different dimension when it is taken by VCF: for example, the administration of the oath, ensuring that the witness understands who is at the local site and what their various roles are, the raising of any objections to the evidence and the use of documents.

4. It should not be presumed that all foreign governments are willing to allow their nationals or others within their jurisdiction to be examined before a court in England or Wales by means of VCF. If there is any doubt about this, enquiries should be directed to the Foreign and Commonwealth Office (International Legal Matters Unit, Consular Division) with a view to ensuring that the country from which the evidence is to be taken raises no objection to it at diplomatic level. The party who is directed to be responsible for arranging the VCF (see paragraph 8 below) will be required to make all necessary inquiries about this well in advance of the VCF and must be able to inform the court what those inquiries were and of their outcome.

5. Time zone differences need to be considered when a witness abroad is to be examined in England or Wales by VCF. The convenience of the witness, the parties, their representatives and the court must all be taken into account. The cost of the use of a commercial studio is usually greater outside normal business hours.

6. Those involved with VCF need to be aware that, even with the most advanced systems currently available, there are the briefest of delays between the receipt of the picture and that of the accompanying sound. If due allowance is not made for this, there will be a tendency to 'speak over' the witness, whose voice will continue to be heard for a millisecond or so after he or she appears on the screen to have finished speaking.

7. With current technology, picture quality is good, but not as good as a television picture. The quality of the picture is enhanced if those appearing on VCF monitors keep their movements to a minimum.

Preliminary arrangements

8. The court's permission is required for any part of any proceedings to be dealt with by means of VCF. Before seeking a direction, the applicant should notify the listing officer, diary manager or other appropriate court officer of the intention to seek it, and should

enquire as to the availability of court VCF equipment for the day or days of the proposed VCF. The application for a direction should be made to the Master, District Judge or Judge, as may be appropriate. If all parties consent to a direction, permission can be sought by letter, fax or e-mail, although the court may still require an oral hearing. All parties are entitled to be heard on whether or not such a direction should be given and as to its terms. If a witness at a remote site is to give evidence by an interpreter, consideration should be given at this stage as to whether the interpreter should be at the local site or the remote site. If a VCF direction is given, arrangements for the transmission will then need to be made. The court will ordinarily direct that the party seeking permission to use VCF is to be responsible for this. That party is hereafter referred to as 'the VCF arranging party'.

9.   Subject to any order to the contrary, all costs of the transmission, including the costs of hiring equipment and technical personnel to operate it, will initially be the responsibility of, and must be met by, the VCF arranging party. All reasonable efforts should be made to keep the transmission to a minimum and so keep the costs down. All such costs will be considered to be part of the costs of the proceedings and the court will determine at such subsequent time as is convenient or appropriate who, as between the parties, should be responsible for them and (if appropriate) in what proportions.

10.   The local site will, if practicable, be a courtroom but it may instead be an appropriate studio or conference room. The VCF arranging party must contact the listing officer, diary manager or other appropriate officer of the court which made the VCF direction and make arrangements for the VCF transmission. Details of the remote site, and of the equipment to be used both at the local site (if not being supplied by the court) and the remote site (including the number of ISDN lines and connection speed), together with all necessary contact names and telephone numbers, will have to be provided to the listing officer, diary manager or other court officer. The court will need to be satisfied that any equipment provided by the parties for use at the local site and also that at the remote site is of sufficient quality for a satisfactory transmission. The VCF arranging party must ensure that an appropriate person will be present at the local site to supervise the operation of the VCF throughout the transmission in order to deal with any technical problems. That party must also arrange for a technical assistant to be similarly present at the remote site for like purposes.

11.   It is recommended that the judge, practitioners and witness should arrive at their respective VCF sites about 20 minutes prior to the scheduled commencement of the transmission.

12.   If the local site is not a courtroom, but a conference room or studio, the judge will need to determine who is to sit where. The VCF arranging party must take care to ensure that the number of microphones is adequate for the speakers and that the panning of the

camera for the practitioners' table encompasses all legal representatives so that the viewer can see everyone seated there.

13. The proceedings, wherever they may take place, form part of a trial to which the public is entitled to have access (unless the court has determined that they should be heard in private). If the local site is to be a studio or conference room, the VCF arranging party must ensure that it provides sufficient accommodation to enable a reasonable number of members of the public to attend.

14. In cases where the local site is a studio or conference room, the VCF arranging party should make arrangements, if practicable, for the royal coat of arms to be placed above the judge's seat.

15. In cases in which the VCF is to be used for the taking of evidence, the VCF arranging party must arrange for recording equipment to be provided by the court which made the VCF direction so that the evidence can be recorded. An associate will normally be present to operate the recording equipment when the local site is a courtroom. The VCF arranging party should take steps to ensure that an associate is present to do likewise when it is a studio or conference room. The equipment should be set up and tested before the VCF transmission. It will often be a valuable safeguard for the VCF arranging party also to arrange for the provision of recording equipment at the remote site. This will provide a useful back-up if there is any reduction in sound quality during the transmission. A direction from the court for the making of such a back-up recording must, however, be obtained first. This is because the proceedings are court proceedings and, save as directed by the court, no other recording of them must be made. The court will direct what is to happen to the back-up recording.

16. Some countries may require that any oath or affirmation to be taken by a witness accord with local custom rather than the usual form of oath or affirmation used in England and Wales. The VCF arranging party must make all appropriate prior inquiries and put in place all arrangements necessary to enable the oath or affirmation to be taken in accordance with any local custom. That party must be in a position to inform the court what those inquiries were, what their outcome was and what arrangements have been made. If the oath or affirmation can be administered in the manner normal in England and Wales, the VCF arranging party must arrange in advance to have the appropriate holy book at the remote site. The associate will normally administer the oath.

17. Consideration will need to be given in advance to the documents to which the witness is likely to be referred. The parties should endeavour to agree on this. It will usually be most convenient for a bundle of the copy documents to be prepared in advance, which the VCF arranging party should then send to the remote site.

18. Additional documents are sometimes quite properly introduced during the course of a witness's evidence. To cater for this, the VCF arranging party should ensure that equipment is available to enable documents to be transmitted between sites during the course of the

VCF transmission. Consideration should be given to whether to use a document camera. If it is decided to use one, arrangements for its use will need to be established in advance. The panel operator will need to know the number and size of documents or objects if their images are to be sent by document camera. In many cases, a simpler and sufficient alternative will be to ensure that there are fax transmission and reception facilities at the participating sites.

The hearing

19. The procedure for conducting the transmission will be determined by the judge. He will determine who is to control the cameras. In cases where the VCF is being used for an application in the course of the proceedings, the judge will ordinarily not enter the local site until both sites are on line. Similarly, at the conclusion of the hearing, he will ordinarily leave the local site while both sites are still on line. The following paragraphs apply primarily to cases where the VCF is being used for the taking of the evidence of a witness at a remote site. In all cases, the judge will need to decide whether court dress is appropriate when using VCF facilities. It might be appropriate when transmitting from courtroom to courtroom. It might not be when a commercial facility is being used.

20. At the beginning of the transmission, the judge will probably wish to introduce himself and the advocates to the witness. He will probably want to know who is at the remote site and will invite the witness to introduce himself and anyone else who is with him. He may wish to give directions as to the seating arrangements at the remote site so that those present are visible at the local site during the taking of the evidence. He will probably wish to explain to the witness the method of taking the oath or of affirming, the manner in which the evidence will be taken, and who will be conducting the examination and cross-examination. He will probably also wish to inform the witness of the matters referred to in paragraphs 6 and 7 above (co-ordination of picture with sound, and picture quality).

21. The examination of the witness at the remote site should follow as closely as possible the practice adopted when a witness is in the courtroom. During examination, cross-examination and re-examination, the witness must be able to see the legal representative asking the question and also any other person (whether another legal representative or the judge) making any statements in regard to the witness's evidence. It will in practice be most convenient if everyone remains seated throughout the transmission.

PART 52

Rule 52.15

Judicial review appeals

52.15 (1) Where permission to apply for judicial review has been refused at a hearing in the High Court, the person seeking that permission may apply to the Court of Appeal for permission to appeal.

(2) An application in accordance with paragraph (1) must be made within 7 days of the decision of the High Court to refuse to give permission to apply for judicial review.

(3) On an application under paragraph (1), the Court of Appeal may, instead of giving permission to appeal, give permission to apply for judicial review.

PART 52 PRACTICE DIRECTION – APPEALS (PARAS 15.3 AND 15.4 ONLY)

Judicial review appeals

15.3 Where the Court of appeal gives permission to apply for judicial review under rule 52.15(3) the court may, hear the application for judicial review. This will be rare, but may be appropriate where, for example, the High Court is bound by authority or for some other reason, an appeal to the Court of Appeal will be inevitable.

15.4 Paragraphs 5.6 and 5.19 above do not apply to cases where the appeal notice seeks permission to appeal a refusal to give permission to apply for judicial review. In such cases the following documents must be filed with the appellant's notice:

(1) one additional copy of the appellant's notice for the Court of Appeal;

(2) one copy of the appellant's notice for each of the respondents to be sealed and returned;

(3) the order refusing permission to apply for judicial review;

(4) Form 86A;

(5) a copy of the original decision which is the subject of the application to the High Court;

(6) any witness statements or affidavits in support of any application included in the appellant's notice;

(7) a copy of the bundle of documents used in the High Court.

PART 54

JUDICIAL REVIEW AND STATUTORY REVIEW

Contents of this part

I JUDICIAL REVIEW

Scope and interpretation

54.1 (1) This Section of this Part contains rules about judicial review.

(2) In this Section –

(a) a 'claim for judicial review' means a claim to review the lawfulness of–

  (i) an enactment; or

  (ii) a decision, action or failure to act in relation to the exercise of a public function.

(b) an order of mandamus is called a 'mandatory order';

(c) an order of prohibition is called a 'prohibiting order';

(d) an order of certiorari is called a 'quashing order';

(e) 'the judicial review procedure' means the Part 8 procedure as modified by this Section;

(f) 'interested party' means any person (other than the claimant and defendant) who is directly affected by the claim; and

(g) 'court' means the High Court, unless otherwise stated.

(Rule 8.1(6)(b) provides that a rule or practice direction may, in relation to a specified type of proceedings, disapply or modify any of the rules set out in Part 8 as they apply to those proceedings)

When this section must be used

54.2 The judicial review procedure must be used in a claim for judicial review where the claimant is seeking–

(a) a mandatory order;

(b) a prohibiting order;

(c) a quashing order; or

(d) an injunction under section 30 of the Supreme Court Act 1981[30] (restraining a person from acting in any office in which he is not entitled to act).

When this section may be used

54.3 (1) The judicial review procedure may be used in a claim for judicial review where the claimant is seeking–

  (a) a declaration; or

  (b) an injunction[(GL)]

(Section 31(2) of the Supreme Court Act 1981 sets out the circumstances in which the court may grant a declaration or injunction in a claim for judicial review)

(Where the claimant is seeking a declaration or injunction in addition to one of the remedies listed in rule 54.2, the judicial review procedure must be used)

(2) A claim for judicial review may include a claim for damages but may not seek damages alone.

(Section 31(4) of the Supreme Court Act sets out the circumstances in which the court may award damages on a claim for judicial review)

---

30 1981 c54.

Permission required

54.4 The court's permission to proceed is required in a claim for judicial review whether started under this Section or transferred to the Administrative Court.

Time limit for filing claim form

54.5 (1) The claim form must be filed–

  (a) promptly; and

  (b) in any event not later than 3 months after the grounds to make the claim first arose.

  (2) The time limit in this rule may not be extended by agreement between the parties.

  (3) This rule does not apply when any other enactment specifies a shorter time limit for making the claim for judicial review.

Claim form

54.6 (1) In addition to the matters set out in rule 8.2 (contents of the claim form) the claimant must also state–

  (a) the name and address of any person he considers to be an interested party;

  (b) that he is requesting permission to proceed with a claim for judicial review; and

  (c) any remedy (including any interim remedy) he is claiming.

(Part 25 sets out how to apply for an interim remedy)

  (2) The claim form must be accompanied by the documents required by the relevant practice direction.

Service of claim form

54.7 The claim form must be served on–

  (a) the defendant; and

  (b) unless the court otherwise directs, any person the claimant considers to be an interested party,

within 7 days after the date of issue.

Acknowledgment of service

54.8 (1) Any person served with the claim form who wishes to take part in the judicial review must file an acknowledgment of service in the relevant practice form in accordance with the following provisions of this rule.

  (2) Any acknowledgment of service must be–

  (a) filed not more than 21 days after service of the claim form; and

       (b)   served on–

          (i) the claimant; and

          (ii) subject to any direction under rule 54.7(b), any other person named in the claim form,

       as soon as practicable and, in any event, not later than 7 days after it is filed.

(3)   The time limits under this rule may not be extended by agreement between the parties.

(4)   The acknowledgment of service–

       (a)   must–

          (i) where the person filing it intends to contest the claim, set out a summary of his grounds for doing so; and

          (ii) state the name and address of any person the person filing it considers to be an interested party; and

       (b)   may include or be accompanied by an application for directions.

(5)   Rule 10.3(2) does not apply.

Failure to file acknowledgment of service

54.9   (1)   Where a person served with the claim form has failed to file an acknowledgment of service in accordance with rule 54.8, he–

       (a)   may not take part in a hearing to decide whether permission should be given unless the court allows him to do so; but

       (b)   provided he complies with rule 54.14 or any other direction of the court regarding the filing and service of–

          (i) detailed grounds for contesting the claim or supporting it on additional grounds; and

          (ii) any written evidence,

       may take part in the hearing of the judicial review.

   (2)   Where that person takes part in the hearing of the judicial review, the court may take his failure to file an acknowledgment of service into account when deciding what order to make about costs.

   (3)   Rule 8.4 does not apply.

Permission given

54.10 (1)   Where permission to proceed is given the court may also give directions.

    (2)   Directions under paragraph (1) may include a stay$^{(GL)}$ of proceedings to which the claim relates.

(Rule 3.7 provides a sanction for the non-payment of the fee payable when permission to proceed has been given)

Service of order giving or refusing permission

54.11 The court will serve–

(a) the order giving or refusing permission; and

(b) any directions,

on –

(i) the claimant;

(ii) the defendant; and

(iii) any other person who filed an acknowledgment of service.

Permission decision without a hearing

54.12 (1) This rule applies where the court, without a hearing–

(a) refuses permission to proceed; or

(b) gives permission to proceed–

(i) subject to conditions; or

(ii) on certain grounds only.

(2) The court will serve its reasons for making the decision when it serves the order giving or refusing permission in accordance with rule 54.11.

(3) The claimant may not appeal but may request the decision to be reconsidered at a hearing.

(4) A request under paragraph (3) must be filed within 7 days after service of the reasons under paragraph (2).

(5) The claimant, defendant and any other person who has filed an acknowledgment of service will be given at least 2 days' notice of the hearing date.

Defendant, etc, may not apply to set aside[GL]

54.13 Neither the defendant nor any other person served with the claim form may apply to set aside[GL] an order giving permission to proceed.

Response

54.14 (1) A defendant and any other person served with the claim form who wishes to contest the claim or support it on additional grounds must file and serve–

(a) detailed grounds for contesting the claim or supporting it on additional grounds; and

(b) any written evidence,

within 35 days after service of the order giving permission.

(2) The following rules do not apply–

(a) rule 8.5 (3) and 8.5 (4)(defendant to file and serve written evidence at the same time as acknowledgment of service); and

(b) rule 8.5 (5) and 8.5(6) (claimant to file and serve any reply within 14 days).

Where claimant seeks to rely on additional grounds

54.15 The court's permission is required if a claimant seeks to rely on grounds other than those for which he has been given permission to proceed.

EVIDENCE

54.16 (1)   Rule 8.6 (1) does not apply.

(2)   No written evidence may be relied on unless–
  (a)   it has been served in accordance with any–
    (i)   rule under this Section; or
    (ii) direction of the court; or
  (b)   the court gives permission.

Court's powers to hear any person

54.17 (1) Any person may apply for permission–
  (a)   to file evidence; or
  (b)   make representations at the hearing of the judicial review.

(2)   An application under paragraph (1) should be made promptly.

Judicial review may be decided without a hearing

54.18 The court may decide the claim for judicial review without a hearing where all the parties agree.

Court's powers in respect of quashing orders

54.19 (1)   This rule applies where the court makes a quashing order in respect of the decision to which the claim relates.

(2)   The court may–
  (a)   remit the matter to the decision-maker; and
  (b)   direct it to reconsider the matter and reach a decision in accordance with the judgment of the court.

(3)   Where the court considers that there is no purpose to be served in remitting the matter to the decision-maker it may, subject to any statutory provision, take the decision itself.

(Where a statutory power is given to a tribunal, person or other body it may be the case that the court cannot take the decision itself)

Transfer

54.20 The court may
  (a)   order a claim to continue as if it had not been started under this Section; and
  (b)   where it does so, give directions about the future management of the claim.

(Part 30 (transfer) applies to transfers to and from the Administrative Court)

II STATUTORY REVIEW UNDER THE NATIONALITY, IMMIGRATION AND ASYLUM ACT 2002

Scope and interpretation

54.21 (1) This Section of this Part contains rules about applications to the High Court under section 101(2) of the Nationality, Immigration and Asylum Act 2002[31] for a review of a decision of the Immigration Appeal Tribunal on an application for permission to appeal from an adjudicator.

(2) In this Section–

   (a) 'the Act' means the Nationality, Immigration and Asylum Act 2002;

   (b) 'adjudicator' means an adjudicator appointed for the purposes of Part 5 of the Act;

   (c) 'applicant' means a person applying to the High Court under section 101(2) of the Act;

   (d) 'other party' means the other party to the proceedings before the Tribunal; and

   (e) 'Tribunal' means the Immigration Appeal Tribunal.

Application for review

54.22 (1) An application under section 101(2) of the Act must be made to the Administrative Court.

(2) The application must be made by filing an application notice.

(3) The applicant must file with the application notice–

   (a) the immigration or asylum decision to which the proceedings relate, and any document giving reasons for that decision;

   (b) the grounds of appeal to the adjudicator;

   (c) the adjudicator's determination;

   (d) the grounds of appeal to the Tribunal together with any documents sent with them;

   (e) the Tribunal's determination on the application for permission to appeal; and

   (f) any other documents material to the application which were before the adjudicator.

(4) The applicant must also file with the application notice written submissions setting out–

   (a) the grounds upon which it is contended that the Tribunal made an error of law; and

   (b) reasons in support of those grounds.

31 2002 c41.

Time limit for application

54.23 (1) The application notice must be filed not later than 14 days after the applicant is deemed to have received notice of the Tribunal's decision in accordance with rules made under section 106 of the Act.

(2) The court may extend the time limit in paragraph (1) in exceptional circumstances.

(3) An application to extend the time limit must be made in the application notice and supported by written evidence verified by a statement of truth.

Service of application

54.24 (1) The applicant must serve on the Tribunal copies of the application notice and written submissions.

(2) Where an application is for review of a decision by the Tribunal to grant permission to appeal, the applicant must serve on the other party copies of–

(a) the application notice;

(b) the written submissions; and

(c) all the documents filed in support of the application, except for documents which come from or have already been served on that party.

(3) Where documents are required to be served under paragraphs (1) and (2), they must be served as soon as practicable after they are filed.

Determining the application

54.25 (1) The application will be determined by a single judge without a hearing, and by reference only to the written submissions and the documents filed with them.

(2) If the applicant relies on evidence which was not submitted to the adjudicator or the Tribunal, the court will not consider that evidence unless it is satisfied that there were good reasons why it was not submitted to the adjudicator or the Tribunal.

(3) The court may affirm or reverse the Tribunal's decision.

(4) Where the Tribunal refused permission to appeal, the court will reverse the Tribunal's decision only if it is satisfied that–

(a) the Tribunal may have made an error of law; and

(b) either–

(i) the appeal would have a real prospect of success; or

(ii) there is some other compelling reason why the appeal should be heard.

(5) Where the Tribunal granted permission to appeal, the court will reverse the Tribunal's decision only if it is satisfied that–

(a) the appeal would have no real prospect of success; and

(b) there is no other compelling reason why the appeal should be heard.

(6) If the court reverses the Tribunal's decision to refuse permission to appeal–
    (a) the court's order will constitute a grant of permission to appeal to the Tribunal; and
    (b) the court may limit the grant of permission to appeal to specific grounds.

(7) The court's decision shall be final and there shall be no appeal from that decision or renewal of the application.

Service of order

54.26 (1) The court will send copies of its order to–
    (a) the applicant, except where paragraph (2) applies;
    (b) the other party; and
    (c) the Tribunal.

(2) Where–
    (a) the application relates, in whole or in part, to a claim for asylum;
    (b) the Tribunal refused permission to appeal; and
    (c) the court affirms the Tribunal's decision,
    the court will send a copy of its order to the Secretary of State, who must serve the order on the applicant.

(3) Where the Secretary of State has served an order in accordance with paragraph (2), he must notify the court on what date and by what method the order was served.

(4) If the court issues a certificate under section 101(3)(d) of the Act, it will send a copy of the certificate together with the order to–
    (a) the persons to whom it sends the order under paragraphs (1) and (2); and
    (b) if the applicant is in receipt of public funding, the Legal Services Commission.

Costs

54.27 The court may reserve the costs of the application to be determined by the Tribunal.

PART 54 PRACTICE DIRECTION – JUDICIAL REVIEW

THIS PRACTICE DIRECTION SUPPLEMENTS PART 54

1.1 In addition to Part 54 and this practice direction attention is drawn to:
    • section 31 of the Supreme Court Act 1981; and
    • the Human Rights Act 1998

THE COURT

2.1 Part 54 claims for judicial review are dealt with in the Administrative Court.

2.2 Where the claim is proceeding in the Administrative Court in London, documents must be filed at the Administrative Court Office, the Royal Courts of Justice, Strand, London, WC2A 2LL.

2.3 Where the claim is proceeding in the Administrative Court in Wales (see paragraph 3.1), documents must be filed at the Civil Justice Centre, 2 Park Street, Cardiff, CF10 1ET.

Urgent applications

2.4 Where urgency makes it necessary for the claim for judicial review to be made outside London or Cardiff, the Administrative Court Office in London should be consulted (if necessary, by telephone) prior to filing the claim form.

JUDICIAL REVIEW CLAIMS IN WALES

3.1 A claim for judicial review may be brought in the Administrative Court in Wales where the claim or any remedy sought involves:

(1) a devolution issue arising out of the Government of Wales Act 1998; or

(2) an issue concerning the National Assembly for Wales, the Welsh executive, or any Welsh public body (including a Welsh local authority) (whether or not it involves a devolution issue).

3.2 Such claims may also be brought in the Administrative Court at the Royal Courts of Justice.

Rule 54.5 – Time limit for filing claim form

4.1 Where the claim is for a quashing order in respect of a judgment, order or conviction, the date when the grounds to make the claim first arose, for the purposes of rule 54.5(1)(b), is the date of that judgment, order or conviction.

RULE 54.6 – CLAIM FORM

Interested parties

5.1 Where the claim for judicial review relates to proceedings in a court or tribunal, any other parties to those proceedings must be named in the claim form as interested parties under rule 54.6(1)(a) (and therefore served with the claim form under rule 54.7(b)).

5.2 For example, in a claim by a defendant in a criminal case in the Magistrates or Crown Court for judicial review of a decision in that case, the prosecution must always be named as an interested party.

Human rights

5.3 Where the claimant is seeking to raise any issue under the Human Rights Act 1998, or seeks a remedy available under that Act, the claim form must include the information required by paragraph 15 of the practice direction supplementing Part 16.

Devolution issues

5.4 Where the claimant intends to raise a devolution issue, the claim form must:

(1) specify that the applicant wishes to raise a devolution issue and identify the relevant provisions of the Government of Wales Act 1998, the Northern Ireland Act 1998 or the Scotland Act 1998; and

(2) contain a summary of the facts, circumstances and points of law on the basis of which it is alleged that a devolution issue arises.

5.5 In this practice direction 'devolution issue' has the same meaning as in paragraph 1, schedule 8 to the Government of Wales Act 1998; paragraph 1, schedule 10 to the Northern Ireland Act 1998; and paragraph 1, schedule 6 of the Scotland Act 1998.

Claim form

5.6 The claim form must include or be accompanied by–

(1) a detailed statement of the claimant's grounds for bringing the claim for judicial review;

(2) a statement of the facts relied on;

(3) any application to extend the time limit for filing the claim form;

(4) any application for directions.

5.7 In addition, the claim form must be accompanied by

(1) any written evidence in support of the claim or application to extend time;

(2) a copy of any order that the claimant seeks to have quashed;

(3) where the claim for judicial review relates to a decision of a court or tribunal, an approved copy of the reasons for reaching that decision;

(4) copies of any documents on which the claimant proposes to rely;

(5) copies of any relevant statutory material; and

(6) a list of essential documents for advance reading by the court (with page references to the passages relied on).

5.8 Where it is not possible to file all the above documents, the claimant must indicate which documents have not been filed and the reasons why they are not currently available.

Bundle of documents

5.9 The claimant must file two copies of a paginated and indexed bundle containing all the documents referred to in paragraphs 5.6 and 5.7.

5.10 Attention is drawn to rules 8.5(1) and 8.5(7).

RULE 54.7 – SERVICE OF CLAIM FORM

6.1 Except as required by rules 54.11 or 54.12(2), the Administrative Court will not serve documents and service must be effected by the parties.

RULE 54.8 – ACKNOWLEDGMENT OF SERVICE

7.1 Attention is drawn to rule 8.3(2) and the relevant practice direction and to rule 10.5.

RULE 54.10 – PERMISSION GIVEN

Directions

8.1 Case management directions under rule 54.10(1) may include directions about serving the claim form and any evidence on other persons.

8.2 Where a claim is made under the Human Rights Act 1998, a direction may be made for giving notice to the Crown or joining the Crown as a party. Attention is drawn to rule 19.4A and paragraph 6 of the Practice Direction supplementing Section I of Part 19.

8.3 A direction may be made for the hearing of the claim for judicial review to be held outside London or Cardiff. Before making any such direction the judge will consult the judge in charge of the Administrative Court as to its feasibility.

Permission without a hearing

8.4 The court will generally, in the first instance, consider the question of permission without a hearing.

Permission hearing

8.5 Neither the defendant nor any other interested party need attend a hearing on the question of permission unless the court directs otherwise.

8.6 Where the defendant or any party does attend a hearing, the court will not generally make an order for costs against the claimant.

RULE 54.11 – SERVICE OF ORDER GIVING OR REFUSING PERMISSION

9.1 An order refusing permission or giving it subject to conditions or on certain grounds only must set out or be accompanied by the court's reasons for coming to that decision.

RULE 54.14 – RESPONSE

10.1 Where the party filing the detailed grounds intends to rely on documents not already filed, he must file a paginated bundle of those documents when he files the detailed grounds.

RULE 54.15 – WHERE CLAIMANT SEEKS TO RELY ON ADDITIONAL GROUNDS

11.1 Where the claimant intends to apply to rely on additional grounds at the hearing of the claim for judicial review, he must give notice to the court and to any other person served with the claim form no later than 7 clear days before the hearing (or the warned date where appropriate).

RULE 54.16 – EVIDENCE

12.1 Disclosure is not required unless the court orders otherwise.

RULE 54.17 – COURT'S POWERS TO HEAR ANY PERSON

13.1 Where all the parties consent, the court may deal with an application under rule 54.17 without a hearing.

13.2 Where the court gives permission for a person to file evidence or make representations at the hearing of the claim for judicial review, it may do so on conditions and may give case management directions.

13.3 An application for permission should be made by letter to the Administrative Court office, identifying the claim, explaining who the applicant is and indicating why and in what form the applicant wants to participate in the hearing.

13.4 If the applicant is seeking a prospective order as to costs, the letter should say what kind of order and on what grounds.

13.5 Applications to intervene must be made at the earliest reasonable opportunity, since it will usually be essential not to delay the hearing.

RULE 54.20 – TRANSFER

14.1 Attention is drawn to rule 30.5.

14.2 In deciding whether a claim is suitable for transfer to the Administrative Court, the court will consider whether it raises issues of public law to which Part 54 should apply.

Skeleton arguments

15.1 The claimant must file and serve a skeleton argument not less than 21 working days before the date of the hearing of the judicial review (or the warned date).

15.2 The defendant and any other party wishing to make representations at the hearing of the judicial review must file and serve a skeleton argument not less than 14 working days before the date of the hearing of the judicial review (or the warned date).

15.3 Skeleton arguments must contain:

(1) a time estimate for the complete hearing, including delivery of judgment;

(2) a list of issues;

(3) a list of the legal points to be taken (together with any relevant authorities with page references to the passages relied on);

(4) a chronology of events (with page references to the bundle of documents (see paragraph 16.1);

(5) a list of essential documents for the advance reading of the court (with page references to the passages relied on) (if different from that filed with the claim form) and a time estimate for that reading; and

(6) a list of persons referred to.

Bundle of documents to be filed

16.1 The claimant must file a paginated and indexed bundle of all relevant documents required for the hearing of the judicial review when he files his skeleton argument.

16.2 The bundle must also include those documents required by the defendant and any other party who is to make representations at the hearing.

Agreed final order

17.1 If the parties agree about the final order to be made in a claim for judicial review, the claimant must file at the court a document (with

2 copies) signed by all the parties setting out the terms of the proposed agreed order together with a short statement of the matters relied on as justifying the proposed agreed order and copies of any authorities or statutory provisions relied on.

17.2 The court will consider the documents referred to in paragraph 17.1 and will make the order if satisfied that the order should be made.

17.3 If the court is not satisfied that the order should be made, a hearing date will be set.

17.4 Where the agreement relates to an order for costs only, the parties need only file a document signed by all the parties setting out the terms of the proposed order.

PRACTICE DIRECTION – SCHEDULE 1, ORDER 54 (APPLICATION FOR WRIT OF HABEAS CORPUS)

THIS PRACTICE DIRECTION SUPPLEMENTS CPR PART 50, AND SCHEDULE 1 TO THE CPR

Terminology

1.1 In this practice direction–

(1) 'Order 54' means those provisions contained in Schedule 1, RSC Order 54 which were previously contained in the Rules of the Supreme Court (1965);

(2) a reference to a rule or Part prefixed with CPR is a reference to a rule or Part contained in the CPR rules; and

(3) a reference to a rule number alone is a reference to the rule so numbered in Order 54.

Scope

2.1 This practice direction supplements Order 54 (which sets out how to apply for a writ of habeas corpus) by providing further detail about the application.

2.2 This practice direction must be read together with Order 54.

2.3 It also lists at paragraph 7 other practice directions which governed procedure relating to Order 54 before 26 April 1999 and which will continue to do so.

Form to be used where court directs claim form to be used

3.1 Where the court directs that an application be made by claim form, under–

(1) rule 2, (on hearing application under rule 1); or

(2) rule 4(2) (application in criminal proceedings ordered to be made to Divisional Court of the Queen's Bench Division),

the claimant must use Form 87 modified in accordance with the guidance set out in the Forms practice direction.

Form to be used for Notice of adjourned application directed by court

4.1   Where the court directs under rule 2 (1) (c) that an application made under rule 1 is adjourned to allow for service of notice of the application, such notice must be given in modified Form 88.

Service

5.1   The party seeking the writ must serve–
(1)   the claim form in accordance with rule 2.2; and
(2)   the writ of habeas corpus ad subjiciendum and notice in Form 90, as modified, in accordance with rule 6.

(CPR rule 6.3 provides that the court will normally serve a document which it has issued or prepared).

The Crown Office List

6.1   When the court directs that an application is to be made by claim form under–
(1)   rule 2 (1) (powers of court to whom application made under rule 1); or
(2)   rule 4 (2) (power of court in where application made in criminal proceedings) the application must be entered in the Crown Office List in accordance with Practice Direction (Crown Office List) 1987 1 WLR 232 [1987] 1 All ER 368.

(In Schedule 1, RSC Order 57 rule 2 provides for the entry of claims in the appropriate office and for the filing of copy documents for the use of the court)

Practice Directions etc, which apply to Order 54

7.1   On and after 26 April 1999, the Practice directions, Statements and Practice Notes set out in Table 1 continue to apply to proceedings under Order 54.

Table 1

Practice Direction, etc.	Content
Practice Note [1983] 2 All ER 1020	Urgent matters outside London-consultation of Crown Office and continuation in London
Practice Note (Crown Office List) [1987] 1 All ER 1184 Practice Direction (Crown Office List) [1987] 1 WLR 232; [1987] 1 All ER 368	Need for accuracy in time estimates Parts of the List
Practice Direction (Crown Office List: Preparation for hearings) [1994] 4 All ER 671, [1994] 1 WLR 1551 (18th November 1994).	Preparation for hearings; Documentation; Time limits; Skeleton arguments; amendment of grounds.
Practice Direction (Crown Office List; Consent Orders) [1997] 1 WLR 825	Consent orders
Practice Statement (Supreme Court; Judgments) [1998] 1 WLR 825, [1998] 2 All ER 638.	Judgments

PRE-ACTION PROTOCOL FOR JUDICIAL REVIEW

Contents
Introduction
A   Letter before claim
B   Response to a letter before claim
C   Notes on public funding for legal costs in judicial review

INTRODUCTION

This protocol applies to proceedings within England and Wales only. It does not affect the time limit specified by Rule 54.5(1) of the Civil Procedure Rules which requires that any claim form in an application for judicial review must be filed promptly and in any event not later than 3 months after the grounds to make the claim first arose.[32]

1   Judicial review allows people with a sufficient interest in a decision or action by a public body to ask a judge to review the lawfulness of:

 • an enactment; or

 • a decision, action or failure to act in relation to the exercise of a public function.[33]

2   Judicial review may be used where there is no right of appeal or where all avenues of appeal have been exhausted.

3   Where alternative procedures have not been used the judge may refuse to hear the judicial review case. However, his or her decision will depend upon the circumstances of the case and the nature of the alternative remedy. Where an alternative remedy does exist a claimant should give careful consideration as to whether it is appropriate to his or her problem before making a claim for judicial review.

4   Judicial review may not be appropriate in every instance. Claimants are strongly advised to seek appropriate legal advice when considering such proceedings and, in particular, before adopting this protocol or making a claim. Although the Legal Services Commission will not normally grant full representation before a letter before claim has been sent and the proposed defendant given a reasonable time to respond, initial funding may be available, for eligible claimants, to cover the work necessary to write this. (See Annex C for more information.)

---

32 While the court does have the discretion under Rule 3.1(2)(a) of the Civil Procedure Rules to allow a late claim, this is only used in exceptional circumstances. **Compliance with the protocol alone is unlikely to persuade the court to allow a late claim.**

33 Civil Procedure Rule 54.1(2).

5   This protocol sets out a code of good practice and contains the steps which parties should generally follow before making a claim for judicial review.

6   This protocol does not impose a greater obligation on a public body to disclose documents or give reasons for its decision than that already provided for in statute or common law. However, where the court considers that a public body should have provided *relevant* documents and/or information, particularly where this failure is a breach of a statutory or common law requirement, it may impose sanctions.

This protocol *will not be appropriate* where the defendant does not have the legal power to change the decision being challenged, for example decisions issued by tribunals such as the Immigration Appeal Authorities.

This protocol *will not be appropriate* in urgent cases, for example, when directions have been set, or are in force, for the claimant's removal from the UK, or where there is an urgent need for an interim order to compel a public body to act where it has unlawfully refused to do so (for example, the failure of a local housing authority to secure interim accommodation for a homeless claimant) a claim should be made immediately. A letter before claim will not stop the implementation of a disputed decision in all instances.

7   All claimants will need to satisfy themselves whether they should follow the protocol, depending upon the circumstances of his or her case. Where the use of the protocol is appropriate, the court will normally expect all parties to have complied with it and will take into account compliance or non-compliance when giving directions for case management of proceedings or when making orders for costs.[34] However, even in emergency cases, it is good practice to fax to the defendant the draft Claim Form which the claimant intends to issue. A claimant is also normally required to notify a defendant when an interim mandatory order is being sought.

The letter before claim

8   Before making a claim, the claimant should send a letter to the defendant. The purpose of this letter is to identify the issues in dispute and establish whether litigation can be avoided.

9   Claimants should normally use the suggested *standard format* for the letter outlined at Annex A.

10   The letter should contain t*he date and details of the decision, act or omission being challenged and a clear summary of the facts* on which the claim is based. It should also contain the *details of any relevant information* that the claimant is seeking and an explanation of why this is considered relevant.

34 Civil Procedure Rules Costs Practice Direction.
35 See Civil Procedure Rules Rule 54.1(2)(f).

11   The letter should normally contain the *details of any interested parties*[35] known to the claimant. They should be sent a copy of the letter before claim *for information. Claimants are strongly advised to seek appropriate legal advice when considering such proceedings and, in particular, before sending the letter before claim to other interested parties or making a claim.*

12   A claim should not normally be made until the proposed reply date given in the letter before claim has passed, unless the circumstances of the case require more immediate action to be taken.

The letter of response

13   Defendants should normally respond within 14 days using the *standard format* at Annex B. Failure to do so will be taken into account by the court and sanctions may be imposed unless there are good reasons.[36]

14   Where it is not possible to reply within the proposed time limit the defendant should send an interim reply and propose a reasonable extension. Where an extension is sought, reasons should be given and, where required, additional information requested. *This will not affect the time limit for making a claim for judicial review*[37] nor will it bind the claimant where he or she considers this to be unreasonable. However, where the court considers that a subsequent claim is made prematurely it may impose sanctions.

15   If the *claim is being conceded in full,* the reply should say so in clear and unambiguous terms.

16   If the *claim is being conceded in part or not being conceded at all,* the reply should say so in clear and unambiguous terms, and:

(a)   where appropriate, contain a new decision, clearly identifying what aspects of the claim are being conceded and what are not, or, give a clear timescale within which the new decision will be issued;

(b)   provide a fuller explanation for the decision, if considered appropriate to do so;

(c)   address any points of dispute, or explain why they cannot be addressed;

(d)   enclose any relevant documentation requested by the claimant, or explain why the documents are not being enclosed; and

(e)   where appropriate, confirm whether or not they will oppose any application for an interim remedy.

17   The response should be sent to all *interested parties*[38] identified by the claimant and contain details of any other parties who the defendant considers also have an interest.

36   See Civil Procedure Rules Pre-action Protocol Practice Direction paragraphs 2-3.

37   Civil Procedure Rule 54.5(1).

38   Civil Procedure Rule 54.1(2)(f).

ANNEX A – LETTER BEFORE CLAIM

SECTION 1. INFORMATION REQUIRED IN A LETTER BEFORE CLAIM

Proposed claim for judicial review

1 **To**
(Insert the name and address of the proposed defendant – see details in section 2)

2 **The claimant**
(Insert the title, first and last name and the address of the claimant)

3 **Reference details**
(When dealing with large organisations it is important to understand that the information relating to any particular individual's previous dealings with it may not be immediately available, therefore it is important to set out the relevant reference numbers for the matter in dispute and/or the identity of those within the public body who have been handling the particular matter in dispute – see details in section 3)

4 **The details of the matter being challenged**
(Set out clearly the matter being challenged, particularly if there has been more than one decision)

5 **The issue**
(Set out the date and details of the decision, or act or omission being challenged, a brief summary of the facts and why it is contented to be wrong)

6 **The details of the action that the defendant is expected to take**
(Set out the details of the remedy sought, including whether a review or any interim remedy are being requested)

7 **The details of the legal advisers, if any, dealing with this claim**
(Set out the name, address and reference details of any legal advisers dealing with the claim)

8 **The details of any interested parties**
(Set out the details of any interested parties and confirm that they have been sent a copy of this letter)

9 **The details of any information sought**
(Set out the details of any information that is sought. This may include a request for a fuller explanation of the reasons for the decision that is being challenged)

10 The details of any documents that are considered relevant and necessary
(Set out the details of any documentation or policy in respect of which the disclosure is sought and explain why these are relevant. If you rely on a statutory duty to disclose, this should be specified)

11 The address for reply and service of court documents
(Insert the address for the reply)

12 Proposed reply date
(The precise time will depend upon the circumstances of the individual case. However, although a shorter or longer time may be appropriate in a particular case, 14 days is a reasonable time to allow in most circumstances)

SECTION 2. ADDRESS FOR SENDING THE LETTER BEFORE CLAIM

Public bodies have requested that, for certain types of cases, in order to ensure a prompt response, letters before claim should be sent to specific addresses.

Where the claim concerns a decision in an Immigration, Asylum or Nationality case:
• The Judicial Review Management Unit
  Immigration and Nationality Directorate
  1st Floor
  Green Park House
  29 Wellesley Road
  Croydon CR0 2AJ

Where the claim concerns a decision by the Legal Services Commission:
• The address on the decision letter/notification; and
  Policy and Legal Department
  Legal Services Commission
  85 Gray's Inn Road
  London WC1X 8TX

Where the claim concerns a decision by a local authority:
• The address on the decision letter/notification; and
• Their legal department[39]

39 The relevant address should be available from a range of sources such as the Phone Book, Business and Services Directory, Thomson's Local Directory, CAB, etc.

Where the claim concerns a decision by a department or body for whom Treasury Solicitor acts *and Treasury Solicitor has already been involved in the case* a copy should also be sent, quoting the Treasury Solicitor's reference, to:

Treasury Solicitor
Queen Anne's Chambers
28 Broadway
London SW1H 9JS

In all other circumstances, the letter should be sent to the address on the letter notifying the decision.

SECTION 3. SPECIFIC REFERENCE DETAILS REQUIRED

Public bodies have requested that the following information should be provided in order to ensure prompt response.

- **Where the claim concerns an Immigration, Asylum or Nationality case, dependent upon the nature of the case:**
- The Home Office reference number
- The Port reference number
- The Immigration Appellate Authority reference number
- The National Asylum Support Service reference number

Or, if these are unavailable:

- The full name, nationality and date of birth of the claimant.

Where the claim concerns a decision by the Legal Services Commission:

- The certificate reference number.

ANNEX B – RESPONSE TO A LETTER BEFORE CLAIM

INFORMATION REQUIRED IN A RESPONSE TO A LETTER BEFORE CLAIM

Proposed claim for judicial review

1. **The claimant**
   (Insert the title, first and last names and the address to which any reply should be sent)

2. **From**
   (Insert the name and address of the defendant)

3   Reference details
(Set out the relevant reference numbers for the matter in dispute and
the identity of those within the public body who have been handling
the issue)

4   The details of the matter being challenged
(Set out details of the matter being challenged, providing a fuller
explanation of the decision, where this is considered appropriate)

5   Response to the proposed claim
(Set out whether the issue in question is conceded in part, or in full,
or will be contested. Where it is not proposed to disclose any
information that has been requested, explain the reason for this.
Where an interim reply is being sent and there is a realistic prospect
of settlement, details should be included)

6   Details of any other interested parties
(Identify any other parties who you consider have an interest who
have not already been sent a letter by the claimant)

7   Address for further correspondence and service of court documents
(Set out the address for any future correspondence on this matter)

ANNEX C – NOTES ON PUBLIC FUNDING FOR LEGAL COSTS IN JUDICIAL REVIEW

Public funding for legal costs in judicial review is available from legal
professionals and advice agencies which have contracts with the Legal
Services Commission as part of the Community Legal Service.
Funding may be provided for:

- *Legal Help* to provide initial advice and assistance with any legal
  problem; or
- *Legal Representation* to allow you to be represented in court if you
  are taking or defending court proceedings. This is available in
  two forms:
- *Investigative Help* is limited to funding to investigate the strength
  of the proposed claim. It includes the issue and conduct of
  proceedings only so far as is necessary to obtain disclosure of
  relevant information or to protect the client's position in relation
  to any urgent hearing or time limit for the issue of proceedings.
  This includes the work necessary to write a **letter before claim** to
  the body potentially under challenge, setting out the grounds of
  challenge, and giving that body a reasonable opportunity,
  typically 14 days, in which to respond.

- *Full Representation* is provided to represent you in legal proceedings and includes litigation services, advocacy services, and all such help as is usually given by a person providing representation in proceedings, including steps preliminary or incidental to proceedings, and/or arriving at or giving effect to a compromise to avoid or bring to an end any proceedings. Except in emergency cases, a proper **letter before claim** must be sent and the other side must be given an opportunity to respond before Full Representation is granted.

Further information on the type(s) of help available and the criteria for receiving that help may be found in the Legal Service Manual Volume 3: *The Funding Code*. This may be found on the Legal Services Commission website at:

www.legalservices.gov.uk

A list of contracted firms and Advice Agencies may be found on the Community Legal Services website at:

www.justask.org.uk

Notes for guidance

NOTES FOR GUIDANCE ON APPLYING FOR JUDICIAL REVIEW

GENERAL

These notes are not intended to be exhaustive but merely to offer an outline of the procedure to be followed. Claimants and their legal advisers should consult Part 54 of the Civil Procedure Rules and the appropriate Practice Direction 54 (issued August 2000).

The procedure set out below applies to applications for permission lodged on or after 2 October. Any case commenced before that date is governed by the provisions of the previous rules.

1.   Judicial review

A claim for Judicial review means a claim to review the lawfulness of an enactment or a decision, action or failure to act in relation to the exercise of a public function. The procedure must be used where the claimant is seeking a mandatory order (formerly known as an order of mandamus), a prohibiting order (formerly known as an order of prohibition) or a quashing order (formerly known as an order of certiorari) – Part 54.1 and Part 54.2.

2.   Commencing the claim

Part 54 claims for judicial review are dealt with in the Administrative Court. Where the claim is proceeding in the Administrative Court in London, documents must be filed at the Administrative Court Office, the Royal Courts of Justice, Strand, London, WC2A 2LL. Where the claim is proceeding in the Administrative Court in Wales (because the claim concerns a devolution issue arising out of the Government of Wales Act 1998; or issue concerning the National Assembly for Wales, the Welsh executive, or any Welsh public body (including a Welsh local authority)) the documents may be filed at the Law Courts, Cathays Park, Cardiff, CF10 3PG or at the Administrative Court Office, the Royal Courts of Justice, Strand, London, WC2A 2LL.

3.   Legal Aid

Neither the Court nor the Administrative Court Office has power to grant legal aid which may only be obtained from the Legal Services

Commission. Application should be made to the appropriate Area Office whose address will be found in the telephone directory, or through a Solicitor, who may advise as to an application for the Board's consideration.

4. Time for commencing the claim

The claim form must be filed promptly and in any event within the period of three months after the grounds to make the claim first arose. Part 54.5.

The Court can extend or abridge time but will only exercise this power where it is satisfied there are very good reasons for doing so. The time may not be extended by agreement between the parties. If an extension or abridgement of time is sought, the grounds in support of that application must be set out in the claim form. Part 54.5.

5. Fees

A fee of £30.00 is payable on lodging an application for permission to apply for Judicial Review. A further £120.00 is payable if permission is granted. (Supreme Court Fees Order 1999 as amended) Cheques should be made payable to HM Paymaster General. Personal cheques are not accepted unless supported by a bankers cheque guarantee card presented in the Fees Room at the time of lodging the application. Any application for a remission of fees must be made in writing to the Supreme Court Accounts Office, Royal Courts of Justice in advance of lodging the application for permission.

6. Form of application

Applications for permission to move for Judicial Review must be made by claim form – Form N461. The claim form must include or be accompanied by–

(1) a detailed statement of the claimant's grounds for bringing the claim for judicial review;

(2) a statement of the facts relied on;

(3) any application to extend the time limit for filing the claim form;

(4) any application for directions; and

(5) a time estimate for the hearing.

Where the claimant is seeking to raise any issue under the Human Rights Act 1998, or seeks a remedy available under that Act, the claim form must include the information required by paragraph 16 of the practice direction supplementing Part 16 of the Civil Procedure Rules.

Where the claimant intends to raise a devolution issue, the claim form must specify that the applicant wishes to raise a devolution issue and identify the relevant provisions of the Government of Wales Act 1998, the Northern Ireland Act 1998 or the

Scotland Act 1998 and must contain a summary of the facts, circumstances and points of law on the basis of which it is alleged that a devolution issue arises.

The claim form must also be accompanied by:

(1) any written evidence in support of the claim or application to extend time;

(2) a copy of any order that the claimant seeks to have quashed;

(3) where the claim for judicial review relates to a decision of a court or tribunal, an approved copy of the reasons for reaching that decision;

(4) copies of any documents on which the claimant proposes to rely;

(5) copies of any relevant statutory material;

(6) a list of essential documents for advance reading by the court (with page references to the passages relied on).

Where it is not possible to file all the above documents, the claimant must indicate which documents have not been filed and the reasons why they are not currently available.

The claimant must file two copies of a paginated and indexed bundle containing the documents referred to above, Civil Procedure Rules Part 54.6 and Practice Direction.

A list must be provided of the pages essential for reading by the Court. Where only part of a page needs to be read, that part should be indicated, by side-lining or in some other way, but not by highlighting.

Where the claimant is represented by solicitors they must also provide a paginated, indexed bundle of the relevant legislative provisions and statutory instruments required for the proper consideration of the application. A claimant who acts in person should comply with this requirement if possible.

Applications which do not comply with the requirements of Part 54 and the Practice Direction will not be accepted, even with undertakings to comply at a later date, save in exceptional circumstances such as urgency. In this context a matter will be regarded as urgent where a decision is required from the Court within 14 days of the lodging of the application. If the only reason given in support of urgency is the imminent expiry of the three month time limit for lodging an application, the papers will nonetheless be returned for compliance with Part 54 and the Practice Direction and if necessary, the claimant must seek an extension of time and provide reasons for the delay in lodging the papers in proper form.

7. Service of the claim form

The claim form (and accompanying documents) must be served on the defendant and any person the claimant considers to be an interested party (unless the court directs otherwise) within 7 days of the date of issue. The claimant must lodge 1 original plus 1 copy of the certificate of service in the Administrative Court Office within 7 days of serving the defendant and other interested parties. The Administrative Court Office will not serve claims.

8. **Acknowledgement of service**

Any person served with the claim form who wishes to take part in the judicial review must file, in the Administrative Court Office, within 21 days of service 1 original plus 1 copy of the acknowledgement of service (Form N462) setting out the summary of grounds for contesting the claim and the name and address of any person considered to be an interested party.

The acknowledgement of service must be served on the claimant and interested persons no later than 7 days after it is filed.

Failure to file the acknowledgement of service renders it necessary for the party concerned to obtain the permission of the court to take part in any oral hearing of the application for permission.

9. **Permission to proceed**

Applications for permission to proceed with the claim for Judicial Review will be considered in one of two ways – on the papers or at an oral hearing in open court:

(i) Consideration on papers

Unless the Court directs otherwise, a Judge will decide whether to grant permission without hearing oral submissions. The purpose of this procedure is to ensure that applications may be dealt with speedily and without unnecessary expense. The decision of the judge (Form JRJ) will be served on the claimant, the defendant and any other person served with the claim form. If permission is granted, the claimant should lodge a further fee of £120.00 with the Administrative Office within 7 days of service of the judge's decision upon him. If such fee is not lodged, the file may be closed. If permission is refused, or is granted subject to conditions or on certain grounds only, the claimant may request the decision be reconsidered at an oral hearing. Such a request must be filed within 7 days after service of the notification of the decision, Civil Procedure Rules Part 54.11, 54.12.

(ii) Oral hearing in open court

At an oral hearing a claimant may appear in person or be represented by Counsel. An oral hearing is allocated 20 minutes of court time. If it is considered that 20 minutes is insufficient, the claimant or his representatives must provide a written estimate of the time required and request a special fixture.

Neither the defendant nor any other interested party need attend a hearing on the question of permission unless the court directs otherwise. Where the defendant or any party does attend a hearing, the court will not generally make an order for costs against the claimant. (Practice Direction)

In a Criminal matter if the judge refuses permission, that decision is final so far as the High Court is concerned. If he grants permission, he may deal with the substantive application then, or adjourn to another date before either a Single Judge or the Divisional Court.

An application for permission in a civil matter which has been refused by a Judge after a hearing, may be appealed to the Court of Appeal Civil Division within 7 days (permission is required of the Court of Appeal) [see para 19 below].

10. Case management directions on permission to proceed

Case management directions under rule 54.10(1) may include directions about serving the claim form and any evidence on other persons and directions as to expedition.

Where a claim is made under the Human Rights Act 1998, a direction may be made for giving notice to the Crown or joining the Crown as a party. Attention is drawn to rule 19.4A and paragraph 6 of the Practice Direction supplementing Section I of Part 19.

A direction may be made for the hearing of the claim for judicial review to be held outside London or Cardiff. Before making any such direction the judge will consult the judge in charge of the Administrative Court as to its feasibility.

11. Defendants

A party upon whom a claim form is served who wishes to contest the claim (or support it on additional grounds) must, within 35 days of service of the order granting permission, file and serve:

(i) detailed grounds for contesting the claim or supporting on additional grounds; and

(ii) any written evidence upon which he relies.

Any party who has done so may be represented at the hearing.

Where the party filing the detailed grounds intends to rely on documents not already filed, he must file a paginated bundle of those documents when he files the detailed grounds.

12. Discontinuance

Discontinuance (withdrawal) of a claim is governed by Civil Procedure Rules Part 38.

There is a right to discontinue a claim at any time, except where:

(i) An interim injunction has been granted or undertaking has been given (permission of court required) (This is applicable to cases where bail has been granted pending determination of the application for judicial review).

(ii) Interim payment has been made by defendant (consent of defendant or permission of court required).

(iii) there is more than one claimant (consent of every other claimant or permission of court required).

The claimant files notice of discontinuance at the Administrative Court Office and serves a copy on every other party. A defendant may apply to set discontinuance aside, within 28 days (Part 38.4). Discontinuance renders the claimant liable for costs until the date of discontinuance. If any other order for costs is required, an order of the court is required.

13.   Hearing of claim

When an application is ready to be heard it will be entered in the Administrative Court Office Warned List and the claimant, defendant and interested parties will be informed by letter. While the Administrative Court Office will give as much notice as possible of the date fixed for hearing, it cannot undertake to accommodate the wishes of claimants, defendants, their solicitors or counsel; in particular the occasional need to list cases at short notice may mean that parties are unable to be represented by counsel of their first choice. Parties may be notified that their case is likely to listed from a specified date – a short warned list. Applications in criminal causes or matters may be heard by a Divisional Court consisting of two or more Judges. Civil cases will generally be heard by a single Judge sitting in open Court but may be heard by a Divisional Court where the Court so directs.

Where the claimant intends to apply to rely on additional grounds at the hearing of the claim for judicial review, he must give notice to the court and to any other person served with the claim form no later than 7 clear days before the hearing (or the warned date where appropriate).

14.   Skeleton arguments

The claimant must file and serve a skeleton argument not less than 21 working days before the date of the hearing of the judicial review (or the warned date, ie, where a case has been identified as likely to be listed from a specified date, the warned date).

The defendant and any other party wishing to make representations at the hearing of the judicial review must file and serve a skeleton argument not less than 14 working days before the date of the hearing of the judicial review (or the warned date).

Skeleton arguments must contain:

(i) a time estimate for the complete hearing, including delivery of judgment;

(ii) a list of issues;

(iii) a list of the legal points to be taken (together with any relevant authorities with page references to the passages relied on);

(iv) a chronology of events (with page references to the bundle of documents;

(v) a list of essential documents for the advance reading of the court (with page references to the passages relied on) (if different from that filed with the claim form) and a time estimate for that reading; and

(vi) a list of persons referred to.

15. Court documents

The claimant must file a paginated and indexed bundle of all relevant documents required for the hearing of the judicial review when he files his skeleton argument.

Two copies are required when the application is to be heard by a Divisional Court.

The bundle must also include those documents required by the defendant and any other party who is to make representations at the hearing.

16. Applications

Where case management decisions or directions are sought after the consideration of the application to proceed, application should be made by way of an application under Part 23 of the Civil Procedure Rules.

17. Determinations without a hearing and consent orders

(i) Without a hearing

The court may decide a claim for judicial review without a hearing where all parties agree – Part 54.18

(ii) Consent orders

If the parties agree about the final order to be made in a claim for judicial review, the claimant must file at the court a document (with 2 copies) signed by all the parties setting out the terms of the proposed agreed order together with a short statement of the matters relied on as justifying the proposed agreed order and copies of any authorities or statutory provisions relied on. The court will consider the documents referred and will make the order if satisfied that the order should be made. If the court is not satisfied that the order should be made, a hearing date will be set. – Practice Direction.

Where the agreement as to disposal (usually by way of withdrawal of the application) require an order for costs or legal aid taxation only, the parties should file a document signed by all parties setting out the terms of the proposed order.

18.   Costs

It is a general rule that the party which loses is ordered to pay the costs of the other side.

19.   Appeals

A. CRIMINAL MATTERS

(i) Substantive application

The Administration of Justice Act 1960 provides:

1(1) Subject to the provisions of this section, an appeal shall lie to the House of Lords, at the instance of the defendant or the prosecutor—

    (a)   from any decision of the High Court in a criminal cause or matter;

    (b)   ...

(2)   No appeal shall lie under this section except with the leave of the Court below or of the House of Lords; and such leave shall not be granted unless it is certified by the court below that a point of law of general public importance is involved in the decision and it appears to that court or to the House of Lords, as the case may be, that the point is one which ought to be considered by that House.

B. CIVIL MATTERS

Appeal lies, with leave of the Court, to the Court of Appeal Civil Division.

In substantive applications, permission to appeal may be sought from the Court determining the application. If an application for leave is not made at the conclusion of the case, the application for permission to appeal must be made to the Court of Appeal Civil Division within 14 days. Civil Procedure Rules Part 52.3 Guidance as to procedure should be sought from the Civil Appeals Office, Royal Courts of Justice.

20.   Advice

If in doubt about any procedural matter claimants, defendants or their advisers should direct their enquiries to the Administrative Court Office, telephone number: 020 7947 6205.

Lynne Knapman
Head of the Administrative Court Office

The Administrative Court Office
Royal Courts of Justice
Strand
London WC2A 2LL

OCTOBER 2001

Notice to Claimants
Application for judicial review

Part 54 of the Civil Procedure Rules and Practice Direction 54

From 4 January 2001 applications for permission to apply for Judicial Review (claim form – Form N461) must be accompanied by additional copies of the claim form which will be sealed by the Court, and returned to you for service on the defendants and any other person you consider to be an interested party.

Please note that copies of all documents served on the Court must also be served on the defendants and interested party with the sealed claim form.

Applications which do not comply with the requirements of the Practice Directions will not be accepted, save in exceptional circumstances such as urgency.

Urgency may be defined as a case in which a decision is required from the Court within 14 days of lodging the application.

If, having read this letter, you have any questions, you should call the General Office on 020 7947 6205 which is available between 9am and 5pm Monday to Friday, or write to the Manager of the Administrative Court Office, Royal Courts of Justice, Strand, London. WC2A 2LL.

GUIDANCE NOTES ON COMPLETING THE JUDICIAL REVIEW FORM N461

Set out [below] are notes to help you complete the form. You should read the notes to each section carefully before you begin to complete that particular section.
Use a separate sheet if you need more space for your answers, marking clearly which section the information refers to.

If you do not have all the documents or information you need for your claim, you must not allow this to delay sending or taking the form to the Administrative Court Office within the correct time. Complete the form as fully as possible and provide what documents you have. The notes to section 9 will explain more about what you have to do in these circumstances.

The Court

CPR part 54 – claims for Judicial Review are dealt with by the Administrative Court.

Where the claim is proceeding in the Administrative Court in London, documents must be filed in the Administrative Court Office in the Royal Courts of Justice,Strand,London,WC2A 2LL.

Where the claim is proceeding in the Administrative Court in Wales, documents may be filed in the Law Courts, Cathay Park,Cardiff,CF10 3PG or in the Administrative Court in London.

Time limit for filing a claim

The claim must be . led promptly and in any event no later than three months after the grounds to make the claim first arose.

If you need help to complete the form you should consult a solicitor or your local Citizen's Advice Bureau.

Section 1 – Details of the claimants and defendants

Give your full name(s)and address(es)to which all documents relating to the judicial review are to be sent. Include contact information, eg, telephone numbers and any other reference numbers.

Section 2 – Details of other interested parties

Where the claim for judicial review relates to proceedings in a court or tribunal, any other parties to those proceedings must be named in the claim form as interested parties. Full details of interested parties must be included in the claim form.

For example, if you were a defendant in a criminal case in the Magistrates or Crown Court and are making a claim for judicial review of a decision in that case, the prosecution must be named as an interested party.

In a claim which does not relate to a decision of a court or tribunal, you should give details of any persons directly affected by the decision you wish to challenge.

Section 3 – Details of the decision to be judicially reviewed

Give details of the decision you seek to have judicially reviewed. Give the name of the court, tribunal, person or body whose decision you are seeking to judicially review, and the date on which the decision was made.

Section 4 – Permission to proceed with a claim for judicial review

This section must be completed. You must answer all the questions and give further details where required.

Section 5 – Detailed statement of grounds
Set out, in detail, the grounds on which you contend the decision should be set aside or varied.

Section 6 – Details of remedy
Complete this section stating what remedy you are seeking:
(a)   a mandatory order;
(b)   a prohibiting order;
(c)   a quashing order; or
(d)   an injunction restraining a person from acting in any office in which he is not entitled to act.

A claim for damages may be included but only if you are seeking one of the orders set out above.

Section 7 – Other applications
You may wish to make additional applications to the Administrative Court in connection with your claim for Judicial Review. Any other applications may be made either in the claim form or in a separate application (Form PF244).This form can be obtained from the Administrative Court Office or the Court Service website at www.courtservice.gov.uk.

Section 8 – Statement of facts relied on
The facts on which you are basing your claim should be set out in this section of the form, or in a separate document attached to the form. It should contain a numbered list of the points that you intend to rely on at the hearing. Refer at each
point to any documents you are filing in support of your claim

Section 9 – Supporting documents
Do not delay filing your claim for judicial review. If you have not been able to obtain any of the documents listed in this section within the time limits referred to on the previous page, complete the notice as best you can and ensure the claim is filed on time. Set out the reasons why you have not been able to obtain any of the information or documents and give the date when you expect them to be available.

ANNUAL STATEMENT BY THE HONOURABLE MR JUSTICE SCOTT BAKER

Lead Judge of the Administrative Court.

1. **Nominated judges**

   There are presently 25 Judges nominated by the Lord Chief Justice to sit in the Administrative Court. They include two judges of the Chancery Division and two of the Family Division who act as additional judges of the Queen's Bench Division when dealing with Administrative Court cases. A list of those currently nominated is attached at Annex A. The Administrative Court now has regular use of six courtrooms – courts 1, 2, 3, 10, 27 and 28. Routinely there are approximately 8 judges allocated to single judge sittings and one or two Divisional Courts sit.

2. **Modern judicial review**

   October 2000 saw the introduction of the Administrative Court and two fundamental changes to the work of the former Crown Office List – the introduction of CPR Part 54 and the coming into force of the Human Rights Act 1998. There has now been time to assess the impact of those changes.

   Part 54 CPR followed the recommendations of the Bowman Review and has reformed the judicial review process. There are two particular areas of note. First, the requirement to serve the defendant and interested parties with the claim form and the ability of those parties to put summary grounds of defence before the Court prior to the Court considering whether permission should be granted to proceed. This change has enabled the Court to dispose at the paper stage of many cases that are bound to fail. Secondly, the introduction of consideration of all applications for permission on paper in the first instance has meant a more structured allocation of cases to judges. Court time is now allocated for consideration of paper applications. The rate of renewal after refusal – an unknown factor in the Bowman recommendations – has stabilised at around 50%. Paper consideration has been a major contributor to the reductions in waiting times achieved over the past year. I shall return to the subject of waiting times.

   Of the cases received from 2 October 2000 to 31 December 2001 some 19% were identified as raising HRA [Human Rights Act] issues. The Act does not, however, appear to have generated a large increase in the receipts. Receipts for 2001 showed an overall increase of 110 in 2000. The increase was attributable to an increase in civil judicial review , in particular in asylum cases (2159 compared to 1876 – an increase of 15%). There have been a number of high profile cases raising Human Rights Issues such as Alconbury – the issue of the planning appeal system and Kebilene – the issue of pre-HRA prosecutions.

3.   Performance of the Court in 2001

During 2001 there were 274 Divisional Court sitting days, 1447 Single Judge sitting days and 102 Deputy High Court judge sitting days.

The statistics for 2001 show an increase in receipts but an improvement in waiting times:

Receipts: 5298 (4407 civil judicial review)
Disposals: 5398 cases were determined in 2001
Adjourned Generally: 85
Determined by Court: 2564
Discontinuance: 372
No motion after grant of permission (pre-Bowman cases): 28
Not renewed: 828
Withdrawn: 1521
Grand Total: 5398

Waiting times during 2001:

The average waiting time for a decision on an application for permission to apply for judicial review was 8 weeks (from lodging to decision).

The average waiting time for a substantive determination (of all types of case) was 20 weeks(from lodging to decision).

Expedited cases are being listed in a matter of weeks.

Legal representatives should bear these figures in mind when preparing cases.

In the light of the performance of the Court a short warned list has been reintroduced to ensure the Court is fully listed and time is not wasted when cases settle at the last minute. Parties in cases which are short warned will be notified that their case is likely to be listed from a specified date, and that they may be called into the list at less than a day's notice from that date. Approximately 6 cases are short warned for each week. If the case does not get on during that period, a date as soon as possible after that period will be fixed in consultation with the parties.

For the benefit of users the current Listing Policy of the Administrative Court is annexed to this statement (Annex C).

4.   User Group

The Administrative Court Users group provides a useful forum for discussion between the court users, the court staff and the nominated judges. Some of the forthcoming initiatives I am about to announce resulted from those discussions.

I intend for the Group to continue to meet each term. I welcome suggestions for the agenda and the feedback which court users are uniquely placed to give.

5. **Use of alternative means of resolution**

I draw the attention of litigants and legal advisers to the decision of the Court of Appeal in *The Queen on the application of Cowl v Plymouth City*, 14/12/2001 [2001] EWCA Civ 1935. The nominated judges are fully committed to resolving disputes by alternative means where appropriate and are exploring ways of promoting this.

6. **Forthcoming Initiatives**

    •   Pre Action Protocol for Judicial review

The protocol was published in December 2001 and comes into force on 4 March 2002. Any claims for judicial review lodged on or after that date must indicate that the protocol has been complied with. Reasons for non-compliance must be given in the claim form. The form is currently being reconsidered in the light of the experience of the past sixteen months and the comments of users. The revised form will be available on the Court Service website shortly.

    •   Urgent cases procedure

CPR Part 54 makes no express provision for urgent applications for permission to apply for judicial review to be made orally. As the result of users' concerns I now issue guidance on the procedure to be applied for urgent applications and for interim injunctions. Advocates must comply with this guidance; and where a manifestly inappropriate application is made, consideration will be given to a wasted costs order. The full terms of the guidance and the form for use in this procedure are annexed to this statement. (Annex B).

1. The Administrative Court currently allocates paper applications for judicial review on a daily basis and one Judge also act as the 'Urgent Judge'.

2. Where a claimant makes an application for the permission application to be heard as a matter of urgency and/or seeks an interim injunction, he must complete a prescribed form which states:

    (a) the need for urgency;

    (b) the timescale sought for the consideration of the permission application, e.g. within 72 hours or sooner if necessary, and

    (c) the date by which the substantive hearing should take place.

3. Where an interim injunction is sought, a claimant must, in addition, provide:

    (a) a draft order; and

    (b) the grounds for the injunction.

4. The claimant must serve (by FAX and post) the claim form and application for urgency on the defendant and interested parties, advising them of the application and that they may make representations.

5. Where an interim injunction is sought, the claimant must serve (by FAX and post) the draft order and grounds for the application on the defendant and interested parties, advising them of the application and that they may make representations.

6. A Judge will consider the application within the time requested and may make such order as he considers appropriate.

7. If the Judge directs that an oral hearing take place within a specified time the representatives of the parties and the Administrative Court will liaise to fix a permission hearing within the time period directed.

- E-mail address for use for urgent post

The Administrative Court Office now has e-mail addresses for urgent post. The addresses are not available for formal filing of documents. When using these addresses the office opening hours must be borne in mind and it cannot be assumed that mail sent after 4.30 p.m. will be opened before 9 a.m. on the following day.

- The e-mail addresses are:

For mail relating to paper applications
Administrativecourtoffice.generaloffice@courtservice.gsi.gov.uk

For mail relating to listed cases
Administrativecourtoffice.listoffice@courtservice.gsi.gov.uk

For mail relating to court orders
Administrativecourtoffice.courtclerks@courtservice.gsi.gov.uk

- Revised renewal form – judicial review

With immediate effect, when completing the form used for renewing applications for permission to apply for judicial review, claimants must set out the grounds for renewal in the light of the reasons given by the single judge when refusing permission on the papers. The revised form is annexed to this statement. (Annex C).

Scott Baker J
1 February 2002

ANNEX A

THE ADMINISTRATIVE COURT
The Hon Mr Justice Turner
The Hon Mr Justice Scott Baker
The Hon Mr Justice Hidden
The Hon Mr Justice Forbes
The Hon Mr Justice Mitchell
The Hon Mr Justice Evans Lombe
The Hon Mr Justice Harrison
The Hon Mr Justice Lightman
The Hon Mr Justice Collins
The Hon Mr Justice Maurice Kay
The Hon Mr Justice Hooper
The Hon Mr Justice Newman
The Hon Mr Justice Moses
The Hon Mr Justice Sullivan
The Hon Mr Justice Richards
The Hon Mr Justice Burton
The Hon Mr Justice Jackson
The Hon Mr Justice Elias
The Hon Mr Justice Silber
The Hon Mr Justice Munby
The Hon Mr Justice Stanley Burnton
The Hon Mr Justice Ouseley
The Hon Mr Justice Wilson
The Hon Mr Justice Crane
The Hon Mr Justice Keith

ANNEX B

THE PROCEDURE FOR URGENT APPLICATIONS TO THE ADMINISTRATIVE COURT

1. In October 2000 CPR Part 54 was introduced which makes no express provision for urgent applications for permission to apply for judicial review to be made orally.

2. The Administrative Court is now issuing the following guidance on the procedure to be applied for urgent applications and for interim injunctions. It is the duty of the advocate to comply with this guidance; and where a manifestly inappropriate application is made, consideration will be given to a wasted costs order.

3. The Administrative Court currently allocates paper applications for judicial review on a daily basis and one Judge also act as the 'Urgent Judge'.

4. Where a claimant makes an application for the permission application to be heard as a matter of urgency and/or seeks an interim injunction, he must complete a prescribed form which states:

   (d) the need for urgency;

   (e) the timescale sought for the consideration of the permission application, eg, within 72 hours or sooner if necessary (see paragraph 8 below); and

   (f) the date by which the substantive hearing should take place.

5. Where an interim injunction is sought, a claimant must, in addition, provide:

   (c) a draft order; and

   (d) the grounds for the injunction.

6. The claimant must serve (by FAX and post) the claim form and application for urgency on the defendant and interested parties, advising them of the application and that they may make representations.

7. Where an interim injunction is sought, the claimant must serve (by FAX and post) the draft order and grounds for the application on the defendant and interested parties, advising them of the application and that they may make representations.

8. A Judge will consider the application within the time requested and may make such order as he considers appropriate.

9. If the Judge directs that an oral hearing take place within a specified time the representatives of the parties and the Administrative Court will liaise to fix a permission hearing within the time period directed.

Administrative Court Office Reference Number: CO/

REQUEST FOR URGENT CONSIDERATION

THIS FORM MUST BE COMPLETED BY THE ADVOCATE FOR THE CLAIMANT

THIS FORM AND THE CLAIM FORM MUST BE SERVED BY THE CLAIMANT'S SOLICITORS, BY FAX AND POST, ON THE DEFENDANT AND INTERESTED PARTIES

NAME OF CLAIMANT:

Name, address and fax number of Solicitor acting for the Claimant

Name of Counsel/Advocate acting for the Claimant

NAME OF DEFENDANT

Date of service of this form and claim form

Fax number served

NAME OF INTERESTED PARTY(IES)
Date of service of this form and claim form
Fax number served

1. REASONS FOR URGENCY

2. PROPOSED TIMETABLE
(a) The application for permission should be considered within hours/days
(b) Abridgement of time is sought for the lodging of Acknowledgments of Service
(c) If permission is granted, a substantive hearing is sought by (date)

3. INTERIM RELIEF
Interim relief is sought in terms of the attached draft order on the following grounds:

SIGNED
ADVOCATE FOR THE CLAIMANT

DATE
NOTE TO THE DEFENDANT AND INTERESTED PARTIES
Representations as to the urgency of the claim may be made to the Administrative Court Office by fax: 020 7947 6802

ANNEX C

LISTING POLICY IN THE ADMINISTRATIVE COURT
February 2002

Fixing substantive hearings
Where a case is ready to be heard substantively, it enters a warned list and all parties are informed of this by letter. Some cases require an early hearing date and take priority over other cases waiting to be fixed – these enter the expedited warned list.

Where counsel has been placed on the court record, their chambers are contacted by the Administrative Court list office in order to agree a convenient date for the hearing. Counsel's clerks are offered a range of dates and have 48 hours to take up one of the dates offered. If counsel's clerk fails to contact the List Office within 48 hours, the List Office will fix the hearing on one of the dates that was offered, without further notice and the parties will be notified of that fixture by letter. Where a hearing is listed in this way the hearing will only be vacated y the Administrative Court Office if both parties consent. Failing that, a formal application for adjournment must be made (on

notice to all parties) to the Court. The same procedure is followed
where a claimant is in person.

Short warned list

Whilst the Administrative Court usually gives fixed dates for
hearings, there is also a need to short warn a number of cases to cover
the large number of settlements that occur in the list. Parties in cases
that are selected to be short warned will be notified that their case is
likely to be listed from a specified date, and that they may be called
into the list at less than a days notice from that date. Approximately 6
cases are short warned for any specified week. If the case does not get
on during that period, a date as soon as possible after that period will
be fixed in consultation with the parties.

Vacating fixtures

There are occasions when circumstances, outside the control of the
List Office, may necessitate them having to vacate a hearing at very
short notice. Sometimes this can be as late as 4.30pm the day before
the case is listed. This could be as a result of a case unexpectedly
overrunning, a judge becoming unavailable, or other reasons. In
deciding which hearing has to be vacated, the List Office will assess
the cases listed for the following day and take the following factors
into consideration:

- Which case/s, if removed, will cause the least disruption to the
  list (the aim is to adjourn as few cases as possible, ideally one).
- How many cases need to be adjourned given the reduced listing
  time available.
- Have any matters previously been adjourned by the Court.
- The urgency and age/s of the matter/s listed.
- Where the parties and/or their representatives are based (this is
  relevant as in some cases the parties travel to London the day
  before the hearing).
- Whether it is appropriate to 'float' the case in the event of
  another listed matter going short (cases will not be floated
  without the consent of the parties).
- The likelihood of a judge becoming available to hear a floated
  case.

After taking these factors into account, the list office decide upon the
case(s) which will have to be refixed and will inform the parties
concerned that their hearing has been vacated. The case record will
be noted that the matter is not to be adjourned by the Court again.
The Court will also endeavour to refix the case on the next available
date convenient to the parties.

Scott Baker J
Lead Judge of the Administrative Court

Index